GLORIANA

The Years of Elizabeth I

GLORIANA

The Years of Elizabeth I

by Mary M. Luke

LONDON
VICTOR GOLLANCZ LTD
1974

NOTE

The front endpaper, *The Coronation Procession of Elizabeth I*, and the back endpaper, *The Funeral Procession of Elizabeth I*, are both reproduced by courtesy of the Trustees of the British Museum.

Printed in Great Britain by
Lowe & Brydone (Printers) Ltd, Thetford, Norfolk

This story completes my trilogy
which has detailed
the history of the House of Tudor.

I dedicate this book
to the memory of its most illustrious member,
who has been a challenging companion,
if, at times, a tyrannical mistress.

I count myself the better for association with the indomitable

Acknowledgments

Gloriana is the culmination of a lifetime interest in the Tudor period, as well as a natural sequel to both *Catherine, the Queen* and *A Crown for Elizabeth.* The Tudor Trilogy is now complete, and I am very aware of the enormous debt I owe to many who, for the ten years during which it was in work, have assisted me so generously.

Particularly, I wish to thank the officers of the Mercantile Library in New York for allowing me to keep materials while my work was in progress. Nearer home, Mrs. Elisha Keeler, reference librarian of the Darien Library, has proved invaluable in seeking and acquiring needed research from libraries and private sources both here and abroad. In England I have had the dedicated assistance of the officials of the British Museum, the National Portrait Gallery, the Courtauld Institute, the Public Record office, the London Library and other venerable institutions. Lord Astor of Hever, who has given me such generous assistance in the past has again been most helpful, as well as provided the rarely published portrait of the Duke of Alençon from the Hever Castle collection. I am also indebted to the well-known Tudor author Neville Williams, deputy keeper of the Public Record office in London, for his kindness in requesting his publishers, Weidenfeld & Nicolson, to provide the negative of Elizabeth's tomb effigy.

I am unusually indebted to the numerous and prolific past researchers of Tudor lore, all of whom are acknowledged in the Bibliography. Much of the work of the oldest researchers, particularly, was accomplished before the day of the typewriter and certainly before the duplicating machine, and it has left me with a tremendous admiration for their unexcelled curiosity and their tireless patience. That latter-day research has often uncovered their all-too-human errors still does not detract from the incredible reality and overall reliability of their labor, which has made it possible for a twentieth-century American cousin to have many facts, quotations, letters and journals available for immediate use. They have my respect and enormous appreciation.

As any *researcher* knows, however, facts are the solid foundation upon which a *writer* builds and interprets. History is time, and where time exists so does place, and in this area, I have made my own research. If the various places mentioned in *Gloriana* still exist, I have seen them and probably more than once. Tudor London itself is very real to me. From the Jewel House in Westminster near the site of the old Palace, I have traced—with the aid of old maps, sketches, descriptions and later Canaletto paintings—the location of almost every site or building mentioned. It does not take much imagination walking down "the Streete"—today's Whitehall—and using the Banqueting House as a focal point, to mentally rebuild old Whitehall Palace with its gardens and courtyards in the shadow of the Holbein Gate. I never cross the site of the Horse Guards Parade without remembering I am treading part of Henry VIII's tiltyard or walk in London's famed parks without blessing Elizabeth's father who, wishing to ride out from Westminster, St. James's or Whitehall to hunt, preserved those acres. Old Henry is even responsible for a beautiful park in the Surrey countryside. Through the kindness of John Dent, Borough Librarian for Epsom and Ewell, I have been guided to the approach and shown the outline of gaudy old Nonsuch Palace, one of Henry's more magnificent whims, the foundations of which Mr. Dent and his colleagues actually unearthed in 1959. I have walked the route which Essex and his companions followed on that fateful Sunday morning when he sought Sheriff Smith in Fenchurch Street, and I have followed him up Seething Lane, hard by Mark Lane and All Hallows Church, where Sir Francis Walsingham lived. The area north-northwest of the Tower around Bishopsgate, Aldgate and Houndsditch was the Belgravia and Park Avenue of Tudor times, and those who did not reside in the beautiful homes on the banks of the Thames lived in large houses with gardens and orchards in areas today more devoted to motor and pedestrian traffic. I have gazed with Sir Walter Raleigh out the Armory window in the Tower at a sad execution taking place below, and through the good offices of Colonel Sir Thomas Butler, the resident-Governor of the Tower of London, have seen several areas not usually shown to visitors. I have followed old Lord Burghley on his painful journey out the Theobalds Road and gone by the river with Elizabeth from Whitehall to Richmond or perhaps only to Chelsea.

Though many monuments to Mary Stuart still stand, her memory is perhaps strongest at all that remains of Fotheringhay Castle—a huge mound above the misty Nene where cattle placidly roam the precincts of the castle and moat. And though she and Elizabeth never met in life, they lie but a few feet from each other in Westminster Abbey, where, nine years after Elizabeth's death, James I brought his mother's body to its final resting place.

However, professional assistance and personal endeavor need the catalyst of someone to bring it all together. In this I have been fortunate in two instances. I wish first to thank my publisher, John J. Geoghegan, for his confidence in and personal encouragement of a new author, which, in the complexity of a modern and competitive business world, is becoming increasingly rare. Mr. Geoghegan's belief that the reader would be interested in the life of young Elizabeth and her brother and sister resulted in *A Crown for Elizabeth*. It was his conviction also that yet another portrait of the great Tudor Queen was viable, especially one concentrated on the personal and intimate, at the same time encompassing the personalities with whom she was surrounded. Mr. Geoghegan's faith in the Tudor Trilogy has made its completion a deep personal satisfaction to the author.

And, last of all, my fond appreciation to a conscientious and gifted associate. For seven years, I have had her generous assistance and constant enthusiasm, and my work bears witness to her dedication, expertise and excellent good taste. Working with Patricia Brehaut Soliman is pleasure as well as privilege, and I am happy to call her friend as well as editor.

Preface

For years Elizabeth Tudor has intrigued scholar and layman alike, much the same as she fascinated her contemporaries of 400 years ago. Yet another work on the forty-five years of her Queenship might understandably produce a feeling of *déjà vu* which would be as unfortunate as it would be mistaken. For each biographer of the last Tudor Queen approaches the subject consistent with his own interest in and understanding of the years in which she reigned. It is his duty also to interpret as well as delineate, and with a greater knowledge of human psychology than our forebears possessed even as little as fifty years ago, it is possible that present-day interpretations of character and events might differ substantially from former accounts.

The material dealing with Elizabeth's long reign—which exceeds even that of her august father, Henry VIII—can quail the heart of a researcher and quench the enthusiasm of the most dedicated historian. So much is repetitive; there is often a misplaced emphasis which has resulted in convictions bordering on caricature. Everyone is familiar with the unfortunate (and mistaken) concept which portrays Henry VIII as Bluebeard-*cum*-buffoon. Another similarly mistaken concept has extended to Henry's second daughter and decreed that she be remembered as an imperious monarch, a political genius and a frigid, sexually impotent woman. Or, given the other side of the coin, Elizabeth is seen as a tense neurotic subject to bouts of semi-hysteria reminiscent of her mother, Anne Boleyn, and with a predilection for boudoir encounters similar to those of her more sensual father. While there is some foundation for all these assertions, they have been over-emphasized by repetition until accepted as fact, at times at the sacrifice of a knowledge more revealing. As often happens, the truth lies somewhere in between, and an author is challenged to choose the material which will—with truth—reveal the most.

To know the woman, one must know the child. As a young girl, Elizabeth had lived in the shadow of her brother, Edward, and her sister, Mary, as they occupied the throne. When she later became Queen, Elizabeth remembered the hazards they had faced and the mistakes they had made. One would be foolish indeed not to realize the advantage this gave to a shrewd young woman who was, undoubtedly, the most intelligent of all the Tudors. Faced with similar risks and challenges, Elizabeth had later only to recall her brother and sister's mistakes. While, during her long reign, she made plenty of her own, she never repeated theirs.

Acknowledging the deprivation—the physical, emotional and spiritual loneliness of her first twenty-five years—it must be remembered that this was no ordinary individual who ascended the throne of England in 1558. Given any other position in life, Elizabeth Tudor would have made her mark, perhaps in the arts and sciences of the day. Given the power of royalty, there was nothing she could and would not attempt. She had had scant security, less love and small hope for most of her life. To Elizabeth, the throne represented *freedom*—freedom to do as she chose as long as she remembered wherein lay her real popularity and strength: in the hearts and affections of her people. She spent forty-five years preserving her subjects' love and her appeal to them. *This preservation of her Queenship was the prime reason for which Elizabeth Tudor lived.* Never, under any circumstances or for any one individual, would she endanger her popularity or risk her royal freedom. Once this is accepted, many of the perplexing questions involving Elizabeth—from her reluctance to marry to her reluctance to make war—become clear and understandable.

While the royal freedom—so alluring to a girl who had suffered imprisonment!—might encompass many things, it also brought responsibility, and in this Elizabeth's subjects were fortunate indeed. For she had inherited the magnificent administrative ability of her father and the prudence and thrift of her grandfather, Henry VII. Measured doses of Anne Boleyn's flippancy and inconsistency marred the performance and brought more than one Councillor, courtier or friend close to the edge of sanity. But remembrance of her insecure childhood and her own pride ensured that Elizabeth consistently gave her best to her people. She blessed the fate which had given her the throne with no successor breathing heavily in the wings. She spent the rest of her life determining there never *would* be any successor and disposing of anyone who might look to her Crown. Understandably, a few heads fell along the way.

Queen Elizabeth presented different faces to many people, yet the mystique of the monarchy was always present. In this modern age where empathy is considered so important, Elizabeth is curiously contemporary. By herself, she was almost a negative character: shallow, opportunistic and incredibly vain. Yet in her relationship with others, in her reaction to various issues or challenges, the Elizabeth-in-depth emerges. It is in this involvement with such as her ladies-in-waiting, her Councillors and churchmen, her courtiers and alleged lovers that the real character of this enigmatic creature is to be found, and not in her behavior toward other monarchs or their ambassadors, where Elizabeth relished being the poseur.

There was one exception. Elizabeth never saw the luckless Mary Stuart, Queen of Scots. Yet it is doubtful if she ever expended as much emotional strength, energy and tears as she did on the misguided Queen who fled to her realm for protection after having thoroughly botched her own life. The following nineteen years were years of despair and frustration for Elizabeth as well as Mary, and even with the ultimate tragedy of the Scottish Queen's death, the trauma did not subside. It was clearly evident, where these two women were concerned, that power and the throne were not compatible with love. Elizabeth always knew this and, in the end, sacrificed her womanhood to the Crown even as Mary Stuart sacrificed her Crown to her womanhood.

Gloriana is very much an evocation of the Elizabethan era. I have adopted a narrative form in an attempt to imbue flesh and blood to people who were a great deal more than mere shadows on history's pages. In presenting Elizabeth in the unimportant as well as the large events of her time—the small happenings as well as the historical crises—it is my hope that we will discover the *real* Elizabeth, the woman behind the grandeur of the Crown, behind the impassive face with the huge ruff, which stares at us from so many portraits. Some of these small events have passed into legend. Not all are attractive or inspiring, but all are human.

Any political, economic, religious or social assessment of the reign of Queen Elizabeth, I leave to the scholars and academicians. If I have completed this book with one strong conviction, it is that man must fight man. It seems a condition of *Homo sapiens* as compelling as the need for food and drink. Modern governments labor for social and political ideologies. In the sixteenth century, while social and political issues abounded, the overwhelming, all-embracing cause for the letting of blood and the sacrifice of countless lives was the cause "of religion." The belief in Jesus Christ as the Son of God had, by the sixteenth century, become so embroiled in side issues, in ritual and creed, as t ⸗

render the original fact itself almost nugatory. Toleration was unheard of; persecution was an encouraged and accepted fact. Elizabeth astounded the monarchs of her time in many ways, but never as much as when she said there was only one Jesus Christ and all the rest "was a dispute about trifles."

In *Gloriana* we will see Elizabeth Tudor as her contemporaries saw her. If, as is true, her critics were numerous, her admirers were legion, and in these pages both will speak for themselves in letters, diplomatic reports, journals and records. All facts have been thoroughly researched, are historically substantiated and referenced for the reader who wishes to delve further. I am convinced it is from the opinion of Elizabeth's contemporaries that we find the germ of truth regarding this controversial woman and not in the estimation of many scholars who have fitted the Queen with a character more in line with their hindsight knowledge of her achievements. Space being precious, I have had to leave out as much as is actually included in the book, and it has been necessary to encapsule some incidents, particularly Elizabeth's marriage negotiations. Her suitors and their representatives were a long-suffering group, but I have not wished to inflict the same condition upon my readers.

Therefore, as people around Elizabeth saw the Queen of England from 1558 to 1603, so shall we. And in this encounter, perhaps the true spirit of this elusive, fickle and, at times, shameless creature—she who was jade and termagant to many—near saint and gracious sovereign to others—who has tantalized the public imagination for centuries will be revealed. It is my greatest hope that when the reader puts aside this book, he will feel he knows Elizabeth of England.

Ridgefield, Connecticut   MARY M. LUKE
June, 1971–April, 1973

Contents

Illustrations follow pages 256 and 512

Prologue

At the "house in the fields," the red-brick palace which an infatuated Henry VIII had built for Anne Boleyn and named for St. James, the crowd which had lingered for the past several days dispersed. In silence they turned their faces into the bitter wind which swept across the marshy ground which had been, before the palace was built, the site of "a house for leper maydens." A safe distance from the busy City, Westminster and Whitehall, the area was as appropriate for royal honeymooners as it was for the diseased occupants who must suffer perpetual exile. Once all traces of the hapless maidens had been swept away, the proud towers of St. James's Palace beckoned in the distance whenever the sovereign and his lady desired a "place of ease" away from the demands and cares of the monarchy. Now, it was a place of comfort for a dying Queen who had asked only to meet her Saviour in peace and with dignity.

The Queen had had her wish. With no pain, she had "seemed only to go to sleep," mercifully unaware that most of the court had deserted and only a faithful few of her ladies-in-waiting remained. Their long vigil at an end, the curious few at the gates left as the royal life within came to its end. If there was no outward display of relief and thankfulness, there was also little regret. They spoke in muffled tones as they bent to the wind and crossed the Park, a part of old Henry's hunting preserve. On past the fields and the conduit near Whitehall, they made their way home.

There were some—with more charity and a remembrance of things past in their hearts—who went into the old Abbey at Westminster to light a candle and pray for the soul of their sovereign, Queen Mary, the unfortunate forty-two-year-old daughter of Catherine of Aragon and Henry VIII, who had died this seventeenth day of November, 1558.

The Queen

I am more afraid of making a fault in my
Latin than of the Kings of Spain, France,
Scotland, the whole House of Guise, and all
their confederates. I have the heart of a man,
not of a woman, and I am not afraid
of anything. . . .

Chapter One

On the day Mary Tudor died, broken in heart, her spirit as blighted as her ravaged body, the heiress apparent to the Crown was at another red-brick palace twenty miles north of London. Daily bulletins had brought her news of Mary's wasting illness, but she needed no official confirmation to know what was happening in the close, dark chamber at St. James's Palace. Once the Queen had taken to her bed, no one assumed she would ever rise again, and the exodus to the stately home of the former Bishops of Hatfield had then commenced. Place seekers and opportunists mingled with the swarms of curious yeomen and honest gentry, anxious only to be present at the great moment when Henry VIII's younger daughter was proclaimed Queen.

Almost to a man, the travelers marveled that she should have succeeded to the throne at all. The middle child of the King, with an older sister, Mary, and a younger brother, Edward, her chances of wearing the Crown had been considered slim indeed. During her younger years, she had suffered abandonment by a father who had ordered her mother's head cut off. She had subsequently been shunted about to a series of dreary royal manors, reminiscent of a royal orphan with whom no one wished to be bothered. Twice she had been bastardized by a compliant Parliament, and once she had been imprisoned for suspected treason against the very woman who, so conveniently, had just died.

From the solarium at Hatfield, Elizabeth Tudor, the heiress apparent, watched the noisy crowd in the courtyard below. In the distance, she could see others converging on the Palace from all directions; the lanes were as crowded as the main road leading to the Palace gate. She remembered the enthusiasm with which her brother Edward's accession had been greeted and the genuine and heartbreaking sorrow when, at sixteen, he had died. Then it had been Mary's turn. The touching and profound sentiment which had heralded the crowning of their beloved Queen Catherine's daughter had soon deteriorated into despair and finally, outright rebellion and hatred at Mary's obstinate insistence on her marriage to the foreigner, Philip, son of the Spanish King. During the following four years, the country had been torn asunder by Mary's determination to return England to the papal fold and her involvement in her husband's Spanish wars, with the recent consequent loss of Calais, the "bright jewel" in the English Crown, the last remnant of English glory in France.

Those four years had been dangerous and uncomfortable ones for Elizabeth Tudor. While her brother was reigning, she had piously and publicly embraced the reformed religion upon which Edward had insisted. Mary, on the other hand, had had a dire time of it, staunchly defending her right to celebrate the Mass and continue her life in the faith in which she had been reared. But Mary had reaped her reward upon her accession, and those who valued their heads and their property—especially the magnificent lands they had plundered from the Church—were quick to conform to the Catholicism of the devout Mary. They had encouraged ill feeling and suspicion on Mary's part toward her younger sister—a suspicion which she had taken to the grave. Knowing the Queen's feelings, Elizabeth had often paced this very room at Hatfield, beginning with the time the rebel Wyatt had dared question Mary's right to wed the Spanish Prince and had led a rebellion into the very City itself. Wyatt had paid for his presumption with his head, and Elizabeth had gone to the Tower for suspected complicity. Two miserable years of restraint at Woodstock had followed before she had been allowed to return to Hatfield. Here she had pursued the scholastic life she loved, safe from the intriguings of the court, the suspicions of her sister and the interferences of the Council.

She remembered the terror of those days and contrasted them with the joyous mingling of the people now below, a joy which was spreading throughout the realm with the news that another Tudor would wear the Crown her grandfather had won from the Plantagenet at Bosworth Field. Already she had been proclaimed in Parliament by Lord Chancellor Heath, and already, in London, bonfires were being laid, church bells were ringing, and ale and wine were being distributed for the night-long celebration. There would be no time to mourn—if, indeed, anyone sincerely mourned poor misguided Mary. There would be only time now to honor their new Queen.

The new Queen. The words still bore the aura of an incredible miracle, and Elizabeth was aware—as never before—of a new security. For almost the first time in her life, she felt *safe*. There was now no one to threaten, to abandon, to incite suspicion. She was Henry VIII's daughter, and if it was not actually wise to mention her mother, there were many who remembered that quicksilver woman who had so charmed a King he had thrown his country and Church into a religious revolution and a political turmoil the like of which they had never before known. Even the Councillors would remember. They would, naturally, compare her with her brother and sister, both of whom had had different mothers. They would be waiting for her to show her hand, to see how she differed; they would assess her strengths and speculate on her weaknesses. She had few illusions about any of them. They, too, had made mistakes during the past few years, and heads had fallen, fortunes been made and lost and reputations tarnished. But they would accept her, for not only was she the heir, but she was also a symbol, a figurehead of the new political and economic movement created by the dissolution of the monasteries and the confiscation of ecclesiastical lands. They would want to keep their holy spoil, just as Mary had wanted to take it from them and return it to the Church. If she, Elizabeth, wanted security, she must win their support.

It was a heady thought: security and support. Both would now be hers! And, she realized, due to her own shrewdness and intelligence, for she had had to trust only in herself. There had been no one to help; instead, there had been many only too willing to harm.

Elizabeth had few real friends. There was old Katherine Ashley, her governess, and the bumbling Parry, who had made such a mess of her household account books the Council had at one time removed him from the post. While she had lived, Elizabeth's greatest friend had been Katherine Parr, her stepmother, who later had wed Thomas Seymour. Elizabeth had every reason to remember Thomas Seymour, the reprobate brother of the erstwhile Lord Protector and of Jane Seymour, whose brief Queenship had ended with her death at Edward's birth. What would Thomas say if he could see her now? As impossible in his enthusiasm as he was lacking in any form of common sense, he would probably sweep her off her feet and, with one of his great oaths, explode with laughter that *she*, "Anne Boleyn's brat," should finally have achieved the Crown of England!

It had been nine years since she had indulged in that shameless flirtation with Thomas Seymour. The flirtation had been one of the many charges leveled against him before his execution. But how he would have enjoyed the fact that the redheaded fifteen-year-old daughter of his old King—the girl he had tried to seduce in his own household—would now occupy the throne! He would have enjoyed the irony and conveniently forgotten the bitterness, fear and suspicion which she herself had experienced in the eleven years since her father's death. *She* would never forget them—those years in which she had castigated herself for her shameless behavior which had led, indirectly, to Thomas' death. It had been behavior unbefitting one of the blood royal. Later she had deliberately adopted whatever pose was convenient—not to save face, as so many had done, but to save her own head. Not to curry favor, but to salvage whatever royal position and privilege she could from the self-seeking and unscrupulous Council which had manipulated her brother and thwarted her sister.

Turning from the window, Elizabeth walked to the stairway. She knew such recollections were best put behind her. Her nobles, Council and her court were waiting. As much as possible, the past was best forgotten—unless it was convenient to remember and avoid the hazards which had beset her brother and sister.

One danger had been the succession, the vital question of who would inherit the Crown when Edward and Mary were dead. Though her father's will had designated each of his children should succeed in turn, the vital religious issues endangered each accession. The Protestants in power at the time of her brother's death did not want the Catholic Mary. And Mary had desperately hoped for a child who might ensure the Catholic faith's triumphing over the reformers who had plagued her short reign. But, to Mary's great personal sorrow and to the despair of her Catholic advocates, there had been no child. On her deathbed, Mary had designated Elizabeth "as the next lawful heir," although as someone hastened to note, the dying Queen had not paid her the compliment of mentioning her by name. But having recognized her successor, within moments she had been deserted by all save a few faithful ladies-in-waiting who had little to lose by leaving their dying mistress. All the rest had hurried to Hatfield and were now part of the crowd in the courtyard below or were mingling with court officials in the Great Hall. It was a shocking display of callousness and, to Elizabeth Tudor (who had had her own share of calculated in-difference), an example she never forgot. She was to spend the remaining forty-five years of her life ensuring it did not happen again.

In the great vaulted Hall, the Privy Council lingered. Holdovers from Queen Mary's reign, they were not too comfortable as they waited with varied emotions for their new mistress. Among them were many who had given Elizabeth Tudor scant comfort and less attention during the years since her father's death. They could not guess the new Queen's reaction; they could merely hope she did not have her father's long memory where similar lapses of support were suspected. Her sister, Mary, had been surprisingly lenient with many who had not championed her claim to the throne. It remained to be seen whether Anne Boleyn's daughter possessed the same compassion—a slender possibility when one remembered the fate of the mother.

William Cecil, Elizabeth's great advocate, had called them together to meet with the new Queen, and as they waited now, small cross-currents of emotion caught at each. Cecil, busy with his everlasting notes, was anxious he had overlooked nothing which deserved immediate attention. It was three days since Heath, the aging Lord Chancellor, had proclaimed Elizabeth in Parliament and couriers had been dispatched to the remotest corners of the land, as well as to Brussels, Vienna, Venice and the northern countries. The ports had been closed and the guard changed at the Tower and the Mint. Garrisons on the Kent and Sussex shores held musters and checked their supplies. Nothing had been overlooked to guarantee a safe transition of the government from Mary to Elizabeth. Even a "safe preacher" had been selected for the following Sunday sermon at Paul's Cross "that no occasion might be given to stir any dispute touching the governance of religion."

Next to Cecil, old Winchester and Sussex reflected on the caprice of fate. Only four years earlier, on Palm Sunday, for her suspected part in the Wyatt rebellion, they had escorted Elizabeth to the Tower and, they were certain, a fate similar to her mother's. Questioned by the late Stephen Gardiner, then Lord Chancellor, she had cried, ". . . you sift me narrowly, my Lords, but you can do no more than God hath appointed, unto Whom I pray to forgive you all!," [2] causing the ever-impressionable Arundel, who had accompanied them, to fall to his knees and beg forgiveness, saying he himself "was sorry to see her troubled about such vain matters." Even after her removal to Woodstock, Elizabeth had continued to protest her innocence in letters begging the Council's intercession with her sister and complaining of her tight restraint and uncomfortable lodgings.

Robert Dudley, son of the John Dudley who had attempted to usurp the Crown for his daughter-in-law, little Lady Jane Grey, during her abortive nine-day reign and lost his head in the attempt, had similar remembrances of Elizabeth. For his part in his father's conspiracy, he too had been lodged in the Tower at the same time as Elizabeth and, on his release, had done what he could to help her cause, even selling some of his possessions for money to bribe officials who might make her detention less wearisome. Their relationship went back many years, for they were of an exact age and once, during the time of her father's marriage to the young and wanton Katherine Howard, Elizabeth had scornfully told her eight-year-old friend Robin that "*she* would never marry!" But now, with a Crown on her head and a throne to safeguard, Elizabeth would be compelled to think differently. That she, a twenty-five-year-old woman, could dominate those sitting at the Council table and deal with the vital issues facing England at this hazardous time was unthinkable.

The door opened, and as the Queen entered, they rose respectfully. Elizabeth was accompanied by two ladies-in-waiting, who discreetly withdrew as their mistress took her place at the head of the long table. Those who had given Elizabeth little thought during the years she had been more of a royal nuisance than a daughter of their former King and a sister of the reigning monarch wished they had been more attentive. It had been so convenient to forget her except when her suspected treasonous activities called for some action on their part. She had had few champions among them. Cecil had been one. At the time of Mary's accession he had wisely retired to his gardens and orchards at Wimbledon. He had dutifully conformed to the outward semblance of the Catholic religion and received an admirable lack of royal notice for his compliance. Amazingly, Philip, the dead Queen's husband, had been among Elizabeth's most vocal supporters, and there had been the usual gossip that his interest was more personal than political. As they sat and watched the new Queen, they all—with the possible exception of Robert Dudley—realized how little they knew of Elizabeth Tudor.

They saw, now, a composed woman who showed no trace of nervousness or anxiety. She sat quietly with hands folded on the table—beautiful hands, with long, slim, tapering fingers, the hands of the mother many of them suddenly remembered with a poignant vividness. She had her mother's oval face and a smooth, fair skin of startling whiteness. The gray-black eyes which in Anne Boleyn had sparkled with mirth penetrated with keen intelligence in the daughter's face. But there the resemblance ended. In coloring, Elizabeth was all Tudor, with her father's auburn hair streaked with brilliant gold. She had the lean, wiry build of her grandfather, Henry VII, and there was also something of old Henry in her cautious, authoritative manner. No one present would have called Elizabeth Tudor beautiful. But the way she carried herself, her tall and well-proportioned figure, her unmistakable aura of presence made mere beauty unnecessary. Their mistress had attained a comely womanhood. There should be little difficulty in getting her a husband; the problem would be to find one *she* would accept!

Elizabeth broke the silence; it was immediately obvious she had given her words much thought. "My lords, the laws of nature move me to sorrow for my sister. The burden that has fallen upon me maketh me amazed—and yet, considering I am God's creature, ordained to obey His appointment, I will thereto yield."

Aware she had her listeners' absorbed attention, the Queen continued. She told the Council that she desired the help of each one, "that I with my ruling and you with your service may make a good account to Almighty God and leave some comfort to our posterity on earth." She said she meant to direct her actions by her ministers' good advice and counsel, especially those of the "ancient nobility . . . and some others [who] have been of long experience in governance. . . ." She also mentioned those who had been "upon special trust lately called" to the service of Edward and Mary and stated, "I shall accept you of my nobility *and such others of you the rest as in consultation I shall think meet and shortly appoint. . . .*" Her intent, she said, was "to require of you all nothing but faithful hearts in such service as from time to time shall be in your powers toward the preservation of me and this Commonwealth." [3]

The Privy Council was composed of the most vitally influential gentlemen in England and was "hardly less important than the Queen in . . . government." [4] To be a member of this body was vastly important. Not only was it a high honor, it was also an open door to privilege, power and profit. There were few among the Councillors who did not feel their authority threatened. Elizabeth sensed their disquiet by an anxious shifting in their seats, and she sought to allay their fears. "For they which I shall *not* appoint," she said firmly, "let them not think the same for any disability in them, *but for that I consider a multitude doth make rather discord and confusion than good counsel.*" [5]

However much tact and diplomacy she had used, the Queen's intent was clear. She meant to reduce the Council which had been so burdensome to her sister, and she rose now, gesturing that they were dismissed. But before they left, she told her ministers, there were two appointments she wished to make. Thomas Parry, her longtime Cofferer, would be knighted and made Comptroller of the Household. There were few present who did not recognize in this reward Elizabeth's appreciation of Parry, who had served her for years, if not always with skill, at least with diligence. Her following words, however, were more disconcerting. Gesturing to one nearby, who immediately stepped forward, she spoke directly to William Cecil:

"I give you this charge"—the Queen's voice rose so that each present might hear her words—"that you shall be of my Privy Council, and content yourself to take pains for me and my realm. This judgment I have of you—that you will not be corrupted with any manner of gifts, and that you will be faithful to the State; and that without respect of my private will, you will give me that counsel that you think best. . . ." Cecil's face was expressionless; only the muscular tightening of his jaw betrayed his emotion as he listened to Elizabeth's final words:

". . . and if you shall know anything necessary to be declared unto me of secrecy, you shall show it to myself only, and assure yourself, I will not fail to keep taciturnity herein." [6]

It was a delicate moment for the Council. The thirty-eight-year-old Cecil was not of the nobility, but the son of Richard Cecil, a Stamford squire of modest fortune who had served Elizabeth's father and grandfather in minor positions. He had brought his son, William, to court at the age of eight to serve as one of the three Pages of the Robes. After Cambridge, and training for the law at the Inns of Court, William had served under the patronage of Edward Seymour and John Dudley, two who had suffered execution for treason during the previous reigns. Yet no guilt by association had clung to Cecil. When he was knighted, just before Dudley's downfall, his friend Sir Henry Sidney had called him, "a most rare man both for his sundry singular gifts of nature, learning, wisdom and integrity." [7] The "rare man" had emerged from the Dudley fiasco, which had ended in the death of the little Lady Jane Grey, quite unscathed. He had been able to dispel any suspicion on the part of the new Queen; Mary Tudor had called him "an honest man." Cecil had quickly retired to his country home, rarely appearing at court. But obviously, there had been communication during those years between him and Elizabeth; he had been the first to inform her that Mary had died. [8]

It would have been surprising to those Councillors who now departed the Hall could they have known that the association of Elizabeth Tudor and William Cecil, officially begun that day, would last forty years, through good times and bad, through crises of state and spirit. They were necessary to each other, for, in his own way, each was fighting for survival. Elizabeth knew that she must have one loyal, dependable and honest servant on her Council. On Cecil's part, he now had the opportunity to compensate for those dull and unproductive retirement years. It was the first time in his life that Cecil had been offered a post of such challenge and responsibility; it was the first important appointment the new Queen had made. For each of them, it was to be the most durable and rewarding association of their lives.

Elizabeth left Hatfield for her capital on November 23. She was attended by the Lords of the Council, her ladies-in-waiting and the royal household retinue, which numbered "a thousand and more." Nearing London, they were met by throngs who had left the crowded City for the small villages outside its walls. At Highgate, a great procession of Bishops, the scarlet-robed Mayor and aldermen awaited their sovereign. Amid loud acclamations, Elizabeth halted the entourage to receive their greetings and oaths of allegiance, graciously extending her hand for each to kiss. As Edmund Bonner, the Bishop of London, came forward, she was seen to withdraw her hand hastily; Bonner had been especially zealous in the burnings which had marred her sister's reign. At the confiscated Charterhouse, "close to the horse-market at Smithfield," where so many of those martyrs had died, the journey ended as the Queen entered the vast building, now the residence of Lord North.

That evening a reception was held in the Great Hall of the former home of the Carthusian monks, several of whom had suffered monstrously cruel deaths during the reign of Henry VIII. In the Hall, which only thirty years previously had echoed to the subdued murmuring and soft footsteps of the holy brothers, the lords of the aristocracy, the foreign envoys and the eminent clergy mingled together to honor the Queen. They saw a young woman, "above middle height and of well-proportioned figure." They noted that she was "pleasing rather than beautiful with golden colored hair, more reddish than yellow, curled in appearance naturally." [9] Gomez Suarez de Figueroa, Count de Feria, the Spanish ambassador, was among those present, awaiting the moment when he might approach Elizabeth. He remembered her as the troublesome sister of the late Queen who had married his King, Philip of Spain, the sister who had counted for so little during the time Mary and Philip had reigned. She had been the focal point of every reforming plot during those years and, he firmly believed, a traitor to Mary in theory, if not in actual deed. The thought that Elizabeth might undo all the Catholic preferments for which Mary had struggled haunted de Feria, and with the elaborate social amenities concluded, he turned the conversation to the Queen's policy regarding the Church and advised, somewhat pontifically, that she exercise much caution "in religious affairs." He was rewarded with a long, cool stare and the somewhat enigmatic reply that "it would indeed be bad for me to forget God, Who had always been so good to me." The appreciative murmur which swept the assemblage at her words left the Count distinctly uncomfortable. He later wrote to Philip somewhat apologetically that "this seemed to me to be rather an equivocal reply." [10]

It would have been possible to proceed directly to the Tower the next day, but the affairs of state—so long neglected during Mary's illness—were more easily and comfortably transacted in the spacious old monastery rooms than in the royal apartments of the Tower. The chief business was the formation of Elizabeth's new Privy Council—that all-important, ever-present body which must follow the Queen, whether at Whitehall or any other royal palace or manor. The Councillors' duty was to advise and serve and, as a main centralized unit, administer the affairs of the realm. The monarch did not always follow their advice, as, indeed, the future was to show. They were also "to preserve order within the country, to defend the realm against foreign powers, to raise enough money to ensure that England was adequately protected and administered." To discharge these vast responsibilities, the Queen had retained the Earls of Pembroke, Derby, Shrewsbury, Bedford, and Clinton, the Lord High Admiral. A few, appointed by Mary and of great Catholic sympathy, felt it wiser to resign than swear allegiance to a monarch not wholly committed to their faith. Others, more worldly than conscientious and ready to accept any theological premise in exchange for power and authority, stayed on. Replacements were swift. Three relatives of the Queen became Privy Councillors: her uncle William Howard; her cousin Henry Carey, the son of Mary Boleyn; and Sir Francis Knollys, another cousin. William Parr, the Marquess of Northampton, a brother of Elizabeth's beloved stepmother Katherine Parr, completed the list. All were known Protestant sympathizers, and the angry de Feria wrote his King the new appointments had followed so fast that "fathers did not know their children!"

Old Archbishop Heath, the Lord Chancellor, was an especial recipient of the tact Elizabeth Tudor could exercise when necessary. A loyal Catholic, he could not envisage anyone but the Pope as head of the Church. It was unthinkable, therefore, that he should officiate at Elizabeth's coronation. The Queen agreed that he might retire with honor, even keeping his title. But custody of the Great Seal and its authority were transferred to Nicholas Bacon, William Cecil's brother-in-law.* William Paget, one of the few remaining old warhorses who had served on Henry VIII's Council, as well as those of her brother and sister, was aged and infirm; his retirement was diplomat-

---

*William Cecil's first marriage was to a sister of John Cheke, a tutor of Edward VI. His wife died after the birth of a son. Cecil then married Mildred Cooke, the erudite daughter of Sir Anthony Cooke. Another Cooke daughter, Anne, married Nicholas Bacon. Their offspring would later be the renowned Sir Francis Bacon.

ically suggested. In the end, eleven of Mary's advisers were retained while seven new appointees, noted for their reforming tendencies, achieved an influential balance. It was a vigorous and competent Council for which Elizabeth and Cecil had striven. If there were a conservative few remaining who might still prove troublesome, they were also getting no younger; Nature would ultimately dispose of them.

Joining the aristocracy in the select Council were several of the rising class of "new men" who had acquired considerable power in the past several years, primarily from the possession of the vast bounty which the dissolution and subsequent confiscation of Church lands had provided. Fattened with their rich loot, they would need time to acquire polish, culture and, it was hoped, a sense of responsibility. Theirs had been the final appointments. Uneasily they had waited several days until the Queen's pleasure was known; Elizabeth seemed in no hurry to alleviate their anxiety. At last their appointments were announced. Their late selection was evidence of the deliberate delay which Elizabeth would later elevate to an art. The Councillors' fervid appreciation of the honor they had thought lost left little doubt of their gratitude. Their inclusion was a unique solution to a problem which had harassed her sister and frustrated her brother—an over-wieldy, self-seeking and aristocratic Council. The vigor and purpose of the "new men" more nearly resembled that of the Queen than the older, more experienced ministers: the infusion of new blood would temper and balance the more reactionary element among her advisers. Of all the Tudors, only Elizabeth was fitted by temperament to be as selective, and the timing of her accession was such that the inclusion of the old with the new was possible.

With the Privy Council complete, the Queen rode on November 28 to take possession of the Tower of London, a traditional obligation honored by every British sovereign. The multitudes had assembled early to watch as Elizabeth, seated in a rich chariot, passed along the Barbican to Cripplegate. There the Lord Mayor received her as the throngs, heady with excitement and exhilaration, pressed from all sides to be nearer the monarch. There Elizabeth—a slim, square-shouldered young woman, whose flaming cheeks belied her outward composure—mounted her horse to enter the City. She wore a riding dress of purple velvet with a scarf of gold looped over one shoulder. Gentlemen-Pensioners clad in vivid red damask bearing gilded axes accompanied her; the brand-new silver "E.R." gleamed on the livery of the other attendants.

Directly behind the Queen rode Robert Dudley, the newly appointed Master of the Horse. The post—that of keeping the Queen and court supplied at all times with suitable transportation, of maintaining the royal beasts, carriages and wagons in excellent condition—was eminently in keeping with Dudley's own superb horsemanship. While Master of the Horse was a responsible position, it was also decorative, and now, on a coal-black charger, he bore out a chronicler's description that "his beauty, stature and florid youth recommend him." Trumpeters blared as the cavalcade passed through streets hung with tapestries, flags and colored bunting. At various street corners, demonstrations of loyalty and affection took place which "the Queen accepted and noted gratefully." At the great citadel of the Tower, the cannon discharged a roaring welcome. It was a moving moment as Elizabeth rode down toward the vast moated fortress. Entering the precincts, she stopped at the Green, her poise momentarily deserting her, and, sinking to her knees, her emotion obvious to all, cried fervently, "Some have fallen from being princes of this land to be prisoners in this place. *I* am raised from being a prisoner in this place to be a prince of this land . . . !" No one doubted her sincerity and many wondered if the Queen might be recalling her mother, "a prince of this land," who suffered execution on the same spot twenty-two years previously. "Let me show myself to God thankful and to men merciful . . ."[11] she whispered. For Dudley, particularly, it was a poignant and affecting moment. He, too, had had his depairing moments in the grim old prison.

Elizabeth remained in the White Tower until December 5. Each day, as her confidence increased, she and her Council laid the foundations for changes which would affect the realm for the next several years. The problems facing the new Queen were summed up by a contemporary:

> The Queen poor; the realm exhausted; the nobility poor and decayed; good captains and soldiers wanting; the people out of order; justice not executed; all things dear; excesses in meat, diet and apparel; division among ourselves; war with France; the French King bestriding the realm, having one foot in Calais and the other in Scotland; steadfast enemies, but no steadfast friends.[12]

Nothing was more true. The vast debt left by Henry VIII had been compounded by his daughter Mary's obedience to her Spanish husband, her willingness to sacrifice the interests of England to the demands of Spain and involve the nation in expensive wars "in which they had neither object to gain nor injury to redress." The Treasury was empty, the currency so debased it had become an object of humor which seriously affected trade. Loans outstanding at Antwerp carried horrendous interest rates, and in addition, famine, plague and destitution had demoralized the people. The middle class, many of whom had risen to wealth on the plunder of monastery lands, had enclosed their holdings for sheep grazing, excluding from employment thousands of yeomen-tenants whose ancestors had tilled the land for centuries. Joined by those who had lost their living in the monasteries—the bakers and gardeners and smiths—they had turned vagrant, creating a multitude of beggars who held little hope of ever regaining a foothold in a secure life.

England's economic peril was aggravated by the vital question of faith and ritual. The religious question, which had so vexed England since Henry VIII had separated the English Church from Rome and declared himself its Supreme Head, was the disastrous inheritance the King had bequeathed to each of his children. Henry himself had died "a good Catholic"—with reservations. Imbuing his asserted supremacy with the force of his own strong personality, Henry could never have visualized the religious excesses which would occur in the reign of his son, Edward Tudor. From childhood, the young King had been surrounded by representatives of the reforming faith. Given that royal isolation which is the lot of princes, it was not surprising that the boy's natural idealism should become tinged with bigotry. Edward had encouraged the Protestant movement which culminated in the publication of his godfather Thomas Cranmer's Book of Common Prayer. During Mary's reign, the Catholic faction had regained their advantage and, on the gallows and at the stake, the reformers and their supporters had died for their beliefs, just as the Catholics had for theirs during the reigns of Henry and Edward. When Cranmer and other noted churchmen suffered hideously at the stake, a popular couplet ran:

> When these with violence were burned to death
> We longed for our Elizabeth. . . .

Only a few days before Mary Tudor's death, the last Protestant martyrs had suffered, and the extent to which the reformers hoped for Elizabeth's accession is shown in another couplet from the same work:

> Six days after these were burned to death
> God sent us our Elizabeth.[13]

The Queen was well aware that a solution to the religious trials which had afflicted English national life for decades must be found. During the past twenty-five years, religious belief and its resultant joy or misery had permeated every facet of her own life. "I know I have a soul to be saved as well as other people have," Elizabeth had once written to the Protector. Yet her abhorrence of any form of religious persecution was undoubtedly the obvious outgrowth of a personality which viewed religion itself as much with the mind as with the heart. Not for Elizabeth Tudor the blind devotion of her sister, Mary, to creed, ritual and faith! When she later tersely told her advisers she would not "open windows in men's souls," she gave full notice that religious excesses were at an end. She herself had suffered harassment and intimidation in her younger, more vulnerable years; her very devotions at the Cross had been ordered, regulated and observed. The religious "disputes and strivings" which had been a festering sore within her realm were a barrier to efforts to foster any sense of national unity, and Elizabeth had small patience with them. "If there were two princes in Christendom," she was later to say, "who had good will and courage, it would be easy to reconcile the differences in religion, for there was only one Jesus Christ and one faith, and all the rest they disputed about were but trifles!" [14]

While realistically accepting that there must be a settled religious doctrine, Elizabeth went one step further. Her goal was nothing less than a national unification of Church and State—a refreshing and startling innovation for the average Englishman, who, four times in twenty-five years, had been told that previous religious settlements were no longer valid. Each change had resulted in an upheaval and redefinition of political and social power and, more important, a redistribution of land and wealth. When the religious orthodoxy of one reign became the treason of the next, the outcome could only be misery, outrage and injustice. It was a situation the monarchy could tolerate no longer.

In order to avert religious dissension Elizabeth compromised on the rewording of the Oath of Supremacy. Instead of the title "Supreme Head of the Church," which had been so tragically contentious during her father's reign, the sovereign became "Supreme Governor of the realm . . . in all spiritual things or causes, as in temporal . . . ,"[15] an obvious attempt to pacify Catholics, yet maintain that spiritual independence from Rome so important to the reformers. "She seriously maintains," wrote one of her bishops, "that this honour is due to Christ alone and cannot belong to any human being whosoever. . . ." [16] When these reformers—Protestant exiles from Mary's reign—rushed home to be later joined by Continental reformers from Zürich and Geneva, they could hardly wait to assist the Queen in furthering the Reformation, which had suffered such a setback under Mary. "Now is the time for the walls of Jerusalem to be built again in that kingdom where the blood of so many martyrs, so largely shed, may not be in vain!" [17] they cried. But they soon realized they had been precipitate; the Queen was in no hurry to accommodate them. Loud in their disappointment that the monarch would not seek to avenge the martyrs' and exiles' sufferings, they began "to sow abroad the doctrine of the Gospel more freely, first in private houses and then in churches, and the people . . . began to flock unto them in great numbers and . . . wrangle amongst themselves and with the Papists." [18] Soon words of their "disputes and strivings" and inciting of the people caused the Queen to act.

Instead of religious persecution, Elizabeth answered her critics with a religious proclamation, and it was a masterpiece of compromise. It directed her subjects to use the Lord's Prayer, the Ten Commandments, the Apostles' Creed and the Epistle and Gospel in English. But the remainder of the religious service was to be in Latin—the Latin so appealing to the Catholics and the older, reactionary English worshiper who had spent a lifetime with the familiar Roman service. Outright preaching—still an innovation in the English Church, where the competent preacher was rare—was prohibited, and "rash talkers of Scripture" were to be silenced. By permitting the use of both the earlier and later editions of Thomas Cranmer's Book of Common Prayer, issued during her brother's reign, Elizabeth gave her subjects a broad choice—one followed the Catholic doctrine that the flesh and blood of Christ was incorporated in the Communion service, while the second denied it. Many had died in the previous reigns for their belief in those doctrines; Elizabeth wished no such sacrifices to disgrace hers.

The Queen's moderation, her refusal to take a definitive stand, a stand buttressed by pressure and persecution, also reflected her own religious sophistication. Certain elements of the Catholic ritual held strong appeal to her emotions, yet the Protestant doctrine appealed to her intellect. The proclamation not only was indicative of Elizabeth's desire for religious uniformity, but also bore evidence of her awareness that she was riding the crest of a political and religious wave which was not going to subside. By the gradual insinuation of a change which would invite cooperation and tolerance more than it would incite resistance, she hoped to achieve the religious peace which had evaded her brother and sister. Mary Tudor had put her Church first and country second. Elizabeth would put her country first and attempt to fit the Church in wherever convenient.

There were many who had anticipated a more dramatic reprisal against former enemies, but the extreme was always anathema to Elizabeth—in this, she and Cecil were indisputably alike. One goal superseded all. Her subjects came first. "Have a care over my people," Elizabeth told her ministers. "You have my people; do you that which I ought to do. They are *my* people. Every man oppresseth them and spoileth them without mercy. They cannot revenge their quarrel, nor help themselves. See unto them. See unto them, for they are my charge. I charge you, even as God hath charged me . . . my care is for my people." [19]

If there were jaded malcontents of the Tudor court who scoffed at what appeared royal naïveté, the Queen seemed not to notice. England came first—no religious sect or theological premise must endanger the welfare of the country and its people. She would take care of her people—and they, in turn, would take care of her. It was an assumption so simple in its premise as to be implausible to many. It would take forty-five years and a dedicated monarch to demonstrate its ultimate feasibility.

Chapter Two

Elizabeth's coronation took place on January 15, 1559, less than two months after her accession. Parliament was to meet on the twenty-third, and Elizabeth was anxious to be crowned before the opening session. In 1544 Henry VIII had placed her in the succession, but there were earlier statutes left unrepealed, which barred her from the throne. Her sister, Mary, in asserting her own legitimacy, had also decreed Elizabeth illegitimate. Only a *crowned* monarch possessed unassailable authority, and Elizabeth was determined that the political minority which still considered her the bastard child of an executed Queen should have little time or opportunity to challenge her right to the throne.

January 15 was designated for other than political expedience. Shortly after her accession, Elizabeth sent Robert Dudley and Blanche Parry, her lady-in-waiting, to Dr. John Dee, a noted astrologer, with the request that he calculate the most auspicious time for her coronation. Elizabeth had been won to her belief in a fortune governed by the stars and planets while still a young princess. Dee had then cast her horoscope—accurately, it seemed—for he predicted her inevitable triumph, though cautiously, he omitted to say how or when it would be achieved.

Once a date had received Dr. Dee's heavenly blessing, Elizabeth and her Council spared no effort or expense to demonstrate to all the importance of the forthcoming coronation. Orders, sending a multitude of craftsmen into a frantic and exhausting activity, issued from the Palace daily. Workmen commenced the building of tiers of planks which would seat the tremendous congregation within Westminster Abbey. The lumber came from the New Forest and the Great Park at Windsor and was pulled on wagons along the miry, often frozen roads.

The menu for the vast banquet which traditionally honored the monarch, occupied more of the Council's time than the interest rates on the monies borrowed from Antwerp which were to pay for all the splendor. And it was soon obvious that splendor was what Elizabeth Tudor had ordered. Couriers were sent to the Continent for cloth of gold, cloth of silver, expensive brocades, damasks and velvets, which were fashioned into wall hangings, banners, clothing and horse trappings. When deliveries of a certain colored cloth fancied by the Queen did not arrive on time, "the customs officers down at the wharves were secretly ordered to impound any crimson silk that was landed, so the Queen could have the pick of them." The royal servants soon discovered that the new monarch expected prompt service with no excuses and that she had an indelible memory and a discerning eye for small details. It was a rare change from the less demanding Queen Mary, of whom they had all taken advantage more than once. The former Queen had also been quick to sympathize with or excuse the recalcitrant servant, two concessions they were not to see again. The winds of change blew not only over all England, but into every nook and cranny of every chamber and hall within the royal residences. Things had not changed so speedily at Westminster since the last ten years of her father's life when his several marriages had brought new Queens in quick succession to the throne.

Elizabeth was determined that nothing—not even the empty Treasury—would spoil her coronation. She knew her people well. In their love of the pageantry and pomp that brought color and cheer into their drab, hard lives, they were like children. There had been little lighthearted gaiety or even goodwill during her sister's years on the throne. The coronation would symbolize the importance of Elizabeth Tudor's accession. She would present the nation with a portrait of a kindly, secure and unchallenged sovereign, one who belonged completely to her subjects, with no ties to any foreign nation or papal prince. She must temper the image of inadequacy, misery and failure which had been Mary's bequest to her people and dispel any lingering impression of feminine incompetence her sister had left. She would give, instead, the appearance of a lavish, generous and loving monarch. It was not for want of personal effort that the Queen's coronation would present a spectacle her subjects would remember for years to come. And when the final cost was calculated and it was found that more than £ 16,000 would be needed adequately to crown Elizabeth Tudor, the new Queen, Cecil and the Council felt it would be worth every penny.

While remembrance of her sister came to Elizabeth's mind as she awaited her great day—for she had lived through similar days with Mary only four years previously—memories of her father also often came unbidden. Many at court noted her resemblance to Henry, particularly in her manner, and they commented on it, to her obvious pleasure. ". . . She gives her orders and has her way as absolutely as her father did . . . !" the Count de Feria wrote somewhat petulantly to King Philip of Spain. What Elizabeth could not know was the similarity of her position, preceding her coronation, to that of her father when, at the age of eighteen, he had ascended the throne as the second Tudor King. Tall, strikingly handsome, with the same vivid red-gold coloring his daughter now possessed, the boy-King Henry VIII and his Spanish bride, the stunning Catherine of Aragon, had presented a magnificent portrait of Majesty which Henry took great pains to cultivate and encourage. His father, the first Tudor sovereign, the formidable Henry VII, had ruled for twenty-four years. However much he had accomplished for England's good, applying the salve of unity and peace to the wounds created by the Wars of the Roses, his reign had been exceptionally noted for its frugality and lack of color and, particularly, for the absence of any personal appeal on the part of the monarch. Subsequently, the court had become a place to be avoided or endured only when necessary. On young Henry's accession, Westminster Palace and Hall became the scene of fetes, jousts, tournaments, lavish banquets and sumptuous pageantry, the like of which no courtier could remember. And the English subjects, not yet taxed to the hilt, had loved it all. Their young monarch could do no wrong, and the power of his personality, his wooing of his subjects, his appeal to them were such that even to the end—through six marriages and countless crises of Church and State—the majority of them had clung to their King. When, later in life and older and wiser, they had viewed him with a more disillusioned eye, the habit of loyalty and obedience was still strong; the monarchy was supreme and the sovereign all-powerful.* It was a lesson Henry had taught his subjects well, but a lesson which the more enlightened generation that followed had challenged during the reigns of Edward and Mary. Plots, intrigues and persecution then seemed to spring into being with a rapidity which weakened the sovereign's power and almost destroyed the emotional response the English always held for their monarch.

For the first time in years, this feeling was stirring again in the

---

*Though there were several minor plots, allegedly treasonous, against Henry during his thirty-seven-year reign, his years on the throne were remarkably free of the intrigues prevalent during his son Edward's reign or of any serious attempts to dethrone him such as had marred the reign of his daughter, Mary.

nation, and it was directed, Elizabeth knew, toward herself. Always her father's daughter, she recognized at once—as her sister and brother never had—that her power and prerogative derived from the people. With their allegiance, there was little to which she could not aspire. Without it, there was nothing. At her death, poor Mary had been stripped of everything a monarch held dear: love, loyalty, power—and freedom. If Mary Tudor had felt the loss of these, perhaps her marriage had made it up to her. For Elizabeth, it did not seem possible that anything could be more desirable than the power and perquisites of royalty. Certainly not a man or a marriage.

On the day before her coronation, Elizabeth made the traditional procession from the Tower to Westminster. The day was icy, for it had snowed in the morning—Dr. Dee not having divined the weather in his heavenly calculations. About two o'clock in the afternoon it had cleared, and as a blast of trumpets rent the cold air of the riverside fortress, the huge royal cavalcade emerged from the Tower gates. People had waited for hours in the freezing weather. This was an event the City had anticipated for two months, and an excitement bordering on hysteria filled the air. As the trumpets echoed and faded, the church bells of the City began their clamor and the pent-up joy of the people erupted. Elizabeth could hear the great shouting long before she could see the people. That morning she had attended services in the Tower, praying aloud, "Oh Lord, Almighty and Everlasting God, I give Thee most humble thanks that Thou hast been so merciful unto me as to prepare me to behold this joyful day. . . ."

She sat, now, in a chariot covered with gold brocade which accented the richness of her robe of cloth of gold, the exact color of a small crown which graced the abundance of coppery hair. A canopy was borne over the chariot, held by four knights. The chariot itself was drawn by two mules, gorgeously caparisoned in gold brocade. Lord Robert Dudley, the Master of the Horse, rode directly behind, leading the Queen's white hackney, draped in cloth of gold which swept the ground. Behind them came thirty-nine ladies-in-waiting, twenty-four on palfreys, the remainder riding in chariots. There was no aloofness in Elizabeth's countenance as she sat amid six cushions of white damask with a matching quilt for warmth. The Queen possessed a friendliness and charming amiability very reminiscent of her father at his best. She responded immediately with smiles and gestures to the roar. As one observer wrote, "As she entered the City, she was received by the people with prayers, welcoming cries and tender words, and all signs which argue an earnest love of obedient subjects towards their sovereign." People dashed to the chariot's side, calling, "God save your

Grace!" or "God bless Queen Elizabeth!" Often, at her signal, the procession halted so that she might speak with several who persisted in running alongside. As the noisy acclaim mounted and the people thronged more closely, it was frequently impossible for the entourage to continue. At such moments, Elizabeth held out her arms to those around her, accepting their homage, and "wonderfully transported were the people with the loving answers and gestures of their Queen!" Before her chariot could proceed, several daring souls rushed to her side and thrust nosegays—unusual in winter—into her lap. While accepting one such offering, Elizabeth noticed an old man in the crowd break down and turn his back so his Queen might not see his tears. A knight, riding close by, gestured toward the man, who, he said, "weepeth and averteth his face." The Queen nodded and smiled. "I warrant you it is for gladness!" [2] she cried.

At Fenchurch Street the pageants began, and here, a fair child, covered in embarrassment, delivered himself of a monologue welcoming Elizabeth to the City. Despite the din, there was a "perpetual attentiveness in the Queen's countenance while the child spake. . . ." At the conclusion, he blurted, "God preserve thee, we pray and wish thee every well!" as she signified her approval by a salute to the relieved boy.

Elated as she was by the joy of her people and the paean of jubilant triumph encountered on all sides, it was not until they had reached the upper end of Gracechurch Street that the Queen was moved to tears. There a "gorgeous arch" simulating an immense family tree stretched from one side of the street to the other. Elizabeth of York and Henry VII, the Queen's grandparents, were depicted with the white rose of York and the red rose of Lancaster intertwined. Elizabeth was nearsighted and did not see the great arch until the chariot passed almost directly beneath. Nothing daunted, she ordered it backed so she could view the spectacle. And there she saw her grandparents and her father amid Tudor roses. And it was there the tears sprang to her eyes as she saw the other figure. It was her mother, Anne Boleyn, receiving honor and homage from her former subjects after a shameful execution almost twenty-three years before.

As the cavalcade rumbled toward Cheapside, it picked up speed, and the Queen's exultation returned. As someone shouted to her, "I remember old King Henry the Eighth!" she waved joyfully to him and others who cheered at the mention of her father's name. The noise of one group of musicians at Cornhill Street blended into the melody of another, as the royal procession finally reached Cheapside. At the Cross, which was "dressed in the richest stuff" the Queen was presented, in the Lord Mayor's name, a purse of crimson satin containing a thousand marks of gold. "I thank my Lord Mayor, his brethren, and ye all . . . be ye assured that I will be as good unto ye as ever Queen was to a people!" she responded to the officials. Another "marvelous shout and rejoicing" reached her as the chariot bore on toward the Little Conduit. There, another pageant depicting an "old man. . . . who sat with his scythe and hourglass" was arranged. On asking who the old gentleman was, Elizabeth was told he represented Time. "Time," she said thoughtfully, "it is Time that hath brought me here. . . ." [3]

The sunlight which had graced the spectacle was fading as the procession advanced toward Temple Bar. At Fleet Street, a small, thin, poorly clad woman had daringly approached the chariot, as it halted for a respite, and thrust a small branch of rosemary into Elizabeth's hands. It was all she had to give, she explained, and the Queen "won many hearts" as she took the offering and thanked the woman, who quickly darted back to safety. "Rosemary for remembrance"—that was the old saying. This day there had been many opportunities for remembrance, for each street in the route of sovereigns through the old City held memories of some sort. Some were proud and happy such as when she had viewed her parents' portraits high above Gracechurch Street; some were bitter and sad as she passed Somerset House in the Strand with its memories of the Seymour brothers, Edward, the Protector, and that reckless, handsome Thomas, who had once so fascinated her. By the time the Cross at Charing Village came into view and the roar of her subjects as the chariot turned into Whitehall became an unbelievable din, she had dropped the rosemary to the floor. The loud ringing of the bells from the Abbey and St. Margaret's Church swept all unhappy thoughts from Elizabeth's mind. As the great procession clattered through the gates of Westminster Palace, where a crescendo of deafening noise greeted the monarch, the Queen was again participating in the tremendous welcome, gesturing and waving to those who had waited so long. When she left the chariot, the branch of rosemary lay forgotten on the floor.

Only one incident marred the coronation plans, for it appeared there was not a bishop agreeable to placing the Crown of England on Elizabeth Tudor's head. The logical choice, Reginald Pole, the Archbishop of Canterbury, was dead. Old Heath, the Archbishop of York and former Lord Chancellor, gathered his conscience like a cloak around him and piously protested he could not crown Elizabeth, even though she had tactfully allowed him to retain his title, if not his duties. Eventually, the timid Oglethorpe, the Bishop of Carlisle, agreed to officiate.

If the difficulty of obtaining a prelate's services to confirm her sovereignty rankled, it did not show on the Queen's radiant face as she appeared early the following morning, January 15, at the end of a triumphal procession which walked on the 702 yards of blue cloth spread from Westminster Hall to the Abbey. The walk itself had been railed in on both sides, and her subjects pressed at the barriers, stamping their feet in the cold, to watch the Queen pass. They saw not only Elizabeth, clad in crimson velvet robe and cap, her long hair streaming around her shoulders, but also the lords spiritual and temporal, gorgeously robed and somber in their appearance as they shuffled along in procession. The Earls of Shrewsbury and Pembroke accompanied the Queen, and the Duchess of Norfolk carried the long crimson train. They were preceded by the Abbey officials and the choir, which sang "Salve Festa Dies." The scarlet-clad and mitered bishops and officers of the royal household were followed by the peers "in their robes and caps of estate, with their coronets in their hands." Nobles proudly bore the regalia—the crown of King Edward the Confessor, the brilliant scepter and orb and the royal spurs and staff—without which no monarch was truly crowned.

And then the Queen herself appeared. Reminiscent of her tremendous success the day before, another roar of acclaim, a triumphant trumpet blast told those already seated in the Abbey the monarch was approaching. Her subjects, who had waited so long in the numbing air, gave full vent to their enthusiasm, and Elizabeth responded with gestures to their homage. "God 'a' mercy, good people!" she cried to those who held out their hands to her from the railed walk.

As she passed into the great Abbey, brilliantly lit with huge wax candles, past the tiers of seated nobles, and mounted the dais for the formal recognition and proclamation, another tremendous fanfare of trumpets split the air. Four times—from different positions on the dais—she was presented to the congregation, and four times the great swelling acclamation "Yea! Yea! Yea! God save Queen Elizabeth!" poured forth.

The remainder of the ancient ceremony, the origins of which were older than the Abbey, was vividly alive to the Queen. On the Protector's orders she had not attended her brother Edward's coronation, but she remembered Mary's. Then she had watched her sister prostrate at the altar and later, when the crown was placed on Mary's head, had felt her own throat constrict with emotion, awe and a biting envy. The emotion and awe were still there but accompanied now by a regal self-assurance which astonished many of the spectators, who, only a few months previously, had denounced her for suspected intrigue against her sister. The poise was evident in Elizabeth's firm enunciation of the coronation oath, in the bearing of the slim figure which prostrated itself, after which her attendants spread a cloth over her gown for her anointment. The actual anointment was spoiled for Elizabeth; later she told her ladies-in-waiting: "the oil was grease and smelled ill!" [4]

At the conclusion of the anointing, the Queen changed her dress behind a traverse and reappeared shortly wearing a dress of cloth of gold, with a long train. Over it was a mantle of the same material completely lined and trimmed with ermine. Around her waist the girdle with the great sword was hung, and bracelets were clasped on the royal wrists. And finally—the crown. Again that tremendous emotion engulfed Elizabeth as the crown of King Edward the Confessor was lowered by Oglethorpe onto her head, being replaced a few minutes later by the small delicate crown of pearls and diamonds especially made for her younger brother, Edward. The coronation ring was slipped on the index finger of her right hand, and as the trumpets blared forth, the scepter and orb were placed in her hands. It was done. The twice-illegitimatized daughter of Henry VIII and Anne Boleyn was truly "Queen of all England, France, Ireland, Defender of the True, Ancient and Catholic Faith, most worthy Empress from the Orcade Isles to the mountains Pyrenee...!" [5] Each peer of the realm then came forward to swear homage and fidelity to the Queen, climaxed by a kiss on her left cheek. "Then the bishop began the Mass, the Epistle being read, first in Latin and then in English, the Gospel the same. . . . When the Mass was done, the Queen retired behind the High Altar and . . . coming forth again with the State Crown on her head, and robed in violet velvet and ermine, and so proceeded to the banquet in Westminster Hall." [6] As she walked the vast length of the Abbey, drummers, pipers and organ swelled together with the blare of trumpets inside and the clamor of church bells outside "as if," wrote one ambassador, "the world was coming to an end."

In the normally icy confines of Westminster Hall, the coronation banquet was laid on amid blazing candles and torches, which helped warm the great room. Elizabeth presided at the royal table, raised on a dais under the huge window at the upper end of the Hall. The Earl of Arundel and the Duke of Norfolk, responsible for the banquet, rode on horseback to each end of the Hall and were soon followed by Sir Edward Dymoke. Dymoke, in full armor and "on a beautiful courser richly trapped with gold cloth," rode into the middle of the Hall to challenge to combat anyone who might dispute Elizabeth's rightful claim to govern the realm. Garter King at Arms read the proclamation, ending with "A largess! A largess! A largess!" as the trumpets blew. Dymoke then cast a gauntlet to the great stone floor. When no one accepted the challenge, a loud roar erupted from the tables. Musicians in the gallery struck up a melody as the servitors strode into the Hall carrying huge platters of food and flagons of wine. Near the end of the feast, the Queen rose and commanded silence. She thanked her noble lords and subjects for her glorious coronation and, raising her goblet, drank their health. Each peer stood and, taking off his coronet, waited as the Queen drank deeply.

The coronation banquet had commenced at three o'clock, some four hours after Elizabeth had first entered the Abbey. It did not conclude until one o'clock in the morning, perhaps justifying a comment made by a foreign ambassador at "the levities and moral licentiousness practiced at the court in dances and banquets." The same pious gentleman directed a verbal reproach to the newly crowned sovereign also as he said, after watching Elizabeth obviously enjoying the merriment, which grew more abandoned as the evening proceeded, "In my opinion, she exceeded the bounds of gravity and decorum!" No one could leave until her Majesty departed, and Elizabeth, whose life until this moment had contained little lighthearted amusement or gaiety, relished the festive grandeur of the coronation banquet to its utmost. A great joust was to have been held the following day, but the exhausted Queen—showing a glimpse of that streak of imperiousness which would grow in time—commanded its cancellation. She was tired, she said, and would remain in her bed. And remain in bed she did, "with a slight indisposition" for two full days.

The first Parliament of Elizabeth I met at the end of January, 1559, and dealt effectively with the vital problems of the succession and a national religion. A statute was passed declaring Elizabeth "rightly, lineally, and lawfully descended from the blood-royal" and pronounced "all sentences and Acts of Parliament derogatory to this declaration to be void." Perhaps there were those with warm memories of Anne Boleyn who might have wished some royal action reversing the Act of Attainder against the dead Queen. But if Elizabeth ever entertained such thoughts, wiser heads prevailed. Once her lawful descent was declared, her own legitimacy and the legality of her mother's marriage were affirmed by implication. There seemed little to be gained in stirring up the painful emotions of twenty-three years past.

Parliament also passed the Act of Supremacy, which restored to the Crown "the ancient jurisdiction over the state ecclesiastical and spiritual ... abolishing all foreign power repugnant to the same." The accompanying Act of Uniformity authorized the use of the second Book of Common Prayer of the reign of King Edward in 1552. Elizabeth and Cecil were adamant: unity of religious doctrine was a necessary principle of the united realm. The Queen was firm—religion had been a cat's-paw too long, to the country's detriment. Elizabeth had no wish to dominate the Church to the extent her predecessors had; she did wish to stabilize it. She wanted a national Church with no tie to Rome and owing nothing to the dogmas of Geneva. Once she had a united Church hierarchy—and she showed herself willing to compromise to attain one—she would let well enough alone. "The law touches no man's conscience," she was later to say, "so as public order be not violated by external act or teaching." [7] Her subjects must now put their country first, their Church second, and such a Church must be, as the Queen considered herself, "mere English." Once such a united Church was established, said the Queen, she would guard its independence, and there would be little interference from royalty. To a nation grown to adulthood on religious change and persecution, it was a startling and incredible precept.

Elizabeth's determination to effect a national unity in the Church resulted in the dismissal of those bishops who refused to swear the Oath of Supremacy to their "Supreme Governor." Their replacements were, of necessity, those who looked more kindly on the somewhat hybrid church services which combined tenets of both the Catholic and Protestant rituals. Elizabeth could be quixotic, however. Walking to services in Westminster at the opening of Parliament, the abbots and monks of the old Abbey met her in broad daylight with tapers burning. The Queen, who had previously been partial to a display of lights during church services, exclaimed loudly, "Away with those torches! We can see well enough!"

In all instances, the new bishops-elect acknowledged lack of any tie to Rome. Noting the Queen's desire to "unite the people of the realm in one uniform order," the new Lord Chancellor, Sir Nicholas Bacon, instructed the bishops to make laws such as might "tend to the establishment of God's Church and the tranquility of the realm," yet they must avoid any measure which would "breed idolatry and superstition." [8] When Sir Edward Carne, the English ambassador at Rome, sent a loyal message to Elizabeth, he received no letter of credence from her, merely the admonition to come home, there was nothing for him to do in Rome. When the Pope later issued a Bull which declared "heretical sovereigns" incapable of reigning, Elizabeth commanded Carne's recall. The Pope, threatening excommunication, forbade his return, and the unfortunate minister—caught in the middle—elected to stay in Rome. In Elizabeth's view, this vastly improved the situation, for official communication between the See of Rome and England was, for the moment, impossible and mainly the result of papal interference. Thus, this first tilt with the Pope ended in Elizabeth's favor. She was not committed to any action and detached herself so thoroughly it immediately simplified a situation which otherwise might have become embarrassing.

One aspect of the situation at Rome was important to Elizabeth, but for reasons other than the religious. This was the effect the affair might have on His Most Sovereign Majesty, the Catholic King of Spain. Shortly before Mary's death, Philip had sent the Count de Feria to England. He reported to Philip that England was "entirely in the hands of young folks, heretics and traitors." The Queen's refusal to identify with any particular political or religious faction enraged the pompous de Feria, who said Elizabeth "does not seem to be too ready to treat with me." Although the Queen had told him at a precoronation reception "that when I wanted anything to speak to her personally . . ." she actually did very little to remedy the situation. Often, she cleverly forestalled de Feria's comments. "She is in the habit of talking to me, of introducing one subject and proceeding with it . . ." he wrote, adding that Elizabeth ended the conversation just as he was about to recite his own complaints.

The ambassador yearned for Philip's intervention, although he recognized that his King's voice had "no more weight with the Council than if he had never married into the realm." Resentment of the Spaniards, so intense during the marriage of Philip and Mary, was now openly flagrant, de Feria wrote. "The people are more free than ever, the heretics thinking that they will be able to persecute the Catholics and those people . . . spread about everywhere that your Majesty in the future will have no more influence here. . . ." His exasperation at his treatment is evident in his closing remark: "Really, this country is more fit to be dealt with sword in hand than by cajolery. . . ."[9]

De Feria's attempt to preserve what remnants of Spanish influence remained in England was further hindered by his failure to obtain lodging at Whitehall Palace. To be near the Queen's person, to have access to those of her court and Council were paramount if he was to produce any justifiable results for Philip. But accommodation in the Palace continued to elude him. "As I am so isolated from them, I am much embarrassed and confused to devise means of finding out what is going on, for truly they run from me as if I were the devil!" he confessed. "The best thing will be to get my foot into the Palace so as to speak oftener to the Queen." But rooms near her Majesty still remained unavailable. "I am trying to get a chamber in the Palace when the Queen goes to Whitehall," he wrote Philip, "although I am very much afraid that they will not give me one, but I have little chance of getting to talk to these people from the outside."[10]

Evidently, both de Feria and Philip had expected Elizabeth, "with neither men, money, leaders nor fortresses," to lean on Spain for protection against further French aggression. When de Feria continued to bombard his royal master with news of England's subtle defection from Catholic Spain—to its probable ultimate ruin, he was sure—Philip sent a proposal of marriage to the Queen of England in which he styled himself "a good and true brother who wishes her well." The proposal was not entirely unexpected. It would be to England's advantage, Philip assumed, to continue the alliance with Spain, and in the negotiations for a settlement with France at Cateau-Cambrésis, he had continued to support the English claim to Calais. Without the protection of Spain, he reasoned, Elizabeth might be forced to turn to France, and, as the Duke of Alva told him, "the French King having Scotland and Calais, will soon be master of England also!"[11] It is possible Philip's interest was as much personal as political; he had always had a lively regard for his young sister-in-law, and she, out of respect, diplomacy or gratitude, kept his portrait prominently displayed in her private chambers.

It took several months and four audiences with the Queen for the situation to be resolved. At first, with suitable modesty, Elizabeth told de Feria of her pleasure at Philip's interest, leading the ambassador to write the King confidently, "If she decides to marry out of the country, she will at once fix her eyes on your Majesty!"[12] Shortly before the coronation, a copy of Philip's instructions to de Feria, advising his minister's handling of the Queen, was read by his English wife, Jane Dormer, and her ladies. Possibly the ambassador had enlisted his wife's support, hoping she and her companions might influence Elizabeth. Eventually, a copy of a specific outline of Philip's letter was given to the Queen prior to de Feria's first visit. In the letter, Philip advised his ambassador, "You will, however, not propose any conditions until you see how the Queen is disposed towards the matter." Philip requested his minister "not to expose him to a refusal which would make his condescension ridiculous." Instead, he must try to determine Elizabeth's feelings before making a definite commitment. Philip noted that he himself was ready "to do anything which his duty to God demanded ... if he could maintain that realm [England] in the religion which, by God's help, had been restored to it." He ended the letter by stating, with just a tinge of the martyr, "I have decided to encounter the difficulty, to sacrifice my private inclination in the service of our Lord and to marry the Queen of England."[13]

Philip had given the proposal and what it would mean to him personally, as well as his country, much consideration. He had previously been married to one Queen of England for four years. In this present instance, however, there were many differences, the main one being that Elizabeth "had not been what she ought to be in religion and to marry with any but a Catholic will reflect upon my reputation," he wrote to de Feria. Elizabeth would have to apply in secret to the Pope "for absolution for her past sins and for the dispensation which will be required for the marriage," he insisted. Also, there was the matter of money; hospitality in England in the past had been a "serious expense," and not for a moment did he think Elizabeth would be as generous as Mary Tudor. And finally, the ticklish problem which had plagued his relationship with Mary. De Feria must make it clear, wrote Philip, that in any marriage between his King and Elizabeth, "she must not expect him to remain long with her." His own subjects would require his return to them "with indescribable anxiety" he insisted, and he would "have to return to Spain whether he left her pregnant or not."[14]

The Spanish King's instructions provided much amusement in Elizabeth's Privy Chamber. The queen was intelligent enough to know she must humor Philip. But her interest went no further. She did not wish to share the Crown with anyone—certainly not her sister's husband! She had no desire to repeat Mary's mistake which had cost England so dearly; she had no desire to marry a Catholic. Yet she must keep the Spanish King as a friend and, at the same time, tacitly apprise him and his minister that Spanish influence in England was at an end. The Treasury was empty; Calais had been lost. The indignation of her subjects at being involved in a conflict in which they had so little to gain had contributed to a moral decay that was eating at the very root of her people's integrity.

However, Elizabeth was equally aware that if she must marry, a Spanish alliance was the most splendid she could make. Even before Mary's death, many foreign emissaries had crowded the court, assessing the chances of their candidates with the heiress apparent, leading Cecil to remark in disgust that the court was "a great resort of wooers!" Even the French King, Henri II, had made overtures of friendship in a magnificent gift of jewels. He had received little in return but a remarkable example of the Queen's fluency in French and a willingness to prolong any negotiations ad infinitum. Even with this knowledge, de Feria continued the suit, unaware that Elizabeth had seen the substance of Philip's proposal. At a subsequent interview, she again spoke of the great honor that had been given her and of her esteem and affection for the Spanish King. But the situation bore all sorts of imponderables, she said, indicating a great willingness to discuss them at length with the puzzled de Feria, without giving him an outright rejection. The "imponderables" bore a mysterious similarity to Philip's own instructions to his ambassador. How, asked the Queen, could His Most Catholic Majesty marry his sister-in-law without a dispensation from the Pope? Especially when that sister-in-law *denied* the authority of the Pope? With a hint of restrained mirth, Elizabeth proudly declared herself a "heretic." And, with a more blatant smile, she told the astonished minister that Philip would be a bad husband. "He would come to England to marry me, then desert me and go home," she said almost petulantly.

At the Queen's criticism of his King, de Feria's bewilderment turned to rage, and in a great pique, he absented himself from the coronation ceremonies. He wrote Philip of the possibility of the Queen's marrying an English subject, and his opinion of Elizabeth's courtiers was blunt. "We can take those whom she might marry here and pick them to pieces one by one which will not require much rhetoric, for there is not a man amongst them worth anything, counting the married ones and all. . . !" He continued, "The more I reflect upon this business, the more clearly I see that all will turn upon the husband which this woman chooses. . . ." At the same time, he was realistic, saying, "I am afraid that one fine day we will find this woman married and I shall be the last man in the place to know anything about it!"[15]

At their next interview, de Feria adopted more aggressive tactics. He painted a dire picture of England's fate once it was cast loose from Spanish protection and at the mercy of France. Elizabeth told him haughtily that "her realm was not too poor, nor her people too faint-hearted, to defend their liberties at home and to protect their rights abroad. . . ."[16] She did not remind de Feria that Spain needed England's friendship as well, if only for the value of their various commercial treaties with the merchants of the Low Countries. Philip could be as good a protector as a friend as he might be as a husband, she said pointedly. And then, regaining her good humor, she brought the session to a close with the remark that marriage was a very serious step. She would have to speak with Parliament on the subject, yet she doubted her people would assent to her marriage with a foreigner.

De Feria waited more than a month for further word, complaining to Philip that Elizabeth was "too wedded to the people" and, lest Philip think he had been lax in producing definite results, wrote, somewhat apologetically, that the Queen seemed reluctant to define the extent of Spain's dominance in England. "I wonder they have not sent me crazy!" he wrote. His patience was nearing its end when the Queen summoned him to a final interview. The French peace negotiations had culminated in an agreement by which Calais would be retained by France for eight years, after which time it would either be returned or a 500,000-crown indemnity would be paid to England for it. As both countries recognized, anything could happen in eight years, but the agreement saved everyone's face, however much it may have lacked in good faith. With that knowledge, and aware the French King was sending an embassy to England to meet with her, Elizabeth was more decisive. She was careful not to give de Feria an outright refusal. She merely repeated what she had said before: she and Philip could accomplish as much together as brother and sister-in-law as they could as husband and wife. For de Feria, who had spent four months trying to keep Elizabeth "pleasant and in good humor" and convince her the future of England lay with Spain, the royal attitude was a bitter jolt.

When later, the French embassy arrived and the first great social occasion of the new Queen's reign commenced with a tremendous banquet in the gardens of Whitehall Palace, Elizabeth's political independence was proclaimed for all to see. Suspecting he had been somewhat exploited during the past fruitless weeks, de Feria wrote Philip. "What can be said . . . is only that this country, after thirty years of a government such as Your Majesty knows, has fallen into the hands of a woman who is a Daughter of the Devil . . . !"[17] Such was his disillusionment that he and his English wife left shortly afterward for Spain, lamenting, "we have lost a kingdom, body and soul!" Before his departure, de Feria had a final interview with the Queen. King Philip, knowing his chances in England lost, had agreed to marry Elizabeth of Valois, the eldest daughter of Henri II and Catherine de Medici of France. The Queen "affected one or two little sighs" and seemed pensive at the news. It did not help de Feria's disposition when she chided him further, saying she had never given Philip an outright refusal. And then, with a much heavier sigh, she said that the Spanish King could not have been very much in love with her since he could not wait four months for her to make up her mind.

Chapter Three

Elizabeth's circumstances, shortly after her coronation and the opening of her first Parliament, were such that the demands on her resources—mental, psychological and spiritual—were pitiless. The vital and challenging issues of religion, finance and the succession, coupled with her reluctance to assume any foreign "protection," led many foreigners to wager that in six months, political strife at home or aggression from abroad would oust her from the throne. Now that Philip was to marry a French princess, it was not inconceivable that Spain and France would move against England, but Elizabeth's policy was always to procrastinate, not anticipate. The Queen abhorred war, not only for the sufferings it entailed, but for the waste and spoliation that accompanied its grim path. She considered Calais a temporary sacrifice for a possible longer peace, recognizing the wisdom of Cecil's remark, "a realm gaineth more by a year's peace than by ten years of war."

Her first successes were marred by tragic parallels. A settlement with the Church had been concluded without friction or bloodshed, and she now had a vigorous Council, as loyal as one could reasonably expect. Yet famine and plague had decimated her realm to the great suffering of the people, for the previous harvest had been ruined by floods. The superstitious interpreted the catastrophe as the punishment of a wrathful God for the hideous sufferings of the Smithfield martyrs near the end of Mary's reign.

There still remained, also, the challenge of the nearly empty Exchequer. Under her father, taxation had been increased, the currency debased and huge foreign loans entailed at ruinous interest rates. Economy now became a byword with the court and Council as tax collectors, judges and sheriffs were dismissed. The Queen made it clear there would be no more foreign subsidies; instead, monies must be found to amortize the crippling loans. Parliament made pecuniary grants to Elizabeth in which, among others, it voted a subsidy of two shillings and eightpence in the pound on all movable goods and four shillings on the land. In this way, the Church and the nobility—the greatest landowners of England—bore the heavier burden of taxation which previously had crippled the lesser citizens such as the yeomen, the farmer and the minor gentry.[1] A clean hand now swept through the bureaucracy which had become rooted in the seventy-four years since her grandfather had occupied the throne and, within six months government expenditures had been reduced by some 60 percent compared with those of the last six months of Mary's reign. While her money problems were not completely solved, Sir Thomas Gresham, Elizabeth's financial genius, now resident at Antwerp, could joyfully write that English credit, so recently an object of derision abroad and anxiety at home, "was that of all other princes." To Elizabeth, whose sense of thrift was that of the canny grandfather who had first won the Crown for the Tudors, who had always managed her own income with prudence—even to the extent of selling produce from her own home garden—this was just as it should be. She now had one large household to manage, and the fact that it was a rich land inhabited by quarrelsome people did not lessen her enthusiasm. She told the French ambassador, "Although I am a woman, nevertheless, I am the daughter of predecessors who knew how to deserve this kingdom."[2]

Despite the recent peace negotiations, the French King, Henri II, had encouraged his sixteen-year-old daughter-in-law, Mary Stuart, daughter of the French Mary of Guise, Queen Regent of Scotland, to assume the arms of England and style herself and her husband, the Dauphin, "King and Queen of England and Ireland. . . ." Prior to her marriage, Mary Stuart had signed a secret treaty by which, in the event of her death without issue, Scotland was to become a French possession and all rights she had or might have to the Crown of England were to follow suit.[3] Though, mercifully, it was impossible to see where this assumption would eventually lead, it was not all arrogant pretense on the part of the French monarch. Mary Stuart, the child who had been spirited from Scotland to France for protection when she was nearly six years old, was the granddaughter of Margaret Tudor, a sister of Henry VIII, whose marriage to James IV of Scotland was to have been the means of uniting the two countries. The legality of her claim by hereditary descent was impeccable. Elizabeth, by contrast, had attained the throne through the will of her father, and despite Parliament's   proclamation   of   legality,   there   were   many—

Catholics especially—who did not believe the Crown could be bestowed by bequest and merely regarded Elizabeth as a usurper. If, for the moment at least, Henri did not intend to press Mary's claim, the threat remained. Elizabeth was aware of the danger and did not mince words when the Spanish ambassador predicted England's ruin because of the Queen's refusal to ally her country with Spain. "Who will bring this about?" she asked him curtly. "Your country or the King of France?"[4]

There was also, in the first year of Elizabeth's reign, a vigorously youthful movement stirring, and those who had grown to adulthood through a Protectorate and had seen a Spanish King married to their Queen now demanded recognition. Cecil was advised by some who could feel the quickening of the national pulse that older conservative civil servants be dismissed and replaced by "men of discretion . . . and younger in years." Should any militia be called, it was recommended that "young gentlemen who would earnestly favor Her Highness" be appointed as officers.[5] Thus began a social antagonism between those who had possessed wealth and power for generations and those who had lately acquired both, mainly from the looting of the monasteries. These "new men," as they were spitefully referred to, were scorned by the peasants as the chief enclosers of the common lands. The nobles despised them as the "creation of a new age," leading one to write, "The wealth of the meaner sort is the very fount of rebellion, the occasion of their insolence, of the contempt of the nobility and of the hatred they have conceived against them. It must be cured by keeping them in awe through the severity of justice and by providing as it were of some . . . channels to draw and suck from them their money by subtle and indirect means."[6] Given a choice—an alternative she disliked and rarely sought—the Queen would inevitably favor the "new men." In some ways, she owed her survival and her accession to them. Though she might feel little for them personally, she recognized their influences which would grow as she grew, and she sought their appeasement and advancement when she could. The older nobility had scorned and imperiled her in past years. There had been exceptions, of course, but for the most part, she owed them little except that respect for tradition peculiar to the English and particular to the monarchy.

In addition to the new, younger influences which many found so provoking, there was the Queen herself. For years, Elizabeth Tudor had existed near the throne in an aura of suspicion. Now, triumphantly, she was Queen, and the court had to adjust to the unique circumstances of a feminine sovereign—and an unmarried one at that. With the exception of her sister, who had remained unmarried only a few months, there was no precedent in England for a Queen who governed alone. Though there were those who scoffed at Elizabeth's capabilities, the majority of her subjects were content with a monarch who so openly adopted the maternal "I will watch over you, my dear people" tone. For the rest, the attitude was to wait and watch. Elizabeth might prove a genuine Lady Bountiful or revert to the scant comfort of her grandfather's court. Only time would tell.

And for Elizabeth, time was sufficient. Her very survival during her hazardous past had given her an unsurpassed talent in the use of time. It puzzled and confused many a courtier or Councillor when the Queen used the device of delay to avoid making decisions. She openly chose to overlook the subtle pressures which others attempted to exert on problems of state. Often this play for time was adopted when she wished to conceal her real feelings. Yet she later had small conscience for any unfortunate results of this delay, for her emotions were ever at the command of her intellect. That intellect was awesome—yet could be maddeningly inconsistent. The Queen's favorite motto was *Video et taceo,* "I see and I am silent." She later told the French ambassador, "It is the custom of evil mouths to say the worse, rather than the better," and later still, the same gentleman was honored by another royal bon mot: "There is no marvel in a woman learning to speak, but there would be in teaching her to hold her tongue."[7]

For those intimately concerned in royal affairs, therefore, the Queen of England was something of a novelty, and a novelty she would remain until her mettle was tested. To the more opportunistic, she represented Majesty which might be approached without interference. Previously, patronage had been dispensed for the most part with the knowledge and approval, and often at the instigation, of a husband and King. It was no secret that Mary had been fearful of making any decisions without Philip's advice. Now there was only Elizabeth.

One thing was certain, Elizabeth Tudor *enjoyed* the exercise of authority. She possessed sufficient perception to know she was momentarily unique—not only to her people, but also to her courtiers and Council. While relishing the thought that she, a woman, held the supreme position at court, she early indicated that she expected the same loyalty, devotion and deference as had previously been rendered a King. She soon made it clear she did not intend to charm as a woman, but to rule as a man, and more than once she was heard to say, "she intended only to maintain herself in her own realm as her father had done."[8] In this respect, she had many gifts, not the least being a tough, resilient young mind. One observer noted her proficiency in dealing with several situations at once. He said, "All her faculties were in motion, and every motion seemed a well-guided action. Her eyes were set upon one, her ear listened to another, her judgment ran upon a third, to a fourth she addressed her speech; her spirit seemed to be nowhere else."[9]

The tangible reality of a virginal young sovereign had its effect on the makeup of the court. Male attendants who had served King Philip were dismissed. The Gentlemen-Ushers, the Privy Chamber and Withdrawing Chamber attendants were relieved of their duties and replaced by ladies-in-waiting and maids-of-honor, the latter being unmarried young girls of good background whose families competed to place their children near the royal person. It was the duty of these feminine companions to accompany the Queen unless she ordered otherwise. Very soon after her coronation, Elizabeth became adept at using their presence to avoid embarrassing confrontations. When she wished, the Queen could always escape to her Privy Chamber, but in the Presence Chamber, where access was relatively easy, she was ultimately at the mercy of all who might gain her presence. During her father's reign, his favorite courtiers, place seekers, professional spies, ambassadors and foreign emissaries had thronged at will. Henry had liked people around him. So did Elizabeth—yet in moderation. At first, the very fact of the Queen's sex made many uncomfortable and unsure of their reception. But in the end, it was Elizabeth's own performance which put them at ease and daily established precedents where none had previously existed, for in the early months of Mary's reign, while she was still single, the "troubles" which attended her marriage had necessitated small audiences. In this, Elizabeth was fortunate, and her performance constantly surprised and pleased many a jaundiced veteran of the court or piqued those who had anticipated a royal toe stubbing owing to inexperience or lack of caution.

Instead, Elizabeth seemed to grasp out of thin air a knowledge of how to conduct herself. While she was "new to the cares of empire," she had spent years in the classroom, and her studies, particularly of history, had given her "experience and knowledge in . . . science beyond what can be acquired . . . by monarchs who have wasted their youthful energies in the pursuit of pleasures. . . ."[10] She had an intuitive understanding of the English people—their strength, tolerances, their prejudices and weaknesses. She knew how to distinguish between those who must be placated and those who might be denied, how to bestow favor with a glance or inspire discomfort with a frosty stare. She was aware that many around her were attempting, with beguiling sophistry, to win places of influence or shine in the royal aura. She found she could play the game as well as they—to their surprise and to her satisfaction.

From her earliest years, Elizabeth had courted popularity—first with the servants in the homes of her older sister, Mary, and later with the gentlemen at her brother's court. Always there had been a silent but strong competition from the child whose mother had died by the executioner's sword and whose father could barely tolerate the sight of her. Now fate and her own shrewdness had brought her the Crown, and of all those involved in the gift, she knew it was her subjects who were the most important. While she must win the affection and support of those who, of necessity, were around her daily, she must also continue to ensure that the tide of pride and love from the people which had surrounded her accession would continue to grow "to the advancement of her power and the defense of her realm." With an almost bankrupt Treasury, it was not going to be easy to present a picture of royal splendor, but what was the ultimate meaning of royalty and majesty if one must live like a menial? Too many of the Queen's years had been passed in conditions bordering on semi-poverty; she was done with them forever.

And yet she would not have been Elizabeth Tudor, with the memory of those perilously quiet years in the shadow of the throne, if she had not quickly recognized the risks inherent in her position. While many around her were friends, there were also the inevitable opportunists all too ready to take advantage of what they regarded as girlish inexperience. She must be constantly on guard lest she inadvertently help or befriend a more sophisticated enemy. She must be alert regarding her own deportment and in her assessment of the attitude of others. It was easy to flatter, to flirt, to offer excessive adulation to a Queen. The very homage normally paid a King became a more personal act, emphasized now by the fact that the monarch was a woman, and an attractive one at that. Elizabeth's attitude was not that of the self-effacing Mary. She possessed genuine wit and a magnificently disciplined intelligence, which had had little outlet for years. The flattery and adulation fell on very receptive ears. It would take time—and many bruised egos—before the court would realize their young monarch would accept their flattery, that she would, in fact, demand it. But having accepted their bounty, she would also make it clear there was no responsibility entailed on her. She would go her own way. While she listened respectfully to the advice of others, particularly Cecil, she ignored the pressure for partisanship, for making quick decisions she might later regret. Time had always been her ally; she could not change her tactics now.

It would take time too before even those closest to the Queen could acknowledge her competence and trust those decisions. Even Cecil was not wholly confident in the beginning where his royal mistress was concerned, for he was once heard berating an ambassadorial messenger for discussing with the Queen "a matter of such weight, being too much for a woman's knowledge."

One problem Elizabeth acknowledged immediately, for she recognized the vital importance of an heir; if she had thought to evade the question of the succession, her ministers soon enlightened her. Parliament was anxious to see its sovereign betrothed. Their mood was echoed in the words of the Queen's uncle Lord William Howard, who said, "Whomsoever she shall take, we will have him and serve him to the death. . . ." Then, remembering the affection-starved childhood of the niece whom, on at least one occasion, he had been forced to bring to what was assumed to be a strict imprisonment, if not worse, he said gruffly, ". . . and the better if he make much of her. . . ."[11] Therefore, it was not unexpected when the Speaker of the Commons, Sir Thomas Gargrave, begged an audience in which he might present the Commons' petition for the Queen to wed. Elizabeth received him in the great Gallery at Whitehall Palace. Gargrave referred to the marriage issue as of "vital importance to the realm" and entreated the Queen to marry "that they might have royal issue to reign over them."

Knowing the interest in the succession which occupied the minds of her countrymen, court and Council, Elizabeth listened patiently to the petitioner. She thanked her subjects "for their thought." But it was evident she had little enthusiasm for the petition and was merely showing royal good manners. She was not about to grasp marriage as eagerly as Mary had, with small profit to herself and disaster to the nation! The heady excitement of flirtation, flattery and courtship, combined with her own royal power, was too precious a reward after all those terrifying years. For the moment, she would make no decision she might later rue. While Elizabeth recognized the importance of a marital alliance, she had only just begun to realize that the subject, with its tremendous political and diplomatic implications, might be almost as satisfying as marriage itself. It was a game in which she held all the valuable cards and was, herself, the greatly desired and sought-after prize. It was a game she was not willing to end too soon.

However, she must placate the Commons. While exhibiting proper appreciation, she said she had long ago decided to remain unwed. "As a servitor of God, I chose this kind of life in which I do yet live, as a life most acceptable to Him wherein I thought I could best serve Him," she added. She frankly admitted the pressure to wed that Mary and Philip had brought to bear on her during their reign. She said the displeasure of her sister and the Spanish King "was constantly before mine eyes." She knew then that only a marriage would redeem her, yet she had, "with God's help," held out. She had remained "in this virgin's estate wherein you see me."

There was a silence in the vast Gallery. The intimacy of the Queen's allusion to her dangerous years in the shadow of Philip and Mary's power embarrassed many who had taken part in her intimidation. Elizabeth sensed this and seemed in little hurry to reassure them. At the same time, she knew she must convince them that hers was no girlish display of modesty, of coyly feminine timidity. She thanked them again for their concern and, drawing the coronation ring from her finger, held it high so all might see.

"Behold the pledge of this my wedlock," she exclaimed. "When I received this ring, I solemnly bound myself in marriage to this realm. Do not upbraid me with miserable lack of children—for every one of you . . . are children and kinsmen to me!" Elizabeth said that if she ever entered on any other course of life, she would "take such a husband as near may be, as will have a great care of the Common-wealth as myself."[12] She continued, "It would be quite sufficient for the memorial of my name and for my glory, if when I died, an inscription were engraved on a marble tomb saying 'Here lieth Elizabeth, which reigned a virgin and died a virgin.' "

Then, returning the ring to her finger, she signified the audience was at an end, saying consolingly, "I take your coming to me in good part and give you, therefore, my hearty thanks." With just a hint of laughter, she ended, ". . . my hearty thanks for your good will and good meaning—more than your message!"[13]

As the assembled throng filed slowly from the Gallery, there were undoubtedly a few who viewed Elizabeth's attitude as fainthearted and modest—an attitude she would be certain to change with any ultimate hardheaded appraisal of her worth in the European marriage mart. Her speech to the Commons, which others regarded as an empty face-saving gesture, was, however, an honest revelation of her most intimate feelings—although it is possible that even she herself did not then realize the depth of her aversion to sharing the Crown. Marriage as a possibility was a game the last Tudor sovereign would enjoy for years to come. Marriage as a *fait accompli* she would spend those same years evading. There was infinitely more pleasure in the pursuit, in Elizabeth's mind, than there would be in any consummation. As long as there was such pursuit, she had all the advantages. "I have let time pass," she would later say, "which I generally find helps more than reasoning."[14]

Elizabeth's aversion to marriage did not indicate any lack of interest in the opposite sex. It was not likely that a daughter of the sensual Henry VIII and the ambitiously capricious Anne Boleyn, who had adequately gauged her worth in the marriage market for six years before she wed Henry, was incapable of desire or passion. Yet the circumstances of her upbringing had offered little or no outlet for any normal adolescent desires. In her earlier years, Elizabeth had received much affection from Lady Margaret Bryan and a succession of govern-esses, resulting finally in the appointment of her own Katherine Ashley. Ashley had given her an unswerving devotion and shared Elizabeth's own time of trial with a period of imprisonment in the Tower. During her very young years, when their father was alive, her sister, Mary, had been almost a mother, visiting Elizabeth whenever she could. On leaving, she had always left a few coins for the child whose father was not always prompt in providing for her household's expenditures. Later, when permitted by their brother's Council to visit Elizabeth, she had brought small gifts such as might delight a young girl—lengths of cloth for a new dress, trinkets or games. Those were the years of royal abandonment as Henry married to beget a son, to satisfy a lust or to placate a political need. The great gulf between Elizabeth and Mary Tudor had not opened until the years when their brother, Edward, was on the throne, when Elizabeth was fourteen and Mary over thirty. Then a subtle rivalry for the boy's affection had begun. Factions within the court and Council did not hesitate to pressure the young King for some sign of favoritism which must result inevitably in the eclipse of one sister. Elizabeth had undoubtedly emerged the vic-tor in that instance, concurring with her brother's religious policies, while Mary obstinately refused to give up the Mass. Mary had many difficult encounters with the boy-King, his Councillors and church-men, while Elizabeth was gaining admiration for her quiet obedience, her modest dress and demeanor and, as a result, enjoyed the privilege of court visits so the King might see his "Sweet sister Temperance."

It was her father's last marriage that had provided a stepmother who had sought and succeeded in giving to all of Henry's children a satisfying maternal love. Elizabeth had had great affection for old Anne of Cleves and often visited her at the riverside Palace of Rich-mond, which had been one of the gifts a grateful King had presented for Anne's enthusiastic cooperation in the matter of a divorce. But Katherine Parr had come on the scene when Elizabeth was not quite ten and, in a matter of months, she had reunited all the royal children, Mary, Edward and Elizabeth, under one roof and for the first time, the isolation which is often the lot of royalty faded. At Whitehall and other royal dwellings, Katherine Parr lavished interest and affection on the three children, only one of whom could remember their own mother to any great extent. Katherine had been married twice before to older men and had remained childless. Now, as wife to an aging and sick monarch, she was not likely to become a mother, and the presence of his children had, undoubtedly, been one of the happier aspects of her Queenship. There had been long, worry-free summer days in Katherine's dower house in Chelsea, an imposing, turreted red-brick manor overlooking gardens which ran down to the Thames.* Originally, it had been built as a royal nursery for Henry's offspring, for it was near enough to Whitehall or Westminster to be convenient, but not near enough to be a burden. There Elizabeth had romped with Mary and Edward, and for one magical summer, after Henry's death, the ill-fated little Lady Jane Grey had joined them.

And then, through her own foolishness and naïveté, Elizabeth had almost lost everything. Two years after Henry died, when she was barely fifteen, she had risked her heart and, as a result, her life. It had begun innocently enough with the advances of Thomas Seymour, the brother of Jane Seymour, young Edward's mother. As Lord High Admiral of England, Seymour had cut a large swath through the court of the boy-King. But envy of his brother, Edward Seymour, the Protector of all England, and greed for more of the perquisites and power both had acquired during their sister's brief Queenship had eaten at Thomas' mind and heart. It festered until he, too, devised a way of obtaining more prestige and what he considered equal authority. In a letter pledging undying love and fidelity, he had asked for Elizabeth's hand, only to be told somewhat demurely that it was too soon after her father's death for her to consider marriage. His subsequent action had shocked Elizabeth, the court and country. Tall, with a lush black beard and bold hazel eyes, Thomas Seymour, Lord Sudeley, instead married the dainty Katherine Parr, the Queen Dowager, and he married her so quickly after Henry's death as to be severely censured. Not only for lack of good taste and reasons of state, but if a child had been born, its parentage might have been challenged. It mattered little to the brilliantly undisciplined Seymour, whose notable proficiency in swearing, drinking and hard living was matched by undoubted courage, great wit and an altogether devastating charm which led even

*Henry VIII's old Manor House "in the comfortable air of Chelsey" was located near Chelsea Old Church and the splendid dwelling of Sir Thomas More which, with its orchards and grounds, covered the area of present-day Beaufort Street. The Manor House was located in the area bounded by today's Lawrence Street, Manor Street and Cheyne Walk.

a detractor to say he was "fierce in courage, courtly in fashion, in personage stately, in voice magnificent, but somewhat empty in matter."[15] Both Seymours, despite their lofty stations, were considered *parvenus* by the older nobility, for until their sister's marriage to Henry, the family had been only minor country gentry.

Now Thomas was wed to an ex-Queen who adored him. In the old manor house at Chelsea, Katherine Parr began a year of radiant happiness for a woman who had had three husbands, yet had been denied happiness with any of them, even though one had been a King. She loved Thomas Seymour with all the pent-up romance that was part of her being. She became pregnant almost immediately and, being well into her thirties and naturally frail, had taken to her bed as a precaution and for ease of sickness. In the meantime, her husband was visiting the chambers of the not quite fifteen-year-old Princess Elizabeth, opening the door in the morning with his own key and awakening the sleeping young girl, tickling her and otherwise indulging in careless horseplay that brought an outraged Ashley quickly to the chamber to still the tittering of Elizabeth's companions, who slept in the next room. The game went on, however, despite Ashley's protests and threats to go to Thomas' wife. Disregarding the fearful warnings of her governess, Elizabeth did not deter the Admiral; indeed, she seemed to encourage him. She would anticipate Thomas' coming in the morning and burrow more deeply under the covers so he must try and get her out. Or else, perversely, she would be up and dressed when he came in. Hiding his disappointment, he would slap her familiarly on the buttocks and then barge into the room next door, enjoying the shrieks of maidenly modesty which his appearance in his robe and slippers caused in those virginal chambers.

It had been little more than a great romp, of doubtful taste and questionable implications, as later events were to show. But it had piqued Elizabeth's curiosity as it would the curiosity of any sheltered and unsophisticated adolescent when someone as flamboyantly elegant as Thomas Seymour chose *her* for his abandoned games. Elizabeth's contacts with the opposite sex had been confined to her schoolmaster, the gentlemen of her household, older members of the court or her younger brother. There were no boys her own age in Katherine's household in Chelsea who would dare approach the sister of the reigning monarch. Since her father's death, she had been allowed to see her younger brother only at the Council's pleasure but never long enough to form any association with those at his court who might have been more desirable. Her marriage had been a subject of constant debate by the Protector and his Council, yet she had never before indulged in the harmless flirtations which others, not restricted by royal blood, would have experienced.

Elizabeth found the stimulation of Thomas' attention a heady affair, for it lent an aura of the forbidden to her days. Her conscience was not bothered, for she had no intention of encouraging him further. Everything had followed in a normal progression until one day, in his usual impetuous fashion, he had openly attempted to embrace her. His timing was unfortunate, for as Elizabeth struggled in his arms, the Queen Dowager, venturing from her sickbed, walked into the room. A lively scene followed, with Elizabeth being sent from the room and, ultimately in disgrace, from the lovely old Thames-side manor home. Before she left, she and Katherine Parr effected a reconciliation. The gesture caused Elizabeth to examine her conscience more closely and write her stepmother she was "replete with sorrow to depart from Your Highness." She meant every word, for she realized too late that she had, by acquiescence, encouraged Thomas in his provocative pranks. Her regret at being sent from her comfortable home and her step-mother was certainly sincere when she wrote the Queen Dowager: "what more can I say than 'thank God' for providing such friends for me."[16]

Her discouragement and sadness were more than compounded by the death of Katherine Parr after the birth of a daughter, two days before Elizabeth's fifteenth birthday. In the month following his wife's death, Thomas Seymour, with his usual brash and thoughtless arrogance, had conspired to overthrow his brother, the Protector, by encouraging active public revolt and poisoning the mind of young Edward against his uncle. He was arrested and imprisoned in the Tower, where thirty-five charges were brought against him, among them his desire to wed the Princess Elizabeth "to the danger of the King's Majesty's person and the peace of the State. . . ." He was con-demned in March, 1549, and later was beheaded on the scaffold outside on Tower Hill. In the sole of his shoe, he had left letters for Mary and Elizabeth Tudor urging further conspiracy against the Protector. Mary had had little connection with Seymour and ultimate-ly dispelled any suspicion. However, for months, rumors had been recurring from Chelsea of Thomas' interest in old Henry's redheaded daughter, and there were many who were eager to believe the worst.

Within weeks of Seymour's arrest, Elizabeth's household had been broken up, her servants dismissed and Thomas Parry, her Cofferer, and Katherine Ashley, her governess, had gone to the Tower. Katherine Parr was gone. Only then had Elizabeth realized the extent of her danger. Her servants were imprisoned, and she herself was held in restraint at Hatfield under the remorseless questioning of Sir Robert Tyrwhitt.

At first, it had been something of a game of wits between her and Tyrwhitt, but as the weeks wore on and especially after Thomas' death, every bit of her talent for dissimulation was brought into use. The continual interrogation only increased tension in the household, and Elizabeth found it difficult to sleep. Eventually, she became shaken and fearful, as no help or relief came from outside. She was refused access to her brother, and during the following weeks the battle of wits between captor and captive continued, as Elizabeth—exercising every ounce of caution—held out. Nothing could break her constant assertion that there had been nothing between her and Seymour.

At last the Council, uncomfortable with the dawning awareness that a teen-age girl was besting them at their own game, attempted one last device to break her will. They informed her that rumors were abroad that she was about to bear Thomas Seymour's child. Perhaps they thought the shameful accusation would shatter Elizabeth's spirit. Instead, outraged, she derided them by letter for their lack of goodwill. She defended her imprisoned servants and strongly recommended that if indeed such accusations were prevailing, she be released from detention to alleviate those "shameful slanders" and come to court "that I may show myself there as I am." The letter was authoritative and explicit for one so young.

With one stroke, Elizabeth repudiated their charges and challenged their ruse, once and for all. But she at last realized the extent of the danger she now faced. When she was told of Seymour's death, of the letter for her in his shoe, Tyrwhitt and others watched her closely. But she did not falter. Realizing how much depended on her performance, she merely shrugged her shoulders and replied noncommittally, "This day died a man of much wit—and very little judgment."

With that, she went into her chamber, and there, in a darkened room, utterly alone, she left adolescence behind. It was not easy, but Elizabeth faced up to herself unsparingly. She, *a princess,* whose mother had been executed for adultery, had foolishly—how foolishly!—allowed herself to be compromised.

For a man's smile and attention, she had endangered her heritage. For a few hours of dubious frivolity which had stricken her stepmother and lost her a reputation, she had risked not only her heart but her life. Elizabeth had been as attracted to Thomas Seymour as a good many had to one of such great charm, looks and wit. Under other circumstances, they might indeed have made a happy pair and enjoyed a life together. All this she realized and accepted, but in those nightmare weeks in her chamber, as she lost appetite and weight, Elizabeth endured the depths of self-abasement and degradation. Her refusal to eat, to emerge for exercise, compounded by fits of weeping, bespoke the breakdown of an overburdened nervous system. She was ill for months. Her studies—long a refuge—were abandoned, and at last her condition became a matter of concern to the Protector and Council. She knew she had outwitted them all, yet the knowledge of how close she had come to sharing Thomas' fate could still terrify her. How dangerous any association with the Crown could be! She had only to look back over the years to realize the extent of the danger she had encouraged. Just in her own lifetime, there had been so many tragedies which had claimed those nearest the Crown. First, her own mother. Then her stepmother, Katherine Howard. Now Thomas was gone.

Not only had she endangered her own life, but she had almost lost her right of succession. She had received no word from her brother. The Protector had seen to that and, with almost unlimited power which could sanction his own brother's death, it was not inconceivable that, despite her father's will, something might be devised to eliminate her from the succession. During those months of solitude the shocked Princess Elizabeth, frightened and ill, took careful assessment. The stress she had known from childhood—of her mother's fate, her father's abandonment and now an attempted seduction by a stepuncle—left a stricken and emotionally depleted young girl. When she emerged from her chambers, she bore little resemblance to the thoughtless, naïve adolescent who had entered. She was nearly sixteen, yet she was no longer a child, but an adult who had learned a hard lesson. She had not spared herself, and she had few illusions concerning those in authority around her. Power was the answer. Power was the means of security, a guarantee of authority and the end hope of all who had once been defenseless and vulnerable. She would never again endanger her chance of attaining and exercising the kind of power which would make her absolutely supreme. There was not a man in the world—or a marriage so splendid—that was worth the loss of the royal power without which her own life would have little meaning. Her next few years were spent in disentangling herself from any of the marriages which were proposed, in safeguarding her own reputation, despite the plots and intrigues during her sister's reign which had utilized her as a focal point. In all that time, as she had progressed from a nubile, sensitive adolescent into a composed and somewhat aloof young woman, she had risked no male association. There had been royal suitors, of course, and once she had been reinstated in the good graces of Queen Mary, there had been opportunities for flirtation at court.

But no foreign suitor, or even those at hand, had succeeded. Elizabeth had learned her lesson well. To the end of her life, she never forgot Thomas Seymour—perhaps not so much for his charm and persuasive personality as for the lesson he had taught her. He had, unwittingly to be sure, taught her to survive and win. And once she had survived and won, the Crown would be the most important thing in her life. Any man would always have to take second place.

The Virgin

I am attracted to perpetual spinsterhood
not by prejudice, but rather by natural
inclination. I call the wedding ring,
the 'yoke ring.'

Chapter Four

Few, however, would have guessed from the Queen's attitude to the men around her, of her inner distaste for the married state. The seed of insecurity which had been placed in a young consciousness had germinated through the years of imprisonment and neglect, of fear and shame. Out of those years of struggle, a remarkable personality had evolved which would prove an enigma to many. For anyone watching Elizabeth Tudor at the court of England in the early summer of 1559, a mere six months after her coronation, would have agreed that never was a young woman more ready for marriage and children, that never had an attractive sovereign more desired and needed the closeness of a family relationship and the physical love and spiritual support of a husband and friend. She was undeniably receptive and flatteringly amiable to the gentlemen of her court, as well as to the foreign ambassadors who came, hat in hand, to offer the heart and homage of their royal masters.

And there were many who aspired to that honor. In the past, there had been suitors from France, Portugal, Scotland, Spain, Denmark and Italy. To these were now added several stalwarts who hid ambition and greed under the guise of love as they viewed the young maiden Queen who they felt so desperately needed the guidance and companionship only a husband and King could provide. Their advent coincided with the earnest determination of her ministers to compel her to wed. "The Council are in an agony to have her married to someone!" wrote the Bishop of Aquila, Alvarez de Quadra, the new Spanish ambassador, to his home court. Every suitor, royal or otherwise, interested the Queen. She was unfailingly attentive to the advice of her Councillors and the foreign emissaries as they extolled the virtues of their candidates. She listened raptly to the blandishments of the court gentlemen who followed her with lovesick eyes. One was Sir William Pickering, a "gentleman of moderate fortune, but comely person" who had fled from England in Queen Mary's reign for his share in the Wyatt rebellion. Pickering was a thirty-six-year-old nobleman of undeniable physical attractions which he had dispensed freely among the court ladies, both wed and unwed, corroborating Bishop John Jewel's pronouncement that he was "highly gifted as to personal qualities." When Sir William returned from duty in Germany and France in May, Elizabeth appeared much taken with him. He was a new face at court and she showed him singular favor and spent much time with him, ultimately giving him lodgings at Greenwich Palace. The royal attention went to Pickering's head to the extent that he spent a small fortune on splendid new clothes and swaggered through the court to the ill-concealed scorn of the older noblemen.

Another suitor was Henry Fitzalan, the Earl of Arundel, who had befriended Elizabeth in the years when a friend was a rarity in her life. When she was first imprisoned in the Tower, he had carried a letter to Queen Mary, begging an audience. Elizabeth had delayed in writing long enough to miss the tide and thus had awaited throughout an anxious night while Arundel saw the Queen. It had been fruitless, but ever afterward, Elizabeth had shown the gentle and not too bright Earl much attention. Such was his enthusiasm that he, too, began to dream of the impossible. Arundel, whom the Spanish ambassador called "a flighty man of small ability," was forty-seven years old, a widower with two married daughters, one of whom was the Duchess of Norfolk. Yet, said the ambassador, he came to court "with a silver wand a yard long . . . looking very smart and clean and they say he carries his thoughts very high!" Arundel borrowed heavily from Italian bankers, "in order that he might present himself before the Queen in an ostentatious manner with fine clothing and lavish expensive gifts upon her ladies."[1] The Queen honored Arundel with a visit to his Palace of Nonsuch in Surrey,[2] which he had leased from Queen Mary. Here Elizabeth was feted with all the lavish ingenuity of masques, a banquet which lasted until three in the morning and entertainment which was provided by the choir of St. Paul's School. Arundel's performance, on high hopes and borrowed money, was the subject of much amusement. He and Pickering soon met head on when Sir William presented himself at the entrance to the Queen's apartments. The Earl restrained him and told him he must await the Queen in the Presence Chamber, that he well knew the Privy Chamber was for peers only. Pickering sneeringly agreed, said he was well aware of the rule and called Arundel an "impudent discourteous knave, which the Earl heard and went out without answering a word, leaving the other to enter."[3] Elizabeth was not above playing one off against the other, all the while greatly enjoying the game, leading a bewildered Cecil to claim, "I would to God her Majesty had one and the rest honorably satisfied!"[4]

The point which eluded Secretary Cecil, the foreign ambassadors and such as Pickering and Arundel was that to Elizabeth it was all a game. She was the prize "for which many great ones did strive," and the game itself was one in which Elizabeth scrupulously observed certain rules. She behaved honorably, flirting a little here and there, as did all the court ladies, but always keeping her suitors guessing—as well as at arm's length. She made no commitments. If they took a smile, a warm glance, the gift of lodgings or some small token as encouragement, the onus of their behavior was upon themselves, not upon her. Elizabeth had her father's compulsion (and talent) for self-vindication, and her past experience had taught her "to bury her emotions beyond the reach of the politicians."[5] There was in the Queen, also, a great deal of Anne Boleyn's enjoyment of the pursuit, of a frivolous, headstrong and willful determination to behave as she chose, as long as the consequences were ones to which she felt equal. Since her heart was not involved, she could play the lover with impunity, for there was little to fear from any of the royal candidates who had been proposed. She must treat their ambassadors honorably and keep their interest alive, while giving little other than a royal congeniality in return. It greatly flattered her vanity—as well as strengthened her diplomatic policy—to keep everyone guessing. In the meantime, the thirsty soul that relished the extravagant compliments and the greedy woman who hungered for admiration enjoyed every move in the game. As for such as Pickering and Arundel, they were merely the first in a long line of courtiers who would spend fortunes —and ruin their nerves and digestions—for the privilege of basking in the aura of royal favor.

Within her first six months on the throne, therefore, the self-discipline Elizabeth had imposed on herself in the ten years since the death of Thomas Seymour was relaxed. The freedom the Crown had brought was compensation for the many years she had been denied male companionship. Now the court was treated to the at times embarrassing spectacle of a young woman, avid for attention and homage, pursuing constant adulation. If the royal dignity became slightly tarnished in the process, it worried her little, nor did it surprise the older element of the court, who were prepared, for the most part, to condone the behavior of one as frisky as a foal, released at long last to the fresh air of freedom after a long confinement. Only her uncle, the shrewd Lord William Howard, who knew Elizabeth better than most, was inclined to scoff. He remembered only too well the years of the Queen's affection-starved childhood, of slight and neglect. At rumors that she might soon select a favorite, or if a court gallant swaggered too broadly after days of Elizabeth's companionship, or the prospect of one foreign suitor seemed to occupy more of her attention than another, Howard was not impressed. Instead, he was frank to say, "She shall never be moved by any. . . ."

Despite the Council's determination that the Queen should wed and the continual presence of foreign ambassadors, Howard was partly correct. Elizabeth was not moved, and she would not be pressured, but she could be most cooperative. Though, mercifully, her Councillors were spared the knowledge, the Queen considered the satisfying marriage game as merely in its infancy, and as long as she delayed in her duty of providing a small redheaded Tudor heir, the coquetry and flirtation might be prolonged indefinitely. The discussion of her personal qualities, the grandeur of her sovereignty, all part and parcel of the diplomatic negotiations, were heady stimulants, as well as a political device, a technique Elizabeth would ultimately raise to an art. She was keenly interested in those suitors who appeared before her in person, for she had been heard to say more than once "she would rather be a nun than marry a man she did not know, on the faith of portrait painters!"[6]

One who braved the royal observation was Adolphus, Duke of Holstein, son of the King of Denmark. Elizabeth was impressed by the handsome young man. She created him a Knight of the Garter, gave him a life pension and expensive gifts—then sent him back to his northern country as soon as possible. Unable to believe her refusal was permanent, Adolphus pursued his passion from Germany, receiving Elizabeth's reply that "she must sing the same song." Prince John, son of the King of Sweden, came to plead for his brother, Prince Eric. He immediately incurred the wrath of de Quadra, who was pressing his own candidate, the Archduke Charles of Austria, and relations between the two became so strained "that the Queen is careful that they should not meet in the palace to avoid their slashing each other in her presence." Prince John found himself so dazzled by the English Queen that he failed to recount the virtues of his brother but offered, instead, his own person for her consideration. John was recalled to face the rage of his brother, who sent an ambassador with tapestries and furs to plead his case, saying he would come in person "to lay his heart at her feet." Elizabeth questioned the ambassador, who, "to demonstrate his King's love . . . wore upon his gown a crimson velvet heart pierced by an arrow."[7] She asked him whether his master would leave his kingdom to marry her, for she could assure him, she said, "she would not leave hers to be the monarch of the world. . . ." Eric was also prepared to be tolerant with religion and said, "as far as he is concerned, every man may believe what he pleased," a fact which appalled de Quadra, who was as much aghast "at the expression of such monstrous views as at the fact that a man could be found to hold them."[8] Bishop Jewel favored Prince Eric, thinking him the most sincere, "for he promises mountains of silver in case of success." As an afterthought, the Bishop added that "the lady, however, is probably thinking of an alliance nearer home."

The good Bishop was not the first to comment on Elizabeth's pronounced preference for a suitor nearby. The departing de Feria had written on April 18, "During the last few days, Lord Robert has come so much into favor that he does whatever he pleases with affairs and it is even said that Her Majesty visits him in his chamber day and night. People talk of this so freely that they go so far as to say that his wife has a malady in one of her breasts and the Queen is only waiting for her to die to marry Lord Robert." Some indication of the ambassador's opinion of the suitor may be seen in his comment: "I can assure Your Majesty that matters have reached such a pass that I have been brought to consider whether it would not be well to approach Lord Robert on Your Majesty's behalf, promising him your help and favor and coming to terms with him."[9]

The gentleman who evoked these remarkable words was Lord Robert Dudley, Elizabeth's childhood friend. He was one of the eight sons and five daughters born to John and Jane Dudley, a family which had risen with Henry VII, fallen with Henry VIII, struggled to prominence again under Edward VI, only to be ruined with the accession of Mary Tudor. Henry VII had employed Edmund Dudley, Robert's lawyer grandfather, as an unscrupulously shady official who "exhumed obsolete crimes and antique flaws in land titles, packed juries and bribed or browbeat judges . . . ,"[10] thereby contriving to transfer an impressive quantity of private property into the Crown coffers. He, with his partner, Richard Empson, had an enviable talent for putting "hateful business into good language." Through an impressive marriage with Elizabeth Grey, daughter of the Viscount Lisle, Edmund Dudley had received control of an extensive estate, and his sons were privileged to claim kinship with old and respected nobility such as the Beauchamps, Nevilles and Talbots. When Henry VIII ascended the throne at eighteen, the public, who had suffered extensively from Dudley and Empson's extortionist methods, clamored for their blood, and young Henry, effectively gauging their hatred for the hapless men who now lacked the former King's protection, willingly complied by sending them, on August 2, 1510, to the scaffold. The families were stripped of their share of the world's goods, and their names were attainted.

The eight-year-old son, John, had grown to manhood with the disgrace of his father's execution before him. By a scrupulous attention to protocol and a patience which must have been a constant frustration, he set about regaining the family's lost honor and fortunes. He served with Henry VIII's forces in France, where he was knighted for conspicuous gallantry. Nine years later he was a close associate of the young King, the very man who had ordered his father's execution. As John Dudley's family grew in size so did the honors which advanced him in royal favor. When the nine-year-old Mary Tudor was sent to Ludlow, it was John Dudley who served in her household and later as Warden of the Scottish Marches. As Lord Lisle, he was appointed Deputy Governor at Calais. He was one of the executors of Henry's will and effectively hid his bitter resentment of Edward Seymour, the boy-King's uncle, who had immediately proclaimed himself Protector of all England. Dudley had given grudging acquiescence to Seymour's pretentions—the title of the Earl of Warwick and Great Chamberlain of all England helped alleviate his envy—for there was little else he could do at the time. But the ruthless ambition which had started him on his upward climb through many minor court positions now had a chance of outright release. For the first time in years, John Dudley could see no limit to what his own ruthlessness and cleverness might bring him and his family.

His was the mastermind behind the Protector's eventual downfall, for he had deliberately poisoned the mind of young Edward against his uncle. The boy had learned to fear the conscienceless Dudley, who, by lies and insinuations, successfully hounded the Protector to the scaffold. Once the unfortunate man was dead, Dudley abandoned all pretensions of selfless service. He, the true son of an extortionist father, had reclaimed the Dudley fortunes with a vengeance. He had created himself the Duke of Northumberland and, as such, became so overbearing, lordly and arrogant that he incurred the loathing of his fellow Councillors, who nevertheless feared him. In a country and an era where crime near the throne was not uncommon and "as an example of the power of sheer unscrupulous genius to get on without popularity, he stands alone in English history."[11]

Upon Edward's death in July, 1554, John Dudley had fought Mary Tudor's accession with all the force and skill of the professional soldier, for he now had a chance to put one of his own blood on the throne of

England. He had married his weak young son, Guildford, to Lady Jane Grey, a grandniece of Henry VIII. And then he had browbeaten a dying Edward into designating Jane the rightful heiress, thus eliminating Mary and Elizabeth from the succession. He had sent his other son, Robert, into Norfolk to apprehend Mary, who was then proceeding to court to comfort her sick brother. But Mary was warned and fled to Kenninghall and then into the vast reaches of Framlingham Castle, successfully eluding Dudley and the certain imprisonment or possible death which awaited her in London. Within weeks the country rose for Mary. The Councillors who had aided Dudley in his enterprise shamelessly abandoned him—only too anxious to absolve themselves as soon as possible. Shortly afterward Mary and Elizabeth rode triumphantly into the City, and John Dudley was beheaded on Tower Hill for his treasonous activity. Jane Grey, though condemned, was kept in comfortable restraint within the Tower, almost certain of ultimate release once the furor died down. Six months later a rebellion led by Thomas Wyatt, which resulted in hand-to-hand combat in the Palace precincts as he and his band of followers struggled to take possession of the City, pointed to the harsh reality of the Queen's ridding herself of any claimant to the throne, even one as innocent as Jane. Mary's advisers were firm in demanding Jane's death, and the Spanish ambassador was insistent that Mary's marriage to Philip would not take place while any threat to the Crown remained alive. The Queen had little recourse other than to sanction Jane's beheading.

Thus did the Dudley ambition claim yet another innocent victim. Though Wyatt exonerated Elizabeth on the scaffold, the suspicion also lingered over the head of the Queen's pretty redheaded sister, and in early March she was summoned to court to explain herself. She had refused to come voluntarily, protesting great illness, which only increased Mary's suspicions. Finally, she was brought under guard only to endure the refusal of her sister to see her until she had confessed her part in the rebellion. Elizabeth obstinately maintained her innocence and thereby incurred an imprisonment which had lasted almost two years before Mary, urged on by her husband Philip, had agreed to a reconciliation.

It was during her imprisonment in the Tower that Elizabeth's friendship with Robert Dudley had revived. They had been born on the same day, September 7, 1533,* and had known each other from

---

*Though later historians give June 24, 1532, as Robert Dudley's birthday, there is no available written evidence to refute the *earlier* historian Camden's assertion that Dudley was indeed born the same day as Elizabeth.[12]

childhood. As John Dudley had grown in power, his children had associated with the royal children, and it is even possible that Elizabeth and Robert shared a classroom. Their mutual imprisonment cemented a relationship of many years' standing, which deepened in Mary's reign when, in decided disfavor, Robert "did sell a good piece of his land to aid her . . . ."[13] a gesture the friendless Elizabeth never forgot.

At the time of their reunion in the Tower, Robert was a married man. On June 4, 1550, some three months before his seventeenth birthday and before his father had reached his ultimate high position at court, Robert Dudley had married Amy Robsart in a ceremony at the royal Palace of Sheen, attended by Edward and the entire court. Amy Robsart was the only legitimate child of a Norfolk squire, Sir John Robsart of Siderstern. She was heiress to considerable property, an attractive inducement to a family as acquisitive as the Dudleys. Robert was well satisfied with Amy, for he coveted the somewhat simple and naïve young lady whose innocence and charm were a refreshing change from the more sophisticated ladies of the court with whom Robert had already demonstrated an ample willingness to dally. Amy was "fair, gentle and trusting," though ill educated in comparison with her contemporaries in London or at the court. What Amy lacked in formal education, however, was more than compensated for in a sweet personality, a dainty figure, feminine and soft, a country belle in every sense of the word. Later her detractors would speak of her as an uncouth provincial not far removed from the dimwitted; their assumptions are almost certainly untrue. For a family recouping its lost fortunes, John Dudley had attempted to wed each son well; he would not have allowed Robert to wed an ungainly girl who would discredit him at court. Nor would Robert, whose later fastidiousness became a byword, have been attracted to one who was repellent either mentally or physically. Amy had property, she had looks, and her parentage, though undistinguished, was acceptable. That was all either Dudley needed.

For more than a year following their marriage, as her father rocketed to fortune and fame over the body and ruined estates of the Protector, Amy and Robert Dudley lived an idyllic life on her father's Norfolk lands. These were the years after Thomas Seymour's execution in which Elizabeth was regaining her reputation. The two young ladies may have met at her brother's court, where the princess, in modest dress and piously sober demeanor, was doing public penance for her part in the Seymour affair. Robert came often to court at his father's prompting, to make new contacts and renew old ones or merely to serve as an attendant for various noblemen. After months of riding the boundaries of his father-in-law's estates to the deferential acknowledgments of neighbors and tenants, association with the powerfully influential men at court must have caused the boy, who had inherited all the limitless ambition of his forebears, to wonder if he was living life to the fullest. He was buried on a Norfolk backwater, with a simple country beauty, whose unsophisticated charm had begun to pall and who had failed to give him children. Amy disliked court life. She accepted with seemingly little regret that she was no match for the challenging and competitively artificial aura surrounding Majesty and was relieved to be left at home. She loved her handsome young husband, and his absence was necessarily painful, yet she could not have overlooked that the only invitations from Robert to have her at court were on the rare occasions when her presence was mandatory.

Inevitably, preferments came his way. He was appointed Master of the Buckhounds and became a Member of Parliament for Norfolk. And when, shortly before Edward's death, he became one of the six Gentlemen of the King's Privy Chamber, he gave up any pretense that he meant to spend his days as an inconspicuous country squire. Thus could a gentleman whose grandfather had been executed for extortion rise in sixteenth-century England if he cut the proper figure, sought the right sponsorship and was allied with the party in power.

Robert Dudley was well on his way to an independent position of influence when Edward died and John Dudley's last aggressive thrust for the Crown had ended in tragedy for the whole family. Again their fortunes were confiscated. Castles and manors and their contents, not only those belonging to the condemned man but also to his sons, went to many of the same rapacious Councillors who had originally approved Dudley's treasonous scheme, but who had pulled away sooner. Again the family name was attainted, and the Dudleys forbidden to inherit or reclaim property. So thoroughly did the Crown deplete the Dudley holdings that at the end only a small part of the mother's original marriage portion remained. Even Amy's dowry was sequestered for the Crown.

Robert's own imprisonment followed, and all the family were certain of death. They remained in the Tower for more than a year, alleviating their boredom with wall carvings which remain to this day. Yet only Guildford—because of his marriage to Lady Jane Grey—was executed. Before he was dragged from his cell, he had carved JANE in tidy letters on the wall. Robert did not carve his wife's name. Instead, he carved his own, ROBART DUDLEY, in strong incisement. Later, with his brothers, he carved a Bear and a Ragged Staff, the emblem of the

Warwicks, and around the badge they wreathed roses, acorns, gillyflowers and honeysuckle—R.A.G.H.—the first initials of the imprisoned Robert, Ambrose, Guildford and Henry Dudley.

Shortly after Mary's wedding to Philip in late October, the remaining Dudleys were pardoned, and each went his own penniless way. Robert returned to Norfolk and Amy; indeed, there was little else for him to do. But after the glitter of a competitive life at court, the daily routine of the country gentry bored the young man, married five years to a woman who no longer interested him. He treated Amy with absentminded kindness which neither helped nor consoled the unhappy woman. She indulged herself in extravagances which were the basis for many quarrels—quarrels which provided a certain outlet for the frustrated Robert, but only frightened the docile woman whose whole experience and upbringing demonstrated the difference between her and the captive *rara avis* who happened to be her husband.

By the time Robert was twenty-two, after having lived what seemed a lifetime in the cataclysmic upheaval of court existence and its attendant perils, he was faced with the necessity of building a new life on the ruins of the old. He accepted the fact that any passion which had once existed between him and his wife had not survived. He might have wondered if seclusion in an inconspicuous Norfolk estate and a dreary wife were all the future held. A true Dudley, he yearned for power, prestige and all the attendant material possessions. He wanted a passionate and attractive partner, as aggressive as himself, who would satisfy the more sensual side of his nature and give him children to inherit the fruit of his labors and pass on with pride the name he felt bound to redeem. If he was to attain any of these things, the virtual abandonment of Amy was a foregone conclusion.

Robert Dudley returned to court in 1557. He reentered by acting, as did his brothers, in the service of Queen Mary when England was forced to help fight Philip's war with France. It was not a popular war with the English people. To endure a Spanish King on the English throne was one thing; to send their sons and spend the nation's funds to fight Spain's wars was another. But to the Dudley men, it was a heaven-sent opportunity. Robert served with the leader of the expeditionary force, the Earl of Pembroke, and distinguished himself in the Battle of St.-Quentin, where he was made Master of the Ordnance. Here his brother Henry was killed. King Philip's attention was caught by the level-headed and disciplined Robert, who had inherited all his father's soldierly instincts and who served tirelessly, thus winning a royal commendation. The Queen's gratitude was demonstrated early in 1558 in the lifting of the attainder against the Dudley name and the restoration of some of Robert's property. When Mary died, eight months later, Robert was in a more solid position than when she had ascended the throne. He had little money, but he had a clean name; he was young, vigorous and handsome. He was as free of all marital obligations as it was possible to be while his wife was still living, for he and Amy had come to terms about their life together. He paid only duty visits to Norfolk, but because "of his mastery of those little attentions" which he continued to show her, Amy was not allowed to forget him.[14] His aim now was to recoup the family fortunes and inject himself immediately into the mainstream of events contingent on the new monarch.

He was one of the first to arrive at Hatfield, where Elizabeth joyfully greeted Robin, the companion of her youth and Tower days. For Robert Dudley, whose past four years had been spent in quiet desperation, her recognition was like drink to a thirsty man. A glimmering of expectation, the possibility of unbelievable vistas of power and privilege, opened before his eyes. His appointment as Master of the Horse was only the first of what he was sure would be rapid advancement. And this time, no aggressive haste, no foolhardy behavior such as his father had demonstrated, nor any greedy thievery such as his grandfather's, would bring down the fortunes of the House of Dudley. He was on his way.

In a court where the illustrious, the distinguished or the merely colorful were commonplace, Robert Dudley shone from the very beginning with his own forceful brilliance. He was "a man of tall personage, a manly countenance, somewhat brown of visage, strongly featured, and thereto comely proportioned in all lineaments of body." His darker complexion led the Earl of Sussex, never one of his admirers, to dub him "the Gypsy." His features were "of sweet aspect, but high-foreheaded, which was of no discommendation."[15] The dark-brown eyes were large-pupiled, appearing almost black. They were piercingly probing, not the eyes of a mortal easily fooled. While smooth-shaven in the country, on his return to court he grew a respectable beard and mustache, for it gave him a look of maturity which his years—for all his unhappy experiences—had not yet bestowed. A jutting, aquiline nose, similar to Elizabeth's, above a sensitive mouth and a determined, angular chin, merely emphasized all that was striking about Lord Robert. The effect was completed by an impressive muscular body hidden under the ornate dress he wore with superb confidence. He carried his shoulders well back and his head high— perhaps an unconscious challenge to anyone who might still wish to sneer at a Dudley. Throughout his life, this effect is noticeable in his portraits: His stance and expression indicate a probable deportment just short of the insolently arrogant.

He typified everything that was good and bad at the Tudor court, which was, at its best, a study in contrasts. He was as greedily self-seeking and vain as many of his contemporaries. He was not of the Privy Council; his finances were limited, and he was burdened with a failing marriage. Robert Dudley, therefore, had further to reach than many, and he was fortunately possessed of many gifts which would help him in the attempt. He was recklessly bold, a born adventurer in every sense of the word, although possessed of an innate caution and shrewdness lacking in his forebears. He was blessed with a fertile imagination and a courage which was as much the product of necessity as it was inborn. Though he could joust, hawk and shoot and was accomplished at all sports, he was never the slave of the hunt or the tiltyard, as were so many of his companions. He was well educated, speaking Latin with ease, although French was to be a painful lifetime experience. An excellent mathematician, with more than a light interest in the sciences, Robert had early won the praise of Roger Ascham, Elizabeth's "scholemaster" who spoke of him as having a "careful mind, even in reading, not only in Latin, but also of the Italian good and sound writers. . . ."[16] It was obvious Robert was not lacking in intellect, although remembering his family's past, the direction that intellect and ambition might take was a source of worry to many.

The advent of Robert's prominence at court coincided with the determination of the Council to see the Queen safely wed. In the past, Elizabeth had distributed her favors impartially, singling out such as Pickering and Arundel for particular notice. She had listened to the importunities of ambassadors and of their candidates. At all the courts of Europe, as well as at home, her marriage was a subject of constant debate and one to which the Queen paid the most devoted attention—particularly if her suitors arrived to woo her in person. The courtship of a Queen might prove a long and tedious business to those not intimately concerned. But to Elizabeth, all the ploys and niceties of the situation were beguiling. And one of the perquisites of Majesty—to distribute the largess of royal interest to a fortunate few and thus ensure a reciprocal and most satisfying attention—was becoming almost a fixation. At first, most of those who knew the Queen well considered her actions properly feminine and harmless as long as she kept the good nature and goodwill of the foreign ambassadors and their suitors. Sooner or later, they felt she would make a choice, for she, as well as others, was aware that the foremost duty of a Queen was to provide heirs. It was unthinkable she would not choose to do so—an offense against nature and a disaster for the nation—for marriage and children were a political objective and a responsibility inherent in the assumption of the Crown. But, as the months wore on and it seemed their sovereign did not have the least intention of choosing even that first requisite, a husband, her ministers and courtiers became uneasy.

It was, then, with understandable dismay that many at court acknowledged Elizabeth Tudor's preference for Robert Dudley. Not only was he a member of a family that had overreached itself on several occasions to the detriment of the Tudors, but he was also a married man. However, by May, 1559, Elizabeth's partiality for Robert could no longer be ignored. In addition to the post of Master of the Horse, the Queen presented her favorite with impressive property at Kew, the sites of the monasteries of Watton and Meux in Yorkshire, the lieutenancy of the Castle and Forest of Windsor and a profitable license to export woolen goods free of duty.[17] Similar honors for his brother Ambrose followed, and she made his sister, Mary Dudley, now married to Sir Henry Sidney, a Lady of the Bedchamber. These measures left little doubt that the Queen was agreeable to replenishing the Dudley coffers and rehabilitating a tarnished name.

By midsummer her blatant predilection for Dudley was the talk of the court. Awards and appointments were one thing; a careless disregard of the proprieties was another. Her preoccupation with Robert was total and all the more stunning considering her lack of interest and experience in the past. She flirted with him outrageously, bullied him, teased him and then, in a quick about-face, adopted a meek and almost servile attitude toward him, which plainly bespoke enthrallment. At court ceremonies and their later attendant festivities, in the royal barge as it skimmed over the Thames, in processions among her subjects or hunting parties on the royal estates, the tall figure of Robert Dudley was never far from the Queen. She would seek him out in a crowd, shamelessly recount his virtues of body and mind and breathlessly defend him should anyone be so bold as to speak disparagingly of a Dudley. She took personal interest, exhibiting an unfamiliar tenderness, in anything that concerned him. Earlier Cecil had tried diplomacy as a means of breaking up a relationship he privately thought was progressing too fast and too soon. He included Robert's name in a list of ambassadors to be sent into foreign service, but when the Queen's permission had been given to the rest, Robert's name was stricken from the list, and he remained at home.

For Elizabeth, open approval and indulgence of Robert were, in themselves, a luxury. She often spoke of his befriending her during the time of her imprisonment. The fact that he, too, had suffered a similar peril, that less than a year previous both of them had been regarded with suspicion and distrust appealed to the Queen's tart humor. She also delighted in shocking, and now it was doubly enjoyable to shock in public after years of furtively concealing her opinions, as well as her emotions. For the first time, as an adult woman, she could openly delight in a man's attention, revel in endearments and glory in having a male confidant and companion. Her unconcealed partiality left no doubt where her heart lay, and for such as Cecil—to whom Dudley's flamboyance was almost a personal affront—their encounters with each other were a source of constant and nerve-racking worry. For a Queen to ally herself so flagrantly with a man who was descended from a family of traitors was one thing. To persist in defending him in the face of all criticism and enriching him with royal patronage could only lead the undeniably ambitious man to think in similar terms. Yet the Queen would have her way. When others derided Dudley, Elizabeth was quick to defend, saying that "she would have no one she did not love." When she chose a husband, said the Queen, she would not pick one who would "sit at home all day among the cinders." Instead, when she married, "it should be a man who could ride and hunt and fight."[18] Her eyes turned to Dudley as she spoke, leading an observer to note that, "like her father, King Henry, she loved a *man*."

Soon, the affair was in full bloom. Even so, there was a curious willingness at court to forgive an indiscretion in the Queen, but the forgiveness did not extend to Robert. Anger and suspicion at the man who was the Queen's age in years, but decades older in experience, soon changed to dismay as the full realization of Elizabeth's emotional involvement became public knowledge. It was with an outraged and stunning disappointment that the people of England and the court at last recognized the extent of their sovereign's infatuation with a man of undistinguished background, with little material resources that had not come directly as a gift from the Crown. Robert Dudley was also a married man. While the wedded state was in no way an unalterable condition in Tudor England, there was a certain nicety of protocol regarding the sovereign in which marriage was held, it was hoped, above reproach. Elizabeth's father had given the people more than their just share of distaste for infidelity and marital excesses. They had expected better of his daughter, and there was an indignant resentment that proud Majesty, who had so far given every indication of possessing an aloofness which would not crumble at emotional pressures mere mortals might find unbearable, was femininely human after all. But in the main, the onus of public shock and disbelief rested on Robert Dudley, and there was a quick, open denunciation of the

Master of the Horse as the cause of all the grief. Even the ambassadors contributed their bit, as when de Quadra wrote, "I have heard great things of a sort that cannot be written about, and you will understand what they must be by that."[19]

But any slander of her favorite made little, if any, impression on Elizabeth. For the remainder of the year, the two were rarely out of each other's sight. If Amy had seen little of her husband before, she now saw even less. Instead, the searching scrutiny of public opinion bore down on the shy and hapless wife of a man who obviously did not want her. Rumors and half-truths penetrated to Norfolk, and Amy now began a season of aimless travel, visiting the homes of friends and relatives, far removed from her father's estates, where the pitying glances of tenants, servants and her own family's silent concern had made life unbearable. There was little to occupy her in a home lacking husband and children. Her solution was to flee.

On June 6, at Windsor Castle, Robert Dudley, in the company of the Duke of Norfolk, the Marquess of Northampton and the Earl of Rutland, was made a Knight of the Garter, the highest honor an English sovereign could bestow on a faithful subject. Whether the honor he shared with the foremost Duke, the only Marquess and one of the most distinguished Earls of the realm was due to Elizabeth's spontaneous generosity or Dudley's insistence is unknown. It was the first in a series of preferences which Robert meant to be only the beginning. That all these stemmed from a woman who intrigued him as much as he did her was fortunate. Elizabeth was everything a man of his age, temperament and ambition could desire. She excited him physically; her brain was a constant challenge, her personality a delight. After years of the bland Amy, the redheaded woman who happened to be his Queen provided a dazzling contrast which could little help but captivate.

Immediately, Robert's ideals coalesced with his ambitions: he had found the right woman, and she was receptive. Now a way must be found for them to be together permanently with the least loss to the royal position and the most gain for himself. He did not dissemble about his position at court or the lack of esteem in which he was generally regarded. He knew that Cecil disliked him and that the Duke of Norfolk, the premier peer of the realm, openly loathed the Dudleys. In the past he had cared little for the good opinion of others; now he set about to mend his social fences. The famed Dudley temper, which did not hesitate at an oath or a drawn sword, now, as one court observer noted, "disappeared into his pocket," and in place was an ingratiatingly handsome and likable fellow who, secure in the royal favor, did not swagger in his importance, as previous suitors had, but wore the mantle of royal approval as an invisible badge of honor. And in the wearing was a subtle scorn for any who might mock or challenge his place in the Queen's affections.

The exact nature of the relationship between Elizabeth and Robert Dudley tantalized the embryo historians of the day, as much as their later successors, who have conjectured everything from a deformed body to a warped psychology as accounting for Queen Elizabeth's preference to remain unwed. There is doubt, however, that at twenty-five, Elizabeth—for all her public protestations of affirmed virginity—actually meant to continue in that state for the remainder of her life. Although her preference was to remain single rather than involve herself in a liaison which would be unattractive personally as well as disastrous politically, she gave every indication with Robert Dudley (and later with one or two other suitors) that she was not psychologically averse to the possibility of intimacy with the male sex. She was not frigid in the modern sense of the word. At this time the rumors which were to plague the Queen all her life commenced. It was the Spanish ambassador who first put it on paper: "If my spies do not lie—which I believe they do not—for a certain reason which they have recently given me, I understand she will not bear children. . . ."[20]

The rumor was picked up by the tavern gossips; they further embroidered the subject with speculation on a physical abnormality or malformation; certainly, at worst, Elizabeth was considered sterile. Such implications, disastrous to ministers and a Council anxious to see their Queen married, were scathingly rebutted by the royal doctors, who told the French ambassador, "The Queen can bear ten children!" William Cecil added his opinion, "Nature cannot amend her shape in any part to make her more likely to conceive and bear children without peril."[21] The most likely refutation of Elizabeth's possible infertility is the degree to which the Council—to whom few matters such as even a Queen's frequency of menstrual periods were secret—attempted to bring about her marriage. On several occasions, they were even willing to suffer another foreign consort for the sake of the heirs which they hoped would come of such a union.

What was more uncertain and actually more secret was that an impediment *did* in fact exist, but it is doubtful if it was recognized as such, even by the Queen herself. It was not physical in nature. Elizabeth often had repeated that marriage was repugnant to her "and she hated it more every day, for reasons which she would not divulge to a twin soul, if she had one, much less to any living creature."[22] There were many reasons why the Queen could regard the so-called advantages of marriage—especially a royal one—with a cynical eye. The sad fate of Catherine of Aragon, who had been ruthlessly cast aside after twenty-four years of marriage, had preceded the tragedy of her own mother. Her stepmother Jane Seymour had died after days of agony in giving birth to a child, and dear old Anne of Cleves had been divorced merely for disappointing royalty in her appearance. Her own kin Katherine Howard had perished on the scaffold for allowing her heart to rule her head. Elizabeth could still vividly remember a similar experience with Thomas Seymour. Her own beloved Katherine Parr had died giving birth to Thomas' daughter. Mary Tudor, her sister, had died with a broken heart owing to a husband's coldness and an inability to bear a child. There was literally almost nothing in Elizabeth's background which exemplified happiness or, more important, *security* in marriage. If there was an obstruction in the Queen regarding the wedded state, it was almost certainly psychological, not physical.

There was also in Elizabeth an attitude which was to grow as she grew in stature and experience. It was a stiff and firm resistance to the idea of Majesty—which was divine in origin—humbling itself in surrender to mere mortal man. It is this inflexible attitude which undoubtedly helped further the rumor of the Queen's frigidity. She was too young at the time of the Seymour affair to contemplate physical surrender; her instinct had been merely to attract and hold attention. Now, as the twenty-sixth birthday of Robert and Elizabeth approached, she might feel every inducement to surrender to the attentions of the handsome courtier who intrigued her mind as much as he stimulated her senses. But something—an aloof sensitivity, a stubborn resistance—held her back. It was a canny Scotsman, Sir James Melville, who first recognized this characteristic in Elizabeth. After she had recounted her Council's efforts to see her wed and her own aversion to marriage, Sir James replied, "I know the truth of that, Madam, you need not tell me. Your Majesty thinks that if you were married you would be but Queen of England, and now you are both King and Queen. I know your spirit cannot endure a commander."[23]

However, as the end of Elizabeth's first year on the throne approached, there is little doubt that she and Robert Dudley carried on as if they were lovers in the fullest sense of the word. They openly caressed each other, shared whispered confidences and laughter in the full sight of the court. One incident which plainly indicates the familiarity of their personal rapport occurred when, as her marriage was being debated as usual, Robert broke off and asked her outright "if she did not think she had some subjects of her own . . . able to make an heir for the kingdom of England?"[24]

While there were many who looked askance at the conduct of the

Queen and her Master of the Horse, it mattered little to the two participants. Robert Dudley knew just how to handle spirited women. His flattery—while not as lavish as others'—struck Elizabeth as more meaningful. He treated her primarily as a woman and then as a Queen—a welcome gesture when the cares of the nation bore heavily on her strength and disposition. He could be amusing, devastatingly charming and indulgent, giving Elizabeth a self-assurance formerly lacking in one who had, as a girl, trod a narrow path with a very careful step. If there is one word which characterizes Elizabeth's attitude toward Robert, it is *freedom*. With him, there was no need to impress. Instead, there was a satisfying lack of self-consciousness and ar-tificiality—two commodities very much in evidence in any royal court—in their relationship.

While the truth of the exact degree of the Queen's intimacy with her courtier went to the grave with them both, there are enough signposts along the path of their thirty-year association to show that what ultimately evolved may *not* have been in either the Queen's or Dudley's mind at the beginning. Certainly Elizabeth was profligate in her atti-tude toward him; certainly her behavior scandalized the more proper of her court and lessened her personal integrity and the dignity of the Crown. Yet it is very probable that she had every intention of marrying Robert as soon as a way could be found for her to do so with whatever honor she might muster from a situation where an unwanted wife must be divorced and a somewhat tarnished husband might be cloaked with sufficient luster to render him suitable for marriage.

These, almost certainly, were her feelings during the remainder of the year as she dallied with her lover, enjoying, for the first time, the heady stimulus of having a love of her own in which she felt secure—one which thrilled and excited her as much for the sense of power as for any other satisfaction. There was never any question of complete physical surrender. Though there were certainly those moments which come to all people in love—kings and commoners share the same nervous systems and impulses—in which her heart might rule her head, she had that invincible core of self-control which her previous history had bestowed. A Queen of England could hardly risk a bastard child; there was enough innate integrity and political percipience in Elizabeth Tudor to know a pregnancy out of wedlock would be a national disaster and a personal catastrophe. If that was her first deterrent—and it undoubtedly was—her second was the knowledge that her dear Robin, for all his exciting masculine imperiousness, would also have to share the Crown with her. One Dudley had already struck at the throne; she would not allow herself to be hurried. She must win the approval of her people and Council where he was concerned. Once that was attained, she had little doubt but that she could handle the situation.

Therefore, in effect, the Queen of England had her cake and the delight of eating it also. There were crises along the way as the mounting clamor of disapproval pierced even royal walls, and Elizabeth understood the weight of her people's dislike for her favorite. First, she laughed at the tales; later, having lost the savor of the first telling, she would rebuke the speakers. When word got around, after the holiday festivities, that the French ambassador had been told by a colleague "that he had been assured by a person in a position to know that Lord Robert had slept with the Queen on New Year's night," there was no denying the rumors were becoming more maliciously pronounced. Some degree of the imperiousness with which Elizabeth and Robert regarded the busybodies' tales is evident in her granting his request for an apartment adjoining her on a floor above ground level to avoid the dampness.

A flood of rumors was unleashed the day he made his move. They were enough to make Katherine Ashley, Elizabeth's old governess and now First Lady of the Bedchamber, go down on her knees and implore her mistress to be more circumspect—or get married. To which Elizabeth irritably pointed to the attendants on duty in the royal apartment. They were there night and day, she said, and asked the stricken woman how even a Queen could possibly misbehave under such circumstances? "Although," she finished in a grim mutter, "if I had the will—or found leisure in such a dishonorable life, from which God preserve me—I do not know of anyone who could forbid me!" To Cecil, busy with foreign and domestic matters and the Queen's marital negotiations, the situation was bewildering. "This sing hath many parts and I am only skilled in plainsong," he lamented.

As the old year ended and a new decade commenced, it would have taken one with the wisdom of Solomon to predict the outcome of the Queen's affair with her courtier. Few, as yet, believed Elizabeth would share her throne with Dudley, even if a way could be found to obtain an honorable divorce from Amy Dudley. As chance would have it, however, it was an event larger than the affair of a Queen and a courtier and a discarded wife which would resolve the situation. The beginning of the end commenced in the courts of both France and Scotland and centered on the figure of a slim eighteen-year-old girl named Mary Stuart, already Queen of Scotland, who, in the eyes of Catholic Europe, was the rightful heir to the English throne.

Chapter Five

As the affair of Elizabeth and Robert heightened in intensity and members of the court and Council assessed their relative positions should a Dudley actually become—as one ambassador already called him—"the King that is to be"—a tragic and far-reaching incident in France became the catalyst which changed forever the destinies of all those involved.

At a joust celebrating the proxy marriage of Philip of Spain to Elizabeth of Valois, Henri II, the French King, was wounded when a lance thrust by a guard captain accidentally entered his visor. It penetrated the eye, a splinter entered the brain, and the monarch was carried, speechless and benumbed, from the field. Ten days later he died in agony. Immediately, his fifteen-year-old son, Francis, and seventeen-year-old daughter-in-law, Mary Stuart, were crowned King and Queen in Notre Dame Cathedral. Watching the ceremony was the dead monarch's widow, the dark-eyed, sharp-visaged Catherine de Medici, now relegated to Queen Dowager. Nearby were Mary Stuart's uncles, two representatives of the powerful House of Guise, the Duke of Guise and the Cardinal of Lorraine. All had something in common, for each—Prince, prelate and Queen Dowager—was determined to run affairs with as little interference from the boy-King and his Queen as from each other.

The early, unexpected coronation of Mary Stuart caused a quick reappraisal by the English of their relationship with Scotland, their unruly northern neighbor. Mary Stuart, with her pretensions to the English throne, had been a troublesome nuisance as Dauphiness. Now, as a crowned Queen of France, one encouraged in further personal and political aggrandizement by a cunning mother-in-law and avidly ambitious uncles, she was a menace not only to England's border, but to Elizabeth's sovereignty.

The threat sprang not only from Mary Stuart's Tudor blood, but also from Scotland's traditional dependence on France as a means of preserving its autonomy. Mary's father, James V, the son of Henry VIII's sister Margaret Tudor and James IV, had died after Solway Moss, where English forces massacred thousands of Scots, with a loss of only seven of their own men. James had snubbed all attempts by his uncle Harry to resolve the differences of the two countries; he effectively cemented his French alliance by marrying the statuesque and beautiful Mary of Guise. Their child, Mary Stuart, was born in December, 1542, as James lay dying after the Solway Moss fiasco. Later Henry had attempted to have the baby sent to England to be brought up as a bride for his son, Edward. But Henry's own death and the later Battle of Pinkie Cleugh, in which the Protector, Edward Seymour, had again decimated Scottish forces, blasted such hopes forever. Mary had been crowned Queen of Scotland at the age of nine months; at six, she was spirited away to France for "protection." There she had grown up, very much under the influence of her two Guise uncles. She retained but the haziest recollection of Scotland and was, in dress, deportment and attitude, a thorough Frenchwoman. She did not see her mother until three years later, when a harassed Mary of Guise had come to France to insist on being named Regent of Scotland. She was accompanied by a group of Scottish nobles of whom Sir John Mason, the English ambassador, wrote, ". . . and such brawling, chiding and fighting make they here for their lodgings and other's quarrels, as though they lately came from some new conquest!" Mary achieved her Regency and returned to Scotland, neither she nor her child realizing they would never meet again.

In an obvious attempt to strengthen the bond between Scotland and France, Mary Stuart had married the French Dauphin less than three months after Elizabeth's coronation. At the insistence of her two uncles and the French King, she secretly signed documents by which, in the event of her death without heirs, Scotland was to become a French possession and all rights she had to the Crown of England were to be honored.[1] The documents were then put away until such time as they might prove useful. In the meantime, with one son married to the Queen of Scotland and a daughter about to be wed to the Spanish King, Henri had felt himself very much in command of the English situation. It would not, perhaps, be too presumptuous to think that his new son-in-law, Philip, might be agreeable to joining forces in a move to subdue the heretic Elizabeth, restore the Catholic faith in England,

and then young Mary would rule as Queen of England, as well as Scotland. A shattered lance and a splinter in the royal brain had changed the participants, but it did not alter the plan.

In England the death of Henri II and the accession of Mary Stuart were viewed with mixed feelings. Though Elizabeth did not know of Mary's yielding of her birthright in the event of her death without heirs, the very act by the French Queen of quartering the arms of England with those of France incurred the royal wrath. When informed that Mary and Francis II were proclaimed King and Queen of England, Ireland and Scotland, Elizabeth swore "to take a husband who would give the King of France a headache and that he little knew what a buffet she could give him!" Scotland was the "postern gate to England." Periodically, such murderous episodes as Flodden, Solway Moss and Pinkie Cleugh erupted, proving once more the English desire to dominate Scotland, either through marriage or by arms, and to rid their northern neighbor once and for all of the troublemaking French retained by Mary of Guise to bolster the Regency until her daughter attained her majority.

The political picture was further muddied by the religious aspect of the two nations—and of the two Queens. As the English Reformation had expanded—and particularly after Mary Tudor's death and the end of her attempt to restore Catholicism in England—many English Catholics regarded Mary Stuart as the legitimate heir. Indeed, most of Catholic Europe had never acknowledged Anne Boleyn's marriage to Henry VIII and viewed the Stuart as the legal claimant. For the majority of the English Catholics, this did not mean active or even anticipated plotting against Elizabeth; only the most fanatical wished any return to the domination of Rome. But throughout England—in the North particularly—there still remained bastions of the "Old Faith" where satisfaction with the status quo might be swayed if reasons were compelling enough. Thus, when a Catholic Scottish Princess—and one of Tudor blood—unexpectedly became the anointed Queen of France, there was good reason to be disturbed. For many Catholics, the prospect that Mary Stuart on the English throne would, in fact, unite England and Scotland and unquestionably restore the Catholic faith was tempting. Others, more worldly and not looking for miracles, realized England would thereby lose the precious independence it had regained with Elizabeth. As England had been dominated by Spain when Mary Tudor reigned, it would be dominated by France if Mary Stuart were Queen. With Elizabeth, at least, they were as free of foreign entanglements as possible—as long as she did not take a foreigner for a husband.

It was well known in England that there was dissatisfaction with the Stuarts in Scotland. The Reformation had moved north, and there, as elsewhere, the Church of Rome was under siege. Unlike England, where its cause had been furthered by royalty and nobles lusting after Church lands and treasures, it derived some from the Scottish people themselves. They were encouraged by John Knox, the acid-tongued preacher who had fled England for the Continent on Mary Tudor's accession. When Elizabeth refused him readmittance into England—his *First Blast of the Trumpet Against the Monstrous Regiment of Women* left little doubt of how he regarded female sovereigns—he returned to Scotland. Coarse and violent in an age which fully appreciated the merits of such characteristics, he preached throughout the larger towns, stirring a religious fervor and dedication reminiscent of the Crusades. His following included many young Scottish nobles, among them Lord James Stuart, Mary's illegitimate half brother. They formed a group calling themselves Lords of the Congregation. Hotheaded charges by the Catholic partisans resulted in retaliation; inevitably, outright rebellion by the Scottish Lords followed. Monks were driven from their monasteries, churches were invaded and their contents smashed and burned, leading the English Protestant Bishop Jewel to write gloatingly:

> Everything is in a ferment in Scotland. Knox, surrounded by a thousand followers, is holding assemblies throughout the Kingdom. The old Queen Regent has been compelled to shut herself up in a garrison . . . all the monasteries are everywhere levelled with the ground; the theatrical dresses, the sacrilegious chalices, the idols, the altars are consigned to the flames. Not a vestige of the ancient superstition and idolatry is left. . . !" [2]

The sick and ailing Mary of Guise was little hindrance to Knox's fervor, and a struggle began now between the two factions as to who would be supreme in Scotland. Again, religion became the stalking horse of those desirous of personal power and national profit.

The Protestant Lords of the Congregation turned to England for help, reasoning that it was as much in Elizabeth's interest to encourage any rebellion which might weaken the influence of the Queen Regent and her daughter. If the French could be ousted, the Catholic influence would also be lessened and the Protestant Lords might then govern Scotland until Mary had attained her majority. Then, buttressed by Elizabeth, they would be in a position to name their own conditions before accepting Mary as Queen.

It was William Cecil, with the experience gained during the former Protector's administration, who first recognized the opportunities implicit in the situation, and he sought to convince Elizabeth of its potential. At first, the Queen showed little enthusiasm. Any outright intervention in Scotland's affairs would be considered a violation of the recent treaty. She could not openly advocate rebellion against a fellow sovereign; all moral niceties aside, it was setting a dangerous precedent. Elizabeth was also skeptical of the Lords of the Congregation's religious integrity. She had seen their counterpart in her own country where any true regard for a religious faith had been subservient to the greedy self-seekers who coveted Church wealth. Once she had helped the Scottish Lords, she doubted they would continue any support of England. Conversely, to prolong the situation was to give the advantage of time to the French to strengthen their hold on a country whose Queen considered herself the rightful Queen of England. Elizabeth listened to Cecil, and eventually the woman who, so far, had aptly lived her motto, "I see and I am silent," agreed to a scheme which was as unorthodox as it was outrageous. There were only three participants: Elizabeth, Cecil and Sir Thomas Parry. The Queen was adamant. If her desire for secrecy were to be effective, even the Privy Council must remain unaware of what was happening. The plan was simplicity itself—England would subsidize the Scottish Lords of the Congregation to fight secretly what England could not fight for in the open, primarily the eviction of French and Catholic influence from Scotland. Sir Ralph Sadler, a trusted emissary, was sent to the Border to negotiate with the Lords. His instructions from the Queen were clear; they authorized him "to confer, treat, or practice with any manner of person of Scotland . . . of any other thing that *may tend to make a perpetual concord betwixt the nation of Scotland and ours.*" What that outward attempt at amity might be, the Queen left to Sadler.

There was also more tangible assistance, and here again, the instructions were explicit. "We do also authorise you to *reward* any manner of person of Scotland with such sums of money as you shall think meet, to be taken of the sum of £3,000 which we have ordered should be delivered unto you in gold; wherein such discretion and secrecy is to be used, *as no part of your doings may impair the treaties of peace lately concluded betwixt us and Scotland.*" The letter, to all but the three in London and the departing Sadler, was a masterpiece of innocent logic. England was to help its neighbor, but only on honorable terms, and good English gold might be distributed to further the cause, yet not disrupt the existing treaty, which had provided a tenuous peace. Sadler well knew that the funds were to be used *only* by those Protestant Lords of the Congregation who had sought Elizabeth's help. It was a situation much favored by the Queen, as it might have been favored by her father. Outward innocent cooperation which, in actuality, was underhanded manipulation, evasive as it was deliberate.

Having thus put into effect the means to muddy further the diplomatic affairs between England and Scotland, Elizabeth sought to deal with the rumors which the French ambassador, François de Noailles, charged were prevalent at the Border. Heatedly, he communicated Mary of Guise's outraged protest of the Border incidents which could only be regarded as provocative English intervention. On the same day as she had authorized Sadler's mission, Elizabeth also wrote to the Queen Regent of her dismay "that certain of our officers on the frontiers have held intelligence with the rebels late in arms against your authority." Her own astonishment was apparent. "We cannot but find it very strange that any of our subjects, and much more that persons in position of public trust, should of their own accord and regardless of our displeasure, have sought to meddle with any such people." And then, strong affirmation of her own innocence. "Forasmuch, however, as at present, we know no particular of these things—but upon being informed, will proceed to punish the offenders, we must entreat you to specify more exactly what you complain of and let us knew the entire truth. . . ." [3] Elizabeth was playing for time, but her deceptive cunning, so insidious in its artfulness, did not fool Mary of Guise. The Queen Regent's wrathful indignation was echoed in de Quadra's comments to Philip. Earlier he had written that "the spirit of the woman is that I can believe anything of her. She is possessed by the Devil, who is dragging her to his own place."

Still Elizabeth continued to maintain that if any of her subjects were meddling with the "evil practices among the Scots," they were doing so without her authority, and she went so far as to order an inquiry, stating that "the Congregation would find they had greatly deceived themselves if they hoped for any favour from her in their foolish enterprise. . . ." Her performance was so skillful, her disdain so apparent, that even M. de Noailles, the veteran French ambassador, was convinced of her innocence. Especially when she challenged him for proof, saying that her signature "was easily recognized—let it be produced if it can be found!" Their discussion occurred in the Gallery at Hampton Court Palace, and to persuade de Noailles of her innocence, she accompanied him to view a portrait of Mary of Guise and praised the "goodness, honesty and virtue" of the Queen Regent and desired him "to present . . . her very affectionate recommendations." [4]

Seeking to strengthen their alliance with Elizabeth, the Lords of the

Congregation proposed she marry the Earl of Arran, head of the House of Hamilton and next in line for the Scottish Crown, leading de Quadra to write dispiritedly, "I have lost all hope in the affairs of this woman. She is convinced of the soundness of her unstable power . . . besides this, her language (learned from Italian friars who brought her up) is so shifty that it is the most difficult thing in the world to negotiate with her. With her, all is falsehood and vanity!" [5] De Noailles, too, was finally beginning to suspect Elizabeth of artifice and reminded her that—according to the Cateau-Cambrésis treaty—she was under oath to arrest Arran if he ventured into England. Elizabeth, poised and unabashed, promised she "would do all in her power to do what her good brother desired" and reminded him "she was not the person to say one thing and do another." But she had never seen Arran, she said, looking him straight in the eye. Which was true enough, although she neglected to mention that the young Earl had been smuggled into the country and was now in hiding, awaiting her summons, at William Cecil's house in Canon Row,* Westminster. The meeting occurred several days later at the Palace of Eltham. Although the marriage would have been the most effective means of dealing with Mary Stuart's ambitions, the handsome, weak and obviously syphilitic Arran had little appeal for Elizabeth. If she would marry the twenty-two-year-old nobleman and make him King Consort, the Scottish Lords would renounce Mary Stuart and unite the two kingdoms of Scotland and England under one sovereign—and that sovereign would be Elizabeth.[6] It was a tempting morsel to dangle before the eyes of a new monarch, but they underestimated the Queen's natural caution, sharpened so acutely during her years of childhood jeopardy. Although Cecil and the Protestant members of her Council were much in favor of the proposal, the political implications of the marriage and the disease which would ultimately doom Arran to forty years of madness made him unfit for the Queen. He was dispatched to Scotland without, typically, any final word from Elizabeth, but "overflowing with zeal . . . . to take his share in the struggle across the Border."[7]

To divert suspicion further and to keep the goodwill of her brother-in-law, Philip, alive, Elizabeth informed the Spanish ambassador she would look with favor on the suit of Spain's official candidate, the Archduke Charles, son of the Holy Roman Emperor. The purveyor of this astounding news was Lady Mary Sidney, Robert Dudley's sister

---

*Canon Row, formerly known as Chanon Row, belonged to the Deans and Canons of nearby St. Stephen's Chapel in Westminster Palace. Called Cannon Row, it still exists today, off Bridge Street, in the shadow of Big Ben. Originally, before the Victoria Embankment was built, it was much nearer the Thames than now.

and one of the Queen's Ladies of the Bedchamber. According to Lady
Mary, the Queen had heard of a plot to kill her; she was embarrassed at
the rumors linking her with Dudley and alarmed at the tension
mounting in Scotland and the resulting bad relations with France.
Lady Mary suggested that if he, de Quadra, broached "the matter of
the match to the Queen now—she was sure it would be speedily
settled." He said Lady Mary swore that "if this were not true I might
be sure she would not say such a thing, as it might cost her her life. . . ."
Later, seeking out Robert Dudley, he questioned Elizabeth's sincerity
and was pleasantly surprised when Dudley informed him the Queen
was entirely agreeable and even offered his own assistance in fostering
the match. "Lord Robert and his sister are certainly acting splendidly
and the King will have to reward them well," wrote the delighted de
Quadra. His delight did not prevent him from seeking Elizabeth at the
first opportunity and challenging her motives. The Queen, as usual,
was evasive. Yet the subject of her marriage and another possible suitor
held its usual fascination. As she and de Quadra tilted verbal lances
—"a long time wasting words," the ambassador described it—Elizabeth
defended her lack of decision. "I am a Queen and I cannot ask a man to
come to England to marry me," she spoke with great plausibility.
"Shall I speak plain and tell you the truth? I think that if the Emperor
so desires me for a daughter, he would not be doing too much by
sending his son here. I do not hold myself of so small account that the
Emperor need sacrifice any dignity in doing it."

It was enough for de Quadra. Knowing Elizabeth's reluctance to
marry anyone she had not seen, the ambassador submitted his recommendations to the home court. Even Cecil gave his reluctant blessing,
expressing his wish to de Quadra that Philip would support England,
to which the ambassador replied that "if this marriage were brought
about . . . the King . . . would do more than was expected!" In another
interview, Elizabeth showed further concern for the rumors involving
herself and Dudley and told de Quadra "that if the Archduke heard
any of the idle tales they tell about her, he might take advantage of
them to the detriment of her honour. . . ." During the next two months
she carried the pretense to the point of farce, restoring crucifixes and
vestments to the Royal Chapel, ostensibly in view of the Catholic
suitor's anticipated arrival, which "greatly horrified the ardent
reformers" and led to many "hot words" between her Councillors and
courtiers. Even the Catholic Earl of Bedford was optimistic of success
and assured de Quadra "that the affair of the Archduke's marriage was
in a very good way and he expected it would be settled." The Emperor
Ferdinand, however, seemed in no hurry to dispatch his son to be

inspected by the Queen of England, and as time went on, Elizabeth's temper shortened under the strain. At a meeting in which the marriage was further discussed, de Quadra reported, ". . . the Queen says the most extraordinary things and I always have a retort for every word, which greatly offends her but does not frighten her. . . ."[8]

As Elizabeth's enthusiasm waned and Robert Dudley's optimism lessened, de Quadra's suspicions were aroused. Suddenly, her Majesty was not as available, and he could readily see "Lord Robert is slackening in our business. . . ." When at last he met with Elizabeth, she told him, with an unusual nervousness, that at present "she did not wish to marry . . . no doubt Lady Mary had meant well but she had spoken without commission. . . ."[9] Which, taken literally, was true as it was Dudley, not Elizabeth, who had inveigled his sister into approaching the ambassador. A scene between the Queen and ambassador followed in which, wrote de Quadra, "I give as good as she brings," and at which Elizabeth seemed "very ill-pleased in being forced to declare herself."[10] When it was at last obvious that Dudley and the Queen had deliberately conspired—even to the extent of using the innocent Lady Mary as accomplice—the outraged minister's wrath was unbounded. "Lady Sidney finds her brother so changed that she had quarrelled with him," he wrote, "but this is not all. I have learned from a person who usually gives me true information that Lord Robert has sent instructions to have his wife poisoned and that all the dallying with us . . . is merely to keep Lord Robert's enemies in play until this villainy about his wife can be executed. I have also learnt certain things as to the terms on which the Queen and Lord Robert stand towards each other, which I could not have believed."[11] De Quadra's estimation of Dudley left nothing to the imagination. "Lord Robert is the worst young fellow I ever encountered. He is heartless, spiritless, treacherous and false. There is not a man in England who does not cry out upon him as the Queen's ruin."[12] Whatever the ambassador's opinion, Elizabeth had gained her objectives: much-needed time, a diversion of attention from herself and Dudley, with her suitor seemingly assuming the role of confidential adviser, intent only on the national welfare. More important, she had gained some inkling of the country's reaction to a Catholic marriage. Though the Duke of Norfolk and others of his party desired the match with the Archduke, when he spoke in favor of it, the English opinion was reflected in Dudley's accusation that Norfolk was "neither a good Englishman nor a loyal subject for wishing the Queen to marry outside the realm." Norfolk, who earlier had professed himself "ashamed of what was going on," had to be restrained from crossing rapiers with Dudley and later said heatedly, "Lord Robert shall never die in his bed unless he gives over his preposterous pretensions. . . ."

The attitude of those who had been so adroitly hoodwinked was summed up by Elizabeth's old adversary, the Count de Feria, who wrote de Quadra, "I should be glad if that woman were quite to lose her head and bring matters to a point, although when I think what a baggage she is, and what a crew she is surrounded by, there is probability enough of my wish coming true. . . ." [13]

When, in October, 1559, the Protestant Lords of the Congregation attempted to depose the Queen Regent on the grounds of introducing foreign troops into the country, William Cecil was adamant that England follow its advantage by an outright invasion of Scotland. As usual, Elizabeth vacillated—from "hour to hour the Queen's humour shifted." How much depended on the firm resistance of the Scots! Time and again the northern people had fought England. Now a smaller portion of them were fighting the greater power of France, and should they lose—and England be involved—England might be lost too. Even the Continent was fearful, for, as the Duchess of Parma, the Regent of the Netherlands, wrote to her brother, Philip of Spain, "The Queen of England is compromising us all . . . if the French once establish themselves in Scotland, England is theirs—and with England they will have the Low Countries." Sadly she admitted her perplexity. "If it be our political ruin to allow France to conquer England, it will be our spiritual ruin to allow that woman to go her own way. If she annexes Scotland and establishes the Protestant religion throughout the island, you know the humour of the Netherlands—you know the peril of the example." [14]

Elizabeth's own Councillors were of little help. In an eight-day debate, during which "ministers quarrelling flung epithets at one another and looked about in a fright for some escape from the terrible decision of necessity," the Queen listened to Cecil's desire "to keep England safe by making a fire in her neighbor's house." He was definite that "such an opportunity would not come again in our lifetime." De Quadra was aghast. "The Queen," he wrote, "is the same as ever. Cecil, who is the heart of the business, alone possesses her confidence and Cecil is obstinately bent on going forward with his Evangel till he destroy both it and himself. I have tried hard to gain him over, for we are the best of friends, but he is possessed with the chimerical notion of uniting Scotland and England under one creed and government and I might as well talk to a deaf adder as try to move him." [15]

Four days after the Council meeting, Elizabeth vetoed any suggestion of open war. She knew her people would abhor another conflict; she had no army worthy of the name and no money for mercenaries. Cecil pleaded that the English Crown was bound "in honour and conscience to defend and protect the realm of Scotland against the French." Elizabeth argued that she had succeeded by secret intervention, and as far as the world might see, her integrity was still intact. There would be no war. Instead, she would battle in secret, and if she failed, then that failure also would remain secret. In the meantime, delay might prove beneficial; she would gamble and wait and see.

In reality, neither the Queen nor her minister was a gambler. Elizabeth, to the end of her days, found it difficult to make a firm decision. Faced with the ruin of his proposal, however, Cecil gambled. In seeming dejection, he gave the Queen the spur she needed:

> It may please your Most Excellent Majesty—
> With sorrowful heart and watery eyes, I, your poor servant and most lowly subject, an unworthy Secretary, beseech your Majesty to pardon this my lowly suit, that considering the proceeding in this matter for removing the French out of Scotland doth not content your Majesty, and that I cannot—with conscience—give my contrary advice, I may, with your Majesty's favor and clemency, be spared to entermeddle therein.

Cecil then pleaded that he could be of little service to Elizabeth in situations where her mind was not agreeable. He was, he considered, "a minister of your Majesty's determinations and not of mine own. . . ." Yet he could not persevere in a course in which he did not believe. His letter continues:

> And, as for any other service, though it were in your Majesty's kitchen or garden, from the bottom of my heart, I am ready without respect of estimation, wealth or ease, to do your Majesty's commandment to my life's end. Whereof I wish with all my poor sorrowful heart, that your Majesty would make some proof, for this I do affair, that I have not had since your Majesty's reign, one day's joy, but in your Majesty's honour and weal.[16]

William Cecil's letter is an early example of the game a great minister and a great Queen would play many times during their association. Both were well aware of how much each needed the other. Cecil was, as he admitted, a creature of Elizabeth's making. He well knew the position of trust he held as her foremost adviser, and—as he was sure she would—Elizabeth yielded.

During Christmas, 1559, Sir William Winter, a young Master of the Ordnance, and fourteen ships of the English fleet were ordered to the Firth of Forth. In effect, Winter was to embargo any French supplies from reaching Mary of Guise. There was to be no outright declaration of war. He was to act on his own authority, with no official commission, and he received no orders, only "that he might provoke a quarrel if he did not find one."[17] If challenged, he was to declare his actions were "his own responsibility." Fortune favored the young adventurer, so willing to embark on such a questionable enterprise. He had the supreme good luck to find the Forth estuary filled with French ships containing munitions. They opened fire immediately on the English, who "drove them ashore on the land held by the rebels, who sacked them. . . ." When the Queen Regent's emissary arrived to ask if the English came as friends or foes, Winter audaciously answered he had come as a friend but, being fired on first, "had found enemies." He had, therefore, "determined with myself to give all the aid I might to the Congregation and to let the French from their wicked practices as far as I might—and that hereof the Queen's Highness, my mistress, is nothing privy."[18]

In the meantime, the French fleet, conveying troops to Scotland, was caught in a tremendous gale. Eight vessels were smashed and lost, their wreckage strewn along the coasts of Holland and East Anglia. The fiasco jarred de Noailles into acceptance of the degree to which Elizabeth had deceived him, and he challenged her interference in Scotland. The Queen answered him sharply, "You do well to look to your affairs and I shall look to mine!" With little attempt to conceal her displeasure, she cried, "Those armies and fleets of yours in Normandy are not meant for Scotland only. . .!" When de Noailles demurred and tried to soothe Elizabeth, saying, "Your Majesty's mistrust is without cause," she replied impatiently, "It may be so, but I find it well to be prepared. In times of danger, it is the custom of England to arm. If we are well-prepared, you will be the less tempted to meddle with us."[19] The confrontation earned a grudging, if somewhat negative, tribute from de Noailles. "She has more dissimulation than sincerity or honesty," he wrote, "few people play the game as well as she!"[20] He added, somewhat as an afterthought, "If you look her straight in the face, she can hardly help blushing, whatever assurance she may possess." The Spanish ambassador, writing to the Count de Feria, was more blunt: "This woman is possessed of a hundred-thousand devils and yet she pretends to me that she would like to be a nun and live in a cell and tell her beads from morning till night."[21]

Following her advantage, Elizabeth sent a further £3,000 north-ward; it was intercepted by the Earl of Bothwell, a young man later destined to play a larger role in history. Incensed, the French ambas-sador in Scotland wrote de Noailles. "You will tell the Queen what we have discovered. She will disavow it all, I suppose; but you will not on that account believe what she may say to you."[22] Lord Grey was sent to the Border with 6,000 foot soldiers and 2,000 horse to reinforce the garrison at Berwick, headquarters of the Duke of Norfolk. Norfolk's heart was not in the campaign. Suspecting Dudley had engineered his dispatch northward, he wrote bitterly to Cecil, "I am a subject and I will obey. . . . I would rather lie in prison than ever come on such a journey. . . ."

The French ambassador hurried to confront Elizabeth with her actions. As he sought to remonstrate with her, the Queen "threw off her mask of concealment" and cried heatedly, "You complain of the fleet and army we have sent to Scotland. What were we to do?" Referring to Mary Stuart's pretensions, she said, "You challenge our Crown; you deny our right to be Queen. You snatch the pretext of a rebellion to collect your armies on our Border and you expect us to sit still like children? You complain that we sent our fleet to intercept your rein-forcements. It is true we did so—and the fleet has done its work. And what then?"

If the minister had thought to discredit Elizabeth, her next words neatly turned the tables. "Those cannon, those arms, those stores which you sent to Leith were not meant only or chiefly for Scotland—they were meant for us! You tell us we are maintaining your rebels—we hate rebels, but the Scots are none. These men whom you call rebels are the same who fought against England at Pinkie Cleugh!" And then, gesturing with one long finger, she pointed to the ambassador. "It is *you* who are at fault—*you* who stole the rule of their country from them, overthrew their laws and sought to govern them with foreign garrisons. *You* have seized their fortresses, *you* have corrupted their money, *you* have filled their offices of trust with greedy Frenchmen, to rob and pillage them . . . till they saw their country about to become a province of France. . . ." When the royal temper had abated somewhat, she told the French minister, "You have given promises upon promises . . . we have forborne long enough. . . ."[23]

The English campaign, however, was not a success. Foul weather and troops grumbling at the insufficient provisions of food and clothing led a distracted Lord Grey to complain that "our men con-tinually run away . . . both by sea and land." At Norfolk's camp, conditions were worse. "Send money!" he wrote scathingly to Cecil.

"English troops will not fight if they are not fed. If they are not paid their wages, they must live by plunder and make enemies of the people!"[24] On the night of April 30, Grey advanced on Leith, and "the English batteries flashed and roared." Yet the town's wall held, and the next day, May Day, the French commander tauntingly festooned "a brave display of maypoles on the garrison's walls." When the rebel Scots besieged the walls, they fared poorly. "You know the Scots will climb no walls!" an English official wrote Cecil. Six days later, as the English attempted the feat, they were humiliated by the fact that their scaling ladders were six feet too short. The jeers of French were accompanied by a disastrous and murderous assault of shot, stones and blazing pitch poured from above.

Two miles away, a dying Queen Regent was carried to the walls of Edinburgh Castle to watch the flaming glow that was Leith. Yet still the town held. "If the French knew how weak we are, it might be dangerous to us . . ." Ralph Sadler wrote Cecil. Several hundred miles away, Elizabeth's concern and the realization of her worst fears did not help the royal disposition. Hearing the threat of mutiny in the English ranks and that " . . . poor men are fain to lie in the streets and can get no house room for money," that the Scots had offered no help to the hurt or wounded and had inflated their food prices so "that our soldiers cannot live on their wages," [25] she stormed at Cecil. After the interview, he wrote to his friend Nicholas Throckmorton in Paris, "God trieth us with many difficulties. The Queen's Majesty never liked this matter of Scotland . . . now the worst comes . . . I have had such a torment herein with the Queen's Majesty as an ague hath not in five fits so much abated!" [26]

It was the death of Mary of Guise at midnight on June 10, 1560, not English valor or military skill, which broke the French defense of Leith. The forty-five-year-old Mary had remained in Edinburgh Castle, her body bloated with dropsy, her spirit fatigued by the despair which left her small will to survive.* She had found little happiness in her marriage and had spent nineteen years of widowhood and exile in a foreign country. Cut off from friends and family, denied the company and solace of her only child, she had served six years as Regent, protecting the rights of a daughter she scarcely knew. She had faced

---

*At the end, Mary's main problem was one of communication with the French forces. Illustrative of her attempts to contact the French commander is the letter she sent to Lord Grey asking that a certain medicine be forwarded from a physician in Leith. Grey was to forward her letter. Instead, he held the letter to the fire, and invisible ink turned black, and the real contents appeared. He destroyed the letter and told the messenger to "tell his mistress that he would keep her counsel, but that such wares would not sell till a new market."

treachery, bloodshed and the insults of many of her subjects rather than falter in that trust.

The victorious Scots treated the body of the Queen Regent with respect; it was sent to France for burial in the soil of the country in whose cause she had spent a lifetime. The good for which Mary of Guise had labored—the maintenance of her faith in Scotland and the securing of the traditional tie to France—was passed on to her daughter, Mary Stuart. Mercifully, at the end, the knowledge of how that child would fare in similar circumstances was denied her.

Chapter Six

The death of the stout-hearted Mary of Guise left the English with a distinct advantage. On hearing of her death, Cecil had hurried to Edinburgh from Berwick; he had departed so hurriedly that, as he wrote the Privy Council in London, "some of us were constrained to lie that night in our clothing." He said the Scottish "hatred of the French is such and the causes so many, the benevolence at this time towards England is so great . . . that I see not that in long time the French shall recover the mind of Scotsmen against us as in times past hath been" and noted "that since the Queen's death, here be none that dare openly show favor to the French." [1]

Cecil had been reluctant to serve as the negotiating commissioner, yet was painfully aware there was no one else to do so. The war he had undertaken in the face of Elizabeth's opposition had turned out well, but the ultimate success was his management of the treaty negotiations and the terms he would obtain. With a few exceptions, he was not sure of his fellow Councillors' loyalty, and he wrote his friend Throckmorton "to write circumspectly, for how he should be judged of in his absence, he knew not. . . ."

On July 8, after sixteen days of negotiation in which Cecil noted, "they may contend about a word, but I mean to have the victory," the Treaty of Edinburgh was concluded, "a victory for the English and Scots on almost every point in dispute." By the terms of the treaty, French forces were to be withdrawn immediately. Mary Stuart and her husband, Francis II, were to relinquish any claim to the English throne and abstain from quartering the arms of England with their own. Elizabeth's sovereignty was acknowledged. The Queen had been adamant that Calais be returned to England, but Cecil held out little hope for such a concession. "I cannot give your Majesty counsel to embrace things so far," he wrote to Elizabeth in London. Unknown to him, as the treaty was being signed, a messenger was hurrying north with a letter from the Queen ordering Cecil not "to abandon the demand and restoration of Calais without payment of an indemnity."

The receipt of the letter left Cecil, as he wrote, in "the deep dungeon of sorrow than ever I thought any letter of your Majesty's should have thrown me." Luck, wisdom and the timely death of the Queen Regent had enabled him to effect the peace that he alone had envisioned. More than the Queen, he was responsible for the victory for which both Englishmen and Scots had fought. They had attempted the eviction of a foreign invader and had won. Had he insisted on the return of Calais, as he wrote the Queen, "the French ambassadors would have departed, the Duke of Norfolk would have to effect a siege at Edinburgh with the possibility of loss and certainly a great deal of casualties . . . and then by what means Calais would have been obtained . . . what means this manner of peace could have hereafter been obtained , I neither see nor can consider." [2] The gentle reproach was lost on Elizabeth. Both the minister and Norfolk were summoned home and, as Cecil wrote his friend Throckmorton in Paris, were "not thanked and not rewarded, sent home with no allowance either in credit or promise. . . ." It seemed to make little difference to the Queen that everywhere her success over the French had resulted in a new respect for England and its young sovereign. Perhaps, quixotically, she disliked acknowledging the victory in a war she had not favored. She had been proved wrong and had done little except give Cecil his head and then complain at the outcome.

Mr. Secretary Cecil returned to court on July 28, exhausted as much by Elizabeth's attitude as by the stress of the negotiations and the tiring journey home. He hoped time had lessened the Queen's displeasure, and that some recognition of the effort would be forthcoming. He had been away sixty-three days, incurring an expenditure of £ 252. Both he and Norfolk were summarily informed their charges would come from their own pockets. The Crown, said the Queen, had received no compensation by the terms of the Treaty! Though Lord Clinton wrote him "that no better service had ever been done to England" and old Lord Paget, retired now from active attendance in the Council, reiterated that "no one shall ever do such service to the realm as you have in concluding this peace. . . .," such gratitude was not reflected in the Queen or in the majority of his colleagues. Many of the Councillors—aware of the Queen's great disappointment regarding Calais—were more guarded in their comments to Cecil. Elizabeth was snappishly petulant with her chief minister. For one who could previously do no wrong, suddenly he could do no right. Even when he recommended, as was customary, that Elizabeth send some small present to the Scottish nobles who had done him good service during the negotiations, "good economy—spending £1,000 to save £20,000 in five years," he called it, she would not listen, sarcastically referring to his Scottish friends as his "brother saints."

William Cecil knew Elizabeth Tudor well. While he realized the extent of her disappointment over Calais—she, like her father before her, did not take denial lightly—he knew there was more to her attitude than political disenchantment. It was William Paulet, the Marquess of Winchester, who helped enlighten Cecil. He had entertained the Queen at his home* during her summer progress, and he now informed the minister that Elizabeth gave "too easy credence to certain back counsels." Cecil did not have to look far to know what the Lord Treasurer meant. Robert Dudley had used his nine weeks to good advantage. His attitude to Cecil was summed up in his remarks describing the Treaty of Edinburgh as "a perfect peace concluded forever—if it lasts so long. . . ." [4] Dudley's partisans and others jealous of Cecil's unusual capabilities, as well as his considerable influence with the Queen, "had persuaded her that she might have covered herself with glory and extorted the surrender of Calais." Their insistence caused Elizabeth to lose the perspective she was later to exercise so skillfully and believe that Cecil had effected too easy a peace to glorify himself personally. Once censured, it was easy to look into all other aspects of his political and personal life and question his moderation and tolerance. For the first and only time in her life, once the steadying influence of her foremost adviser and confidant was removed, the Queen succumbed to the attentions of her handsome Master of the Horse, neglecting her royal duties and allowing his influence to dominate. If there was to be a sacrifice to Dudley's overweening presumption, it was obviously destined to be William Cecil.

It was not long before news of the minister's fall from royal favor was known abroad, and Nicholas Throckmorton hurried to his friend's defense. "The worse hath been cast of his absence from hence by his friends," he wrote from Paris, "I know of none who love their country better!" And then, daringly, "I would the Queen's Majesty could love it so well. . . ." [5]

---

*Elizabeth, ever the coquette, complimented the seventy-year-old Marquess of Winchester who had been her host. "She liked so well my Lord Treasurer's house, and his great cheer at Basing, that she openly and merrily bemoaned him to be so old, "for else, by my troth," said she, "if my Lord Treasurer were a young man, I could find in my heart to have him to my husband before any man in England!"

Cecil was also concerned about Elizabeth's health. He noted she lacked the sparkle he had come to take for granted. "She is not so gay as usual," one court ambassador noted. She was also easily aroused to petty response, complaining of imagined faults and slights and exhibiting all too many unattractive feminine traits formerly lacking in the more regal monarch.

Once the court had returned from its summer progress in Hampshire, she continued her absence from the Council chamber; nor was there any access to her presence by foreign emissaries. Even her courtiers saw little of the Queen, unless they were the privileged few accepted as companions by Robert and Elizabeth. The two hunted and picnicked from morning till night. When the weather kept them inside, Dudley engrossed the Queen and "kept her shut up with him." On one occasion, while abroad in the court, she exclaimed, "she would be married ere six months were up," leaving her eager listeners to wonder whether she meant the Archduke, whose suit was under way, or her handsome Master of the Horse. Dudley, in a fit of elation, happily told his friends, "that he would be in a very different position a year from now. . . ."

And still her anger at Cecil did not abate. She neglected to use his services, and mortified, Cecil contemplated withdrawal from court. He was in despair at the scandal her conduct was causing, at the gossip permeating every corner and chamber of the royal residences, gossip bawdily shouted in the inns and taverns of the City and carried to the shires—to be greatly enlarged in the telling, he was in little doubt—by every courier on horseback or foot. "I dare not write that I might speak," he wrote Throckmorton, "God send her Majesty understanding which shall be her surety. . . . I omit to speak of my comfort in service that in this journey have for her honour oppressed myself with debt and have no consideration made me. . . ." [6]

After a month of royal rudeness and observing, in addition, the slackening of government procedures which needed a sovereign's attention, Cecil's depression—compounded by anxiety—inevitably turned to a deep and genuine fear. As a younger man, he had been exposed to the political exigencies of Henry VIII's reign; he had seen many heads fall. He had been involved personally in the tragedies of the Protector and Northumberland during the reigns of Edward and Mary. Prudent withdrawal and a bland demeanor had preserved his prestige and saved his possessions in those days. Royal disenchantment was often the prelude to royal condemnation. Cecil's solution, as before, was an inclination to disentangle himself from all court activity. He wrote the young Earl of Bedford, ". . . therefore, I do mean to leave it as I have too much cause, if I durst write all." There was, however, enough professional concern in Cecil to think of his replacement. "As soon as I can get Sir Nicholas Throckmorton placed, so soon I purpose to withdraw myself, which if I cannot do with ease, I will adventure some small displeasure, for so have I cause rather to do than to continue with a perpetual displeasure to myself." [7] On August 29 he decided to resign his office.

By the middle of the first week in September he was considering ways and means by which his departure might be effected. He had reached the end of his patience—and his courage. Elizabeth's shameful personal treatment of him was one thing; her disregard for her royal position and its ensuing responsibilities was another. Meeting with the Bishop de Quadra, with whom, despite their different religious and political policies, he had always had a warm relationship based on their mutual respect for each other's talents, Cecil unburdened his soul. The extraordinary conversation illustrates the minister's wretched despondency. In an outburst rare for one usually so self-controlled, he revealed his feelings to de Quadra, perhaps hoping the ambassador might shock Elizabeth into an awareness that he, Cecil, had been unable to achieve. De Quadra wrote in full to the Duchess of Parma, the Regent of the Netherlands and a sister of Philip of Spain. The letter is dated September 11. After writing, "I came to Windsor where the Queen is, five days ago," de Quadra continued:

> Since my last letter to your Highness so many great and unexpected matters have taken place here, that I think it right to give you immediate information of them.
> On the third of this month, the Queen spoke to me about her marriage with the Archduke. She said she had made up her mind to marry, and that the Archduke was to be the man. She has just now told me drily that she does not intend to marry and that it cannot be.

This marriage was the union proposed earlier for which Dudley and the Queen had used the guileless Lady Sidney as emissary. According to the letter, Elizabeth had changed her mind in a period of eight days, but his "just now" might have been even earlier—on the sixth, for instance—when he arrived at Windsor. Unfortunately, he does not refer to definite dates in the remainder of his letter:

> After my conversation with the Queen, I met with the Secretary Cecil, whom I knew to be in disgrace. Lord Robert, I was aware, was en-deavouring to deprive him of his place.
> With little difficulty, I led him to the subject and, after many protesta-

tions and entreaties that I would keep secret what he was about to tell me, he said that the Queen was going on so strangely that he was about to withdraw from her service. It was a bad sailor, he said, who did not make for port when he saw a storm coming and for himself he perceived the most manifest ruin impending over the Queen through her intimacy with Lord Robert. The Lord Robert had made himself master of the business of the State and of the person of the Queen, to the extreme injury of the realm with the intention of marrying her, and she herself was shutting herself up in the palace to the peril of her health and life. That the realm would tolerate the marriage he said he did not believe; he was, therefore, determined to retire into the country, although he supposed they would send him to the Tower before they would let him go.

He implored me for the love of God to remonstrate with the Queen, to persuade her not utterly to throw herself away as she was doing, and to remember what she owed to herself and to her subjects. Of Lord Robert, he twice said he would be better in Paradise than here.

De Quadra had told Cecil that he was "deeply grieved" and reiterated his concern for the Queen's well-being, pointed out how he had labored for the union with the Archduke, to what avail Cecil well knew. After a few remarks about the internal affairs of the country, his letter continues:

> Last of all, he said that they were thinking of destroying Lord Robert's wife. They had given out that she was ill, but she was *not* ill at all. She was very well, and was taking care not to be poisoned. God, he trusted, would never permit such a crime to be accomplished, or allow so wicked a conspiracy to prosper.
>
> This business of the Secretary cannot but produce some great results, for it is terrible. Many men, I believe, are as displeased as he, especially the Duke of Norfolk, whom he named to me as one of the most injured by Lord Robert and most hostile to him.
>
> The day after this conversation, the Queen on her return from hunting told me that Lord Robert's wife was dead or nearly so, and begged me to say nothing about it. Assuredly it is a matter full of shame and infamy, but for all this I do not feel sure that she will immediately marry him, or indeed that she will marry at all. . . .

De Quadra then prophesied that "the country will not have a woman over them anymore and this one is likely to go to sleep in the palace and to wake with her lover in the Tower. . . ." He said nothing could be expected but "revolution and change" and boasted that "if I made up to them, they would trust me and tell me all. . . ." At the end came the devastating news:

Since this was written the death of Lord Robert's wife has been given out publicly. The Queen put in Italian, *"Que si ha rotto il collo."* (She has broken her neck.) It appears that she fell down a staircase.[8]

This letter, encompassing the candid facts of Elizabeth's involvement with Dudley, her disregard for her responsibilities and his intention to dissociate himself as quickly as possible, shows the depths of Cecil's despair. Estranged from Elizabeth, certainly unable to convince her of the folly which would deprive her eventually of any royal dignity, if not the throne, his one hope lay in the intercession of the Spaniard for whom he knew Elizabeth had a high regard. There is no other answer for his imprudence. He could not know, however, the extent to which his words would compromise the Queen of England for centuries.[9]

The Spanish ambassador's letter is misleading. In the phrases "after my conversation with the Queen, I met with the Secretary Cecil" and "the day after this conversation" his chronology becomes blurred. If de Quadra meant to imply—as it appears—that he spoke with Elizabeth on the sixth, with Cecil immediately afterward and again on the following day—which would have been Saturday, the seventh—then Elizabeth told him that Amy "was dead or nearly so" *before the accident had even occurred*—a fact so incredibly unbelievable as to negate itself. If, however, the Queen's comment meant that Amy was dying of cancer, the phrase was innocent and becomes meaningful only because Lady Dudley was found dead later under very suspicious circumstances. If, on the other hand, de Quadra arrived at Windsor on the sixth, met with the Queen on the seventh, with Cecil on the eighth and then, "the day after," learned from Elizabeth of Amy's accident—her fall from a flight of stairs—then the chronology works out correctly and de Quadra's attempt at somehow implicating the Queen of England in Lady Dudley's death is not valid. Actually, his phrase "since this was written" at the end implies the ambassador wrote the letter over a period of several days, as news became available from different sources. "The day after," therefore, was more likely Monday, September 9, when news of Amy's accident had just reached Windsor—news which had not as yet been verified.* If the conversation took place beforehand, then Elizabeth was probably referring to Lady Dudley's cancer. But the incredible timing of Cecil's comments—and de Quadra's eager willingness to recount them suggestively—gives the

---

*Latter-day historians have agreed in this instance that de Quadra employed what Professor Pollard called "a deft economy of dates."

impression that Elizabeth knew of the mishap before it happened. Yet the letter does not reveal this to be actually so—it is only implied, deliberately or otherwise. Sometime during that fateful weekend, Elizabeth mentioned Amy Dudley as being near dead, and she wisely asked the ambassador to say nothing until later. And then de Quadra *had* to wait until the news of Lady Dudley's death was made public, which certainly occurred by Tuesday, September 10, at the latest. There is no other explanation for his having waited until the eleventh to write the horrifying news, *if he had actually known of it on the seventh*, which impression he gives in his letter. Presumably he spent some time recounting what had happened with Cecil and his conversation with the Queen and, on the eleventh, added that "since this was written the death of Lord Robert's wife has been given out publicly . . . it appears she fell down a staircase." He obviously had been waiting to hear what the announcement would be; all he had previously from the Queen was that "Lord Robert's wife was dead or nearly so. . . ."

The death of Amy Robsart Dudley, which became a *cause célèbre* that rocked England and the Continent in the autumn of 1560, has intrigued generations of scholars, amateur criminologists and modern medical experts. Each century has contributed to its own interpretation consistent with the accumulated knowledge of the time and each adherent, pro or con, seeks to strengthen his argument at the expense or lessening of his opponents'. Still, essentially, the fact remains that on Sunday, September 8, 1560, the body of Lady Dudley was found at the foot of a staircase, and only a handful of letters exist to tell what occurred.

The beginning of the end for Amy Dudley commenced about four years after her marriage, when she left her parents' home in Norfolk. It was then that Robert Dudley had made inquiries about purchasing an estate of his own, but the acquisition was never completed. This, in itself, is a large part of the Amy-Robert puzzle. As yet Dudley did not possess any great wealth, but his prospects in 1558 were bright indeed, and by 1560 he was well in a position to afford an estate of his own consistent with his rank and one that might contribute, through its farm leases, to his own purse. His home at Kew was a gift from the Queen; he lodged for the most part at court. After almost eleven years of marriage, both he and Amy must have realized that they were not destined to have children. It is also possible he thought Amy incapable of helping to administer an estate when, during his long absences, someone in authority other than a paid Household Steward would be an absolute necessity. The only extant letter from Amy, which she wrote to a "Mr. Flowerdew" in August of either 1559 or 1560, illuminates her relationship with her husband:

MR. FLOWERDEW—

I understand by Grise that you put him in remembrance of what you spoke to me of concerning the going of certain sheep at Siscombe, and although I forgot to move my lord therefore before his departing, yet notwithstanding, knowing your accustomed friendship towards my lord and me, I neither may nor can deny you that request in my lord's absence of mine own authority, yea and it were a greater matter, as if any good occasion may serve you, so try me.

Desiring you further that you will make sale of the wool so soon as is possible, although you sell it for six shillings the stone, or as you would sell for yourself; for my lord so earnestly required me at his departing to see those poor men satisfied as though it had been a matter depending upon life! Wherefore, I force not to sustain a little loss thereby, to satisfy my lord's desire; and so to send that money to Grise's house to London, by Bridewell, to whom my lord hath given order for the payment thereof. And thus I end, always troubling you, wishing that occasion serve me to requite you; until that time, I must pay with thanks.

And so to God I leave you, from Hayes, this 7th of August,

Your assured during life,

AMYE DUDLEY[10]

In this letter, Amy's concern and affection for her husband are apparent. Their relationship was still a personal one, and in this instance, when she had been remiss in completing the sale of some wool referred previously through her to Lord Dudley, her anxiety is evident. Now she is concerned enough to sell even "to sustain a little loss" so that the money can be forwarded to London for payment so Dudley may "see those poor men satisfied." Her husband's preoccupation with court matters could also still disturb Amy. Since his responsibilities as Master of the Horse were always dispensed capably and with little fuss, the "weighty affairs" which "sorely troubled" him can only have been the possibility that one royal suitor for Elizabeth's favor might prove more successful than another, an eventuality Dudley had come to dread. Amy was sufficiently sensitive where Robert was concerned to be "not altogether in quiet for his sudden departing." If, as was rumored, she was ill, then her dismay is even more understandable. Her husband came infrequently and rarely stayed more than one night. She must have missed the man from whom, for several years, she had had closer companionship.

By September, 1560, Amy was living at Cumnor Hall, six miles north of the market village of Abingdon and four miles from Oxford. Cumnor had once been a monastery and was situated idyllically amid a pleasance of trees and lush shrubs; ponds and terraces overlooked a magnificent view of the Downs. The property was owned by William Owen, son of Dr. Owen, Henry VIII's personal physician, to whom the King had given the monastic lands; they had since been leased by Anthony Forster, a Steward of Lord Robert Dudley's. By the terms of the lease, the Owens still occupied one section of the venerable building, Forster lived in another part, and the remainder was given over to Lady Dudley and her servants.

Amy's life at Cumnor was quiet. Presumably she had the companionship of the Forsters, of the Owens and of a Mrs. Odingsells, a friend of the Forsters'. The entire household and its living arrangements were eminently respectable, not unlike hundreds of others. In this case, the lacking element was suitability. For the wife of the Queen's Master of the Horse to be living as a paying guest in another's rented home was entirely inconsistent with Amy Dudley's rank and lent itself to its share of gossip. Other rumors were also prevalent. Those which emanated from the court—of the Queen's consuming interest in Robert Dudley—also filled the Gallery and damp scullery of Cumnor Hall. They could only have further injured Amy's pride, warping her spirit as they broke her heart. If she actually had "a cancer in one of her breasts," then her mental agony was only compounded by a crippling and painful ailment. If it is true, as was said, that Amy was taking care not to be poisoned, then the chilling element of fear was probably also present.

Immediately after the news of her death reached the court, Robert Dudley was sent to his house at Kew to be confined at the Queen's pleasure, for tradition demanded that anyone suspected of a crime be removed from the royal presence. Previously, he had received news from Cumnor regarding Amy's health which had "disquieted him," and he had sent a kinsman, one "Cousin Blount," to make further inquiries.[11]

Windsor, September 9, 1560.

Cousin Blount,
    Immediately upon your departing from me there came to me Bowes, by whom I understand that my wife is dead, and, as he saith, by a fall from a pair of stairs. Little other understanding can I have of him. The greatness

and the suddenness of the misfortune doth so perplex me, until I do hear from you how the matter stands, or how this evil doth light upon me, considering what the malicious world will bruit, as I can take no rest.

And, because I have no way to purge myself of the malicious talk that I know the wicked world will use, but one, which is the very plain truth to be known, I do pray you, as you have loved me, and do tender me and my quietness, and as now my special trust is in you, that you will use all devices and means you possibly can for the learning of the truth, wherein have no respect to any living person; and as by your own travail and diligence, so likewise by order of law, I mean, by calling of the coroner, and charging him to the uttermost, from me, to have good regard to make choice of no light or slight persons, but the most discreet and substantial men for the juries; such as for their knowledge may be able to search honorably and duly, by all manner of examinations, the bottom of the matter; and for their uprightness will earnestly and sincerely deal therein without respect. And that the body be viewed and searched accordingly by them, and in every respect to proceed by order and law.

In the meantime, cousin Blount, let me be advertised from you by this bearer, with all speed, how the matter doth stand; for, as the cause and the manner thereof doth marvellously trouble me, considering my case many ways, so shall I not be at rest till I may be ascertained thereof; praying you ever, as my trust is in you, and as I have ever loved you, do not dissemble with me, neither let anything be hid from me, but send your true conceit and opinion of the matter, whether it happened by evil chance, or by villainy; and fail not to let me hear continually from you. And thus, fare you well in much haste.

Your loving friend and kinsman, much perplexed.

R. D.

I have sent for my brother, Appleyard, because he is her brother* and other of her friends, also, to be there, that they may be privy and see how all things do proceed.[12]

Robert Dudley's letter clearly stands as his own best defense against the prevalent suspicion that he had conspired his wife's death. His disbelief, anxiety and shock are evident throughout; his words ring with a veracity which would be almost impossible to simulate. Dudley had many talents, not all of them worthwhile or attractive, but artful literary composition was not one. Now, under restraint at Kew, remembrance of his past imprisonment and the possible loss of his honors, preferments—perhaps even a Crown—overwhelmed him, and his words convey his incredulity. He was very aware of what the "malicious world" would think and does not deny that therein lay a great deal of his distress. In begging the help of his kinsman, he was

*John Appleyard was a half brother to Amy Dudley.

surely aware that few of those friends he could count on would risk any taint of association with him under his present circumstances. He did not hypocritically mourn his wife. Never, then or during the following months, did he affect any sorrow for the dead woman. Instead, he insisted "that the body be viewed" and that there be a thorough investigation to determine "whether it happened by evil chance, or by villainy." His concern is such that he asked that Amy's brother, Arthur Robsart, and her half brother, John Appleyard, "and other of her friends" be summoned "to see how all things do proceed." He himself might have had serious suspicions that Amy had indeed been murdered. Certainly he accepted that the world would consider it so. How better to discredit such suspicions than by insisting that her friends and family be there?

Blount, mindful of Robert's trust, diligently pursued his commission. Riding to Cumnor Hall, he had met Bowes, the messenger, carrying the tragic news to the court. He wrote to Dudley immediately afterward. "The present advertisement I can give to your Lordship at this time is, too true it is that my Lady is dead; and, as it seemeth, with a fall, but yet how or which way I cannot learn." He told the anxious Dudley that once he had heard the news, instead of proceeding directly to Cumnor, he had stayed overnight at Abingdon, "because I was desirous to hear what news went abroad in that county. At my supper I called for mine host [the innkeeper] and asked him what news was thereabout, taking upon me that I was going into Gloucestershire. He said, 'there was fallen a great misfortune within three or four miles of the town.' I asked him by what chance? He said, 'He knew not.' I asked him what his judgment and the judgment of the people? He said, 'Some were disposed to say well and some evil.' " Blount then asked the innkeeper what he himself thought and was relieved to hear the answer: " 'By my troth,' said the man, 'I judge it a misfortune because it chanced in that honest gentleman's [Forster's] house. His great honesty doth much curb the evil thoughts of the people.' " Blount next asked the innkeeper what the servants who lived at Cumnor Hall thought or what "they who had waited upon her should say . . . to this." And out of the servants' stories grew the details of Amy Dudley's last day on earth, details as mystifying as the woman herself.

Sunday September 8, 1560, was a festive day, for it was the opening of a local fair in the village of Abingdon. When Amy Dudley appeared at breakfast, she announced that all her household must go to the fair. As her own servants were numerous, this meant there would be none left in the house except those employed by Mr. Forster. She was insistent that *all* should go and became, in the words of one of them, "very angry with any of her own sort that made reason for tarrying at home." The servant explained that by "her own sort" Amy had meant the gentlewomen such as Mrs. Odingsells and Mrs. Owen. Mrs. Odingsells remarked that it being a Sunday, the "vulgar sort" would be at the fair and "it would be better for a gentlewoman to go tomorrow." At this, there was a further display of Amy's temper. She retorted that Mrs. Odingsells "might choose and go at her pleasure, *but all hers should go.*" When one of the servants ventured to question her unreasonable insistence and asked "who should keep her company if they all went?" Amy remarked tartly that she would dine with Mrs. Owen in another part of the house.

Amy had had her way. One by one, the servants left for the fair. Old Mrs. Odingsells remained in her apartment; Mrs. Owen was in her rooms; the Forsters were away. When the servants returned that evening, the body of Amy Dudley was lying at the foot of the stairs, with a broken neck. Presumably, once her servants had departed, no one from the other sections of the building had entered the part reserved for Lady Dudley. Amy's body bore no bruises, and the hood on her head was still carefully arranged and firm on her hair.*

Blount questioned one Pinto, Amy's maid. "She was a good and virtuous gentlewoman," the distraught maid replied, which was not surprising since Pinto was known to "dearly love" Lady Dudley. "She would daily pray upon her knees," continued the talkative woman, and "divers times," she said, she had heard Lady Dudley pray to God to "deliver me from desperation!" When Blount suggested suicide, Pinto was insistent that such an evil thought had never entered her Lady's mind. "No, good Mr. Blount," she countered, "do not judge so of my words. If you should so gather, I am sorry I said so much."

As Blount wrote to Dudley, "My Lord, it is most strange that this chance should fall upon you, as it passeth the judgment of any man to say how it is, but then the tales I do hear of her make me to think she had a strange mind, as I will tell you at my coming." When Pinto was queried about her own explanation for Lady Dudley's bizarre end, she noted that by her faith, "she did judge the death of her Lady to be very chance and neither done by man nor by herself."[13]

An inquest was held, and Blount confirmed Dudley's hope that the jurors were "as wise and as able men to be chosen on such a matter as any men . . . as ever I saw. . . ." No witness could be found to give any information how Amy Dudley had fallen down the stairs, and after a full inquiry, the jury rendered the only possible verdict: accidental' death.[14]

*This fact, however, was not given out until twenty-four years later.

At Kew, where he remained in exile from court, Lord Robert's days passed in agonizing frustration and suspense. Although he was measured and fitted out for mourning clothes, by tradition he could not attend Amy's funeral, even had he been able to do so. His profound anxiety for his reputation had been unrelieved by any word from the Queen. But she did send William Cecil, who, only days before, had contemplated resigning, primarily because of the "mischief" engendered by the very man he was now sent to visit. It is tantalizing to conjecture Cecil's feelings in view of his recent words to de Quadra; undoubtedly he was glad to see for himself first hand the emotional climate at Kew. The occupant faced continual disfavor, imprisonment or worse, in which case Cecil could be helpful in sentencing. If, as was still possible, Amy's death left the way clear for a future marriage between his sovereign and Dudley, then Cecil wished his association with the man to be firm. Faced with the courtier's obvious bewilderment and distress, Cecil undoubtedly decided to regard him as innocent until further proof was forthcoming, and his visit did much to console the tormented Dudley. Out of gratitude he wrote Cecil expressing his appreciation "for the great friendship you have shown towards me, I shall not forget." He asked Cecil's continued support and said, "I am sorry so sudden a chance should breed me so great a change for methinks I am here all this while as it were in a dream and too far, too far, from the place I am bound to be . . . ," [15] meaning most certainly the court and the Queen.

Never in one instance did Dudley evince any remorse or mourn the loss of his wife. The calm, almost offhand acceptance of Amy's death by all involved is most noticeably illustrated by the reaction of Dudley's brother-in-law Lord Hastings. In his home at Ashby de-la-Zouch, he was writing Lord Robert homey incidents of country life as the news of Lady's Dudley's death was brought by messenger. He added a few pious sentiments and then stated that Robert would understand what he was attempting to say better than he could say it and then continued with his letter. Again, there was no false mourning, no attempt to alleviate a sorrow or suffering he knew would be absent in Amy's husband. Amazingly, there was not even a message from his wife, Amy's sister Katherine, who plainly did not feel her sister's death merited any comment. This incident, along with the attitude of other contemporaries, shows clearly that Amy's death—aside from its appalling manner and even more appalling implications—was regarded by many as a release and a convenience all round.

It is this attitude, more than anything else, that offers a more logical solution to the puzzling death of Amy Dudley. Always there had been rumors of her "uncouthness," her "simplemindedness" or, as Blount put it, "her strange mind." This did not necessarily refer to a lack of intellect. Amy was no fool, and her one extant letter shows she was properly educated for her time and place in life. However, these statements—made in the parlance of their own era—might have meant a very different condition. In the words of modern usage, they might have meant that Amy was an emotionally unbalanced person, a "social misfit" as she might be called today, one who was "her own worst enemy." Once the physical aspect of their marriage had deteriorated, this, more than anything else, would have driven Dudley from her side. It can account for his refusal to burden the woman with an estate to manage, knowing she could never cope with the myriad household problems which confronted every sixteenth-century housewife. It would account for his refusal to bring her to court, where her precarious emotional balance might prove costly to him, with unexpected social scenes and political risks which would be as embarrassing as they were unnecessary. It would account for the attitude of her family, who seemed to waste few tears or empty words on their relative, who, very possibly, had done little to endear herself to them. It would account for her constant need for change—the incessant traveling and visiting. No money was spared to keep her comfortable; her husband's account books are ample testimony to his generosity.

Yet even money could not buy Amy a permanent home, which she probably did not want, presuming instead to inflict herself on relatives and friends who could not or dared not refuse her accommodation, no matter how much a nuisance she might have been. It also accounts for her strange actions on the day she sent everyone to the fair. By that time the idea of suicide may have entered her untidy mind. In that strange emotional climate in which she existed—fed by the rumors and gossip she heard—she might have realized there was little point in continuing to live. Since she knew of her husband's involvement with the Queen, some climax was inevitable, and prolonging her life was only an open invitation to murder or slow poisoning. If Amy was indeed precariously balanced, the fear and dread of such a fate would not help. In her overwrought condition, there might have been one moment of supreme anger when she decided on suicide as the only way she could thwart the Queen of England's desire and Robert Dudley's ambition. In a supreme gesture of defiance and despair, she would avenge herself for Robert's neglect and attain in death what she could not in life: she would thwart irrevocably any chance of her husband marrying Elizabeth. Or, in a magnificent gesture of love, she would remove herself from the scene so thoroughly that he *could* wed the

Queen. Or perhaps—in those last lonely moments—she simply decided that *anything* was better than living a life that was only a sham. She was going to die anyway; the pain from the breast cancer was getting worse all the time, and this, combined with her distraught condition, could account for Pinto's overhearing her prayerful plea to "deliver me from desperation!"

There still remains, of course, the possibility of accident, murder or a natural death. A more recent theory advances the probability that one suffering from advanced breast cancer is prone to a spontaneous collapse of the spine, which has grown extremely brittle, a result of the disease itself.* This may have occurred at a time when Amy, in a fit of pique, had ordered her servants out of the house and, in one of fate's more magnificent coincidences, suffered a collapse on the stairs while alone. Alternatively, she might have been deliberately misled by any number of ruses. It might not have seemed odd to one of a "strange mind" to be asked by someone she trusted to release her servants for the day and then find, once alone, that he who had duped her was a murderer in the pay of those who realized how greatly the death would compromise Dudley and the Queen or, conversely, how it might result in Elizabeth actually marrying Dudley, who would, in turn, greatly reward them. But a fall downstairs is no way to kill anyone, and a professional murderer would have sought a method more certain. Yet Amy, if bent on suicide, might have thought it a very good method indeed—and had succeeded beyond her wildest and warped expectations.

Whatever the reason for the death of poor, misguided Amy Dudley, there is no verifiable conclusion other than the jury's ultimate decision of accidental death. Despite the horror her death had generated and the suspicion that pointed so strongly to the Queen and her Master of the Horse, one fact remained. Robert Dudley was now free to wed, and it remained to be seen if the woman whose heart had so indisputably been given into his keeping would follow her desire, even at the expense of her honor.

*Professor Ian Aird, in *English Historical Review*, 1956.

The Coquette

*I have never been able to be so allured by
the prospect of advantages or so terrified by
misfortunes, swayed by honours or fettered
by affection, nay, not even so smitten by the
fear of death, as to enter upon marriage.*

Chapter Seven

For Elizabeth Tudor, the death of Amy Dudley was a personal disaster. It changed the course of her life, her relationship with Dudley and, inevitably, the history of her country. Had Amy lived, there might have been an annulment or a divorce and a subsequent marriage to Dudley. Given the Queen's unpredictability, the chance is there. If Dudley had, in fact, become King Consort, there is no way of concluding what his influence on the nation and its Queen would have been except that it would have been considerable; the antagonism of his peers alone would have constituted a formidable threat. Few possessed the wisdom of Elizabeth's longtime partisan the Earl of Sussex, whose dislike and distrust of Dudley were well known. Yet, said Sussex, everyone desired a "blessed prince." The surest way to get one, he advised, was to let Elizabeth "choose after her own affection. Let her take the man by the sight of whom her own senses are aroused by desire (*omnes ejus sensus titillarentur*) and whomsoever that man might be," Sussex promised, "him will I love and honour and serve to the uttermost."[1] But Sussex stood alone. His powerful colleagues would have used their considerable influence against Dudley, and civil war between rival political and religious factions would have been an open invitation to French and Spanish aggrandizement.

But Amy had not lived. Instead, she had died in a manner many considered criminal. In three days the news was known all over England and there, as on the Continent, suspicion—ugly in its strength—pointed at Lord Robert and through him to the Queen. In France, Mary Stuart exemplified the prevalent outcry when she laughed shrilly and said, "The Queen of England is going to marry her Horsekeeper who has killed his wife to make room for her!" Englishmen abroad considered themselves shamed by the appalling news, which only confirmed rumors that had been filtering through the back rooms of royal dwellings for months. Whenever unexpected violence occurred, murder was the answer, and this sixteenth-century rationale is summed up in the reaction of Nicholas Throckmorton, who wrote from Paris complaining to Lord North that he could only wish himself dead or away from the Frenchmen. "One laugheth at us, another threateneth, another revileth the Queen . . ." he noted abjectly, "and some spoke of the Queen and some others that which every hair on my head standeth at, and my ears glow to hear." Catholics needled Throckmorton. "What religion is this that a subject shall kill his wife and the Prince not only bear withal, but marry him?" they asked. He cried that "all estimation the English had girt is clean gone. . . ." From Scotland, the English ambassador, Thomas Randolph, echoed a similar shame, writing that "the news so passioneth my heart that no grief ever I felt was like unto it." From dozens of pulpits English preachers, infinitely preferring the Scottish Arran to Dudley as a match for their Queen, exhorted their congregations. A Coventry preacher named Lever wrote to Cecil "of the grievous and dangerous suspicion and mutterings of the death of her that was the wife of my Lord Robert Dudley." Even de Quadra, not without some satisfaction, proclaimed, "She is in a fair way to lie down one evening the Queen and wake next morning plain Madame Elizabeth, she and her paramour with her." [2]

The distressing awareness that again she was an object of suspicion bore upon Elizabeth. For months she had been the popular cynosure of all eyes, secure in the protective grandeur of the Crown. The attention remained but was now of a very different aspect. She had suffered obloquy before. She had been imprisoned, spied on and suspected of treason. At that time, her demeanor had saved her in the face of a predicted final abandonment to prison or the scaffold. Even as shock, disbelief and a chilling apprehension enveloped her at the news from Cumnor, Elizabeth recognized at once the compromising position in which she, as Queen, was placed. And it was as an outwardly secure and inviolate Queen, not as a frightened woman, that she acted.

It would be within the realm of possibility if—perhaps for only a brief moment—Elizabeth might have wondered if Robert were guilty of complicity in his wife's death. Her interest in her Master of the Horse had extended to a discussion of marriage. A Crown, Elizabeth well knew, was a powerful inducement to justify any action to bring its realization closer. The effect of the hateful gossip, the growing suspicion of her personally and, indirectly, of the Crown itself would be tremendous, and she did not minimize its impact. While she accepted with satisfaction the fact of her personal popularity, there was no guarantee that her subjects' affection could or would withstand such a scandal. As head of the state and particularly of the Church—that Church she had so shored up it now had its greatest chance for survival—she must be above reproach. If her subjects judged her, the possessor of the Crown, guilty, they would consider that guilt theirs also. Their resentment that their Queen must suffer such iniquity she knew to be compounded by the fact that it was caused by such as Robert Dudley.

Guilt, however, was an alien feeling to Elizabeth Tudor. Morally, she was as guilty as if she had pushed the unfortunate Amy down the stairs. She had enticed Lady Dudley's husband from her side, loaded him with honors, preferments and material possessions. She had taken advantage of her own royal position to bind Dudley as closely as possible without the disadvantage or legal inconvenience of a marriage. She had given little or no thought to Amy's position or feelings.

If Elizabeth regretted her former imprudence—and it is doubtful she did—her great pride would not allow her to admit the fact or necessarily alter her conduct which might be considered a shamefaced admission of error. Given any occasion—and there were to be many in her life—when remorse might have overcome her, she inevitably emulated her father's masterly performance in a display of self-righteous justification. Now, with so much in the balance, she exceeded herself, yet in her action there was a tacit support of Robert. In public and private she remained calm. While Robert was under restraint at Kew, there had been no contact with the court except his visit from William Cecil. If she was frightened, it did not show in her reaction, and this, perhaps more than anything else, helped convince those who could witness her performance that the Queen was innocent. She absorbed herself and others in work at the Council table, at the same time demanding to be informed of each and every happening in the Dudley case. She ordered the court into mourning, and on September 22, two weeks from the day of Amy's death, services were held in the royal Chapel, after which she was buried in a funeral "which would cost better than £2,000."[3]

In each and every instance, Elizabeth's manner proclaimed for all to see that Majesty was incorruptible—and innocent. Though a servant of the Crown had been defamed by a puzzling and shameful tragedy, under no condition must that suspicion fall on the Queen.

As in similar circumstances during her adolescence, the effort took its toll of Elizabeth. Nicholas Throckmorton, annoyed and frightened beyond endurance at the malicious rumors prevalent at the French court, sent R. J. Jones, his secretary, to Greenwich "to advertise her Majesty of such things as might touch her . . . to be opened but to herself." Elizabeth heard Jones patiently, interrupting him at one point to say, "I have heard of this before, and he [Throckmorton] need not have sent you withal." When Jones launched into a recital of Dudley's background "the point that touched his race," Elizabeth could not contain her amusement. She smiled, "turned herself first to one side, and then to the other, and set her hand before her face." She informed the secretary that Dudley had been at the court on the day of Amy's death. "The matter," she said, "had been tried in the country and found to be contrary to that reported . . . it would neither touch her own honour nor his honesty." She added almost gently that "the ambassador knoweth somewhat of my mind in these things." Jones watched Elizabeth intently, however, and wrote Throckmorton, "The Queen's Majesty looketh not so hearty and well as she did, by a great deal, and surely the matter of my Lord Robert doth much perplex her. . . ."[4]

To deflect suspicion—and to take advantage of Elizabeth's sudden penchant for work—Cecil and the Council worked again for her marriage. Matthew Parker, the Archbishop of Canterbury, and his fellow Bishops of London and Ely, wrote their sovereign it was her stern duty to give herself in wedlock so she might bear a child which would guarantee the Protestant succession. The Council and clergy's great zeal for and insistence on her marriage were counterbalanced by a complete lack of regard for or understanding of Elizabeth's position at a moment when she was especially vulnerable. While she had previously relished the feminine satisfaction of being an object of desire, she was now impervious to any thought of marriage, and her temper revealed her irritation at the manner in which her royal person was bartered in the marital and diplomatic market. She knew that eventually she might be compelled to endure what she could view only as a degrading sacrifice, but in her mind the time was not yet. So once more the responsibilities of her sovereignty and the yoke of public opinion settled on a personality which, in the past several months, had experienced for the first time the love of a man who had aroused the normal yearnings of her sex. Those few months were all Elizabeth Tudor was ever to have of a free courtship and of an even freer response. She had had the satisfaction of a triumph in the Scottish conflict—a conflict in which she had privately placed little hope. But such satisfaction had eluded her where her innermost feelings were concerned—those feelings which, in themselves, were still something of a startling novelty to acknowledge and display openly.

So once more it was necessary to submerge her emotions. She heard her Councillors and churchmen with inward resentment and outward compliance. Few recognized what the effort cost, but the effect—combined with worry over Dudley—was apparent in the harassed-looking woman who confronted Throckmorton's secretary. The seeming disregard for Elizabeth's personal inclinations was not all the Councillors' fault. There was little or no precedent for the ministers to act on, for in a personal way the whole state of Queenship was unique with Elizabeth. While her sister had lived, when single or married, Mary's feelings had always been evident on her plain face and apparent in her deep voice. And, thirty-five years before, when Catherine of Aragon, Mary's mother, had fought for her honor and her husband against the advances of Elizabeth's mother, Anne Boleyn, the demands of state and subjects were outwardly satisfied in the person of Henry VIII, their father. The private feelings—or even the personal prerogatives—of any Queen had little impact on the nation other than the emotional, for she was expected to subjugate her feelings to the necessities of husband, Church and State. And, should the King wish some source of satisfaction other than a Queen often provided by reasons of state, rather than personal choice, no one would think him the worse if he took a mistress.

It was now that Elizabeth realized, as she never had before, that she could not remain impervious to the demands of state; the challenge of the monarchy required an inviolate Queen of unquestioned honor. If Majesty was Divine—and all the Tudors firmly believed it was—the baser reactions of the common person were forbidden her. One more sophisticated than Elizabeth would not have made such a display of herself as she had in the past few months. Her unorthodox behavior bespeaks not only a self-indulgence, but a naïveté and vulnerability of which Dudley took full advantage and which would disappear only with experience. Her fling with her Master of the Horse, while Cecil was away, was not unlike that of a cloistered adolescent kept in restraint too long. When authority in the person of her chief minister vanished, she could throw caution to the winds and behave like a child whose parents had left on a journey.

There may never have been one particular moment when Elizabeth realized she could not marry Robert Dudley; inevitably the decision was borne in on her over many months. It was not until after two coroners' inquests and a governmental inquiry had vindicated him that he was allowed to return to court, anxious to establish himself again in the Queen's favor. In this is the strongest repudiation that Elizabeth was Dudley's mistress or a conspirator in Amy's death. If both factors had been true, it would have been much easier (and wiser) to have imprisoned, exiled or murdered Dudley than to have allowed his return to court, free to add emphasis to the already scurrilous rumors. In allowing him freedom, Elizabeth proclaimed her belief in his innocence and, at the same time, silently challenged anyone to prove otherwise. Though many thought it evidence of her continued romantic interest in her courtier, it was two changed people who met again. A shaken and subdued Dudley was reunited with a Queen who greeted him warmly and sympathetically, her manner providing a defense against those nobles who barely hid their contempt for the infamous Master of the Horse.

Yet when papers for the Earldom she had promised Robert and the restoration of the Warwick title to his brother Ambrose were presented, she gave vent to her feelings. Remembering the three Dudleys who had perished on the scaffold, as well as the fact that they were allegedly descended from an insignificant great-grandfather who had been a carpenter, she also remembered the attempt of those who sought to defame Robert by saying that "he was the son of a Duke, the brother of a King,* the grandson of an esquire and the great-grandson of a carpenter, and that the carpenter was the only honest man in the family and the only one who had died in his bed."[5] Angrily she ran a knife through the patent, muttering that "the Dudleys had been traitors for generations." She offered no excuse for her action, only clapped Robert on the cheek and said, with measured flippancy, "No, no, the Bear and Ragged Staff [the emblem of the Warwicks] is not yet so soon overthrown!"

She was still drawn to him and showed him great favor. She was still willing to accept his attentions and caresses but gave him no encouragement that there would ever be anything else. At other times she was, quixotically, noncommittal, vague and unresponsive. She was conscious, as never before, of an inner strength which precluded any submission to the whims of passion. It became almost a game to her—and a puzzle to Dudley—how much she might be tempted and yet remain "at all times the mistress of her passion."[6]

When those closest to her asked if she would now wed Dudley, she would "pup with her lips," declaring she would never marry a subject, for then "men would come and ask for My Lord's Grace." Told she only had to make her husband a King, she replied that "this she would in no wise agree to."[7] Elizabeth, remembering her sister Mary's emotional enslavement to Philip, meant to be dominant, as Dudley learned to his discomfort. She turned on him shortly after his return to court

---

*Guildford Dudley, married briefly to Jane Grey, the Nine-Day Queen.

when he had peremptorily rescinded some minor order and cried, "God's death, my Lord, I have wished you well, but my favour is not so confined to you that others shall not share it with you! I will have but one mistress and no master here!"[8] Dudley's humility was apparent for days as, abashed, he brooded sullenly over the fate which had freed him to wed and, in so doing, seemingly moved the object of his desire farther away than ever. He could not know that the seed of doubt placed in Elizabeth's mind during the previous weeks needed time to germinate, and in its flowering—which would prove her glory—lay his own supreme disappointment.

Although Mary Stuart had empowered commissioners to represent her at the time the Treaty of Edinburgh was negotiated, when ratification was sought, she refused to comply, perhaps hoping that "internal dissatisfaction" in England and Elizabeth's expected loss of popularity would prove such action unnecessary. The young Queen had small regard for her Scottish subjects, "who do their duty in nothing," she told Throckmorton. "I am their Queen and so they call me, but they use me not so!" Mary complained further. "They have sent hither a poor gentleman to me, who I disdain to have come in the name of them all in such a legation. They have sent great personages to your Mistress. I am their sovereign, but they take me not so. They must be taught to know their duties...."[9] Her uncle, the Cardinal of Lorraine, told Throckmorton grimly that Mary "hath the name of their sovereign, but your Mistress [Elizabeth] hath the effect and obedience." The refusal of the French monarchs to ratify or even concede such a point as eliminating the arms of England with France led Throckmorton to write sadly, "These doings are very far from the terms that we were in when our men were before Leith, and our navy strong on the sea...."

Mary had cause for complaint. The "poor gentleman" sent to her had been a common courier, while the "great personages" who journeyed to England were the Scottish Earls of Morton and Glencairn and William Maitland, the Laird of Lethington. In their first formal visit since the French defeat, the commissioners brought with them their grateful appreciation of Elizabeth's intervention and a proposal that she now marry the Earl of Arran in order to cement the alliance even more firmly. The Queen was happy to find the Scots appreciative and told them she was glad "her money had not been wholly thrown away." But with the Arran proposal, she merely repeated her dislike of marriage. She did not doubt that their offer was well meant and that

Arran "was the choicest person they had to offer." But, said Elizabeth, for the time being she could not oblige them and the Earl must consider himself free "to make any other connection which might appear to him desirable."[10]

Within a matter of weeks, fate had unexpectedly solved the situation. Shortly after Throckmorton's letter was written, Francis—always a feeble youth—suffered the effects of an extremely bad cold accompanied by a fever, "an indisposition," wrote Surian, the Venetian ambassador at the French court, "to which he is subject and said to have inherited from his father and grandfather. . . ." On December 5, 1560, the sixteen-year-old boy-King, Francis II, died, leaving, wrote Throckmorton, "as heavy and dolorous a wife as of right she had good cause to be, who, by long watching with him during his sickness, and painful diligence about him . . . is not in best tune of her body, but without danger."[11] It was three days before Mary Stuart's eighteenth birthday. Francis' successor was his ten-year-old brother Charles, the Duke of Orléans, "of handsome presence, gracious and high and noble spirited." The accession of Charles, which might ordinarily have caused little change in the internal affairs of a country where one youth of the same family replaced another, was, in this instance, a very different matter. Control of the state, Treasury and Church had formerly been in the grasping hands of Mary's two French uncles, the Cardinal of Lorraine and Francis, the Duke of Guise, brothers of her dead mother. Their iron dominance had resulted in two Princes of the blood, Anthony, the Duke of Vendôme and King of Navarre, and his brother, Louis, the Prince of Condé, both of the powerful ruling House of Bourbon, allying themselves with the religious zealots who constituted the followers of the reformer John Calvin. Their prime purpose was the overthrow of the Guise and, through the Guise, of the Catholics. An aborted Conspiracy of Amboise the previous March had resulted in the imprisonment of Condé, now under sentence of death. A religious purge was expected to eliminate the more noisome Calvinists, who included many of the French nobility willing to undertake any cause to effect the downfall of the hated Guise. Now death had accommodated them by removing the young King, the source of that power they had used "solely as a means of gratifying their pride and avarice." Between them and their former prestige now stepped the formidable Florentine Catherine de Medici, mother of the monarch. For several years, as Queen Dowager, powerless against her daughter-in-law's family, she had waited her chance. She ordered the release of Condé and hundreds of others who now called themselves Huguenots and placed herself square in the middle of the religious and political breach that Francis' death had caused. Those militant Catholics, represented by the Guise and backed by Philip of Spain and the Pope, were now arrayed against the Protestant followers of Condé and his brother. In the minority was a national party, headed by the Constable de Montmorency, which dreaded civil war and, instead, proposed moderation and toleration in the hope of preserving the unity of France. Any such thought was lost in the religious fanaticism of the Guisian Catholics and the Huguenots. Catherine de Medici was now in a position to play one off against the other, avenge herself of all past wrongs and reap an enviable harvest for the future.

One of the few who seemed genuinely to mourn the young King was his widow. Throckmorton wrote of Mary Stuart, "who being no less noble-minded than beautiful and graceful in appearance, the thoughts of widowhood at so early an age and of the loss of a consort . . . who so dearly loved her, and also that she is dispossessed of the Crown of France, with little hope of recovering that of Scotland, which is her sole patrimony and dower, so afflict her that she will not receive any consolation, but brooding over her disasters with constant tears and passionate and doleful lamentations, she universally inspires great pity."[12] Later Throckmorton would concede that possibly Mary's tears were for her lost authority and already she was looking for a husband who would guarantee "the continuation of her honors and to marry one that might uphold her to be great. . . ."[13]

Elizabeth had little pity for Mary and protested her shock at her Scottish cousin's refusal to ratify the Treaty. There was some consolation in Throckmorton's contention that the "House of Guise does seem here to bear small rule." In their difficulty was England's opportunity. For, with the release of the imprisoned Huguenots, the assumption of power by Catherine de Medici and the Bourbons, the political forces which only a few weeks previous had been in the minority were now in the ascendancy. Throckmorton was brightly optimistic that "the true religion [Protestantism] is very likely to take place in France and so consequently throughout all Europe where Christianity is received." A General Council was planned to promulgate this "true religion," and he desired the Queen to send some "learned men" to the Council and devoutly wished, since it was but three months since Amy Dudley's death, that their arrival would be unmarred by the effect of gossip concerning Dudley and the Queen. He admonished Cecil, " . . . if her Majesty do so foully forget herself in her marriage as the bruit runneth here, neither think to bring anything to pass here or elsewhere. I would you did hear the lamentations, the declamations, and sundry affections which have course here for that matter!"

Cecil, busy with the tremendous implications Mary Stuart's widowhood had made on Scottish-English affairs, had little patience with Throckmorton's overanxious, patronizing concern evident in the letter's ending: "My duty to her, my goodwill to you both move me to speak plainly. . . ." Cecil spoke equally plainly in his answer: "I must advise you not to meddle with the matters of this Court, otherwise than ye may be well advised from hence." His own awareness of the Queen's capriciousness was apparent in his final comment: "Writings remain, and coming into adverse hands may be sinisterly interpreted. . . . Servants or messengers may be reporters to whom they list, and therefore, I cannot safely give you so plain counsel as I wish, but, in one word, I say—'contend not where victory cannot be had' "[14] Politically, the situation in France was more attractive than the situation at home, and he chose not to dwell on it. His zeal for the reformers is evident in his remark "The knowledge of Christ against the anti-Christ of Rome . . . now is the time for Calvin and all such noble men as have fetched their knowledge thence, to impugn and suppress the tyranny of the Papists."[15]

The death of Francis II and the return of Robert Dudley to court while still in the shadow cast by the manner of his wife's death emphasized the need for settling Elizabeth's marital future. Early in 1561, William Cecil approached de Quadra and stated that the Queen might be amenable to further overtures on behalf of Archduke Charles of Austria. The once-bitten de Quadra, still smarting from the occasion when Elizabeth, with the cooperation of Lady Mary Sidney, had blasted similar hopes, was not so easily persuaded. He surmised, correctly, that Cecil and the Queen were attempting such strategy as a threat to the French at the moment when, following the death of the King, their internal affairs would be in confusion. The Emperor, Charles' father, was unmoved. He had sent three ambassadors in the past, he said. He had forwarded a portrait of the Archduke at the Queen's request. But the young man himself would never come to England without a binding promise to wed. Elizabeth's natural evasiveness and reluctance to commit herself guaranteed a quick cessation of further commitments in that direction.

At the same time, her remarkable capacity for overlooking what she did not wish to see had led to a resumption of Robert Dudley's influence at court and with the Queen. Their extraordinary rightness for each other was very evident. He was as captivated by Elizabeth's personality as he was amused by her temper which he compared "to summer storms." He respected her political insight and her perceptive attitude toward her subjects. They had great pride in each other; he in her sovereignty, she in his overwhelming masculinity. He did not demean her tremendous vanity. It was as much a part of Elizabeth as his regard for his own capabilities and potentialities. If their temperaments clashed—and this was due more to the disparity in their positions than to any temperamental differences—their outlook on life, particularly *their* life, was much the same. To emphasize this extreme complementing of each other, Elizabeth gave Robert a nickname other than the Robin she called him in conversation. He was her "Two Eyes," she said, and she often referred to him as such, while he invariably signed any letters to her ⊙⊙ . Not that he spent much time from her side; he had easy access to the Privy Chamber, and there were few contents of the most secret state dispatches with which he was not familiar.[16]

Suitors came and went, yet Robin remained. He, more than any of the others about Elizabeth, shared her sophisticated, cutting humor. He could and did match the great royal oaths, and he dared presume where others merely hoped. If he could not be her husband, Robert gave Elizabeth a companionship, a friendship and a trust that—with the possible exception of William Cecil—she shared with or extended to no one else. While he was very much a creature of her making—a fact she did not hesitate to remind him of when their differing opinions reached the exploding point—Robert had blossomed into such a splendid example of magnificence that Elizabeth made little effort to hide her pride in him. The Queen's behavior with Robert was the old suitor game carried to more personal and intimate heights in the privacy of her own chambers. With the exception of sexual union and the giving of his name, Robert rendered all the satisfactions of a husband and a dear companion. It was unfortunate, in the view of many, that this feeling had settled on the one member of her court whom she could not marry, for she had more than once said she would never wed "without the consent and goodwill of her people who have the right of controlling the public actions of their sovereigns; she did not wish to prejudice this right by marrying without their consent."[17] She never underestimated her people's dislike of Dudley. Apart from her own aversion to sharing the Crown, it had been her foremost reason for delaying a decision.

Such a delay was, understandably, not easy for Robert. Though he never fully erased the stigma of Amy's death, his return to court had been earlier and easier than many had anticipated. Elizabeth's total preference for her lover was blatant. "She is infatuated to a degree which would be a notable fault in any woman, much more in one of her exalted rank," said de Quadra, disapprovingly. It was only a matter of time, everyone was sure, before Elizabeth succumbed to the Dudley charm. This enthrallment was what lay behind Cecil's advice to Throckmorton, "contend not where the victory cannot be had," or, as he later wrote, "there was no point in swimming against the stream." Therefore, it was not surprising that at the end of January, 1561, another move toward marriage was made, not with the Archduke Charles, but with the Master of the Horse, Robert Dudley.

The emissary to de Quadra, the Spanish ambassador, on this occasion was Sir Henry Sidney, husband of the guileless Mary, Robert's sister. Sidney was an ardent Catholic, whom de Quadra respected "as a very sensible man and better-behaved than any other courtier." Sidney's proposal was explicit—and incredible. He requested that de Quadra write King Philip of Spain, suggesting Robert Dudley as a husband for the Queen since "it was a love affair, the object of it was marriage and there was nothing illicit about it." If King Philip would show himself agreeable to Elizabeth's marriage to Dudley, Sidney explained, he was sure the Queen's husband "would hereafter serve and obey your Majesty like one of your own vassals. . . ." He was surprised that neither de Quadra nor Philip had thought of this themselves.

De Quadra merely ventured the wry comment that neither the Queen of England nor her Master of the Horse had blessed him with their confidences, that "he had no means for guessing the thoughts of the Queen who hitherto had not taken the advice Philip had given her so that there was no opportunity of offering advice again."

Sidney chose to overlook any implied reproof or sarcasm in the ambassador's attitude. Instead, he said he was satisfied that the death of Lord Robert's wife "was accidental . . . although he knew that public opinion held to the contrary." He said the Queen was fearful of public demonstrations which her questionable behavior and the religious unrest and open criticism now emphasized by the Scottish Queen's attitude toward the controversial Treaty.[18] He said that "the Queen and Lord Robert were determined to restore religion by means of a General Council," and he left the definite impression that if Philip would help Dudley accomplish his marriage to the Queen, both would be willing to restore Catholicism to a country where the Protestants had been the recipients of royal favor in the three years since Elizabeth's accession.

The thought that religion was being used as bait caused de Quadra to say somewhat stiffly that he considered it improper "to bring the religious question into these transactions. . . ." He reminded Sidney forthrightly "that he knew what happened with his wife in the matter of the Archduke when the Queen had deceived both of us." He was adamant he would not write Philip unless the Queen authorized him to do so, to which Sidney replied that if he introduced the subject to her, he "might be sure that she desired nothing more than the countenance of your Majesty to conclude the match. . . ."

Impressed despite himself, de Quadra wrote Philip of Sidney's suggestion. He said Elizabeth's Comptroller and great friend, Sir Thomas Parry, had recently "died of sheer grief" at Elizabeth's involvement with Robert and the debacle of Amy Dudley's death, and "there is not a person without some scandalous tale to tell about the matter and one of the Queen's Gentlemen of the Chamber is in prison for blabbing."[19]

During the next few weeks, de Quadra observed the court atmosphere as much as possible. He wrote Philip he did not think Queen Elizabeth "was anxious to commend her affairs to your Majesty out of any wish or goodwill of her own, but forced thereto by the persuasion of Lord Robert. . . ." Both Robert and possibly Sidney were bringing their not inconsiderable influence to bear on the Queen. Before committing herself, however, Elizabeth asked the advice of Lord Paget, the distinguished old relic of her father's Council. Paget came out of retirement to advise the girl he had known since her birth to "make a firm peace and alliance with France, to appeal particularly to the Protestant element there and then she could treat with any monarch on any subject more effectively." Elizabeth dispatched the Earl of Bedford to France to ask for ratification of the Treaty of Edinburgh and to contact the Bourbon party "to bring about good understanding . . . with the heretics of the French court."[20]

On February 13, de Quadra met again with Sidney, who brought Dudley himself to the meeting. Robert begged the ambassador to speak with Elizabeth. "He repeated all that Sidney had told me," wrote de Quadra, "and thanked me with a great many compliments and humble words for the answer I had sent; he besought me, in your Majesty's name, to commend the Queen to marry him and he would promise to render to your Majesty all the service his brother-in-law had told me and much more."[21] Suddenly, it did not seem at all impossible that a change of events might return England to the Catholic fold. Scarcely able to conceal his excitement, de Quadra hurried to the Presence Chamber.

The Queen was most amiable. She listened with apparent pleasure to de Quadra's wish that she marry and see "her government firmly and tranquilly established." He pledged Philip's support and friendship. Elizabeth seemed to hesitate and then, haltingly, said she wished to make a confession. "She told me," wrote de Quadra, "that she was no angel. She did not deny that she had some affection for Lord Robert for the many good qualities he possessed. But she certainly had never decided to marry him or anyone else, although she daily saw more clearly the necessity for her marriage, and to satisfy the English humor that it was desirable that she should marry an Englishman." Before de Quadra could reply, she stammered and asked, "What your Majesty would think if she married one of her servitors . . .?[22] De Quadra replied he would write with all diligence to Spain, but he believed Philip "would be pleased to hear of her marriage . . . and of the advancement and aggrandizement of Lord Robert as I understood that your Majesty had great affection for him and held him in high esteem." At this Elizabeth appeared very pleased and seemed on the verge of further confidences. But de Quadra, without as yet any advice from Philip, merely uttered some general phrases, for "I did not care to carry the matter further for fear of making a mistake. . . ."[23]

The next day Dudley thanked the ambassador and said the Queen was much pleased and begged de Quadra to seek another interview to "refer to the subject as he knew that it was only fear and timidity that prevented the Queen from deciding." He told de Quadra that if a representative at the forthcoming General Council of Trent were needed, "he would go himself." Dudley's astonishing opinion—that the religious compromise Elizabeth had successfully effected could so easily be put aside—did not allay de Quadra's fears. He did not wish to compromise his dignity by too easy acceptance; nor did he wish to lose the opportunity by delay. He told Dudley he would do everything as far as his commission permitted, but what Robert and Elizabeth did about religion must be justified "by their own conscience." He wrote Philip, "I am thus cautious with these people because, if they are playing false, which is quite possible, I do not wish to give them the opprtunity of saying that we offered them your Majesty's favour in return for changing their religion. . . ."[24]

It was more than a month before de Quadra heard from Philip. Courier service was much at the mercy of winter storms and gales. The Spanish King hoped Sidney's proposal "might extract good from evil." Nevertheless, he insisted that anything the Queen and Dudley wished should be put into writing and signed by Elizabeth. "This is necessary," he told the ambassador, "as her words are so little to be depended upon and you know by the experience you have had of her that this is always the course she pursues when she has no intention of fulfilling what she says. . . ."[25] In the meantime, Robert had endeavored to have Elizabeth send an envoy to Spain. She had refused, but, to pacify him—and to gain time—at last she sent William Cecil to de Quadra to ask in her name that Philip send the Queen of England a letter, advising her not to delay her marriage any longer and to choose "a gentleman of her own country" and to promise "to be a friend to whoever may be chosen for a husband."

The arrival of William Cecil on the scene was all that was needed to convince de Quadra of Elizabeth's sincerity. Whether at that point, the Queen's Secretary knew of Dudley's offer to restore the Catholic religion in exchange for King Philip's support is questionable. What he *did* realize immediately was the extent to which Dudley and Sidney had gone in even negotiating with the Spanish King. He supported Elizabeth's request for a letter, and his momentary acquiescence was necessary until he could ascertain the extent of the Queen's commitment. He knew that to challenge Elizabeth's fancy and her infatuation, for Dudley was a lost cause. At the slightest disparagement of Robert, she would spring immediately to his defense. And so, unless he wished ultimately to acknowledge Robert Dudley as Consort—which he could clearly see was the aim behind the negotiations—his own opposition must be against an issue, not a controversial personality. He must avoid any incident that would provoke Elizabeth's wrath, yet he must do something to thwart Dudley's ambition. His performance was masterful and worthy of his position and the trust Elizabeth reposed in him. After reiterating that the Queen would, indeed, be pleased to receive a letter from Philip, he said that he himself would then present it to both houses of Parliament, which would, presumably, be packed with cooperative members who would give their quick sanction to the marriage. He told de Quadra that Elizabeth was a "modest maiden" and disliked making the proposals herself "which would make her look like a woman who sought to carry out her desires and went praying people to help her. . . ." After the conversation, de Quadra wrote Philip that Dudley was very displeased by the Queen's reluctance to "take a stand. . . and throw herself entirely on your Majesty's favour. . . . but I do not think that he has been able to prevail upon her. . . ."[26]

Philip's final acceptance of the Sidney-Dudley proposal carried a high price. He insisted that to show good faith, Elizabeth must liberate all imprisoned Catholics. She must agree to send only Catholic ambassadors and Catholic bishops to the Council of Trent and "to submit herself unconditionally to its decisions." Then her marriage would have his blessing. He added that one Abbé Martinengo would carry the Papal Bull announcing the General Council to the Queen and that the Pope—apparently apprised of the Queen of England's romantic intentions and their interesting possible conclusion—had ordered the Abbé to contact the Bishop of Arras "to see what progress is being made with Sidney's negotiations . . ."[27] before requesting entry to England.

In England, de Quadra awaited the arrival of the Papal Nuncio and, with the permission of the Queen, even moved to Greenwich so that any reception of the Legate might not be disrupted by unfriendly Londoners. Somehow word had leaked from official sources that the Pope's emissary was just across the Channel awaiting permission to see the Queen. Once the formal request was made, Londoners were stunned. "Here hath been no small ado to refuse this Popish messenger. The Bishop of Aquila had won more with former practices than was easy to overtake . . ."[28] Cecil wrote to Throckmorton. Quickly the news traveled, and in the Catholic North, arms were made ready if needed to support the Nuncio, if the sovereign so indicated. In the City, additional mobs roamed the streets and attacked known Papists. At the news of the trouble the Nuncio's arrival was causing, Dudley took to his bed, "ill with vexation"; the uprising and temper of the Londoners promised a stormy reception at best.

Everyone, Protestant and Catholic alike, now awaited Elizabeth's reply to the Nuncio's demand for entry, for her answer would serve notice to everyone, from Pope to commoner, whether "she regarded her breach with Rome beyond repair."[29] Those who had helped accomplish her settlement with the Church advised outright refusal. Many of the ancient nobility, several of the Council and powerful Northern representatives, hoped she would at least accept the invitation—which carried no ultimate responsibility for agreement—with some display of royal good manners. Now Elizabeth was firmly in the middle of a religious situation where pacification of one group would only enrage and alienate the other. Disliking the troublesome middle position, she made one halfhearted attempt to delay any action. She asked the Earl of Bedford at the French court to enlist the support of Catherine de Medici in requesting a more impartial Council, where Protestant representatives might not be coerced by the majority of Catholics. Catherine wished no alliance, however, with one as controversial as the English Queen, although had it served her purpose, she would not have hesitated. Instead she declined, and Elizabeth, left to the resolving of a problem she had helped create, acted characteristically.

Immediately, the Nuncio in Flanders carrying the Pope's invitation to his "Dearest Daughter in Christ" was bluntly refused permission to enter England. Immediately, the Protestant effusion of joy was evident at court. De Quadra could scarcely believe the news, and enraged and humiliated, he hurried to see Cecil and the Queen. With an outward firmness he was far from feeling inwardly, Cecil explained. There had been a Catholic plot, he said, which luckily had been discovered in time. Subversive correspondence between imprisoned Marian bishops had been uncovered. Several instances of the Mass being celebrated had been found. The old chaplain of Mary Tudor's great friend Sir Edward Waldegrave had been hauled before the Council for saying Mass daily in Waldegrave's house; ultimately Sir Edward and his Lady would enter the Tower for a short duration. Other priests had allegedly "conversed with the Devil" in having the Queen's horoscope cast to learn how long she might live. The fact that such activities had been tolerated or ignored for several years in the hope that Elizabeth's religious compromise would become strengthened was not mentioned.[30] All such activities had been related to the coming of the Nuncio, and "dangerous hopes had been awakened with agitating rumours," the minister said, and if, for the moment, Mr. Secretary Cecil chose to make a very huge mountain out of a very small molehill, the stakes were correspondingly high. Secure once more in the Queen's trust, even if momentarily uncomfortable in his conscience, he told the unnerved de Quadra that such Catholic conspiracy could not be tolerated in England. There was little he could suggest other than that de Quadra talk with Sidney, Dudley or the Queen.

Sidney had earlier realized that once the scheme passed into Cecil's hands, there would be little hope of success. At its ignominious end, Sidney told de Quadra he had been ordered by the Queen to Wales, where he was to serve as President of the Council. He "had been the first instrument in the negotiation and his presence was inconvenient."[31] he told de Quadra sadly. He said the Queen had changed her mind, she "would act like a woman," and the blame would be thrown on Lord Robert Dudley, still languishing in his bed in mortified disillusionment. Cecil accurately assessed Dudley's position when he wrote Throckmorton," . . .I can see no certain disposition in her Majesty to any marriage, and any other likelihood doth not the principal (Dudley) here find, which causeth him to be perplexed."

Since neither Cecil, Sidney nor Dudley could accompany him, de Quadra faced Elizabeth alone. At first she seemed "embarrassed, confused and evidently frightened," he later wrote to King Philip. But as they spoke, she seemed to gain confidence and did not appear as the vulnerable young woman whose destiny he had hoped to direct. When he spoke of the Nuncio's rejection, the Queen replied that "when she had spoken to me about the Council, she had assumed it would be a 'free Council'. . . ."[32] When de Quadra taxed her with the fact "that she had led me to expect a different result . . . and had made me ridiculous in your Majesty's [Philip's] eyes," Elizabeth only said she was grateful for the King's interest, but she refused to accept any implication of conspiracy at all. She refrained from answering why she had forbidden the Nuncio admittance to her kingdom. Majesty, she reminded the baffled de Quadra, need not explain. If he wanted reasons, he must go to her ministers who had assisted her in the decision. She owed neither him nor Philip any explanation.

De Quadra was not so easily dismissed. Angrily, he demanded to know why she had sent Dudley to broach a marriage in the first place. Why should he bother his King if he had not thought the Queen privy to the plan? Elizabeth's answer and her cool manner did not help allay de Quadra's hot Spanish temper.

She, said the Queen, had given no approval to any such plan, and she could not imagine how de Quadra had thought otherwise. Granted they *had* discussed such a possibility, but, she challenged the hapless ambassador, had *she* personally ever asked his help or Philip's? They had discussed her need to marry and her affection for Robert Dudley, that was all. If it had gone further than that between de Quadra and others, it certainly was no affair of hers and not her fault! If Philip's championing of Dudley had become public, then the ambassador's servants must have talked too much and too soon. She had asked no religious concessions in exchange for her choice of a husband, and to turn the knife a bit more sharply, she pointedly reminded the ambassador of his own comment that any religious settlement should not be linked with marriage. She implied, rather crossly, that she could not be held responsible for every harebrained scheme those around her might concoct. Her courtiers were free agents; she was not bound by their actions. Obviously, the ambassador had been taken in? It was not her concern.

It took every ounce of self-control and remembrance of diplomatic courtesies for de Quadra, stung to the quick, to refrain from uttering epithets unbefitting a servant of God and King from escaping his lips. Such self-discipline had its effect, and with pounding heart, short of breath and silently calling on saints and Saviour to curse "this devilish woman, this Jezebel," who had outwitted him again, he left the court. As he climbed into his litter and proceeded down the muddy Strand to his Durham House lodgings, the heavenly hosts accommodated with a fiery bolt of lightning which, before the humiliated ambassador's eyes, tore the steeple from St. Paul's Cathedral and burned the spire down to the stonework. It was all there was to soothe the man whose frustration and anger had no other outlet. Perhaps it was enough.

Out of the farce which had played itself out at the English court for almost half a year, some enlightening events helped Elizabeth Tudor resolve one of the most difficult decisions of her life. She had willingly consented to Dudley's scheme to enlist the help of the Spanish King. De Quadra's earlier comment that she had not at first been eager for the scheme was later buttressed by his statement that Robert had persuaded Elizabeth only when he had convinced her that her life was in danger. Fear may have been present, but whether she knowingly encouraged Dudley in *every* proposal he submitted to de Quadra is something that remained a standing quarrel between them. Given Elizabeth's natural evasiveness, her genius at implying without actually permitting, combined with Robert's own desperate desire to produce *anything* which would tip the scales—and Elizabeth's mind—in his favor, the chances are that she always knew what was going on, without involving herself too far, knowing that the final decision always rested with her.

Dudley had not scrupled to promise "to hand the whole government to the King of Spain and fully restore the Catholic faith."[33] Elizabeth had not scrupled to use a dear and intimate friend when it had served her own purpose. If Dudley had practiced deceit, Elizabeth had been doubly deceptive. Robert now exhibited little shame or conscience and loudly complained he had been used as a decoy. If he had, Elizabeth argued, he had instigated the procedure himself, so why blame her? She had allowed the incident to unfold, perhaps honestly hoping that *something* might occur that would permit a marriage, should she ultimately choose to wed. It was only when Cecil took charge and a final showdown with the Nuncio and Parliament became inevitable that courage had failed her. And her people's response had shown what her action must be. In the end, one thing was certain. She held herself blameless. She had, said the Queen, merely concurred with everyone, that yes, she did have great affection for Dudley, and yes, she would like to marry him—sometime. She had, in truth, committed herself no further than that. Cecil had realized this quicker than the hopeful Dudley. He had answered Throckmorton's anguished disbelief that the Queen might actually be going to marry Robert by writing, "I see no small declensions from former dealings; at least, I find in Her

Majesty by diverse speeches, a determination not to marry one of her subjects."[34]

In the intrigue in which she had not hesitated to use friend, lover, minister and ambassador, Elizabeth gained valuable knowledge. It increased the resourcefulness and self-reliance nurtured by danger in her youth; it confirmed her judgment of men and their motives. While her final decision blasted de Quadra's hopes and left a papal delegate stranded in Flanders, everything that would prove helpful to the Queen coalesced at home. The Protestants were more firmly welded to their monarch than ever before, and the Catholic reaction was amazing. Disappointed as they were, once the story behind the Nuncio's rejection became public, they saluted the Queen for her stand, if not for her religious "heresy." For their own part, they might hope for a return to Catholicism and even, ultimately, be willing to rebel for it, but at the moment they were, first and foremost, Englishmen, and to have a foreign King help foist a husband for the Queen on them was just one more instance of Spanish arrogance. And that the choice be *Robert Dudley!* Catholics grew purple at the thought and blessed the good sense with which their monarch had ended the whole disastrous episode. At that moment, a fortunate bit of information reached London that yet another Papal Nuncio, Father Wolfe, was in Ireland urging Irishmen to rebellion, and in England, Catholic and Protestant drew together in a unity as remarkable as it was brief. William Cecil had the last word when he wrote Throckmorton:

> What the matters be, the writing will declare, howsoever the end is, the way thereto was full of crooks. . . . the Bishop of Aquila [de Quadra] had entered into such a practice with a pretence to further the great matter here, meaning principally the church matter and percase, accidentally, the other [Dudley] matter also, that he had taken faster hold to plant his purpose than was my ease shortly to root up. But God, whose cause it is and the Queen's Majesty whose only surety therein resteth, hath the one by direction, the other by yielding, ended the matter well. . . .[35]

For Elizabeth personally, the episode confirmed what she had always intuitively known. By inference, implication and suggestion, she had permitted Robert Dudley to be used as a political and religious pawn and had provoked a solution she could never have gained in any other way. She could have her "Robin," her "Two Eyes," with Spanish consent, with Spanish support and a blatant sacrifice of the religious settlement she had effected. She could have Dudley if she were willing to place Catholic against Protestant, risk civil war and owe the delights

of married life to a Spanish King. There was no other way. She had
discovered what she wished to know and, in so doing, had manipulated
Spain into seemingly offering the husband of *her* choice for the religion
of *its* choice. Her subjects' reaction had been one of anger and distrust,
and Robert Dudley, who had hoped to win the greatest prize of his life,
had become, instead, an unwilling sacrifice. From that, Elizabeth knew
she would never marry Dudley, probably knew she would never marry
at all.

If there was any satisfaction in the sacrifice, in the fact that she had
upheld her coronation oath to keep peace in the realm, it was a Queen's
satisfaction. And it was to be primarily as a Queen, free for every
possibility of greatness, not as a married woman, that she must live her
life. While absorbing the knowledge that the desires of Queen and
woman are rarely compatible, she set herself to nursing the stricken
Dudley. Bitter and resentful, he threatened to sail away from her
kingdom "to the King of Spain's wars." It came to nothing. Once more
he accepted the inescapable fact that he was Majesty's creature and, as
such, subject to Majesty's whims. Several weeks later, on Midsummer's
Day, while abroad on the Thames in the royal barge, where Elizabeth
had thoughtfully invited the still-brooding de Quadra, both the Queen
and Dudley "began talking nonsense which she likes to do much better
than talking about business," the still-smarting ambassador wrote
later. Suddenly, Dudley jokingly suggested that if Elizabeth were
agreeable, the ambassador might marry them then and there. To
which the Queen, in an offhand way, merely replied that she did not
think the Spanish Bishop knew enough English for the purpose.

Chapter Eight

The City of London and its environs of Whitehall and Westminster formed a fitting and splendid background for the magnificence which Queen Elizabeth encouraged for the benefit of her court, herself and, indirectly, her subjects. The City was an irregular semicircle of about one square mile with its Cathedral of St. Paul's, monasteries, government buildings and more than 100 parish churches; all were enclosed by the City wall and its seven great gates of Aldgate, Aldersgate, Cripplegate, Ludgate, Bishopsgate, Moorgate and Newgate.[1]

Within the gates, the old City conformed to the medieval pattern of tortuously twisting narrow streets, sufficient in a day when London had been less populous and less successful as a trading center. Now, with a population approaching 200,000, the streets, lanes and roads were congested with porters, pack animals and horses, merchants, artisans, draftsmen, apprentices and ordinary citizens. The busy streets often bore the name of their commodity; thus the housewife knew just where to shop in Bread Street, Milk Street, Honey Lane, Fish Street or the Poultry, before proceeding to the great markets in Leadenhall, Smithfield and Cheapside. The streets were lined by timber-framed buildings, the smaller ones made all the more squalid and darkly crowded by the projecting overhang of second and third stories. Inside, the rooms bore a great similarity. There was an almost complete lack of hygiene and drainage, and the windows, which were rarely opened, guaranteed an absence of light and air and contributed to the rich smell of continual human habitation unrelieved by the rushes on the floor. Water was difficult to obtain and had to be carried from the Great and Little Conduits in Cheapside. Cooking, sleeping and family living were often carried on in one or two small rooms. In the more enlightened homes, the verminous dried grasses on the floor had given way to "Turkey" carpets and cushions or, more startling still, a bare floor kept clean by frequent sweeping.

The broader thoroughfares of Cheapside, with its great Eleanor Cross,* and Fleet Street, with the small bridge over the open Fleet Ditch, were always noisily crowded with throngs seeking the more open areas to shop, to watch the royal, church or civic processions or to indulge in the petty thievery which plagued merchant and citizen alike. Just outside Temple Bar, Fleet Street melded into the narrow Strand, always busy, aways muddy but less raucous, for here were the back entrances to the great homes of the nobles and prelates of England. To the west of the Strand was the small village of Charing, with its crossroads and the last Eleanor Cross.

North of the Strand were the broad open fields and pastures used by laundresses for drying the clothing they pegged to the ground. They were dotted with windmills, small farms, cottages and dairies. Near Holborn and Ely Place, the busier Smithfield Market gave way to the open fields of Finsbury, Moorfields and Spital, all outside the City gates and used by the City dwellers for recreation and amusement; for hunting, hawking, football, jousting on the spongy earth of Moorfields and skating on the frozen pool of Smithfield with skates made from animal shinbones.[2] More than 200 archery butts were in constant use by citizens and soldiers. Among the gardens, orchards and pastures outlying the City, the small churches of St. Giles and St. Martin's were solitary in their fields. The green land was unspoiled, especially the great hunting preserve of St. James, where, by royal proclamation in July, 1546, Henry VIII had forbidden any hunting "of the King's game" from Westminster to Hampstead Heath. He was desirous, said the old King, "to have the game of hare, partridge, pheasant and heron preserved in and about his honour at his Palace of Westminster, for his own disport and pastimes to St. Giles-in-the-Fields, to Our Lady of the Oak, to Highgate, to Hornsey Park, to Hampstead Heath . . ." and his subjects were forbidden to hunt or hawk within the precincts unless they wished to risk "imprisonment of their bodies and further punishment of His Majesty's will and pleasure. . . ."[3] The air was as pure in the fields as it was stinking in the City. The great open ditches of the Fleet River, of Moor Ditch, Shore Ditch (a corruption of "Sewer Ditch") all spewed their refuse—animal and human—into the Thames.

---

*The Eleanor Crosses marked the funeral route of Eleanor of Castile, Edward I's Queen, who died at Harby in Nottinghamshire in 1290. They were commissioned by her devoted husband to denote the resting places where the funeral cortege stopped enroute to Westminster Abbey. There were thirteen Crosses in all, from Harby to the last one in the little village of Charing.

One ditch became so clogged with dead dogs it was dubbed "Hounds Ditch."

The most traveled route in all London was its river, the mighty Thames. The wharves, harbors and stairs were crowded with barges, fishing boats, eel boats and numerous wherries—the slight small row-boats used as water taxis—which were summoned with the cry of "Oars!" The watermen of London, a tough, coarse lot, delivered their charges upstream, downstream or across the water to the public foot stairs or to the many private water stairs. They shared the river with all manner of small and large craft, including the ornately gaudy Lord Mayor's barge and the Queen's stately gilded barge manned by oars-men in Tudor green and white livery. The royal swans—proud in their sacrosanct status—were usually given the right-of-way. The oarsmen were expert at their trade, especially at guiding their craft through the arches of London Bridge at high tide, when the water boiled and swirled around the piers. "Shooting the bridge" was not for the fainthearted; more than one passenger left his boat at the Three Cranes in the Vintry and picked up the same conveyance at Billingsgate after it had passed safely under the bridge.

Westward from the Tower, the watermen rowed past the Steelyard toward Queenhithe and the gloomy pile of Baynard's Castle. On past the Blackfriars, the Bridewell, the Whitefriars and the Temple, the river teemed with traffic which often numbered 2,000 craft at one time. After the Temple, the great river mansions came into view, the Strand buildings which had once been the homes of proud provincial Bishops. The plunder of the Reformation was evident in the names of the owners which now included royal favorites or wealthy laymen: Paget Place, Arundel House and Somerset House, built by the dead Protec-tor, Edward Seymour, the brother of Henry VIII's third Queen. The ancient Savoy Palace, hard by Durham House and Ivy Lane, marked the curve of the river which led to Whitehall and Westminster. At Whitehall the traffic was greatest. The vast building, formerly owned by the See of York, had been rebuilt by Cardinal Wolsey, only to be seized by Henry VIII in 1529. It was actually a mélange of many buildings added to without plan at Henry's whim; thus, it rambled on both sides of "The Streete." The royal whim was also evident in the gardens, which were meticulously maintained, with an ornate sundial which allegedly told the time in thirty different ways. As the unwary visitor examined the sundial, it was possible for a companion to step on a concealed hose which sent a shower over the other to the great merriment of the observers. The sundial was surrounded by neat flower beds, large topiary bushes and tall gilded columns atop which reared the Queen's beasts. Smooth lawns bordered all this magnificence, and two great gates kept the curious out.

Across the road, those of the court might joust in the tiltyard, gamble in the Cockpit and enjoy tennis or bowling in the adjacent buildings. Farther down "The Streete" was the vast and gloomy Westminster Hall, built by a Norman King, as well as the decaying Palace of Westminster, which had partially burned in 1512. Opposite was the ancient Abbey of Westminster, enlarged now by the Chapel of the Queen's grandfather, Henry VII; the newer stonework had not yet blended with the old. The Abbey offered sanctuary and was a place for repose and reflection, as well as daily religious ceremonies and observances. From the water stairs of Westminster Palace, watermen plied their trade, discharging passengers across the river at the gemlike Lambeth Palace, its deep blood-red brick a solitary outline in the fields. Below the venerable structure, whose walls were lapped by the river, was the landing where horses were ferried across the water to the Horseferry Road. From the landing along the bank of the Southwark side of the Thames, there was less crowding, less magnificence—and less respectability. The Paris Garden, a pleasure park, gave way to the Bankside's open-air theaters-in-the-round, where live horses and bears were baited by packs of hungry dogs, "scaffolded about for the beholders to stand safe." From the Bankside, one might glance downstream to the aged London Bridge*, one of the sights of Europe. A thirteenth-century construction, it had a church, shops and houses —often several stories high—on either side and, at its narrowest, was only twelve feet wide. What it lacked in width it more than gained in color, noise and confusion. For more than 300 years, it had been the foot passage from the City to Southwark and was the gateway to all southeastern England. It had witnessed the welcome of foreign dignitaries, the reception of Kings and Queens and Princesses arriving as marriage pawns. Rebels had trod the path the pilgrims had walked to the shrine of Thomas à Becket at Canterbury, and Englishmen had gathered here to welcome a victorious king returning from Agincourt. At the Southwark end, near the Church of St. Mary Overy, could be seen the rotting heads of traitors, the gruesome bounty of the Tower executioner.

In all its phases, the medieval City[4] with its great solitary bridge over the crowded river—the London of Queen Elizabeth—was a growing hurly-burly of a city of courtiers, merchants, squires, yeomen and the

*London Bridge, built in 1209, stood with various rebuildings until 1832. Its successor, built about 100 feet west of the original, was in service until 1970, when it was dismantled, shipped to the United States and reassembled at Havasu, Arizona.

thieves who waged a daily deadly war on all. It was a city of Guilds and
Corporations numbering thousands of apprentices and master
members, who controlled all crafts and food distribution within the
"liberties" of London's walls. It was a city of fair houses, great mansions and squalid hovels, of fairs and parade grounds, of gibbets,
executioners' scaffolds all back to back with open fields, small cottages,
windmills, dairies and farms. It was a city graced by venerable
churches from the now spireless St. Paul's to the parish churches with
the outlandish but meaningful names of St. Andrew's Undershaft, St.
Michael's-in-the-Corn, St. Mary Axe, St. Mary Woolchurchawe and
St. Andrew's-by-the-Wardrobe. It was a city of great ladies who
inhabited the noble mansions on the Strand, with the broad lawns,
gardens and orchards running down to the Thames.

Across the river were the wretched prostitutes who lodged in the inns
and grubby hovels of "the stews." Within shouting distance of the
lordly residence of the Bishop of Winchester,* these "sisters of sin,"
their bawds and pimps often spent a night in "The Clink" or the
Marshalsea Prison for disturbing the peace. Adjacent to Winchester
House was the magnificent Church of St. Mary Overy, and nearby the
splendid Suffolk House, the residence of the late Charles Brandon, the
commoner who had married Henry VIII's younger sister, Mary, the
"Tudor Rose." With its ponds, orchards and great vineyard, it was a
showplace fitting to grace the neighborhood which had otherwise
spawned an inordinate number of inns and taverns: The Spur, the
Christopher, the Tabard, the King's Head and the George were there
for the refreshment and accommodation of travelers. Many had stood
since the Canterbury pilgrims had wended their way over the bridge to
Becket's Shrine.

To this ever-changing and burgeoning metropolis, the court of
Queen Elizabeth contributed its color and life. From her earliest appearance as Queen to the end of her reign, Elizabeth followed a pattern
which brought the splendor of royalty into the less glittering lives of her
subjects. It was not surprising, therefore, that much of her people's lives
came into the Queen's. Both were better for the contact, and from the
beginning Elizabeth encouraged a mutual participation. After years of
forcibly restraining her feelings, of eternally calculating the risk of any
displays of emotion which might affect brother, sister, Protector or
Council, it was a *relief*—a veritable boon of which Elizabeth almost
never tired—to give vent to her feelings. On emerging from the

*Because the See of Winchester owned the land upon which the brothels and inns of ques-
tionable repute were housed, a famous latter-day Elizabethan, one William Shakespeare, later
referred to the harlots of the area as "Winchester Geese."[5]

anonymity of a neglected and captive Princess, she reveled in freedom. It took form in the words which left her lips as she responded to her subjects' welcome, repeating, "God love you, good people!" as she walked among them. It was evident in the smiles and beckoning gestures she bestowed on them. She was generous with her hand which might be kissed—the hands of which she was so vain that she took every opportunity to uncover them that all might see the long slim fingers, the unblemished skin, the elegant tapering ending in pale, rounded nails. The performance which grew in depth as Elizabeth grew in maturity, won the love of the masses and at least an outward deference from those who wished to oppose her religious or political views. Often, to their surprise, these recalcitrants later found their feelings for the Queen had undergone a genuine change. Elizabeth possessed her father's theatricality and her mother's flamboyance. These traits, combined with the hardheaded practicality of her Tudor grandfather, Henry VII (who had rarely concerned himself with his subjects' opinions), resulted in her subjects' pride in the handsome Queen who reveled in her "mere Englishness" and possessed, in truth, more English blood than many of her predecessors.

Away from the City, the magnificent river palaces of Windsor, Richmond, Greenwich and Hampton Court beckoned, and when these had to be vacated for the necessary cleaning or "sweetening," the royal manors of Nonsuch, Woodstock, Oatlands and Eltham provided Elizabeth with the physical background against which the pageantry that etiquette demanded—and in which the Queen frankly gloried— was played. Thus, when she went to Greenwich[6] just a few miles downstream from the City, she was accompanied by the entire court which embarked at Whitehall Stairs to the accompaniment of beating drums and blaring trumpets. At a civic tournament held at Greenwich during a hot July day, 1,400 men-at-arms "clad in velvet and chains of gold with guns, Morris pikes, halberds and flags . . . marched over London Bridge into the Duke of Suffolk's park at Southwark where they mustered before the Lord Mayor." All night the men bivouacked in St. George's Fields, setting out the following morning "in goodly array" and entering Greenwich Park to await the Queen. It was not until late in the afternoon that Elizabeth appeared. She came into the gallery of Greenwich Park Gate with ambassadors, lords and ladies. The Marquess of Northampton (Katherine Parr's brother), her uncle Lord William Howard and Robert Dudley were in attendance, and they reviewed the muster, "which was to set their two battles in array to skirmish before the Queen, with flourish of trumpets, alarm of drums and melody of flutes, to encourage the counter champions to the fray." Guns were discharged, each combatant gripped his weapon, "and then they fell together as fast as they could, in imitation of close fight, while the Queen and her ladies looked on." At the conclusion, Elizabeth "thanked them heartily . . . whereupon was given the greatest shout ever heard, with hurling up of caps and the Queen showed herself very merry."[7]

Similar games were indulged in at court or Westminster Hall, and here again Elizabeth's early policy and inclination were to allow, as much as possible, the participation of her people, if it included only the viewing of the knightly spectacle. On all such occasions, Elizabeth insisted her subjects must share in the pleasure. "If ever any person had either the gift or the style to win the hearts of the people," says an earlier historian, "it was the Queen."[8] Once the tournament was complete, the court would retire to the Banqueting Hall or often, in good weather, to tents or eating pavilions built "of fir poles, decked with birch branches and all manner of flowers, both of the field and garden, as roses, July flowers, lavender, marigolds and all manner of stewing herbs and rushes." Simple refreshments or "a goodly banquet" often followed, after which everyone danced a masque; with fireworks and a great firing of guns, the festivities ceased at midnight.

The Queen enjoyed close contact with her subjects, whether prince or pauper, noble or peasant. One "sturdy countryman" who had suffered the not unusual abuse of having his livestock sequestered for court use by a royal purveyor and then paid less money than his produce warranted took the matter directly to the Queen. He eschewed the proper channels of communication, and instead, while Elizabeth was visiting Greenwich (and having informed himself of her habits), he "conveniently" met her as she engaged in her morning walk. Upon her appearance with her ladies, he cried, "Which is the Queen?" As Elizabeth turned, he cried in mock astonishment, "You!—you are one of the rarest women I ever saw, and can eat no more than my daughter Madge, who is thought the properest lass in our parish . . . the Queen Elizabeth I look for devours so many of my hens, ducks and capons that I am not able to live . . ." he finished sorrowfully.

Never unable to resist a compliment, however oblique, Elizabeth inquired into the matter. She asked the purveyor's name and promised the countryman that redress would be made. Good to her word, she found the purveyor had indeed swindled the farmer in direct violation of statute book laws against just such an abuse, and later he was hanged.[9]

Elizabeth loved to exhibit her learning. She flaunted her proficiency in languages, and, as Roger Ascham, her schoolmaster, wrote, "there

were not four men in England, either in church or state, who understood more Greek than her Majesty." He related, with all the pride of
a teacher for pupil, "that he was once present at court when she gave
answers at the same time to three ambassadors—the Imperial, the
French and the Swedish—in Italian, French and Latin, fluently and
gracefully and to the point."[10]

New Year's Day was eagerly anticipated by the Queen. Never having forgotten the semi-poverty and neglect of her childhood, she accepted her New Year's gifts with appreciation and excitement.
Elizabeth encouraged the giving of plate, clothes and sundries as much
for reasons of economy and practicality as for any other. For the most
part, she realized her courtiers' gifts were not only custom, but a bid for
attention and royal favour; her purse might as well be augmented in
the process. Thus, standing cups of silver and gilt mingled with petticoats and embroidered sleeves. Gorgeously bejeweled brooches accompanied simple fans, scarves and cunning comfit boxes. Cushions
"of tawney cloth of gold," pots of green ginger and lemon rinds came
from the lesser palace servants and one royal baker always presented
his mistress with "one fair pie of quinces, oranged."[11]

Among the carcanets, bodkins and the elaborate toilette articles, one
gift impressed the woman, as well as the Queen. Her Majesty's silk-
woman, Mistress Montague, brought for her New Year's gift an
unusual pair of knit black stockings made of silk. After wearing them
for a few days, the Queen professed herself well pleased and asked
"from whence they came and if she could have more?" The silk-woman
promised she would "set more in hand," earning Elizabeth's grateful
reply: "Do so, for indeed I like silk stockings well because they are
pleasant, fine and delicate and henceforth, I will wear no more cloth
stockings." And she never did.

Stockings were merely the beginning of the Queen's collection of
finery, to which she added all her life. In the earlier years of the reign,
the ruff had not yet exploded into the monstrous ornament it would
later become, symbolizing to Puritan eyes all that was decadent,
wasteful and useless in the monarchy. In those earlier years, the Queen
wore dresses in the black and white she preferred, simpler in design, cut
and execution than they later became. For state occasions or any
public appearances, she wore cloth of gold, silver or tinsel; satin or silks,
trimmed with gold or silver and adorned with sables. Fur, velvet,
bright embroideries and jewels—often pearls—added a touch of sumptuousness to royalty's splendor. Very feminine, Elizabeth preferred the
colors that enhanced the reddish gold of her hair—the russets and
tawnies, orange and marigold, peach and "lady blush"—a delicate

pink. Soft colors in pale shades—these were the Queen's pleasure, and her dressmakers and ladies-in-waiting learned to select the colors she preferred. They made her pretty embroidered sweet bags, sachets full of lavender and other sweet-smelling preservatives, and these were tucked into the furs, lap mantles of plush or muffs of swansdown Elizabeth used in colder weather.

Elizabeth reveled in her appearance before her subjects. She celebrated her Maundy by washing the feet of as many poor women as she had years, giving a gown to every one, and later dispensed public alms of twopence each to upwards of 2,000 poor men, women and children in St. James's Park. On St. George's Day, a day of national festival, the court was at Greenwich, and there "all her Majesty's chapel came through the hall in copes, to the number of thirty, singing 'O God, the Father of Heaven,' the outward court to the gate being strewn with green rushes." Accompanied by heralds, the Master Dean of the Chapel in robes of crimson satin and eleven Knights of the Garter followed, and then, as Sovereign of the Order, "came the Queen . . . in her robes and all the Guard following in their rich coats to the Chapel. After service, they returned through the Hall to her Grace's chamber. The Queen and the Lords went to dinner, where she was most nobly served, and the Lords, sitting on one side, were served on gold and silver. After dinner, two knights were elected, viz: The Earl of Shrewsbury and Lord Hunsdon."[13] Henry Carey, Lord Hunsdon, was the oldest child of Mary Boleyn, a child born shortly after Henry VIII had forsaken the caresses of the more docile Mary for those of her bewitching sister, the black-haired Anne.

In all these encounters with her subjects and courtiers, the central figure was always the Queen, and her obvious delight in such prominence augured well for its continuance. There was never any abruptness, impatience, aloofness or ennui in Elizabeth's attitude toward her people. Unlike many of royalty who had been so exposed to adulation since birth that it had become commonplace, the Queen never exhibited any reluctance to put herself at the head of a procession, to visit with her subjects, to talk, to flatter, to bestow, to participate. In hundreds of ways, the rejected child, a prisoner of the Tower, Woodstock and Hatfield, gloried in demonstrations of loyalty and love which wrapped her in the enviable cocoon of security she had lacked for twenty-five years. The affectionate "Gloriana" which a native poet* would give his sovereign was still a quarter of a century in the future, but the inclination to glory and greatness was evident on

*Edmund Spenser in *The Fairie Queen.*

every occasion when the Queen left her Palace, her dais or her litter to mingle with her people, to charm with a word, a gesture or a smile. It became, over the years, a performance so professional that many privately thought the Queen guilty of artful pretense. They were very wrong. Until the day she died, Queen Elizabeth and the majority of her subjects maintained an attachment and regard which, born in the earlier years, grew in depth and was as reciprocal on the Queen's part as it was in her countrymen. It would change as she matured, as theirs would wax and wane, but it would never die. It was fostered and kept alive by a woman who deliberately kept herself in public view. It was strengthened by a monarch and a woman who cared for her subjects' esteem. In these respects, she was vastly different from her father, her brother and her sister. In 1559, when Elizabeth entered London for her coronation, William Birch wrote "A Song Between the Queen's Majesty and England."[14] One line—"Here is my hand, My dear lover England, I am thine both with mind and heart"— accurately described the unique rapport which existed between a Queen and her subjects or, perhaps more important, between a woman and her friends

Elizabeth Tudor was to become a much-traveled monarch. Henry VIII had journeyed to the Continent for such diplomatic extravaganzas as the Field of Cloth of Gold and to participate in war maneuvers. Several times he had inspected English coastal defenses; on one occasion he had gone as far as York. Otherwise, his traveling was limited and set the example followed by Mary and Edward, who rarely ventured from the court. Elizabeth, however, reveled in change. The woman whose freedom had been so restricted as a child never seemed to weary of the prerogative now hers: She could come and go as she pleased. And thus, for the first time in years, the older palace servants, accustomed to less energetic royal inclinations, were frequently heard to complain among themselves that "the Queen will be off again!" Then wagons were loaded, chests must be stuffed, the royal bed was dismantled and its mattress covered in protective sheeting. The Queen's gowns were packed, the jewels safely coffered. All was bundled into wagons, carts and litters; then the nobles and courtiers, the ladies and gentlemen of the court and Council, numerous servants and attendants joined the procession which lumbered down a long winding avenue, leaving only rising dust and faint echoing cries behind. More than one retinue of royal servants, caretakers or an exhausted host and hostess collapsed in grateful but tired triumph before the Queen's entourage was out of sight.

Elizabeth wished to participate in everything. Urged on by William Cecil—and her own keen financial perception—one of her first endeavors, "which neither Queen Mary nor King Edward would durst attempt," was the restoration of English currency to sterling value. In the previous reigns the coins had been so clipped and debased by the substitution of a high percentage of alloy that their worth was an object of derision. The low intrinsic value of the "base money," as it was called, accounted for most of the highly inflated prices which increased the cost of government, and the merchants complained continually that the "state of the currency had an adverse effect on foreign exchange."[15]

Elizabeth had proposed her own method for the revaluation. "The Opinion of Her Majesty for Restoring the State of the Coinage," Cecil wrote at the top of her suggestions. There were, apparently, many conflicting opinions which angered Elizabeth. Some harried noblemen bore the brunt of the royal temper, as a memorandum from Paulet, the Lord Treasurer, and Sir Thomas Sackville indicates, for Paulet wrote Cecil to give his thanks "for removing from the Queen's mind that they had deceived her in the coinage."[16] Eventually, Sir Thomas Gresham, Elizabeth's financial genius who had managed her foreign loans, worked out the exchange wherein £700,000 of old money was returned. Each person received the nominal value of the coin in new sterling money, with the government theoretically bearing the loss. With an improved exchange rate, however, the transaction actually bore a £45,000 profit for the Queen, of which fact she was undoubtedly aware from the beginning. Each newly minted coin bore a portrait of Elizabeth crowned and in armor and ruff, her hair disheveled and flowing over her breast. A popular couplet of the time ran:

The gold and silver, which was so base, that no man could endure it scarce, Is now coined with her own face.[17]

When the new money was ready, Elizabeth came by water to the Tower and thereby to the Mint, where "she coined certain pieces of gold with her own hands, giving souvenir pieces to her cousin, Lord Hunsdon and the Marquess of Northampton." It was a day of national celebration, and William Cecil, whose purse had begun to bear the fruit of the Queen's largess,* was host at his fine new house being built

---

*Elizabeth's appreciation of Cecil commenced after the death of Amy Dudley. Heretofore she had mocked his Scottish peace and even denied him legitimate expenses. Now she awarded him the Stewardship of Westminster and later bestowed on him the lucrative post made vacant by Thomas Parry's death, the Master of the Court of Wards and Liveries.

in the Strand. Here he waited by torchlight with the Council and many lords, knights and ladies, and as he later proudly wrote in his diary, "The Queen supped at my poor cottage in the Strand before it was finished. . . ."

It was at this time that Elizabeth began a lifelong habit of visits or "progresses." They were her very real delight, as they were the despair of those who had to accompany her and whose labors contributed to the royal comfort and safety. Notice of the coming of the Queen was as much a message of despair as of joy, particularly for those who constituted the welcoming committee in the various cities, towns or villages. It was customary to greet her Majesty with a display of courtly grace as unusual as it was trying, and the ceremonies often reduced more than one town official to mumbling numbness. On the more practical level, the acquisition of sufficient funds to pay for all the festivities was nerve-racking.

One of Elizabeth's first progresses was made into Essex and Suffolk; it was forever commemorated as an introduction to Colchester oysters which afterward were purveyed for the royal table at her request.[18] A visit to Ingatestone Hall, the many-gabled home of Sir William Petre, one of her Secretaries and a Privy Councillor, followed. Sir William, "a man of approved wisdom and exquisite learning," was a West-country man. He had come to court early in the reign of Henry VIII and had served as knight, Privy Councillor and one of the two principal Secretaries (the other was Cecil) during young Edward's reign. He had been one of Thomas Cromwell's commissioners during the dissolution and had paid the Abbess of Barking a "fair market price" of £849 : 12 : 6 for her manorial hall at Ingatestone, which he had subsequently enlarged. The old gentleman had weathered all the religious and political storms of previous reigns and escaped the block, the Tower, house arrest, disgrace, fine, exile or enforced retirement which had claimed so many of his contemporaries. Now deaf and unable to move about except with discomfort, he said of himself, "I account myself unfit to be in any company," yet he spared nothing to welcome Elizabeth. Proud of the beautiful home he had built, he showed the Queen the marvel of Ingatestone Hall: an elaborate system of water pipes and drains, making "divers vaults and gutters of brick, very large, underground, round about the whole house, conveying the waters from every office"—a system which was a precursor of a more modern drainage system previously lacking in houses where the outside privy was more the norm.

After three days at My Lord Petre's, Elizabeth journeyed to Harwich, where the court enjoyed the clear sea breezes for three days. The small town gave its sovereign a lavishly warm welcome, and when departing, Elizabeth asked the nervous Mayor if she could do anything for Harwich in return. After a moment of suitable reflection, the Mayor bowed and said that "they did not require anything at the time." On the journey from the town, the Queen stopped the entourage, looked back at the small cluster of buildings and steepled churches and said, with a trace of amused pride, "A pretty town—and wants nothing."

At Ipswich, things began to go wrong. Attending religious services, Elizabeth found great fault with the clergy who were not wearing surplices and with "the general want of order observed in the celebration of Divine service."[19] In the various cathedrals and colleges visited previous to her progress, she had noted many wives and children, "contrary to the intention of the founders and much tending to the interruption of the studies of those who were placed there." When the Archbishop of Canterbury, Matthew Parker, remonstrated with her, taking the privilege of one who had once been Chaplain to her dead mother, and chided his sovereign for her "Popish tendencies," Elizabeth said that "she repented of having made any married bishops." Later the Archbishop told Cecil, "She took occasion to speak in that bitterness of the holy estate of matrimony that I was in a horror to hear." It seemed to escape everyone that the gall and wormwood of a woman continually urged to marry—and yet deprived of the one man to whom she was drawn and with whom she was in constant association—might occasionally rise to the surface, especially when she was confronted with servants of God who, only a few years ago, had been required to lead celibate lives.

The Queen's animosity was evident when she visited Lambeth Palace, the residence of the Archbishop of Canterbury and his wife. They had endeavored to entertain her with warmth and elegance. On her departure, as the moment came to render thanks, the Queen looked at the Archbishop's wife and said, testily, "And you—Madame I may not call you; mistress I am ashamed to call you, and so I know not what to call you. But, howsoever, I thank you."* There were others, however, who gave as good as they got, such as the noted Puritan preacher, David Whitehead, who later summed up the opinion of many who disliked Elizabeth's preferred spinsterhood. When the Queen com-

---

*Elizabeth's resentment of the married members of her clergy was carried to a high point that summer, when Pilkington, the Bishop of Durham, settled £10,000 upon his daughter as her marriage portion. This was the exact sum that Henry VIII had settled upon Mary and Elizabeth as their dowries. Resenting the Archbishop's affluence, the Queen immediately increased the annual tax of the See of Durham by £1,000 and transferred the money to her garrison at Berwick.

mended him by saying, "I like thee better, Whitehead, because thou livest unmarried," the intrepid minister replied, "In truth, Madame, I like you the worse for the same cause."

It was at Ipswich, as the Queen grew so pale in the heat and so tired at the strain of the unending receptions one observer said that "she looked like one lately come out of childbed," that one of Elizabeth's worst fears was realized. For three years she had been harried to wed, to bear a "blèssed prince," an heir who would carry on the Tudor name. For three years, afraid to share her hard-won authority and Crown with the only man with whom she could ever contemplate a union, she had evaded her responsibilities, secure in the knowledge that there were no claimants with whom she did not feel equal to deal. At Ipswich, she was belatedly told the incredible news that Lady Katherine Grey was pregnant and, as heiress presumptive to the throne by the same will that had placed Elizabeth in that enviable position, might now be ready to bear the "blessed prince" so eagerly desired by all England.

Chapter Nine

Though Elizabeth did not reveal her increasing awareness that her
true strength as a monarch would lie in an unshared Crown and bed,
she had begun to accept that there would be little diminution of
authority in a woman who was willing to spend every waking moment
in the dispensation of her realm's responsibilities, who seemed to
require nothing but affection from her people instead of a husband and
relished every act that brought her closer to them. She seemed willing
to sublimate the instincts which would normally have found a natural
outlet with husband or family and to direct her enormous energy
toward the demands of government and countrymen. A great deal of
attention was expended in the daily routine, in the pleasant and
satisfying life now hers, and some of this attention had begun to take
shape in an extreme interest in the cult of virginity. Elizabeth, with her
knowledge of astrology, was proud she had been born under the sign of
Virgo on the eve of the Feast of the Nativity of the Virgins. Indeed, the
very chamber at Greenwich in which she had been born was known as
the Chamber of the Virgins because of the tapestries depicting a
history of the Wise and Foolish Virgins which hung there.[1] Virginity
was a shelter, a protection wherein Elizabeth felt strongest and safest.
It was startling that a child of Henry VIII and Anne Boleyn should
possess this willingness to hold herself aloof and untouched, should
encourage it, use it and, ultimately, carry the precept to a high form of
endeavor. Her only mistake, however, was in thinking that principle
which she found so desirable might be shared by her most intimate
companions, her maids-of-honor and ladies-in-waiting.

One of the great conceits of the Queen was to surround herself with
young and beautiful women—"stars in the presence of the sun" the
French ambassador called them—to whom she was pleased to extend

the royal patronage in exchange for their loyalty, trust and support. There is no doubt that Elizabeth regarded her maids-of-honor and ladies-in-waiting as minor extensions of herself—lacking many privileges, of course. They were expected to share the luster and glory of Majesty, but they must not infringe on it. Her attitude toward them was based a great deal on custom, but it was custom carried to a further extreme than by any of her predecessors. The majority of the royal ladies-in-waiting were there for a purpose—to serve the Queen in the myriad everyday tasks of living, from the time she arose at six and gathered them together for a brisk walk along the dew-laden garden paths of the Palace until she retired at night. They were there to give her whatever companionship she desired, to provide the important and useful function of listener, sounding board and, in some rare instances, confidante. In the past, ladies-in-waiting had carried great weight in the royal chambers. Elizabeth was not endowed by nature or upbringing to permit many—with the possible exception of Ashley, her old governess—to become intimately close. What she *did* require was an undisputed and uncluttered deference and a flattering acknowledgment of her position, as well as an appreciative acceptance of the favor she had extended to each young noblewoman who might preen in the royal aura.

Not all the young ladies around the Queen shared her enthusiasm or her attitude. By tradition, they must be as well educated as possible, must speak or understand enough of several languages if they were to be fit companions for a woman whose clever brain and facile tongue caused her to speak as the occasion might demand. They must be deft needlewomen, possess adequate musical ability, be graceful dancers and good horsewomen. Above all, they must possess the desire to please their mistress, to be discreet when necessary, virtuous at all times, to refrain from meddling in any political issues and—equally important as affection for the Queen—remain aloof from any effort to bribe them or use them by any who might wish to take advantage of their position near the monarch. Depending on the point of view, this was not always easy. The young women were constantly about the court and were often cajoled or manipulated into seeking favors from Elizabeth, perhaps not always realizing how much they were used. Some courtiers, perhaps not as successful in their attempts to sway the young women, compared them to witches—"they could do hurt, but they could do not good."[2] The ladies were not averse to gossip, and information gleaned from the courtiers with whom they associated daily often supplied the Queen with intelligence others had hoped to keep from her. Even Cecil was at times chagrined that his royal mistress knew more about a subject than he did when it came under discussion.

When Elizabeth was crowned, the first and foremost woman around the Queen was Katherine Ashley, the governess who had once suffered Tower imprisonment for her sake. Ashley was the nearest to a mother figure in the Queen's life, and she now became First Lady of the Bedchamber and, indirectly, the "mother" of the ladies-in-waiting. Next in influence and affection was Blanche Parry, who had rocked the newborn Elizabeth and first roused an interest in the studies of the heavens. Blanche Parry dabbled in the occult, read palms, consulted her crystal ball, and many a rainy day was spent in the Privy Chamber before a roaring fire with credulous young women and an equally impressed Queen—all consulting the statuesque older woman as she divined their fortunes.

In quick succession, others had appeared at court. All bore illustrious names, impeccable lineage being a requisite. Many had immediate forebears who had been prominent at the courts of Elizabeth's father, brother and sister. Several of the Queen's cousins were among her companions. Katherine and Philadelphia Carey, daughters of Henry Carey, Lord Hunsdon, were Elizabeth's first cousins. His sister, Catherine, had wed Sir Francis Knollys, and their children, Lettice and Cecilia Knollys, as well as another relative, Mary Howard, completed the family group. Even more prominent, though not nearly as favored, was Lady Katherine Grey, sister of the executed Jane Grey.

Though Elizabeth had at first shown little partiality among the group, her attitude toward Lady Katherine was almost certainly tinged with the awareness that if she, Elizabeth, did not marry and died without issue, her legal successor would be Katherine Grey. In his will, Henry had left the Crown first to his own children and, after them, to the children of his younger sister Mary and her descendants, two of whom were very much present in the figures of Katherine Grey and her dwarfish younger sister, Mary.

These granddaughters of Henry's sister, Mary Tudor, the "Tudor Rose," and her handsome, though dissolute, husband, Charles Brandon, had lived sad, neglected lives in the midst of royal privilege. Katherine Grey had been born in August, 1540, at the family home in Dorset Place in London, three years after the birth of her older sister, Jane. Though always somewhat fragile, Katherine enjoyed the sports so beloved of her mother, the red-faced, hard-voiced Frances Brandon Grey, Duchess of Suffolk. While her clever sister Jane became the martyr of the schoolroom and the pet of the reformers for her youthfully erudite and brilliant espousal of the "new learning"—while Jane was practicing her handwriting and dipping into Plato's *Dialogues* and the *Orations of Demosthenes*—Katherine hunted, rode, enjoyed children's games and joined the family in their incessant traveling from the family seat in Leicestershire to London or to wherever the court was in residence. While Jane was being consciously molded as a bride for young King Edward, Katherine was left to the pursuit of her own pleasure, which an unfortunate lack of imagination rendered almost nonexistent. She was a thin, whey-faced girl with her mother's lack of charm and her father's narrow-minded arrogance. When it was obvious King Edward was dying, her father had hurriedly arranged that ill-fated marriage for her sister Jane to Guildford Dudley, son of the Duke of Northumberland, who had become a virtual dictator during the boy-King's minority. Between them—via their children—Jane's and Guildford's fathers hoped to rule England. At the same time, the ambitious Henry Grey had contracted Katherine to the eldest son of the Earl of Pembroke, a monstrously cruel and selfish man who had so delighted in the expulsion of the Abbess and nuns from the Abbey near the family seat in Wilton that he had struck at them with whips and cried, "Go spin, ye jades, go spin!" When the abortive nine-day reign of poor Jane had ended in imprisonment for the luckless girl, Pembroke had heatedly repudiated the marriage contract between Katherine and his son, so there might be no tinge of guilt by association; the marriage was later annulled. When the country rose for the dead King's sister, Mary Tudor, the new Queen had been tolerant: Jane had suffered a mere protective imprisonment, and her father had gone free. Even Pembroke immediately exchanged his staunch Protestant faith to become so fervent a Catholic that he stood bareheaded in the rain and watched the nuns of Wilton, whom he had so abused, return to their old domain.

Because their continued existence seemed only to incur rebellions of which they were the focal point, a sorrowful Mary Tudor had eventually been compelled to sign the death warrants of Jane Grey and her father. Katherine, by comparison, had suffered very little. Her mother had—to the eternal laughter of the court—married her groom, Adrian Stokes, some fifteen years her junior, only a few weeks after her husband's death. She had given birth to a daughter, Elizabeth, scandalously close to nine months later. Mercifully, the child had died. Content with her young husband, Frances Brandon, the erstwhile powerful Duchesss who had made life such a hell for her daughter Jane while the child had lived, had little time for her remaining children and was delighted when Katherine and Mary Grey went to court to become Queen Mary's companions in the Privy Chamber. Katherine was well versed in the politics of the time and—a true daughter of her mother and father—regarded her sister's death for what it actually was, a matter of public policy, not personal revenge on the part of the Queen. Her father's estates had been confiscated, and her mother made little provision for her daughters; thus the £80 Mary paid them yearly was a welcome substance. Queen Mary had allowed Katherine and Mary the precedence accorded Princesses of the blood, and they walked before all the great ladies of the court, with the exceptions of Elizabeth and Anne of Cleves. Katherine Grey later said that her time at the quiet court of Mary, with its numerous religious observances and colorful processions, the needlework, card playing and music, and the company of ladies of similar character, was the happiest she had ever known. Some of that protective feeling had been lost when Mary wed Philip of Spain and there were more Spaniards about the court to confuse the not very bright Grey sisters with their outlandish language and customs.

But it was then, shortly before Mary and Philip returned to London, that Katherine had again met Edward Seymour, the young Earl of Hertford, son of the dead Protector, whom she had not seen in several years, and a courtship began. Hertford was as penniless as Katherine, for his family's possessions, too, had been confiscated when his father had been beheaded. The deepening friendship of Katherine Grey and Edward Seymour, the innocent children of two powerful fathers who had suffered traitors' deaths, would undoubtedly have culminated in marriage had Queen Mary lived. After her death, a shaken Katherine had returned to her mother's home at Sheen—she literally had no other place to go—but motherhood not being one of Lady Frances' more endearing traits, it was not a pleasant experience. Upon Elizabeth's accession, both Katherine and Mary Grey had been given apartments at Whitehall befitting their rank, yet the difference in their status was felt daily in a dozen different ways. Queen Mary had made them Ladies of the Privy Chamber, where only those closest to her might be admitted. Elizabeth bore none of her late sister's affection for the Grey sisters, yet deemed it politic to keep them under surveillance. She made them Ladies of the Presence Chamber, a slight which Katherine, whose pale red-gold Tudor hair bespoke a matching temper, did not take lightly. The girl was not overly endowed with common sense, and not realizing the good fortune which had put her in the royal orbit once more, even if in a less intimate position, she "spoke arrogant and unseemly words" in the presence of the Queen. With a vanity unsubstantiated by great beauty or intelligence, she was a ready prey to the advances of Ambassador de Feria and, later, de Quadra even obtained her promise not to marry without at least consulting him. Elizabeth was not blind to Katherine's position or her inclinations; she herself had been in a similar circumstance for too many years. But she did not think Katherine Grey any great personal threat.

When Katherine's mother died and Elizabeth gave her the tremendous funeral a niece of Henry VIII's merited, she attempted to placate the girl, assuming an affectionate regard which, she hoped, might induce a reciprocal attitude. Where formerly "she could not abide the sight of her," Elizabeth now went to great lengths and "makes much of her in order to keep her quiet," wrote de Quadra; she even spoke of formally adopting the twenty-year-old girl. It all came to nothing, and the barely hidden animosity of the two was replaced, over the course of several years, by a token politeness, which in Katherine, at least, was near the breaking point. Her relationship with young Hertford had progressed to talk of marriage, but his fear of the Queen's reprisal held him back. At one point, before her death, Frances Brandon had framed a letter to the Queen, "asking her goodwill that he might marry the Lady Katherine, her daughter. . . ." But the young man would not allow the letter to be sent, "for he took fright at the boldness of it and said he would not care to meddle any more in the matter."[3] Still Katherine Grey persisted, and with the help of her dear friend Jane Seymour, Hertford's sister, the boy's fears were overcome. During the holidays of 1560, as the Queen prepared to hunt at Eltham, both Katherine and Jane pleaded illness. Katherine bound her face with a handkerchief and announced the anguish of a toothache, and Jane said that "she could not go a-hunting for she was sick with a bad headache." The unsuspecting Elizabeth excused them from attendance and was scarce on the river before the two excited ladies-in-waiting, like two schoolgirls on a lark, stole from the court. Disdaining the more open thoroughfare of "The Streete," where they would meet intimates, they waited until the tide was out and, braving the blasts of icy wind and the oozy mud and slime of the Thames, stole along the river's edge to Canon Row in Westminster and the house of Edward Seymour, Earl of Hertford. There, with his servants dismissed and a priest hurriedly summoned from his quarters near the Abbey, Katherine and Edward were married by candlelight with Lady Jane as the only witness. Edward gave Katherine a plain gold wedding band, and since he had not thought of a fee, his sister paid the clergyman—whose name they did not think to ask—the sum of £10. There was wine and food to celebrate, but now that the deed was done, Lady Katherine "was too unnerved to drink." Realizing they must not be out of the Palace too long, the two girls, hugely satisfied with the success of their venture, made preparations to return and, finding the tide had risen, were obliged to hire a boat back to their chambers.

Incredibly, the secret was kept. Three months after the marriage, on March 20, 1561, Lady Jane Seymour, always fragile and in ill health, died suddenly in her Whitehall apartment. Elizabeth was very attached to the girl who was a niece of the late Lord Admiral Thomas Seymour, who had figured so prominently in *her* young girlhood. She was shocked by the loss and ordered a funeral of great splendor with more than 200 mourners prior to the burial in St. Edmund's Chapel, Westminster Abbey. Jane's death robbed Katherine Grey of her only confidante, and though she continued to meet her husband at his Canon Row house, there was no one else to share her happiness. A month after Jane's death, the bridegroom was ordered with the younger son of William Cecil into France, where they seem to have distinguished themselves chiefly with "gaieties and jaunts" rather than the "legal studies and meditations" which were the principal excuses for the journey.

Shortly after his departure, Katherine Grey Seymour found she was pregnant. Her husband was gone, and she had carelessly mislaid the deed of jointure assigning her £1,000 which he had settled on her. Her dearest friend, her husband's sister, had died. At last the pressure of her secret, which must so soon come into the open, led her to confide in another court lady, one Lady Saintlow who would later go down in history as the redoubtable "Bess of Hardwick." Mistress Saintlow, however, was a long way in experience and wealth from her future privileged position of authority, and upon hearing the young woman's startling disclosures, she reproved Katherine for her thoughtlessness in making her the recipient of her secret folly. In a fearful rage, she ordered Katherine from her chamber. After several hours in which to think, the distraught girl, now nearly hysterical with fear and self-pity, entered the bedroom of Robert Dudley, the brother of her dead sister Jane's husband. Throwing herself at his bedside, she woke the sleeping man, and "shaking with sobs and in a most awesome state of mind," she confessed her secret and asked Robert's intercession "requesting him to be a mean to the Queen's Highness for her. . . ."

Elizabeth's own sleeping apartments were very near Dudley's; she was used to visiting him at all hours when she herself was a victim of insomnia. These nocturnal visits were no secret to the Palace servants, who often witnessed the comings and goings and, at times, remained discreetly withdrawn within the chamber itself. Fearful his Queen might find his erstwhile sister-in-law in tears at his bedside, Robert calmed the overwrought girl and, hoping to ease her hurriedly from his quarters, promised to do his best. He did what he could, but on hearing his story the following morning, Elizabeth acted predictably. Any member of the royal family wishing to contract a marriage must, of necessity, obtain the consent of the Queen and Council. Not only had Katherine flouted tradition, but her actions for one so near the throne were deemed by Elizabeth as nothing short of a challenge. They also conveniently served as a catalyst by which the royal temper might be assuaged. In a frenzy, the pent-up emotion of several years in which she had tolerated the Grey girl's arrogant impudence exploded, and she ordered Katherine to the Tower. Hertford's mother, the Duchess of Somerset, was apprised by Cecil of the situation and—again predictably—replied in a letter beseeching him to believe she had had no part in the affair and begging Cecil to remain her friend "that the wildness of mine unruly child do not diminish Her Majesty's favour towards me." The Duchess's fears were not unfounded. Professing she was "not well quieted with the mishap of Lady Katherine," Elizabeth also ordered the recipient of the girl's first disclosures, Lady Saintlow, to the Tower for not having revealed the matter sooner. At the Tower, Sir Edward Warner was ordered "to examine the Lady Katherine very straightly, how many hath been privy to the love between her and the Earl of Hertford from the beginning, and let her certainly understand that she shall have no manner of favour except she will show the truth not only what ladies and gentlemen were privy thereto, but also what lords and gentlemen for it doth now appear that sundry personages have dealt herein."[4] Elizabeth's indignation was apparent in every word.

At the Tower, Katherine was exhibiting an obstinacy as galling as it was pointless. Elizabeth had ordered that the girl be made comfortable, and thus bits and pieces of shabby furniture, hangings and carpets—relics of her sister Jane's imprisonment, possibly of Elizabeth's own—were brought into her apartment. She was allowed the company of the parrots, monkeys and lapdogs which had cluttered her apartments at Whitehall. Meanwhile, the unsuspecting bridegroom had been ordered home. It was not until his arrival at Dover that he was informed of his arrest, lodged in the castle, deprived of his servants and left a prey to his fears regarding the Queen's revenge. On September 5 he was brought to the Tower and committed to apartments separate from his wife. A commission, which included the Archbishop of Canterbury and Sir William Petre, waited on him with questions regarding "his infamous proceedings with Lady Katherine Grey." The brutal questioning reacted on Hertford, who staunchly defended his actions, saying he had lawfully married Katherine which the commission sought to disclaim. The clergyman who had officiated either could not be found or was himself intimidated from appearing. The only witness, Lady Jane Seymour, was dead, and the deed of jointure settled by Hertford on his wife was still missing.

Katherine, in floods of tears and now obviously terrified, was also examined by the commission. The procedure was interrupted by the birth of a son on September 21, 1561. He was baptized five days later in the Church of St. Peter-ad-Vincula within the Tower grounds, near the moldering bones of his executed relatives—his Aunt Jane; both grandfathers: Henry Grey and Edward Seymour; and his uncle Thomas Seymour. Katherine had not had an easy confinement, and broken in spirit, as well as weakened in body, she remained tearful and listless in her rooms. There were many, including William Cecil, who sought to reason with the Queen that her treatment, while understandable, was harsh, and they dared suggest some measure of compassion for Katherine or at least, her removal to a private home, where she might be kept under surveillance. It was all useless. Elizabeth remained firm: Her honour and her Crown had been touched, she said, when one so near to her in position and blood had used the royal indulgence so outrageously. Beneath the Queen's harshness may be seen an even deeper emotion. Katherine had reacted as a woman to satisfy a normal woman's desire for a husband and children. In so doing, she had flouted Elizabeth, who might never possess either, and in the doing, there was an implicit challenge to all Elizabeth actually *did* possess—her Crown. Katherine was the first of many to learn that when her sovereignty was challenged, Elizabeth Tudor could be merciless.

Eight months later the commission which investigated the matter declared "there had been no marriage between the Earl of Hertford and Lady Katherine Grey." Their son was, in effect, a bastard and presumably no threat to the succession. And all three were ordered to remain in the Tower at the Queen's pleasure.

At the time Katherine Grey was undergoing her ordeal, her cousin* across the Channel was preparing to leave France. Mary Stuart had spent the traditional forty days of mourning cloistered at Orléans, and on emerging from the stuffy, dimly lit rooms, she journeyed to the Abbey of St. Pierre-les-Dames at Rheims to visit her powerful Guise relatives. Here the most important topic of discussion was a future

*As Mary Stuart was the granddaughter of Henry VIII's sister Margaret, so Katherine Grey was the granddaughter of his younger sister Mary.

marriage. For Mary Stuart of Scotland and France was now—with Elizabeth Tudor of England—one of the most sought-after marital prizes. The choice of suitors—Eric of Sweden, Charles of Austria and Don Carlos of Spain—was identical for both Queens, although the merits of each were debated by Mary and her family with considerably more interest than the English Queen exhibited. The most desirable union was with Catholic Spain, an alliance dreaded by both the Huguenots in France and the Protestants in England. But nowhere was the future position of the widowed Queen of more importance than in her own country.

"We all begin to enter into some devotion to our sovereign Lady . . ." wrote Maitland, the Laird of Lethington, to William Cecil. He was quick to state that Scotland had not forgotten its debt to Elizabeth, but that for the moment "all men's minds were stirring and their own Queen must now be their primary object of attachment." There was a trace of irony in Maitland's remark, for the Scots had been provoked by Elizabeth's refusal to marry the Earl of Arran. As the English ambassador, Thomas Randolph, wrote Cecil, "there is such resentment at the rejection . . . that the Scots hold themselves almost absolved from all their obligations. . . ."[5] Now Arran was being considered as a husband for Mary Stuart. It seemed to matter little to the ambitious syphilitic Earl *which* monarch he married. If Elizabeth would not have him and Mary would, they might even work together to dethrone the English usurper.

Couriers and deputations from both the Protestant and the Catholic factions of Scotland visited Mary in France. One emissary, John Leslie, bore the fealty of powerful peers such as Huntly, Atholl, Bothwell, Seaton, Crawford and Caithness—strange, unfamiliar names to Mary. He suggested her arrival at Aberdeen, where she would be met by 20,000 loyal Catholic followers, who would escort her to Edinburgh. He urged her quick return before the intrigue besetting an absentee monarch could deepen.

The Protestant representative was Mary's illegitimate half brother, the twenty-eight-year-old Lord James Stuart, a tall, black-haired, handsomely rugged Scotsman, who brought with him the good wishes of the Scottish Parliament. He spoke of her prominent Protestant supporters—Maitland, Argyll, Kirkcaldy of Grange—all strong members of the Congregation. Mary's uncles made tantalizing offers to Lord James to switch his loyalty from the Congregation and England, and they offered him the Regency of Scotland in Mary's absence if he would accept. But Lord James, aware of where Scotland's real strength lay, refused. Her peers offered a warm reception and a true loyalty, provided she showed due regard for the reformed religion, said Lord James. If, in her youthful piety, Mary conjured up visions of a girl-Queen fervently fighting to restore her faith in her native land, her more practical family—with Mary Tudor's experience bright in their memory—soon informed her otherwise. The Scottish Congregation had assured Mary she might worship as she pleased, James promised. The state religion, however, must be Protestant. Since Mary was eager to assume a Queen's mantle again, she realized toleration and moderation were part of the bargain.

At eighteen, Mary was more preoccupied with her Queenship than with any emotional concern for the land she would rule. Her sorrow at her husband's death mingled with the daily discontent of her drastically changed circumstances. Her consideration of Scotland bore no warmth of recognition or familiarity. She felt her mother's life had been sacrificed to keep her country secure until she herself could return; even so, the Scottish people had not hesitated to diminish her sovereignty. She had but the faintest memory of the stark hilly country of her ancestors; the splendor of the Highlands, foggy and remote, the magnificent lochs and deep valleys were all unknown. Taken to France to escape the designs of the English Protector, Edward Seymour, to bring her to England as a bride for young Edward VI, she had spent her childhood and adolescent years cosseted and pampered in the silken luxury of French palaces, surrounded by the elegant courtesies and secure comforts only a sophisticated and cultured court could offer. By temperament, Mary was more Guise than Stuart. She was—and was forever to remain—a thorough Frenchwoman, more at home in the shining chambers of French chateaus with their jewellike tapestries than in the dark, drafty and ill-smelling rooms of Scottish dwellings with their somber, heavy furnishings and incessant dampness. She would forever be happier amid the wonders of Fontainebleau, where glowing Titians and da Vincis lined the walls, where the works of Cellini, Del Sarto and Primaticcio were admired or handled daily, where libraries filled with Petrarch, Machiavelli, Tasso and Boccaccio were side by side with the works of Ronsard, du Bellay and Rabelais. Mary had been educated as a future Queen of France, Scotland and, it was hoped, England. Her French was faultless; she spoke Latin and several other languages with ease. She was proficient musically, especially on the lute, and as graceful a dancer as she was a competent rider. Many of her accomplishments were not considered desirable in Scotland, a nation which was viewed—too charitably, many thought—to be at least 100 years behind other European courts in culture, manners and general standard of living. Of all the many

talents she possessed, it is indicative that the only one later truly
admired in her homeland was Mary's ability to handle a horse.

While anxious to please her uncles and more than eager to resume a
sovereign role, Mary did not relish the thought of leaving France, the
only land she truly considered home and where she had been so happy
for twelve years. She later said, "I desired a hundred times more to
remain in France, a simple dowager and content with Touraine and
Poitou for my dowry, rather than go to a savage country, but messieurs,
my uncles . . . counselled me to go." As preparations were made, she
sent to England for a safe-conduct through that realm—a not
unreasonable request in view of weather conditions which might cast
her on English shores and a courtesy usually extended by England to
friendly powers.

Elizabeth received the request from M. d'Oysell, Mary's minister, in
the midst of a crowded court. For more than a year, Mary had delayed
ratification of the Treaty of Edinburgh, and Elizabeth now took the
opportunity to unburden herself of her chagrin. Angrily she berated
d'Oysell "that the Queen of Scots should ask no favours until she has
ratified the Treaty . . ." and the humiliated minister was left with little
to do but gather the shreds of his dignity and leave. Elizabeth also left
the Scottish Parliament in no doubt of her feelings; Mary had not
behaved honorably in leaving the treaty unsigned. "We must plainly
let you all understand that this manner of answer without fruit, cannot
long content us," she wrote, "our meaning to your sovereign has been
good. We stayed her realm from danger and have kept peace hitherto,
as we promised. We think it strange she has no better advice . . . if you
support her breach of solemn promise, we shall accept your answer and
doubt not but by the Grace of God, you shall repent it. . . ."[6] As for the
safe-conduct, she could hardly offer the hospitality of her shores to
someone who had acted so negligently. The Queen's action seems to
have surprised no one except d'Oysell. Even the French ambassador
told Cecil Elizabeth had reacted exactly as he had expected.

Mary's youthful pride was touched by the Queen's treatment of her
minister, and she was scornful of Elizabeth's attempt to bargain a
safe-conduct for a treaty ratification. In this instance, the first of many,
seeds of distrust destined to bear such ill fruit in future years were sown.
With almost prophetic candor, Mary's half brother, James Stuart,
summed up the essence of what was to become such a heartbreaking
reality, when he wrote Queen Elizabeth: "You be tender cousins, both
Queens in the flower of your ages, much resembling the other in most
excellent and goodly qualities. . . ." He said he wished his half sister
had never accepted the advice of uncles and husband to claim

Elizabeth's title, "for I am fully persuaded that you would have been and continued as dear friends as you be tender cousins . . . but now I fear that unless the root may be removed, it shall ever breed unkindness between you. Your Majesty cannot yield and she may on the other part think of it hard, being so nigh of the blood of England, to be made a stranger from it. . . ."[7]

The news of her cousin's discourtesy reached Mary at St.-Germain. Further rumor that several ships of the English Navy had been sent to intercept her passage only added to Mary's wrath, and she summoned Sir Nicholas Throckmorton. Their interview took place in July, 1561, and the English ambassador, feeling the summer heat, did not relish the summons. Dutifully he presented himself at court, steeling himself against Mary's ill humor, and was immediately impressed, as he had been dozens of times before, by the feminine appeal so lately apparent in Mary as she had passed from adolescence to young womanhood. Even in her widow's weeds of black and white, the beauty, grace and charm that would later cause men to risk their lives for her were obvious. Mary was, like her mother, very tall and gracefully slender; an erect stature only emphasized her well-endowed figure. Her face was a delicate and piquant oval, with clear skin and abundant chestnut hair. The almond-shaped eyes, alert and intelligent beneath a smooth clear brow, offset the too thin mouth and sharp nose. Normally her manner was soft and gracious. It was difficult not to be swayed by such loveliness, and often, in these encounters, Throckmorton found himself affected despite his strong Puritan dislike of everything Mary was and represented. Repeatedly his correspondence indicated a firm opinion of Mary and later—the result of an interview—a softened opinion would demonstrate her appeal to his masculinity and his concern for her circumstances. It was ever Mary's gift—in whatever state she might be at the moment—to induce in men a compassion for her distress. She invited a desire to protect and help; in no other way were she and Elizabeth so completely dissimilar. The mere thought of the English Queen appealing for protection and using her sex as a means of obtaining it would have made the least intelligent English courtier speechless with mirth.

When Throckmorton was ushered into Mary's presence, her disdain, as well as her beauty, was apparent. She showed little graciousness, for she had been stung by Elizabeth's refusal to grant a safe-conduct and even more touched by the insulting reception accorded her minister. Never was her sensitivity more apparent as she waved away those around her, saying, with pointed sarcasm, if she were to be "transported by her passions as the English Queen had, she did not wish witnesses to her loss of control." The perspiring Throckmorton sought excuses for his Queen, stating it had been more than a year since the Treaty lacked ratification. It was for "this unamicable and indirect dealing" that Elizabeth had refused Mary. He said if Mary would ratify, then Elizabeth "would not only give you and yours free passage, but also will be most glad to see you pass through her realm, that you may be accommodated with the pleasure thereof. . . ." Mary listened with ill-concealed annoyance. Bitterly she replied, "there is nothing that doth grieve me more than that I did so forget myself as to have asked of her favours which I could well have done without. I came here in defiance of the attempt made by her brother Edward to prevent me and, by the Grace of God, I will return without her leave. . . ."[8] When Throckmorton protested that Elizabeth regarded Mary "as a Queen, her next neighbor and her next kinswoman," Mary ignored his comment. Heatedly, she said, "I need no more to have made her privy to my journey than she doth me of hers. I may pass well enough home into my own realm, I think, without her passport or license. . . ." Mary repeated she was not to be charged with the delay in the ratification, that the decision was made "in the late King's time" and that she must now be advised "by the Council of my own realm." She said she could not be held accountable for the actions of others and continued, "As God favors me, I did never mean otherwise unto her than becometh me to my good sister and cousin, nor mean her any more harm than to myself. God forgive them which have otherwise persuaded her. . . ."[9] Rising, she asked Throckmorton, looking at him directly, "What is the matter, pray you, Monsieur l'Ambassadeur, that doth so offend the Queen your mistress, to make her thus evil affected to me? I never did her wrong, either in deed nor in speech. . . ."

Throckmorton, distinctly uncomfortable, answered his only commission was "to have no more to say to you, but to know your answer for the ratification of the treaty." But Mary could not leave the ambassador without an answer and her strange young intensity, her obvious groping for some solution led him to the truth. He told Mary of Elizabeth's anger at the French monarchs' assumption of the arms of England, saying that "if anything can be more prejudicial to a Prince than to usurp the title and interest belonging to them, Madam, I do refer it to your own judgment . . . ," for Mary's claim was tantamount to declaring Elizabeth illegitimate. Again Mary declared that her father-in-law, husband and uncles had commanded such action, that it was not her doing. At the same time, she pointedly emphasized that her grandmother was Henry VIII's sister, "and, I trow, the eldest sister he had. . . ." Mary stated she was determined to return to Scotland, "to adventure the matter whatsoever come of it." She told Throckmorton, "I trust the wind will be so favorable that I shall not need to come on the coast of England, Monsieur l'Ambassadeur, for if I do then . . . the Queen your mistress shall have me in her hands to do her will of me and if she be so hard-hearted as to desire my end, she may then do her pleasure and make sacrifice of me . . . peradventure that casualty might be better for me than to live . . ."[10] she ended almost prophetically.

When Throckmorton's letter reached England, Cecil urged Elizabeth to grant the safe-conduct. By withholding what was, after all, a formal act of courtesy, the English Queen had not deterred the Scottish Queen. Instead, one woman had only offended another's female pride. It was ever one of Elizabeth's many strengths that when more might be obtained by compromise, she could yield. The safe-conduct was duly sent, but too late, for Mary Stuart had sailed with the royal rudeness still rankling.

Mary was escorted to Scotland by her three Guise uncles, Claude, René and Francis. With her also, were her ladies-in-waiting, the "four Marys," Mary Seton, Mary Beaton, Mary Livingstone and Mary Fleming. Accompanying the royal party were numerous pages, poets, musicians and noblemen, companions to make life in Scotland bearable for the Queen. Sailing from Calais, a tearful Mary Stuart gazed around the harbor at the country she loved so well. She watched from the stern until nightfall, when, at her request, a makeshift couch was set up on the deck so she might view the French coast on awakening. At daybreak she was found watching the receding green land. Plaintively she whispered, "Farewell, France, farewell. . . ." She watched through tears until the North Sea mists enveloped her galleon, cutting off the sight of land, before turning dispiritedly aside. Midway, the English ships waylaid one of the Scottish convoy carrying the royal horses; in the fog, the remaining two vessels quickly sped on their way. The English did not give chase. As Cecil later wrote to Throckmorton, "The Queen's Majesty's ships that were upon the seas to cleanse them from pirates saw her [Mary] and saluted her galleys. . . . " Mary Stuart ultimately sailed safely to her realm but not, however, without the galling knowledge that the Queen of England had allowed her the privilege of passage.

To refute the poor impression she had given her Scottish cousin, Elizabeth invited those who had escorted Mary to pass through England on their return to France. Thus, more than 100 nobles, including Mary's Guise uncles, visited the English court, and Elizabeth spared no expense or personal effort to impress her distinguished visitors. One whom she particularly beguiled was the courtier Brantôme, later to become a celebrated biographer. Years later he recounted the royal entertainment in his memoirs:

> The Queen gave us all one evening a supper in a grand room hung around with tapestry representing the parable of the ten virgins of the Evangelist. When the banquet was done, there came in a ballet of her maids-of-honor, whom she had dressed and ordained to represent the same virgins. Some of them had their lamps burning and full of oil, and some of them carried lamps which were empty; but all their lamps were silver—most exquisitely chased and wrought—and the ladies were very pretty, well-behaved, and very well dressed. They came in the course of the ballet, and prayed us French to dance with them, and even prevailed on the Queen to dance, which she did with much grace and right royal majesty, for she possessed then no little beauty and elegance.[11]

The fete, honoring Elizabeth's birthday, gave the Queen an opportunity of reaffirming her affinity for the virgin state. But even as she danced and swayed with her maidens, religious and political forces were coalescing and various private persons around her were pursuing somewhat treacherous ambitions to thwart the sovereign of her most valuable possession, her Crown.

Once the French delegation had left her shores, it was obvious the Queen's health was declining. Her physical condition was as much a source of worry to her intimates as it was an immense interest to those like the Spanish ambassador, de Quadra, who observed: "The Queen is becoming dropsical and has already begun to swell extraordinarily . . . she is extremely thin and the color of a corpse. . . ."[12] This inclination of Elizabeth's was usually evident when stress was present. Her personal habits often gave cause for concern. She ate sparingly—too sparingly, many thought—and only when she was hungry, at times impatiently waving food from sight. She avoided the tiresome ceremonial of eating in public in the Presence Chamber whenever she could, preferring instead to eat in her own Privy Chamber, where she might dine overlooking the Thames or the gardens below. Many times, to the despair of the royal cooks and servitors, she ordered a table set for herself and a few intimate companions in some secluded arbor of the gardens, and there she would eat the small portions she preferred. She drank a moderate amount of good English ale or beer and always mixed water with her wine. She seemed to need little rest, never retiring before midnight, to the discomfort of her ladies, who were less hardy, who knew they must be up by six o'clock to help dress the Queen and walk with her in the gardens. There, amid dripping hedges and outlandish topiary specimens laden with dew, in the morning air often filtered with fog, Elizabeth liked to stride briskly "to catch herself a heat." If the weather was particularly forbidding, she and her maidens often availed themselves of a new contraption, an *umbrella*. Because of her penchant for such exercise, she had caused the building of a new terrace at Windsor Castle where she might walk when the weather was inclement, but most of all—in rain or sunshine—she enjoyed a walk in the cold air, especially if there was a frost. Then indoors to a breakfast of bread and ale, before settling down to the affairs of state with her Councillors and ministers, to attack with obvious relish the mountains of papers and discuss the myriad problems of her country, Treasury and people. In the Privy Chamber, Elizabeth met with ambassadors, as well as friends, and once the royal duties were concluded, she played cards or sat on cushions with her ladies and watched the court dancing, often rising to join expertly in a galliard or a pavane.

Other than the pretensions of the Scottish Queen and some envious relatives, serious intriguing or conspiracy against the Queen had been slight. There were plots, some more rumor than real. De Quadra wrote of one instance when the Queen had been threatened with poison. Although Elizabeth preferred to treat it humorously, William Cecil apparently was not so certain. De Quadra wrote, "I know however that it was not looked upon at all as a joke at first and that Cecil himself was waiting at a door for many hours on the watch for two men . . . who were to be arrested. This would not have been done, at least by Cecil himself, if they had not taken the thing seriously."[13] Cecil's precautions led him to urge Elizabeth not to place any clothing next to her skin until it had been examined. She was to inhale no perfume which came from any stranger and consume no food unless it was cooked by her own servants. Even the guards were reinforced at all entrances to the Queen's apartments.

If fear or disillusionment at times plagued Elizabeth, she needed only an encounter with her people to restore her spirit. When she returned from her summer progress, she came to London from Enfield, and from Islington on, "all the hedges and ditches were levelled to clear the way for her and such were the gladness and affection manifested by the loyal concourse of people who came to meet and welcome her that it was night when she came over St. Giles-in-the-Fields."[14] It was also days before the glow of her reception left the Queen's tired features and anxiety appeared again.

The progress had been more wearing than she had anticipated. It was only a year since the Scottish conflict had been resolved and the notoriety of Amy Dudley's death had seemingly been laid to rest. Her cousins Mary Stuart and Katherine Grey had contributed to her concern. Each had touched Elizabeth Tudor in a very different way, but all had been judged in the light of her sovereignty. The pressure on her to marry continued, a relentless pressure she could not wave away with a command. Always she must pay strict attention to her Council's advice, to judge the merits and values of her different suitors, to weigh the advantages of a marital alliance with one country over another. And always just outside the Council door was the only man she truly wished to be with *if* she were ever to wed. He was an Englishman born and bred, ready to whisk her to the hunt, to the archery butts, onto the Thames or perhaps just a walk in the quiet, secluded royal gardens, where they might talk in low whispers or embrace without their companions looking on.

Robert Dudley had returned to court, any chastening bestowed by the debacle of his Spanish negotiations disappearing daily as Elizabeth again restored him to favor. Their relationship had deepened, which in itself is indicative of Elizabeth's innocence of any wrongdoing in Amy's death and her belief that Robert also was guiltless. She would hardly have borne his continued presence in a court where, presumably, knowledge of her complicity could have been used as a threat in a dozen situations in which Robert yearned for more power. Although she still refused him an Earldom, she honored his brother Ambrose by restoring to the Dudley family the Earldom of Warwick.

At the Christmas holidays, Robert was dubbed "Constable and Marshal of the Court of Merriment." An observer at the fete called him "a man of a flourishing age and comely feature of body and limbs . . . tall and singularly well-featured, of a sweet aspect, but high-foreheaded, which was of no discommendation. . . ."[15] Not everyone regarded Robert or his influence on Elizabeth so favorably. His familiarity with the Queen was irritating to others, if not to her personally. Such tolerance on the Queen's part quite naturally led Dudley, at times, to exceed the limits of royal endurance. On another occasion, when a rumor swept London that Elizabeth had wed Dudley at Baynard's castle, the home of the Earl of Pembroke, she humorously told the assembled court that "they must not believe everything they heard." Robert told de Quadra the Queen had, instead, *"promised* to marry him, only not this year." She had often told him, replied the

Spanish ambassador, that *if* she should marry an Englishman, "it should be only Robert."

Elizabeth still delighted in receiving the diplomats anxious to further her marriage, although some at court were beginning dimly to perceive how reluctant the Queen would be to dispose of the important marital weapon which might, over a period of time, be made to carry as much importance as a marriage itself. When one such minister arrived to renew the King of Sweden's suit, a fearful Robert Dudley did not hesitate in an attempt at intimidation. When he was unable to meet the Swede, he contrived to have him imprisoned on some minor fault, and the hapless visitor was "warned to take heed—his cutters look as though they would do some hurt."[16] When Elizabeth learned of Dudley's outrageous behavior, she summoned him to court, and there in her Presence Chamber, with all her courtiers looking on, her anger erupted. White with rage, she icily told her Master of the Horse she would never marry him; his birth was too mean, his family too treacherous. Her anger continued as she warned Robert not to interfere again in her diplomacy and reminded him once more his preferments came from her, *the Queen!* He, no more than anyone else, must not abuse her generosity or goodwill. Stung by her open denunciation, Robert begged her leave to depart the country and go to sea. With a wave of her hand, the Queen scathingly waved him away. "Begone, then. . . .!" But by nightfall Robert was still there, the royal anger had cooled, and the two were whispering with heads together over a shared goblet of wine. It was confusing, irritating, aggravating—and hopeless. If many viewed Elizabeth's conduct disapprovingly, if their attitude showed they might have wished behavior more royal from their sovereign, it was equally apparent that neither Dudley nor the Queen cared one whit what any of them thought.

While none, with the possible exception of Ashley, might remonstrate with the Queen over her disgraceful behavior with Robert Dudley, there were many who did seek to spare her some of the burden of statecraft and its attendant drain on her well-being. But while Elizabeth was prepared to delegate responsibility, she was unwilling to delegate authority; consequently, she had to be apprised of everything that contributed to the welfare of her realm or her own royal person. This, combined with the emotional frustration of her relationship with Dudley—a relationship of the deepest intimacy which lacked only the actual fact of intercourse to complete it—had resulted in the thin, tense and nervous creature who presented herself daily to conduct the business of her country. Therefore, when the scheming of Margaret Douglas, the Countess of Lennox, was brought to her attention,

Elizabeth might justifiably have uttered one of her great oaths or—more unlikely—burst into tears and thrown up her hands in disgust and despair. Instead, emulating her father, she dispatched her orders and awaited the results.

A poor relationship had always existed between Margaret Douglas and Elizabeth. Margaret was Henry VIII's niece. She was the daughter of Margaret Tudor, the King's older sister, by her second marriage* to Archibald Douglas, the Earl of Angus. Henry had excluded Margaret Douglas and her descendants from the succession because of their Catholic faith and named, instead, the descendants of his younger sister, Mary. Margaret Douglas was tall with the erect stature of the Tudors; her deep voice and forbidding manner were reminiscent of her Scottish forebears. She had married Matthew Stuart, the Scottish Earl of Lennox, who had forfeited his estates in Scotland and France when he wed the King's niece; Henry had subsequently given them vast holdings in Yorkshire.

From her earliest childhood, Elizabeth had suffered the attempts of Margaret Douglas to intimidate her. The Countess had always been contemptuous of Anne Boleyn, scornful of Henry's divorce and all the emotional and religious havoc that had resulted for England. Her scorn extended to Anne and Henry's daughter, and during all her adolescent years, Elizabeth—depending on whether her status was currently legitimate or illegitimate—had had to give precedence to the Countess. Margaret Douglas had been an intimate of Mary Tudor's during her reign. They shared the same faith and were more of the same age. And, Elizabeth knew, Margaret had never ceased to poison Mary's thoughts with her own opinion of her sister's allegedly treasonous activities; she was even reputed to have urged Elizabeth's execution. At one point, as Elizabeth had been returned from Wood-stock after a long imprisonment for suspected complicity in the Wyatt rebellion, she had been lodged in a small apartment at Whitehall. Worry, restraint and privation had reduced the shattered girl to a perilously ill state, and with ragged nerves and a mind made almost hallucinatory by lack of sleep, her discomfort was aggravated by activity in the apartment directly overhead. When she inquired, she was told it was occupied by the Countess of Lennox's staff. Daily and well into the night, the noise overhead reduced Elizabeth to tears of frustrated rage. There was "casting down of logs, pots and vessels," people walking back and forth, chairs scraping and continual talk and

*Margaret Tudor's first marriage had been to James IV of Scotland, who was killed at the Battle of Flodden Field. Their son, James V, was the father of Mary Stuart, Queen of Scots.

laughter. Elizabeth sent word via a servant to ask for the Countess' sympathetic intercession. Yet nothing had happened; if anything, the conditions became worse. This, and the remembrance of the years when, as a child and later as a young girl, she had been compelled to suffer the Countess's insolent stares, had not helped matters. Yet on her accession, Elizabeth had exhibited a tolerance which did not come easily. She had received Margaret Douglas at court and given her the precedence her rank required. Even so, the Countess had paid her the merest deference, coupled with such condescension, that their relationship was one of only surface politeness. Margaret spent much time at Temple Newsam, the Yorkshire estate where the family castle was a focal point for discontented Catholics or anyone harboring malice against the Crown. One servant, out of either fear or a grudge against the Lennoxes, finally saw fit to inform the Queen of the ambitious Countess soliciting the aid of the northern Catholics in favor of her son, Lord Darnley, as a husband for Mary, Queen of Scots. He also brought the titillating information of Elizabeth's being referred to as "that fool bastard" when the family's fool was urged to disparage the Queen as Robert Dudley's mistress during the evening festivities.

At first the Queen chose to overlook the implications, but she could not overlook the Countess' plotting with de Quadra in favor of her son or the constant political activity at their residence. When repeated evidence was set before her, Elizabeth lost little time. She summoned the Countess and the Earls of Northumberland and Westmorland to court, allegedly to pass the festive holidays with her. In the meantime, the Countess's tall seventeen-year-old son, Henry Stuart, a weak and spoiled individual, had gone to France. Handsome in a puerile way, Darnley combined the blood of the Tudors with that of Stuart and Hamilton, and he sought to further his suit for Mary Stuart's hand with her Guise uncles. When confronted with her family's activities, the Countess hotly defended her right to consider her son as a husband for the Scottish Queen. Mary Stuart was her niece, she said; she wished "to marry her son, by which the succession of the kingdom would be secured to the Scottish Queen and all reason for strife would be avoided in case of the Queen [Elizabeth] dying without issue. . . ." The Countess could not have chosen a worse defense, for, as de Quadra wrote the Spanish King, "The Queen, however, bases her security on there being no certain successor to whom people could turn if they were to tire of her rule, and I understand she is in great alarm about this business."[17]

Elizabeth ultimately provided a master stroke of retaliation. She "recalled" that the marriage of Margaret Douglas' mother, Henry's sister, had been annulled by the Pope—an action that proud Prince sorely regretted when Henry Tudor later petitioned for a similar convenience. The marriage to Margaret Douglas' father had been dissolved. Therefore, said the Queen, since her parents had never been properly married, Margaret Douglas was illegitimate, and her offspring of no importance as possible heirs. And to have opportunity to mull over her new status in private, she ordered the Countess into the custody of Sir Richard Sackville at Sheen, and her husband, the Earl, joined Katherine Grey in the Tower.

The Diplomat

There seems to be something sublime in the words and bearing of the Queen of Scots that constrains even her enemies to speak well of her.

Chapter Ten

Elizabeth's successful excursion into Scotland had given her no taste for war. As a monarch she loathed the waste of funds; as a woman she hated the tragedy, suffering and sorrow of armed conflict. Mediations at the Council table and the craft and cunning of diplomacy were more practical. There was also less risk of a Treasury enlarged by chronic frugality being depleted in very short order. Elizabeth was realist enough, however, to know that the blessings of peace are enjoyed by those who are prepared. She was the first English monarch to order the home manufacture of the gunpowder her predecessors had always purchased abroad.[1] The coastal fortifications her father had built or strengthened, as well as those along the Border, were kept in good repair. She increased the wages of her mariners and soldiers to discourage desertion and, with an eye to the future, set forth a ship-building program which led de Quadra to write petulantly, that Elizabeth "was determined to make herself Mistress of the Seas." While her predecessors had hired needed ships from the Germans or Italians, the Queen would accept nothing but stout English vessels, and she encouraged men from the Devon coast to build and man them. The sixteenth-century game of international politics, combined with the religious friction of several decades, was a murderous device fraught with a cruel potential, and Elizabeth, who did not possess the gift of quick decision, always looked for ways to circumvent any challenge which might lead to war. Therefore, when an incident occurred which was to ignite the terrible conflagration of the religious wars in France, the quick reaction of the English Queen was all the more surprising.

On a frosty Sunday in March, 1562, the Duke of Guise, Mary Stuart's uncle, complained, as he attended Mass in the tiny French village of Vassy, of the lusty singing of a group of Protestants in their small church nearby. Asked to desist from such outrageous behavior so his Grace might attend his devotions with more piety, the reformers only sang the louder. Incensed, the Duke's retainers surrounded the small church and set it on fire. More than 60 died in the flames; more than 200 were cut down or wounded when they fled the building. The Queen Mother, Catherine de Medici, had attempted some toleration for the Huguenots, "but they injured their cause by forthwith demanding greater privileges."[2] The atrocity caused an eruption of the bitter feeling existing between Catholics and the Protestant Huguenots. It reverberated throughout the Continent, and in England Elizabeth, horrified and shaken, proclaimed the Guise as murderers and looked the other way when Frenchmen were harried and abused in the London streets. The English Reformation movement felt itself imperiled by the attack on their brothers-in-faith in France, and the Queen made no attempt to hide the fact that she shared the popular feeling. The Duke of Guise seized the boy-King and Catherine and sent them to Paris. The immediate result in England was the arrival of emissaries from Condé, the Huguenot leader, to plead for English help. Condé reminded Elizabeth of the help he had rendered her in driving the Guisian French from Scotland. Now *she* must help *him*, else the Protestant cause might founder forever in France.

As usual the English Council was divided. Conservative and hard-working Sir Henry Sidney was sent to France to confer with Catherine de Medici, who, fearful for her son's throne, was too busy maintaining what little power she possessed to be of much help. The overwhelming fear among the Councillors and the Queen was that Philip of Spain, now married to a French Princess "and in respect of the conservation of the Christian religion," might form a Catholic majority with Catherine de Medici and Mary Stuart, thus inciting the English Catholics to rise too. At last the Council advised against any intervention. Cecil reminded the Queen of her father's foolhardy expedition into Boulogne. He was not adverse "to building fires in neighbor's houses" by surreptitious aid or diplomatic manipulation, but he disliked the idea of armed intervention. In the meantime, German and Swiss Protestants flocked to the aid of Condé and his followers. They seized Lyons, Tours, Montpelier and Grenoble, yet the Guise had triumphantly entered Paris and was appealing to Spain for help. The Netherlands were in sympathetic revolt, and Cecil perceived the great threat to England. "It shall be like a great rock of stone that is falling down from the top of a mountain which—when it is coming—no force can stay," he wrote his friend Throckmorton, who was now contending with the Guisian followers in Paris. Daily messages of atrocities were brought across the Channel. Six weeks after Vassy, Throckmorton wrote that the Catholics had slain more than 200 Protestants at Sens in Normandy and that at Blois, women and children were torn to pieces. Protestant church services were interrupted and the ministers blinded as their eyes were torn from their sockets and thrown into a fire. In retaliation, the Huguenots plundered the tomb of St. Martin and burned the saint's bones. If Elizabeth did not intervene, said Throckmorton, her own turn would come. She must take the opportunity offered "for her surety and perhaps her profit . . ." he said.

And so it went, with rumor adding horror to murderous fact. Elizabeth was determined to aid Condé, and when her Council did little but debate, she—whom they had had to prod into the Scottish conflict—took the initiative and overrode her advisers. Enraged at their lack of enterprise, she told them "if they were so much afraid that the consequences of failure would fall upon them, she herself would take all the risk. . . ."[3] In July ten ships of the Royal Navy were victualed, and the southern and eastern seaboard counties ordered to levy troops. Throckmorton was recalled, and by August plans were under way to join the Huguenot forces at Newhaven.* One by one, the Council came around so that Cecil could write that "it hath been seen meet to the Queen's Majesty by the advice of all her Council, to set her foot and to preserve the miserable state of her poor neighbors in Normandy with a buckler of her defence."[4] On September 20, 1562, the Treaty of Hampton Court was signed by which Elizabeth agreed to send troops and money to France; the restoration of Calais would be her repayment. To Catherine de Medici, she proclaimed no animosity for the French Crown—only "for the Duke of Guise, our sworn enemy. . . ."

The unfortunate timing of Guise's assault on the Huguenots resulted in the cancellation of the meeting between the Queen of Scotland and the Queen of England. Ever since Mary Stuart's return, negotiations had been under way for a meeting of the cousins. Anxious to redeem herself after the blunder of the safe-conduct, Elizabeth had sent Lord Bedford to Edinburgh with a startlingly personal letter for the Scottish Queen in which she begged Mary to accept her friendship and "bury all unkindness." They would forget past disagreements and "remain good friends and sisters," said Elizabeth, since "you shall see we require nothing but justice, honour and reason." Mary replied, "We will deal frankly with you and wish that you deal friendly with us. We will have no judge at present . . . but yourself." As for the tiresome treaty, "so far as it concerns us, we will do all that within reason may be required, or

*Newhaven-The modern LeHavre.

rather enter into a new one, such as may stand without our prejudices in favour of you and the lawful issue of your body, provided that our interest to that Crown . . . may be put in good surety." At the end she wrote frankly, "We, having written thus to show the bottom of our mind nakedly, trust to be answered in like fashion."[5]

Mary's conciliatory attitude pleased Elizabeth, who liked nothing better than to give advice. Her cousin, so lately a thorny subject, was now behaving like a docile lady-in-waiting, anxious only to please. Not everyone was as satisfied. "I find a great desire in both these Queens to have an interview," wrote Cecil, "and knowing the diversity of both their intents, although I wish it, yet I know it is dangerous to be any singular doer therein." The relationship between the two sovereigns, however, had never been better, and a meeting was set for August, in the Midlands. To seal the bargain, Mary sent Elizabeth a ring "with a diamond fashioned like a heart," saying, "that above other things I desire to see my good sister and next that we may live like good sisters together. . . ."[6] Elizabeth, whose normal frugality was already attaining more than respectful regard, showed she could be extravagant when warranted. She chose "a diamond like a rock" to send to Mary. Each Queen claimed an extreme curiosity about the other, a condition viewed by both Catholics and Protestants with mutual apprehension. The Catholics, particularly, believed Mary's papal devotion might be bargained away under the pressure of Elizabeth's strong personality. The Scottish people hoped Elizabeth would recognize Mary as her heir. The peace of both realms would then be secure, and the Scottish Protestants, particularly Lethington and James Stuart, would be stronger than ever.[7]

If the English had any of the same fears, they need not have worried. The furthermost idea from Elizabeth's mind was any recognition of Mary Stuart's claim; instead, she hoped for a treaty ratification which forbade any such assumption by Mary in her lifetime. Whatever their own private motives, the visit had been much anticipated by both women. Therefore, when Sir Henry Sidney journeyed northward in July to postpone the August meeting, the reaction on Mary Stuart's part was understandable, for, said Sidney, "it drove her into such a passion as she did keep her bed all that day."[8] Elizabeth had wisely decided she could not yet meet with the woman whose uncle was now her chief enemy in France. Cecil said that "the Queen may not, by any interview, give countenance to the House of Guise. . . ." Yet, said the Secretary, Elizabeth did not blame Mary personally. "I find the Queen's Majesty so well disposed to keep amity with the Queen of Scotland as surely the default of their agreement shall not grow from the Queen here."[9] Elizabeth herself, anxious to keep Mary placated, wrote of her own disappointment. She mentioned her Councillors' first indecision. "But when I saw that my Councillors and subjects thought me too much beguiled, my intellect gone astray and mind improvident, I awoke from slumber thinking myself unworthy to govern my kingdom if I could not be Prometheus in my affairs. But, remembering how it gently touched yours, my God!—how I felt at heart...!" Elizabeth then said she hoped her aid to the Huguenots might not be misinterpreted, that "these old sparks may fan this new fire...." She said England must guard its shores from peril, its houses from spoil. "For what hope can be in strangers when cruelty so abounds in the family? I pass over in silence the murders on land, the burials in water and say nothing of men cut in pieces, but pregnant women, strangled with the sighs of infants at mothers' breasts, pierce me through. What drug of rhubarb can purge the bile which these tyrannies engender? In these broils, my own subjects have lost their goods, ships and lives, and received a new name, formerly unknown to me *c'est Huguenots.*' "[10] She mentioned Mary's relatives in France, "My letters from the King and Queen Mother show me he is only King in title. I cannot suffer such evils, as a good neighbour. You shall have no occasion to charge me with deceit having never promised what I will not perform. If I send my people to these foreign ports, I have no other end than to help the King ... my hot fever prevents me writing more."

Elizabeth's allusion to "my hot fever" foreshadowed the first serious illness since her accession. The stress which had been evident for almost a year had left the monarch a tense and nervous woman. She had sent 6,000 troops to France under the command of Ambrose Dudley, the Earl of Warwick, and then, awaiting news at Hampton Court in the early fall of 1562, had taken a bath to relieve her tension. Elizabeth had small patience with uncleanliness. She did not hesitate at any unwelcome odor to reprove an offender with a "Tush, man! Your boots stink!" and those around her spared themselves such criticism by daily application of soap and water. But complete immersion in a bath was something of a novelty and adopted for medical or pleasurable reasons by the more affluent. After her bath, the Queen had walked in the brisk air of the Palace gardens, the result of which was a chill and high temperature. Ordered to bed by her physicians, she surprisingly followed their advice. As her temperature mounted, her cousin Lord Hunsdon brought his own physician, the immigrant Dr. Burcot to attend her. Upon examination, the little German was explicit. "My liege, thou shalt have the pox," he said. Elizabeth gazed at him unbelievingly. The pox!—the scourge of the age, the curse of fine, unblemished skin! Angrily she shouted at those around her, "Have this knave out of my sight!," following her comment with a well-aimed cushion. Yet daily her condition worsened, and periods of unconsciousness followed as her temperature continued to rise. In her few moments of lucidity, Elizabeth was able, with great effort, to raise the hands of which she was so vain and peer at them in the gloomy darkness of her chamber to see if they were still free of the pestilent red blemishes. The effort cost her dearly. Weakly, she would lapse into a semi-coma in which her loud, fevered breathing could be heard by the guards on duty outside. At last the court physicians told Cecil he must prepare for the worst. Immediately, the Council was called. Elizabeth had left no heir, and she had named no successor. The private fear of every minister was now an appalling reality. They gathered at her bedside to await the worst.

When, after fours hours of unconsciousness, Elizabeth next awakened, she could hardly speak. As Mary Sidney bent to moisten her lips and brush the sweat-stained red hair from her forehead, the Queen saw her ministers gathered around her bed. It must be the worst. She felt like death, and her Councillors would not be there if they thought she was going to live. While they might have been contemplating their fate should the Queen die, their main concern was with the succession. Even in her extremity, Elizabeth realized this, and thinking she had little strength or time left, she spared them any lengthy speech. Instead, she asked that they appoint Lord Robert Dudley "Protector of my realm. . . . with £20,000 a year." Before anyone could interrupt, she added that she wished Tamworth, the servant who slept in his room, to be given £500 and that her own servants also be taken care of. Even in her weakened and feverish state, Elizabeth recognized her Councillors' doubts. "My lords, I am facing my Maker," she whispered, "I have always loved Sir Robert dearly . . . yet, it is the truth, nothing improper has passed between us. . . . " With that supreme effort, as her ministers gazed at each other, she turned her face aside.

These words, stark in their simplicity and guiltless considering the circumstances, undoubtedly state the truth of Elizabeth Tudor's relationship with Robert Dudley. She loved him dearly, "yet . . . nothing improper has passed between us."

Unwilling to accept the death of his sovereign and kinswoman, Lord Hunsdon remembered the doctor who had so enraged Elizabeth. Hurriedly, he sent for Dr. Burcot, whose professional pride had been insulted by the royal reaction. He refused point-blank to leave his house, saying that "the Queen had called him a knave. If she were going to die, she were going to die," he muttered, lapsing into his native

German. A knife pressed into his side by one of Hunsdon's messengers immediately changed his mind. In a short time, the group arrived in the sick chamber. One glance, and the doctor's professionalism reasserted itself. "It is almost too late, my liege," he whispered to the feverish woman whose breathing had so depleted her strength. Quickly he ordered the fire to be built up and someone to bring a long length of red flannel. When it arrived, the thin, hot form of the Queen was wrapped like a mummy, and as she asked for water, a bottle was held to her lips. Elizabeth drank eagerly, saying that "it were very comfortable." The doctor insisted that one hand be left outside the tight wrappings of red cloth. There, in the heat of the fire's glow, one by one, small red spots began to cover the hand. Elizabeth saw them. "What is this, good doctor?" she cried. With no effort to soften the blow, the doctor answered soberly, "It is the pox. . . ." And, as Elizabeth began to cry and writhe within the tight wrappings and her voice rose to a lament, the physician's patience disappeared. "God's pestilence!" he cried, "is it better to have the pox in the hands and in the face—or in the heart and kill the whole body?"

Dr. Burcot's quick treatment saved Elizabeth's life. Eruptions appeared on her features, her arms and hands, but mercifully, they left no deeply pitted scars. Only one woman, Robert Dudley's sister, Lady Mary Sidney, suffered disfigurement. Sir Henry Sidney returned from Scotland to find his wife ill. "I left her a full fair lady—in mine eyes, at least, the fairest," he said sadly, "and when I returned I found her as foul a lady as the smallpox could make her. . . ." Lady Mary's disfigurement was so complete that she asked permission to leave the court for Penshurst, the family home in Kent. Mary was dear to Elizabeth, both as the sister of her lover and the wife of a trusted friend. But, all too well, she understood the woman's sensitivity and granted her leave. Mary Sidney spent the remainder of her life in the darkened chambers of her home, refusing to visit the court where she had been one of its most admired and loved members.

It was six weeks before Elizabeth, shaken and weak, emerged from her apartments. Hoping to make restitution to the good German doctor who had saved her life, she awarded him lands and a pair of her grandfather's golden spurs. After receiving the congratulations of her court, she left for Windsor Castle so Hampton Court might be cleansed of its impurities. At Windsor, she was reconciled with Robert Dudley. They met in Windsor Park, where Lord Robert was engaged in an archery match. There the Queen, with her cousin Kate Carey and several others, all dressed as simple maids, stole upon them as the courtiers' attention was engaged at the butts. Dropping behind her companions, the Queen was the last to be seen by the gentlemen, and amid the greetings of welcome, Elizabeth was heard to whisper to Robert "that she had passed the pikes for his sake . . . therefore he was beholden to her. . . ." Several days later Robert Dudley was sworn as a member of the Privy Council, but to balance his influence, Cecil insisted—and held out—for the appointment also of Elizabeth's kinsman the Duke of Norfolk.

In her campaign to aid the Huguenots, Elizabeth had concentrated her strength on the coastal towns, yet had succeeded only in clearing French commerce from the Channel. From the beginning, things had gone wrong on land. In December, the Battle of Dreux ended with 6,000 dead and the Prince de Condé, the Huguenot leader, taken prisoner. "Except Almighty God show His arm and power, this web is undone and new to begin," wrote Cecil to Sir Thomas Smith with the English forces in France. One of Mary Stuart's Guise uncles, the Duke d'Aumale, was wounded; another died in the cold of battle. Quickly Angers, Tours and Bourges fell. Indiscriminate massacre added to the horror as inhabitants were hacked to pieces, young girls and women repeatedly raped before being hung out of windows as targets for the soldiers below. Others wandered the streets, naked except for leaves torn from the Geneva Bible as their only covering.

Catholic forces sought to capture the English-held Newhaven. Even Robert Dudley's nerve failed him when the Council—terrified to a man to inform the Queen of her potential loss—chose him to impart the news. The best he could do was merely hint at the possibility. Undaunted, Elizabeth took pen in hand and inscribed a warmly encouraging note to Dudley's brother the Earl of Warwick in command in France, hoping her words might inspire a miracle. The note is illustrative of Elizabeth at her best:

MY DEAR WARWICK,

If your honour and my desire could accord with the loss of the needfullest finger I keep, God so help me in my utmost need, as I would gladly lose that one joint for your safe abode with me. But, since I cannot that I would, I will do that I may, and will drink in an ashen cup that you and yours should not be succoured both by sea and land, and that with all speed possible.

And let this, my scribbling hand witness it to them all.

Yours, as my own,

E.R.

Two months later, on February 18, 1563, the Duke of Guise was shot from behind a hedge in Orléans by a nineteen-year-old assassin and died six days later. With the Catholic leader dead and the Protestant leader, Condé, imprisoned, the French Queen Mother gathered the remaining members of the warring factions, and together at Amboise, they came to terms. They effected their settlement without any consultation of the English Queen. Warwick still held Newhaven by which Elizabeth hoped to effect the restoration of Calais as payment for her aid. When Catherine de Medici reminded Elizabeth that her previously announced intention had been only to help safeguard the French Crown and that such "protection" was no longer needed, the English Queen's answer was to send Lord Admiral Clinton and ships of the English Navy to aid Warwick. The English ranks, however, were decimated by the plague. The original garrison "died like flies," and reinforcements suffered similarly. By July Warwick had received a leg wound which had ulcerated, but he refused to leave his men, saying sadly "that the plague of deadly infection had done more for them than that which all the forces of France could never have done."[12] Clinton's ships arrived in time to help the small group of survivors surrender Newhaven. Led by Warwick, his wounded leg wrapped in a "large red taffety bow," they returned to London, bringing with them the plague germ, which claimed 20,000 lives the first summer and was regarded by many as a visitation from God for England's unwise intervention in France. Peace was declared the following month; it brought nothing to England. "God help England and send it a King" wrote one outraged citizen, "for in time of women it has got but a little!"[13] Though profiting nothing but a deadly infectious scourge, Elizabeth had learned a formidable lesson. Intervention on foreign soil was a dangerous and risky business. It would be much easier in the future—and more in keeping with her own natural instincts—to sponsor and encourage antagonism between enemies than to undertake the support of one at peril to herself and her country.

Elizabeth's narrow escape from death emphasized all the more England's acute need for an heir. Before her illness, her ministers had hoped for a marriage which would give the Queen a child. Now they were sufficiently perturbed to consider those claimants to the succession as well. Even as the writs for Elizabeth's second Parliament went out, members of her Council met at the Earl of Arundel's house in the Strand and there, in a session lasting until 2 A.M., discussed the succession. Most of those present favored the Suffolk line in the person of Lady Katherine Grey, still imprisoned in the Tower. When she heard the story, Elizabeth "wept with rage." She summoned Arundel, who did not deny his action or its import; instead, he strongly taxed the Queen with her negligence in settling so important a matter.

She was prepared, therefore, to face the challenge of the Parliament which met in January, 1563. The tone was set by a service preceding its opening. Dr. Alexander Nowell, the Dean of St. Paul's, then solemnly related that "all the Queen's most notable ancestors commonly had issue to succeed them, but her Majesty yet none . . ." and, turning to address Elizabeth directly, asked, "if your parents had been of your mind, where had you been then?" The Queen's face did not change expression. She bore out William Cecil's statement made before the service: "I think somewhat will be tempted to ascertain the realm of a successor . . . but I fear the unwillingness of her Majesty to have such a person known will stay the matter."[14] The Secretary knew his sovereign better than most.

When petitions from the Parliament echoed the Dean's sentiments, Elizabeth gave her answer. In a letter to Thomas Williams, the Speaker, she thanked him for the Commons' advice. Referring to her illness, she said, "I know as well as I did before that I am mortal. I know also that I must seek to discharge myself of that great burden that God hath laid upon me. For of them to whom much is committed, much is required." At the end, she said, "I am determined in this so great and weighty a matter to defer mine answer till some other time, because I will not in so deep a matter wade with so shallow a wit. . . ." In the meantime, should her Saviour take her, she could "assure you all that, though after my death you may have many stepdames, yet shall you never have a more natural mother than I mean to be unto you all."[15]

When the deputation from the Lords arrived a few days later with a similar request, noting that "factious, seditious and intestine war" would follow if the Queen did not have a designated successor or heir, Elizabeth showed her impatience. She who had faced death was quite weary of having its possibility pointed out to her, she said tartly. Pointing to her face, she cried "that the marks they saw on her face were not wrinkles, but pits of smallpox and that although she might be old, God could send her children as He did to St. Elizabeth!" She would not, she reiterated, appoint a successor. "If I do, it will cost much blood to England," she said soberly. She had had some experience of being the heir, she reminded the Lords sharply. She remembered those "who had run after her when she was Princess." She would designate no successor who would become the focal point of intrigues against the Crown. It would mean her own death and the ruin of all she had accomplished which she firmly believed was for England's good. When Sir Nicholas Bacon sought to touch the woman's heart, even if it left the sovereign unmoved, by saying, "If your Highness could conceive or imagine the comfort, surety and delight that should happen to yourself by beholding an imp of your own . . ." the Queen replied that marriage was a personal matter and a personal choice. Regarding the succession, she said, "I have good record in this place that other means than ye mention have been thought of, perchance for your good as much and for my surety no less . . ." although she did not care to enlighten her Lords on just what the means were.

A distinct advantage had come to them while Parliament was in session. In February, as Elizabeth was hearing her ministers' petitions, the imprisoned Lady Katherine Grey had given birth to another son—the result of a meeting with her husband in the Tower, arranged by a sympathetic Lieutenant Edward Warner. Alarmed, the Queen berated the Lieutenant and resisted all attempts of Cecil and others to soften her attitude toward the girl. As the plague had begun its deadly work, she ordered Katherine Grey out of London to the custody of her uncle Sir John Grey at Prygo. Her husband, the Earl of Hertford, appeared before the Star Chamber and was fined £15,000 "for seducing a virgin of the blood royal." Both children were declared bastard, and any further meetings between husband and wife sternly prohibited. Despite the pitiful letters Katherine wrote and the many requests for leniency the Queen received—even from Cecil—she remained unmoved. When the royal dictum was flouted, Elizabeth could be pitiless.

During midsummer, William Maitland, the Laird of Lethington, was expected at the English court to offer Mary Stuart's services as a mediator at the cessation of French hostilities. He also would bring pressure to have Mary's claim to the English throne recognized. If she, Elizabeth, were to circumvent this necessity, she must have "another string to her bow." As she prepared to receive Maitland, the Queen at last felt sure of her answer—an answer which would give England an English heir, yet lay no claim to the Crown while she herself was still alive.

The two years Mary Stuart had spent in Scotland seemed endlessly long to the twenty-one-year-old woman who was making the best of what she regarded—with some justification—as a bad bargain. From being Queen "of the mightiest King in Christendom" she was now husbandless, sovereign of a sorry land of bitter cold, unpredictable storms and fogs which only made her long more intensely for the green, sunny provinces of France. Remembering the warmth, spaciousness and light of the chateau rooms of her youth, she had sought to make the austere royal apartments in Holyrood reminiscent of the polished,

cultured court of that happier time. Here she installed the finest
Gobelins, Turkey carpets, great gilded beds, portraits and all her finely
bound books. Here, to the scandalized observation of the Protestant
preachers who regarded any levity as consistent with the worst sins and
vices, she spent much time at the masques and games she so much
enjoyed. Here her French minstrels played the madrigals and roun-
delays of the French court, and here French poetry and song echoed
through the chambers long after dusk. Outside, a selected group of
Scottish nobles listened to music of their own—drums, fiddles and the
incessant caterwauling of the bagpipes; others joined in hymns and
discordant folk songs. There were occasions when the two factions
came together, such as at the wedding of her half brother, Lord James
Stuart. Then, bonfires were lit in the streets, and at Holyrood there was
music and dancing, running at the tilt and casting of fireballs. The
celebration continued for several days, to the disgust of many of the
Protestants to whom "the greatness of the banquet and the vanity used
thereat offended many godly."

Life in Scotland had considerably matured the Scottish Queen.
After hearing of her uncles' deaths in France, a sorrowing Mary told
Randolph, the English ambassador, "that she perceived now the world
was not that which men would make it, nor they the happiest that lived
the longest in it."[16] She had promised religious toleration to Scotland,
and she meant to keep her word. It was soon apparent, however, that
many of her subjects did not appreciate her intent or reciprocate her
feelings. During her state entry into Edinburgh, she was affronted by
the mock burning of a priest until a disgusted nobleman ordered the
offensive sight removed from her eyes. Wherever she traveled, during
her first months in her native land, insulting pageants, invective and
harassment greeted her, drowning out the genuine acclamation of
others pleased at the sight of their youthful Queen. Mass was
celebrated in her Chapel, but not without risk, for members of the
Congregation had dared invade her devotions with drawn swords,
crying that "the idolator priest shall die!" before the frightened prelate
was hurried to safety. Boys carrying Mass candles were often badly
beaten, and always the muttering of the Protestants was whetted by
the fanatical haranguing of the overzealous John Knox.

A swarthy, stocky Scotsman, with penetrating black eyes above an
unkempt beard, John Knox typified all the best and worst of the
Reformation preacher. A bigoted and demagogic reformer with all the
zeal of an Old Testament character, but lacking compassion, tolerance
or understanding, John Knox had fathered the reformation of the
Scottish Kirk, an achievement he expected to maintain by an un-

swerving domination of its members and an unceasing display of arrogant authority, unleavened by either humor or humanity. Knox considered himself a prophet and a supreme saver of souls. Randolph, the English ambassador, wrote of Knox with some evident awe: "I assure you the voice of one man is able in one hour to put more life in us than 500 trumpets continually blustering in our ears."[17]

John Knox had attended the University of Glasgow, where he studied scholastic philosophy and theology. Ordained a priest in 1530, he became a philosophy teacher at St. Andrews. During the next ten years, his religious convictions had been severely shaken by the "new learning," and by 1542 he was an avid reformer; later he was declared a heretic. He had been condemned to eighteen months of hard labor in the galleys of a French ship as a prisoner of state. The iron of his cleaving ring was not unlike the iron in his narrow prejudiced intellect, and this, combined with a formidable command of rhetoric and an absolutely fearless genius in the pursuit of his religious ideal, had made him one of the most turbulent presences in Scotland. He had been the guiding force behind the Protestant movement which had resulted in desolated churches and monasteries, the humiliation and physical assault of priests and other ecclesiastics which had preceded the establishment of Scottish Protestantism.

Mary had not been in Scotland long before Knox made his presence known. Naïvely, she had anticipated that preachers, along with other of her subjects, would honor and reciprocate her promise of religious freedom. However, Knox's opinion that "one Mass is more fearful to me than if 10,000 armed enemies were to land and suppress the whole religion" set the tone for Mary's religious reception. Though the Scottish Parliament theoretically supported her, the rank and file, incited by Knox's thundering, did not. Daily, small incidents of calculated rudeness pricked the conscience and temper of the young Queen, who, from childhood, had experienced only compliance and subservience. Such an upbringing had resulted in a woman as relatively free from bias as was possible in her era, with a refreshing lack of arrogance and a willingness to compromise—up to a point. Counterbalancing this was Mary Stuart's absolute conviction in the supremacy of her royalty, in the dignity and queenliness of her position, although, unlike Elizabeth, she never realized it carried a corresponding responsibility. Mary could never understand or accept the limits on her sovereignty imposed by popular feeling or traditional and conceptual national laws. Yet her demeanor impressed many. Maitland wrote Cecil, "The Queen, my mistress, behaves herself so gently in every behalf as reasonably we can require; if anything be amiss, the fault is rather in ourselves. You know the vehemency of Mr. Knox's spirit, which cannot be bridled, and yet doth sometimes utter such sentences as cannot easily be digested by a weak stomach. I wish he should deal with her more gently. . . ."[18] But guilelessness—or tenderness—was not Knox's gift. Ultimately, his continued assaults on the royal religion were something Mary could no longer tolerate. She asked that the preacher be summoned; Knox was eager to confront his royal mistress. It was a meeting neither was ever to forget.

Mary was prepared to be forbearing, never doubting that her queenliness and her dignity would impress the stoic old Calvinist. When the gloomy-faced man was ushered into her presence, the silence in the chamber was broken by the clear young voice of the Queen, who recounted Knox's offenses against the Crown: his book against the "monstrous regiment" of females who occupied thrones, his incitement of the Scottish people against the royal authority and his outrageous disrespect to her own religion. She requested him "to use more meekness in his sermons," asking if he as a subject "should resist his Prince?" With great self-righteousness Knox lapsed into a parable wherein a father, with murderous intent, might slay his family. Only then must the family defend themselves. "Even so is it with Princes who would murder the children of God that are subject unto them. . . !" he thundered.

His reply set the tone for the remainder of the meeting, which soon degenerated into a purely religious disputation in which there could never be agreement. Knox lost his temper and harangued against Rome and the Mass and lectured Mary that as a sovereign "she must protect and foster the pure Church of God. . . ." The Queen was now angry; angry at the presumption of the shabby and inflexible man in front of her and annoyed at herself for allowing her own regal poise to be ruffled. "But you are not the Church that I will nourish," she cried passionately as tears welled in her eyes. "I will defend the Church of Rome, which I think the true one . . ." she trailed off ineffectually, as Knox, seizing the moment and gesturing at her, cried, "Your will, Madam, is not reason; neither does your thought make the Roman harlot the true immaculate spouse of Jesus Christ! Wonder not, Madam, that I call Rome a harlot—for that Church is polluted with all kinds of spiritual fornication in doctrine and manners!" There were some witnessing the historic meeting who sympathized with Mary and denounced Knox, "who knocked so hastily upon her heart that he made her weep," Randolph, the English ambassador, wrote to Cecil. As her temper mounted, Mary, enraged and humiliated, had waved the minister from her presence, hardly justifying his comment that "in communication with her I find such craft as I have not found in such an age. . . ."[19]

Not only were Mary Stuart's days marred by Knox's constant needlepricks against her authority, the endangering of her religious faith, but also by the petty quarrels—important only to themselves—of her self-seeking nobles, with whom she had nothing in common and found lacking as any source of pride or comfort. Many years before, her own father, James V, had written of his courtiers that "there is not a nobleman in my realm as has not been seduced from his ally by promises and bribes. Even my person is not safe; there is no guarantee that my wishes will be performed or if the existing laws will be obeyed."[20] Later a French ambassador had said, "Money and personal advantage are the only sirens to whose voices the Scottish Lords will lend an ear. To try and bring them to a sense of their devotion towards their Prince, to talk to them of honour, justice, virtue, decent and reliable negotiations, merely incites them to laughter."[21] The rude, uncouth and invariably unwashed group—the Maitlands, the Craw- fords, the Lennoxes, the Lindsays, the Argylls—were constantly quarreling among themselves. Their fondness for murderous cliques and factions had spelled disaster for any sort of national unity. They were accountable only unto themselves and their families; they were naturally suspicious of any sovereign, and this attitude doomed any display of love, affection or support for Mary such as Elizabeth received from her people.

If Mary Stuart was forever to be a stranger in the dark forbidding woodlands of her northern realm, the fault was as much that of her nobles as herself. She quickly understood their lack of trust and the challenge to her own authority; her one strong support was her half brother, Lord James Stuart. It was also true that while Mary always attempted to play the gracious sovereign, she had little real interest in her people's customs, their history—or their future. She did not under- stand her subjects, and she did not regret it. She did not expect to remain only their Queen for the rest of her life. Scotland was to be a stepping-stone to a Crown as great as the one she had been forced to relinquish. The depth of Elizabeth's devotion to the welfare of her people and to England would have puzzled Mary Stuart and mystified her Scottish people. This was forever to be one of the many differences between the two Queens, and it was a difference which made any real understanding impossible. Elizabeth might be forced to marry in due time, but in the meantime, love, husband and children were well lost for the privilege of ruling over her island kingdom. Mary Stuart, on the other hand, who had been genuinely fond of and happy with her first husband, candidly admitted to Randolph, "Not to marry—you know it cannot be for me. . . ."

From the moment of her return, her marriage had been debated as heatedly as Elizabeth's. The suitors were the same; only the Queens were different. Mary was anxious to make the marriage which would solve her predicament as unhappy Queen of a miserable nation with a group of brawling clansmen arrogant in their ill-smelling authority, and she consoled herself with thoughts of the future. She shed "many a salty tear," wrote Randolph, at the death of her uncles. Yet around her, many openly laughed and showed their pleasure at the news. Throughout the following months, relations between Knox and the Queen worsened. "He hath no hope that she will ever come to God or do good in the commonwealth," wrote Randolph to Cecil. Knox feared that "new strangers might be brought into this realm . . ."; he feared that Mary might make a Catholic marriage wherein "a number shall come to possess this realm again as before. . . ." Knox still "inveighed sore against the Queen's dancing and little exercise of herself in virtue or godliness," which finally brought the exasperated woman to summon him again, at which time she raged at him, "I have borne with you in all your rigorous manner of speaking both against myself and my uncles; yea, I have sought your favours by all possible means. I offered unto you presence and audience whensoever it pleased you to admonish me and yet I cannot be quit of you. I vow to God, I shall be once revenged!" At which point, Knox later wrote proudly, his Queen again lapsed into tears "and 'owling" before departing.[22] However, the implacable preacher's attitude had an effect. Mostly through fear, said Randolph, Mary had "laid aside much of our dancing." On Christmas Day, 1563, none of the court musicians would sing either at Mass or Evensong; they had been so terrorized that Mary "knoweth not where to turn." It was in this frame of mind that she dispatched William Maitland to England ostentatiously to offer her services as mediator at the cessation of French hostilities. Maitland was also to speak of her marriage, the marriage which would take her forever from the ungracious land she would count well lost. With her marriage would go the Catholic domination of Scotland. Everyone—including Maitland and Elizabeth—recognized the potent threat it constituted to the Protestant Queen south of the Tweed.

This was the situation confronting Elizabeth as Parliament closed its stormy session on Easter Eve, April 10, 1563. The birth of Katherine Grey's second son had added fuel to the argument of the succession, and the possibility of Mary Stuart's marriage and a subsequent Catholic heir was the torch which might incite conflagration. The issue plagued Elizabeth constantly. In her handling of it may be seen the genius which often derived from blind instinct, although that instinct was often assisted by chance. But for the most part, it was the genius of a Queen who loved her country, understood its customs and traditions and cherished her countrymen. She took good care of her people with the not surprising result that they, too, loved her personally and regarded the Crown respectfully.

The arrival of William Maitland brought to the forefront not only the succession question, but also the question of a husband for the Queen of Scots. As for the first, Elizabeth was firm. Maitland had an enlightening interview with the English Queen in which she expressed herself fully and clearly on the dangers facing any monarch who recognized a successor in her lifetime. She did not question Mary Stuart's right, she said, and she would prefer to have her sister of Scotland the heir. "But, " she told the Scotsman frankly, "so long as I live, I shall be Queen of England. When I am dead, they shall succeed me that have the most right."[23] She told Maitland that "if I mean to do anything to hurt her rights, the Scots need only ask her to reform it." But they must not ask her to designate Mary Stuart her heir; that "would require me in my own life to set my winding sheet before my eyes." She recounted the hazards of her position during her own sister's rule. As heir she had been hopelessly exploited by those who disliked Mary Tudor's government. Had she been truly interested in plotting against her sister, said Elizabeth, "I know what enterprises would have been attempted to bring it to pass."[24] She spoke of her people's idiosyncrasy, not with anger but with understanding, *"Plures adorant solem orientalem quam occidentalem,"* she said, "for the most part they worship the rising rather than the setting sun."

Elizabeth was more interested in Mary's marriage than in the succession. If Mary wanted action, Elizabeth wanted delay. She also recognized that she held the trump card for, if Mary wanted her endorsement as heiress presumptive, her marriage must carry the blessing of the English Queen. Elizabeth knew the weakling Archduke Charles "was too nearly a Lutheran" for any serious consideration.[25] She knew there was little eagerness in France for Mary's return. Mary had once labeled Catherine de Medici *la grossa Caterina*, referring to her as "the daughter of a Florentine pawnbroker," and the Queen Mother's aversion to having the Queen of Scots marry another of her sons was well known. Elizabeth advised Maitland that she would look with pleasure on Mary's marriage to a member of the Scottish or

English aristocracy, wherein the balance of power would be maintained. Mary, mindful of her need to keep the English Queen's friendship, later replied to Maitland's suggestion that she was desirous of following her dear cousin's advice and, with just the right touch of levity, requested Elizabeth to tell her explicitly which suitors she had in mind? "I shall be guided by your wishes and shall be careful not to marry any man of so high a rank that my position, my well-beloved sister, will overshadow yours," she wrote soothingly.[26]

When Maitland visited the Spanish ambassador, he told a different story. De Quadra fully expected Maitland to propose King Philip's son, Don Carlos, as a husband for Mary Stuart. Despite the fact that Don Carlos was an epileptic whose idiocy bordered on criminal lunacy, it would be the proudest match she could make. But he did not hesitate to tell Maitland that, in his opinion, "there was no other remedy for the Queen of Scotland but to marry a husband from this Queen's [Elizabeth's] hand, *in which case she would be declared her successor."* Maitland pointed out "that there were two difficulties in this course —namely that the Queen his mistress would never marry a Protestant, even if he were lord of half the world, as he well knew, for he had resorted even to the use of threats to get her to change her resolve in this respect but without success." The second difficulty was that Mary "says she will not take a husband, Catholic or Protestant, from the hands of the Queen of England, even if by this act alone she could be declared her successor. . . ." Mary also lamented that no one "had yet dared to suggest to her a husband less great and powerful than the one she has lost." De Quadra spoke of Elizabeth's fear that Mary would wed Don Carlos. "They expect your Majesty will play them a fine trick when they least expect it," he wrote King Philip. Such a union would only incite the English Catholics in Mary's favor. Maitland had spoken scornfully of England's brand of Protestantism as compared with Scotland. He told de Quadra, "Elizabeth cared little for one as for the other." He said their religion in Scotland was very different from the English, "as here they have removed the sacrament and names from the Anglican Church without reforming the abuses and irregularities. . . ."[27]

Ten days after de Quadra's letter, Maitland again met with Elizabeth. She had been fully apprised by Cecil's spies of his visits to the Spanish ambassador's Durham House residence and could guess the reason. He was now going to France, where he might confront Catherine de Medici with the threat of Mary's Spanish marriage, whereby Catherine might prove more agreeable about her son. His last meeting with the English Queen proved his most successful—and most surprising. Elizabeth was in great good humor, as if she had finally arrived at a happy conclusion to a vexing problem. She received Maitland with much ceremony and, after some parrying about his mission to France, informed the Scotsman she had a candidate for Mary's hand and said "that if his mistress would take her advice and wished to marry safely and happily, she would give her a husband who would ensure both . . . one who had implanted so many graces that if she [Elizabeth] wished to marry him she would prefer him to all the princes of the world." Taking his cue, Maitland responded lightly, inquiring the name of this man of all virtues. Settling back in her chair, Elizabeth unleashed her surprise. The man's name was Robert Dudley.

If it had been her intention to shock, she succeeded beyond her own expectations. Maitland was speechless until his diplomatic training won out, and recovering his poise, he said in a light tone matching the Queen's that "this was a great proof of the love she bore to his Queen, as she was willing to give her a thing so dearly prized by herself." But, he continued, "he thought the Queen, his mistress, even if she loved Lord Robert so dearly as she [Elizabeth] did, would not marry him and so deprive her of all the joy and solace she received from his companionship. . . ." Elizabeth, relishing the confused Maitland's performance, said, "I wish to God the Earl of Warwick, his brother, had the grace and good looks of Lord Robert, in which case we could each have one. . . !" Amid general laughter, Elizabeth hurried to say that Warwick was not ugly or ungraceful, "but his manner was rather rough and he was not so gentle as Lord Robert." But he was "brave, liberal, magnanimous, truly he was worthy of being the husband of any great princess."[28]

Now more in control—and anxious to bring the baffling session to a close—Maitland jokingly said that Mary Stuart was still young and Elizabeth might yet marry Lord Robert herself and have children by him. "Then, when it should please God to call her to Himself, she could leave the Queen of Scots heiress to both her kingdom and her husband!" Only in this way, Maitland finished triumphantly, "would it be impossible for Lord Robert to fail to have children by one or the other of them, who would in time become Kings of these two countries. . . ." He added some humorous pleasantry, and then, satisfied he had acquitted himself well in an embarrassing situation, gratefully made a quick escape.

Three days later Maitland left for France. Before he departed, he took formal leave of the Queen, and this time, levity aside, Elizabeth "commanded him to tell his mistress that she had heard of negotiations having been commenced for her marriage with both Don Carlos and the Archduke Charles." She told Maitland that if Mary "married either one of them . . . she could not avoid being her enemy and she consequently charged her to consider well what steps she took in such a matter." On the other hand, said Elizabeth, "if she married a person to her satisfaction, she would not fail to be a good friend and a sister to her and make her her heir . . . instead of being, as she otherwise would be, her mortal enemy. . . ."[29] It was the message Maitland ultimately took to Scotland; it was unlike anything he had hoped to bring back. Underlying all his concern was whether or not the Queen of England was sincere.

Chapter Eleven

If Elizabeth had any ulterior motive in suggesting the man she could not marry herself as a husband for the Queen of Scots, it was not evident in public. She was enthusiastic and firm; she had offered Mary the choicest gentleman she knew, one acceptable to herself. By implication—although as yet unofficial—with Dudley would be granted what Mary desired most: her ultimate recognition as heiress to the Crown of England.

The Queen's public attitude and her private disposition were, however, two very diverse aspects which often puzzled her Councillors, mystified her courtiers and perplexed her subjects. Never was Elizabeth's talent for dissimulation more evident than in her handling of Mary Stuart's marriage. Following her suggestion to Maitland, she seemed content to let the matter alone and await results. She would rely, as she was often to rely in the future, on a blind instinct which came from some generous well of feminine intuition unsoiled by more adult perceptive reasoning. She had shocked not only the Scottish Maitland with her suggested candidate, but own ministers as well. Yet she had shocked no one more than Robert Dudley himself.

Lord Robert had considerably less enthusiasm for the scheme than the Queen. He was now a member of the Privy Council, where, if he was not always supported, his words were listened to respectfully. The handsome young nobleman—both he and Elizabeth were just thirty years old—of twice-attainted blood, had grown in stature and respectability at court. He very much desired to marry a Queen, but not the Queen of Scotland. Despite the reports of the resident English ambassador of Mary's highly agreeable physical gifts—obviously designed to stimulate Robert's sexual curiosity—he was dismayed by Elizabeth's action. He had no wish to go into exile even as King Consort of a land he personally thought ungovernable, no matter how it improved his fortune or prestige. He privately doubted his head would long remain on his shoulders once the profane northern clansmen were browbeaten into momentarily accepting an English Master of the Horse as their monarch. He had had enough experience with the Scots to know his chances of a long life would be slim.

There were arguments in Elizabeth's private chambers with the Queen, appealing, explaining, pointing out the merits of her proposal, telling him that he was the *one* man—"her Eyes"—that she could trust. She appealed to his chivalry, common sense, pride and then, at his continued lack of enthusiasm, lost her temper and pointed out disagreeable alternatives to his refusal. She emphasized he was "her creature"; without her he was nothing! *She* would never marry a subject—she hammered the point home—she might yet marry out of the realm, she might be forced to. But she would never marry a subject! And then, becoming a woman in love, she appealed to Robert's manhood to assist her to help protect her country and Crown. She agreed their own love was perfect, but they could never be husband and wife. Losing him would be intolerable, but at least the loss would ensure a safer England; *she* was ready for the sacrifice. Why then should he dislike rendering her and his country this great service?

Her whole performance left Robert in a great dilemma. He had no desire to be a royal sacrifice, and he could have argued—with much merit—that the love between him and Elizabeth was far from perfect. She might be perpetually susceptible, but she was also perpetually evasive. He had been kept dancing attendance for almost five years. Yet he had never actually possessed her, and he accepted now, as it would have been impossible to accept only a year or so ago, that Elizabeth was not going to be the pliable sexual partner he desired. Other women were not so unwilling, and each new experience only emphasized the iron control with which Elizabeth regulated the limit of their relationship. Its effect on the virile Robert had at times been exhausting. Not only did the constant deprivation of a natural fulfillment leave him edgy, irritable and indignant, but there was also Elizabeth's attitude. In all these encounters, she retained her heart —and her power. He had nothing except what came from her; he had no power except what she chose to extend him. And his heart—and its desires—must be constantly at her command so that she controlled his emotional being, as well as his material position. It would have galled any masculine ego less strong and healthy than Robert Dudley's.

But as long as he remained at her side, there was hope. If he remained in England, perhaps circumstances—and the royal heart and will—might change. During the next few weeks, as they thrashed the question further, however, Elizabeth remained inflexible, and ultimately, as she probably never doubted, the sovereign's will transcended the woman's pleading. It was not a happy occasion, with Robert sober and depressed; their parting left heartache. But she had won her point. If Mary would have him, he would go. To sweeten his enthusiasm, she gave him Kenilworth Castle in Warwick—a poignant reminder of his father, for Kenilworth had once belonged to John Dudley, the executed Duke of Northumberland. She would do even better than that, she told Dudley. Mary of Scotland must have a more suitable husband than a mere nobleman. She would make him Earl of Leicester, that long-awaited prize she had previously denied. And so that he might play the part of an absent suitor more appropriately, she ordered him to send four handsome geldings from the royal stables to the Scottish Queen. But there Robert's courtesy ended; he did not involve himself further, leading the English ambassador, Randolph, to write Cecil complaining and, for his pains, receive Mr. Secretary's opinion that "of my knowledge of these fickle matters, I can affirm nothing that I can assure will continue. . . ."

Once Maitland returned to Scotland, there was a silence of many months. He chose to regard Elizabeth's suggestion as something of a royal joke, a momentary aberration or indulgence on the Queen's part. Eventually, Elizabeth instructed Randolph to commence negotiations. Maitland, therefore, privately told Mary who Elizabeth's choice was. When she met with Randolph, the Scottish Queen admirably held her temper. Before Dudley's name was revealed, Mary had thought the suitor might be either the Duke of Norfolk or Lord Darnley. Both were Catholic, of noble birth, in every respect proper candidates for her hand. When Randolph eventually disclosed Dudley as Elizabeth's choice, Mary answered angrily. "Is it conformable to her promise to use me as a sister or daughter—to marry me to a subject?" With a rising voice she said, "What if the Queen my sister should herself marry and have children? What have I then gotten?"[1]

When Maitland pointed out that an acceptance of Dudley would bring an official recognition as Elizabeth's heir, Mary, still affronted, said more graciously that "for the person himself she could have no misliking of him of whom the report was so good and her good sister so recommended."[2] To her intimates, however, she continued to express her indignation and asked "who would hardly agree that I should abase my state so far as that!" With a frankness her sister Queen might have admired, she wasted few words on Randolph, saying coolly, "Now tell me, good Mr. Randolph, doth your mistress in good earnest wish me to marry Lord Robert?" The subject was the butt of much merriment at dinner, to Randolph's great discomfort, when he was asked by various Scotsmen why "instead of troubling our Queen," Elizabeth did not marry Dudley herself? The ambassador had little hope of Mary's consent; he said her "noble stomach can never imbase itself so low as to marry in place inferior to herself." He continued to urge her to accept Dudley, even pointing up the plight of "her four Marys," for, as he said, "her four companions have vowed never to marry until she does."

After weeks of debate at the Scottish court, Maitland and Lord James Stuart triumphantly told Randolph that should the acceptance of Dudley carry official recognition of Mary's succession, they would recommend the suit to her. Once they had expressed agreement, there was, oddly, little action from the English court, only the usual letters and diplomatic instructions. "Gentle letters, good words and pleasant messages be good means to begin friendship among princes, but I take them to be slender bands to hold it long fast!" Maitland chided Cecil, as he urged a definite action before Mary or her advisers changed their minds.

Several weeks later Mary went on progress to the Western Highlands. While there she received word from de Quadra, in England that Philip—notoriously slow and indecisive as ever—had regarded her proposed marriage to his son, Don Carlos, more seriously. The Queen's spirits soared. Marriage to another "proud Prince"—albeit a lunatic—would be an eloquent answer to the Queen of England and her cast-off lover! Should Philip prove uncooperative, she might even use the remote possibility of a Spanish match for engendering enthusiasm in France or Austria! Mary's elation remained. Again the proud Guise and Stuart blood asserted itself; she would marry no one "in a lower station." Instead, she would ally herself with strength and power wherein she would be strong enough "to assert by force her right to the Crown of England," and once that was done, she would restore her faith to that heretic country. That would be her answer to the archheretic, Elizabeth.

By midsummer the plague was at its height in London, and one of its first victims was the Spanish ambassador. De Quadra had longed to return home. "Public affairs here and my own private troubles and necessities force me to beg your Majesty to be pleased to allow me to leave this island . . ." he wrote pleadingly to King Philip. The crafty old Spaniard had had an unhappy final year in England. His household had been raided by authorities for allowing other than his own servants to hear the Mass. His correspondence was detained, opened and read—and provided the Queen and her Council with some illuminating ambassadorial opinion of the royal person and policies. Sick and chronically short of funds, de Quadra pronounced himself "totally ruined; I am suffering much in health and all else." Toward the end he sat in the little turret room of Durham House, the brooding old mansion which had so long been associated with Spain. Sixty years previously, from that very room overlooking the gray Thames, a frightened Spanish princess, Catherine of Aragon, had sat writing her parents, Isabella and Ferdinand of Spain, begging funds to keep her small group of Spanish servants together in the face of Henry VII's financial negligence. De Quadra could look back over his many years in England and wonder just what he had accomplished. He was not satisfied and perhaps at the end admitted to himself—undoubtedly crossing himself and begging his Saviour's pardon—that Philip's chronic caution and timidity had greatly hampered his own effort and ability. The power of an ambassador was limited by a monarch's decisiveness. In the end it mattered little. "I can do no more," he wrote and in mid-July surrendered to the plague.*

De Quadra's successor, Don Diego Guzmán de Silva, the Bishop of Toledo, arrived in England several months later. A cultured sophisticate, de Silva was of a much broader stamp then the provincial de Quadra. His natural elegance delighted Elizabeth, who strongly desired to better her relations with Spain. De Silva was received with much cordiality and ceremony at Richmond, where he was escorted by Lord Darnley to the Presence Chamber. There he found the Queen surrounded by her ministers and a somewhat chastened Countess of Lennox, now released from her wearisome detention in the Tower. The account of his meeting with the English Queen is typical of the enthusiasm Elizabeth could invariably arouse when she chose to exert her natural graciousness and charm:

As I entered, someone was playing a harpsichord. Her Majesty rose, advanced three or four steps to meet me, and then giving me her hand, said in Italian she did not know in what language to address me. I replied in Latin, and after a few words, I gave her your Majesty's [King Philip's] letter. She took it, and after first handing it to Cecil to open, she read it through.

She then spoke to me in Latin also—with easy elegance—expressing the

---

*The Spanish ambassador was so in debt that his creditors would not release his body for more than a year until friends finally collected enough funds to have it returned for burial in Spain.

pleasure which she felt at my arrival. Her court, she said, was incomplete without the presence of a minister from your Majesty; and for herself, she was uneasy without hearing from time to time of your Majesty's welfare. Her "ill friends" had told her that your Majesty would never send an ambassador to England again. She was delighted to find they were mistaken. Her obligations to your Majesty were deep and many, and she would show me in her treatment of myself that she had not forgotten them.

After a few questions about your Majesty, she then took me aside and inquired about the Prince [Don Carlos, Philip's son], how his health was, and what his character was. She talked at length about this, and then falling back into Italian, which she speaks remarkably well, she began again to talk of your Majesty. Your Majesty, she said, had known her when she was in trouble and sorrow. She was much altered since that time, and altered, she would have me understand, much for the better.[3]

Elizabeth outdid herself to make the Spaniard feel welcome, even—to his surprise—embracing him when he departed. That de Silva's astuteness was superior to de Quadra's is seen in his appraisal of William Cecil, whom Philip continually tried to discredit in Elizabeth's eyes, even advising de Silva "if you can crush him down and deprive him of all further share in the administration, I shall be delighted to have it done." The ambassador was frank in his report to Philip, saying Cecil was "well disposed to Spain and shows himself well affected towards your Majesty." He said Cecil was "lucid, modest and just, although he is zealous in serving his Queen (which is one of his best traits), and is amenable to reason." And then, tendering him the highest compliment, he wrote, "I can say nothing except that I wish he were a Catholic. . . ."[4]

De Silva was the recipient of many startling royal confidences during his first months in England. Discussing the religious problem which had confronted Elizabeth, she told him, "she had to conceal her real feelings to prevail with her subjects in the matter of religion, but that God knew her heart, which was true to His Service." Daringly, the ambassador told her that many ministers "spoke ill of her because she had a Cross on the altar in her chapel" and that he considered their attitude "a disrespect to her person." Elizabeth did not refute his tone. "They charge me," she told him confidingly, "with a good many things in my own country and elsewhere and, among others, that I show more favour to Robert than is fitting, speaking of me as they might speak of an immodest woman." Elizabeth attempted to explain to de Silva: "I ought not to wonder at it. I have favoured him because of his excellent disposition and for his many merits. But I am young and he is young and therefore we have been slandered. God knows that it is a great iniquity and the time will come when the world will know it also." A trace of irritation showed in the Queen's manner as she concluded: "My life is not in the dark and I have so many witnesses that I cannot understand how so bad a judgment can have been formed of me. But what can we do? We cannot cover everyone's mouth but must content ourselves with our duty and trust in God, for the truth will at last be made manifest. He knows my heart which is very different from what people think, as you will see some day. . . ."[5]

Her comments show Elizabeth's awareness of the gossip which attended her relationship with Robert Dudley. Such slander might bite into a feminine soul, but it must not be allowed to dent a sovereign's armor. The Queen was anxious that the ambassador—newly arrived in England—receive her own statement before the insidious rumors worked their poison. It proved a wise course. In the weeks that followed, de Silva, privileged with others to observe Elizabeth and Robert at close quarters, agreed that while their intimacy was unusual, that the Queen was not Dudley's mistress. He did not doubt that she loved her handsome Master of the Horse. Neither did he doubt that she loved her Crown and scepter more.

The death of de Quadra left Mary Stuart heartsick. He had been her sole link with Spain, the secret instigator of that correspondence by which Philip had shown some encouragement for her marriage to Don Carlos. It would be months before she could renew the clandestine negotiations. Yet even then Philip was showing characteristic vacillation. He was not anxious to see his son wed to Mary; he knew the English temperament sufficently well to know that such a union would result in war with that country which his empty Treasury would render difficult to win. If he allowed himself to be used as a lever to propel Mary into a wedding with the French King, her former brother-in-law, France would prevail on him to invade England in the Catholic restoration. "To be at war on other people's account is not at all to my liking . . ." he had said more than once. He much preferred to leave Mary to the Austrian archduke, for with little money or power between them, they would prove less troublesome than otherwise.

Mary's despair was compounded by the rebellion of one of her foremost noblemen, the Earl of Huntly. For one day on her progress, her very life had been in danger, and she realized again the futility of her role as a husbandless Queen, dependent on the protection of her half brother, Lord James Stuart. But she had kept her despair to herself. She had helped quell the rebellion, hanged one of its leaders and set his head on the castle battlements at Inverness as a warning. Randolph wrote admiringly, "In all these garboyles [turmoil], I . . . never saw her merrier, never dismayed, nor never thought that stomach to be in her that I find. She repententh nothing, but when the lords and others came in from the watch, [told them] she wished she were a man to know what life it was to lie all night in the fields. . . ."[6]

Back in Edinburgh, her elation disappeared. She became ill and kept to her bed for weeks. Randolph said bluntly that "the Queen's sickness is caused by her utterly despairing of the marriage of any of those looked for; they abroad being neither very hasty"—as much a reproach to Elizabeth and Cecil as he allowed himself—"nor her subjects here very willing. . . ." Randolph was right. Faced with the collapse of her marital hopes, Mary had been "at divers time in great melancholy, her grief being marvelous secret, and she often weeps when there is little apparent occasion."[7] She showed a renewed interest in the proposal of Robert Dudley and, despairingly, sent Sir James Melville to England "to confer and treat upon all matters of greatest importance, as should be judged to concern the quiet of both countries and the satisfaction of their Majesties' minds." He was to show no interest or enthusiasm for the Dudley marriage until Mary's rights in the succession were acknowledged. One "great matter" which Melville carried with him was to establish communication with the Countess of Lennox, who had a marriageable son in the agreeable person of Henry Stuart, Lord Darnley. Though Mary had previously said "she had no desire to match with that race," a union with Darnley would unite two Catholic claims to England's throne.

At the same time as Melville left, Darnley's father, the Earl of Lennox, applied for Elizabeth's permission to return for the first time in many years to Scotland since Mary Stuart had promised to reinstate the estates he had forfeited when he wed Margaret Douglas. Many in the Council advised the Queen against permitting him to leave. Elizabeth vetoed the Earl's request that his wife and son accompany him and, eventually overriding her ministers, allowed Lennox to depart. Once in Scotland, he was received in great state at Holyrood and, happy to be back in his native land, set about to recoup his prestige by distributing lavish gifts of jewels, ornate clocks and mirrors. Randolph wrote that "his cheer is great and his household many." He accompanied Mary to Mass and, careful not to show affront to the Lords of the Congregation, also attended "the sermon," later enjoying himself thoroughly by "banquetting the four Marys and other delicate dames."[8] Randolph was uneasy at Lennox's conduct. Mysteriously, Elizabeth appeared unconcerned. So Lennox remained, and Randolph observed, not realizing he was witnessing the first step in a royal drama which would not end until some twenty-three years later in the Great Hall of Fotheringhay Castle.

Mary's emissary, Sir James Melville, arrived at the English court to be greeted by an affable Queen of England. With Elizabeth again were the Countess of Lennox and Lord Darnley, the former basking in the glow of royal favor once more, the latter anxious to show himself to good advantage of this visitor from his Scottish cousin's court.

As with de Silva, Elizabeth took great care to welcome and impress Melville. She had made a careful toilette for the eyes of the man who would carry his impression of her north to her cousin. The red hair was softly curled around her high forehead; the white skin glowed with good health once more and showed only the faintest traces of the pox. The Queen had disdained too formal attire on the ground she was treating of "a family matter" with her dear cousin's representative. She wasted little diplomatic ritual in asking if Mary had sent any answer "to the proposal of marriage made to her by our Mr. Randolph . . . ?" To which Melville bravely told the truth, "My mistress thinks little or nothing thereof. . . ." Undismayed, Elizabeth spoke of Robert Dudley, whom she said "she esteemed as her brother and best friend, whom she would have herself married if she ever minded to have taken a husband." She told Melville honestly her reasons for wishing him as Mary's husband, "for being matched with him, it would remove out of her mind all fear and suspicion, to be offended by any usurpation before her death, being assured that he was so loving and trusting that he would never suffer any such thing to be attempted during her time."[9] What his own private thoughts were on how such action might benefit Mary Stuart, Melville mercifully kept to himself.

A summer progress, including a state visit to Cambridge, was planned during August. William Cecil, as Chancellor, although suffering from the "unhappy grief" of gout in the foot, journeyed to the University to see the Queen's reception. He found the venerable seat of learning in an uproar. Already there were rivalries in full blast as to who would greet the monarch, what entertainment might be offered, where the Queen would lodge, who would be the royal escort? Sir William chastened the scholars and dons that "two things may especially appear in the University: order and learning." Taking the hint, reverend doctors and professors returned to business while poets and orators burned much midnight oil composing elaborate offerings. Behind the scenes workmen erected stages and platforms; cooks laid in supplies and extra labor, and, one and all prayed for appropriate weather to bless the auspicious event.

The visit was a great success. Elizabeth arrived at Cambridge "dressed in a gown of black velvet pinked and had a caul set upon her head with pearls and precious stones, and a hat that was spangled with gold and a bush of feathers." She was welcomed by Sir William Cecil, who waited while, "the beadles kneeling, kissed their staves, and delivered them to Mr. Secretary, who, likewise kissing the same, delivered them to the Queen's hands." Elizabeth could not hold them all, and somewhat nonplussed, "her Grace gently and merrily re-delivered them willing him to 'minister justice uprightly or she would take them into her own hands and see to it.' "

Following Cecil's welcome, the King's College orator, after three deep bows, made an oration in Latin, praising all the royal virtues which, as they seemed endless, caused Elizabeth several times to mutter, *"Non est veritas."* When, however, he ended by praising her acknowledged virginity, she exclaimed, "God's blessing on thine heart—there continue!" The speech lasted nearly half an hour and, being all committed to memory, earned the Queen's comment "that she would answer him again in Latin but for fear she would speak false Latin and then they would laugh at her. . . ."

There followed several days of sermons, prayers, music, plays and other entertainment. On one occasion, a disputation was held at St. Mary's Church on "whether the monarchy were better than a republic." Only scholars who had taken a degree were permitted to appear. In caps and gowns they knelt in place, as "at the ringing of the university bell" the Queen appeared and they shouted in glorious unison, *"Vivat! Vivat! Regina!"* The three disputants were on an elevated platform. They could be seen easily, but as soon as their arguments were under way, it was evident they could not be heard. Repeatedly, the Queen called on them *"Loquimini altius!"* ("Speak higher!") When conditions did not improve, she did not hesitate to leave her seat and, somewhat to the discomfiture of the participants, settled herself at the very edge of the stage. Once the disputation was over, both the Duke of Norfolk and Robert Dudley humbly desired her Majesty "to speak something to the University in Latin." Though she had a speech already prepared, Elizabeth feigned reluctance, replying "that if she might speak her mind in English, she would not stick at the matter." Yet, she said, since she understood that it was the custom to speak in Latin, she would comply and so made "a very sensible speech." At the conclusion those assembled, "being marvellously astonished," rose and again a tremendous *"Vivat! Vivat!"* soared throughout the vast building. Elizabeth was so pleased at her reception she told Cecil "that if there had been greater provision of beer and ale, she would have remained until Friday!"[10]

In all these encounters, whether at a great university or riding over dusty roads at the head of a huge procession through small towns and villages, it was very evident that all exhaustion or dispiritedness was soon alleviated when Elizabeth Tudor came into contact with her subjects. Whether they were great nobles, knights, merchants, country gentry or simple yeomen, the warmth of public acclaim and personal involvement with her people worked a magic on the Queen that nothing else seemed to bestow. She appeared to draw strength and sustenance from such encounters, and always these meetings with her subjects acted as a stimulant from which Elizabeth appeared to gather a radiant strength. She never tired of greeting them; they never became bored with welcoming her. Though others in the royal retinue grew gray with fatigue or ennui, the redheaded woman at the procession's head did not lessen in her display of cordiality, appreciation or enthusiasm. It was not an assumed pose. With people on all sides calling their affectionate goodwill, something in the Queen responded, and it was to grow in intensity as she herself grew in stature and experience. *They were her people.* Their love, acclaim and trust were all she needed; she could not imagine living without them. And to the end of her life, she would give many indications that—should she ever lose it—she would not consider life worth living.

On Michaelmas Day, 1564, at St. James's Palace, the investiture of Robert Dudley took place in the presence of the entire court. Both Melville and de Silva, the Scottish and Spanish emissaries, were present on the occasion when Dudley, in preparation for the great role he was to play in Scotland, was created Earl of Leicester and Baron of Denbigh. The court assembled in the Presence Chamber, the peers in their robes of state, the heralds standing nearby with trumpets ready. As the patent was solemnly read, Elizabeth stood waiting, regarding the handsome man "sitting on his knees" in front of her. Perhaps as the words ennobling the man "she loved as a brother" were read from the crackling parchment, her mind ranged back over the quarter century of their association, from children, to prisoners, to lovers, to Queen and Earl. As the ceremonial mantle of miniver and ermine was handed to her, she smiled "at the great gravity" on Robert's face and gently laid the mantle across his shoulders. As he prepared to rise, suddenly, in a gesture of spontaneous affection, she allowed her fingers to tickle the neck of the new Earl, ignoring the uncomfortable red flush which crept into his face. The ceremony over, the embarrassed Dudley rose to his feet, and his hand in Elizabeth's, the Queen turned to ask Melville, who was standing nearby, "And how do you like our new Earl?" Melville, ever the adroit diplomat, termed Dudley, "a worthy servant. . .who had a princess who could discern and reward good service." Elizabeth would not be put off by Melville's unctuous answer. "Aye," she replied, "yet you like better of yonder long lad," pointing with one slim finger toward Lord Darnley, who, as first Prince of the royal blood, bore the sword of honor before the Queen. Melville shook his head, saying, that "no woman of spirit would make choice of such a man who resembled a woman more than a man."[11] The "handsome, beardless and ladyfaced" Darnley never had any admirer in James Melville.

Because she had been "well informed of the Queen's natural temper," Mary Stuart had advised Melville, "to leave matters of gravity sometimes and cast in merry purposes," lest Elizabeth be wearied. He had expected entertainment but not an astonishing performance by the Queen of England herself. It commenced shortly after the investiture of Robert Dudley. In his *Memoirs* Melville later wrote an account of Elizabeth's behavior following the ceremony.

> She took me to her bed-chamber and opened a little cabinet wherein were divers little pictures wrapped within paper and their names written with her own hand upon the papers. Upon the first that she took up was written "My Lord's picture." I held the candle, and pressed to see that picture so named. She appeared loath to let me see it, yet my importunity prevailed for a sight thereof, and I found it to be the Earl of Leicester's picture. I desired that I might have it to carry home to my Queen, which she refused alleging that she had but that one picture of him. I said, "Your Majesty hath here the original," for I perceived him at the furtherest part of the chamber, speaking with Secretary Cecil. Then she took the Queen's [Mary Stuart] picture, and kissed it, and I adventured to kiss her hand, for the great love evidenced therein to my mistress. She showed me also a fair ruby, as great as a tennis ball. I desired that she would send it, or my Lord of Leicester's picture, as a token to my Queen. She said that if the Queen would follow her counsel, she would in process of time get all that she had; that in the meantime, she was resolved in a token to send her with me a fair diamond. It was at this time later after supper. She appointed me to be with her the next morning by eight of the clock, at which time she used to walk in her garden. . . .[12]

Elizabeth's curiosity regarding Mary Stuart seemed unquenchable. She asked after Mary's clothing and said she herself "had clothes of every sort, which every day thereafter so long as I was there, she changed," wrote Melville. "One day she wore English clothes, another the French and another the Italian, and so forth." She asked Melville which of them became her best. Melville told her he preferred the Italian, "which answer I found pleased her well for she delighted to show her golden colored hair, wearing a caul and bonnet as they do in Italy. Her hair was rather reddish than yellow, curled in appearance naturally." Elizabeth asked Melville "whether his Queen's hair or hers was the best and which of them two was fairest?" Put to the test, Melville answered evasively, "the fairness of them both was not their worst fault," which Elizabeth would not accept and earnestly asked him "to declare which of them I judged fairest!" The envoy answered somewhat lamely that Elizabeth "was fairest Queen in England and mine in Scotland. . . ." "And which was the taller?" asked the Queen, to which Melville could truthfully say that Mary was taller than Elizabeth. "Then she is too high," replied the satisfied Queen of England, "for I, myself, am neither too high or too low." Asked if Mary was musical and if she played any instruments, he answered, "reasonably well for a Queen."

Later that evening, after dinner, Lord Hunsdon drew Melville to a gallery of the Palace from which music could be heard. It was Elizabeth playing the virginals, Hunsdon explained. Melville, wondering what would now be expected of him stood silently, listening to the excellent tones. Then, venturing into the chamber, he "stood a pretty space" until the Queen, turning, saw him. "She appeared surprised to see me and came forward, seeming to strike me with her hand, alleging that she used not to play before men, but when she was solitary, to shun melancholy. . . she asked me how I came there?" To which Melville rising handsomely to the occasion, which had so obviously been planned, answered that he had been passing her chamber door and "heard such melody as ravished me, whereby I was drawn in. . . ."

During the next few days, Mary Stuart's admonition to James Melville to "lay aside gravity" became a live reality. Elizabeth hated to have him out of her sight. In her Privy Chamber she herself put cushions at his feet to make him comfortable and then asked more of the Queen of Scots. She never wearied of hearing what language Mary spoke, how Mary spent her time and "what kind of books she most delighted—whether theology, history or love matters?" The Scotsman soon wearied and attempted to speak of business, to which Elizabeth answered coquettishly that "I was sooner weary of her company than she of mine." Undaunted, Melville protested that he must soon return to Scotland, that "his mistress' affairs called him home." But Elizabeth would not have it. "Therefore," he wrote in great irritation, "I was stayed two days longer, that I might see her dance." The occasion over, Elizabeth inquired of him "whether she or my Queen danced best?" to which Melville answered that Mary "danced not so high or disposedly as she (Elizabeth) did." Repeatedly, Elizabeth spoke of her wish to meet with Mary until, realizing he would be safely away in a matter of hours, Melville jokingly offered "to convey her secretly to Scotland by post, clothed like a page, that under this disguise, she might see the Queen. . . ." He embroidered the tale, suggesting that her presence in England need not be noticed "if her chamber might be kept in her absence as though she were sick. . . ." Elizabeth was entranced; she clapped her hands and, "appearing to like that kind of language, only answered it with a sigh saying 'Alas, if I might do it thus!' "[13]

The following day she reluctantly said good-bye to the minister, asking Lord Darnley to escort Melville to Dudley's barge awaiting at the river's edge. Lord Robert accompanied Melville to London. In halting words he asked for Mary Stuart's opinion of their proposed marriage. Melville demurred, whereupon Dudley began "to purge himself of so proud a pretence as to marry so great a Queen. . . ." Despite his recent ennobling, Dudley still felt his unsuitability. With a tired gesture he blamed William Cecil, "who was trying to ruin him in the eyes of both Queens at once." He entreated Melville "to excuse him at her Majesty's hands and to beg in his name that she would not impute that matter to him, but to the malice of his enemies."[14] Harassed at the part he was playing, he told Melville his position was unbearable. "If I should have seemed to desire that marriage, I should have taint the favour of both Queens," he said. He would offend Mary by his presumption and incur the jealousy of Elizabeth by any display of enthusiasm. It was evident to Melville that the new Earl of Leicester was indeed in an unenviable position.

Once home, Melville found Mary Stuart eager for his impressions of Elizabeth and the marital question. He left the Scottish Queen in little doubt of the English Queen's intentions. "There was," he told Mary, "neither plain dealing, nor upright meaning, but great dissimulation, emulation and fear."[15] Melville also had carried home the good wishes, affection and great hopes of the Countess of Lennox and her son, Lord Darnley. On the surface there was great enthusiasm in Scotland for the match with Robert Dudley, especially among the Scottish Protestants, and to allay any suspicion, Mary pretended similar interest, completely deceiving Randolph, the English ambassador. He left for London shortly afterward, convinced of her sincerity and devoutly hoping to bestir the Earl of Leicester to more enthusiasm for his intended royal bride.

Mary also asked that Elizabeth allow Lord Darnley to join his father "in order that his right to the entail of his estates should be recognized." At first, Elizabeth seemed agreeable, but the protestations of her Councillors caused her to change her mind for some weeks. In the end she could see no reason to restrain Darnley, and he was given permission to visit Scotland for three months. The Lennox estates in England were much richer than those in Scotland, and Elizabeth reasoned that the Earl and his son would hardly risk their confiscation by the Crown by any disloyal venturings away from home.[16] Only Cecil and Leicester—each for different reasons—agreed with the Queen. To a man the rest of her Council thought she had taken leave of her senses. The Countess, Darnley's mother, was in transports of joy over his good fortune and never thought to look to the motives of the monarch, which were just as strong as her own. Darnley crossed the Border about the same time as Randolph returned from London, where he had all but completed negotiations for Dudley's betrothal to Mary Stuart. He was mystified by Darnley's ease of access to Scotland, where he was received with the great pomp and ritual reserved for royalty. In London he had chided Dudley for his lackluster attitude toward Mary Stuart, telling him he thought him "overslow and careless for his own weal and the profit of his country. . . ." Back in Scotland, he could only wonder what possible purpose Darnley could serve, and he regretted "that any comfort should be taken here by any as to think that through his presence, my purpose here should be subverted. . . ." He wrote Cecil, "My mind was ever to obey unto her Majesty's will, but how to frame or fashion this. . . .I know not yet what to think or how to behave myself. . . ."[17]

As the year 1564 drew to a close, Philip of Spain vetoed Mary Stuart's marriage to his son, Don Carlos. While his rejection was made with the same secrecy as the negotiations, the King's action stung Mary to the quick. Her despair was compounded over the fact that her own Guise relatives and Catherine de Medici had agreed in the decision. "Truly, I am beholden to my uncle," she exclaimed bitterly, "so that it will be well with him, he careth not what becometh of me. . . ."[18] With shattered pride—and little expectation—she viewed her future through gloomy eyes. There was no proud Prince waiting outside her door. Instead there was only the Queen of England's lover, newly clothed in shining vestments and ennobled with a rich title amply buttressed by material endowments. Yet he was still only Robert Dudley of attainted blood and doubtful ambitions. Although she had sworn "never to match with that race," Mary Stuart now anticipated the arrival of Lord Darnley with more enthusiasm than she had formerly shown. He was young; he was royal; he was Catholic. She needed and wanted a husband, and since the demented Don Carlos was not available, she might yet choose her own mate and, in so doing, snap her fingers at the Queen of England.

Chapter Twelve

At the celebration of the New Year in 1565, it was noted that the complement of the Queen's ladies-in-waiting and maids-of-honor had changed since Katherine Grey had married and been imprisoned. Elizabeth's cousin Lettice Knollys had married Walter Devereux, the Viscount Hereford, and Ann Russell had wed Ambrose Dudley, the Earl of Warwick. Mary Dudley Sidney still remained at Penshurst, the poxmarks on her face a disfiguring remembrance of her devotion to the Queen. Her sister, Catherine Dudley, Lady Huntingdon, had taken her place. At the New Year gift-giving ceremony, each of her ladies handed a gift to Blanche Parry, the Keeper of the Jewels, as Elizabeth smiled and nodded her appreciation. Often she singled out one such as her cousin Kate Carey for "six handkerchiefs edged with gold, silver and silk" which the girl had made. Each of the maids-of-honor presented gifts which had challenged their imagination as much as it had strained their resources. Some gave gold enameled toothpicks to complement the tooth cloth which the Queen used daily. Others gave buttons, clasps, jewels or tassels of gold to adorn the Queen's clothing. They were well aware of Elizabeth's inclination to lose such small items, for they were often taxed with finding a lost pair of gloves, a misplaced purse, a jeweled feather or fan or other adornment from the royal gowns. All such losses were duly noted by Blanche Parry in the Keeper's records: "Lost, from her Majesty's back, the 17th of January . . . one aglet of gold enamelled blue. . . ." Or it might be "one small acorn and one oaken leaf of gold." Shortly after Robert Dudley became the Earl of Leicester, the item appeared in the royal records, "Lost at Richmond, the 11th of February, from her Majesty's back, wearing the gown of purple cloth. . .one great diamond out of a clasp of gold, given by the Earl of Leicester. . . ."[1]

While several had left the Queen's household for reasons of health or family responsibilities, in many instances, when a maid-of-honor wed, she returned as a lady-in-waiting and, as such, continued to serve the Queen. One New Year's Day, a vacancy being available, Sir Humphrey Radcliffe came forward and, to the amusement of the court, presented a unique New Year's gift—his daughter, Mary. A strong friendship between her new maid and the Queen blossomed at once. Mary had a caustic wit and a sharp tongue—two attributes much savored by Elizabeth—and seemed to share the royal aversion to marriage. She laughed outright at those who flocked about the Queen and her ladies, aptly judging their worth and intentions and not lacking to tell one "that his wit was like custard, nothing good in it but the sop, and when that was eaten, you might as well throw away the rest."[2]

It was at Ann Russell's wedding to Ambrose Dudley that an item of clothing destined to revolutionize English dress made its first appearance. Lace ruffs had long been worn at court functions. Modest in size, they were held in place by wire "supportasses." When one Mistress Dinghen, a Dutchwoman, came to England, she brought with her the merits of a commodity called "starch" and, for a five-pound fee, offered to instruct anyone in the process of starching a ruff whereby, with long steel or silver "poking sticks," the delicate lace ruffs could be made higher, wider and stiffer. In the shop of one Higgens, a tailor, the ruffs or "picardels" were further "clogged with gold, silver or silk lace . . . wrought over with needlework . . . speckled here and there with the sun, the moon, the stars . . . and other gew-gaws so pestered, as the ruff is the least part of itself."[3] Higgens' work with the "picardels" became so popular that his shop gave his name to an area: Piccadilly. Traffic inside and outside his shop was viewed by the more conservative reformers, now dubbed the Puritans, as monstrous. Starch was labeled "the devil's liquor," and those who indulged in the ludicrous fashion were guilty of the sins of vanity and pride. It little bothered the Queen. Once she and her maids had adopted the starch and glorified ruffs, everyone else at court did also, and there was even a special servant, Mistress Boonen, whose sole duty it was to take care of Elizabeth's ruffs.

As the plague continued to claim victims, it was thought prudent for the court to leave London for Windsor. Great precautions were taken to prevent the plague from spreading to the castle precincts, and all entry to the little town was expressly forbidden "upon pain of hanging without judgment." A nearby gallows lent emphasis to the threat "to hang up all such as should come there from London."

Elizabeth had never liked Windsor, much preferring her river palaces of Richmond or Greenwich. The castle was drafty, in many chambers there were holes in the ceiling and in the floors, and those who accompanied the Queen complained bitterly among themselves. Once the great wagons and that new invention the coach, "which put both horse and man into amazement," arrived with furniture, tapestries, cooking utensils, hangings, quilts and bedsteads, the place became more habitable, although many still protested because "the partitions that are made of boards . . . should be made higher, for the servants look over!"[4]

When poor weather continually prohibited her exercise, Elizabeth set her steward to planning the building of an enclosed terrace where she might walk with her ladies. On fair days there was riding and hunting, for the royal park was full of deer and smaller game. Elizabeth gloried in the chase. It had been said of Henry VIII that "hunting with Henry was no pastime but a martyrdom instead," and Elizabeth, ever her father's daughter, wore out her beasts and companions. She shared her spoil with those who did not have the opportunity to hunt, and on one occasion, after a particularly successful chase, Robert Dudley wrote the Archbishop of Canterbury that the Queen "hath commanded me to send you a great fat stag, killed with her own hand, which because the weather was wet and the deer somewhat chafed and dangerous to be carried so far without some help, I caused him to be parboiled for the better preservation of him. . . ."[5]

Despite his nomination as a husband for the Queen of Scots, Robert Dudley, now the Earl of Leicester, continued in apparent great favor with Queen Elizabeth. At de Quadra's death, he had obtained the lease of Durham House, and now, only minutes from the court, he was constantly at Elizabeth's side, her intimate companion, "her Eyes," her "dearly beloved brother. . . ." When during a winter so cold the Thames froze over "and people walked upon it as they do the streets," the Spanish ambassador, de Silva, wrote that the Queen caught "a catarrh. . . she has also had an attack of the pains in the head to which she is subject." While she was ill, Dudley remained constantly at her side. Observing the pair with eyes uninfluenced by long association, de Silva wrote King Philip, "I understand she bears herself towards him in a way that, together with other things that can be better imagined than described, makes me doubt sometimes whether Robert's position is irregular as many think." De Silva never accepted the contemporary belief that Elizabeth was Dudley's mistress, and the Queen herself left him in little doubt of her own view. Previously she had said that she was "attracted to perpetual spinsterhood not by prejudice but rather by natural inclination," and now she enlightened de Silva further. "The world, when a woman remains single, assumes that there must be something wrong about her, and that she has some discreditable reason for it," she told the ambassador. "They said of me that I would not marry because I was in love with the Earl of Leicester, and that I could not marry him because he had a wife already. Yet now he has no wife, and nevertheless I do not marry him, although at one time, the King [Philip] advised me to do it. . . ."[6]

The Queen still hoped for Dudley's acceptance as Mary's husband, yet the corresponding necessity of designating Mary as her heir was a factor which seemed to make for endless delay in negotiations. "I see the Queen's Majesty very desirous to have my Lord of Leicester placed in this high degree to be the Scottish Queen's husband . . . but when it cometh to the conditions to be demanded, I see her then remiss of her earnestness," wrote William Cecil, aptly gauging the true extent of his Queen's feeling for Dudley versus her Crown.

Dudley was, at this time, in an unenviable position. Offered by the one woman for whom he professed sincere devotion as a husband for another—an involvement he regarded more apprehensively as each week brought its fulfillment nearer—he had prevailed repeatedly upon de Silva to ask King Philip's influence in bringing about his own marriage with Elizabeth. Yet though very willing to share his leisure moments, listen to his opinions and join in his activities, the Queen remained as unattainable as ever.

The elevation to an Earldom had not outwardly affected Robert's behavior; his attitude had always been one of outrageous self-confidence. Yet it rankled with others of the court. There were some who sincerely doubted that Elizabeth ever meant to sacrifice her beloved and send him northward as the husband of a sister monarch. She frankly told the French ambassador, ". . . I could not be without him once a day. He is like my little dog, so much so that when they see him enter anywhere, they say at once that I am coming. . . . ."[7] In the meantime, Dudley's display of devotion—and its subsequent evident response from the Queen—only piqued the jealousy and pride of some not so well favored. Their constant association often placed both Elizabeth and Robert in situations which invited trouble. Once, during a respite from Windsor, they journeyed to Hampton Court so the great tennis court built by Henry VIII might be used. At the end of a match in which he had participated with great vigor, as he stood near the Queen, Robert reached out and thoughtlessly took Elizabeth's handkerchief, "and, being very hot and sweating . . . wiped his face." Nearby, the Duke of Norfolk witnessed the act and, infuriated at the familiarity of the gesture, bore down on Dudley threatening to smash his own racquet over the offender's head. As Robert looked on in unabashed surprise, Elizabeth, with a great oath, separated the two with evident exasperation and impatience. Instead of chastising Dudley, she taunted Norfolk with being "saucy."

Her exasperation was echoed by Randolph, the English ambassador at the Scottish court, to whom the news was relayed with relish by an observer. Randolph deplored the fact that good news took so long to reach him, but bad news traveled fast. "We lack no news, so for what is most secret among you is so soon at this Queen's [Mary Stuart's] ears, that some would think it should be out of the Privy Chamber door where you are!" Randolph was zealous in keeping Elizabeth informed of all that passed between him and the Scottish Queen. The negligence of Elizabeth, Cecil and the Council in reciprocating did not simplify his task. Elizabeth's dislike of making any positive decision wearied the tidy Randolph as it hampered the dispatch of his ambassadorial duties. Mary Stuart did not hesitate to tax Randolph for such royal malingering, and on his return from London, he wrote of his reception.

He found the Scottish Queen at St. Andrews. Emulating Elizabeth, she declined to be decisive with Randolph. Mary was in a holiday mood and was living, as an ordinary citizen—temporarily forsaking her royalty—in a modest home. "Her Grace lodged in a merchant's house, her train very few . . ." he wrote Elizabeth. He was ordered by a blithe Mary "to make merry" in the plain surroundings as Mary and her companions were doing and then spent several days awaiting Mary's disenchantment with native simplicity. "Having thus spent Sunday, Monday, Tuesday, I thought it time to utter to her Grace your Majesty's last command by Mr. Secretary Cecil," he wrote. When he was finally admitted to Mary's presence, she was still acting the role of commoner and had only light words for Randolph's stubborn desire to discuss business. "I see now well that you are weary of this company and treatment," she jested with the ambassador. "I sent for you to be merry and to see how like a bourgeois wife I live with my little troop and you will interrupt our pastimes with your great and grave matters!" Adopting the tone of a "bourgeois" wife, she said, "I pray you, Sir, if you be weary here, to return to Edinburgh and keep your gravity and great embassy until the Queen come hither, for I assure you, you shall not get her here, nor I know not myself where she is become. . . ."[8]

Later, after dinner, Mary became serious. Riding with Randolph, "she talked most of the time with me of France and the honour she received there to be the wife unto a great King. . . ." Mary was still wounded by the abandonment of her Guisian relatives and her rejection by King Philip, and she now taxed Randolph with Elizabeth's laxity. "I find in her no resolution nor determination. . . !" Mary complained. "And therefore, this I say—and trust me, I mean it—if your mistress will, as she hath said, use me as her natural born sister or daughter, I will take myself either as the one or the other as she please and show no less readiness to obey and honour her."As Randolph began an explanation, Mary, wearying of the conversation and anxious to return to her friends, interrupted, "But if she will repute me always as her neighbour Queen of Scots, how willing soever I be to live in amity and to maintain peace, yet must she not look for that at my hands that otherwise I would, or she desireth . . . My meaning unto her is plain and so shall my dealing be. . . . " When Randolph began to answer with "fair words," Mary lost patience and said, waving him away, "I am a fool thus long to talk with you; you are too subtle for me to deal with. . . ." Before departing, he mentioned the negotiations for the marriage with Dudley, earning Mary's reply: "My mind towards him is such as it ought to be of a very noble man, as I hear say by a good many and such a one as the Queen . . . doth so well like to be her husband if he were not her subject, ought not to mislike me to be mine. . . ."

The fine edge of sarcasm was not lost on Randolph. Unknown to him, Dudley himself had written several letters to Mary in which he protested his worth to be her husband. He also questioned Elizabeth's interest in offering him as such, informing Mary the English Queen's intent was to delay the occasion so she, the Scottish Queen, might select a husband.[9] Mary had a final word for Randolph, which indicated her awareness of a situation so fraught with unwelcome potential. "How much better were it," she said, "that we two Queens so near of kin, neighbours and living on one isle, should be friends and live together like sisters, than by strange means divide ourselves to the hurt of us both. . . ."[10]

Encouraged by Mary's amiability, Randolph hurried to write Robert Dudley. "That matter [the marriage] which I have in hand, I am assured, if it take effect, shall turn your Lordship to the greatest honour that you can be called unto. . . ." Striving at anything to ignite some enthusiasm in Dudley, he continued, ". . .it may please your Lordship to understand that this Queen is not content to give good care unto the Queen's Majesty suit in your behalf. . . . By reports she hath heard so much good of your Lordship that she judgeth you worthy of any place of honour. . . ."[11]

Privately, however, Randolph was puzzled. His valiant efforts to spur some definite action seemed destined for failure. Always there were delays in communication, and the reasons given for indecision seemed foolish and pointless. In the meantime, the arrival of Lord Darnley had put an entirely different complexion on the whole issue. Randolph could see, with some consternation, the growing attraction between Mary and her cousin. The young woman, once the Queen of a great and powerful nation, had lacked the company of agreeable and handsome young men. Her stay at the Scottish court had not given her any new diversions which included the presence of an attractive suitor. Darnley had ingratiated himself not only with Mary, but—recognizing where the real power lay—with James Stuart, her half brother. Stuart heartily disliked the young Englishman on sight, not only for what he saw as a vain and dangerously weak personality, but also for what the young man represented: a Catholic presence near the throne of a country rapidly embracing a Reformed religion.

One of the deterrents in completing the marriage negotiations of Mary Stuart and Robert Dudley lay in the terms of the marriage contract. Elizabeth had promised to name Mary and her heirs her successor if the Scottish Queen accepted Dudley. That was the bait for Mary, as it was bitter gall for Elizabeth. No matter what her former intent, when it actually came to naming a successor or relinquishing one small portion of her sovereign power, Elizabeth Tudor would balk. Any designated heir would provide a rallying point "round whom all present discontent and potential rebellion would assuredly gather."[12] Such had always proved true and in this instance would be made more disastrous since Mary considered herself the rightful heir to Elizabeth's Crown. So there were constant fine points to debate, counter proposals to make, all of which took much time while Mary fumed and Randolph continued baffled. What had commenced in apparent good faith had, for nearly two years, become an exercise in circumlocution, and in the end the negotiations foundered on such subtle ramifications as Elizabeth's intent and her determination not to make an outright declaration on Mary's succession "until she, herself, had married or notified her determination never to marry."[13]

The Scottish Queen was not easily deceived. She had waited long to little avail; she allowed herself a tearful outburst "and wept her fill." The harassed Randolph wrote Dudley in masterful understatements. "I could not so cunningly handle the matter, nor temper it with such terms, but I might perceive in her, in my tale-telling, that altogether she grew discontented." It did not help when Elizabeth suggested that if Mary wed Dudley and they lived in England, she, the English Queen, would pay the expenses of both households! The sturdy Randolph, beginning to grasp that his mission entailed the responsibility of a referee between two female sovereigns engaged in a battle of wits —and endurance—attempted to placate Mary with excuses that "matters were great" that "time was required" that "judgment must be observed in order that nothing was prejudicial to her cause." Mary left him in little doubt of her own attitude. "I have had warning enough of your doings," she said, "I accuse not your mistress, though she be loath to give unto me my desire in that which perchance any would be loath to do; but, so long a time to keep me in doubt, and now to answer me with nothing, I will find great fault, and fear it shall turn to her discredit more than to my loss!" And then, with a supremely feminine acquiescence—so different from his own sovereign's manner—she said, "I will content myself with my small portion and maintain that as God will give me grace. . . ."[14]

However, Mary's patience was wearing thin as Elizabeth's appeared inexhaustible, and her attitude was reflected in Lord James Stuart and many others at court. Dining with Randolph, Stuart told the English ambassador that Elizabeth should act quickly before Mary "turned to enemy hands." It was no secret that when Maitland, the Laird of Lethington, had gone to France, "that he went a-wooing or seeking a husband for his mistress. . . ." Stuart was firm. "If she marry any other, what mind will he bear me that knoweth how much I do mislike therewith? If he be a Papist, either we must obey or fall into fresh cumbers, and *I* ever be thought the ringleader!" he said indignantly. The Laird of Pitarrow sought Randolph and echoed her brother's fears that Mary might seek a Papist husband. The Protestant Pitarrow told Randolph Elizabeth should seize her opportunity promptly. "Remember," said the fierce old Scotsman, "how earnestly she [Mary] is sought otherwise," a reference to several ambitious Scottish nobles to whom the Queen had paid little attention. "You know her years, you see the lustiness of her body, you know what these things require. . . loss of *her* time is *our* destruction. . . ."[15] When Elizabeth's negotiations seemed to have reached an impasse, James Stuart accosted Randolph and said threateningly, "The devil cumber you . . . our Queen does nothing but weep and write. Amend this betimes or all will be naught. . .!"[16] When still no news arrived from the English court, "in so great a storm of snow. . . as I could not put my head out of the door," wrote Randolph, James Stuart somehow reached the ambassador's lodgings and "cursed me that could guide a Queen no better when I had her in my will. . . ."

Unable to communicate anything other than Elizabeth's suggestion that Maitland travel to London, Randolph, being "chafed on all sides" by Mary and James Stuart, erupted in despair. The recipient of one of his last letters on the subject was Sir Henry Sidney, Dudley's brother-in-law. Undoubtedly he hoped his imploring words would reach the reluctant bridegroom-to-be.

> I have brought it unto that pass, that now that I have gotten the Queen's goodwill to marry where I would have her, I cannot get the man to take her, for whom I was suitor! How good an end I am like to make of my business in hand your Lordship by this may easily conjecture. . . . If she were unknown or never seen by your Lordship you might well marvel what divine thing it is by whom this great felicity may be achieved.

Sidney had met Mary Stuart earlier but lest he had not informed his brother-in-law of the Scottish Queen's charms, Randolph ventured to elaborate further:

> To that which yourself hath been judge of with your eyes, there is now so much added of perfect beauty that in beholding the selfsame person when you come again, you shall neither find that face nor feature, shape nor making, but all turned into a new nature far excelling any (our own most worthy Queen alone excepted) that ever was made since the first framing of mankind. How many countries, realms, cities and towns have been destroyed and souls have suffered to satisfy the desire of wilful man! But he whom I go about to make as happy as ever was any, to put him in possession of a kingdom, to make him prince of a mighty people, to lay in his naked arms a most fair and worthy Lady, either nothing regardeth the good that shall ensure unto him thereby, the honour that shall be to his name and race, the profit that shall redound unto his country—but so uncertainly dealeth that I know not where to find him, nor what to speak or promise, that I shall not be forced to alter or call back again.

Randolph spoke of Lord Darnley "that ever looked so lofty in the court. . . ." He was apprehensive of the impression the young Englishman was making. "I know not what alteration the sight of so fair a face daily in presence may make in our [Queen Mary's] heart but hitherto I have espied nothing, yet I am somewhat suspicious, or more peradventure fearful or jealous than a wise man would be. . . ." Having offered his counsel and voiced his fears, his hope of any amendment was apparent in his ending, "To make this matter shortly off or on. . .Lethington repaireth to the court. There shall we have our two fine secretaries [Cecil and Lethington] matched together, a couple as well matched to draw in a yoke as any two that ever wrote with a pen. . . ."[17]

At Lethington's departure, Lord Darnley became ill with the measles. His chief visitor, who did not disdain the task of nursing him, was Mary Stuart. "The Queen's familiarity with him breeds no small suspicion. . ."wrote Randolph to William Cecil. "It is now commonly said, and I believe is more than a rumour, that this Queen has already such good liking of him that she can be content to forsake all other offers of suitors, and content herself with her own choice." The young Englishman had made an agreeable first impression on the Scottish court and Queen. Henry Stuart, Lord Darnley, was a very tall and extraordinarily graceful young man. Despite Melville's opinion of him as "lovely, beardless and ladyfaced," Darnley, with his fair hair, large, round eyes and smooth complexion, was a very different image from the more uncouth Scots about Mary in the past. He was accomplished in all the courtier's graces and "well liked for his personage," and his bland countenance successfully hid a powerful ambition, which carried with it little awareness of any corresponding responsibility. He had been reared from birth to believe—his granduncle Henry's will to the contrary—that as a Prince of the blood royal, he stood very near the throne. Unusually privileged in his upbringing, he had the nature of an eccentric, spoiled, willful young man, whose one great skill was an ability to conceal his deficiencies. Unencumbered by any great intelligence, he had followed his parents' lead in manipulating his own peculiar aptitudes to the further enhancement of his family's fortunes. His journey to Scotland was a tremendous opportunity he did not mean to endanger, and his first success there was amply borne out in Randolph's report: "His courteous dealing with all men deserves great praise and is well spoken of."[18]

Mary had first met Darnley at Wemyss. "Her Majesty took very well with him, and said that he was the properest and best-proportioned long man that ever she had seen," wrote James Melville, who observed the meeting. In the next few weeks, they were constantly together at court functions, riding and hunting during the day, dancing a galliard or enjoying other evening festivities. It was inevitable that Mary should be charmed. Darnley's physical attractions, his soft-voiced, tender regard soon aroused a genuine passion in the Queen—a passion which had remained unawakened throughout her two-year marriage to a King who was little more than a boy at the time. She was gayer, happier and more relaxed than she had been previously; her very response to Darnley was also heightened by the lure of the forbidden. She was—or soon would be—espoused to the Earl of Leicester, and *that* marriage would carry the blessing of the Queen of England, as well as the succession. But in the interim Darnley was there in her own country, and the Queen wished to make the most of the visit. What she hadn't anticipated was that she might fall genuinely in love with the fascinating man who, like herself, was of royal blood and happily shared the same faith.

Randolph was anxious about Mary's preference for Darnley. Not only was he fearful for the political disaster which might result, but it was evident he was heartsick for the plight of the young woman herself, a feeling which often expressed itself in his letters and aptly reveals Mary's unfailing appeal to the vulnerable male. "I know not what Lethington knows or will utter," he wrote Cecil, "but I am assured that, with the best of his country, he partakes their griefs of the inconveniences and dangers like to ensue. He can more easily find how far they have gone." The "inconveniences and dangers" were very much on the mind of the Scottish nobles and Parliament, now firmly committed to Protestantism. Mary's Catholicism had been warily tolerated. Her nobles strongly desired that she wed someone of the Reformed faith; in this, Robert Dudley had won grudging approval. The Scots were puzzled, therefore, why Darnley had come to Scotland, and Randolph echoed their complaint that Elizabeth had allowed him passage, "to match the Queen meanly and poorly, rather than live long in amity. . . ." The ambassador was anxious, always, to relieve his sovereign of such dishonor. "My whole care is now to avoid the suspicion that the Queen's Majesty was the means and worker thereof," he noted. He could not deny Darnley's impact, however, and told Cecil, "What is thought of Darnley himself, his behaviour, wit and judgment, I would there were less spoken than is, or less occasion for all men to enlarge their tongues as they do. . . ."[19]

Elizabeth's response was to inform Randolph that she would send Sir Nicholas Throckmorton to reason with Mary and impress on Darnley the magnitude of his actions. "But," wrote de Silva, the Spanish ambassador, "day by day goes by and he does not depart."[20] Nor could he find out just who or what was preventing the ambassador from undertaking his journey to Scotland. It was not until weeks later, when the banns for a marriage between Mary Stuart and Lord Darnley were published, that Throckmorton went north.

Darnley's conquest of Mary Stuart had not taken long. When he recovered from his illness, she made him Earl of Ross, by which he swore allegiance to a Scottish monarch, choosing to overlook the protests of Elizabeth's ambassador and the Scottish nobles' ill-concealed disapproval. "The Queen was stricken by the dart of love, by the comeliness of his [Darnley's] sweet behaviour, personage, wit and virtuous qualities. . ." observed a visiting French ambassador. These enviable qualities lessened daily in the eyes of the Queen's half brother James Stuart, and his fellow courtiers. Stuart bluntly prophesied, "If she takes fantasy to this new come guest [Darnley], then shall there be sure of mischief, sedition and debate at home."[21] The religious temperament of the country which had—on the surface at least—remained quiescent since the first months of Mary's return—now erupted visibly. "Such discontent, large talk, and open speech I never heard in any nation," wrote Randolph, ". . . it must burst into great mischief, for the Queen is suspected by many of her nobles and her people are discontented for her religion, this matchmaking without advice. . . their talk of this marriage is so contrary to their minds, that they think their nation dishonoured, the Queen shamed, their country undone. A greater plague to herself and them there cannot be. . . . She is now almost in utter contempt of her people and so far in doubt of them that without speedy redress, worse is to be feared."[22]

Nicholas Throckmorton ultimately arrived in Scotland near the end of May. He carried a document signed by all the English Privy Councillors stating that a match with Darnley "would be unmeet, unprofitable and perilous to the sincere amity between the Queens and their realms."[23] In an afternoon audience he met with the Scottish Queen, who read of Elizabeth's dislike of the "hasty proceedings with Lord Darnley," and he told Mary, surrounded by her nobles, that she "erred by unadvisedness and rashness. . . ." Argyll, Morton, Atholl, Glencairn—staunch Protestants all—openly nodded their approval of the royal remonstrances. Ignoring their conduct, Mary did not yield. Instead, in firm tones, she told Throckmorton that she "marvelled not a little because she did but use her choice. . . ." She noted that Elizabeth had said "she might take her choice of any person within the realm of England and Scotland." Mary added a subtle taunt to her words saying she thought "none might be more agreeable to your Majesty [Elizabeth] and the realm of England. . .than the Lord Darnley, he being your Majesty's kinsman and hers. . . ."[24] As he observed her firmness, the flush of her cheeks when she spoke of Darnley, her apparent disregard of her nobles' attitude, it was Throckmorton's opinion "that this Queen is so far passed in this matter with Darnley, as it is irrevocable." Throckmorton said, "I find her so captivated either by love or cunning (or rather to say truly by boasting or folly) that she is not able to keep promise with herself. . . ."

Throckmorton's observations were seconded by Randolph, who, from longer association with Mary, felt great pity for the young woman whom he personally liked so well. It was the ambassador's opinion that Darnley, with a prospect of greatness before him such as he had never believed possible—and so easily attained!—was beginning to show an insufferable arrogance. "He is grown so proud, that to all honest men he is intolerable and almost forgetful of his duty to her. . . that has adventured so much for his sake," Randolph wrote. Darnley's inclination to drink heavily had manifested itself in several court scenes, and, said the English emissary, "he spares not also, in token of his manhood, to let some blows fly where he knows they will be taken. . . ." Warily Randolph's concern for Mary grew. "I know not how to utter what I conceive of the pitiful and lamentable estate of this poor Queen," he wrote Robert Dudley, "whom ever before I esteemed so worthy, so wise, so honourable in all her doings. . . ." He spoke regretfully of the growing breach between Mary and her people. He said he found her "so altered with affection towards the Lord Darnley that she hath brought her honour in question, her estate in hazard, her country to be torn in pieces. . . the Queen in her love is so transported. . . . What shall become of her or what life with him she shall lead, that already takeneth so much upon him as to control and command her, I leave others to think. . . ."[25]

James Stuart, whose fortunes were irrevocably tied to the Protestant movement, regarded his sister's obsession with the Catholic Darnley as a personal catastrophe. He also lamented the "great familiarity between her and Rizzio, her Italian secretary." They finally had it out in an emotional scene in which Stuart, "who by his plain advice to his sister got nothing but ill will, resolved to leave the court, so that he might not be thought the author of what was acted there." Other Protestant nobles emulated his action. "The godly cry out that they are undone. . . no hope now of the sure establishment of Christ's true religion, but all turning to confusion . . ."[26] wrote Randolph in despair.

In London, when the ambassadorial reports were read, the Queen of England allowed herself the luxury of a thorough eruption of temper. Dudley had often commented on Elizabeth's changeable moods, her sudden transition from quiescence to fierce reaction. Now the Queen was succinct in her comments of the fool for which she had been played. She had allowed Darnley to go to Scotland—now the whole world would see how she had been outwitted! She threatened both Darnley and his father with outright confiscation of their English estates. They, with greater honors at hand, ignored her summons, and Darnley impertinently replied, "I find myself very well where I am and so purpose to keep."[27] Elizabeth retaliated by returning the Countess of Lennox, Darnley's mother, to the Tower cell she had inhabited only a few years previously. There was a confrontation with the Privy Council that left even Cecil shaken. The Councillors drafted a message which declared any marriage between Darnley and Mary Stuart as "strange." They offered Queen Mary instead "a free selection of any other of the nobility in the whole realm. . . ."[28] In the end the Queen extended to Mary the offer for which she had waited through two long years. Wed the Earl of Leicester, said Elizabeth, and with the marriage, Mary "would be accounted and allowed next heir to the Crown as though she were her [Elizabeth's] own born daughter."

But Mary had gone too far. Her love for Darnley was such that she could flout Elizabeth's proposal with justifiable disdain. She resented the English Queen's "overlordship," she said. For two years she had been "trained with fair speeches and beguiled in her expectations." Now she had found the man of her heart, and regardless of Elizabeth's decree or the loss of the Lennox possessions, she would wed whomsoever she chose, and Elizabeth must seek to interfere no further. Mary's convictions had worked a strange change in her usually reasonable self, so that Randolph, in all seriousness, reported, "The saying is that surely she is bewitched . . . she is now so much altered from what she lately was, that who now beholds her does not think her the same. Her Majesty is laid aside, her wits not what they were . . . her beauty another than it was. A woman more to be pitied than ever I saw—such a one now has neither her own regard, nor she takes count of any that is virtuous or good." Randolph's ultimate despair is evident in his lines: ". . .I protest before God I never wrote a thing with worse will in my life than presently I do this. . . . I wish that it were not known to creatures alive, and would God that what imperfections soever be in her, had before been known, than now to burst out to so great a grief of many men's hearts. . . ."[29]

While events in Scotland were unfolding toward their disastrous conclusion, Elizabeth visited Robert Dudley at Kenilworth Castle. She spent a day at Coventry, receiving a purse with £100 in gold from the Mayor and other notables. Pleased with the gift, the Queen smiled at her companions and said, "It is a good gift—£100 in gold. I have but few such gifts." To which the Mayor chivalrously replied, "If it please your Grace, there is a great deal more in it." When Elizabeth asked what else was in the cup, the Mayor answered, ". . .the hearts of all your loving subjects." To which the Queen responded, "We thank you, Mr. Mayor. It is a great deal more indeed. . . ."[30]

Elizabeth enjoyed the respite at Kenilworth, where the new Earl of Leicester was beginning the construction of a vast range of buildings to be added to those built by John of Gaunt and King John. It was at Kenilworth that the more astute observers about Elizabeth and Robert first noticed a growing coolness between the two. They rode and hunted during the day and were together at the court entertainme.1t in the evening. On the surface their relationship seemed the same as ever, leading one French visitor to say archly that the Queen "could do nothing better for the welfare, repose and content of her kingdom than to espouse one of the greatest peers in England . . ." with a meaningful glance at Dudley. To which Elizabeth, with some asperity, replied "that even if she espoused a person without extensive possessions, his marriage with her would give him the means of engaging in pernicious schemes and intrigues. . . ." It was an uncomfortable moment for Dudley, who might possibly have wondered if his letters to Mary Stuart had come to Elizabeth's knowledge. The Queen left the Frenchman in little doubt of her mind. "For this reason," she said, "I will never concede to a husband any share in my power—that but for the sake of posterity and the good of my realm, I would not marry at all!" The royal refrain was becoming familiar: The Queen would not share her power. The lessons of a deprived childhood—too many executions of those dear to her—had etched their meaning more deeply than many realized into the personality of Elizabeth Tudor. She would trust no one—not even Robert Dudley, one of those dearest to her.

It was, therefore, doubly distressing when the Queen lost the companion of those dangerous years. During the midsummer, only a day after Elizabeth had visited her, Katherine Ashley died, and the Queen's grief, said the Spanish ambassador, "left her prostrate." Elizabeth was, indeed, inconsolable at the loss of the woman whose unflagging friendship and love had been the one steadying influence during her adolescent years. Ashley had, from her earliest memory, always been there to listen to childish confidences and, later, to adolescent fears. She had shared Elizabeth's triumphs and hazards, the Queen could recall more than a quarter century of close, sweet involvement. With Ashley's death, she knew an era in her life was over. Even if the opportunity presented itself, a monarch did not form such close, personal alliances. The risk was too great. Perhaps in the end she had been luckier than she knew to have had the solid affection, support and trust from a beloved personality for so long.

Depressed at the loss of Ashley, Elizabeth needed all her resources when news reached the English court in July, 1565, of a wedding in Scotland. In the face of firm opposition from the Scottish Parliament, from her nobles and people, Mary Stuart had wed Lord Darnley; she had also married him against the express wish of the Queen of England. The Catholic Queen had taken a Catholic husband and, in so doing, had not only risked the friendship of England, but civil war in her own country as well. It was also not lost upon Elizabeth, who stormed and railed at Cecil, the Council or anyone else who would listen, that the marriage represented a tangible viable hope to the English Catholics.

Those at court, only too familiar with Elizabeth's temper, gave her wide berth when possible. There were several, however, more astute, observant and sophisticated, who silently applauded the Queen's strategy. For they recognized—as some more intimately concerned did not—the great risk Elizabeth had taken and the long time in which she had outwardly worked against what she inwardly intended to happen every step of the way. Suddenly everything fell into place: Darnley's ease of access to Scotland, the delay of the negotiations for the marriage of Robert Dudley and Mary Stuart, the poor communications between the English and Scottish courts, the deliberate restraint of Throckmorton, kept waiting in London while he could just as easily have started north had the Queen really wished him to go. Elizabeth had, with her own superb awareness of human nature, correctly assessed a situation which had been under the very noses of the more professional politicians. With her own cool courage—and completely conscienceless heart—she had precipitated a situation and then awaited its natural outcome. Long before anyone else had evaluated the possibilities, the Queen had perceived Darnley was her way out. Darnley was the bait, Darnley was the sacrifice, and Mary Stuart was the victim. She had let a young man—whose worthless character she knew only too well—go to Scotland and see the Queen. From then on, only a capricious fate knew what would happen. The worst would be that Darnley might be unacceptable to Mary, but Elizabeth would have gained valuable time in the interim. The best would be that Mary would wed him—as she had done. Elizabeth counted her loss of face before the world as a price well worth paying. If the world wished to believe Mary had outwitted Elizabeth and flung Dudley in her face, the Queen was well content.

As Catholic response poured into Edinburgh from all over the world—as the faces of those around her grew longer with forboding (excepting Dudley, who felt reprieved), Elizabeth continued in her denunciation of the unfortunate alliance. Superficially, her demeanor was in direct contrast with an inward satisfaction. She knew only too well the moral worth of the young man who would be King of Scotland. She had always felt more than equal to coping with him or his family; that satisfaction now extended to his young wife also. The marriage of Mary Stuart and Lord Darnley was an extraordinary testament to Elizabeth's perception, her cunning ability to judge human nature and her almost incredible patience to let a situation evolve. If, as she sat depressed and disconsolate over Ashley's death, pondering the loss of one era, she could only have viewed the Scottish Queen's marriage as the beginning of another.

The Sister Sovereign

*The right of succession to my throne shall
never be made a subject of discussion. It
would cause disputes as to the validity of
this or that marriage.*

Chapter Thirteen

The marriage of Mary, Queen of Scots, emphasized anew the vulnerable position of England's virgin Queen. The Catholics of northern England were blatant in offering their support to Mary and Darnley should they attempt to salvage England from the Protestant scourge. King Philip of Spain, considering Mary's claim to the English Crown, "to which Darnley also pretends," promised "to assist and aid them in the aim they have in view." Yet when Elizabeth's own fearful Protestant ministers counseled her to help the Scottish rebels, as she had done once before, she refused. She had helped them oust the French from Scottish soil, but now Scotland's rightful Queen sat on her throne, and she, Elizabeth, would offer no challenge to an anointed sovereign. She was also convinced that left alone, time would resolve the situation. Already this belief was being confirmed. "I may well say that a more wilful woman and one more wedded to her own opinion without order, reason or discretion, I never did know or hear of," wrote Randolph. "Her husband, in all these conditions, and many worse, passeth herself; her Council are men never esteemed for wisdom or honesty. . . ." [1] Many who had heretofore advised Mary had been dismissed. When James Stuart, now the Earl of Murray, reminded Mary she could not make her husband King without the consent of Parliament, both he and William Maitland, the Laird of Lethington, were banished from the Council and their estates confiscated. Murray was later outlawed as a rebel. They had gone into exile with other Protestant leaders of the Congregation who could not sanction their Queen's Catholic marriage. Murray, particularly, was "grieved to see the extreme folly of his sovereign," and he lamented "the state of the country that tended to utter ruin." [2] In their place were David Rizzio, Mary's Italian secretary, and James Hepburn, the Earl of Bothwell, a

Border Lord noted more for fearless soldiery than diplomacy. Their appointment earned Randolph's comment that "I would hardly believe that she is so much changed in her nature that she beareth only the shape of that woman she was before." Randolph, clearly, did not see the determination of a woman in love to have her way even at the risk of imperiling the tenuous religious and political security of her country.

While Elizabeth had publicly forbidden any express assistance to Mary's rebellious Lords, when the banished James Stuart arrived in England, he was not disappointed. He was welcomed by William Cecil, at whose home he was a guest, and the following morning played his part in a scene before the Queen of England and two French emissaries. On his knees before Elizabeth, he received a strong tongue lashing for presuming on her friendship and appealing for support against his sovereign. "Her Majesty spake very roundly to him before the ambassador, that whatsoever the world said or reported of her, she would by her actions let it appear she would not, to be a Prince of a world, maintain any subject in any disobedience against the Prince, for besides the offence of her conscience which should condemn her, she knew that Almighty God might justly recompense her with the like trouble in her own realm."[3] There was more than a modicum of truth in the Queen's belief, even though, as everyone present guessed, the scene had been presented for the Frenchmen's benefit particularly. Once they had departed, James Stuart was received more warmly, and later an ample purse was sent to the exiled Scots at Newcastle.

With Mary's marriage the public clamor for Elizabeth to wed increased. The matter of Mary Grey had burst in an untimely inconvenience upon her court. Mary was the sister of the dead Lady Jane Grey and Katherine Grey, still imprisoned with her husband and two sons in the Tower. A dwarfish, unattractive girl, Mary had served as one of Elizabeth's maids-of-honor, receiving £80 a year and lodging in the Palace. She was freckled and redheaded as both her sisters but, unlike them, was only a little over four feet in height, with a "crooked back and very ugly," the Spanish ambassador noted. It was her size—as well as her proximity to the throne—which made her selection of a husband all the more incongruous. Mary's choice was Master Thomas Keyes, a Sergeant-Porter at the Watergate of Westminster Palace. Keyes was over forty years old, the father of a vast brood of children by a deceased wife, "was over six feet six inches tall without his shoes" and of correspondingly ample girth. "Here is the most unhappy chance and monstrous" wrote William Cecil. "The Sergeant-Porter, being the biggest gentleman at this court, hath secretly married Lady Mary

Grey, the least of all the court." [4] The fact that the lonely Mary had formed a genuine attachment to the tall, jovial Keyes—one of the few people in her unhappy young life who had been honestly kind to her—was overlooked by all who were quick to condemn the girl who had wed without the royal permission.

When informed of the marriage, Elizabeth was scandalized and angry. She "took the matter of the Lady Mary very much to heart," said her uncle Lord William Howard. Mary not only had flouted the royal authority, even when faced with her own sister as an example, but had also made herself and her relatives a laughingstock by her unfortunate choice. With her known distaste for marriage, especially without her permission, Elizabeth's reaction was predictable. Mary was one of her near kinswomen and, after Katherine Grey, was regarded by the Protestants as the heiress to the throne. Elizabeth did not wish Mary Grey to duplicate her sister's folly. She would have "no little bastard Keyes," the Queen said grimly. Less than two weeks after the marriage ceremony, Thomas Keyes was sent to the Fleet Prison and the tearful bride ordered into custody of one William Hawtrey of Buckinghamshire, who was ordered "to take into his charge and custody the Lady Mary Grey and convey her forthwith to his house 'the Chequers'; without permitting her to hold conference with anyone. . . ."

The marriages of Mary Stuart and Mary Grey and the inevitable contrast with the Queen of England, who seemed so hesitant to enter holy matrimony, only increased the importance of Elizabeth's choosing a mate. Her subjects' enthusiasm—which some viewed as an opportune moment for the Queen to take advantage of her affection for Dudley—coincided instead with a noticeable coolness between the two. Heretofore they had been virtually inseparable, and at Mary Stuart's marriage Leicester had let his hopes soar, telling de Silva, "Since the Queen is marrying only Lord Darnley, she [Elizabeth] might now accept me." Two months later it was obvious Leicester's hopes had been premature and de Silva noted, "Lord Robert seems lately to be rather more alone than usual, and the Queen displays a certain coolness towards him." Cecil confirmed this attitude in a letter to Sir Thomas Smith in Paris. "The Queen's Majesty is fallen into some misliking of my Lord of Leicester, and he therewith much dismayed . . . the Queen's Majesty letteth it appear in many overt speeches that she is sorry of her loss of time, and so is every good subject. What shall follow of this, God knoweth. . . ." Cecil, whose attitude toward Dudley was always warily tolerant, did not seek to demean the fallen favorite. Instead he wrote, "For my part, I will do what becometh an honest man, not to procure harm to him, though I know he hath not lacked procurers for my harm. But God forgiveth them! . . . if I were as evil disposed to others I could make a flame of this sparkel. . . !" [5]

Cecil's forbearance was not emulated by others, who noted "the Queen is much offended with the Earl of Leicester. . . ." Always relishing any good contest between courtiers for royal favor, partisans of both Leicester and the Queen were now treated to a comedy of manners in which the stakes were high. Elizabeth's conduct was observed as anxiously as Leicester's reactions. "She has begun to smile on a gentleman of the bedchamber named Heneage which has attracted a good deal of attention," wrote de Silva. He said Heneage was married "and is a young man of pleasant wit and bearing, also a good courtier"—qualities to which Elizabeth was always receptive. The fact that he was also a good friend of Leicester's appealed to Elizabeth's humor as much as his more obvious attractions, and the Queen was adept at playing one off against the other, earning de Silva's impatient comment that she "was vain and would like all the world to be running after her. . . ." As an afterthought he added, "Lord Robert is still doing his best to win her. . . ." [6]

Doing his best had become a familiar endeavor for the Earl of Leicester. For almost eight years his main desire had been to wed Elizabeth Tudor. Since Amy's death, it had been eminently possible except for the caprice of the Queen, who insisted on his obedience and adoration in exchange for his favored position. She had adequately compensated him for his efforts with privileges, material honors and preferments. Yet Robert at thirty-three still found his ambition and his determination as strong as ever. The game the Queen played with his emotions, the sexual frustration which caused him to seek release in the arms of the more willing ladies in and out of the court seemed never to tire her as it exhausted his own spirit, made him question his physical prowess and insulted his virility. He was also uneasy that his attitude toward his proposed marriage to Mary Stuart had been found wanting. To please Elizabeth was not easy and, where her ego was concerned, almost impossible. To display eagerness to wed Mary would have enraged Elizabeth, the woman. To display reluctance would have angered the Queen, his sovereign. It had been a delicate and tight situation, and he was weary of being in the middle. He had tried to resolve it in a somewhat amateurish fashion by his letters to Mary—letters which he was sure were not unknown to Elizabeth. It would be typical of her to keep him wondering. The same reasoning applied to any of her own proposed marriages. Should he support her alliance with any suitor, it would make her think, as he told the Duke of Norfolk in great stress, that "he had relinquished his suit out of distaste for her—and so turn her regard to anger and enmity against him, which might cause her, womanlike, to undo him." The remark is revealing, for it shows quite plainly Leicester's hold on the Queen to be less firm than if she had actually been his mistress.

All in all, after eight years, he felt there had been too many situations where he could not do right for doing wrong. They had taken their toll of him, and now, after weeks of Elizabeth's contemptuous attitude and outrageous behavior with Heneage, the fierce Dudley pride at last asserted itself. If the Queen, after their many years of devoted friendship, sought to humiliate him at court, frighten him with the loss of her favour and its accruing material benefits, he would not play the meek lapdog she had once compared him to and allow any sickening display of continued abasement. When he enlightened Sir Nicholas Throckmorton on his position, it was that worthy's opinion that Leicester "should make love to another lady and see how the Queen took it. . . ." [7] The game that less illustrious couples practiced the world over was now to be performed before the court of England.

Robert was quick to seek out the lady of his choice, and she was not hard to find. Lettice Knollys, the Viscountess Hereford, was first cousin to the Queen* "and one of the best-looking ladies of the court." She was the mother of several children but, with a husband soldiering in Ireland, was more than receptive to Leicester's attentions. In addition to her beauty, Lettice was bright, witty "with high spirits," and her response was balm to Robert's frustrated soul. For weeks they were together at the court. Elizabeth, missing nothing, but pretending not to see, paid equal attention to Heneage, who basked in the royal limelight while his wife sulked at home. When, being admonished by Throckmorton that absence did indeed make the heart grow fonder, Leicester asked to leave the court, Elizabeth, "in a very great temper and very bitter words," showed her displeasure. Several months of such verbal tiltings left the court in a dizzying disturbance, which came to a head one day during the holiday season as, during a game of questions and answers, the question was put to the Queen, "which was the most difficult to erase from the mind—an evil opinion created by a wicked informer or jealousy?" The question was forced—not too innocently—on Leicester by Thomas Heneage, who had supplanted him in his usual role as Master of Festivities during the holiday season. Enjoying predominance, Heneage insisted Robert ask the question of the Queen.

*Lettice Knollys was the daughter of Sir Francis Knollys, who had married Catherine Carey, the daughter of Mary Boleyn, Anne Boleyn's sister.

When he had done so, as the court grew quiet, aware of the obvious contest between the fallen and the favorite, Elizabeth answered that both were hard to displace, but in her opinion, jealousy was the most difficult. Once the game was over, Robert sought Heneage and threatened him with a beating, to which Heneage jauntily replied that should he make good his threat, he would be met with a sword. Since dueling was expressly forbidden by royal decree, he was safe, as he knew. When Elizabeth heard of the scene, she angrily sent Heneage from court and told Robert to refrain from entering her presence. In an angry exchange of words, she threatened that "if by her favour he became imprudent, she would soon reform him and that she could lower him just as she had raised him"—an echo of a remark her father had once made to her mother.

The whole performance wore on Leicester's nerves. He was edgy in the Council chamber, so much so that Elizabeth had again to scold him in public for taunting the Earl of Sussex at the Council table. Sussex, a true aristocrat, always had small use for Leicester. On his deathbed he would say, "Beware of the Gypsy, for he will be too hard for you all . . . you know not the beast as well as I do."

In the midst of these conflicts of personality, William Cecil sought to keep a level head, cool emotions and a nonpartisan outlook. It was not always easy, for the struggle within the Council to remain in the good graces of Elizabeth often bore heavily on political decisions. Underlying his words written to Smith in Paris "there are sundry rumours that the Lords here do not accord together" lay annoyance as the result of Elizabeth's often intemperate bestowing of favor which encouraged animosities and latent jealousies. Yet Cecil loyally would say, "but I trust hereof no harm indeed shall follow, for all these Lords are bent towards her Majesty's service, and do not so much vary amongst themselves as lewd men do report." It was often difficult, however, for Cecil not to show his own partiality, especially for the Duke of Norfolk, of whom he said, "I think England hath not had in this age a nobleman more likely to prove a father and a stay to this country . . . he is wise, just, modest, careful, *et times Deum.*"[8] Cecil's own rise from a less exalted background, his survival through several reigns which had proved disastrous to other ambitious noblemen invariably led him to favor the more illustrious members over such as Leicester and Heneage.

Elizabeth's continued prickings aimed at the dejected Leicester finally bore fruit. Many at court seemed to avoid him; no one wished the taint of association as the erstwhile royal favorite continued his decline. He finally asked Elizabeth's permission to leave the court, "as other men did," but when it was given, he merely retired to his chambers in a raging ill humor. He remained there, in pettish sulkiness for days, and the messages which came from others at court did not alleviate his anger or anxiety. Elizabeth, he was told, had been extremely angered by his petulance and, perhaps missing him more than she wished to admit, had waspishly told her cousin Lord Hunsdon, "My Lord, it hath often been said that you should be my Master of the Horse, but it is now likely to come true. . . ." [9] Hunsdon, knowing his sovereign's changeability and guessing the motive behind the remark, wisely did not respond. But the loss of the appointment meant a great deal to Robert. While it was not as lucrative as other preferments which had come from the Queen, he loved the post which placed him nearest the sovereign in royal processions. He hurried back to court at once. In the meantime, Cecil and, oddly, the offended Lord Sussex had tried to act as mediators between the willful lovers. Once Robert was admitted to the royal presence, they wisely withdrew before the eruption of anger from within. A blazing quarrel commenced, with Elizabeth accusing him of improprieties with Lettice Knollys and Leicester, nothing daunted, giving as good as he received, with unflattering remarks about that scoundrel Heneage. As quickly as it had happened, it was over. Mutual recriminations were put aside in favor of reconciliation, and, as de Silva later wrote, "both the Queen and Robert shed tears. . . ." [10]

Though the French ambassador could later write, "The friendship and favor of the Queen towards the Earl of Leicester increases daily," the Council was still debating Elizabeth's marriage. Pressure was again being exerted for her to wed, and the Queen, whenever cornered, inevitably resumed her negotiations with the Hapsburg court, which was duly informed that "whereas heretofore she had always purposed to die a virgin, nevertheless at the pressing instances of the Estates of her realm, she had now decided to marry. . . ." [11] But, as Cecil wrote to his friend Sir Thomas Smith, the great obstacle was "that the Queen's Majesty will needs see before she marry. . . ." The fact that the father of the Archduke Charles, now Emperor, repeatedly refused to let his son come to England for appraisal by the Queen was only one of the many items which might be deliberated endlessly while time was wasted pleasantly and unproductively with Elizabeth maintaining her unwedded state. "She is so nimble in her dealing, and threads out of this business in such a way," said de Silva, "that her most intimate favourites fail to understand her, and her intentions are therefore variously interpreted." [12]

Equally obstructing, although not as familiar to the Queen as it was to her negotiators, was the Emperor's small enthusiasm for a woman whose scandalous relationship with one of her foremost noblemen was common knowledge in the European courts. Cecil was constantly besieged by such rumors, again writing his friend Smith, "Briefly, I affirm that the Queen's Majesty may be by malicious tongues not well reported, but in truth, she herself, is blameless and hath no spot of evil intent." [13] While Cecil's propriety was often assaulted by the Queen's lack of taste regarding her male favourites, he knew her better than anyone else in the court, with the exception of Leicester. Cecil was not one to put an imprudent word to paper. When his convictions were strong, he could express himself with great logic and forethought. When his beliefs were uncertain, it was easier to evade comment. Had he truly believed Elizabeth guilty of adultery, his oft-stated belief that while the Queen was careless in her actions, she was not improper reflects a more judicious opinion than was apparent in the echo of court and City gossip.

This acute perception—and consequent deductive reasoning—is nowhere more apparent than in an appraisal of Leicester and the Archduke which Cecil drew up concerning the matrimonial advantages of each.[14] Leicester came off somewhat the poorer in the comparison: It is evident where William Cecil's preference lay. And as the news from Scotland worsened, he could only hope that whatever conviction was guiding the Queen of England in her strong determination to remain unwed, that the headstrong Tudor sovereign might ultimately prove more amenable. For not only was Mary Stuart's marriage proving unhappy, but the Queen of Scotland was pregnant. If the Queen of England did not wed and provide an heir, Mary Stuart's child would be regarded by more than half of Elizabeth's subjects as their future monarch.

Mary's marriage had deteriorated almost from its very beginning. Within two short months, the Scottish Queen's highly passionate desire and love for her husband had not survived the brutal assault of a shallow, aggressive youth with small capacity for understanding his wife's sensitivity and no vocation whatsoever for sovereignty. Randolph hurried to write the English court: "He [Darnley] looketh now for reverence to many that have little will to give it to him, and though some there are that do give it, that think him little worthy of it. . . ." His continual drinking inflamed an arrogant, weak and suspicious nature which fastened on the gentler person of twenty-eight-year-old David Rizzio, Mary's personal secretary, as the cause of all his troubles. Upon arrival in Scotland, Darnley had sought the friendship of the little Piedmontese who so influenced the Queen. Rizzio was anxious to

WILLIAM CECIL'S CHART[14]

To Be Considered In The Marriage

Convenient Person	Charles	Dudley
In birth	Nephew and brother of an Emperor.	Born son of a Knight, his grandfather but a Squire.
In degree	An Archduke born	An Earl made
In age	Of-and never married	Meet
In beauty and consideration	To be judged of	Meet
In wealth	By report, 3000 ducats a yr.	All of the Queen and in debt.
In friendship	The Emperor, the King of Spain, the Dukes of Saxony, Bavaria, Cleves, Florence, Ferrara, and Mantua	None but such as shall have of the Queen
In education	Amongst Princes always	In England
In knowledge	All qualities belonging to a Prince—languages, wars, hunting and riding.	Meet for a courtier
In likelihood to bear children	His Father, Fernando, hath therein been blessed with a multitude of children. His brother Maximilian, hath plenty. His sisters of Bavaria, Cleves, Mantua and Poland have already many children.	*"Nuptia steriles."* No brother had children and yet their wives have—Duchess of Norfolk. Himself married and no children.
In likelihood to love his wife	His Father, Fernando, *ut supra.*	*Nuptiae carnales a laetitia incipiunt et in luctu terminanter.* *
In reputation	Honored by all men.	Hated of many. Infamed by his wife's death.

*"A carnal marriage begun in pleasure and ended in sorrow."

press Darnley's cause with Mary in order that the Catholic monarchs might work together to reestablish that faith in Scotland. Now that he was wed to Mary, Darnley regarded with hatred Rizzio's secretive Latin manner and soft, lilting voice. "The suspicion of this King towards David is so great that it must shortly grow to a scab amongst them,"[15] wrote Randolph. Darnley's feelings were also tinged with envy. The hardworking little Italian, with large, round eyes and "very black in visage," had the affection, trust and confidence of the Queen, while the Queen's husband had neither.

Darnley's drunken behavior in and out of the royal residences had become public knowledge. His dictatorial aggravation of the Scottish ministers and advisers, his lack of restraint in dealing with all other courtiers, his pursuit of women of the court and in the brothels of Edinburgh were no secret from his wife. "He could not be persuaded upon to yield the smallest thing to please her," wrote Randolph, "what shall become of him, I know not, but it is greatly to be feared that he can have no long life among this people." [16]

Within weeks the magnitude of her mistake was borne home to Mary. Daily she saw her ideals and goals—one of which encompassed the Crown of England—endangered by her unfortunate choice of a consort. The aura of passion and devotion with which Mary had entered her union with Darnley was soon stripped clear in intolerable scenes which shamed her in public, as much as in private. Once at a merchant's home in Edinburgh, wrote Randolph, "she only dissuading him . . . from drinking and enticing others, in both of which he proceeded, and gave her such words that she left the place in tears . . . these jars arise, among other things, from his seeking the crown-matrimonial which she will not yield to."[17] Randolph said that "she is very weary of him, and, as some judge, will be more so ere long." Their continued battles beat the Queen's pride raw and often left her either in tears or contemptuous silence. Her one great solace was that she was with child.

When, eventually, the pregnant Mary refused Darnley's sexual advances, the young man became convinced that Rizzio was the recipient of his wife's favours and that he himself "had suffered the greatest dishonor that can be inflicted on man." [18] Mary often sought the company of the Italian so that he seemed indispensable to her, and this, together with his Catholicism, made him hated by many in and out of the court.

By the first week in March, 1566, matters had come to a head. Darnley's insistence on sharing the crown-matrimonial, by which he would rule jointly and be made King for life, continued to be refused by his wife. All state papers were now signed by Rizzio with an iron stamp bearing Darnley's signature, and the coinage, which bore both his and Mary's portraits, had been recalled. Fearing his son would be degraded further, the Earl of Lennox rushed to Darnley's side, inflaming the small, drunken mind of the twenty-year-old boy with stories designed to incite suspicion. From spies around the court, the exiled Protestant Lords correctly assessed the situation. Lennox was joined by Argyll, Glencairn, Morton, Rothes, Boyd, Ochiltree and, finally, the exiled James Stuart, the Earl of Murray. Darnley was an easy prey to their whispered insinuations regarding Rizzio. Mary had given her secretary rich clothing, he had his own retinue of servants, and he alone was entrusted with the Great Seal of Scotland. It was even rumored that Mary might make him Chancellor. The Lords had many reasons for hating Rizzio. Primarily they disliked his religion, but his very closeness to the Queen, his intimate knowledge of her private papers and state dispatches—knowledge formerly shared by them— fanned their hatred. It was Mary and Rizzio who stood between the return of their Church lands and vast revenues, and they implied to Darnley that it was Rizzio who stood between him and his wife. An agreement—shocking in its intent—was drawn up on March 1. In it the Lords, who had nursed so many grievances, promised—as if they were accomplishing nothing more significant than an increase in the price of wool—to assassinate Rizzio, noting ". . . they shall spare neither life nor death in setting forward his [Darnley's]honour according to the word of God." For removing Rizzio's undesirable presence from around the Queen, Darnley was to guarantee the return of their confiscated lands and monies. They, in turn, would help him to attain the crown-matrimonial which the Queen had so long denied.

Darnley had added one note to their intentions. He insisted the deed be done in the Queen's presence.

The design of the rebellious Lords and the Queen's husband was an ill-kept secret. Although Rizzio had not been mentioned by name, five days after the signing, a copy of the infamous agreement—or Bond as it was called—was on its way to London, and Randolph wrote in a covering letter, "I know now for certain that this Queen repenteth her marriage—that she hateth him and all his kin. . . . I know that there are practices in hand, contrived between the father and the son, to come by the crown against her will. I know that if that takes effect which is intended, David, with the consent of the King, shall have his throat cut within these ten days. Many things more grievous and worse than these are brought to my ears. . . ." [19]

On the evening of Saturday, March 9, as Mary dined at Holyrood with several guests in a small turret supper closet off her bedchamber, she was joined by Darnley, who, by prearrangement, had agreed to appear before the crime was committed, possibly to absolve him of any complicity. His arrival cast a pall over the gay little party which had eaten a comfortable dinner, drunk well from the French wine gleaming in the light from the single large silver candelabrum on the heavy table. They had been listening to a resplendently garbed Rizzio, "in a nightgown of damask, furred, with a satin doublet and hose of russet velvet, with a jewel about his neck and his plumed cap upon his head." [20] He was singing in a deep baritone voice, accompanying himself on the lute.

Within moments of Darnley's seating himself, the door was flung open, and silhouetted in the doorway was the heavy figure of Patrick, Lord Ruthven, a terrifying sight in full armor. Behind him, Mary could see many other figures in the dusky light. Ruthven demanded that Rizzio leave. Instead, the terrified man leaped to Mary's side as the Queen cried, "It is by my will that he is here!" Ruthven told the Queen that they meant no harm to her and again demanded that Rizzio come forward. As one of the guests made ready to challenge Ruthven, the door was flung back, and the remaining conspirators entered with drawn swords and daggers. In the scuffle the table was knocked over, the candelabrum seized by a distraught Lady Argyll, one of the guests, as it fell forward, and in the flickering shadows a screaming Rizzio, calling, "Save me, Madame! Save me!" was dragged toward the door. Mary started forward, but Darnley, his face twisted with hate and fear arose, and forcibly held his wife's shaking figure against the wall. Sickened by the scene, with tears streaming from her eyes, Mary could only listen to the screaming of her friend as he was hacked to pieces in the hallway outside and the thud of his slight figure as it fell down numerous stone steps, to be flung through a window into the open courtyard below. Once released by her husband, she turned on him, crazed with grief and terror, shouting her hatred and rage, her disdain of the weakling. She called him traitor, coward, every epithet her wretched mind could remember, crying, "I shall be your wife no longer, nor lie with you any more and shall never like well till I cause you as sorrowful a heart as I have at this moment. . . ." [21]

The next morning a sober Darnley presented himself in his wife's apartments. Mary had spent a sleepless night, torn with grief for her murdered friend and a burning hatred for her husband. In great humiliation, she recognized she was now a prisoner of her own nobles, the very ones she had cast aside several months previously. Much as she detested her husband, she needed him now to use as he had used her.

With great insight, she preyed on the weak man's fears. She recognized his doubts about how he might fit into a Protestant-dominated Council. His jealousy and lust for Rizzio's blood had disappeared with the onset of his early-morning sobriety, and Mary now taunted him that the powerful Lords would use him and then possibly dispose of him as they had disposed of Rizzio. With trickery worthy of a Guise and the courage and resourcefulness of a Stuart, she said they had used him, and David had been the sacrifice. Now he must choose between them and her, or *he* might prove a further sacrifice. Caught in the middle, the cowering Darnley sought the safety and refuge which Mary and the Crown represented.

Within hours, Mary had communicated with the Catholic Earl of Huntly and his brother-in-law, James Hepburn, the Earl of Bothwell. During the late-evening hours, disguised in long dark cloaks, she and Darnley passed down a secret spiral staircase, through a subterranean cellar of the Chapel out into the quiet darkness of the adjacent churchyard. As the pair crossed to where the horses were waiting, they trampled the soft mound of earth which marked David Rizzio's last resting place. The horrified Mary broke into sobs and muttered "that a fatter than he should lie near it ere one twelve months was at an end. . . ." [22] The Queen could not leave the precincts fast enough, but once she was away, her common sense reasserted itself. She was then six months pregnant, and she begged Darnley to ride more slowly. To which her frightened and unsympathetic husband only jeered that if she lost the child, "they could always beget more. . . ."

Five hours later they rode into the formidable castle at Dunbar. Within days the conspirators who had killed Rizzio—lacking Darnley's protection—had fled the country, "some one way and some another," and her own supporters—Atholl, Huntly, Bothwell and some 8,000 others accompanied Mary and Darnley back to the safety of Edinburgh Castle. Here, meeting with her estranged half brother, James Stuart, the Earl of Murray, the Queen threw herself into his arms. In the gesture was her tacit acceptance and recognition that if she were to retain her Crown, it would be with a Protestant-dominated Council—not, as she had hoped, with a strong Catholic husband and King at her side.

When news of the Rizzio murder reached the English court, Elizabeth immediately wrote Mary a "private letter with her own hand," earning Mary's grateful reply, which also asked that Elizabeth refuse shelter to the fleeing Lords who had killed her secretary. She asked that Elizabeth act as godmother for her child, ending, "I will not weary you further at this time. Excuse me if I write so ill, for I am so *grosse,* being well advanced in my seventh month, that I cannot stoop, and even so, I am ill with what I do. I therefore kiss my hands to you, Madame, my best sister, and I will pray God that he may give you as much prosperity and as long life as I would desire for myself." [23]

On one occasion the Spanish ambassador found Elizabeth with a portrait of the Queen of Scotland, "hanging from her waist by a gold chain. . . ." The Queen's sympathies were with Mary, and she proclaimed Darnley, still protesting his innocence, a liar. Since the fleeing Lords had sent Mary the infamous Bond signed by Darnley, Elizabeth was pleased to hear from her own ambassador, Randolph: "The King is in the worst case for the Queen has no good opinion of his attempting anything against her will, nor the people that he hath so manifestly denied a matter proved to be done by his commandment, and now himself to be the accuser and pursuer of them that did as he willed them!" She told de Silva that Mary had written her so much "and that so many things had happened that it would take her three hours to tell me. . . ." [24] She said had she been in Mary's place "she would have take her husband's dagger and stabbed him with it. . . ." Perversely her reason was not for the murder of a helpless man, but for the disrespect shown her own royal person. She spoke at a meeting in which de Silva was urging her to accept the Archduke Charles in marriage, and in sudden humor, Elizabeth turned to him, put her long fingers on his arm and said he must not think she would treat her suitors in such a fashion. As for marriage itself, she continued, "If I think of marrying, it is as if someone were tearing the heart out of my body . . . nothing but the welfare of my people would compel me to it!" The French ambassador, to foil de Silva's plan for the Archduke, later hinted broadly to Elizabeth that it would greatly benefit her country if she would marry one of her own noblemen. He pointedly told the Queen it was taking her longer to marry than it had taken God to make the world. To which the Queen dryly replied that God was a greater artist than she—and her people would just have to be patient.

Elizabeth's humor often lit up the weightier moments at court. She had inherited her mother's quick wit and daring and could jest with a servant or a King's ambassador with ease. She liked Guzmán de Silva, the Spanish ambassador, as much as she disliked Dean Man, the Bishop of Gloucester, her own envoy to the court of Spain. She wrote King Philip that as he had sent her a "Gooseman" (Guzman), in return, she had sent a "Man" not a whit better than a goose. . . ." [25] When, in full reconciliation with Leicester, she made a summer progress to Oxford University, of which he was Chancellor, as Dr. Laurence Humphrey, noted for his Puritan stiffness, made ready to kiss her hand on arrival, she said to him with a smile, "Mr. Doctor, that loose gown becomes you well. I wonder your notions should be so narrow!" On the same visit, as another learned Doctor proceeded to dispute at great length on an interminable subject, Elizabeth wearily asked him "to make an end of his discourse without delay." The Doctor proceeded for another half hour as Elizabeth fidgeted and her anger mounted. When, at the conclusion, she baited him with "presuming to go on with his discourse to so unreasonable a length, after she had sent her command for him to bring it briefly to a close," the poor man could only say he had learned the speech by rote and could not, without shame to himself and the university, shorten it as she had commanded. The Queen, who could speak extemporaneously quite well, threw back her head and laughed at the doctor's innocence and frankness. The next day she made a special point of stopping during her own discourse to ask someone to bring a stool to William Cecil, who suffered badly from gout. And she waited until the seat had been obtained and placed under the relieved man—with a special glance at the long-winded speaker of the previous day—before continuing her talk as if there had been no interruption.

Elizabeth was quickly clever at the contemporary game of rhyming people's names or fashioning rebuses. A rhyme on an extravagant gentleman named Noel quickly found as much favor out of court as in:

> The word of denial, and letter of fifty ['No" and the Latin L]
> Is that gentleman's name, that will never be thrifty.[26]

Another time, observing several knights visiting from Nottingham, she whispered to one of her maids, "Gervase, the gentle; Stanhope, the stout; Markham, the lion—and Sutton, the lout." [27] Few were spared her caustic wit, not even the "lazy scamps," the Bishops, of whom Elizabeth said, "Two or three are enough for a whole country." When the Catholic Bishops protested such treatment, Elizabeth told the French ambassador, "I wish one could see my heart as if it were a picture that could be sent to Rome so that all could see what it was like." When de Silva later told her that should she wed, the Pope would be very pleased, "that he had a very exalted idea of her ability," Elizabeth was quick to respond, "I think he and I should get married. . . ." [28]

There were also occasions when the royal defenses were down and the Queen's façade of bravery and wit deserted her. Such was observed the evening of June 23, 1566, when William Cecil threaded his way through a throng of merrymakers at Greenwich Palace and spoke in the ear of the Queen. Elizabeth's face turned ashen, and for a moment, she missed a step before groping for a chair where she quickly sat down. Asked by one of her women what was wrong, Elizabeth struggled to compose herself and said, "The Queen of Scots is the mother of a fair son." And then, in a more strangled voice, "and I am of barren stock!" Though she had expected it, the actual words whispered in her ear induced a physical shock in the Queen. She retired early but, by the next morning, had recovered her composure sufficiently to play the gracious sovereign and "show a glad countenance" to James Melville, who had brought the news to court. With recovered poise and once more the practiced diplomat, she welcomed the Scotsman "with a merry *volte*," the opening steps of a French dance then much in fashion. She extended her warmest congratulations to Mary and agreed to act as godmother to Mary's son, James, delegating the Countess of Argyll to act as her proxy. She appointed the Earl of Bedford to represent her and sent Mary a baptismal font of gold worth £1,000. She told Melville if the baptism were delayed and the child too grown, "you may observe that our good sister has only to keep it for the next." [29]

In the autumn the Queen was forced to summon her second Parliament. During the 1563 session, Elizabeth had half promised to marry, but three years later that marriage which would hopefully provide the country with an heir seemed more elusive than ever. Mindful of the risks the country faced in a disputed succession, the members who assembled had one thing in common: they wished the Queen wed so as to avoid a civil war and to guard the still-shaky bastion of Protestantism against the more ancient citadel of Catholicism.

Elizabeth had been reluctant to summon Parliament, for she was as determined as its members not to be forced to declare a successor which the more Protestant Commons—not favoring the Scottish claim of the Catholic Mary Stuart—devoutly wished. She had the always dependable crutch of negotiations with the Archduke Charles to buttress her alleged willingness to wed—eventually. She would much have preferred that Parliament remain prorogued, but the financial state of her Treasury after the French war demanded a subsidy which could only be secured with its consent.

The Queen was not unmindful of her Parliament's temper. She knew that with the birth of Prince James, the Scottish claim was now stronger than ever, that only her life stood between a Scottish monarch on England's throne or a disputed succession which might involve several claimants such as Katherine Grey. Her marriage was a subject of debate in the City as much as at the Council table. For the first time since Mary Tudor's reign, broadsheets were left in the streets, in the churches and even in the Queen's own private chamber, chiding her laxness in dealing with the succession question. Law students at Lincoln's Inn argued that since Mary Stuart "had been born outside the realm . . . [she] could not succeed to the Crown even if she were the nearest in birth and the ablest." [30] There were many who questioned Elizabeth's wisdom in summoning her lawmakers at the precise moment when public clamor was so loud. But the condition of the Treasury left little alternative.

From the very tenor of the first sittings, however, it was soon apparent that Parliament would not consider additional funds until the Queen had decided on a more important subject: her marriage. When Sir Edward Rogers, Elizabeth's Comptroller, spoke to the Commons "that the Queen had emptied the Exchequer as well in the late wars as in the maintenance of her ships at sea, for the protection of her kingdom and subjects . . ." there was a loud outcry, and one member leaped to his feet, saying "that he saw no occasion nor any pressing necessity which ought to move Her Majesty to ask for money of her subjects. . . ." [31] Mr. Secretary Cecil tried vainly to keep the Parliament to its business, accounting for the war expenses. Still the members would have none. Instead, a motion was made "for the reviving of the suit for the succession. . . ." One member noted that the Queen had received funds in the last Parliament, had promised to wed or declare a successor. The funds were gone, he said, and the Queen was still a spinster. As far as he and his fellow members were concerned, they would vote no money till the Queen gave them an answer. Sir Ralph Sadler, a Privy Councillor, sought to intervene, saying that "it is not fit for us to deal with it [the succession] at this time, especially not to mix or mingle it with the matter of the subsidy . . ." but he was shouted down. As the arguments continued, tempers rose as partisan members exchanged blows before it was decided "to go to the Queen and let her know our intention. . . ."

The commission waited upon Elizabeth in the Privy Chamber. They made it clear "they were unanimously resolved to deal with the subject before treating a subsidy or any other business. . . ." If the Queen would not declare her mind on the subject, they said, they might as well go home. Elizabeth's reply was brief. "The Commons," she said tightly, "are very rebellious. . . ." It was not for them to impede her affairs, and it did not "become a subject to compel a sovereign." They little realized, she said, what they were asking in demanding that she designate a successor. It would be digging her grave before she was dead, she emphasized, and belligerently she told them they would never have dared been as presumptuous in her father's lifetime! She was a Prince, she reminded them and it was not fit for subjects to meddle in a Prince's affairs. Marriage was *her* affair, not a political obligation. She promised, somewhat grimly, if she needed protection from her own Parliament, she'd marry someone—someone whom perhaps they would not like or desire. The commission retreated, a bit chastened, but pointedly did no further business. The House of Lords, anxious at the break between the Queen and her Commons, sought some reconciliation between the two. Elizabeth waved away their deputy, saying, "My Lords, do what you will. As for myself, I shall do nothing but according to my pleasure. All the resolutions which you may make can have no force without my consent and authority . . . I will take counsel with men who understand justice and the laws, as I am deliberating to do. . . . I will choose half a dozen of the most able I can find in my kingdom for consultation. . . ." Her parting remark was that the whole issue was much too important "to be declared to a knot of harebrains." [32]

The royal attitude did not help. The rebellion passed to the House of Lords, where the nobles, headed somewhat aggressively by the Duke of Norfolk, Elizabeth's cousin, was heard to say the Queen was foolish for refusing "to take any other advice than her own." The Lords joined forces with the Commons and proceeded to wait it out in a battle of wills with the Queen, while Elizabeth, enraged, threatened Norfolk with arrest for his impertinence and denounced him a "traitor."

Norfolk was undoubtedly right in his assessment of the conflict, and his comment was sound. On any other issue, Elizabeth would have listened more impartially to her lawmakers. But neither Norfolk nor her Parliament could know the depth of the Queen's aversion to marriage. The attitude of the eight-year-old child who had told her friend Robin Dudley, "I shall never marry," had been grounded in self-preservation. Her attitude was still the same, only now it was strongly reinforced by *fear*. The Crown was hers and had been for nearly ten years. She had been an effective monarch who possessed the love of her people. She would not risk both Crown and popular support for one man, either nobleman or monarch. Her solution was silence.

For several days the impasse remained. The quiet in the court was oppressing. The Council Chamber was empty; the Presence Chamber vacant. People spoke in whispers among themselves, repeating the latest gossip from the Parliament, gossip which could also be heard in the City's inns and taverns. Elizabeth, alone with her ladies, appeared taciturn and withdrawn. Although she showed no signs of relenting, the expressionless face hid the nervous agitation of a woman whose preoccupation with her needlework barely concealed the terror which she tried to keep at bay. She felt cornered. Being forced to comply or compromise, which would only endanger her safety and peace of mind, was a constant fear. The nightmare image of her childhood, the isolation and imprisonment of one close to the throne or—the inevitable fate of too many Queens—exile or death on the scaffold, was not easily forgotten. The actual physical aspect of surrendering not only her body, but that intimate private refuge of safety which she prized more than anything else in the world—her sovereignty, her divine privilege—gnawed at Elizabeth's composure. Marriage among monarchs as she had observed it with the eyes of a child held nothing but peril and risk. It was not for her.

It was the first major impasse between the nobles, the Commons and the Council arrayed on one side and the sole person of the thirty-three-year-old sovereign on the other. The lawmakers, unaware of the depth of the Queen's aversion and fear, regarded her silence as foolish and unwise. As for the Queen, she was virtually powerless to cope; she literally *could not* accede to their demands. Her fright and despair were such that she could act or respond in the only way compatible with her own innermost emotional resources.

William Cecil echoed Elizabeth's despair. His distress at the Queen's predicament was apparent when he wrote his absent friend Sir Henry Sidney, "I do with all my heart condole and take part of sorrow to see your government so great. . . . I feel myself, being also here wrapped in miseries and tossed, with my small vessel of wit and meanness, in a sea swelling with storms of envy, malice, disdain, suspicion. . . . What discomfort they commonly have that mean to deserve best of their country!" [33]

When at last Parliament adjourned over a weekend, Robert Dudley, the Earl of Leicester; William Parr, the Marquess of Northampton; Elizabeth's uncle Lord William Howard; and the Earl of Pembroke begged an audience to intervene for Norfolk, with whom Elizabeth still remained at odds. Their intention was to apologize for Norfolk's peremptory action in the Parliament, to assess the Queen's intention and, hopefully, soften or placate her and end the deadlock.

It was the first Elizabeth had seen of her ministers in several days, and the result showed in the Queen's strained appearance as they met in the Privy Chamber. Days of isolation had induced a pent-up anger, and she welcomed the release of words. Tersely she spoke of the situation as she understood it, censuring the Duke of Norfolk for his critical remarks and leading toward what she hoped would be a more palatable discussion of the troublesome question. The Earl of Pembroke attempted some rebuttal and "remarked to her that it was not right to treat the Duke badly, since he and the others were only doing what was fitting for the good of the country, in advising her what was best for her, and if she did not think fit to adopt the advice, it was still their duty to offer it." Elizabeth brushed aside his remarks and accused him of speaking "like a swaggering soldier," which momentarily silenced the loquacious gentleman who had a great reputation of being overly fond of his own words. To William Parr, Marquess of Northampton, whom she had known since childhood, she was more personal. Parr had previously been deeply involved in matrimonial affairs, even to the point of having Parliament settle his marriage contract at one time. Elizabeth now accused him of being "no account." Fiercely, the Queen said he "should not mince words with her." Rather than talk about *her* marriage, she advised "he had better talk about the arguments used to enable him to get married again, when he had a wife still living. . . ." As Northampton shifted uncomfortably, her eyes lit on Leicester, who, more than anyone else, should have known her horror and fear of marriage. "You! My Lord!" she cried excitedly. "You! If all the world abandoned me, I thought that *you* would be true . . . !" Overwhelmed, Leicester vehemently protested his devotion. He went down on his knees before her and said he "would die at her feet. . . ." To which Elizabeth, almost on the verge of tears, impatiently told him to get up and snapped "that had nothing to do with the matter. . . ."

For their pains, both Leicester and Pembroke were banned from the Presence Chamber "for furthering the succession question in the Parliament without the Queen's allowance. . . ." They all departed with nothing accomplished except the alleviation of tension and the release of the royal temper; they had not changed the Queen's mind.

Two weeks later, on hearing that a petition would be sent her from the Parliament, Elizabeth decided to forestall the measure. She summoned thirty members from each House to appear before her and, for days, worked on the speech which would attempt to explain her position to her lawmakers. As the somber delegation stood before her, she set the tone by referring to their performance as a "traitorous trick," and she "mused how men of wit can so hardly use that gift they hold. I marvel not much that bridleless colts do not know their rider's hand, whom bit of kingly rein did never snaffle yet."

For the next several moments, the onlookers were treated to expressive bits of Elizabeth Tudor's eloquent philosophy. The Queen rarely had any trouble expressing herself, and she vigorously lamented what she considered the disgraceful conduct of her Parliament. Regarding the petition to marry, she angrily told them that "it was a sorry business" that they would barter her happiness in exchange for money to run her kingdom. Her natural affront arose as she regarded her lawmakers' stoic expressions. She had spent their money wisely and well, she said, and then, casting aside her speech, she spoke to them directly. "Was I not born in this realm?" she asked testily. "Were my parents born in any foreign country? Is there any cause I should not alienate myself from being careful over this country? Is not my kingdom here? Whom have I oppressed? Whom have I enriched to other's harm? What turmoil have I made in this Commonwealth that I should be suspected to have no regard to the same? How have I governed since my reign? I will be tried by envy itself. I need not to use many words, for my deeds to try me. . . ."

Her speech had been overlong, and the Queen sought to end it. She reviewed the terrors peculiar to an heir which she had experienced during her sister's reign, *and so shall never be my successor,* she said firmly. She reiterated that she knew she was mortal. "And though I be a woman, yet I have as good courage, answerable to my place, as ever my father had. I am your anointed Queen. I will never be by violence constrained to do anything. I thank God I am endued with such qualities that if I were turned out of the realm in my petticoat, I were able to live in any place in Christendom!" [34]

As for her marriage, Elizabeth said that "she had not bound herself by any vow of celibacy never to trade [*i.e.* participate] in that kind of life called marriage. . . ." For herself "she thought it best for private women—but for a Prince, she endeavoured to bend her mind to it. . . ." As for the succession, she said, "I will deal therein for your safety and offer it unto you as your Prince and head, without request." She told them firmly that "it is monstrous that the feet should direct the head" and then, dismissing them, promised "that they should have the benefit of her prayers. . . ." [35]

Neither House was satisfied, although a great deal of their vigor had been dissipated by the Queen's firmness. Eventually, Elizabeth resolved the impasse although it cost her part of the badly needed funds. She promised to request only two-thirds of the required subsidy. This would pay her war expenses and allow her shipbuilding program to continue, and she stated that the part remitted "would content her as she considered that money in her subjects' purses was as good as in her own Exchequer." [36] The Parliament enthusiastically accepted the Queen's compromise and, once the Subsidy Bill was drawn up, contented itself with gaining the last word by incorporating in the preamble the royal promise to wed. When Elizabeth saw it, knowing it would ultimately be made public, she ordered it stricken from the Bill. She scrawled "in her running hand" at the bottom, "I know no reason why any of my private answers to the realm should serve for prologue to a subsidy vote. Neither yet do I understand why such audacity should be used to make without my licence an Act of my words. . . ." Her opinion of the Commons was obvious in her last words, "If these fellows were well answered, and paid with lawful coins, there would be no fewer counterfeits among them!" [37] Eventually the debated preamble was reworded to indicate the Queen had graciously allowed she would marry at her convenience. And with that the members had to be content.

The 1566 session "was the decisive Parliamentary conflict of the reign,"[38] and through her tact, skill and courage, Elizabeth had kept firm control over her lawmakers. Between them, she and Cecil had molded the two Houses—which had taken the incredible step of censuring their Queen's actions—to their own ends. But the opposition had given firm notice that their patience might not be inexhaustible. Elizabeth had won, but time—her great ally, as she always said—might eventually prove, where her marriage was concerned, to be her greatest enemy.

William Cecil
Lord Burghley
attributed to Marcus Gheeraerts I

Queen Elizabeth
The famed "Pelican Portrait,"
from Pelican jewel above hand.
Attributed to Nicholas Hilliard

James Stuart
Earl of Murray
Mary Stuart's
half brother
Artist unknown
*The National Galleries
of Scotland*

William Maitland
Laird of Lethington
Artist unknown
*The National Galleries
of Scotland*

James Hepburn
Fourth Earl of Bothwell
Artist unknown
*The National Galleries
of Scotland*

David Rizzio
A posthumous
portrait
*Holyrood
Amenity Trust*

Mary Stuart
Queen of Scotland
Artist unknown
*The National
Portrait Gallery,
London*

Henry, Lord Darnley
Age seventeen
and brother
Charles, age six
*Courtesy of
Her Majesty
Elizabeth II*

Thomas Howard
Fourth Duke of Norfolk
From a private collection

Robert Dudley
Earl of Leicester
Artist unknown
*The National
Portrait Gallery,
London*

Queen Elizabeth
Age thirty
Artist unknown
*The National
Museum,
Stockholm*

Blanche Parry
Artist unknown
The National Museum of Wales

Lady Katherine Grey and Son
*Courtesy of the Duke of Northumberland
and "Country Life" magazine*

Sir Nicholas Throckmorton
The National Portrait Gallery, London

François, Duke of Alençon by Clouet
Courtesy of Lord Astor of Hever

Chapter Fourteen

While Elizabeth was dealing with her Parliament and, through graceful yielding, strengthening her sovereign prerogatives, Mary Stuart was continuing in the headlong process of losing hers. Outwardly the relationship between the cousins was amicable, but the letters carried by weary couriers between them often bristled with outraged feminine complaints. Elizabeth was pained that Mary had secretly aided the Irish outlaw Shane O'Neill, as well as a rebel Papist, Christopher Rokesby. She wrote Mary advising her to "Remove these briars ... lest some thorn prick the hand of those who are to blame. ..." She said she considered the Scottish Queen's actions as "full of venom as [are] your words of honey" and frankly warned Mary: "If you are amusing yourself at my expense, do not think so poorly of me that I will suffer such wrong without avenging it. Remember, my dear sister, that if you desire my affection, you must learn to deserve it." [1] Either Mary or her minister inevitably conjured up a bland reply. The quickest way to deal with England, they had learned, was to adopt Elizabeth's own policy of underhand maneuverings, all the while protesting outward conciliation.

The rapport between the two Queens was not enhanced by the intelligence which arrived from Scotland. William Cecil had deftly turned the services of Rokesby to good account by offering "pardon and profit" if he would act as a spy at the Scottish court. Accepting the bargain to "call to remembrance things that were done," Rokesby delineated his conversations with Scottish ministers and, particularly, with the Queen. He saw Mary on several occasions, on which she imprudently recounted her efforts to win the support of Catholics in northern England. Familiar names rolled off Mary's tongue—Sir Thomas Stanley, Herbert, Darcy, the Earls of Derby, Northumberland, Westmorland, and Cumberland. She recounted her hope of restoring Catholicism "and thereby win the hearts of the common people." Toward that end, she had "tried to have two of the worshipful in every shire of England" look kindly on her efforts and had sent one Father Lascelles letters with blank superscriptions which he would direct to such as would prove faithful on the day Mary assumed power in England. The Queen's further plans were "to cause war to be stirred in Ireland whereby England might be kept occupied." Then "she would have an army in readiness and herself with her army to enter England . . . and [be] proclaimed Queen. . . ." She assured Rokesby that "her soothsayers do tell us that the Queen of England shall not live this year. . . ."* [2]

Mary's great ambition was hindered by her marriage. Darnley's complicity in Rizzio's murder had only increased her detestation for her husband. While others remained in exile, Darnley, the one most responsible for the assassination, was still at her side—a fact which incurred the enmity of the exiled Lords and their friends both at court and in exile. Darnley had promised his fellow conspirators immunity but, by cravenly clinging to Mary for protection, had turned on them earning their undying contempt. He held himself clear of any complicity in Rizzio's murder, and on March 20, the good citizens of Edinburgh were confronted with a proclamation upon which they might read that their King "declared upon his honour, fidelity and the word of a Prince that he never knew of any part of the said treasonable conspiracy . . . ," a public betrayal that stunned even the hard-bitten Scottish Lords to whom treachery was a way of life. The reaction was not what Darnley had hoped. "The King is in the worst case," Randolph wrote Cecil in early April, "for the Queen has no good opinion of his attempting anything against her will, nor the people, that he hath so manifestly denied a matter proved to be done by his commandment, and now himself to be the accuser and pursuer of them that did as he willed them!" [3] When Mary defiantly hired Guiseppe Rizzio, David's brother, to fill his place, at the same time disinterring the dead man's remains and burying him in the Royal Chapel, the Lords and Darnley might well wonder what they had actually accomplished.

In the months following the tragedy, Mary, humiliated and longing for release from her marriage, discussed with her half brother, Murray,

---

*Rokesby's original letters to Cecil were found in his lodgings in Scotland, and as a result, he spent almost two years as a prisoner in Spynie Castle. Thus the incredible naïveté of Mary in confiding, as she did, in someone virtually unknown to her came to the knowledge of the English Council *after* Rokesby's release and just about the time the Scottish Queen fled to England for Elizabeth's protection.

and Lethington how she might rid herself of her unstable husband. "It is heartbreak for her to think that he should be her husband, and how to be free of him she sees no way. I see betwixt them no agreement, nor appearance that they will agree thereafter. How soon, or in what manner it may change, God knows," wrote Lethington. Both he and Murray were quick to advise that any divorce, so soon after the birth of her child, would only lend credence to the scandalous rumors of its paternity which had circulated at Rizzio's murder. She must stay with Darnley for the present and give the appearance of a reconciled couple. The thought of living with the man she loathed was unbearable, however, and once out of childbed, Mary took young James to Alloa, the estates of the Earl of Mar. In doing so, she served notice to Darnley that she would not live with him, and when he later followed, penitent as a puppy, he was repulsed so thoroughly he stayed but a few hours. Her attitude was emulated by others, and thus, less than fourteen months after his marriage the King of Scotland found himself barely tolerated by courtiers, dismissed from the Council, snubbed by his wife and scorned by most of his subjects. The knowledge that he alone was responsible for his misery did not help the mental or moral condition of the young boy who had been given power and privilege too soon and subsequently possessed little of either. He was desperately lonely, his pride was constantly assaulted, and behind all, he bore a latent fear that those indignant Lords he had abandoned and betrayed might seek revenge. In particular, he hated Murray, the Queen's half brother, because of her dependence on him, and he feared that Murray's influence would cause Mary to pardon the exiled Lords, who would seek vengeance on him. Spitefully, he absented himself from his son's baptism in December, 1566, remaining in his chambers throughout,* and later he took the only course open to him. He returned to his father's estates in Glasgow and announced he would "fly to Flanders and publish his grievances to the world." [5]

Alarmed by his intentions which would present to all the courts of Europe the spectacle of a Queen abandoned by her husband—and lend support to the persistent rumors regarding her child's paternity—Mary summoned her Council to deal with the situation. When Darnley returned to Edinburgh to end his affairs, his distrust and fear were such that he refused to enter Holyrood while any of the Lords were present, apparently fearing a fate similar to Rizzio's. When Mary learned of Darnley's attitude, she dismissed the Council, and guards and any

---

* The French ambassador gave two reasons for Darnley's behavior, saying he was jealous that more attention was paid to Mary than to him as King and also, since "the person who came from England . . . will take no notice of him, he is afraid of receiving a slight."[1]

citizens near the Palace walls were the diverted by the sight of the Queen of Scotland emerging to greet the King and induce him to enter his residence. Mary insisted Darnley's suspicions were unfounded and, realizing what she must do, enticed the young man inside and "so conducted him to her own apartment where he remained all night. . . ." Darnley, convinced he had lost her by his foolish actions, was only too glad to be apparently reconciled with such a loving wife. In a few days he was as much in her thrall as ever, but still undecided on his reception by the Lords. His uncertainty was short-lived. One morning he was peremptorily ordered before the Council, where the Lords endeavored "to understand from the King . . . whether he had formed a resolution to depart by sea out of the realm, and upon what ground and for what end." The meeting was conducted in the presence of the French ambassador so the truth might be relayed to his home court. When Darnley did not answer their question, the Councillors remonstrated with Darnley that his honor, the Queen's honor and the honor of Scotland were at stake. They said if he should "abandon the society of her to whom he is so far obliged . . . if he should act in this sort, the whole world would blame him as an ingrate. . . ."

Mary then "spoke affectionately to him, beseeching him that . . . he would at least be pleased to declare before these Lords where she had offended him in anything." Why did he wish to leave? What had she done? Taking him by the hand, she "besought him, for God's sake, to declare if she had given any occasion for this resolution" that he must leave Scotland. As Darnley, taken by complete surprise, stood silent, biting his lips and wondering what to say, the Queen's words were emphasized, as one by one her Councillors asked how he could leave "so beautiful a Queen and so noble a realm?" Darnley's emotions were ever prevalent over his wit. Instead of frankly stating his complaints: the snubs and scorn, his lack of any real authority and a wife who so disregarded him—the wretched young man waited what seemed an interminable length of time, which embarrassed the ambassador and Councillors. He realized his wife had put him on the defensive publicly, and there was really no way he could explain the situation, which was well known to all present, without also resurrecting the Rizzio murder and his part in it. Finally he turned on Mary, realizing at last why she had agreed to their reconciliation. His face was white as he struggled to keep his composure and retain some semblance of dignity. At last he spoke, "Adieu, Madame, you shall not see my face for a long space," he said and then turning to the Lords, spoke again, "Adieu, Gentlemen," and bowing, left the room.

At his departure, Mary looked relieved. Her reputation was safe.

Before the evening was over du Croc, the French ambassador, would write his version of the meeting. She had pleaded publicly for an understanding with her husband, who had declared he could find no fault in her, and the Lords affirmed they would bear witness to Darnley's declaration. Mary dismissed the meeting with a satisfied smile, and du Croc later wrote, "I never saw Her Majesty so much beloved, esteemed and honoured, nor so great a harmony among all her subjects, as at present is by her wise conduct. . . ." [6]

Mary had other reasons to smile. The attentions of James Hepburn, the Earl of Bothwell, were noted with alarm by his fellow nobles, who, much as they admired the warrior in the tough Border Lord, disliked his Protestantism and his overweening ambition. Randolph, the English ambassador, particularly distrusted the swarthy noble, calling him a man "whose power is to do more mischief than ever he was minded to do good in all his life; a fit man to be made a minister to any shameful act, be it either against God or man. . . ." [7] Bothwell's followers, impressive in number, were held in similar disrepute; they were an unscrupulous, unsavory lot, who had resorted to piracy on the sea and brigandage on land on more than one occasion. They were, however, undaunted in their allegiance to their resourceful leader. At thirty years of age, Bothwell was darkly handsome, broad-shouldered, with jet black hair and mustache. With a fierce countenance lit by an arrogant, sensual smile, he was outstanding among Mary's nobles. His exploits in battle were impressive; none questioned his competence as a soldier. He was well educated, came of an influential family, possessed a fearless nature and a seemingly inexhaustible self-confidence. He differed from his fellow nobles in that he had never accepted English bribes and had been dedicated in his devotion to Mary of Guise, the Queen's dead mother. He surpassed his fellow courtiers in one other way also. His reputation with the ladies was as impressive as the virile strength which dominated his personality. In a court where male canniness, brutal strength, plain talk, light amours and easy morals were the norm, James Hepburn, the Earl of Bothwell, seemed to embody them all.

Bothwell had recently wed Lady Jane Gordon, a sister of the Earl of Huntly. Mary Stuart had attended the wedding, and though she instinctively trusted him more than the other Lords, she had not unduly favored him. Bothwell, in turn, had never seemed impressed, with the Queen, even saying bluntly that "Mary Stuart and Elizabeth Tudor rolled together would not suffice to make one proper woman." [8] But after the Rizzio tragedy particularly, Bothwell had become a main source of strength and protection, so much so that the visiting Earl of

Bedford noted, "Bothwell carries all credit in the court," with the predictable result that "he is one of the most hated men among the noblemen in Scotland." Later Randolph wrote, "His influence with the Queen excels that of all the others," and many, resentful of his growing authority, could compare his position only to that of the hated Rizzio. Mary Stuart had never learned—as Elizabeth had learned early in life—that small delegations of authority, of impartial favoritism, paid large dividends. One could not play factions off against the other unless one knew, as Elizabeth always did, the strengths and weaknesses of both sides. Mary saw only the end result, the attainment of something very personally desired. How it was acquired and who got hurt or lost in the process really did not perturb the Scottish Queen. Mary had championed Rizzio in the face of popular disapproval. Her open favoring of Bothwell was one more example of the willful obstinacy of the Queen, who could not compromise. In short, the tragedy of Rizzio seemed imminent again.

Except this time there was a great difference. Rizzio had never been Mary's lover, despite the scurrilous rumors surrounding their relationship. But in the months following her child's birth, as the husband who was to have helped her to the English scepter sulked at his father's castle, Bothwell and Mary were constantly together. Her unhappy marriage, the horror of her secretary's murder, the pain attendant upon her child's birth and the restriction of her convalescence had left the pleasure-loving Queen, so used to flattery, pampering and indulgence, thirsting for the fun and freedom which now, for the first time in months, seemed possible. Freed from the company of her husband, her child safely placed with a guardian, Mary was suddenly less fettered than she had been for a long time. There was more than a little of the temptress and flirt in the Queen, as several at court had found to their sorrow. One of her larger mistakes—and so indicative of her inability to assess another's susceptibilities—was to underestimate her effect on Bothwell. Always completely in command of himself, fearing no one, he had taken his pleasure as he found it, with few refusals or reproaches. He had great loyalty to the monarchy itself and, presumably, respect for the person of the monarch. He had watched Mary's attempts at flirtation with amused tolerance. That she was a pretty and very feminine woman could hardly be overlooked, and as the weeks passed and Mary's coquetry continued, he became intrigued in spite of himself. It was typical of both Bothwell and Mary that where their own desires were concerned, they thought little of the consequences. The Earl was a bridegroom of seven months; Mary, estranged from her husband, the mother of an infant son. Yet neither condition lessened the fact that as Bothwell's power had increased in the court, so had his attention to his Queen.

There came a day in the late autumn when Mary was at the "Checker House in the Cow Gate" in Edinburgh, where she often stayed when it became necessary to supervise her financial accounts. In this particular instance, she wished to provide funds for the care of her young son. Bothwell as usual was in attendance, and as Mary proceeded to the business at hand and others of her retinue drifted away to await her departure, the Queen urged the Earl to stay. Possibly Mary may have meant only to spend a pleasant hour or so trifling with the handsome Earl, after which she would dismiss him at the proper moment. After some time on her accounts, Mary pushed the books away and, glancing at the personable courtier, began to flirt, quickly feigning indifference when Bothwell looked receptive. The Earl humored the Queen, who responded with a captivating smile. Mary was aware of what she was doing, and she found herself enjoying the performance hugely. She could always end it whenever she chose—or so she thought.

Bothwell could guess Mary's inclination. She would lead him on and then dismiss him with a laugh and a wave of her hand, as he had seen her do with others. He had watched her husband's sorry performance, and he realized the Queen's married life left a lot to be desired. But as Mary rose from her chair to leave, all reasoning suddenly left Bothwell, and he was only aware that the woman before him was not only his sovereign, but one desperately in need of fulfillment. The thought became the catalyst which aroused his passion even as it cast caution aside. Mary had been offering him an invitation for days; it was obviously up to him to respond.

Quickly he embraced the Queen, who appeared startled by his fervor and then, laughing, ordered him to release her. When he did not do so, she became more insistent and, suddenly, sensing that Bothwell was serious, struggled to free herself. None of those waiting outside would come without her summoning them, as she and Bothwell both well knew. To scream would be to cause a scene which would only demand embarrassing explanations. And with Bothwell's hand at her back, his lips warm on her neck and his other hand caressing her intimately, she felt her own desire rise and her struggles lessen. Even so, she did not give in. Some proud inner core of Majesty and reserve could not surrender completely, even as she recognized that Bothwell would not be put off. Still resisting, she was soon overpowered and in tears lay on the hard floor while the Earl of Bothwell promptly raped her— "forced her against her will," as she was later to say—with seemingly little more thought than he would have given to the ravishing of a serving wench.

Or perhaps, with his tremendous insight, knowledge and experience of the opposite sex, he knew exactly what her response would be. Mary had been wed to a fifteen-year-old boy and a fumbling and ineffective youth of nineteen. Her marital experience had been more one of surrender than participation. Duty compelled the gift of her body, and she had passively acquiesced. To her, as to Elizabeth, flirtation without surrender was heady excitement. But with Bothwell there awoke in the Queen a passion which became a living thing, for which she was willing to overlook her past, forget her present and risk her future, her Crown and her life. In characteristic, headlong abandon, Mary did not hide her passion. While visiting the Castle of Drummond and Tullibardine, "Mary and Bothwell were chambered during their stay in these two houses [where] many found fault with but dared not reprove. How lascivious also their behavior was, it was very strange to behold. . . ."[9] In a fiery ecstasy, which continued rendezvous only inflamed, Mary's careless, profligate love for Bothwell was deepened, strengthened and finally became all-consuming. For her now there was this love without restraint, without pride, without moral scruple of any sort. Time and again she gave herself to her lover asking nothing, and everything, her heart and mind closed to the risks.

Eventually, there was a price to pay. Inevitably, as the first wanton abandon was dissipated, her conscience became as assaulted as her body. Five months after the birth of James Stuart, she was again pregnant,* and the enormity of her actions was finally brought home in compelling fashion to the Queen, who had dared everything for moments unlike any she had ever before experienced. Now larger issues loomed before her—honor and dignity, her religion and sovereignty. She accepted that she had now placed herself outside respectability, and the result was to be seen in the highly emotional and exhausted creature who spent her days in bed, sobbing, asking only the release of death. As she desperately sought an answer to the problem which no Queen in honor could face, she spent weeks in isolation, her moodiness and irritability tinged with hysteria, and, when she finally recovered, those around the Queen noticed she had become a "different person." She appeared more mature; there was less fretting, and she exhibited an altogether new and unusual firmness.

*Details of Mary's pregnancy are virtually unknown. When she conceived and when she gave birth have never been factually verified. But with a leeway of a month or two, her actions forecast her secret. There is no other explanation for all her subsequent behavior, after the December christening of her child, other than the fact that she was pregnant.

During her illness she had reviewed her position. She was married, and her husband was a King. Bothwell was married, and his wife was the sister of one of her foremost Catholic nobles. How could their illicit love ever be recognized—and how could she account for the pregnancy which no one in their right mind would attribute to Darnley, for whom she had not had a kind word or thought in months? How long might it be before James Hepburn, whose ambitions were as limitless as his sexual indulgences, become weary of a too-willing Queen, especially a pregnant one, if their affair brought nothing but an eager body that he could have for the asking in any chamber in the Palace or bedroom in Edinburgh? How long would it be before he tired of her?

The heart-stopping thought was all that was needed to spur the Queen to action. At a meeting with her brother, Murray, Lethington and Huntly, she referred to her illness and said "that unless she might by some means or other be dispatched of the King, she would never have any good day; and if by no other way she could attain it, rather than she could abide in such sorrow, she would slay herself." Seizing the opportunity, Lethington smoothly suggested, "If it please your Majesty to pardon the Earl of Morton, Lords Ruthven and Lindsay, and their company, we will find the means with the rest of the nobility to make divorcement between your Majesty and the King, your husband, which shall not need your Grace to meddle therewith." [10] Mary answered that she was agreeable under two conditions: that her divorcement be made lawfully and that it not prejudice her son's title; otherwise she "would rather endure all torments and abide the perils that might chance her in her lifetime. . . ."

Bothwell, standing nearby, helpfully noted that his own parents had been divorced, but "he had succeeded to his father's heritage without any difficulty. . . ." Lethington promised that the nobility "shall find the means that your Majesty shall be quit of him without prejudice of your son." Gesturing to her brother, who had remained silent, he said, "And albeit that my Lord of Murray . . . be less scrupulous for a Protestant, nor your Grace is for a Papist, I am assured he will look through his fingers thereto, and will behold our doings, saying nothing to the same." When Mary reiterated that "nothing by which any spot may be laid to my honour or conscience" must happen, Lethington quietly advised she leave the method to them.[11]

There could be no mistaking their meaning. Both the Queen and Darnley were Catholic, and they had a child and heir. They had received great support from Catholic France and Spain, and at their marriage the Pope had sent money, as well as his blessing. No one in the room—including Mary—believed divorce would be the answer. But the Queen, as well as the others, would be compelled to "look through her fingers" and not be too squeamish at the method of dispatching her husband if she wished to be free. In her compliant attitude—despite her lofty self-justification—Mary Stuart only accelerated her descent on the downward path she had chosen with her impetuous and ill-fated marriage.

In January, 1567, Darnley was at his father's castle in Glasgow. It was his purpose, he said, to "retire out of the Kingdom upon the sea"; a ship was then awaiting in the Clyde to convey him to Flanders. In one of those tremendously inconsequential and seemingly mundane moments when fate overrules the plans of mortal man, Darnley contracted smallpox. As he lay in bed, feverish and uncomfortable, he was startled to learn that his estranged wife was at the gates, seeking admittance. His father, the Earl of Lennox, was suspicious of Mary's sudden appearance, but Darnley's longing to see his wife overcame Lennox's objections, and once inside, Mary hastened to her husband's bedroom. The pleasure of the young King was apparent, for, as Mary later wrote, "he said that he did dream and that he was so glad to see me that he thought he should die. . . ."

In his weakened condition, Darnley was very willing to accept Mary's excuse that she had only recently heard of his illness and her determination to return him to Edinburgh. He said her cruelty "was the cause of his sickness," for Mary had not accepted his "offers and repentance." Darnley could not castigate himself enough. "I confess that I have failed in some things and yet greater faults have been made to you sundry times, which you have forgiven. I am but young, and you will say you have forgiven me divers times. May not a man of my age for lack of counsel, of which I am very destitute, fail twice or thrice, and yet repent and be chastised by experience?" Mary could only answer that she was sorry for his sickness, but why must he take ship and leave Scotland? Darnley said he had nothing to sustain himself or his servants, "as she well knew," but he was obviously eager to take advantage of her presence to work for a reconciliation. He asked her forgiveness for all his past actions, saying, "I crave your pardon and protest that I shall never fail again. I desire no other thing but that we may be together as husband and wife. And if you will not consent thereto, I desire never to rise forth of this bed. . . ."

The fervent pleas touched even Mary's heart. Though her whole being had been given into Bothwell's keeping, the desperate woman could still feel misgivings, as well as resentment, at the necessity for her conduct. The growing duplicity of the role she was undertaking with her credulous young husband wearied her. Later that evening, after she had left the protesting Darnley, she wrote Bothwell. In the flickering candlelight, she penned the first of several letters[12] which would forever after haunt her life and later damn her name:

> He would not let me go, but would have me watch with him. I made as though I thought all to be true, that I would think upon it, and have excused myself from sitting up with him this night, for he sayeth he sleepeth not. You have never heard him speak better nor more humbly; and if I had not proof of his heart of wax, and that mine were not as a diamond, no stroke but coming from your hand could make me but to have pity on him. But fear not, for the plan shall continue to death. . . .

Her remarks, which bordered on callousness, were often interspersed with flashes of conscience, of rebellion, as her spirit flared out at the man for whom she was risking so much. "You are the cause thereof!" she wrote Bothwell abruptly. "For my own revenge, I would not do it. . . . You make me dissemble so much that I am afraid thereof with horror and you make me almost to play the part of a traitor. Remember that if it were not for obeying you, I had rather be dead. My heart bleedeth for it. . . ." The manner of death planned for Darnley haunted Mary, and she pleaded that since she was to take her husband to the baths at Craigmillar "to be purged and cleansed of the sickness," Bothwell find some invention more secret by physic . . ."—presumably poison.

A bleeding heart, however, would not long conceal her secret, and time was very much Mary's enemy. She continued at her husband's bedside, even feeding him with her own hands. When she urged his removal to Craigmillar, the beguiled Darnley said he would go "if they might be at bed and board as husband and wife, and she to leave him no more, and if she promised this on her word, he would go where she pleased. . . ." Mary replied, saying that "if she had not been so minded, she would not have come so far and gave him her hand and faith of her body that she would love and use him as her husband. . . ."[13] Later, again writing Bothwell, her words and actions would haunt her. "I do here a work that I hate much, but I had begun it this morning. Had you not list to laugh to see me so trimly make a lie, at the least dissemble, and to mingle truth therewith?" Then her conscience would momentarily assail her as she wrote, "God forgive me and God knit us together for ever the most faithful couple that ever he did knit together. This is my faith; I will die in it. Excuse me if I write ill, you must guess the one-half. I cannot do withal, for I am ill at ease, and glad to write unto you when other folks be asleep, seeing that I cannot do as they do, according to my desire, that is lie between your arms, my dear life, whom I beseech God to preserve from all ill. . . ." [14]

The next day irritation had replaced her momentary concern for her husband, and she wrote, "Curse be this pocky fellow that troubleth me thus much. . . . He is not much worse, but he is ill-arrayed [disfigured]. I thought I should have been killed by his breath, for it is worse than your uncle's breath, and yet I was set no nearer to him than in a chair by his bolster and he lieth at the further side of the bed." When her husband tried to caress her, Mary was wretched, although Darnley was "the merriest that ever you saw." Plainly she had to convince him to leave the safety of Glasgow while he was in a receptive mood and while his disease still prevented any resumption of their marital relationship. At last he acceded to her wishes and, five days after her arrival, confidently left the Castle, his face swathed in a cloth to hide the pock marks.

In Edinburgh great preparations had been made for his arrival. Not at Holyrood or Edinburgh Castle, but, because of the contagious nature of his disease, Darnley was to be lodged at the desolate Kirk o' Field, the site of a demolished Dominican church and monastery. The small house was built over an arched crypt, and both were in semi-ruinous conditions. Its shabbiness had been concealed by tapestries and rich hangings brought from other residences and a great bedstead, belonging to Mary of Guise, set up for the young King's use in one of the large rooms on the upper floor. A smaller, less sumptuous room had been prepared for Mary on the ground floor.

If Darnley was surprised at his isolation, he made no complaint. He was installed with four servants, one a bodyservant, who would sleep in his room. Mary divided her time between Kirk o' Field house and Holyrood—spending just enough time with her husband so that he could write his father, seven days after his arrival, that his health was greatly improved owing to "the loving care of my love, the Queen, who doth use herself like a natural and loving wife." [15] It was the last communication the Earl of Lennox was to have from his son. The date of the letter, February 7, 1567, was also the last date on which Mary slept at Kirk o' Field. On the ninth she had the great bed dismantled and a more ordinary one put up, telling her husband that they "should lie together in the rich bed . . ." when they were back at Holyrood. That morning her brother, the Earl of Murray, had suddenly decided to visit his sick wife at Fife, some distance from Edinburgh. Later in the day Mary went to see her husband and remained in the house until nearly eleven o'clock. On the night of the ninth two couples were to be married at Holyrood, and a double wedding supper was to be given by the Queen. Using the wedding festivities as an excuse to leave, Mary noted, as she made ready to depart, that it was nearly a year since Rizzio had been murdered. Darnley suddenly remembered her prophecy made at the grave that "a fatter than he should lie near it, ere one twelve months was at an end."[16] Shortly thereafter she took leave of her startled husband and, with a retinue following bearers carrying lighted torches, made her way to Holyrood.

The young King, suddenly apprehensive at her quick departure and curious remark about the dead Rizzio, talked to his servant, and after a cup of wine, he sang a psalm as the servant prepared him for bed.* Once he had retired and the candles were extinguished, Darnley was unable to sleep. Hearing footsteps in the garden, he rushed to the window, where he saw armored figures stealthily approaching. Once they had disappeared into the lower room, the frantic young man climbed out the window, followed by his frightened servant, hoping to escape before they returned. But there were others he had not seen; more than fifty men were by then on the premises. His slight figure was seized, "and he was strangled with the lace sleeves of his shirt," the servant suffering a similar fate. Their bodies were then flung into the garden, probably because by that time the gunpowder was due to explode and no one wished to risk returning the corpses to the inside.

At two in the morning of February 10 the townspeople of Edinburgh were awakened by a tremendous explosion in the direction of the ruined Kirk o' Field. In the shambles of what had been the garden, the two bodies were discovered. Women living in nearby almshouses spoke of seeing cloaked figures entering the premises and of hearing Darnley's muffled pleas for his life. Others who had rushed to the scene had noticed rich costumes and velvet shoes under the plain cloaks of the intruders; one of the shoes was left behind in the owner's haste to flee. It was later remembered that several nobles attending the wedding festivities—including the Earl of Bothwell—had slipped away when the Queen reappeared at the Palace. The great explosion, "as if five and twenty cannon had been fired simultaneously," not only sounded the death knell for a King, but also proved the tocsin by which a much-abused fate served notice that time was running out for a Queen.

Within the next few days, the unbelievable news that the young

*These details were revealed by Thomas Nelson and Anthony Stadon, two of the servants who escaped and later allegedly revealed the details to the Earl of Lennox, Darnley's father.

King of Scotland had been strangled and left to be blown up in an
Edinburgh slum was carried to the courts of Europe. "The matter is so
horrible and strange, as we believe the like was never heard of in any
country," wrote Mary to Archbishop James Beaton, her emissary at
the French court. There, as in other courts where political assassination
was not unknown—and tolerated if the results were sufficiently justifiable—there was stunned and silent disbelief. That Darnley had been
a blatant sacrifice by nobles who barely acknowledged him and by the
wife who had no further use for him was quickly recognized, if not
exactly approved. A subtle poisoning, a tragic hunting accident—any
other manner of removal—might possibly have been more acceptable.
But for months, Mary's attitude toward her husband and her liaison
with Bothwell had been common knowledge, and once the Queen
forfeited the protection of the royal aura she was a lost woman. For one
of her birth to have allied herself so openly and so disastrously with
such a reprobate as Bothwell sealed her fate as surely as the crumpled
and charred figure of her husband blackened the proud Guise and
Stuart names.

The monarchs of France and Spain maintained a telling silence; the
Pope lamented his "lost daughter," and across Scotland, the unbelievable horror of Darnley's death spread. In the towns and cities,
highlands and lowlands, the castle strongholds bordered on misty
lochs, the death of a King and the sin of a Queen were discussed by
indignant Scotsmen, "who abhor the detestable murder of their King
. . . and shame . . . to the whole nation. . . ." [17]

There was one voice which did not accuse. The Queen of England,
genuinely shocked at her cousin's violent death, told de Silva that she
could not believe "that the Queen of Scotland can be to blame for so
dreadful a thing. . . ." When Sir Robert Melville, brother of Sir James,
brought the disastrous news to England, Elizabeth reacted as a friend
and kinswoman and wrote Mary Stuart in her own hand:

MADAME,
    My ears have been so astounded, my mind so disturbed, my heart so
shocked at the news of the abominable murder of your late husband, that
even yet I can scarcely rally my spirits to write to you; and however I
would express my sympathy in your sorrow for his loss, so, to tell you
plainly what I think, my grief is more for you than for him.
    Oh, Madame, I should ill fulfil the part of either a faithful cousin or an
affectionate friend, if I were to content myself with saying pleasant things
to you and make no effort to preserve your honour. I cannot but tell you
what all the world is thinking. Men say that, instead of seizing the
murderers, you are looking through your fingers while they escape; that

you will not punish those who have done you so great a service, as though the thing would never have taken place had not the doers of it been assured of impunity.

For myself, I beg you to believe that I would not harbour such a thought for all the wealth of the world, nor would I entertain in my heart so ill a guest, or think so badly of any Prince that breathes. Far less could I so think of you, to whom I desire all imaginable good, and all blessings which you yourself would wish for. For this very reason I exhort, I advise, I implore you deeply to consider of the matter—at once, if it be the nearest friend you have, to lay your hands upon the man who has been guilty of the crime—to let no interest, no persuasion, keep you from proving to everyone that you are a noble Princess and a loyal wife. I do not write thus earnestly because I doubt you, but for the love I bear towards you. You may have wiser councillors than I am—I can well believe it—but even Our Lord, as I remember, had a Judas among the twelve; while I am sure that you have no friend more true than I, and my affection may stand you in good stead as the subtle wit of others.[18]

ELIZABETH [18]

Elizabeth's concern is plain, and it extended to the bereaved Countess of Lennox, Darnley's mother, still incarcerated—albeit very comfortably—in the Tower of London. The Queen sent Lady Cecil and Lady Howard to break the news to the woman who had had such high hopes for her son and lived to see their realization—and the subsequent doom to which her ambition had brought him. The Countess became so overwrought that Elizabeth sent her own doctor to attend her, and later she was removed to the home of Sir Richard Sackville. There she saw Sir Robert Melville, and hearing his account of the tragedy, "she used words against his Queen," whom she suspected "to have had some hand in the business. . . ." The Spanish ambassador, de Silva, reflected the Countess' suspicions and said the English Catholics were divided, "the friends of the King holding to the Queen's guilt, and her adherents to the contrary." There was no doubt in the mind of Darnley's father, the Earl of Lennox, who, in great anguish, demanded vengeance for his dead son. From his Glasgow stronghold, Lennox thundered at the silence and inaction surrounding the murder, at the lack of inquiry on the part of her who should have been the first to demand its solution.

Lennox was more than justified in his suspicions. When the Queen was informed of her husband's death, "she was in great grief and kept her chamber all that day." That was about the extent of Mary Stuart's official mourning. Instead of the weeks or months of keeping to her chamber, of insisting on a formal investigation into the crime and locking up any and all suspects until the inquiry, the Queen was silent. If ever subterfuge, caution, pretense and sheer courage were called for, it was immediately after Darnley's death as the smoke and grime of the Kirk o' Field explosion still hung over the city. Had the Queen shown herself outraged or prostrate with grief, had she lamented her husband's death and instigated a prompt and thorough investigation, all might have been well.

Instead, she did nothing.

Mary's silence—if one wishes to be charitable—may also have stemmed from pure violent shock and, possibly, some lingering remorse. Not for Darnley's death but for the position in which it had placed her. Tense, harried, knowing she had involved herself to such an extent that no retreat was possible, she required perhaps more physical strength than she possessed to lament a death for which she could only feel relief. Perhaps there were stirrings of conscience. When one Cullen, one of the alleged assailants, later confessed, "The King was long a-dying and in his strength made debate for his life," Mary might have lingered over Darnley's last moments, wondering if he had guessed the degree of her implication, remembering how she had led him, by sweet words and promises, to his death. Worn out with misgiving and tension, still clutching the secret of her pregnancy, she could do little but maintain a stoic silence. Mechanically, she went through the routine of signing dispatches to the courts of Europe, giving her carefully worded version of the tragedy, intimating that it was an act of God she had not died also, "for we assure ourselves it was designed as well for ourselves as for the King. . . ." This, too, added to the Queen's guilt, for it was well known by citizens and foreigners alike that Mary, on leaving Darnley, had proceeded through the streets of Edinburgh with lighted torches—which the murderers well knew also.

Perhaps each day, as she went through the motions of living, the Queen convinced herself she would be believed. Mary Stuart never possessed the genius that was Elizabeth Tudor's: a capacity to relate to her subjects, to know their thoughts and feelings and anticipate their reactions. Perhaps Mary convinced herself that her words were enough, that by describing her husband's death as "horrible and strange," her callousness would be accepted as shock. Perhaps in that tight little world of royal privilege in which she had always dwelled —again so different from Elizabeth, who had suffered deprivation and imprisonment in her youth—she was convinced that her story offered very little reason for objection by her people or her fellow monarchs. She was the Queen; she had spoken. Her nobles were behind her and just as deeply implicated. She had no fear. She was now free to wed her lover, give birth to his child and enjoy the destiny fate had handed her.

But it was not enough. Edinburgh citizens expected some official retribution, and daily the Queen of Scotland's guilt—or at least her complicity and knowledge of the crime—was proclaimed by her actions. People stood at the Cow Gate, near the Tolbooth, at the Market Cross, women in shawls clutched against the February wind and murmured to their neighbors against the Queen. Their husbands, tight-lipped, repeated the bits of gossip which had infiltrated the town. How, as the Queen had left Kirk o' Field, she had met one of her servants, a Frenchman nicknamed Paris, as he emerged from the cellar and had said, in merry conspiratorial fashion, "Jesu, Paris! How begrimed you are!" Women near the site who had seen many figures enter and had heard Darnley's last words, "Oh my brothers, have pity on me for the love of Him who had mercy on all the world!" told and retold their story. The Scots were a proud and defiant people; they talked of the dishonor the Queen had brought to them, engulfing the country in disgrace. Few of them had cared for Darnley personally. But a King was a King, and once dead, the weak and unpopular young man, who had been such a source of contention for all his brief stay in Scotland, became a martyr. Perversely in death, Darnley assumed the importance he had never enjoyed in life.

Incredibly, there was no state funeral. Darnley's body was left in a humble lodging near Kirk o' Field in the care of a groom, Sandy Dereham, and on February 15 he was buried in the royal tombs near Mary's father, James V. The next day Mary went to Seton and, with ill-disguised pleasure, enjoyed herself in games of golf and archery. She was joined several days later by Bothwell and several of the incriminated Lords.

When this news was relayed to England, Elizabeth was aghast. Memories arose of a similar occasion when *she* had been the target of suspicion, when all eyes were on her and tongues had wagged to implicate her in the death of Amy Robsart Dudley. She knew how she had saved her Crown during that unhappy time. She had promptly dispatched Lord Robert to seclusion, ordered an inquiry and then stood on the fringes and attended to her royal duties. Sir Henry Killigrew, whom Elizabeth had sent to Scotland to see first hand what impact Darnley's murder had made, wrote "that there was a general misliking among the Commons and others, which abhor the detestable murder of their King, a shame, as they suppose to the whole nation. . . ." [19] When the Earl of Lennox wrote Elizabeth asking that she insist on the inquiry for which Mary showed so little interest, she was quick to agree. It was inconceivable to Elizabeth that Mary should treat her Crown so lightly, and she urged her cousin to cooperate. Had Mary, at this point, made *any* gesture, much might have been forgiven, but her cold indifference, her complete withdrawal only infuriated the people and puzzled those not implicated in the crime.

But what could Mary do? She could not summon the Council to seek lawful revenge when many of its members were as guilty as she. The Queen's hands were tied. She could not arrest Lethington or Bothwell; she could not implicate those of her nobles who had known of the plot, yet done nothing to stop it. And so she, too, did nothing. And daily, instances of Mary's perverse behavior titillated listeners in the inns and taverns. Priests harangued from their pulpits and hinted at responsibility "in high places." Overnight placards appeared in the Market Place and nailed to the Church doors, placards which bore Bothwell's name and portrait, labeled "Bloody Bothwell" and the words "Here is the King's murderer." When Archbishop Beaton wrote Mary that the murder was a *cause célèbre* in France and advised Mary to "take a rigorous vengeance thereof, that rather than it be not actually taken, it appears to me better in this world that you had lost life and all . . ." [20] Mary felt compelled to make some gesture. She offered £2,000 to anyone who had information of the crime, but none dared claim it, as Bothwell had been heard to threaten he would "wash his hands in the blood of anyone who dared accuse him." When, ultimately, Catherine de Medici said that if Mary did not attempt to revenge the death of the King, "they [the Valois] would not only think her dishonoured but would be her enemies," Mary fixed April 12 as the inquiry date. Because of Bothwell's threats and the emotional atmosphere existing in Edinburgh, the Earl of Lennox could hardly expect an impartial hearing, and he sought Elizabeth's help once more to seek a postponement. In response to his appeal, the English Queen again wrote to Mary from Westminster on April 8. There is a noticeable coolness and irritation present in this letter not apparent previously:

MADAME,

I should not have been so inconsiderate as to trouble you with this letter had it not been that the bond of charity towards the ruined and the prayers of the miserable constrained me.

I understand that a proclamation has been issued by you, Madame, that the trial of those suspected of being concerned in the murder of your late husband and my late cousin, would take place on the 12th of this month. This is a thing which it is most necessary should not be hidden in mystery or craftiness, which in such a case might happen, and the father and friends of the dead gentleman have humbly requested that I should pray you to postpone the date because they are aware that these iniquitous persons are contriving by violence what they could not do normally. Therefore I cannot do otherwise, for the love of you, whom it touches most and for the consolation of the innocent, than exhort you to grant this request which, if it be denied, will turn suspicion largely on you.

For the love of God, Madame, use such sincerity and prudence in this matter which touches you so nearly that all the world may feel justified in believing you innocent of so enormous a crime, which, if you were not, would be good cause for degrading you from the rank of Princess and bringing upon you the scorn of the vulgar. Sooner than that should befall you I would wish you an honourable grave rather than a dishonoured life.

You see, Madame, I treat you as my daughter and assure you that if I had one, I would wish for her nothing better than I desire for you, as our Lord God may bear witness, and to Whom I pray with all my heart that He will inspire you to do what will be most to your honour and to the consolation of your friends.

With my very cordial recommendation as to the one for whom one wishes the greatest good that may be possible in this world.[21]

ELIZABETH

Mary never received Elizabeth's letter, and it is questionable that it would have made any difference to her actions if she had. The letter was given to the Provost Marshal at Holyrood, who informed the messenger the Queen was asleep. Ultimately Lethington passed it to Bothwell, who pocketed it while cursing the messenger "for bringing the English villain that sought to procure the stay of the trial."

The inquiry proceeded as planned, and the forthright denunciation by Lennox of the Queen's lover deemed it a failure from the beginning. The next day, on April 12, Bothwell left Holyrood as a foolish Mary waved gaily to him from a window. In a mockery of justice, he rode along Canongate with arrogant confidence toward the Tolbooth with sword and dagger apparent, accompanied by a huge force of followers, "their iron skull caps gleaming dully." Conversely, by tradition, the returning Lennox could not bring any more than six men with him when he reentered the City and, being apprised of the situation which he would hardly leave alive, was forced to send a representative to read his protest, thereby losing his case by default. Compounding the fiasco so obvious to all were the judges. They had been selected from the nobles or from the Council, and either bribed, intimidated or, to some extent, involved in the crime themselves, they gave the only verdict possible: Bothwell was exonerated from "any art and part of the said slaughter of the King" on the mere ground that "no accusation had been brought against him."

Daily the cancer of resentment and suspicion grew in Edinburgh, and Mary, by her imprudent actions, did nothing to check it. She presented Bothwell with additional church lands, her mother's furs, jewels, monies and even—the ultimate sacrilege—her dead husband's rich clothes. When she insisted that Parliament pass an act making it a crime "that set up any writing that speaks anything of him," James Stuart, the Earl of Murray, had had enough. Murray had allegedly tried to arrest Sir James Balfour as one of the instigators of Darnley's murder, and Bothwell had prohibited his doing so. Murray could well see where Mary's actions were taking her and, wishing to leave before the holocaust, asked his sister's permission "to see Venice and Milan." Several weeks later he was telling all who would listen at the English court that he felt dishonored to stay any longer in a kingdom "where so strange and terrible a crime remained unpunished."

Mary was past redemption. Everything that had happened previously was of little consideration beside the fact of her obsessive love for Bothwell and her pregnancy. She was so enthralled by her lover she was heard to say that "she cared not to lose France, England and her own country for him, and will go with him to the world's end in a white petticoat, rather than leave him."[22] Her one aim now was to recover whatever she might of the shreds of her life, to retain whatever honor and dignity she could before the full scope of her folly was evident. She must wed Bothwell, and soon. Yet she must have ample public reason for doing so other than the private one which remained as yet unknown. Her resort—extreme in its folly and lack of regard for her royal position—was virtually the only thing the distraught woman could imagine. A Queen could not have an illegitimate child; therefore that child must be given some semblance of legitimacy. Mary's solution was to allow herself to be kidnapped publicly by her lover. On a visit to see young James, she was apprehended near Gogar Burn at Almond Bridge, between Edinburgh and Linlithgow. There Bothwell, with 100 followers "with lifted pikes and bared swords," blocked the Queen's train, threatening to attack unless she willingly came with him. Mary, firmly insisting "she wished to avoid bloodshed," complacently left her retinue to go with Bothwell to alleged captivity at Dunbar. There she remained for twelve days, presumably dishonored and ravished—with the only solution that she must wed very soon.

The plot, shoddy and incongruous, fooled no one. Kirkcaldy of Grange wrote the Earl of Bedford, "This Queen will never cease till she has wrecked all the honest men of this realm. She was minded to cause Bothwell to ravish her to the end that she may sooner gain the marriage which she promised before she caused the murder of her husband. . . ." [23] Bothwell's entry into Edinburgh, "leading the Queen's Majesty by the bridle as captive," on May 6 only helped increase her degradation. "It is pitiful," wrote another of her countrymen, "to watch this excellent Princess hastening to destruction without anyone calling her attention to the danger. . . ." Three days later Mary appeared before her Lords and said she had "formally pardoned her captor," assuring them she was "a free agent." The Lords refused to listen and told the Queen they would never consider her free "so long as she be in the Earl's company, albeit he may persuade her Majesty to say otherwise." [24]

Mary had had her last chance. Had she even, at this late date, forsaken Bothwell, she might have kept her Crown, somewhat tarnished to be sure, but with time and another marriage, much might have been forgiven. But the Queen of Scotland was lost; if her devouring passion for Bothwell could be put aside, the fact of her pregnancy could not. When the banns for her wedding were published just three months after Darnley's murder, even the Lords were shocked. It was one thing to wish for a husband's death and connive for it; in this they were as guilty as the Queen. It was another to wed one of his murderers, and their rather politic sense of honor was more affronted at this than at the manner of the King's death. They had kept their bargain, but the Queen had not kept hers. She had not taken them into her full confidence. Had she wanted Bothwell as a lover, they would have "looked through their fingers." But they would not accept the arrogant Border Lord as King Consort, with power over them.

The court and citizens of Scotland were speechless at the affront. Their horror was reflected in the minister's comment: "I took heaven to witness that I abhorred and detested that marriage, as odious and scandalous to the world. . . ." With adequate bribery, a quick divorce had been secured from Bothwell's accommodating wife, and on May 15, 1567, Mary Stuart—she who had been the wife of two Kings—knelt at midnight "in utter abasement" in the Chapel at Holyrood and, in a Protestant ceremony, married James Hepburn, the Earl of Bothwell, rapist, Border brigand and murderer.

Until the moment of her wedding, Mary and the Lords might have salvaged something from the Kirk o' Field ruins. They were all equally guilty, and between them, memory might have been shortened and the monarchy saved. They had agreed to rid her of her husband. They had never intended, however, to help her to another. And to have her choice be Bothwell, of all the nobles of the realm, was an insult they could and would not tolerate.

The ink was scarcely dry on the wedding documents before it was evident that in raising Bothwell higher than any other noble, Mary Stuart had flung the last hope of sovereignty—and redemption—away. In her condition, she could do little else. But from the moment she took her wedding vows, the final decision was no longer hers.

Chapter Fifteen

Along with the rest of the civilized world, Elizabeth was scandalized by the Queen of Scotland's precipitate marriage. Even though Mary had tarnished her religious beliefs by marrying a divorced man in a Protestant ceremony, the blow to Catholicism did not—in Elizabeth's eyes—lessen the blow to the Scottish monarchy itself. As she walked with Randolph in the garden at Whitehall, Elizabeth unburdened herself, telling of her "great misliking of the Queen's doing, which now she doth so much detest that she is ashamed of her...." She told Randolph of her fear "lest Bothwell, having the upper hand ... will reign again with the French and either make away with the Prince or send him into France...." [1] While Mary's marriage had certainly diminished her personal stature, as well as the threat to Elizabeth's throne, there was still young James to consider. He must never fall into French hands, as Mary had in her youth.

The disastrous union of the Queen of Scots and Bothwell again emphasized the necessity for Elizabeth's marriage. Never, for one moment, did the relentless pressure to wed lessen. Everyone's hopes were revived when the Queen sent the Earl of Sussex, a devoted subject, to the Austrian court to meet her perennial suitor, the Archduke Charles. The choice of Sussex was inspired, for he was recognized as an intense opponent of the Earl of Leicester, and this doubtless played some part in his selection, for again Elizabeth was delaying making any decision. In a long letter to his Queen, Sussex extolled Charles' virtues:

> His Highness is of person higher, surely, a good deal than my Lord Marquess [Northampton]; his hair of head and beard, a light auburn; his face well-proportioned, amiable, and of very good complexion, without

show of redness or over-paleness; his countenance and speech cheerful, very courteous, but stately. His body is very well shaped, without deformity or blemish; his hands very good and fair; his legs clean, well-proportioned, and of sufficient bigness for his stature; his foot as good as may be. So as, upon my duty to your Majesty, I find not one deformity, misshape, or anything to be noted worthy of misliking in his whole person; but contrariwise, I find his whole shape to be good in all respects, and such as is rarely found in a Prince.[2]

This paragon also spoke German, Spanish, Italian and Latin. Sussex's visit had impressed the Habsburg court, which had previously regarded Elizabeth's intentions as "frivolous," and Charles himself seemed awed by the emissary from the great English Queen. His natural fear of rejection led him to say, "I have always had good hope of the Queen's honourable dealing in this matter, yet I have heard so much of her disposition not to marry, as might give me cause to suspect the worse. . . ." But Sussex allayed all fears. The Archduke even agreed, upon marriage, to attend the reformed services of the English church, provided he might have a small chapel for his own use, where no Englishman need be present at the Mass. This restriction presented Elizabeth with the opportunity for endless rebuttal. Sussex, at the Austrian court, bitterly denounced the influence of Robert Dudley, the Earl of Leicester, saying that "he knew who was at work in the vineyard at home, but if God should ever put it to his dear mistress' heart to divide the weeds from the grain, she would reap the better harvest here."

The astute Sussex was right. Robert was once more secure in Elizabeth's affections, although, as some courtiers had noted, it was "somewhat toned down." After the debacle invited by his flirtation with Lettice Knollys, some did not trust his rapid return to the Queen's favor. So much so that de Silva, the Spanish ambassador, was frankly astonished when, as he left the Privy Chamber after an audience, "the Queen . . . called me back and said she would be glad if I would show some love and friendship to Lord Robert, as I was wont to do."[3] Others, such as Cecil and the Duke of Norfolk, deplored his influence with Elizabeth, especially regarding marriage. While Sussex negotiated and waited, Leicester did not hesitate to point out to the Queen how her sister's marriage had "put England in danger of the Spanish yoke." For a Queen to marry a foreigner, she must be "continually conversant with strange customs and a strange language," and he said "that the children of a foreign bed had generally an odd inter-mixture in their composition." Playing on the Queen's pride in her "mere Englishness,"

Leicester emphasized that "she would only add strength and increase to her husband's dominions" while, at the same time, having to subject herself to another's command "and lay open the secrets of her kingdom to a stranger. . . ." [4] Leicester's reasons were not entirely unselfish. He still hoped to wed Elizabeth and often reminded her that her own father had elevated an English subject to the nobility and married her in preference to a foreign union. There was just enough common sense and logic in his argument to appeal to the woman desperately seeking to evade marriage, and she was only too willing and ready to believe his contention that "England had no need of foreign aid, but had strength enough to defend itself against any exterior force." [5] Well might Sussex lament "he . . . who was at work in the vineyard at home."

As the tenth year of her reign approached, Elizabeth could feel pride in her countrymen and in her Crown. Her stewardship of England—that privilege which made all else commonplace and consequently of little importance—had been rewarding. "Lack of money is the principal sickness in this court," wrote Cecil to Sir Henry Sidney. Yet while the Queen knew she would never be rich, her frugality and her talent for spending each penny where it would do the most good, had resulted in a solvent Exchequer. Though religious dissension remained quiet, she realized that such dissension would probably outlive her; the teachings of centuries could not be replaced in a few generations. If there was no nationwide enthusiasm for Protestantism, there had been no great violence during her ten years' sovereignty either.

Trade was flourishing, although the fishing industry had suffered—the unexpected result of a new religious creed which allowed meat on Friday. Young King Edward, during his short reign, had prescribed "due and godly abstinence [from fish] as a means to virtue to subdue men's bodies to their soul and spirit." Thus those who lived "by the trade and mystery of fishing" had to seek other means of livelihood, and England was now in the odd position of having its own waters fished by Frenchmen and Flemings, while parts of Ireland were fished by Scots and Spaniards. A new breed of English mariner was being born in these same coastal waters. Merchant seamen, they called themselves, while "water thieves" or "pirates" seemed more apt to those who crossed their watery path. Young Englishmen who had fled the Protestantism of Edward or the religious excesses of Mary's reign had gathered together in the inlet waters of the Irish coast or across the "broad ditch" of the English Channel along the coast of France and the Low Countries. Proud West Country names—Carews, Tremaynes, Horseys and Killigrews—they attracted similarly adventurous souls possessing exuberant spirits with nonexistent consciences and embarked on outright piracy. Even Elizabeth's childhood infatuation, the Lord High Admiral Thomas Seymour, the husband of Queen Katherine Parr, had had his fling with piracy in the Scilly Isles.

Commerce was expanding in a manner Elizabeth's father and grandfather would have regarded as incredible. Freed from the demands of Catholicism and not yet dominated by Puritanism's tyranny, the average Englishman had access to luxuries either heretofore unobtainable or else so expensive as to be possible for only a few. Funded by private monies, ships crammed with English goods, particularly wool, challenged the trade monopoly of Spain and Portugal, a practice not easily tolerated by those two mighty nations. In exchange for their wool, the English returned with perfumes, spices, rice, cotton, indigo and jewels from India. Other ships entered the great Pool of London with "Turkey" carpets, velvets, damasks, cloth of gold and silver and "robes wrought with diver colours" from Persia. From Russia came ermines, sables, wolf and bearskins, as well as the more mundane ropes, cables, pitch, tar and masts for yet more new ships. Cargoes from the New World contributed sugar, rare woods, gold, silver, lemons, oranges, oils and even pearls. While this brought a variety of wealth, luxury and comfort to the once-austere home of the average Englishman, it disturbed Elizabeth's minister William Cecil that the wool which paid for such luxury was obtained by withdrawing workers from agriculture, while landowners continued to turn their lands and tenants over to the more profitable sheep raising. The import of wine "four times as much in a year as in 'ancient times' " Cecil considered particularly irksome, because "it enriched France whose power England ought not to increase." Taverns multiplied and were "an evident cause of the disorder amongst the vulgar." [6]

In the beginning, Spain and Portugal tolerated the efforts of an upstart England for daring to infringe on their territories.* England had, in the past quarter century, sent William Hawkins to the coast of Guinea. Sir Hugh Willoughby had sailed in search of the "Isles of Cathay," landing to an ill-fated end in the Arctic instead. Other explorers had been to the Levant, to Constantinople and Jerusalem. Independent mariners, merchant adventurers as they called them-

---

*In 1493, Pope Alexander VI had drawn a line from pole to pole "one hundred leagues west of the Azores." All lands to be discovered east of this line belonged to Portugal, those discovered west of this meridian belonged to Spain.

selves, disdained by the established Guilds, loaded their ships and, in a spirit of adventure sparked by the lust for gold and glory, sailed wherever the wind and a market would take them. They did not hesitate to dabble in the slave trade which had previously been the monopoly of Spain and Portugal. Such infringements had not helped relations between England and the two great Catholic nations. In 1567, young John Hawkins and a relative, Francis Drake, lay at San Juan de Ulúa, the roadstead to Veracruz in the Gulf of Mexico. Alongside were five Spanish ships, and the sailors taunted the Englishmen on the size of their smaller vessels. One word led to another, and to the Spaniards' surprise, the English accepted the challenge and fought heroically, escaping with two ships. But the gauntlet had been flung, and its repercussions would be far-reaching. From that moment, military and seafaring men all over England "fretted and desired war with Spain," and every Spanish ship was fair game for the stout men of Cornwall and Devon, who valued Thucydides' claim that the ancient Greeks had practiced piracy and "the employment carried no disgrace with it, but rather glory and honor . . ." [7] as an excuse for their larceny. Later two ships, the *Dragon* and the *Swan* commanded by Francis Drake, went searching for revenge in Spanish waters, capturing "a few goodly barques laden with merchandise." As Elizabeth had closed her ears and eyes to her sailors' pleas to revenge the national honor by a war with Spain, so she closed her ears and eyes as her men towed their stolen prizes home. She could do little else; often she was a financial partner in the ventures.

Not all were so lucky. In 1563, William Cecil estimated that twenty-six English sailors had been captured, suffered questioning by the Spanish Inquisition and were burned at the stake. Nor did the English adventurers stop at Spanish ships. During the same year, a quarrel broke out between English and French sailors at Gibraltar, and the English, unable to resist, let cables slip from three or four of their vessels, "opened fire and attempted to run the Frenchmen down." It was an incredible breach of the peace, an insult to both France and Spain, and this time the English were taken prisoner. Spanish authorities decided to make an example of them and sentenced some 240 to a slow death as galley slaves. Eventually, after long negotiations, 80 men who had survived their savage punishment were returned to England. Their arrival only induced the desire for revenge, and as one incident piled upon another, it was evident a new age of piracy was abroad on the seas. By late 1567 de Silva could angrily confront Elizabeth and say, "Your mariners rob my master's subjects on the sea, and trade where they are forbidden to go. They plunder our people in the streets of your towns, they attack our vessels in your very harbours, and take prisoners from them!" He said that "we have borne with these things, attributing them rather to passion or rudeness of manners than to any deliberate purpose of wrong. . . ."[8] Yet despite his intense recriminations, little was done. Elizabeth considered that piracy in some form had been going on since her father's time, and what protest she did make to please de Silva was "a sop to irate victims of the pillage" with little actual outright redress.

However she might overlook the shortcomings of her mariners, Elizabeth could not close her eyes or ears to the deteriorating condition of her cousin, Mary Stuart. Within a month, abandoned by Spain, France and the Pope, who termed her marriage "dishonourable to God and to herself," a storm of controversy was stimulated by the discontented Lords. Those few who remained by the Queen's side, such as Huntly and Lethington, were alternately cajoled or threatened. Balfour, one of those most deeply implicated in Darnley's death, abandoned Mary with the promise of the Keepership of Edinburgh Castle at the appropriate time. The Lords were concerned with the fate of Mary's baby, and when the Queen commanded the return of her son from Stirling Castle, she was told the child would be surrendered only into a custody which excluded Bothwell. Incensed by their action, Mary became even more distressed as the days passed. Bothwell's jealousy led to many scenes which emphasized the melancholy change in her life in which she had seemingly surrendered child, honor and power.

But she still deeply loved the man for whom she had risked so much—and she still had her Crown. Money was dangerously low, and afraid the Lords might make some attempt against her husband, she was "driven thereunto by necessity" to melt down her plate. When that proved insufficient, Mary was forced to have the splendid gold font which Elizabeth had sent for James' christening also melted. As it was done, some glimmer of what she had sacrificed was borne home to the luxury-loving Mary, and as one English observer noted, "the Queen wept bitterly." It all had its effect. Du Croc, the French ambassador, who had hoped to counsel Mary, wrote, "The Queen was the most changed woman of face that in so little time without extremity of sickness they have seen. . . ."[9]

Within three weeks, the emotional climate in Holyrood was such that neither Bothwell nor Mary felt safe within its confines. On June 5 they left Edinburgh for Borthwick Castle, "four leagues from Edin-

burgh," from which Mary commanded a muster at Muirhead Abbey
for "all noblemen, knights, esquires, gentlemen and yeomen . . . with
six days' victuals, and every man to come in warlike manner," for her
defense.[10] Bothwell similarly sent word to his supporters to collect at
Melrose. The contempt in which the Scottish people held the Queen's
marriage—and the Queen's husband—was seen in the pathetic few
"with no hearts to fight in that quarrel" who responded to their
monarch's call. Taking advantage of the situation, the Lords, led by
Hume, Lindsay and Mar, besieged the Castle, calling for Bothwell,
"bidding him come out!—'traitor, murderer, and butcher.' " [11] At his
wife's urging, Bothwell slipped out "by the postern gate among the
trees," as Mary, "wanting other means for her revenge" and to keep the
Lords distracted, reviled them from the battlements. When du Croc
sought to intercede and bring about a reconciliation between the
Queen and the Lords, Mary was loyal to Bothwell, saying that "if the
Lords meant to attack her husband, she desired no agreement with
them." [12] Later that evening, dressed in men's riding clothes, booted
and spurred, Mary also abandoned the Castle and joined Bothwell at
a prearranged hiding place. Several hours later, dusty and tired, they
arrived at Dunbar Castle at three o'clock in the morning.

At Edinburgh, the returning Lords entered the Market Place and
publicly declared their intention "to pursue their revenge for the death
of the King." Their forces had been augmented by 800 horsemen,
retainers of that Lord Mar in whose custody Mary's son had been left.
Edinburgh Castle was surrendered by the new Keeper, Sir James
Balfour, "a very traitor!" wrote du Croc. "No one in the town offered
any resistance . . . which makes us think that the plot was a large one
and well understood by those concerned in it," noted the despairing
Frenchman.

By the end of the week Mary had mustered some 600 horsemen,
hackbuteers and three portable field guns, and when these were joined
by 3,500 of Bothwell's followers, the decision was made to try to regain
control of Edinburgh Castle. With anticipated support from Lord
Fleming and the Hamilton clan, Mary and Bothwell left Dunbar en
route to Edinburgh. The heat was oppressive; the land was so parched
even the heather had shrunk in the heat. For ease in riding, the Queen
had dressed in a white linen blouse, "its sleeves tied with points," and
a short red plaid kilt and red velvet hat. She was heartened by cheers as
she passed through small villages where people brought drinking water
and welcome refreshments. Their gestures lifted Mary's tired spirits.
Her first month of married life had been one of disappointment,
heartache and discomfort; anxiety was a constant companion. It did

not abate when news was brought from Edinburgh that hearing of Mary's journey, the rebel Lords were advancing to meet her.

On June 15, 1567, the two forces met at Carberry Hill overlooking the little town of Musselburgh. The rebel force was commanded by Kirkcaldy of Grange, a particularly bitter antagonist of the Queen's. A banner, consisting of a sheet spread between two spears held aloft, was in the vanguard. On it lay a dead man crumpled under a tree. Nearby a child on its knees cried, "Judge and Revenge my Cause, O Lord!" Had Mary been able to discern the banner at a distance, she would have recognized the figures of her husband and child.

Once they had come within sight of each other, both forces maneuvered defensively. At the same time, du Croc, who had arrived at the scene after giving the Lords a three-hour start "so it would not look as if I supported them," was pressed into service. Under a flag of truce and accompanied by fifty horsemen, the French ambassador crossed the brook which separated the two forces to where Mary rested on a rock. The Queen was pathetically glad to see him, but less enthusiastic at his message. The Lords were willing to negotiate a truce, he told the tired woman, if she would abandon her husband. Mary's response was fierce. The Lords had vindicated Bothwell "of the deed of which they now accused him," she cried, and she would receive them only "if they would acknowledge their fault and ask her pardon!"[13] In the meantime, Bothwell joined them and "in a very loud voice . . . and with a very bold manner" asked "if he was the one they wanted?" Belligerently, he asked what harm he had done the Lords? "He declared," wrote du Croc later, "that he had never thought of displeasing anyone, but rather desired to please everybody, and that they were only envious of his greatness. Fortune, he said, was to be won by anyone who chose, and there was not one of them who would not like to be in his place!" Bothwell, however, knew his former confederates well, and he realized they would never have proceeded so far if they had not thought victory possible. When he offered to meet any one of his enemies "of suitable rank" in a single combat, Mary quickly interrupted and cried, "I will not suffer that!" Bothwell then begged du Croc ". . . for the honour of God . . . to put an end to the trouble in which he saw the Queen, whose suffering was extreme. . . ."

In the meantime, several of the rebel Lords, perhaps not trusting the ambassador, had ventured into the brook, and Bothwell, glancing nonchalantly at them, likened du Croc "to that go-between who, unable to bring about a peace between the two armies of Scipio and Hannibal . . . took up a position where he had watched the greatest pastime he had ever seen. . . ." His bantering tone did not deceive the ambassador, who, realizing that both the Queen and Bothwell were adamant, prepared to leave. While never any admirer of Bothwell, du Croc was impressed with Mary's consort in spite of himself. He later wrote, "I must say that I heard him speak with the confidence of a great captain who would lead his army gallantly and wisely, and . . . estimated that he would have the best of it if his men remained faithful. I praised him that he was in no way perturbed at seeing his enemy resolute, while he could not be assured of half his own men. . . ." [14] Mary did not share Bothwell's strength; her eyes were wet with tears as she watched du Croc rejoin the forces on the opposite side of the brook.

Owing to the heat, both forces remained quiet during the morning. The Lords maneuvered for position; they were fearful of the Queen's safety if they attacked. In Mary's camp, Bothwell's men, faced with the long delay in which they had time to think (and observe the enemy close at hand), lost what little inclination they had to fight and spoke of asking for terms. Some of those on the fringes melted into the glades, where not a leaf turned in the whisperless heat. Others commenced to drink at the brook's edge, after which they crossed to meet friends and relatives in the rebel ranks. Mary sent for Kirkcaldy, who soon joined her under a flag of truce. The Queen asked "if there were no means of making some agreement for the safety of the Duke?" When the old Scotsman answered, "We have all sworn to die or to obtain possession of him," Mary realized she was beaten. Her one thought then was to see Bothwell safe. Kirkcaldy said the Lords would submit and profess allegiance to her once more if she would leave her husband. Surprisingly, he also promised "to do his utmost to prevent him from being pursued" if Bothwell would then flee.

When more activity was noticed in the rebel ranks, Mary became frantic. Though Bothwell had not appeared eager to run, he was at length overcome by the Queen, "who persuaded him to absent himself for a time till the issue of the coming Parliament should be known." Undoubtedly both of them believed that once Mary had regained her authority, she would possess enough power to arrange a return to her side. Her one thought now was to accept the Lords' offer of loyalty in exchange for her husband's safety. Taking her at her word, Bothwell embraced his wife, mounted his horse and, accompanied by thirty spearmen, left the field. It is unlikely either he or Mary even vaguely sensed they would never see each other again.

Brokenhearted and drooping in spirit, Mary accompanied Kirkcaldy to the waiting Lords. Crossing the brook, they passed through the ranks of soldiers, where a rumbling sound greeted her appearance. The rumble broke into a roar as several voices commenced calling obscenities to Mary. "Burn the whore!" several shouted as Mary, her face a study in grief, looked at them disbelievingly. A few of the Lords attempted to quiet the outburst and "rode up and down striking at the speakers with the flat of their swords to silence them." But it was useless. The men had spent hours in the merciless heat while their sovereign Lady dallied on the opposite bank, and they now had little pity. As the Queen passed between the ranks, they waved the banner with Darnley's crumpled figure in her face. Mary had not eaten since the previous night and "could scarce be held in her saddle for grief and faintness." Her weakness gave way to rage as she flung a hand outward to avoid being touched by the banner. She rode on, clutching whatever dignity she could in the humble dust-stained and rumpled riding clothes. Du Croc wrote that "I would have expected the Queen would have been gentle with the Lords and have tried to pacify them, but on her way from the field, she talked of nothing but hanging and crucifying them all. . . ." As the rude gestures became more obscene and the rude comments even louder—a harassment the Lords seemingly could not check—she asked for Lord Lindsay's hand and, taking it, cried, "By this hand, which is now in mine, I will have your head for this!" [15]

For the next four hours, surrounded by her Lords, their arrogance somewhat subdued by the fact that they were leading their sovereign as a captive, Mary endured the agony of the return to her capital. As they passed through small towns and villages, over baking heathlands, people pressed forward. Not in admiration or in love, as before, but now reviling the Queen with such foulness Mary wished to hold her hands to her ears. Instead, she looked straight ahead, as the Lords beat at those who ventured too close.

Near Edinburgh, word went ahead that the Queen was returning, and by the time she reached the outskirts of town a crowd had assembled and saw their sovereign, "her face now disfigured with dust and tears," led past the charred Kirk o' Field ruins. Disheveled and rumpled, Mary attempted to muster some remnants of strength to face the crowd, which greeted her with cries and screams of revenge. Riding up the Canongate, the soldiers closed ranks around her to protect her from the wrath of the people, who scornfully shouted epithets and threats as she was led in a slow procession to the home of the Provost of Edinburgh in the High Street. She was lodged in the ground-floor room with only a stout window between her and the murderous mob, their fury unleashed by the sight of their Queen. The infamous banner of her murdered husband had been thrust into the ground outside her window, where she might see it each time she looked out.

All night long her subjects thronged about her prison. "Burn her, she is not worthy to live! Kill her! Drown her!" were shouted into the room by faceless tormentors behind flaring torches and dinned into the ears of the Queen, who was by now hysterical with fear and trembling with such shame so that she screamed back—all the while unconscious she was doing so. "She came to the window sundry times in so miserable a state, her hair hanging about her ears, and her breast, yea, the most part of her body, from the waist up, bare. . . ." [16] In such a state, hungry, faint and cold, the Queen of Scotland answered the reviling of her subjects until humiliation and terror finally overcame her shattered body and she lay, senseless, on the bed.

Early in the morning, before the dawning mist gave way to the heat of the day, when most of the tired and sated mob had dispersed, "and to avoid crying out of the people," Mary was rescued by Morton and Atholl. Fearing they would be torn to bits earlier, they had not dared approach the Provost's house while the infuriated people thronged outside. Mary was too tired to rail at her captors when, silent and in shock, she was taken to Holyrood at one o'clock in the morning. Later that night a force of 1,000 men, with the banner of the murdered Darnley at their head, took the Queen to Lochleven Castle in Kinrosshire. The Castle was virtually impregnable, being in the middle of the lake and had the further advantage of being owned by a former mistress of Mary's father, Lady Douglas, the mother of James Stuart, the Earl of Murray. It was one of the first of many prisons the Queen of Scotland would endure in exchange for a month of married love.

If Mary's marriage had shocked Elizabeth, the English Queen was aghast at her imprisonment. She had foreseen trouble with Darnley and had, indeed, contrived the marriage in preference to a foreign alliance for Mary. But never, in her most extreme expectations, had she seen the far-reaching, conclusive events which resulted in a dead King, an imprisoned Queen and a country in the hands of rebellious Lords. At once that deep, shrewdly feminine intuition which was the core of Elizabeth Tudor's strength and spirit assessed the effect on England, on her Crown and herself personally. What she saw and ultimately realized was to prove, for the next twenty years, a threat to her sovereignty, a challenge to her diplomacy and a deep personal hell for her as a woman.

Mary Stuart had always claimed to be the legal heir to the throne of England. As such, she held the love of England's devout northern

Catholics. Secure in their mountain strongholds, powerful as any Scottish clan or medieval lord, these nobles possessed the last remnants of feudal barony in England and presented an implacable barrier to any incursions by the Protestant faith. United by their Catholicism and intermarriage, they were also supported by thousands of retainers who swore a fealty which to them was more realistic than that sworn to their monarch in far-off London. In the remote and thinly populated North, Elizabeth Tudor was tolerated while Mary Stuart—because of her Catholicism and her descent from Henry VIII's sister, Margaret Tudor—was almost venerated.

The imprisonment of the Queen of Scotland by her own subjects opened a vast Pandora's box of political and religious implications. Elizabeth recognized the grave issue—almost without precedent—must be met head on before Scotland was plunged into civil war with clan fighting clan and religious factions assaulting each other, with Mary's Crown as the prize. On a broader scale, should conditions worsen, Catholic France would almost certainly intervene on behalf of the heir, young James Stuart. And with the Border being the "postern gate" into England—and those partisan Northern Catholics on the English side of the Border—what chance would there be that civil and religious strife might be averted? What chance would she, Elizabeth, the heretofore-bastardized daughter of a disputed marriage, have then of retaining her Crown?

Almost to a man, Elizabeth's ministers condemned Mary Stuart and argued for her continued restraint. Cecil, Leicester, Sir Francis Knollys—all pointed to Mary as a lost woman. They advised that Elizabeth woo the friendship of the Scottish Lords who would further advance the Protestant cause and with their fiercely won independence—and that with the help of the English Queen—be unlikely to yield to French influence.

But Elizabeth would not hear of abandoning Mary. Deep within her, the great personal pride of sovereignty, of dignity and power, was affronted by the gross spectacle of an anointed monarch of Divine origin, roughly handled, condemned and imprisoned. Elizabeth had suffered imprisonment, and she, better than any of her advisers, could imagine the depth of Mary's grief, if not her shame. Her kinswoman, whom she had promised to use "as a sister or natural daughter," had suffered a fate so ignominious that the royal mind could scarce accept it. Therefore, when Cecil and others advised the Queen to recognize the rebel Lords' government, they were dismayed at the strength of her refusal. In frank terms and a strong voice, she relegated Mary's Lords to the status of scoundrels who had disgraced the person and position of the woman to whom they had sworn fealty. Instead of attempting to revive her own influence in Scotland at the expense of its now-defenseless Queen, Elizabeth promised—to the consternation and disappointment of her ministers—to assist Mary Stuart.

The Queen needed no counseling to understand the Scottish situation and its subsequent effect in Spain and France. Philip kept a silent voice—albeit a cautious eye—on the situation. Catherine de Medici had, in effect, washed her hands of Mary, but she had invited the good wishes of the rebel Lords, hoping that Mary's son might be sent to France for his upbringing. A friend visiting in France wrote Leicester, "Have an eye that no French ships steal thither to convey the Prince away, for not long since such a matter was a-brewing . . . some of their merchant ships under color of a voyage shall do the deed. . . ."[17] While this too was Elizabeth's fear, her first thought was of Mary. Two weeks after the debacle of Carberry Hill, she wrote the imprisoned Queen a letter remarkable for its frankness as it is revealing of Elizabeth's ability to convey her thoughts with refreshing candor whenever she chose to do so:

MADAME,
   It hath been always held for a special principle in friendship that prosperity provideth, but adversity proveth friends; whereof at this time finding occasion to verify the same with our actions, we have thought meet—both for our professions and your comfort—in these words to testify our friendship, not only by admonishing you of the worst, but also to comfort you for the best.
   We understood by Sir Robert Melville such things as you gave me in charge to declare on your behalf, concerning your estate, and especially of as much as could be said for the allowance of your marriage.
   Madame, to be plain with you, our grief hath not been small, that in this your marriage, so slender consideration hath been had, that we perceive manifestly, no good friend you have in the whole world can like thereof; and if we would otherwise write or say we should abuse you, for how could a worse choice be made for your honour, than in great haste to marry such a subject, who besides other notorious lacks, public fame hath charged with the murder of your late husband, besides the touching of yourself also in some part, though we trust in that behalf falsely? And with that peril have you married him that hath another wife alive, whereby neither by God's law nor man's yourself can [you] be his lawful wife, nor any children betwixt you legitimate! Thus you see plainly what we think of the marriage, whereof, we are heartily sorry that we can conceive no better, what colourable reason soever we have heard of your servant to induce us thereto.

Elizabeth then reminded Mary of the advice given when Darnley had been assassinated—"to have searched out and punished the murderers" whereby "there might have been many more things tolerated better in your marriage than that now can be suffered to be spoken of." Darnley had been her kinsman too, noted the Queen, and there was Mary's son and heir to be preserved "for the comfort of you and your realm." Yet, by her actions, Mary had let her husband's murderers go free and endangered her son's inheritance. Elizabeth's letter continues:

> Now for your comfort in such adversity as we have heard you should be in—whereof we cannot tell what to think to be true—we assure you, that whatsoever we can imagine meet to be for your honour and safety that shall lie in our power we will perform the same; that it shall well appear you have a good neighbour, a dear sister, a faithful friend; and so shall you undoubtedly always find us and prove us to be indeed towards you; for which purpose we are determined to send with all speed one of our trusty servants, not only to understand your state, but also, thereupon, so to deal with your nobility and people, as they shall find you not to lack our friendship and power for the preservation of your honour and greatness.[18]

Elizabeth's letter stands as its own best testament to her desire to befriend and support Mary, the Queen, even as she censured the impetuous actions of Mary, the woman. In so doing she was alone. Other Kings, Queens and the Pope had abandoned Mary, and in taking up her cause, the English Queen did so in the face of the best advice of her own Council. Nothing is more indicative of Elizabeth's shrewd reasoning, her political ingenuity and, at this point at least, what was a genuine compassion for her stricken cousin.

Two weeks after Carberry Hill, therefore, Sir Nicholas Throckmorton, disliking his task and lamenting to all who would listen, left the English court to assess Scottish affairs. He was to promise Elizabeth's aid in restoring Mary to liberty either by persuasion, treaty or force. Next, Mary must promise to renounce Bothwell and punish Darnley's murderers. Third, the young Prince must be sent to England for royal protection and, Elizabeth promised, "as good safety therein . . . as can be devised for any that might be our child, born of own own body. . . ." The Queen had heard rumors of Mary's pregnancy and told Leicester that "it will greatly touch her, appearing so soon after her marriage; whereby it will be thought all was not well before. . . ."[19] Even so, her advocacy did not diminish. Throckmorton also carried the English sovereign's words to Mary's rebellious Lords that "she neither would nor could endure for any respect, to have their Queen and Sovereign imprisoned or deprived of her estate or put in peril of her person." She castigated the Scotsmen, stating "she had changed her intention of silence" and was determined "to aid and relieve her [Mary] by all possible means to recover her liberty. . . ." [20] For Mary herself there was also a message. Compared with Elizabeth's former frank letter of a week before, this communication reveals the influence of William Cecil and the Council:

Richmond
June 30, 1567

MADAME,

Our perplexity is such, both for your trouble and for the occasion thereof, that we cannot find the old way which we were accustomed to walk in, by writing to you with our own hand. And yet therein we mean not you should conceive on our part any lack of our old friendship. Wherefore, we send this bearer, Sir Nicholas Throckmorton, that he understand truly your state, and thereupon to impart to you our own true meaning at fuller length than we could to your own faithful servant, Robert Melville, who, though he did—as, we believe according to the charge given him—use much earnest speech to move us to think well and allow of your doings. Yet such is both the general report of you to the contrary, and the evidence of sundry of your acts since the death of your late husband, as we could not by him be satisfied to our desire. Wherefore, we desire you to give to this bearer firm credit in all things, as you would give ourselves.

And so we end. [21]

To the Lords themselves, Elizabeth was more succinct. She wrote Throckmorton that "the more she considers the rigorous and unlawful proceedings of those Lords against the Sovereign lady, the more she is determined to relieve the Queen, her sister, and is determined to spare no charge to impeach their further proceedings. . . . For, as she [Mary] is a Princess, if they continue to keep her in prison, or touch her life in person, she will not fail to revenge it to the uttermost on such as shall be in any wise guilty thereof." [22]

There was strong resentment by the Lords at the English Queen's attitude, which made little effort to conceal her contempt for their actions. Theirs was an indignation, tempered by surprise that Mary, abandoned by those to whom her religion if nothing else should have provided a strong and protective tie, should be championed by one whose Crown she had coveted. It was a revelation—unexpected and undesired—that Elizabeth's threat to hold the Lords accountable for any violence done to her cousin was the one firm security at which the imprisoned Queen might grasp. It was a shock to all—and a three-day wonder at the Scottish court—that the staunchest advocate the Queen of Scotland now possessed was the Queen of England.

Elizabeth's personal compassion for Mary was certainly tinged with adroit political expediency. She wished for a nonaggressive Scotland, a northern neighbor presenting little threat or challenge to her Crown or country. She had no desire to subjugate for political, economic or religious reasons and had been content to let the factions north of her Border work out their own problems and destiny. Her Council and a competent network of spies kept a collective eye open to see that only the desired end resulted. Whatever happened with a free Queen, a dissenting Council and an unruly people were Mary Stuart's problems—provided she did not seek to influence the English Catholics or seek French aid in her ambition. But with an imprisoned Queen, a rebellious Council and an inflamed people, the situation became understandably perilous and demanded the strongest—and the most careful—handling.

From Scotland, where he had been refused permission to visit the imprisoned Mary at Lochleven Castle, Throckmorton wrote that the Lords "which have her in guard, do keep her very straitly, and as far as I can perceive, their rigour proceedeth . . . because the Queen will not by any means be induced to lend her authority to prosecute the murder, nor will consent by any persuasion to abandon the Lord Bothwell for her husband, but avoweth constantly that she will live and die with him. . . ." [23] Bothwell had obtained sanctuary at the Orkney Isle estates of his brother, the Earl of Caithness, and Mary's continued espousal of her husband led Throckmorton to say, "Queen Mary will never have any more power in Scotland . . . the Lords could not permit her any longer to be put in peril by her disorders."

Throckmorton said he had "found the means to let her know that your Majesty [Elizabeth] hath sent me hither for her release." Throckmorton was certain the Lords meant to rid themselves of Mary, by legal means or foul. "The Queen is in very great peril of her life, by reason that the people, assembled . . . do mind vehemently the destruction of her," [24] he wrote Elizabeth. When threats of Mary's execution continued, the English Queen fiercely threatened retribution which would result in an invasion compared to which Flodden, Pinkie Cleugh and Solway would be games for children. Not surprisingly, the belligerent Lords, equally furious, denounced Elizabeth's attitude and proclaimed it only imperiled Mary more.

Throckmorton maintained that Elizabeth's inflexibility and staunch support of Mary were, however, having their effect. He wrote William Cecil, "As far as I can perceive, to be plain with you, they find more peril to grow with them through the Queen's Majesty's dealing than they do by the French or by any contrary faction amongst themselves. For they assure themselves the Queen will leave them in briars if they ruin her [Mary's] fortune. . . ." [25] And so eventually, with the presence of her emissary, with continued persistence and an undaunted declaration of grievous retaliation should Mary be injured, a less violent attitude toward the Queen of Scots was soon noticed. "Whether it were fear, fury or zeal, which carried these men to the end they become to, I know not," wrote Throckmorton to Leicester in late July, "but I dare boldly affirm to your Lordship, albeit I could neither obtain access to this Queen nor procure her liberty . . . yet, I have at this time preserved her life, to what continuance, I am uncertain." Throckmorton spoke of his own uncomfortable situation. "I am in a town guarded by men of war which do visit all men that do enter and issue. I have no horses, but must depend upon these Lords for the furthering of me and my train. I cannot depart but at their pleasure. . . ."[26] Later Sir Robert Melville corroborated Throckmorton's belief, saying, "To be plain with your Majesty, the greater number was so bent in rigor against my mistress, that extremity had been used if your Highness' ambassador had not been present, who did utter both his wisdom and affection to your Majesty. . . ." [27] Melville told Elizabeth that Mary "would rather herself and the Prince were in your realm, than elsewhere in Christendom." While Elizabeth would have delighted in receiving Scotland's heir, such a welcome did not extend to his controversial and dishonored mother, and she wrote Throckmorton in alarm, "We find her removal into this realm or into France not without great discomfort to us." It was evident that while Mary, the Queen, had Elizabeth's strong support, Mary, the woman, retained—under her present circumstances—equally strong censure for her actions from the English Queen.

Yet none could deny that Elizabeth's persistence, derived from her own innate belief in the supremacy of the monarchy, the rapid spate of letters, cajoling, threatening, reasoning, combined with the calm and persuasive influence of Throckmorton, swung the balance in favor of Mary. Had Elizabeth too joined in the general denunciation which greeted Mary's marriage, had she shown no threat of retaliation, there is little doubt the Scottish Queen could have escaped execution.

Instead there was a price: abdication. On July 17, 1567, James Stuart, the Earl of Murray, returned to Scotland from the journey he had undertaken two months previously when the farce of Bothwell's "trial" had occurred. It was ever Murray's way to absent himself from dubious situations and return in time to pick up the pieces and, by virtue of his position, grasp authority. He did so now and confronted the Lords, who had, in the meantime, come into possession of a silver casket with the incriminating letters and sonnets written by the enthralled Mary. They provided the Lords with just the required assurance and vindication to insist on the Queen's abdication. Copies were made and distributed, each disclosure strengthening the moral position of the men who had made a Queen captive. The Casket Letters provided an unalterable answer; each sheet of scrawled writing was the means by which the last pretense to sovereignty of Mary Stuart withered and died.

Several days after his return, Murray visited Lochleven, his mother's castle, where his half sister threw herself sobbing into his arms. She had recently miscarried of twin children* and, weakened by her condition, was in a highly emotional state.

Murray's purpose, to insist on her abdication, did not help. When Mary remained stubborn, Murray threatened disclosure of the Casket Letters, and the appalled Queen then realized how deeply she was implicated. Murray insisted she had no choice. If she did not sign, civil war might result and her child would be ferreted away to France, as she herself had been years before. At the very worst, both of them might be assassinated. She had absolutely no chance of regaining power, he maintained, to which Mary could only cry, "But I am only twenty-five years old. . . !" If she had expected consolation from her brother, Mary was severely disappointed. Murray had small patience with the woman whose folly had brought dishonor to her Crown and their name. He told the sobbing Queen he would attempt to salvage what he could from the debacle created by the disclosure of the casket and its letters, which Mary begged him to retain and not make her foolish indiscretions public. If she abdicated, she asked that he become Regent to act for her young son during his minority. On those sad words, he took his leave.

Several days later Sir Robert Melville and Lord Lindsay brought three sheets of parchment to Mary. One consented to the coronation of her son; the second created a Regency of the realm; the third designated her brother, Murray, to act as Regent. Since her brother's visit, Mary's strength had returned and with it some semblance of stub-

*The date of birth of Mary's twins is unknown but it was certainly before the July 25 date of her abdication. Another story, never authenticated, is that Mary's child was a girl, that it was born in February, 1568, and "was taken to France, where she became a nun at Notre Dame de Soissons." [28]

bornness, and she viewed the papers with distaste. Again that proud nature, the inviolable inheritance from her ancestors, her lifelong acceptance of a power and privilege which answered to no human restraint manifested themselves. Spiritedly she denounced her visitors. Obviously she had not yet accepted the complete vulnerability of her position. But the Queen was bluntly informed that if she did not sign, she would be charged with the breach of the "laws and decrees of the realm," specifically adultery with Bothwell "and others"—although who "the others" were her visitors did not say. She would also be charged with the murder of her husband, Henry Darnley. Lindsay, a weak bully, buttressed his charges with the comment that "if she did not sign . . . she would compel them to cut her throat, however unwilling they might be." [29] In great anguish, seeing she could do little else, the tearful Mary signed a scrawling *"Marie"* at the bottom of the sheets, contenting herself by saying that since her signature was being obtained by force, "she would respect the deeds only so long as she remained in captivity."

On July 29, 1567, Mary's son, James Stuart, was crowned James VI in the great church at Stirling, and in Edinburgh, wrote Throckmorton, there were "a thousand bonfires. The Castle shot off twenty pieces of artillery, the people made great joy, dancing and acclamations, so it appeareth they rejoiced more at the inauguration of the new Prince than they did sorrow at the deprivation of their Queen. . . ." [30]

Yet, apparently, James Stuart did not trust his imprisoned half sister, who might still challenge his Regency. If Mary were to remain powerless, even though confined, her reputation must be forever compromised. Several months later he, who had promised to retain some remnant of respectability and honor for his sister, consented to having the compromising Casket Letters read aloud in the Scottish Parliament. Here they were examined by friends and foes alike, and the handwriting was declared to be genuine. Copies were then sent to all the foreign courts so others might understand the moral indignation in the Scottish court which justified imprisonment of a Queen.

In England, Elizabeth was confronted by a *fait accompli,* and she took out her ill humor on her chief Councillor and the absent Throckmorton, to whom Cecil wrote, "This afternoon about five o'clock the Queen sent for me hastily and entered into a great offensive speech that nothing was thought of for her to do to revenge the Queen of Scots' imprisonment and deliver her. I answered as warily as I could, but she increased so in anger against these Lords that in good earnest, she began to devise revenge by war. Nothing I said satisfied her but I must in all haste make a letter. . . ." [31]

It is doubtful if Elizabeth ever honestly meant to invade Scotland in support of Mary. She was astute enough to accept—as her Councillors certainly repeatedly informed her—that such action would ensure a quick death for Mary. But by hectoring and intimidation, she had won her end. While she had not saved a Queen's honor, she had saved her cousin's life.

But it had not all been feminine compassion and political opportunism. One who knew her well recognized a deeper motive. As William Cecil told Throckmorton, "I see two special causes move her Majesty, one that she be not thought to the world partial against the Queen. The other, that by this example, none of her own be encouraged. . . ."

In essence, this was Elizabeth's fear. Should the Scots successfully depose or execute their monarch, other nations might be encouraged to follow their example. Possession of a Crown was worth more than anything else in the world, and Elizabeth Tudor would ever go to any lengths to preserve its sanctity and uphold the mystique of royalty. It was only right that monarch support monarch against crude usurpation by the commonalty. While Mary's sovereignty was gone and now vested in her son, Elizabeth had—through the power of her Crown—preserved her kinswoman's life. The English Queen would find comfort in this when, twenty years later, the shattering events at Fotheringhay continued to haunt her for the rest of her life.

The Mistress

It will be very easy to agree about the conditions for my marriage when it is settled who is to be the bridegroom.

Chapter Sixteen

As the Queen of England faced her thirty-fifth birthday, still a spinster, with no prospect of a husband to say nothing of an heir, her health was of much concern and speculation. Elizabeth was not as prone to illnesses as Mary and Edward had been. At thirty-five her one noticeable deterioration was due to her propensity for reading and studying. The Queen never ceased her quest for knowledge—at sixty she would make English translations of the first five books of *Boethius On The Consolation of Philosophy*.[1] Now she read dispatches and other state papers, often in a bad light. She practiced her music, read poetry or did needlework for relaxation; consequently, she had developed a tendency toward shortsightedness and suffered mild headaches.

But she had been marked in other ways. That childhood trauma—the knowledge of her mother's fate and the ensuing semi-abandonment by her father—had resulted in an introspective melancholy, which, especially as she grew older, manifested in severe nervous reactions. Such melancholia took the very real form of weeping for no apparent reason, painful migraines which differed from her headaches caused by overwork and—imaginary or real—a shortness of breath. Such prolonged apprehension resulted in spates of hysteria, "a spice of the mother," as it was called, which left her exhausted and spent. Few in her household were privy to these occurrences. Ashley, while she was alive, and later Blanche Parry both were familiar with Elizabeth's emotional disturbances and, with hot or cold compresses, a variety of herbal concoctions, soothing words and undisputed affection, had invariably nursed the ill woman back to health.

As Elizabeth grew older, a good deal of the tendency to severe emotional stress disappeared. Authority is a marvelous medicine, and Elizabeth Tudor had it in great measure when the Crown was firmly set upon her red hair. She deeply believed God had placed her in a position to minister to her country, and from the moment of her coronation, the most meaningful aspect of her life was her Queenship. Everything else lessened beside this fact. She let it be known that no detail was too small for her attention; every Councillor from Cecil on down must prepare a list of things to be done and submit them to Elizabeth for her perusal. In times of urgent decision, she did not hesitate to confine her entire Council to her chamber, and there they remained until they—and she—had completed their business. She would have them awakened at two, three or four o'clock in the morning if she desired an opinion, and it was understood that she herself must be awakened the moment any important news arrived at her Palace gates. She worked day, night and weekends throughout the year amd insisted that those who wished to assist the Crown do the same. If they did not or could not, they were free to go elsewhere.[2]

In ten years, such devotion to duty had won its rewards. Her subversive maneuvers in Scotland and the more aggressive war with France had impressed more firmly on Elizabeth what she had always intuitively recognized: peace was prosperity while war was a costly misadventure. The national currency had been stabilized and English credit held in the highest estimation of the Antwerp moneylenders. The Queen had kept taxation at a minimum; if nothing else, her experience with her last Parliament had shown her that future subsidies would be pried from her lawmakers only with more cooperation from their sovereign regarding a marriage. Religious tolerance for Catholic, Protestant and the even more critical Puritan seemed flexible and lenient. Reflective of her own love of letters, she had fostered a great interest in education and so that her great universities might be competently administered had placed the two men nearest her—Cecil and Leicester—as Chancellors of Cambridge and Oxford. By every estimation, her ten years on the throne had been admirably productive, and as a result, there was a national pride on the part of the people in their sovereign.

Everyone, it seemed, had an opinion about Elizabeth Tudor, and the opinions were as varied as the Queen's moods. While "Jezebel" and "The English virago" were favorite terms employed by earlier Spanish ambassadors, she had de Silva's greatest respect. He called her "a great chatterer" and said her frankness frequently distressed the "aristocracy" but acknowledged that in the eyes of her people, the Queen could do no wrong. The French ambassadors, rarely bestowing a compliment if there was any chance otherwise, said, "She is a great Princess who is ignorant of nothing," and noted "that the government depends upon the Queen," a comment supported by Cecil, who claimed that "no one of her Councillors could tell her what she knew not . . . there was never any great consultation about her country at which she was not present. . . ." The Venetian ambassador was frankly in awe of Elizabeth and reported, "Her intellect and understanding are wonderful," while another Frenchman threw caution to the winds and reported, "She is one of the wonders of the world!" Even the Pope said of the heretical monarch that Elizabeth and he himself "were the only rulers capable of their tasks."

Such devotion to her country and Crown had worked wonders for the mercurial personality who had ascended the throne. Her slight frame, plagued with anaemia, was marvelously tough nevertheless, and she sought to keep it in good condition by prudent intake of wine and food and by judicious exercise. She seemed incapable of fatigue and still "could hunt all day, dance or watch masques and pageants all night, till the knees of strong men trembled under them as they wearily watched in attendance upon her person. . . ."[3] Elizabeth resisted serious infections fairly easily even withstanding the onslaught of smallpox twice. The common cold was tolerated, but she often complained of "pains in the stomach and all over the body" with "very bad catarrh and some fever." She was very thin, so much so that de Silva noted that "a doctor who had seen her tells me that her bones may be counted"—a condition which worried everyone. Yet her abstemious habits, love of the out-of-doors and intellectual curiosity kept her alert and responsive and preserved her bodily health normally and naturally in an age when disease made terrifying inroads on the majority.

But mental health was something else again. Those very childhood deprivations which had followed her mother's death—the shame, humiliation, slander, imprisonment—had marked her psyche as firmly and irrevocably as the pox had left faint marks on her skin. These psychological failings were not as visible as the more physical blemishes, yet they were very evident to a few. Those closest to her, such as Cecil and Leicester, aware of her adolescent ordeal, recognized the severe emotional insecurity traceable to her younger years, when the possibility of a traitor's death faced her and reduced the girl to shaken numbness.

But there was, literally, almost no one who would have recognized the apprehension which often now beset Elizabeth when an emotional crisis confronted her sovereignty or femininity. Should she suffer betrayal by an errant lady-in-waiting, should a noble abuse her trust, should a servant take advantage of her kindness or infringe on

Majesty's patience, then foreboding and self-doubt rose in varying degrees. Then she must call on all her resources to stifle the suspicion and anxiety—or rage—that threatened. Elizabeth was even deprived of the satisfaction of admitting her apprehension to those who might comfort of reassure her, for she would have suffered the most painful death rather than admit to weaknesses. In the face of the gigantic task to which she had dedicated her life—the ruling of her beloved England—there must be no human frailty or feminine lack. But it was there—even if not greatly evident—and it accounted for what many of her era, and the later times as well, considered Elizabeth's somewhat foolish and vain foibles, which often bordered on the absurd.

One was the Queen's consummate vanity, which became a compelling mania as the years passed. Like her mother, Elizabeth's appeal lay in the brilliance of her personality rather than in any perfection of face or form. Her pale skin and startlingly red hair provided an agreeable background for the elaborate dresses, the jewels, the fans, the feathered ornaments with which she sought to enhance the features and figure of a Queen who knew she lacked a true and perfect beauty. She was very conscious that several of her own maids-of-honor or ladies-in-waiting possessed more comely features or pleasing expression than she; it was not coincidental that the Queen's warmer relationships with such women were often with those of a plainer cast. But what she did possess—the lovely skin and flaming hair, the piercing black eyes and the beautiful, long-fingered hands—she well knew how to use. All the artifice of the knowledgeable feminine coterie around Elizabeth was evident in introducing the latest colors, fabrics and scents so the Queen might use them. Elizabeth was as eager to experiment with the newest cosmetic, hairpiece or fashion as her youngest maid-of-honor, and her selections invariably set court fashion for the moment.

Since she had done her share, as it were, in gilding the royal lily, it was now her courtiers' obligation to do theirs. Dwelling in regal isolation, Elizabeth relied on those around her to justify that feminine sense of worth which her poorer but wedded subjects took for granted. Splendid gowns, elaborate cosmetics and costly jewels, coupled with intelligent conversation and quick wit on the Queen's part, must be lavishly acknowledged by everyone. Compliment must follow compliment— on her dress, her beauty, her grace and charm—all must be noted, spoken of and discussed in her hearing. The habit, once commenced, was to grow over the long years of her reign until it became a subject of jest with even those closest to her. To be handy with the right compliment was a talent as desirable in a new ambassador as an ability to represent his home court. With Elizabeth, the tendering of such compliments approached a fulsome extravagance which at times mocked the respect and deference expected by royalty. But it served its purpose: It bestowed on the woman who did not possess the warm physical love of husband and children to whom she might have given affection a sense of self-esteem which had nothing to do with her sovereignty. If she did, as she often noted, consider all the English as her children, then it was also required that they regard her with the admiration for her vigilance, which was superbly feminine before it was maternal.

Husbandless and childless, Elizabeth had the inclination and the time for interests which an older, busier matron with family responsibilities might have forsaken. She had always been drawn to the occult and had, from childhood, been fascinated by astrology. Her great friendship with Dr. John Dee resulted from this interest. John Dee was in his forties during Elizabeth's first years on the throne. A man of "superior attainments," he took his degree as a Master of Arts at Cambridge in 1548 in astronomy and geography. He left, "being accused a sorcerer," in the same year and, returning later, was imprisoned under Mary for drawing a horoscope more favorable to Elizabeth than to Mary herself. At Elizabeth's request, he had fixed her coronation date, and she often consulted him, even sending him her doctors when he was ill. Dr. Dee frequently visited at court, along with Cornelius Lannoy, a Dutchman, who practiced alchemy and vowed he could convert base metal into gold, as well as an elixir which promised "perpetual life and youth." Incredibly, even Elizabeth's own strong intelligence was momentarily duped, but when Lannoy failed to deliver his questionable potions, he found himself lodged in the Tower.[4]

On September 17, ten days after Elizabeth's thirty-fifth birthday. Dr. Dee wrote in his *Diary*, "The Queen's Majesty came from Richmond in her coach, the higher way to Mortlake field. . . ." There she "beckoned me to come to her coach side," he continued, "where she very speedily pulled off her glove and gave me her hand to kiss and, to be short, asked me to resort to her court and so give her to know when I came there." Dr. Dee, a tall skeleton of a man, looked the part of an esoteric. A long black robe and a skullcap on his bald head, a long, flowing beard gave his appearance an air of the forbidden. His study at Mortlake, full of "parchments, gloves, scales, crucibles and other outward signs of occult mysteries,"[5] was often visited by Blanche Parry and others of the Queen's ladies-in-waiting. There they breathlessly viewed his "magic glass," a mirror possessing such supernatural powers that Elizabeth's ladies could scarcely discuss it in sensible terms. At last the Queen must see for herself, and ultimately, "The Queen's Majesty, with her most honorable Privy Council . . . came purposely to visit my library . . . ," wrote Dee. The funeral of his wife had taken place only four hours previously, and when Elizabeth was informed of this, "her Majesty refused to come in, but willed me to fetch my glass so famous, and show unto her some of the properties of it, which I did. Her Majesty being taken down from her horse by the Earl of Leicester, Master of the Horse . . . did see some of the properties of that glass* to her Majesty's contentment and delight."[6] Whatever it was that Elizabeth saw in the mirror—if indeed she saw anything other than her own image—it apparently did not reflect anything sinister. Or perhaps at the moment she peered into the polished surface, Robert Dudley made sure his own features were near hers so their reflections appeared simultaneously.

The ardor of the Earl of Leicester had been dampened, though never extinguished, by Elizabeth's repeated vows of constant virginity. He told de Silva "that the Queen had put him off so long that he began to fear she would never marry him at all . . ." but this did not preclude an intimacy that still tantalized the crowned heads of Europe, as well as her own subjects, and made for endless rivalries within her court. The new French ambassador, Bertrand de Salignac de la Mothe-Fénelon, was a penetrating observer and a vivid reporter of Elizabeth's activities and conduct at this period. He wrote his home court that the long-standing feud between the Duke of Norfolk, the young premier peer of the realm, and Leicester had deepened when Norfolk castigated Robert on his uncircumspect behavior with Elizabeth, accusing the Earl of fondling and kissing the Queen "too often when he was not invited thereto." Norfolk said such familiarities disgraced the Crown. Fénelon noted that Norfolk was supported by other nobles, all of whom deplored the fact that Leicester entered the Queen's bedchamber before she arose, "and that he took upon himself the office of her lady-in-waiting, by handing to her a garment which ought never to have been seen in the hands of the Master of the Horse."[7] All of which was probably very true. But it was not primarily the intimacy of Elizabeth and Leicester which bothered Norfolk and his kind, as Leicester well knew. Rather it was jealousy of his unique position near the person of Majesty with its constant privilege and potential of even greater power. However, he presented a bland countenance as the Councillors quibbled: if the Queen meant to marry him, all was well

*This same mirror was sold in the summer of 1841 by the estate of Horace Walpole for fifteen guineas. It has since disappeared.

and good, they said, and even offered "to unite their influence . . . to sanction their honourable union and stop all this scandal." Norfolk and the others knew they were safe in promising cooperation and that Elizabeth was not going to marry. But the Earl, carrying through the charade, assured the Duke "that he had, by this offer of assistance, laid him under the greatest obligation in the world . . . and he would never forget the same." The time was rapidly approaching when both Leicester and Norfolk would have a good chance to remember those words.

Even the Archbishop of York undertook to remonstrate with the Queen of England regarding her conduct with Leicester. Whereupon Elizabeth turned on the prelate, and, in the words of de Silva, the court was treated "to one of those royal rages for which she is famous . . . and with roughness and hard words she threatened to prosecute him" before the Earl intervened. The ambassador later wrote, "The Queen greatly favours Leicester's party, but all her near relatives, whom she esteems, are on the other side," causing the Spaniard to reflect momentarily that "it must be all a trick to retain them both. . . ."

Still Robert continued to covet his Elizabeth. It cost him dearly in his colleagues' estimation, for jealousy has small limitations. Both he and the Queen possessed awesome tempers, yet his responses were invariably hampered by the fact that he was dealing not only with the woman of his choice, but his Queen as well—a fact which always gave Elizabeth the final advantage. When, as in many instances, he retreated from court to lick his wounds, he could write, petulant and self-willed as a child, "I see I need not to make so great haste home where no good opinion is conceived of me. Either a cave in a corner of oblivion or a sepulchre for perpetual rest, were the best homes I could wish to return to,"[8] indicating that my Lord Robert was also capable of dramatic twinges of self-martyrdom.

Yet they were always reunited, and Robert's hopes would soar that Elizabeth *might* change her mind. In the meantime, they enjoyed each other's company at the endless masques, tiltings, bearbaitings and other social functions of the court. Leicester worked hard for his Queen and his country, for which his devotion was the equal of any other courtier, with the exception of William Cecil. Elizabeth's willingness to sacrifice him as a husband for Mary Stuart illustrates her faith that even as a Scottish Consort, he would have been accommodating of England's welfare. As Chancellor of Oxford University, he "lost no time in instituting a better order for the advancement of true religion, virtue and learning."[9] If, as is true, he was accused of looking to his own pocket for profit by accepting bribes for head academic offices or placement of scholars, which "is as common as buying and selling of horses in Smithfield," he was no better or worse than many of his fellow nobles in indulging in one of the less meritorious practices of the time: selling the prerequisites of his position for his own personal gain. All of Elizabeth's ministers engaged in rendering "services" in exchange for "commissions," and the practice extended throughout the government, as well as the Church hierarchy. Wherever patents, charters, licenses, social patronage, guardianships or such were in the hands of one man, the profit inevitably remained one man's also.

Robert was a great patron of the arts and sciences; he maintained Leicester's Players, one of the first theatrical groups in England headed by James Burbage, the father of a latter-day famous Hamlet. The Players themselves were the worthy progenitors of the group which later included Shakespeare. In additon to serving as a drama patron, Leicester was Constable of the Castle and Forest of Windsor, the Ranger of Snowdon, and to the day of his death, he never relinquished the post he loved most: Master of the Horse. Outside the explicit duties of the post, he undertook the breeding and improving of the royal stock. As Master of the Horse, he was often called on to represent the Queen in greeting the splendid royal visitors, eventually escorting them to her presence. Later he hunted in forest and field with the distinguished travelers and their retinues before the evening's entertainment, when he, dressed in "white satin embroidered with gold a foot broad very curiously, his cap black velvet with white feather, his collar of gold beset with precious stones . . ." became for everyone as great a sight to see as the Queen herself. The brilliant Leicester—handsome, erudite and haughty—merited the *Dominus Factotum* nickname by which many at court referred to him—not always complimentarily—as well as "The Great Lord," the appellation many of the visitors carried home with them.[10]

It was a life for which he was ideally suited by temperament, appearance and an all-consuming ambition: to glorify the Leicester name in honor of his love and his Queen. Leicester was never far from Elizabeth's side; if he was absent too long, Elizabeth became edgy, asking when he would return. Their letters show an acceptance and intimate knowledge of each other, a familiarity resulting from a quarter century's friendship. While Robert could ingratiate and flatter with the best of those at court, he paid his Elizabeth the compliment of a comfortable prose which illustrates the almost prosaic tenor of their rapport. Once he wrote from Kenilworth, where "your poor thralls" (he and his brother, the Earl of Warwick), "your Ursus Major and Ursus Minor," were visiting. "Now if it please your Sweet Majesty that

I return to my manner," he wrote, "your Old Eyes ⊙ ⊙ are in your old lodging here, very well and much the better for the comfort I have lately received . . . of your healthful estate, which is what I most pray for. . . ." Robert's concern for Elizabeth's health was often voiced in his letters: "Thanks for sending so graciously to know how your poor Eyes ⊙ ⊙ doth. I have hitherto so well found myself after my travel, as I trust I am clearly delivered of the shrewd cold that so hardly held me at my departure from you. I have always found exercise with open air my best remedy against those delicate diseases gotten about your dainty City of London, which place, but for necessity, I am sorry to see you remain about. . . ."[11]

Yet invariably a relationship in which final consummation is completely and irrevocably denied must attain a level at which both participants require a change of partner. Elizabeth's vanity was such that the attention of one suitor alone could never satisfy; she missed few new faces at court, and more than one handsome young nobleman was often rendered gawky and self-conscious as a country clod as the Queen singled him out for attention. It might last two days, two weeks or two months before he found himself abandoned and back in obscurity's shade after preening in the brilliance of royalty's favor. Leicester certainly had affairs in and out of the court which satisfied his physical desires as Elizabeth satisfied his ego. Both would probably have admitted their relationship had many disadvantages even as they also agreed that they could not do without each other. Elizabeth was scornful of the rumors and gossip which attended her feeling for her ⊙ ⊙. Along with Cecil, Robert Dudley was one of the few about the court whom she trusted. She also loved and needed him. Everything else was superfluous; her conscience was clear.

Elizabeth's conscience regarding her possible successors might have justifiably been troubled during January, 1568, when Lady Katherine Grey ended her seven-year imprisonment. The girl who had surreptitiously wed Edward Seymour, the Earl of Hertford, without royal consent and borne him two sons had spent her last years in a captivity which seemed not only to deplete her own frail strength, but also that of her custodians. Four years previously, she had been sent from plague-ridden London to the custody of her uncle John Grey at his country seat near Havering-atte-Bower in Essex. Lady Katherine arrived with her oldest son (the other being in the custody of the father), several attendants and baggage which included her collection of monkeys, parrots and small dogs. Though she had traveled in one of the Queen's coaches, the long journey had been over ill-kept roads, and her own health was such that the fatigued woman was in bed for days.

While John Grey was happy to have his niece released from the Tower, his joy did not extend to her being in his custody, for the girl's physical and emotional condition interrupted the peaceful routine of his well-run household. He lamented his plight to Cecil, saying that " . . .the thought and care she taketh for the want of Her Highness' favour pines her away; before God I speak it. If it come not sooner, she will not long live thus—she eateth not above six morsels in the meal. If I say unto her, 'Good Madame, eat somewhat to comfort yourself' she falls a-weeping and goeth up to her chamber. If I ask her what the cause is she useth herself in that sort, she answers me: 'Alas! Uncle, what a life this is to me, thus to live in the Queen's displeasure; but for my Lord and my children, I would to God I were buried.' "[12] Sometime later Katherine's husband, still in the house custody of his mother, wrote Leicester asking his intercession with the Queen. "I still crave your especial and most humble means of desire to her Majesty that we may be unburdoned of her Highness' intolerable displeasure, the great weight whereof hath sufficently taught us never to offend so merciful a Princess." The "merciful Princess," however, remained unmoved, and neither Cecil nor Leicester's protests were of any help. During the stormy session of the last Parliament, Lady Katherine Grey had been prominently mentioned as Elizabeth's successor should the Queen any longer defer that matter herself. The last thing Elizabeth wished was to have Katherine Grey and her husband once more about the court. Even when her uncle John Grey died ("his friends report that he died of worry, but his gout was sufficient to have ended his life") and hopes ran high for Katherine's return, she went instead to Ingatestone Hall, the Essex home of Sir William Petre, who died shortly thereafter. Katherine was then taken to Sir John Wentworth's home, Gosfield Hall. Sir John, like his predecessors, complained of his unwelcome guest and called himself a "most unmeet man to receive such a charge, being of years above three score and sixteen and of late much visited with sickness."[13] The poor gentleman had little sympathy with either the Queen or Katherine, and her arrival with her grotesque entourage eventually hastened him into an early grave within a matter of months.

Katherine Grey's last abode was Cockfield Hall at Yoxford in the custody of Sir Owen Hopton. Elizabeth wrote Sir Owen, "Do not suffer her to have any conference with any stranger, nor that any resort be made unto her other than by yourself and of your household." The Queen need not have worried. Sorrow, anxiety and melancholy had severely depressed the woman who, for seven years, had lived in unhappy restraint in various houses, as unwanted as she was unwelcome. Upon her arrival, Hopton wrote, "She is now come to such weakness that she hath kept her bed these three days being not able to rise and take little sustenance. . . ." It almost seemed as if the wretched girl was willing to die, for when Lady Hopton kindly urged her to get well, she replied, "No, no, my Lady, my time is come and it is not God's will that I should live longer. . . ." When Sir Owen joined his wife in the sickroom and asked Katherine "how she did?" the girl weakly replied, "Even going to God, Sir Owen, even as fast as I can." Before her strength gave out, she made him promise "that you yourself with your own mouth, will make this request unto the Queen's Majesty which shall be the last suit and request I ever shall make to her Highness, even from the mouth of a dead woman." Katherine's wishes were simple: she asked the Queen "to be good unto my children and not impute my fault unto them. . . . I desire her to be good unto my Lord [her husband] for I know this my death will be heavy news to him." Asking for her jewel box, she showed the Hoptons her wedding rings, fondling them carefully and asking they be given to her husband. Lying back on her pillow, she said, "Welcome, death . . . " whereby Sir Owen, knowing the end was near, asked that the church bell be rung. The girl seemed to slumber, awakening at nine o'clock for only a moment to utter the same words her sister Lady Jane Grey had said fourteen years previously, "Into thy hands I commend my spirit. . . ." She was only twenty-seven years old.[14]

Elizabeth's persecution of Lady Katherine Grey was not judged harshly.[15] In the eyes of her contemporaries, her long detention was a wise and necessary political ploy. It removed a major figure—a frail and not very bright young woman—from stage center to the wings and thus effectively prevented her from serving as a focal point for intrigue against the monarchy. It was her subjects' opinion that the Queen had merely availed herself of the opportunity incurred by Katherine's own foolish actions to protect her Crown. And even as she did so, events in Scotland and in other parts of her island kingdom were stirring which would sorely test her patience and courage. The tragedy of Katherine Grey was now to be played again. This time, however, the participant was a dishonored Queen, Mary Stuart, and her tragedy would unfold on a wider stage which would encompass the full remainder of her lifetime.

After almost eleven months of captivity, Mary Stuart escaped from the island castle of the Douglases at Lochleven. Plans were seemingly well laid, commencing with Mary winning the devotion of the Regent's younger half brother George Douglas, who, according to

Melville, "was in a fantasy of love with her." When he engineered one escape plan which aborted, his family banned George from the island so that Mary might not work further "witchery" on him. He carried letters the frantic captive had written to Catherine de Medici in which Mary pleaded for her former mother-in-law to "have pity on me—for if you do not take me by force, I shall never go from hence, of that I am sure. . . ." Mary begged Catherine to send French troops, indicating that many noble Scots would revolt against Murray "if they have but the means of gathering themselves together."[16] The Queen wrote this letter—which breaks off in mid-sentence—the day before her dramatic escape; it is obvious she did not know of the final plans until the last moment.

George Douglas had remained in the Lochleven neighborhood quietly mustering support for the Queen. A plan was worked out in which a sixteen-year-old foundling, adopted by the Laird and given the name of Willie Douglas, would secure the gate keys and row the Queen to the opposite shore. Not only did Willie secure the keys by the ruse of dropping a napkin over them as they lay beside the Laird's plate at dinner, but he also locked all the gates behind him as he left. Previously he had thoroughly punctured all the boats so they might not be followed. Willie met Mary, who, by prearrangement, was waiting with a young maid in her chamber. Together they stole along the corridors where the sounds of diners could be heard, across the courtyard, through the last gate, which Willie locked behind him. Quickly the Queen and her companion sprang into a waiting skiff while Willie dropped the keys into a nearby cannon. In a moment they were off.

George Douglas was waiting with horses for Mary and her companions. Eagerly the Queen mounted; it had been nearly a year since she had had the pleasure of being astride a horse, and all her senses responded to the simple miracle of being free. Now with the others, she rode fiercely throughout the night. At Lord Seton's house at Long Niddry at midnight, "while men were stretching their aching legs," Mary was feverishly sending dispatches, making plans, the joy of her freedom reflected in the features which showed no sign of fatigue or fear. At sunrise they were off again, bound for the castle of the Hamiltons, some four leagues from Dumbarton, where Mary wrote to Elizabeth, to the Cardinal of Lorraine, to de Silva in London begging Philip's help and to the King of France asking for arms.

In Glasgow, Murray learned of his half sister's escape and hastened to issue a proclamation in the name of her son, the King, asking subjects to muster with fifteen days of provisions "for the preservation

of the King's person and authority and the establishing of quietness."
Murray's Regency had borne its share of disillusionment. Morton,
Mar, Glencairn, Lords Hume, Lindsay, Ruthven "and many of the old
professors of these parts" were still with him, but others—such as the
powerful Hamiltons—had fallen away. They resented the Regent's
usurpation of power; more practically, his prudent and austere use of
that power had set ill with those who had expected more from him. He
had helped himself liberally to Mary's jewels, gowns, furniture, plate,
tapestries and beds, giving some to his wife and putting others up for
sale,* which "colded many stomachs among the Hamiltons especially."[17] Mary had always intended that her personal jewels would
be added to the Scottish Crown jewels, but the Regent was desperate
for funds, and many of Mary's outstanding collection were now lost
forever to the nation.

Within ten days, Mary had rallied the support of a small army of
between 5,000 and 6,000 including the Earls of Argyll, Cassilis, Eglin-
ton, Rothes and Lord Herries. Joyously, feeling again the power of a
sovereign and anticipating the further fruits of freedom, she set out on
the morning of May 13 for Dumbarton, where she had hoped "to draw
to me again, little by little, my whole subjects." In the meantime,
Murray had stationed his forces on a hill near Langside overlooking
Govan Moor just outside Glasgow. Informed of their presence, Mary
hesitated and again suggested going to Dumbarton. There at least the
sea would be her last avenue of escape. But the Hamiltons, anxious to
have this chance of unseating Murray from the Regency and over-
confident because of their larger forces, "must needs hazard battle then
and there." They also thought "to be masters of the Queen, to command and rule all at their pleasure. . . ."[18]

Mary sat astride her horse and watched from the height overlooking
Langside one-half mile away. From the beginning, her forces were at a
disadvantage, having to push through the fringes of Langside village,
through hedges, buildings and enclosures to the high open ground,
where they met the full body of the Regent's attack. At once the
initiative was lost, and they, who in a more offensive position might
have won, were at a supreme disadvantage. At the first shock, Patrick
Campbell, the Earl of Argyll, became so frightened "for fault of
courage and spirit" that he fainted in the saddle. The panting clans-

*On the very day that the Scottish Queen was writing to Elizabeth of her escape, the English
Queen was gazing in awe at Mary's famous pearls. They consisted of six rows of extremely large
pearls the color of muscat grapes. Elizabeth's fondness for pearls was well known. They were sold
at considerably below their value to the English Queen, even though Catherine de Medici also
tried to obtain their return. They may be seen in many of Elizabeth's later portraits.

men, climbing to meet the foe, lacking direction and leadership, were no match for their better disciplined opponents, who, aware they were outnumbered, fought savagely and brilliantly under the direction of Kirkcaldy and Morton. Soon Mary's forces degenerated, and the battle became a rout. After three-quarters of an hour, "with the slaughter of six score or thereby of the chief Hamiltons, they were overthrown." The survivors abandoned their artillery and left their dead and wounded on the field. The spectacle sent Mary fleeing in panic "in so great fear that she rode away at full speed." She could barely comprehend the bloody slaughter she had witnessed and now possessed only one thought: safety. With sixteen others, including George Douglas and Lord Herries, she rode without a backward glance into the comparative safety of the Catholic southwest, never stopping except for horses until she had put some ninety miles between herself and the carnage at Langside. On May 15 she was at Dundrennan Abbey near Kirkcudbright on the Solway Firth. It was the first anniversary of her marriage to Bothwell.

From Dundrennan, Mary assessed her position. As she later wrote her uncle, the Cardinal of Lorraine, "I have endured injuries, calumnies, imprisonment, famine, cold, heat, flight, without knowing whither, ninety-two miles across the country without supping or alighting. And then I have had to sleep upon the ground and drink sour milk and eat oatmeal without bread and have been three nights like the owls, without a female, in this country." To Elizabeth she wrote piteously, "I am now forced out of my kingdom and driven to such straits that, next to God, I have no hope but in your goodness. I beseech you, therefore my dearest sister, that I may be conducted to your presence, that I may acquaint you with all my affairs." In closing Mary wrote, "To remind you of the reasons I have to depend on England, I send back to its Queen this token the jewel of her promised friendship and assistance."[19] Accompanying the letter was the heart-shaped diamond Elizabeth had previously sent as a pledge of her friendship and support.

The Regent Murray had no thought of permitting his sister to remain at large. Mary realized she had to make the most of her brief respite. Before the web of captivity was drawn tightly around her once more, she must make her decision. Already several of the nobles who had accompanied her were wondering how to make their peace with the victorious Regent. Mary, in turn, was wary of their loyalty; they might buy their own safety by surrendering her to Murray. When Lord Herries ventured to ask, "Why she would not remain in Scotland and trust to a better fortune in the future?" Mary bitterly answered that "it was impossible for her to remain in any part of her realm, not knowing whom to trust. . . ."[20]

Several of her companions advised her to take ship for France or Spain, but Mary was reluctant. Philip and the Pope would have no wish to support her. Politically she had lost Scotland to the Reformation. Personally, she had married a heretic in a Protestant ceremony, a man everyone considered Darnley's murderer. Above all, Mary would not hear of returning to France "with the equipage of an exile or fugitive where she had formerly appeared in so much glory and splendour" to bear the malice of *la grossa Caterina* or else be cloistered in some religious shelter for her remaining years. Instead, Mary looked across the Solway for succor and haven. In England, as a descendant of Margaret Tudor she would still be regarded with respect. It was the English Queen who had threatened English fire and sword if one hair of Mary's head were touched during her imprisonment. She would seek the protection of Elizabeth, her cousin, forgetting momentarily the years in which she had also claimed that cousin's Crown.

Therefore, Mary Stuart made her decision. She had arrived at the edge of her realm facing the shores of a country through which she had once been denied safe-conduct from storms. Now storms of her own making had forced her—she who had known splendor, sorrow and ecstasy—to seek refuge. Grandeur and luxury—known to only a few in life—also had been hers. Three husbands, two kingdoms, many close and dear friends she would never forget and many treacherous, self-seeking others best forgotten had filled her twenty-five years. If ambition and a foolish self-indulgence had brought her to this end, Mary might bitterly have wondered at this moment at the folly of her predicament. Yet never for one moment did she doubt but that Elizabeth would joyously receive her, a sister sovereign, and help reinstate her on her throne. Finally, she could wait no longer. With little intact but her pride, on the morning of Sunday, May 16, 1568, Mary, Queen of Scotland and the Isles, crossed Solway Firth and landed at the village port of Workington on the Cumberland coast of England. It was the first step in the unfolding tragedy during which she would spend tedious hours embroidering her prophecy "In the end is my beginning."

The news of Mary's arrival in England created great consternation at the English court. While the northern counties, "swarming with Catholics," were celebrating her escape with bonfires and ringing of church bells, the situation in London was very different. Immediately, Elizabeth called a meeting of her Council, before whom "she spoke strongly for Mary." The Queen's first instincts were to befriend the woman now dethroned and dishonored, but few of her Councillors agreed. They insisted that Mary's presence in England was a threat to their sovereign and argued that Elizabeth's assistance would entail arms and money to help Mary regain her Crown. It would be an affront to the Regent, as well as the Protestants of both countries. De Silva aptly summed up the English government's quandary when faced with Mary's defection when he wrote: "I think they must be somewhat embarrassed as this Queen has always shown good will to the Queen of Scots and the Council, or a majority of it, has been opposed to her and lean to the side of the Regent and his government." Elizabeth, however, had refused to recognize James' Regency;* to do so would concede that Mary was no longer the sovereign. De Silva maintained that: "If the Queen has her way now, they will be obliged to treat the Queen of Scots as a sovereign, which will offend those who forced her to abdicate, so that, although these people are glad enough to have her in their hands, they have many things to consider. If they keep her as if in prison, it will probably scandalize all neighboring princes, and if she remains free and able to communicate with her friends, great suspicions will be aroused. In any case, it is certain that two women will not agree very long together.[22]

The astute de Silva had probed to the heart of the royal dilemma—a dilemma which would test the endurance of two monarchs for almost a quarter of a century. The presence of the Queen of Scots indeed placed the Queen of England in a singularly embarrassing position. For years, Elizabeth had pledged to regard Mary as a "natural sister or daughter." She had used her royal authority to effective advantage at Mary's first imprisonment, and her envoy, Throckmorton, said his presence and Elizabeth's aggressive support had saved Mary's life. Now the woman had escaped and was in her own land under circumstances in which such promises would be expected to be honored. At once Mary had put her hand to paper to remind Elizabeth of her past assurances. Two days after her arrival, the Scottish Queen wrote to Elizabeth from Workington, recounting the events leading from Rizzio's and Darnley's death, to her marriage and subsequent imprisonment. Her letter continued:

Afterwards, by God's guidance, I escaped out of prison and being guarded with the flower of nobility, which gladly flocked to me from all parts, I put my enemies in mind of their duty and allegiance. I offered

*Yet while Mary was at Lochleven, Cecil was secretly writing Murray and urging him vigorously to settle the problem of his royal half sister and the Catholic party in Scotland once and for all.[21]

them pardon, and propounded that both parties might be heard in an Assembly of the Estates, lest the commonwealth should be rent any longer with civil combustions. Two messengers I sent about this matter—both of them they cast in prison. Those which aided me they proclaimed traitors and commanded them by public proclamation that they should presently leave me. I prayed them that the Lord Boyd might upon public faith and assurance treat with them about a compositon, but this also they flatly denied. Yet I hoped that by your mediation, they might have been recalled to their duty. But when I saw that I must have undergone either death or a new imprisonment, I resolved to go to Dumbarton. They in the way opposed themselves against me, slew and put my men to flight in battle. I betook myself to the Lord Herries with whom I am come into your kingdom, trusting assuredly in your singular kindness, that you will assist me, and excite others by your example.

I do therefore earnestly entreat you that I may be forthwith conducted unto you, who am now in very great straits, as I shall more fully inform you when it shall please you to take pity on me.

God grant unto you a long and safe life and to me patience and consolation which I hope and pray that I may obtain of Him by your means.

MARIE[23]

Mary's letter raised the first of the countless twinges of insecurity, doubt and resentment of which Elizabeth Tudor was to experience many during the next nineteen years. She had rejoiced in Mary's escape, writing, ". . .my hand has seldom performed its office toward you since your unfortunate captivity. I could not write to you without pain. But hearing the joyful news of your escape, affection for you as my near relation and my sense of what is due to the honour of a Queen, constrains me to send you these few words. . . ." The "few words" became quite lengthy since Elizabeth could not refrain from lecturing her cousin for her lack of regard for "that state and that honour" that it was to be a Queen. The messenger bringing the letter was instructed to amplify further Elizabeth's insistence that Mary abandon Bothwell and prove her own innocence in Darnley's murder. She had ended her letter saying, "Remember that those who have two strings to one bow may shoot strongly, but they rarely hit the mark . . .," an undoubted reference to Mary's claim to the English Crown as well as the one she had lost.

But now, faced with a fugitive Queen on English soil, Elizabeth's own common sense, strengthened by her Councillors' advice, led to a less personal evaluation of the situation. Her ministers recounted Mary's past sins: she had openly made challenge to the English Crown, "not as a second person after the Queen's Majesty, but before her." She had never ratified the Treaty of Edinburgh. She had kept contact with those staunch English Catholics in the North and boasted of their partiality for her cause. It was easy to recount Mary's failings, but not so simple to decide what was to be done with her. Political assassination, while still prevalent, was not as easy or as highly regarded as it once had been. One of the first things Elizabeth commanded was that Mary's food be prepared by her own servants who ultimately joined and remained with her, lest any accidental illness or death be imputed to her personally. To return Mary to Scotland and the Regent Murray was tantamount to execution or a long and more rigorous imprisonment. To lead an army to assist her to regain the Scottish throne was foolhardy and an endeavor her Protestant government and subjects would scarcely stand for. To let her remain free in England and to act as a lure to every Catholic, as a magnet for intrigue, as a pivot for the schemes of France and Spain was an old, old story, one very familiar to Elizabeth. To bring her to court—where it was apparent Mary felt she had every right to be—the woman who for years had carried England's arms and called herself England's rightful Queen—was unthinkable. But what to do with Mary Stuart?

It was, inevitably, Mary herself who provided the answer. Mary had been escorted to Carlisle Castle, where, as the unbelievable tidings spread across the hills, bright with the new green of an early spring, the pilgrimage started. Everywhere Catholics of high and low degree, attracted as by a lodestar, went to pay their respects to the Queen of Scotland. Mary had nothing in the way of suitable clothing, and one wealthy merchant, Henry Fletcher, came bringing thirteen yards of crimson velvet, while Mary awaited Elizabeth's response to her plea to send suitable clothing, jewels and ornaments for her use. She was soon joined by John Leslie, the Bishop of Ross, and members of the Livingston and Fleming family who left Scotland to be with her. And Mary Seton, the last of the "four Marys" also was joyously reunited with the Queen.

Officially, Elizabeth sent Sir Francis Knollys, her Vice-Chamberlain, and Lord Scrope, Governor of Carlisle and Warden of the Western Marches. Sir Francis carried a parcel of clothing from Elizabeth for the Scottish Queen, and even his fine Puritan sense of fitness was jolted when he observed the miserable torn remnants which constituted the package Mary eagerly opened. Lamely, he apologized, stating the contents must have been intended for one of her serving women, while the Queen gazed, stricken and speechless, at the contents.

For the next several days a stream of letters from Sir Francis and Lord Scrope left Carlisle. At first, both were plainly impressed by Mary, writing, ". . . we found the Queen of Scots in her chamber of presence ready to receive us. After . . . our declaration also of your Highness' sorrowfulness for her lamentable misadventures and inconvenient arrival . . . we found her in her answers to have an eloquent tongue and a discreet head, and it seemeth by her doings she hath stout courage and liberal heart. . . ."

The emissaries delivered Elizabeth's letters in which she stated that she could not receive Mary until the circumstances of Darnley's death had been resolved. After reading the eagerly awaited communications, Knollys reported that Mary "fell into some passion with the water in her eyes, and therewith she drew us with her into her bedchamber, where she complained unto us, for that your Highness did not answer her expectation for the admitting her into your presence forthwith. . . ." Mary passionately declared that she had come into England "not of necessity" but only of goodwill and asked that Elizabeth either aid her or "give her passage through your country into France, to seek aid at other Princes' hands, not doubting but both the French King and the King of Spain would give her relief. . . ."[24]

Neither Knollys nor Lord Scrope pointed out the pitiable lack of reality in Mary's statement that she had not come "of necessity" into England or the fact that both the French and the Spanish Kings were something less than enthusiastic in their desire to assist her. Instead, they said they would "advertise her determinations with all speed" to Elizabeth, and with the letter went their own careful appraisal of the situation. They said that "many gentlemen of diverse shires . . . have heard her daily defence and excuses of her innocency. . . ." To keep such an "innocent" Queen in restraint would win Elizabeth little admiration, and Sir Francis reflected "whether it were not honorable for you in the sight of your subjects and of all foreign Princes, to put her Grace to the choice whether she will depart back into her country . . . or whether she will remain at your Highness' devotion within your realm here. . . . For, by this means, your Highness shall stop the mouths of backbiters, that otherwise blow out seditious rumors, as well in your own realm as elsewhere, of detaining her ungratefully."

But apparently both Knollys and Lord Scrope were mystified about Mary's true intentions. The letter continues: "And yet I think it is likely that if she had her own choice, she would not go back into her own realm presently, nor until she might look for succor of men out of France to join with her there. . . ." The Englishmen were mindful, as was Mary, of the danger of the Regent's forces. But, said they, "she cannot be kept so rigorously as a prisoner with your Highness' honour, in mine opinion, but with the devices of towels or toys at her bedchamber window, or elsewhere, in the night, a body of her agility and spirit may escape sooner, being so near the Border." The letter ended prophetically: "And surely to have her carried further into the realm is the highway to dangerous sedition. . . ."[25]

Mary's emissary, Lord Herries, who had assisted her out of Scotland, was sent by the Queen to London to plead for a safe-conduct into France, so that Mary "might seek succour from other Princes and friends, my allies, without any prejudice to the ancient friendship between us two. . . ." Mary exhibited her first awareness, some tremor of fear at her restraint, when she wrote to Elizabeth belligerently "that there was nothing to prevent me from applying to them, but this detention, which I think rather harsh and strange, considering I came so frankly into your country, without any condition, or any distrust of your friendship, promised in your frequent letters. . . ." If Mary's frank and somewhat derisive tone was meant to stir Elizabeth to some. decision, it only had the predictable result of giving the English Queen an opportunity to delay. She wrote, acknowledging Mary's desire "to justify yourself in my presence of the things charged against you." She understood that desire, she wrote, emphasizing her own similar feeling. "Oh Madame, there is no creature living more desiring to hear it than I, or who will more readily lend her ears to such answer as shall acquit your honour. But whatever my regard for you, I can never be careless of my own reputation. I am held suspect for rather wishing to defend you herein, than opening my eyes to see things these people condemn you in. . ."[26] As Mary read Elizabeth's rather pious words, some remembrance of the English Queen's own brush with iniquity in the matter of Amy Dudley's mysterious death must have entered her mind and embittered her even further.

Lord Herries arrived in London, carrying Mary's letters to Elizabeth; he protested violently that since his arrival he had been watched as if he were a prisoner. He demanded a prompt audience with the Queen, complaining after a three-day interval "he could not suffer the long delay usual here, nor would the nature of his business permit it. . . ." He wished to see Elizabeth, he stated bluntly, to discern whether "as she had always promised. . .she would help his Queen. . . ." If Elizabeth were to continue to hold herself aloof, he told her Councillors, "then he would go and beg the aid of the King of France, the Emperor, the King of Spain and the Pope," to which the Earl of Bedford, a noted Puritan, dramatically held his hands before his eyes and cried distastefully, "The Pope?" as Herries tartly ended,

"Yes, and even the Grand Turk... seeing the need my Queen is in...!"[27]

Herries' venture was fruitless. Not only did Elizabeth remain indecisive, but she also refused passports for either Herries or Lord Fleming to go into France, saying she "was not so wholly bereft of her senses as to allow the chatelaine of Dumbarton to introduce the French into the country." Mary was bitter at Elizabeth's reaction and "burst into great passion and weeping," crying that only God was her judge and no one else "could take upon them to judge Princes." She said caustically that "it appeared that the Queen's Majesty would be more favourable to my Lord of Murray and his than she would be to her." The Regent, said Mary resentfully, had access to Elizabeth, yet the Queen would not receive her own cousin, who had come "only to purge herself." Had Mary accurately assessed the reality of her position—or had she known Elizabeth better—she might have exercised more patience, restraint and self-discipline. She might have adopted a meeker attitude, a softer approach to Elizabeth, allowing the English Queen to play the self-righteous forgiving sister sovereign, for she did not know as yet how impossible it was for Elizabeth to bestow anything which was demanded. And so Mary did none of the things which might have placed Elizabeth in a less rigid position. Instead, letter followed letter—to the Kings of Spain and France, to Catherine de Medici and to the Pope. And with Elizabeth's constant refusal to admit Mary to her presence, her refusal to allow the Scottish emissaries abroad, Mary's own passionate pride erupted. In a letter written less than a month after her incarceration, she wrote:

Carlisle, June 13, 1568

MADAME, MY GOOD SISTER,

I thank you for the dispositon which you have to listen to the justification of my honour, which ought to be a matter of importance to all Princes, and especially to you, as I have the honour to be so near of kin to you. But it seems to me that those who persuade you that my reception would turn to your dishonour manifest the contrary. But alas, Madame, when did you ever hear a Prince censured for listening in person to the grievances of those who complain that they have been falsely accused? Dismiss, Madame, from your mind, the idea that I came hither to save my life; neither the world nor all Scotland has cast me out; but to recover my honour, and to obtain support to enable me to chastise my false accusers, not to answer them as their equal, for I know that they ought not to enter into engagements against their sovereign, but to accuse them before you, that I have chosen you from among all other Princes, as my nearest kinswoman and perfect friend....[28]

Mary's pride is apparent in every line. She had conveniently forgotten her former words, "I am now forced out of my kingdom and driven to such straits that, next to God, I have no hope but in your goodness. . . ." Her passionate words may have helped alleviate that wounded pride, but they made little sense from a woman who had fled as one possessed across her border to the safety of a neighboring realm. Now she chose conveniently to forget those words, stating with a touch of remembered arrogance that "I supposed it an honour" to be called the Queen's restorer, who hoped to received this kindness from you, giving you the honour and the glory all my life, making you also thoroughly acquainted with my innocence, and see how falsely I have been led." Mary then threw Elizabeth's fine words in her face, stating, "I see, to my regret, that I am mistaken. . . ."

Mary's letters abroad had promised that "she would be Queen of England in three months if an armed force were sent to her assistance."[29] As the weeks passed, however, and Elizabeth made no definite move, as the Scottish emissaries were refused permission to travel abroad and did not, as yet, dare return to Scotland, Mary's optimism began to fade. She wrote revealingly to her uncle the Cardinal of Lorraine, "If you have not pity upon me now, it is all over with my son, my country and myself."

Interim

Chapter Seventeen

H ad it been possible in early 1568 to view the reign of Elizabeth I as a whole, the five years commencing with the detention of the Queen of Scots would have been seen to be decisive. Those years constitute a natural division, a period in which all of Queen Elizabeth's personal energies, formidable intelligence, malleable conscience and remarkable staying power were called into play. During those years, political forces which had been steadily increasing in authority reached the peak of their strength. Luckily, through her devotion to hard work and the constant exercise of her native perception, Elizabeth had similarly grown in stature, knowledge and experience. She had successfully passed the first difficult hurdles with which any monarch is confronted. With the exception of minor forays into Scotland and France, her realm had been largely at peace, and the Protestant cause had been energized in England, as well as on the Continent. She had kept the balance of power and the tenuous friendship of two powerful nations, France and Spain—a notable achievement considering the infringement her sailors were continually making on Spanish shipping and her concern for the Huguenot cause in France. She had known when to compromise and when to stand firm. She had been fortunate, as Cecil continually reminded her, at the same time expressing his opinion that such good fortune could not last forever.

Personally, Elizabeth believed that such "good fortune" was the result of shrewd planning, an awareness of her opponents' advantages and a willingness to take a chance when the rewards loomed large. In this respect her ability to estimate the potential worth of a subject—or an ally—was superior to most of her Councillors, whose main ambition often seemed a consistent desire to oppose one another. Her ability to involve herself in a situation, appraising it as a whole, was a trait her more narrow-minded ministers eventually came to regard with respect. Over the past years, she had honed this astuteness to a remarkable fineness, vigorously applying it to any situation, large or small.

Never, under any circumstances could Elizabeth be guilty of *laissez-faire*. By 1568 her ten years on the throne had seen an early vigilance, the offshoot of her youthful vulnerability, replaced by an optimistic self-confidence which came naturally instead of being assumed to hide her inner wariness. She had acquired additional poise and learned to give full vent to her naturally dominating and aggressive personality, although vacillation and an inability to make up her mind continued to vex her associates. She had firmly grasped the mantle of sovereignty and authority. She was supreme in the court and in the nation, and her awareness of a justly earned power was a great and secure personal satisfaction. More important, she knew her subjects, Councillors and courtiers recognized it also and that the other crowned heads of Europe rendered her a grudging esteem. It was during these subsequent five years, after 1568, that the true stature of the Queen of England emerged, when the foundations for that tremendous outburst of creativity, of industrial and social expansion which led to the creation of an English empire were laid.

These were the years which would see the first serious danger to her Crown, a challenge to her policies, a threat to her very life. From the moment that Mary Stuart had crossed the Solway, Elizabeth recognized—and Cecil emphasized—the menace constituted by the Scottish Queen. Her detention was the stimulus which provoked immediate political and religious dissension, while Mary Stuart herself evoked anger, pity, resentment or pride, depending on one's point of view and one's religion. Mary was to be the catalyst—and eventually to assist in every way possible—by which a threat to the English sovereign and to English power might result in her own succession and the advancement of her Catholic faith. Indeed, for the next eighteen years, the problem of the Queen of Scots was to be the prevalent topic in English politics.[1]

Struggling to find some answer to the perplexing dilemma of Mary Stuart, William Cecil had, as usual, drawn up a concise paper, "Things to be Considered on the Queen of Scots' Coming to England," in which he listed her willingness to enter England "trusting Elizabeth's many promises of help." She had, wrote Mr. Secretary, been "unlawfully condemned . . . imprisoned . . . refused leave to answer in person or by advocate in the Parliament which condemned her." She was a Queen, Cecil noted, and "not bound by law to answer her subjects" and had offered, once in Elizabeth's presence, "to acquit herself." Contrary to all these compelling declarations was the fairly substantial recognition that "she had procured her husband's murder," had protected Bothwell, causing him to divorce his wife, and then "feigned to be forcibly taken by him and then married him, increasing his power to a point that none of her nobles dared abide about her," all the while refusing the aid of any noble who might have rescued her.[2] Mary Stuart must, said Cecil, be adjudged guilty or innocent and, if blameless, restored to her throne. If proved guilty, she could hardly be returned to Scotland or allowed entry into France to enlist aid in recovering her lost Crown. And, as heiress presumptive—even if unnamed—to the Crown of England, she would use all her considerable influence with the English Catholics to assert that claim. It was a dilemma without precedent, which taxed all of Cecil's native wisdom. Such was the situation which faced Elizabeth and all England during midsummer of 1568, when the problem of the Scottish Queen, with its varying religious and political implications, occupied the mind and emotions of everyone.

Elizabeth kept in constant touch with Mary's custodians. At Carlisle Castle, Sir Francis Knollys' daily visits with Mary, whom he called a "notable woman," were revealing and piqued Elizabeth's natural curiosity regarding this cousin who had muddied her life so thoroughly that she had lost her Crown. Knollys wrote William Cecil that Mary "seemeth to regard no ceremonious honour beside the acknowledging of her estate regal." (For one so used to Elizabeth's constant insistence on "ceremonious honour" paid to her own royalty, Mary's lack in this respect must have been startling.) His letter continued:

> She showeth a great desire to be avenged of her enemies; she showeth a readiness to expose herself to all perils in hope of victory; she delighteth much to hear of hardiness and valiance. . . .The thing that most she thirsteth after is victory, and it seemeth to be indifferent to her to have her enemies diminish, either by the sword of her friends or by the liberal promises and rewards of her purse, or by divisons and quarrels, raised among themselves, so that for Victory's sake, pain and perils seem pleasant unto her. . . .

Sir Francis had asked Cecil, "Now what is to be done with such a Lady and Princess. . . . I refer to your judgment." Knollys feared that Mary would seek French aid. Unwisely, the Scottish Queen, too, played on this fear; Knollys wrote that "no fair semblance of speech seemeth to win any credit with her. . .this cold dealing will not satisfy her fiery stomach and surely it is a great vanity, in mine opinion, to think she would be stayed by courtesy, or bridled by straw, from bringing in of the French into Scotland. . .to satisfy her bloody appetite to shed the blood of her enemies." Mary had also told Knollys that "unless she be removed as a prisoner," she would not "be removed further into the realm, to be detained from her Highness' presence." It was plain that Sir Francis found the situation wearing. He complained that the couriers were lax, the charges excessive, and then, almost irrelevantly, that Mary's "loathsomeness to be removed further into England" also indicated that "some practices of escaping were not out of her heart, not yet out of her hope." Elizabeth had ordered that Mary "be treated with all honour" and her diversions were ample. She watched a game of football on the Castle's playing green; she walked abroad "with divers gentlemen and other servants" for company; she rode "hunting the hare. . .galloping so fast" that Knollys continued uneasy that "some of her friends out of Scotland might invade and assault us . . . to rescue and take her from us. . . ."[4] In the end Knollys declined to comment further, saying, "But I speak like a blind buzzard and therefore will leave these matters to you that have judgment." He wrote that the return of Lord Herries from London was unwelcome, that "he seeth to the bottom both of your doings and ours and he will stir coals at his coming hither accordingly, neither will there be any end of her [Mary's] perilous practices."[5]

As time went on, Mary's "fiery stomach" asserted itself even more, and her determination to resolve her situation became more evident. She told Knollys that she would "not any longer be delayed, for I will require the Queen, my good sister, that either she will let me go into France, or that she will put me into Dumbarton, unless she will hold me as a prisoner," a condition Mary did not actually believe would happen. Neither did she believe Elizabeth would "of her honour, put me into my Lord of Murray's hands." With understandable ill humor, yet little wisdom or tact, she told Knollys that she would seek aid of the French King and the King of Spain, and, as for England, "she said she had found that true, which she had heard often or before her coming hither, which was that she should have fair words enough, but no deeds." Knollys' own comment to Cecil was: "And surely all deeds are no deeds with her unless her violent appetite be satisfied." He repeated Mary's barely hidden threat, "I have made great wars in Scotland and I pray God I make no troubles in other realms also," and said if she were "detained as a prisoner, we should have much ado with her. . . ."[6] Lamenting the slowness of the courier service, Knollys suggested that Cecil concern himself with "increasing the posts with increasing of their wages for this busy and necessary time."

On July 11, 1568, Knollys was ordered to remove Mary to Bolton

Castle, and he was apprehensive of her reaction. Mild threats had been made to the Scottish Queen, whose letters abroad had promised "she would be Queen of England in three months if an armed force were sent to her assistance."[7] When Elizabeth learned of such tactics, she wrote advising Mary to refrain from making trouble; she was a guest in the realm and would be treated as befitted her rank, but she must seek no foreign aid whatsoever. She was also told that all visitors would be prohibited unless she quietly accepted the move; Sir Francis believed that such threats "that made her more pliant herein than otherwise she would have been." Knollys complained of lack of sufficent horses and litter for the journey and again needled Cecil that "the posts are grown very slack." He said Murray had sent Mary "three coffers of apparel," none of which the Queen considered sufficent, and therefore "we have sent . . . for her desired apparel remaining in Lochleven." He said Mary had "offered our messengers nothing for all their pains and charges," and therefore Elizabeth "is like to bear the charge thereof also." Clearly, Sir Francis' enchantment with the situation was wearing very thin. On the day after the removal to Bolton, during which Mary was "very quiet, very tractable and void of displeasant countenance," he also said she had firmly stated "she will not remove any further into the realm without constraint. . . ." He added, "If I should declare the difficulties that we have passed before we could get her to remove instead of a letter I should write a story and that somewhat tragical!" he lamented. Harassed and fearful, he wrote Cecil that if Mary were to be removed further, "the removing will easier be done, if it be taken in hand by better personages than we are!"

At Bolton, Mary tried another approach. She manifested an interest in the Protestant ritual, disarming Knollys, for she "heareth the faults of Papistry revealed by preaching or otherwise with contented ears and with gentle and weak replies. . . ." The Regent Murray, her half brother, was less impressed and caustically wrote Lord Scrope, Mary's co-custodian, that "her resorting to the Kirk of England did but serve her turn to move godly men to conceive a good opinion of her conformity and towardness."[8] That Murray was correct is shown in one of Mary's own letters to de Silva, the Spanish ambassador, in London, in which she noted the great danger to the remaining Catholics in Scotland and England if she should honestly forsake her religion. "Though for my own part, I would sooner be murdered, yet you had better consider the possibilities and send word to the King, your master," she threatened. When Catholics in the neighborhood—their spontaneous joy at her being in their midst evaporating—reproached her for such tactics, Mary had second thoughts and proudly made a public declaration that she was still staunch in her faith. When Sir Francis, abashed and disappointed, accused her of "backsliding," Mary taunted him, "Would you have me lose France and Spain and all my friends in other places by seeming to change my religion, and yet I am not assured that the Queen, my good sister, will be my friend to the satisfaction of my honour and expectation?"[9] It was clear the situation had to be resolved, and eventually, Knollys wrote Elizabeth that he wished Mary back in Scotland and the Queen, "must deal plainly and sharply with her."

To deal "plainly and sharply with her," Elizabeth had first to deal with her Council and ministers, especially Cecil, whose view of Mary differed strongly from that of his royal mistress. Elizabeth had previously been enraged at Cecil's willingness to treat with the Regent Murray, and her attitude was such that he wrote, discouraged, that he feared "the likelihood of the loss of the fruits of six or seven years of negotiations with Scotland."[10] To Elizabeth, Mary Stuart was still a Queen, the rightful sovereign of Scotland, and Murray was a usurper. To Cecil, Mary was a disgrace to her country and throne, a threat to his own monarch and a serious impediment to the full flowering of Protestantism in Scotland. He regarded Murray as the "savior" of that northern land, and when Elizabeth had procrastinated, finally urging Murray to relent in his treatment of the imprisoned Mary and her followers, Cecil had privately sent a messenger north with instructions urging Murray to haste in resolving the situation once and for all, before his, Cecil's, hands were tied.

Elizabeth's first inclination to be charitable and magnanimous where Mary was concerned had diminished daily; here again the insistence of Cecil and his colleagues ultimately proved correct. Many times in the privacy of her chamber, Elizabeth had attempted to put herself in the Scottish Queen's place. She too had been imprisoned, had suffered calumny, despair and a terror of what the next day might bring. But there had been a tremendous difference. Then she had had only the prospect of a Crown, not its blessed actuality. She had not been an anointed Queen, merely the unfortunate sister of the reigning monarch, the hopeful answer to the political and religious activists who had used her for their own profit, much to her own peril. But Mary Stuart had possessed the Crown of Scotland since she was only a few days old. She had grown up with the privilege and security which royalty bestowed, even acquiring the Crown of France in the interim. To have lost her birthright so shamefully and shockingly—and for a *man*—was an eventuality of which Elizabeth could barely conceive. She had lost respect for Mary's native intelligence and perception when she had wed the fool, Darnley, and her subsequent behavior had done nothing to elevate her in Elizabeth's or anyone else's view.

But it was virtually impossible for Elizabeth to imagine herself placed in Mary's predicament; the reactions and motives of both the Queens were so different as to make any such assessment futile. Mary's presence in the North—a younger, more beautiful woman only too anxious to be a figurehead for those of similar religious faith—posed a threat to Elizabeth which conjured up frightening visions of an abandonment by her subjects similar to that which she had suffered by her father. Rebellion, conspiracy, *treason*—these were old words to Elizabeth, only now *she* had much to suffer and lose should Mary be in any position to claim her rights in the English succession. Elizabeth realized also that continued detention without some cause would only incur more Catholic pity and be an additional reason to ask for French and Spanish assistance. One of her Councillors, Arundel, remarked that "one that has a Crown can hardly persuade another to leave her Crown because her subjects will not obey. It may be a new doctrine in Scotland, but it is not good to be taught in England!" The unfortunate plight of a Queen under restraint—without due cause—was one in which Elizabeth knew she could not assist. Mary was her kinswoman and sister sovereign, however dishonored, and the Queen could not remain deaf to her pleas to come personally to Elizabeth to defend herself. She wrote Mary:

> Oh Madame, there is not a creature living who more longs to hear your justification than myself; not one who would lend more willing ear to any answer which will clear your honour. But I cannot sacrifice my own reputation on your account. To tell you the plain truth, I am already thought to be more willing to defend your cause, than to open my eyes to see the things of which your subjects accuse you.

Elizabeth told Mary she had been warned "to be on her guard" by those who felt Mary's sympathizers might attempt harm to the English Queen. Nevertheless, said Elizabeth, since Mary had committed herself to her cousin for protection, "you may assure yourself I will have that care both of your life and honour, that neither yourself nor your nearest relation could be more concerned for your interests. . . ."

To Mary's persistent plea to meet with Elizabeth, she answered:

> Does it seem strange to you that you are not allowed to see me? I entreat you put yourself in my place! When you are acquitted of this crime, I will receive you with all honour; till that is done, I may not. But afterwards, I

swear by God, that I shall never see a person with better will, and among
all earthly pleasures, I will hold this to be the first. . . ."[11]

As the Scottish Queen bitterly railed at her misfortune and
demanded "to come in person and lay my complaints before you to
justify myself . . . " or, conversely, be allowed to go into France, discussions were held daily in the Council to resolve the perplexing
situation. And again, it was Mary Stuart herself who helped make the
ultimate decision.

By October, as letters arrived daily from Mary, as letters left Bolton
Castle for the Pope, for Charles of France, for Philip of Spain, a scheme
was evolved which was a testament to the political inequities and
unprincipled maneuverings of the sixteenth century, wherein social
and legal justice might be corrupted or twisted to suit immediate and
pressing needs.

Elizabeth's solution to the vexing problem of Mary Stuart was an
offer to act as a mediator between Mary and her half brother, the
Regent Murray. She would hear both sides, said the Queen, and render
an opinion—although what good an opinion only was going to do
under the circumstances no one could say. Murray had privately
shown copies of the Casket Letters to several English representatives in
order to justify his action in imprisoning Mary; theoretically, at least,
they were a powerful denunciation of the Scottish Queen. The Regent
had had sufficient experience, however, with Elizabeth's noted
"lapses" of memory, her inconsistencies and rapid changes of mind and
felt little confidence in her policy where Mary was concerned. Before
the inquiry, he wrote to Elizabeth, asking point-blank what the purpose of accusing his sister would be "when we are not assured what to
prove, or, when have proved, what shall succeed?" In other words, if
Mary were to be proved innocent of any complicity in the Darnley
murder, she would eventually have to be restored to her throne. And
there was little doubt in Murray's mind of the vengeance she would
then wreak on him and his supporters. If, on the other hand, Mary
were to be so dishonored before Scotland and the world that her
restoration was a virtual impossibility, then Murray was anxious to
commence in and cooperate with any proceeding which would bring
about such a desirable end. Disclosure of the Casket Letters was his
solution.

Within weeks, Elizabeth had seen what she must do, and once faced
with the necessity, she pocketed her conscience, stifled some natural
stirrings of compassion, rallied every posture of artifice and cunning
possible and set to work. She well accepted she had no legal authority

for bringing Mary Stuart to trial; it was unthinkable the Scottish Queen would even lend herself to anything resembling a judicial inquiry. But Elizabeth, needing the justification of an open "conference" of sorts before she made any decision, assured her cousin that some sort of "device" must be put forth which would give Mary an opportunity to be heard. Murray, on his part, must justify his usurpation of the Regency, and the Lords of the Congregation would be summoned to answer for their conspiracy and rebellion against their lawful Queen. It was a mere formality, Elizabeth told Mary, and once the inquiry was over, she would be restored "under certain specific guarantees for future peace" and "to stop the mouths of factious, murmuring subjects." She repeated the same substance—that the Queen would be restored to her throne—to de Silva, to Fénelon, the French ambassador, and to Mary's emissary, Lord Herries. However, two weeks before the inquiry opened, she assured Murray that though he would hear such talk of restoration, "should the Queen of Scotland be found guilty, it would behoove her [Elizabeth] to consider otherwise of her cause." Cecil was more succinct. In notes meant to clarify the English position, he wrote, "that it was not meant, if the Queen of Scots should be found guilty of the murder, to restore her to Scotland, however her friends might brag to the contrary."[12]

Mary's first reaction that she must answer for anything was supreme indignation. No Prince should be compelled to answer the charges of rebels! She wrote to Elizabeth, saying, "I will never plead my cause against theirs unless they stand before you in manacles! Madame, I am no equal of theirs and would sooner die than by any act of mine behave as if I were."[13] She denounced the Casket Letters as "impudent forgeries" and declined to attend the inquiry. When informed that default was as damning as an outright accusation, she changed her mind, chose to accept Elizabeth's insistence that the inquiry was a "mere formality" and with false bravado wrote the Kings of Spain and France (who had done nothing to assist her) that her sister Queen was coming to her aid.

Mary chose her confidential secretary, John Leslie, the Bishop of Ross, and Lord Herries to represent her at the conference which opened in October, 1568, at York. The English commissioners comprised the Duke of Norfolk, the Earl of Sussex and Sir Ralph Sadler. The Scottish representatives were William Maitland, the Laird of Lethington, and the Earl of Morton. The varying motives and hopes of all concerned made for an artificial climate of secrecy and distrust in a situation where there were, seemingly, to be no accusations and no judgments, but merely a passive recitation of unsubstantiated facts which might be heard by both sides. Neither Mary's nor Murray's representatives were at their best. Lethington and Morton were too intimately concerned in the crime under discussion to be comfortable. John Leslie privately believed Mary to be guilty (as he would admit several years later), and Lord Herries, Mary's staunch advocate, was extremely concerned what he might recoup from the debacle on his return to Scotland; already his estates had been confiscated.

The English representatives were well aware of Elizabeth's inward and Cecil's outward determination that Mary be so disgraced that her restoration would be impossible. Her continued detention—once Elizabeth's face was saved by an "open inquiry"—was the only answer which solved all the problems represented at the conference table. The Casket Letters were duly produced, and Mary's heart, soul and presumed guilt laid bare to the scrutiny of those present. All were predictably horrified and, just as predictably, affirmed that such evidence of guilt must be more fully explained before Mary's future might be decided.

There was one representative at the conference table who was less enthusiastic in his denunciation. Thomas Howard, the thirty-four-year-old Duke of Norfolk, had, before Darnley had gone to Scotland, been considered as a husband for Queen Mary. On the basis of his landed estates alone, Norfolk was the wealthiest man in England,[14] as well as the premier peer of the realm. His grandfather, the illustrious Lord Treasurer and old war-horse of Henry VIII's Council, had commenced acquiring the vast holdings which comprised the Norfolk Liberty, and the young Duke's subsequent marriages to wealthy widows—and Elizabeth's generosity—had increased his properties in Suffolk, Sussex and Essex. His father, Henry Howard, Lord Surrey, the brash young poet peer, had been beheaded weeks before the death of Henry VIII for his presumptions concerning who would reign after the old King's death. Norfolk was related to Elizabeth; the mother of Anne Boleyn had been Elizabeth Howard, the old Lord Treasurer's sister.

From his family estate at Kenninghall, from the new Howard House now emerging from a renovated old Charterhouse in London, or from the vast fortress of Framlingham Castle, Howard directed the fortunes of his considerable family and, in all places, "lived as a high and mighty Prince." In addition to brothers and sisters wed to other distinguished noblemen, Norfolk possessed a covey of children, either his own or stepchildren acquired from his previous wives, all of whom had died in childbirth. In 1568, recovering from the depression caused by the death of his third wife, he returned to court at the same time as

Mary escaped from Lochleven. His sister, Lady Scrope, was the wife of Mary's co-custodian at Carlisle Castle, and as the months passed, with no decision forthcoming on what Mary's future might hold, more than one English peer, with Catholic leanings and vitally concerned with the succession, concluded that one way of resolving the difficult situation would be to wed Mary to an Englishman. Elizabeth obviously did not favor matrimony or the eventual blessing of an heir, and there were many subjects, particularly Catholics, who looked on Mary as the rightful Queen and her son, James Stuart, as their future monarch. Although Norfolk was a Protestant by virtue of expediency, the Howards originally had been of the Catholic aristocracy, and their Protestantism "sat lightly upon them."

When the official inquiry commenced, it was the Duke of Norfolk who presided. After much deliberation, the Casket Letters were produced and, in Norfolk's estimation, at least were genuine, "the matter contained in them being such as could hardly be invented or devised by any other" than the Scottish Queen. Norfolk further stated the Letters revealed "such inordinate love between her and Bothwell, her loathsomeness and abhorring of her husband that was murdered, in such sort as every good and godly man cannot but detest and abhor the same." Norfolk requested that Murray suppress the letters and "that the Queen should not be accused, nor dishonoured for the King her son's cause and for the respect to the right they both had to succeed to the Crown of England. . . ."[15] As the first surreptitious encouragements were now being tendered to profess Mary as his wife, Norfolk undoubtedly considered the Casket Letters lent little credit to a prospective bride, even a royal one. In the face of Mary's incarceration and an inquiry debating the escapades which had resulted in a murdered husband and the loss of a Crown, even Norfolk might have hesitated. But he was a weak, yet gentle man, easily led, lacking in discernment, and his own natural arrogance and pride led him eventually seriously to consider marrying an alleged adulteress, whose one outstanding attraction in his eye was that she was a Queen. In his optimism he looked no further than Mary's Crown; he gave little thought to the Crown of his own monarch.

Norfolk was not the only Englishman under consideration as a husband for Mary Stuart. Young George Carey, the son of Lord Hunsdon, Elizabeth's cousin, had also been mentioned. As for Queen Mary, it seemed to make little difference. Bothwell had escaped to Norway. There he had been captured by King Frederick, the joint sovereign of Norway and Denmark, who refused to extradite him to

Scotland or allow him to embark for France. Eventually, Bothwell would die insane in his foreign prison.*

From the moment of her own incarceration, however, Mary's interest in and concern for Bothwell lessened considerably. Before the conference at York, she had agreed to a divorce. At the time of the inquiry itself, Norfolk was certainly pondering the thought of marriage with the Scottish Queen and this despite the phrase in his commission which warned that anyone advising or contracting such an alliance for or with Mary "shall be *ipso facto* adjudged as traitorous and shall suffer death." Apparently some inkling of what was going on reached Elizabeth in London, and when she heard from Norfolk that "this cause is the doubtfullest and dangerous that ever I dealt in; if you saw and heard the constant affirming of both sides, not without great stoutness, you would wonder!"[16] she abruptly terminated the inquiry and adjourned it to Westminster. Cecil wrote to Sir Henry Sidney, not without satisfaction, that "The Queen's Majesty is now at the pinch so careful for her own surety and state as I perceive the Queen of Scots shall not be advanced to greater credit than her cause will serve!"[17]

Elizabeth's quandary was reflected in the various courses open to her. She could hope Mary might ratify her abdication and thenceforth, powerless, live in England. Mary might rule jointly with her son, James, or be restored with certain limitations with security for the Regent Murray. It was even suggested at one point that the young Prince be "brought to live in England and eventually succeed to the English Crown," a measure which, in her heart, Elizabeth found difficult to approve.[18] But each and every proposal depended on Mary's cooperation, and she staunchly resisted every effort to tamper with her sovereignty or in any way conciliate Murray. When suggestions concerning Norfolk were whispered to her, she was receptive; Elizabeth had once wished her to marry an Englishman, this same Norfolk. Perhaps it would be the most expedient way out of her troubles.

Elizabeth had selected Norfolk for his "fidelity and circumspection" and because, basically, she trusted him as much as she permitted herself to trust anyone. They had had their differences in the past, and she hadn't failed to call him traitor, conspirator and "words of similar flavour" when he had strongly supported those in the last stormy Parliament who had insisted on the Queen's settling the succession or

*The Earl of Bothwell died in 1578 after almost ten years of imprisonment which broke his health and—because of the increasingly harsh conditions of his confinement—eventually contributed to his insanity. His mummified remains may be viewed in the vault of Faarvegle Church about twenty miles from Dragsholm Castle in Dragsholm, Denmark.

selecting a husband. Withal, as her foremost nobleman and kinsman, she held Norfolk in some esteem—an esteem tempered with an intimate knowledge of his capabilities, ambition and pride. When stories reached the court—as they inevitably did—of his matrimonial interest in Mary, Elizabeth confronted the Duke with her knowledge upon his return from York. Dismayed, he denied any interest in such a marriage, saying "that the project had not originated with him and that he had never given it any encouragement," a partial truth adequately clothed in wishful thinking. Elizabeth persisted, attempting to bait him by saying, "But would you not marry the Scottish Queen if you knew it would tend to the tranquillity of the realm and the safety of my person?" Flustered, the Duke could not reply in the evasive or jocular vein the situation demanded, but instead noted firmly that "no reason could move him to like of her that hath been a competitor to the Crown, and if her Majesty would move him thereto he will rather be committed to the Tower for he never meant to marry with such a person, where he could not be sure of his pillow . . . ," an oblique allusion to Lord Darnley's fate.[19] Outwardly, Elizabeth appeared relieved and "did well allow his vehement disliking of that marriage."

In this atmosphere, on November 25 in the Star Chamber, the conference reopened. Here the English representatives were increased by the addition of Cecil, Bacon, Leicester, Clinton and Arundel. Mary had had some information about the Casket Letters' being submitted as evidence, and she wrote her commissioners, "Ye shall affirm in my name I never wrote anything concerning that matter to any creature and if such writings there be, they are false and feigned, forged and invented by themselves."[20] Her outrage had little effect. Again the Casket Letters were produced for the fascinated eyes of the sober-faced commissioners "and were compared for the manner and writing and fashion of orthography with other letters before written by the Queen of Scots, in the collation whereof no difference was found."[21] Cecil, Leicester, Sir Ralph Sadler and Bacon were convinced. Others, with a bit more conscience and Catholic leanings, expressed room for doubt and stated "they had no right to be her judges."

The main desire of Elizabeth and her representatives was to gain as much justification for themselves from the proceedings, the only merit of which was to disallow Mary's restoration. When no unanimous opinion could be reached, the commissioners were asked if Elizabeth should receive Mary. To this the Lords answered "that they had therein seen such foul matters as they thought truly in their consciences that her Majesty had just cause to refuse to see her, until some answer had been made, first, tending in some way to clear the weight of the charge. They could not think it meet for her Majesty's honour to admit the said Queen to her presence as the case did stand."[22]

On December 14, 1568, at Hampton Court, with Elizabeth herself presiding, the conference was officially adjourned. Nothing had outwardly been resolved. Elizabeth had no official authority to condemn. Yet to acquit and release Mary would encourage Norfolk and the English Catholics, encourage civil war in Scotland, if not in England itself, and leave Mary free to pursue her right in the succession. Elizabeth remembered Cecil's warning that "the Queen of Scots is and always shall be a dangerous person to your estate." Outright vindication being impossible—there was too much substance in the accusations regarding Mary for that—Elizabeth sought to temporize. The last thing she wished was to keep Mary prisoner, to plot and conspire. What she did desire were concessions from Mary both for herself and for the Regent Murray. Therefore, several weeks later, Elizabeth announced that "there had been nothing sufficiently produced nor shown . . . against the Queen . . . whereby the Queen of England should conceive or take any evil opinion of the Queen, her good sister, for anything yet seen." In typical fashion, Elizabeth rendered an inconclusive decision that was "no decision," a result which left Mary Stuart aghast. Knollys reported that "she stood upon her rights" that "she would live and die a Queen!" When Elizabeth's letter reached her stating that "we cannot but let you understand . . . that as we have been sorry of long time for your mishaps and great troubles, so we find our sorrows now doubled in beholding such things as are produced to prove yourself cause of all the same . . . ," Mary assailed Knollys and cried that "she would make all princes know how evil she was handled, she had come on trust to England; she could not believe the Queen would condemn her, hearing her adversaries and not hearing her!"[23]

What everyone carried in his mind at the conclusion of the trial that was no trial was a word no one had uttered: *captivity*. By keeping the Queen under restraint—however much it was to her own personal disliking—Elizabeth had it both ways. Although the decision that was no decision never satisfied her, she could refuse to receive Mary, and more important, Mary's open advocacy of her claim to the English throne was now no longer possible in Parliament.[24] Elizabeth could also threaten Murray and the Scots themselves with Mary's restoration if at any time their actions ruffled the Queen of England's temper.

At the conclusion of the inquiry, Elizabeth sent Mary's commissioners, Lord Herries and the Bishop of Ross to explain the decision to the imprisoned Queen. They carried a letter from the English sovereign in which Elizabeth sought to impress her unfortunate captive with the risk Mary invited by attempting to ally herself with Norfolk or any English Catholic. On January 20, 1569, she wrote to Mary Stuart:

> It may be, Madame, that in receiving a letter from me, you may look to hear something which shall be for your honor. I would it were so—but I will not deceive you. Your cause is not so clear but that much remains to be explained. As I understand it, my heart which directs my hand forbids me to write, because the fruit of a sorrowing spirit is bitter, and I had rather write something else than pen of mine should shed such drops on you.
>
> Your commissioners will tell you what has passed. If they do not tell you also what sincere goodwill I have myself shown towards you, they deceive you and they do me too much wrong. Only let me advise you this: Let not the fine promises, the pleasant voices, which will do you honor through the world, wrap you in clouds and hide the daylight from your eyes. Those do not all love you who would persuade your servants that they love you.
>
> Be not over confident in what you do. Be not blind nor think me blind. If you are wise, I have said enough.[25]

In her chambers at drafty Tutbury Castle, Mary Stuart perceived what had happened. By consenting to the inquiry, she lost what little shreds of immunity her royalty had provided; she had put herself on the defensive. She had been duped by others who decided her fate while she herself remained unheard. Elizabeth and her advisers had betrayed her and broken their promises of nonpartisan involvement; similar damning charges against Murray and his confederates had resulted in no official reaction. Too late Mary recognized she had been beguiled into assent. Murray and others implicated in the Darnley murder had seen the Queen, yet Mary herself, a sister sovereign, was denied admittance to the royal presence.

If Mary was actually guilty of the charges against her, Elizabeth was equally guilty in utilizing a political inquiry in judgment regarding the conflict between Murray and Mary, between Mary and her people and the murder of Darnley. Her first generous impulse to help the Scottish Queen had been stifled. Repeatedly her ministers had pointed out that to admit Mary to her presence was a tacit recognition of her right to be restored to the Scottish throne,[26] and England had neither the men, money nor inclination to participate in such a venture. By keeping Mary in "honourable custody," the threat to her own Crown would be removed, and presumably peace would prevail in Scotland, where further entrenchment of Protestantism would result. Well might old Archbishop Matthew Parker cry, "Now our good Queen has the wolf by the ears!"

It certainly appeared that Elizabeth Tudor had gained an impressive, bloodless victory, but it was to be a victory for which the English Queen would daily have to account. Up to this point she had been supreme in England, but now there was another Queen—a younger, more beautiful sovereign and one made more appealing by the very nature of her confinement. By restraining Mary, Elizabeth encouraged resentment and intrigue which would never have existed had she not resorted to her unjustified course of action. Had she briefly received Mary and sent her on her way, she would have condemned the Scottish Queen to an existence dependent on the charity and goodwill of other Continental monarchs. With the revelation of the Casket Letters, it is doubtful they would have fought for her restoration, as Cecil and his colleagues believed. But by imprisoning Mary Stuart, Elizabeth assisted in "equipping her with the halo of martyrdom."[27]

Even more important, Elizabeth had provoked a reaction in Mary Stuart which would lie quiescent for years. Mary was dazed by the inquiry's decision and castigated herself that she had so far demeaned her sovereign position as to comply with Elizabeth's request in the first place, and her bitterness overflowed. Too late she realized what had happened and, for the first time, understood the full extent of her peril. For the first time also, she recognized the underhanded measures by which she had cooperated in her own restraint. She had expected more honorable dealing with the English sovereign, but she would expect nothing more in the future. Whatever that future might hold, it would be as much of her own shaping as her limited powers and confinement permitted. Elizabeth might never receive her, but until the day she died she would never be allowed to forget that somewhere in her realm another Queen was living—and waiting.

Before he returned to Scotland, Murray had the audience with Queen Elizabeth which Mary still so desperately desired. Previously he had discussed the issue of his sister's marriage with the Duke of Norfolk. Aware of the risk he was incurring in contemplating such action without his monarch's approval, Norfolk spoke freely to the Regent. "Earl of Murray," he said, "thou knowest that thing whereunto I will make none in England nor in Scotland privy, and thou has Norfolk's life in thy hands. . . ."[28] Even with Norfolk's words ringing in his ears,

Murray did not now hesitate to use his first opportunity of revealing to Elizabeth the extent of her great nobleman's ambitions. He returned home with £ 2,000 and the Queen's gratitude. Ironically, Norfolk had been the one to request that Elizabeth assuage Murray's chronic need of cash. He remained unaware that Murray had so broken his trust.

At the conclusion of the Westminster inquiry, dissatisfied by Elizabeth's and the Council's attitude toward the imprisoned Queen, Norfolk's varying motives and desires coalesced. Mary, ready to grasp at any scheme which would guarantee her freedom, was now addressing Norfolk letters promising faithfulness to "Mine Own Lord." Yet when the English Council sent the Bishop of Ross to question her about a future marriage, she said, "My fortune has been so evil in the progress of my life, and specially in my marriages, as hardly I can be brought to have any mind to like of a husband. . . ." She said by marrying such as Norfolk, "I am sure to lose all my friends beyond the seas, France and Spain and all other Catholic princes. This is the greatest loss I could lose." But that Mary was willing to risk such a loss for the regaining of her freedom and possibly her throne is evident in her words: "If I should give consent to my Lord of Norfolk in this behalf, I would know how my good sister's will and consent may be had to the same. . . . I would be glad to know not only if my good sister would like thereof, but also how friendly those of the nobility would deal with him. . . ."[29] Whether Elizabeth consented or not, she did not wish to lose the opportunity, writing to "My Norfolk," "Our fault were not shameful. You have promised to be mine and I yours; I believe the Queen of England and country should like of it. . . ."[30]

Norfolk had yet formally to seek the Queen's approval. As the weeks passed and the warnings of his worried colleagues went unheeded, he even put aside his friendships with Cecil and Sussex. His concern was such that for the first time, he refused to leave London and the court during the summer, hoping to find just the right moment to inform Elizabeth of his plan and secure her consent.

Shortly after Mary Stuart arrived in England, Guzmán de Silva was recalled to Spain. Elizabeth deplored his return; she and de Silva had formed a remarkably satisfying association owing in no small part to the dexterity of the sensitive ambassador, whose talents had proved equal to the handling of a temperamental and difficult woman. Yet at times even de Silva, so used to the jaded and self-serving attitude of other monarchs, could be genuinely touched by Elizabeth's reaction. Once, as they returned to London from Hampton Court, riding through the streets in her usual open carriage so that people might see their sovereign, de Silva commented on the passionate enthusiasm and warm cries which greeted her appearance, saying what pleasure it must give her. To which Elizabeth replied that her people loved her because "while the other nations of Europe were tearing each other in pieces, they alone, under her rule, were living in safety under their own vine and fig tree." The Queen attributed her success to Divine inspiration. "To God she owed it," the ambassador later wrote, "it was the marvellous work of His hand."

Elizabeth knew that de Silva had been in communication with Mary Stuart, and she contemplated that now, perhaps having inaugurated some conspiracy with the Scottish Queen, he was leaving England to avoid exposure. When he took his leave at Hatfield, Elizabeth paid him the compliment of complete frankness, telling him their relationship had always "been agreeable and she would have been well pleased if he had remained—and she trusted in God that there was no mystery in his going." De Silva recognized her fears and, concerned that he should leave with the Queen's highest regard, replied that "he had been recalled at his own request because the English climate disagreed with him."[31] As a tribute to the many months of his ambassadorship and typical of the warm regard of the Queen of England, Elizabeth surprised the Spaniard with an overly generous and handsome gift of plate at his departure.

DeSilva had had great success with Elizabeth because of a highly bred natural intelligence, immense charm and a sensitivity laced with prudence and consideration. Above all, he was of a relatively unsuspicious nature with small inclination to troublemaking or intrigue. The Queen was not to be so lucky with his replacement in the person of Don Guerau de Spes. De Spes was inferior to de Silva in most ways; his outrageous manners, thoughtless remarks and genuine capacity for troublemaking soon made him highly unpopular. No one was exempt from his remarkable ability to annoy, not even William Cecil. Discussing their countries' mutual affairs one day in the chief minister's chambers, de Spes later triumphantly wrote, "I let him talk on, and when he had done, I waited a little for him to recover somewhat from his rage, and then went up to him laughing and embraced him, saying that I was amused to see him fly into such a passion."[32]

Cecil's reaction may also have been due to more than de Spes' jibes. Coinciding with the ambassador's arrival in England and with the Duke of Norfolk's advancement toward Mary Stuart was a definite movement within the government to unseat William Cecil. He had concurred in the Queen's decision to detain four Spanish ships which had sought shelter from French pirates in Plymouth, Falmouth and Southampton waters. En route to the Netherlands, their holds con-

tained sixty-four stout chests of silver destined to pay the salaries of the
Duke of Alva's troops. The new ambassador, de Spes, quickly asked
Elizabeth's "protection" of the treasure, and the Queen lost no time in
ordering the rich cargo worth £ 85,000 to be brought to London. There
she commandeered it, saying that since it was actually the property of
a group of Genoese bankers, she herself would borrow it and "if the
King of Spain could prove it belonged to him, she would restore it."
Such a flagrant act of piracy—and the huge amount of the windfall—
stunned Philip. Alva promptly laid an embargo on all English
property and subjects in the Netherlands, and Elizabeth, in retaliation,
arrested all Spaniards in London. Even de Spes, for once speechless,
was put under house arrest. The full brunt of the displeasure of the
English merchants, who in the suppression of their trade were losing
valuable markets—while sharing not one iota in the Spanish plunder—fell on Cecil as the key figure involved in the seizure. Immediately
all the previously hidden animosities against the Queen's chief
minister erupted. Fénelon, the French ambassador, wrote at the end of
December, 1569, "It is Cecil who rules us all now and prompts the
villain tricks which trouble us. No words can tell the depth of Cecil's
heresy; and as he sees the Protestant cause going to the ground, he
grows more furious as if possessed by ten thousand fiends."[33] De Spes,
still under house arrest concurred: "The chief of the Council is Cecil, a
man of low extraction, cunning, false, malicious, full of all deceit, and
so true an Englishman that he thinks all the sovereigns of Christendom
cannot conquer this island. He it is who governs all. He is diligent,
acute, and never keeps faith of words. He thinks we are none of us a
match for him; and so far as he has succeeded but now he is verging to
his fall."[34]

The foreign ambassador's feelings were reflected in the attitude of
many of Cecil's colleagues. Leicester had always felt that the minister's
influence worked against him in his great ambition to marry the
Queen—a supposition which does not say much for Robert Dudley's
perceptive knowledge of Elizabeth Tudor. The Duke of Norfolk considered Cecil—and rightfully so—as too severe in his judgment of the
Queen of Scots. Others of the Council disliked his unabashed support
of the Huguenots in France and the Protestant Netherlanders. They
decried his lack of effort in keeping a strong Spanish alliance. Earlier in
the year, de Spes had said that Cecil "would declare open war against
us, but for the remonstrances of the Council." His firm loyalty to the
Reformed church meant little to others who switched their spiritual
affiliations easily. His adamant insistence that Elizabeth deal effectively with the threat of the "Popish Landlords," those arrogant and

powerful Catholics who lived north of the Humber, whose life-style resembled that of a monarch on their vast estates, with life and death sway over their tenants, had angered many Councillors.

But in the main the Council's most severe complaint against Cecil was the extent of his influence with the Queen—an influence arising out of her respect for his intelligence, his honesty and his great capacity for hard work. It had all had the inevitable result: Jealousy was rife, and mixed with their envy of the man personally was their dislike of his "middle-class ideas" and their distrust of how they might affect them personally. They decried his growing prosperity through his Master of the Court Wardships and other government perquisites and his continued avowed preference for the Suffolk succession in the person of the diminutive—and still-imprisoned—Mary Grey. Many of his fellow Councillors secretly favored Mary Stuart as Elizabeth's successor. For the most part, it was a case of older, wealthier gentry, the like of a Norfolk, of an Arundel, Lumley or Pembroke, envying the competence and domination, the hard-won efficiency and prosperity of a "new man" like William Cecil. In time others such as Northampton and Winchester joined their ranks. In this select group, the Earl of Leicester seesawed in and out, always aware his opinions and actions must in the end coincide with those of the Queen, the woman he still hoped to wed.

By the middle of 1569 Elizabeth was certainly aware of the rumblings of discontent within her Council and recognized at whom they were aimed. She could well understand her Council's misliking of her Secretary. Cecil was no saint. He could be as perfidious, devious and brutal as any one of her ministers. She had no illusions otherwise, except to know that he was also cautious, brave and politically brilliant. But there was one difference between Cecil and the others. All of Cecil's considerable talents—redeeming or otherwise—were exercised for the benefit of the Queen of England and her subjects, the English people. The same could not be said for her other ministers, whose main motives were usually to look to their own welfare first. For that reason, if for no other, it would have been prudent of her Council in attempting the downfall of William Cecil to accept that they must first deal with a powerful adversary in the person of Elizabeth Tudor herself.

Her ministers' furtive manipulations, coupled with the furor over the confiscated Spanish treasure and the consequent crippling embargo, troubled the Queen. She had been saddened by the death of the wife of Sir Francis Knollys. Fénelon, the French ambassador, met with the Queen at Hampton Court and found her "full of sorrow for the death of Lady Knollys, her cousin, whom she loved better than all the women in the world. . . ." Elizabeth herself, he thought, appeared drawn and strained; the pressure of the past few months had been severe on her always-sensitive nervous system. She complained, with apparent wounded vanity, of the activity of de Spes, saying that the Duke of Alva had been "too hasty" in believing the Spanish ambassador and putting the embargo into effect. She said, angrily, that "the Duke was neither so great, herself so little, nor the affair so unimportant, but that he might have troubled himself to write more at length to her, and to have made proper inquiries before he attempted such an outrage at her and her subjects!" Fénelon attempted to placate her by agreeing that the Duke was naturally irritated at the loss of his troops' monies and was now facing mutiny. He said that Philip, "once more a widower and in search of a suitable consort, would not for the world offend an unmarried princess like her . . ." to which Elizabeth, disdaining the bait, replied tartly "that she could be very well assured of the friendship of the King of Spain as she might have married him at the beginning of the war, if she had chosen."[35]

The commercial crisis was another charge which the Council hoped to lay at Cecil's door, and ultimately, even Norfolk, irresolute and dreaming his own private dreams of grandeur which encompassed a somewhat tarnished Scottish Crown, worked also to unseat Cecil. Norfolk's partisans urged that the Netherlands embargo stand, although English merchants were already suffering a severe business depression. It did not seem untenable or immoral to them to urge that the great fleet carrying English products to the city of Hamburg—a prime initial venture in English commercial shipping—be captured by either French or Spanish pirates in order to discredit Cecil further. They seemed to care little how their own countrymen, whose hopes and monies were sailing with the fleet, would suffer in the loss.

Once their influence had worked on other wavering members, the Council contemplated the physical restraint of Cecil. In a situation similar to the removal of Henry VIII's minister, Thomas Cromwell, it was hoped that Cecil might be apprehended at the Council table and forcibly removed to the Tower. In this way, although they meant no dishonor to the Queen, they felt her main prop would be removed and they—wishful thinkers all—would then be in a stronger position to force her to their own way of thinking. They would insist she change the direction and content of her policy regarding her marriage, religion, the succession, the matter of the Queen of Scots and just about every other subject over which they had experienced discontent in the past months.

Cecil was intensely aware of what was going on. If nothing else, the evasion and cool aloofness of those whom he had regarded as good friends were a warning. Elizabeth herself had heard the veiled and then the more open threats and complaints which often degenerated into outright harangues. It all came to a head one evening when Leicester and Cecil disagreed violently and Leicester, upset, brazenly told Elizabeth "that her throne would never be safe until Cecil's head was off his shoulders." Angrily, the Queen swore at Leicester, saying she would send *him* to the Tower instead! She had not lowered her voice, and at the opposite end of the room, the Duke of Norfolk observed that Leicester was in high favor only so long as he echoed Mr. Secretary's opinions but now, with one of his own, he was to go to the Tower! "By God!" he cried, "it shall not be . . . some remedy shall be found for this!" To which another Councillor added, "Pray God it may be so. . . ."[36] The Duke went to the Queen and asked that "when her anger had cooled," she would reflect on Mr. Secretary Cecil and the need for making better provisions for her own and her subjects' safety. He advised that he and his fellow Councillors, "faithful servants all," would consider what ought to be done. At which Elizabeth, "in obvious distress," turned her back and left the chamber.

She spent the next several days, ill and tensely overwrought, but the time gave her opportunity to muster her very considerable emotional resources. A great demand had been made on her personally for the past several months. She was not honestly satisfied with the settlement of the Queen of Scots issue. She had deplored the confiscation of the Spanish treasure "and wished the Devil had flown away with it" as many times as she had noted her good fortune in obtaining it. She was heartsick and resentful at the involvement of her foremost peer, Norfolk, who was working so secretly to marry the Scottish Queen. Yet she knew, intuitively and firmly, that once she allowed her Council to dictate to her, she would no longer be Queen. She liked, respected and had affection for William Cecil. He had done his job, which was more than she could say for many of those so ready to accuse him. She, better than her Councillors, knew what was best for England, and as their innuendos broadened to almost outright accusations and insistence that she deprive Cecil of his office, the Queen's own obstinacy grew in similar measure.

Within the next few weeks, the little intrigue played itself to a natural and not too surprising conclusion, as the Queen and her minister gave her Councillors repeated opportunities to do their worst. At one point, it was decided that Easter, 1569, would be the occasion to accuse Cecil in full Council and order him to the Tower. But, unexpectedly, Elizabeth arrived, in fine form, in good humor, full of state business which she and Cecil promptly dispatched; she allowed no intrusion of debatable subjects to enter the conversation. Once the business was completed, she abruptly adjourned the session.

Twice after that, there were plots to kidnap Cecil, and then, questioning who among them would do the job, the Councillors found a good deal of steam evaporating from the proposal. Each time their determination dwindled, their scheme lessened until, at the end, it became a somewhat embarrassing display of bluster. At that point, Cecil stepped in and diplomatically obtained a favorable decision for Norfolk in a legal issue over property left to one of his stepchildren. It enriched Norfolk, angered and embittered his opponent, the Northern Lord Dacre, and cut the Council conspiracy in half as Norfolk withdrew his enmity against Cecil. When the great English fleet, carrying the produce as well as the dreams and energies of English farmers, merchants and artisans, sailed successfully across the North Sea protected by the guns of the English Navy, landing at Hamburg, to the relieved cheers of the English representatives, Elizabeth and Cecil could snap their collective fingers at the Netherlands embargo.

The tide had turned, and suddenly the man who had faced arrest or worse and the Queen who everyone had predicted would find herself considerably less influential without him were the celebrities of the hour. All London was joyous as the church bells announcing the arrival at Hamburg rang out. William Cecil must have heard those bells with thankful prayer; he was well aware of what he had faced. That he also knew whom to thank for his deliverance is shown in a letter he wrote to an old friend, Nicholas White:

> It may be you may on my behalf be troubled with bruits unpleasant . . . .I will give you a rule to measure both sorts of reports, be they good or bad. I am, thanks be to God, in good health. I am in quietness of mind as feeling the nearness and readiness of God's favour to assist me with His Grace to have a disposition to serve Him before the world. And therein have I lately proved His mere goodness to preserve me from the clouds and mists, in the midst whereof I trust mine honest actions are proved to have been lightsome and clear. And to make this rule more proper and special to be applied, I find the Queen's Majesty my gracious good lady without change of any part of her old good meaning towards me. And so I trust only in God's goodness to deserve the continuance. . . .[37]

Yet Norfolk's intention to wed Mary Stuart still remained firm, and in Northern England the union occupied the energies of many nobles and their companions. Even Murray, the Scottish Regent, pretended, or appeared to pretend, to favor the marriage. The Northern Catholics realized as the months passed that Cecil was now stronger than ever and Elizabeth virtually impregnable, while Mary Stuart had not fared so well. The English Queen had intercepted a letter which Mary had written "requiring some of the Lords of her country to take up arms" to rescue her, and Elizabeth was fierce in her denunciation. She told the French ambassador that while she herself "had no cause to change her pale hue for anything . . ." she wished to God "that the Queen of Scots had no more occasion to blush at that which could be seen of her." She told Fénelon that "she had taken pains to be more than a good mother to the Queen of Scots, yet she had continually practised intrigues in her kingdom against her, and that those who did not know how to behave to a good mother merited no other than the cruelest stepdame." She took the opportunity also of unburdening her resentment of some Councillors present who favored the royal captive, threatening "that she would make them shorter by the head."[38]

The Spanish ambassador, de Spes, had promised that King Philip would support Norfolk's marriage to Mary Stuart if the Duke would work for the Catholic restoration in England. Encouraged by this success, the Northern Lords—restive at how little Mary's cause was being forwarded—began to rally. Norfolk was urged to obtain Elizabeth's formal approval, which was, in everyone's eyes, the crux of the whole affair. At a subsequent Council meeting at which Elizabeth was not present, Norfolk—feeling stronger as the days passed—officially presented his intention to wed the Scottish Queen, an intent long known to those present. Many felt the marriage a logical solution to a vexing problem, and even Cecil, in newfound rapport, promised to do whatever he could, provided Elizabeth approved. Leicester, particularly, was enthusiastic and generously offered his support. He felt his influence with Elizabeth would be considerable, and he was ever hopeful that other marriages might similarly inspire the Queen. No one had mentioned the possibility that Elizabeth might not agree, and they assumed that Norfolk's considerable prestige and formidable backing would cause her to think twice before refusing the Duke. Only Cecil—who knew Elizabeth Tudor better than most—thought she might have a very different reaction.

As no one had previously wished to be chosen to apprehend Cecil, so now the brave souls on the Council were equally insistent that *they* should not be the ones to inform her Majesty of Norfolk's marriage intentions. When Leicester suggested a committee, the idea was thought superlative until no one could be found to serve on it. Leicester then advised that "he thought it not well to have it broken to Her Majesty by a number because he well knew Her Majesty's nature did well like better to be dealt with by one or two."[39] He then offered to confront Elizabeth personally, provided Cecil accompanied him. It was then noticed that the chief minister had discreetly retired and could not be found for days. Leicester then promised to approach Elizabeth singly, to assess her mood and will, but seemingly he wasted opportunity on opportunity while the hesitant Norfolk waited, between bouts of apprehension and sudden misgiving. When the Duke ultimately questioned Leicester on what progress he was making, his reply was that Elizabeth "had been out of quiet," and the right moment had not yet occurred. Clearly, my Lord of Leicester's self-assurance was also less than he had originally indicated. Eventually, hoping to conclude the matter once and for all, Norfolk gathered his courage, approached the Queen, nerves on edge but full of good intentions. Elizabeth, well aware of what was going on, gave him every opportunity, but the Duke became flustered, his thoughts muddled, his courage evaporated, and he went home ill and without dinner. The next day the Queen went to Richmond.

Resolving to do better, Norfolk rose early the next morning and promptly followed the royal party. Near Kew, he came upon the Earl of Leicester, lost in thought, placidly fishing in the Thames. He inquired of the Queen's humor and how much she might know of his intentions, to which Leicester replied, somewhat distantly, that "some women at the court had blabbed" of the affair, telling Elizabeth that indeed "the matter was already concluded!" He advised Norfolk to make a clean breast of things at the earliest opportunity and most seriously consider the Queen's reaction if he wed without her knowledge. Apparently, Leicester preferred to go no further himself.

Later, meeting with Cecil, Norfolk received similar advice, and by the time he was admitted to the Queen's presence he was in a highly nervous state. Elizabeth greeted him affably, however, and inquired "what news was abroad?" There was a moment's silence. It was the perfect opportunity for the Duke to follow his friends' advice "to make a clean breast of everything." Instead, he gulped, felt fearful and, ignoring the Queen's obvious wish to give him an opening, replied, "None."

It was too much for Elizabeth. She rounded on him in angry disappointment and said caustically, "None? You mean you come from London and can tell me no news of a marriage?"

The effrontery of her remark left Norfolk speechless. Any attempt at a quick followup was mercifully interrupted as Lady Clinton approached to show the Queen a basket of flowers. Elizabeth, who loved nothing better than to tuck a choice specimen into her ruff, sleeves or fan, turned to admire the blossoms. The interruption caused Norfolk's words to fly from his head; quickly, he excused himself and withdrew.

Again several weeks passed as Norfolk waited for Leicester to smooth the path to royal approval. Elizabeth then took the initiative and asked the Duke to dine with her when she stopped at Farnham. Unaware of what Leicester had told Elizabeth, Norfolk again appeared tongue-tied. At the conclusion of the meal the Queen appeared sympathetic. Still disappointed at his uncommunicativeness, she balled her fist and gave him a not unfriendly nip on the ear and, with some humor, recalled his own words, saying, "I wish you to take good heed to your pillow. . . ." Her forthrightness cowed Norfolk, who later testified, "I was abashed at Her Majesty's speech." Even though it was most apparent that Elizabeth was, at this point, more troubled by Norfolk's lack of frankness than his intent, the Duke thought "it not a fit time nor place there to trouble her. . . ."

With the situation remaining unresolved, Norfolk returned to London, brimming with marriage plans, seemingly unconcerned that he had not taken the Queen into his confidence. He told one friend "that before he lost that marriage he would lose his life," and he enthusiastically encouraged the Northern Lords in their plan to rescue Mary from her captivity as a prelude to the wedding. Once the Duke signaled, the whole North would rise to his undertaking, he was told. Feeling stronger by such evidence of support, he again rode to join the Queen, determined at long last to tell Elizabeth everything.

Previous to his arrival, the Queen had had a message from Leicester that he was seriously ill at Litchfield. Elizabeth flew to his side, concerned and affectionate, to find him in bed, but more "counterfeiting the sick" than really ill. There in the intimacy of his bedroom, Leicester poured out to Elizabeth the whole scope of the Norfolk-Mary, Queen of Scots, endeavor, using his pretended illness as a reason for his revelations, for "he could not die in peace without confessing his faults and obtaining her pardon for his guilt." Elizabeth proved, as he had expected, compassionate and grateful, and that same day she accosted Norfolk and sharply reprimanded him and "commanded him, on his allegiance, to give over these pretensions." To which the Duke, taken by surprise, promised immediate compliance. With great bravado, he sought to demean his interest in Mary by stating "that his estate in England was worth little less than the whole realm of Scotland . . . and that when he was in his own tennis court at Norwich, he thought himself as great as a King."[40]

The following day Elizabeth assembled her Council and roundly trounced them for treating with Norfolk without her knowledge. She told them if she consented to such a union, "she would be in the Tower within four months." She watched the faces of those she had appointed to advise her; their countenances betrayed little. How many had encouraged Norfolk? How many would, in their secret hearts, be overjoyed to see her in the Tower and the Scottish Queen in her place? Her anger and resentment grew, and when one Councillor read a petition from the Spanish ambassador for Mary's liberation, the Queen's own façade of civility crumpled, and she cried "that she would advise the Queen of Scotland to bear her condition with less impatience, or she might chance to find some of those on whom she had relied shorter by the head."[41]

It all had its effect. Suddenly the marriage everyone had viewed as a means of solving so many domestic problems did not seem that simple a matter. Within days, enthusiasm cooled, and the proudest peer in England found himself in such disfavor with his friends that he was shunned and regarded with such disdain that his own courage waned. He told Cecil, "I am sorry that no man can keep me company without offence . . ." and within the next week, without formal permission, he left the court for London.

His departure was the signal for Elizabeth to act. Recognizing that whatever the direction of the plot, possession of the Scottish Queen would be paramount, she sent her cousin the Earl of Huntingdon to remove Mary Stuart from Wingfield, where she had been removed for safer keeping, back to Tutbury Castle. Hastily, she ordered the ports closed, alerted the militia and commanded that the Duke of Norfolk, on his honor, return to court. She herself would go to Windsor, where she felt secure enough to face any siege if it should come to such an end.

At this point, there was still the slim chance that by a quick return to the royal presence, the Duke might have redeemed himself. With a fine and a year of his sovereign's coolness and perhaps less favor in the future, eventually, he might have wound himself back into her good graces. But Norfolk's courage had deserted him. He pleaded an ague and, on September 23, fled to Kenninghall.

Everyone at court assumed he had gone North to signal the rebellion, which had been simmering for months. Having done all she could, Elizabeth, too, waited, and "all the whole court hung in suspense and fear lest he [Norfolk] should break forth into the rebellion. . .," an unprecedented condition that had not faced Elizabeth in the years she had been Queen. During her sister Mary's reign, there had been the disastrous Wyatt rebellion; at the end of her brother Edward's reign there had been the tragedy of Lady Jane Grey's claim which had caused the death of its perpetrator, John Dudley, Leicester's father. But Elizabeth had given her country eleven years of peace. There had been few undercurrents of uneasiness in her court and Council to which she was not privy. In most instances, her own tolerance and intelligence had guaranteed their quick resolution. But now she was expected to deal with the result of one man's arrogant ambitions and the direct effect of another younger and more beautiful Queen on English soil. And in her own efforts lay the answer to the question of who would wear the Crown of England.

In the North, everything hinged on Norfolk's participation. Everywhere Catholics were massed, waiting the signal from East Anglia. Puzzled by Norfolk's silence, they could not know his own courage had deserted him. He had not answered his summons to court, and the silence from that direction was discomforting. Days in which he had done nothing passed. Instead of marching northward, he wrote Elizabeth on September 24 that "he was grieved to hear that her Majesty was displeased with him and he took to God to witness that he had never entertained a thought against her Highness, her Crown or her dynasty." But "finding cold looks at court. . . he feared that he would not be able to show his innocence to her Majesty, and therefore had preferred to withdraw." Again he protested "I never dealt in the Queen of Scots cause further than I declared. . . ."[42]

His letter crossed one from Elizabeth again commanding, "without manner of excuse," his return to court. She also said, somewhat enigmatically, she did not intend "to minister anything to you but as you should in truth deserve." While Norfolk was anxiously reading her words, soldiers of the Queen had entered Mary Stuart's chambers at Tutbury and, over her outraged protests, examined her coffers and other boxes, but found nothing. Her custodian, the Earl of Huntingdon, said that "she pleadeth greatly her innocency to the Queen's Majesty, of whose dealing she speaketh bitterly." Huntingdon added his own wish that God would give spirit of wisdom and fortitude of mind to the Queen and her Council, "which two things were necessarily required," he wrote, "considering the person they had to deal with."[43]

On September 30, Norfolk, still torn by indecision, informed the Northern Earls that they must cancel the uprising, "for if they did not, it would cost him his head as he was going to court." Leicester had written him that "he had nothing to fear in submission, but would be proclaimed a traitor by disobeying" his Queen's commands. Therefore, still attempting to stifle the bewildering doubts which assailed his conscience, Norfolk rode to court on October 1 over the remonstrances of his friends and family at Kenninghall. On his departure, his servants were so overwrought with anxiety they "held him by the knees and clung to his stirrup-leathers as he mounted his horse. . . ."[44] But the Duke realized he could do nothing else, and during the journey he managed to convince himself that once he could see Elizabeth, he could explain the situation fully and, he hoped, secure her understanding forgiveness. Never was a venture more hopeless; never was there a more valid testament to one man's inability to evaluate a situation realistically. Norfolk had "lived like a King" too long.

Elizabeth had broken off her summer progress; she had not dared go too far from any point where she could not be easily reached. She returned from Hampshire to Windsor, and when Norfolk arrived at court on October 8 she refused to see him. She still regarded his fearful retreat to Kenninghall as an act of defiance. Summoning her Council, she stunned her ministers, including Cecil, who had been privy to the conspiracy for months, by her orders: The Duke of Norfolk was to be remanded at once to the charge of Sir Francis Knollys and taken to the Tower. His close confederates, Arundel, Pembroke and Lumley, were placed under house arrest. In one gesture, she removed the focal point of any rebellion and dissipated the strength of the conspiracy. The remaining Councillors, feeling as a group somewhat reprieved, sighed with relief that nothing more would be expected of them—or proved against them.

Thus, at dusk on an October evening, the only Duke in England was taken by water to the Tower of London. Great crowds lined the banks between Westminster and London Bridge and were, according to the French ambassador, "vociferous in their expressions of displeasure," for Norfolk had always been popular. Arriving at the Tower, he was escorted respectfully, as befitted his rank, into the Constable's Lodgings. Ironically—or perhaps deliberately—he was ordered into the same chambers his grandfather, the third Duke, had occupied during the last year of the Queen's father's life.

Chapter 18

In the North the impatient Earls waited. Eager to commence the great undertaking which would rid the Council of undesirable influences, which would give its heiress presumptive in marriage to the nation's foremost nobleman and would, with God's help, aid in the restoration of the old faith, they awaited only Norfolk's signal to commence the uprising. He would join them to secure Mary herself, and together they would ally with the forces Spain would surely send to combat those of the Crown. Hadn't Mary Stuart said that if the King of Spain would help, "I shall be Queen of England in three months"? Once massed, with whatever recruits they might gather from those who always waited to see which side would prove the ripest pickings, they would be a formidable threat to Elizabeth and her Crown.

When Norfolk was apprehended, the dismay in the North was understandable. In London the general belief was that with the Duke under restraint, the rebellion would dissipate for lack of purpose. The Earl of Sussex wrote from York, "I trust the fire is spent with the smoke," and said the rebellion, "the cause of which is yet unknown . . . ," was undoubtedly at an end. Elizabeth was not so certain. Neither did she entirely trust Sussex himself, and she resolved the situation by ordering that Northumberland and Westmorland, "the Earls who were old in blood, but poor in force," as she said, return to court. Both refused, Westmorland saying, "I dare not come where my enemies are without bringing such a force to protect me as might be misliked. . . ."

Before either the Queen or Sussex could proceed further, matters were taken out of their hands. On the night of November 9, 1569, the church bells of Topcliffe, a little village in Northumberland County, began to ring backwards—a prearranged signal—and by the next day a full-scale rebellion was at hand. The followers of the powerful Catholic Lords were not concerned in the petty squabbles which plagued the minds of ministers, Councillors and Queen in the South. They had many complaints dealing with the matter of their religion, their traditions, their feudal privileges, and once their leaders asked for a delay, they rose as one great mass in proud refusal. Clad in their uniforms of Crusader blue with a red cross on the front, and bearing a banner depicting the Five Wounds of Christ, these simplehearted Englishmen—children of those who had participated in the ill-fated Pilgrimage of Grace thirty-three years previously—were again on the march. Swearing allegiance to their beloved monarch, they proclaimed they would resist by force the "evil disposed persons about the Queen's Majesty, [who] have, by their subtle and crafty dealings to advance themselves, overcome in this our realm the true and Catholic religion . . . dishonoureth the realm and now lastly seek and procure the destruction of the nobility. . . ,"[1] an undoubted reference to Norfolk and the precarious position of Northumberland and Westmorland. The proclamation, practically a duplicate of the one of the Pilgrimage of Grace, ended "God save the Queen!" In their naïve idealism, they still expected help from Norfolk's forces and from Spain to teach their monarch and her advisers a sorely needed lesson. On November 14, led by seventy-one-year-old Richard Norton, a relative of Queen Katherine Parr's, carrying the Banner, they entered Durham Cathedral, burned all books representative of the Reformed religion and proceeded to celebrate Mass. One group aimed for York, another went to free the Queen of Scots at Tutbury, and another marched to Hartlepool to await, in vain, help from Spain. Up to this point, the rebellion looked formidable. All that was needed was the person of the Queen of Scots and many Englishmen would rise to assist Mary to the English throne.

Panic hit London, and de Spes exulted, "Never was there a fairer chance of punishing the men who had so long insulted Spain, or of restoring the Catholic religion!"[2] Remembrance of the Wyatt rebellion, when men had fought in the streets and the Queen's sister, Mary, had bravely gone to the Guildhall to whip the fearful citizens into a display of courage they were far from feeling, was still ripe in many memories. Now it was Elizabeth's turn to display that same tenacious attitude which made followers of wavering dissenters, which taught courage through leadership and respect by example. The Queen did not disappoint her subjects. When the rebels reached Tutbury, they found Mary had been removed farther south to Coventry, riding by night "to avoid the fond gaze and confluence of the people." Rumors of an armed force en route North, headed by Lord Clinton and the Earls of Warwick and Hereford, reached their camps, and in East Anglia the retainers from the great estates of the imprisoned Norfolk, fearful for their own skins now that their Lord was in the Tower, refused to join in the cause. When the rebels reached Hartlepool, instead of Spanish help, it was the Queen of England's ships that fired on them. And, a final blow, word reached them that the Duke of Alva now regarded the whole undertaking as "foolhardy" and refused the assistance which the reckless Ambassador de Spes had promised.

At once the rout began. Winter had reached the North, an unusually severe one, and the rebel's return was as uncomfortable as it was hurried. Many returned safely to their homes, but Northumberland fled into Scotland and Westmorland into Flanders, causing Cecil to write that "the vermin be fled into foreign coverts." Northumberland eventually was returned by the Scottish government and died on the gallows; Westmorland later died in exile.[3] The futile rebellion, "the last armed stand in England against the secular spirit,"[4] was over. No one had been killed; little property had been damaged; the rebel's sole crime had been proclaiming their wish to "restore all ancient customs and liberties to God's Church and His whole realm."

In London the strain had begun to tell on the Queen. Whom could she trust? Too many had been privy to Norfolk's and Mary's plans. Leicester was told he had "greviously offended" and begged forgiveness on his knees. Even Cecil himself incurred days of royal displeasure for his foreknowledge of the scheme. Elizabeth's wrath was such that she informed the Scottish Regent she would conspicuously favor him if it could be found that the Duke of Norfolk, not the Scots, had actively promulgated the initial scheme.[5] Daily the vision of her cousin's treachery expanded, and she knew no peace. When Cecil somewhat hesitantly informed her that under the Treason Statute of Edward III, the Duke was not subject to any penalty of the law by any overt act of treason, she was so overcome that she cried hysterically, "Away! What the law fails to do, my authority shall effect!" Increasingly, Elizabeth was subject to what Leicester called "some *spice*, or show, of hysteric fits. . . ." Her suspicions were often aroused that those whom she must trust might ultimately betray her. Now, almost ungovernable in her rage, she swooned, sinking to the floor, while Cecil's shouts for aid brought an attendant with some "vinegar and other stimulants to recover her."[6]

During the next few weeks, word reached the English court of the shocking assassination on January 23, 1570, of James Stuart, the Earl of Murray. The thirty-five-year-old Regent had been ambushed by one of the Hamiltons of Bothwellhaugh and shot through the stomach, the bullet passing through him to kill a horse on the other side. He lingered for several hours, during which time he gave the care of the young King to Lord Mar, and then, "without speaking a reproachful word of any man," died before midnight.[7] From Coventry, Mary Stuart professed great delight at her half brother's tragic end and wrote the Archbishop of Glasgow to give young Hamilton a pension.

One immediate effect of Murray's death was the infiltration along the Border into England of hundreds of Scots anxious to help prolong the Northern uprising. Elizabeth had been prostrate with shock at Murray's murder, and "the blow told with terrible power." Assassination, the private nightmare of every highborn or political figure, was a threat with which the Queen lived daily. But, as she knew she must, she put fear and apprehension behind her and rose to deal with the situation.

One prominent holdout, Lord Dacre, was still confined to Naworth Castle, and Elizabeth vowed she would know no peace until he had been taken. She sent her cousin Lord Hunsdon to bring him to court, and on February 9, 1570, with blazing beacons lighting the route, the snowy hills of the North Country were "full of men, horse and foot, crying and shouting as if they had been mad." It was reported that Dacre had twice Hunsdon's strength, but the emplacement of Hunsdon's forces was superior. The Borderers, anxious to start the battle, took the initiative. "They gave the proudest charge that I ever saw!" Hunsdon wrote Elizabeth admiringly, but it proved futile for the rebels. The royal forces stood their ground and in withering fire mowed down the first onset of troops while those in the rear struggled in confusion or retreat. Dacre fled into Scotland "like a tall gentleman and never looked behind him till he was in Liddisdale." With their leader gone, the Borderers scattered, and the Castle was surrendered. More than 300 dead were on the field, with many wounded and taken prisoner.

Responding to her cousin's account of the battle which, if it had been successful, might have inspired the straggling remnants of the uprising to join together once more, Elizabeth wrote Hunsdon in her own hand:

> I doubt not, my Harry, whether that the victory were given me more joyed me, or that you were by God appointed the instrument of my glory. And I assure you that for my country's sake, the first might suffice, but for

my heart's contentation, the second more pleased me. It likes me not a little that with a good testimony of your faith there is seen a stout courage of your mind that more trusted to the goodness of your quarrel than to the weakness of your numbers.

But I can say no more. *"Beatus es ille servus quem cum Dominus venerit invenient faciendo [sic] sua mandata."* And that you may not think you have done nothing for your profit, though you have done much for your honour, I tend to make this journey somewhat to increase your livelihood, that you may not say to yourself, *"Perditur quod factum est ingrato!"*

Your loving kinswoman,
Elizabeth R.[8]

Elizabeth kept her word, and Hunsdon later was given a ripe picking of the confiscated lands of the Earl of Northumberland.

Once the Hunsdon victory was assured, the power went out of the uprising. Disillusioned, the Queen, whose nerves had been tortured with misgivings reminiscent of the dark memories of her youthful imprisonment, turned a deaf ear to the plea of such as Sussex who sought sympathy for the rebels. Consideration, understanding and tolerance had not brought her the Crown, and they would not keep it for her, Elizabeth told herself and anyone else who dared ask for mercy for her Northern subjects.

It was at this unpropitious moment that Pope Pius V chose to publish his oft-threatened *Regnans in Excelsis*, the Bull of Excommunication, which cut off "that servant of all iniquity, Elizabeth, pretended Queen of England . . . . from the unity of the Body of Christ." Elizabeth had often promised that she would not interfere with men's consciences "as long as they shall in their outward conversation show themselves quiet and not manifestly repugnant and obstinant to the laws of the realm. . . ." It was one of the pitiful ambiguities of the Bull that it created just the opposite of its intended effect. It now made it impossible for the Queen to separate—where Catholicism was concerned—the religious from the political. The Bull stated "that all peers, subjects and people of the said kingdom, and all others upon what terms soever bound unto her [Elizabeth], are freed from their oath and all manner of duty, fidelity and obedience."[9] Ironically, the Bull served only to make Catholicism in England even more untenable, for now the increasingly Puritan-minded government might logically label a practicing Catholic a traitor to the Crown. Elizabeth's oft-repeated wish "to make no windows into men's souls" was now rendered unrealistic by the Pope's action, for leniency and tolerance were impossible when challenged by a Bull which absolved her

Catholic subjects from any fealty to their Queen. Theoretically, all Catholic monarchs were also now enemies of Elizabeth's. In actuality, the Bull "met with unanimous reprobation from the crowned heads of Europe."[10] As one wit wrote, "The Pope had given England to anyone who will undertake to come and get it," but neither Spain nor France wished to undertake to depose the "heretic Queen," and the Bull merely completed the breach between Rome and England. It proved disastrous for many wavering English Catholics, who now despairingly joined the Anglican Church; others left England for good, and for those who remained staunch in their faith, life was to be made increasingly difficult.

Publication of the Bull also hardened the Queen's determination to punish the rebels. After what she had endured, with subjects rising against her, with her foremost nobleman in jail and countless Catholics ordered to absolve themselves of any fealty to their anointed monarch, Elizabeth felt small compassion for the conspirators. One observer had written to Cecil, "I beseech Almighty God that Her Majesty may take such order as the punishment of these rebels may be an example to all others in this age. I would not have thought to have found any corner in England where God and the Queen is so little acknowledged." The Queen concurred. Cecil might spout of lack of lawful proof which would stand inspection in a courtroom, but to Elizabeth there was no lack of lawful evidence. Men had marched against her, and when Sussex and others hung back from active retaliation she did not hesitate to write them caustically "that she somewhat marvelled that she had as yet heard nothing . . . of any execution done by martial law as was required."[11] Sussex then gave in, replying, "I guess it will not be under six or seven hundred that shall be executed of the common sort. . . ."

And so it happened. In an act reminiscent of her father, who had wreaked similar vengeance for the Pilgrimage of Grace uprising, Elizabeth now ordered the misguided wretches and conspirators, whose main crime was a "feudal faithfulness to their Lords" as well as their Church, to pay the ultimate price. And as usually happens, those whose staunchness to their faith was the truest in the land—the peasants—suffered the most brutal retributions. Ultimately more than 750 rebels were executed at Durham, York, Carlisle, Darlington and Barncastle. Rotting corpses hung in gibbets at every turn of the road, and mutilated segments of quarters were exhibited on all public buildings. At Durham Cathedral, the priest who had celebrated Mass for the rebels was hanged in front of the cathedral doors.

Not all the suffering was limited to the activists. Sir Henry Percy, loyal to the Queen, returned to the family castle of his uncle, the exiled Earl of Northumberland, to find the Earl's two small daughters, "in hard case, for they neither had any provisions nor one penny to relieve themselves with." He asked that they be removed "for their want of fire is so great, and their years may not well suffer that lack." In addition to being near frozen and half-starved, the young Percys also suffered being exposed to the appalling spectacle of the dangling corpses of the family servants swinging from estate trees.

Eventually all such sights would disappear from view. More enduring were the legal acts which followed the rebellion. Many of the clergy were deprived of their benefices, and the vast estates which had been family possessions for centuries were confiscated by the Crown. Pardons and reprieves were given freely to nearly all who could purchase them. Elizabeth's chronic shortness of ready cash, her constant necessity of "much ado to procure money" for her defense made her nearly wild with anxiety. She had spent eleven years accumulating funds to keep her realm solvent; there was no provision for armies to subdue civil acts of violence. Those who could buy their freedom now assisted the thrifty Queen in paying the cost of quelling the disturbance. Many of the wealthiest were brought to trial to be legally declared traitors, instead of executed outright; in this way, their lands automatically fell to the Crown.[12] It followed, therefore, that eventually her subjects themselves paid for their misdemeanor—with their lands, their monies or, having nothing else, their lives.

At the end a shaken Queen knew herself victorious. While many foreign powers had thought she might not prove equal to the task, she had successfully weathered the threat caused not only by religious differences, but, at its core, by the pride of the nobility and its one member who wished to wed Mary, Queen of Scots. A good deal of Elizabeth's natural sympathy for Mary vanished; she was more aware than ever of the menace the Scottish Queen would be to her sovereignty and authority. She also knew exactly to whom she owed her victory. Not her Councillors, her courtiers, or even soldiers like her good cousin Hunsdon. She owed her victory to no one but herself. She had risked the danger of the Catholic coalition which would almost certainly have formed on behalf of Mary Stuart had the uprising been even moderately successful. She had, with little aid from her ministers, affirmed that there would be no compromise with noble privilege. She had insisted on allegiance and an undisputed faith in the Crown, that what the Crown ordained was good for all England. She alone, while many others had wavered, had had the courage of her own conviction.

There might be those who spitefully insisted that the royal wrath was exerted in order to protect her own sovereign person from future danger. And in this Elizabeth Tudor would have agreed. But she would have taken it one step further; her life and her Crown must be spared, for they were what was best for England—not the bumbling assumptions of others of less courage and character who thought otherwise. That the Queen was correct in her thinking would be proved later in her reign: the Northern uprising marked the end of any similar disturbances. Never again would such a display of armed rebellion in her own country confront Elizabeth. The gruesome corpses swinging amid the leafless trees—many of them executed for slight reasons—were potent examples of a monarch's angry retaliation. In this direct and brutal response, the last backbone of quasi-feudal resistance was broken forever in England. Thirty-three years previously, the idealistic Pilgrimage of Grace marchers had brought similar tragedy to the North. The Rising in 1569–70 completed the havoc and paradoxically, resulted in the opposite of its proclaimed intent.

It did not cement loyalties or restore religion. Instead, it dispersed lands, broke family alliances and erased forever the medieval concept of lordly patronage and isolated privilege. No more would the Northern counties be bound to the service of a Percy, a Neville, a Norton or a Swinburne; no more would such as a Norfolk or a Dacre sway minions to their own way of thinking. There would be no further opportunity for the assumption of individual authority to work against the Crown. For the power of the North had been broken. It was never to rise again—or be the same as before.

And when it was all over, Elizabeth sat at her desk and, by candlelight, exorcised her anger and sadness in the sonnet which bestowed on Mary Stuart, Queen of Scots, an immortal anonym by which she would be forever remembered:

> Those dazzled eyes with pride, which great ambition blinds,
> Shall be unsealed by worthy wights, whose foresight falsehood binds.
> *The Daughter of Debate,* that eke discord doth sow,
> Shall reap no gain where former rule hath taught still peace to grow.[13]

As the Northern Uprising swept to its tragic conclusion, Elizabeth elevated Sir William Cecil to the peerage, creating him Lord Burghley. The title derived from the Abbey which had been the new peer's share of the loot of the Reformation and was a gesture of his royal mistress' confidence in her chief minister. They had spent thirteen years together, in which Burghley had learned as much from his sovereign as she from him. Elizabeth had her father's appraising eye for competent public servants. She and Burghley had worked well together; neither had sought to dominate the other, and therein probably lay the secret of their long mutual success. Each recognized the peculiar capabilities of the other, and to a day near his death when the Queen would feed him with her own hands, Burghley could and would be surprised by her reactions or opinions. That he could take advantage of what was often an impulse on Elizabeth's part—an inspiration from her shrewd, intuitive mind—and mold it into durable national policy benefited everyone. That the Queen, in turn, allowed herself to be guided and led in areas where she was uncertain or lacking—or merely, as was often the case, unable to make up her mind—was a testament to her faith in the solid and satisfying presence of the new Lord Burghley. They were both working for the same thing: a strong and secure England.

The ceremony took place in the Presence Chamber at Westminster in the presence of the whole court. There, escorted by the Earl of Leicester and Lord Cobham, Elizabeth listened to the words in the letters patent: " . . . for the long services in the time of our progenitors, Kings of England, as also for the faithful and acceptable duty and observance which he hath always performed from the very beginning of our reign, and ceaseth not daily to perform many ways . . . also for his circumspection, stoutness, wisdom, dexterity, integrity of life, providence, care and faithfulness . . ." which created William Cecil, Baron of Burghley. After the reading, she took the Baron's cloak from Lord Hunsdon and wrapped it around Cecil's shoulders. The trumpets blew, and the new Lord accepted the congratulations of the court before escorting the Queen to her dinner.

The appointment meant a great deal to Cecil, although he "affected to take the matter lightly." Elizabeth was not generous with titles; only three peers had been created before his own ennobling,[14] and Cecil was very aware of the honor that had come to him. With his usual modesty and fine sense of fitness, he wrote to his friend Nicholas White, "My style is Lord Burghley if you mean to know it for your writing, and if you list to write truly, the poorest Lord in England . . .!"[15] Burghley's affirmation of poverty was another illustration of the minister's own basically simple, prudent nature, but it was not evidenced in his manner of living. In addition to his house at Wimbledon, his home at Canon Row in Whitehall, his newly built mansion in the Strand, Burghley had begun enlarging Theobalds. It had originally been a small country retreat but over the years became larger presumably because the Queen visited so often. Elizabeth loved the area and had spent much time there as a child; she called it Tongs. Now, said Burghley, his enlarging was "rather for the Queen and her great train . . . not the pomp or glory." Theobalds ultimately became

an imposing mansion with fountains, walks and gardens about which
Burghley jogged comfortably on a mule during his all too infrequent
visits. The road to Theobalds from London ran straight as an arrow
and became known as the Theobalds Road. The building, once
completed, demanded the services of twenty-six to thirty persons in
constant residence, and each day twenty or thirty poor were fed at its
gates. Burghley, despite his great cares of state, usually found time to
review his household accounts and to discuss with his steward the
rotation of crops, the sale of garden produce, the breeding of stock and
the replenishment of gardens.[16] Only his younger son, Robert,
remained at home, and Theobalds was intended as his inheritance,
although, as Burghley said, "it would be too big for the small living he
could leave his son." At the age of fifty-one, often sick and martyred
with gout, Burghley might have thought he had reached the peak of his
career. His friend Nicholas Throckmorton, who died shortly after the
ennoblement, had cautioned him to lighten his burden "so to use your
service as you may long serve."[17] He would never know that the
minister's career would last almost another quarter of a century.

Possibly the greatest challenge to the new peer's responsibility was to
occur in the following months after the Queen permitted the release of
the Duke of Norfolk from his Tower prison. Although comfortably
lodged by comparison with lesser prisoners of state, confinement had
deteriorated Norfolk's health, which had never been robust, and it had
further exacerbated his resentment against the Queen and her
ministers, particularly the new Lord Burghley. Norfolk had been one of
the prime movers in the attempt to unseat William Cecil. He had kept
in touch with friends during his confinement, working out a cipher so
messages might be passed back and forth in leathern bottles. Against
the direct orders of the Queen, he had continued to receive messages
from Mary Stuart, who encouraged him to participate in any measures
which might result in freedom for them both, "for if you and I could
escape . . . we should find friends enough," she wrote, "being free and
honourably bound together, you might make such good offers for the
countries and the Queen of England as they should not refuse. . . ."[18]
She signed herself, "Your Own Mary" and spoke of the diamond she
wore at her neck, a gift from the Duke. She was waiting, she said, only
"until she could give it again to the owner of it and me both . . ." and
ended with "Your Own Faithful until Death. . . ."

Once the plague hit London and the "noxious airs" around the
Tower were at their worst, Norfolk would have been endowed with an
unearned martyrdom had he succumbed; therefore, it seemed
expedient to remove him to safer lodgings. After he had made a voluntary

submission, vowing "never to deal in that cause of marriage to the Queen of Scots, nor in any other cause belonging to her" and begging Elizabeth for release "out of the dungeon of your displeasure," he was remanded to his own Howard House to the custody of Sir Henry Neville, still a prisoner, but in comfort and some degree of safety from the plague. William Cecil thoughtfully suggested his widowed sister-in-law, the wealthy Lady Hoby, as a wife for the Duke. His enthusiasm might have been tempered had he realized that imprisonment had not lessened Norfolk's ambition; Mary Stuart herself had read his "submission" before he presented it to Queen Elizabeth.

Glad to be rid "of yonder pestilant house," Norfolk busied himself with improving stately Howard House. He received limited visits from friends or family and, on occasion, gave his opinion on state matters by messenger to Cecil. He implored the minister's help. "I have omitted nothing that lay in me to do to recover Her Highness' favour, without which I wish no life," he wrote.[19] Still the Queen refused to receive him or to communicate with him personally. She could not find it in her heart to excuse or pardon Norfolk. From the time of the York Conference, he had been partial to Mary Stuart's cause. Consistently he had lied and broken his word. She had given him every chance; she had warned him, tolerated his disloyalty, and he had repaid her with treachery. She had saved him from worse than imprisonment, but as a near kinsman, who should have safeguarded her person and Crown, he had acted in an appalling manner. She would give him limited freedom—in time, perhaps his complete freedom—but she would not receive him, and she would never trust him again.

Eventually, such treatment had its effect on the irresolute Duke. Bored within the confines of his palatial home, he was soon immersed in another conspiracy encouraged by Roberto Ridolfi, a Florentine who had brought the copies of the Papal Bull excommunicating Elizabeth to England. A true student of espionage, the Florentine banker possessed a capacity for intrigue as great as his lack of caution in furthering his conspiracies. He was well known about the court, often lending money to nobles notorious for their lack of ready cash. He was convinced that with the publication of the Bull, the English Catholics would rise if Mary Stuart were freed. Toward that end, he engaged the attention of Pope Pius V, asking that the Duke of Alva, still smarting from Elizabeth's appropriations of his troops' funds, provide men and money and, if they would do so, to "undertake with the help of the Catholics to deliver the Queen of Scots out of the hands of this Queen and re-establish religion in this realm."[20]

Ridolfi's optimism was contagious. Everyone concerned in the original plot to wed Mary to Norfolk—including several of Elizabeth's Councillors—was sure that now, with a formally excommunicated Queen, Alva and Philip would assist and the Pope would bless any attempt to dethrone Elizabeth. Ridolfi was smuggled into Howard House to talk with Norfolk, who, though he refused to sign any incriminating documents, gave his full moral support to the scheme. His own inclination was not to supplant Elizabeth; he wished only to restore Mary Stuart to her throne and her rights in the English succession. But others in the plot, Ridolfi primarily—and certainly Mary herself—had greater ideas than this, and "the enterprise on the person of Elizabeth" involved deposition at least and, should any attempt be made to restore her, murder at the end.[21]

The Bishop of Ross, Mary's emissary in London, and de Spes, the Spanish ambassador, assisted in drawing up letters to the Pope, to the Duke of Alva and to King Philip of Spain. Ridolfi then presented himself for an audience with the Queen at Greenwich, where he obtained a passport for Italy "on private business." To the jubilance of all concerned, he was allowed to leave the country to deliver personally letters which involved active treason against the Queen of England, thoroughly justifying Norfolk's prophetic remark: "I hold the wolf by the ears. I can neither let go without danger nor hold without peril!"

The letters promised that the Duke of Norfolk would supply an army of at least 20,000 soldiers and 3,000 horses against the Queen of England if Alva would furnish further "men, money and munitions." Mary and Norfolk would, on Mary's release, wed at once and "restore religion." The Duke ordered the sale of part of the family plate and jewelry for ready money for horses, arms and bribery and, on his somewhat tarnished honor, assured the Pope, the Duke and the King, "I faithfully promise not only to do all my endeavour so far as my powers may extend, but also to hazard my life for the glory of God."[22] What glory Norfolk might have envisioned was doomed from the start; the hazard to his life was to prove all too real.

Mary Stuart had, in turn, followed Norfolk's example and written letters of credence for Ridolfi, inspiring the Spanish ambassador's comment: "She certainly seems a lady of great spirit, and gains so many friends where she is that, with a little help, she would be able to get the kingdom into her hands. . . ." But the "little help" was not enough. Though Mary had even promised the King of Spain a marriage between her young son and one of Philip's daughters and that the Prince himself might be sent to the Spanish court "to be educated in virtue and the Christian faith," Ridolfi was not warmly received by anyone except the Pope. Pius exhibited great enthusiasm, and on Mary's assertion that she had met with great "ill-treatment . . . from my subject, the Earl of Bothwell," who had "detained her against her will," the Pope promised a timely divorce, and wrote the Spanish King that Ridolfi should be assisted.

The Duke of Alva was not impressed. "I do not like Ridolfi," he wrote Philip, "He is a babbler . . ." and he had little to offer the Florentine. He still hoped to retrieve the Spanish treasure by the use of diplomacy.* Alva said he would support Ridolfi only if the English Catholics instigated the deposition or murder of Elizabeth, and if they should inspire successful rebellion for forty days, he would then look with favor on the "enterprise of Elizabeth." He wrote Philip, "The first steps must not be taken by us. . . ."

Undaunted by Alva's sensible practicality, Ridolfi continued his journey and met with the Spanish King at Madrid. Philip promised £50,000 and indicated an Italian in his employ, Chiapin Vitelli, the Marchese of Cetona, who volunteered the assassination of Elizabeth. The English Queen, he said, was noted for her lack of personal security and was "notoriously easy of access." Philip, who had lived in England as the Queen's brother-in-law while married to her late sister, Mary, was not so sure but gave the plot his uneasy blessing. Well might he have been uneasy. While traveling from Rome to Madrid, Ridolfi had foolishly "babbled" of the plot to the Grand Duke of Tuscany, who thoughtfully sent detailed information of it to Elizabeth in England.

At the same time, William Cecil had discovered wisps of plot and intrigue, and in Rome, Brussels and Madrid a myriad of English spies soon uncovered more. Letters to the Duke of Norfolk, to the Bishop of Ross, to Mary Stuart and others had been intercepted, and when a messenger carrying £600 and a cipher to the Scottish rebels was captured, the substance went out of the conspiracy. †

In London agents of the Queen entered Howard House, from which Norfolk had only recently requested release so he might seek "a change of air" for reasons of health "or else my poor body is not like to endure." He had his wish sooner than expected, but not the one he had anticipated. Whereas there had previously been no legal means of charging Norfolk, Cecil now had documents which daily brought the full scope of the conspiracy to light. The pieces that were missing were

*Negotiations for this treasure went on for years. Cajolery, bribery and appeals to English honor were pointless, and envoys returned home empty handed. Eventually, the property dwindled and was so eaten up in parcels that little remained.[21]

†Ridolfi, needless to say, did not return to England. He journeyed to Rome and was created a Papal Senator by the Pope and lived another forty years, "making a comfortable income from his financial dealings," in his native Florence.

soon attained. One of Norfolk's servants—threatened with the thumbscrew and the rack—revealed one of the Duke's hiding places "under the mat, hard by the window side in the entry towards My Lord's bedchamber where the map of England doth hang," where an inflamatory letter from Mary Stuart was discovered. The cipher itself was later discovered "betwixt two tiles in the roof."

The Bishop of Ross, Mary's representative, was also apprehended and "seeing everything discovered beyond his expectations . . . fell faint-hearted, avowed himself penitent for his evil practices and made some important confessions." The confessions were damning indeed, as Dr. Wilson, the interrogator, wrote to Cecil. "The Bishop seemeth to me to be very glad that these practices are come to light," Wilson wrote, "he sayeth . . . that the Queen his mistress is not fit for any husband. For the first, he sayeth, she poisoned her husband, the French King, as he hath credibly understood. Again, she hath consented to the murder of her late husband, the Lord Darnley; thirdly, she matched with the murderer and brought him to the field to be murdered. And, last of all, she pretended marriage with the Duke [Norfolk] with whom, as he thinketh, she would not long have kept faith, and the Duke should not have had the best of days with her. . . ." It was all too much for the simple Dr. Wilson, and his comment was one of astonished bewilderment. "Lord what people these are!" he exclaimed. "What a Queen —and what an ambassador!"[24]

On Friday, September 7, 1571, the Queen's birthday, after almost a year of relative freedom and comfort at Howard House, the Duke was again conveyed to the Tower "for the first time on a horse in eleven months."[25] Elizabeth, distraught and shaken by the extent of the conspiracy, gave full vent to the fury which consumed her, and the chambers and halls of the royal residence rang with her invective. Ironically, while the search for incriminating evidence had been proceeding in London, the Queen had been visiting Audley End, the home of Norfolk's son, Thomas,* "whereby great means were used to give Her Majesty to put Norfolk in full liberty . . . whereunto Her Majesty seemed to give favorable ear, especially upon asseverations that it was thought that he would become a good subject and that he had forsaken the matter of the Queen of Scots. . . ." Immediately, her orders went out. An invitation to foreign power, a promise to seize or murder the sovereign were the rawest kind of treason. The Queen's attitude pointed the way for others at court who had been partial to Norfolk. Even Leicester, who had once encouraged the Duke in his

---

*Thomas Howard was the oldest son of Norfolk's *second* marriage to Margaret Audley, from whom he inherited the title Lord Howard of Walden. Later he was created Earl of Suffolk.

marital ambitions, realized he was now a lost man and switched his allegiance. All of which seemingly justified the Duke of Alva's bitter comment: "For my own part, I looked for nothing better with such light people to deal with!"[26]

With the Duke's second incarceration in the Tower, the Crown moved to appropriate his estates. At Howard House, Kenninghall, and all the vast properties of the Norfolk Liberty inventories were taken of livestock, tenants, buildings, wardrobes, plate, jewels, tapestries, "Turkey" carpets, portraits, baubles, books, some of which the servants —"Very sorrowful for the Duke in his trouble"—had begun to package preparatory to consigning them out of danger to other members of the family. Norfolk's eldest son and heir, Philip,* was distraught at the arrival of the investigators. The boy was fourteen, and the brutal plunder of beloved family possessions caused him to claim that "it doth make me greatly fear that the Queen is much displeased with my Lord, my father." At the end of several days of diligent effort, the Queen's agents could proudly say, "We have not left to our knowledge any closet or coffer of the Duke unsearched."[27] In the end the gates of Kenninghall Palace, where he had "lived like a King," were closed for good. His children, stepchildren, retainers, household officers, grooms, maids, stablemen, porters, laundresses and other women were ordered to find other lodging and employment.

On January 16, 1572, in Westminster Hall, the scene of the previous state trials of many great nobles—the "Good Duke," the Protector Somerset; of John Dudley, the Duke of Northumberland; and of a Chancellor of England, Sir Thomas More—the Duke of Norfolk stood trial. He was brought from the Tower by water, "between seven and eight o'clock in the morning which had not been seen in any time." There he heard an indictment charging him with conspiring the deposition and death of the Queen, with endeavoring to bring foreign armies into England and with having sought to wed Mary Stuart, "knowing she laid claim to the Crown," and thus alter the religious establishment of the realm. Before twenty-six of his fellow peers, many to whom he was related by marriage and of whom he was senior in birth, prestige and wealth and in kinship to the Queen, he awaited the verdict, "oft biting his lips" in nervousness. Previously when Cecil had asked him for his confession, Norfolk had been reduced to tears, saying that "he could write nothing more concerning the matter."

The verdict was a long time coming. Each juror wished to justify in his own conscience the verdict expected of him. It was not until a

*Philip was the Duke's eldest son by his *first* marriage to Mary Fitzwilliam and was heir to not only his father's title but, by right of his mother, the lands and title of the Earl of Arundel.

quarter to seven that evening that they concurred—a testament not to their perversity, but to the mountains of evidence to be reviewed. Then, as darkness enveloped Westminster Hall, and a large crowd, tired and depressed at the long wait, began to break up, the Earl of Shrewsbury asked each peer for his opinion. Each answered "guilty." Whereupon, at the conclusion of the roll call, the Earl addressed Norfolk: "The Lords, thy peers, have found thee guilty . . ." and the Duke listened to the same monstrous words his father had heard twenty-five years previously. "Thou shalt be hanged and, being alive, thou shalt be cut down quick, thy bowels shall be taken forth of thy body and burnt before thy face; thy head shall be smitten off; thy body shall be divided into four parts of quarters; thy head and thy quarters to be set up where it shall please the Queen's Majesty to appoint; and the Lord have mercy upon thee. . . ." Norfolk, shaken and in tears, said, "This is the judgment of a traitor and I shall die as true a man to the Queen as any liveth. . . ." He said he would not petition the Queen for his life. "I trust shortly to be in a better . . ." he said miserably and then turned to follow the guard, who, with the ax turned toward him, escorted him outside. Those who had waited long, seeing the turned ax, groaned and wept at the fate of the popular Duke. As Norfolk, his face impassive, obediently followed the guard, he heard the session within the hall end with the glad cry "God save the Queen!"

The tormenting presence of Mary Stuart in England was to create a deep emotional hell for the Queen of England as the months and, ultimately, the years passed. Always there was the constant awareness that lodged in a castle in the deep countryside was another anointed sovereign who claimed the English Crown, who bore the religion still beloved of many Englishmen. As long as she remained in custody, it was virtually impossible that the religious issue should remain quiescent. Sir Henry Norris wrote from France, "The open talk at Paris was of war with England, for the release of the Queen of Scots and the toleration of Papistry." Catherine de Medici referred to the Northern uprising as God's way of warning Elizabeth, who had favored the Scottish Regent over the Scottish Queen. Norris wrote that the Cardinal of Lorraine, Mary's uncle, had engaged several assassins to destroy Elizabeth, after which the Duke of Alva supposedly would "make a diversion into Scotland," while the French moved on London and captured Mary, who would then wed a French Prince. "I pray you assure yourself that except they fail of their purpose, they intend the ruin of her Majesty. As you tender her Majesty's preservation, let the Queen of Scots be removed out of the country!" he advised.[28]

Elizabeth would have liked nothing better, but after Murray's assassination, any thought of releasing Mary was remote. Scotland's government now bordered on anarchy as Catholics and Protestants, embodied in the great clans, fought for supremacy. When the Earl of Lennox, Darnley's father, was traveling north to accept the Regency, several of the Lords begged Elizabeth to deliver Mary to them, an act which would almost certainly have resulted in her death. Elizabeth was tempted, and she asked for some guarantee which would absolve *her* of any complicity or responsibility in Mary's fate. Typically, she would not put her desire in plain words. Instead, she wrote the Scottish emissary, "I believed you were a wise man. You would press me to speak what is no wise necessary. You know that, for my honour, I must require pledges. But I think you may judge of yourself what might be best for me. . . ."[29] But the Scots would not cooperate, and ultimately, common sense won out, and Lennox went alone.

Murray's death had eliminated the main Scottish Protestant tie with England. The arrogance of those now in power was seen in the presence of the Northern rebels, Westmorland and others, who "sat in Council" with the Scottish Lords. Elizabeth's emissary, Thomas Randolph, wrote that Sussex had spoken with the Scottish Lord Lindsay to arrange for the nobles' return to England and punishment. "I find he hath a great eye to his own profit," wrote Randolph, "and yet very desirous to be quit of them, for the great trouble and charge that he is at, but to any resolute point, he will not grow, more than that he would gladly be quit of them. He would the Queen should pay for them. . . ."[30]

Eventually, the situation worsened as civil war broke out in Scotland. Marauders prowled the Border, scavenging and burning, provoking the tenuous peace between England and Scotland. After Norfolk's imprisonment, conditions became intolerable as those left of the Queen's party threatened reconciliation with France unless Mary Stuart were restored. When the English demand for the return of the rebel Earls was consistently ignored, an enraged Elizabeth sent 4,000 soldiers to Berwick. Randolph hurriedly left Edinburgh and joined the commander Lord Sussex, who vowed "before the light of the coming moon was passed to leave a memory in Scotland whereby they and their children should be afraid to offer war to England."[31]

Sussex was true to his word. While many of her noblemen waited word of the venture, while Leicester went to Kenilworth, where he employed "many workmen to make it strong and doth furnish it with armour, munitions and all necessaries for defence," the valiant English leader and his army, accompanied by another force under Sir John

Foster, passed Teviotdale in two bodies on either side of the river, "leaving neither castle, tower nor town undestroyed" till they came to Jedburgh, where every stone building, large and small was blown up. At Fernihurst, Hawick, Branxhole, they "rent and tore" every solid building "so that no man nor beast might use it for refuge or shelter." They stripped thatch from cottages and set it on fire. They burned orchards and granaries, and what would not burn was blown up. At the end of the foray, "ninety strong castles, houses and dwelling places, with 300 towns and villages," had been utterly destroyed.

As the bells of England tolled the victory, as Elizabeth reaped the congratulations due for the "honourablest journey that ever was made into Scotland, with so few men, with so safe a return," she sought to deal once more with Mary Stuart, hoping to wring some concessions from the Scottish Queen and force her to renounce her claim to the English throne. Lord Burghley and a companion were selected to confer with Mary, an assignment which, said the new peer, had "thrown him into a maze." He invoked God's guidance, "for neither of us like the message!" Neither he nor Mary chose to leave a recorded account of their meeting, nor did Burghley ever give any direct appraisal of the Scottish Queen. However, the Bishop of Ross wrote the imprisoned Norfolk that the minister had dealt with Mary "firmly, in such sort that he has promised to be her friend." Burghley had, apparently, told Ross that he "liked her nature very well and confirmed his opinion . . . which was that the Queen of Scots was of a clement and gentle nature and was disposed to be governed by counsel of them in which she reposeth her trust. He promised to travail that she and the Queen of England shall speak together and hath given her counsel how she should behave herself in that case to win the Queen of England's favour."[32] Certainly, no one was better instructed to advise Mary toward that particular end than Elizabeth's most intimate adviser. Both Mary and her visitor undoubtedly showed their best aspects to each other. The unfortunate truth was that in the end Burghley could never answer directly for Elizabeth, and Mary would have forsaken any advice or broken any promise to be free.

Upon his return to court, Burghley could claim a modest success. Mary had agreed to a compromise. In the clause whereby she renounced her claim in favor of Elizabeth and her issue, she insisted on the insertion of the word "lawful" preceding "issue." As she agreed to the insert, Elizabeth could not refrain from saying tartly, "She may, peradventure, measure other folks' dispositions by her own actions!" However, she made certain she had the last word. As the insertion of the word "lawful" was allowed, Elizabeth insisted that the word "pretended" be inserted before Mary's title to the accession. All of which left the new Lord of Burghley to ruminate on the vagaries of his burgeoning career which allowed so seemingly eminent a statesman to act as moderator between two sovereigns who happened to be female and had difficulty in sheathing their claws.

The effects of the Northern Uprising and the Ridolfi plot, which had brought the foremost peer in England to his knees, had one great effect. After the disastrous revelations became public, the people rallied closer to their Queen. Countless churches were thronged in extra services in grateful thanksgiving that Elizabeth had escaped the evil danger which had threatened her Crown and her life. Various assemblies in the London streets were noisy with threats against those, such as Mary Stuart and the King of Spain, who had conspired against their sovereign. And for the Pope, they asserted "he was more full of Bulls than money."[33]

The Ridolfi conspiracy proved to be the last combined effort of the English aristocracy to undo the Reformation "and strangle the new order of things before it grew too strong for them." But once the facts were known, it was not only the aristocracy which mattered, for everywhere the common people of England demanded revenge. Delegations from the City, from the counties, even from Parliament waited upon Elizabeth with their insistence that Mary Stuart suffer a fate similar to Norfolk's. The Queen, whose first natural pity and compassion for Mary had long since disappeared, could find her only release in anger. When Fénelon attempted to justify Mary's complicity in the Norfolk-Ridolfi disaster, Elizabeth was nearly beside herself and "burst into the most furious rage and dwelt very strongly on the evils which . . . were brought upon this country by the Queen of Scotland." The French ambassador wrote that "she screamed this out with so much vehemence that everybody in the Palace could hear her."

Others heard Elizabeth also, particularly those who came pleading for Mary's blood. Point by point the English Queen recounted how she had attempted to protect the Scottish Queen, who was a guest in her realm, from the result of her own provocative actions. Yet Mary had —all the while with smooth words glossing over the fact that she was conspiring with Elizabeth's own kinsman and various Continentals— continued to intrigue and plot. When she was heatedly advised, even by Burghley, "to make short end of traitors once and for all," Elizabeth pleaded that Mary should be spared as "she was a Queen's daughter." To which her chief minister replied that Elizabeth was "a King's daughter and our own Queen" and should act like Majesty and not a wavering female who could not pronounce sentence and see it carried out.

Often Elizabeth was half persuaded. She was heartily sick of her unwanted guest and wished her out of England, where she was causing such trouble. She knew that Mary would forever be the pivot of the opposition and the center of organized resistance. The longer she remained in the Kingdom, the more sympathy she incurred. Wearily, Elizabeth could look with optimistic favor on the possibility of Mary's death—as long as she was not blamed for it. Where, previously, she had refused to publicize Mary's dishonor, she now allowed the translation and publication of the *Detectio* by George Buchanan, the Scots' version of the Mary Stuart-Lord Bothwell-Lord Darnley affair. To it, she had allowed the Casket Letters to be appended. But that was as far as Elizabeth would go, causing the usually more taciturn Burghley to write that God could not be pleased with "such slowness . . . such stay in resolution in the highest person. . . ." Burghley said he was so "overthrown in heart, as I have no spark almost of good spirits left in me to nourish health in my body." The gout which had begun in his middle years was taking its toll, and he said he was "forced to be carried to the Parliament House and to her Majesty's presence."[34] Elizabeth was adamant that Mary, Queen of Scots, would remain where she was and she herself would stand between her and the wrath of Protestant England.[35] Her Councillors and the Parliament recognized Majesty's invincible obstinacy when they saw it. Mary had flown to her realm "as a bird that had flown to her for succour from the hawk," said Elizabeth. No matter how insidious her plotting and how persistent her hatred, Mary was a Queen. And one Queen could not sentence another to death, she said. And with that her ministers had to be content.

Elizabeth's indecision had also extended to the Duke of Norfolk. In the Tower on the day before the expected execution, the Duke occupied himself in writing a long letter to his children. In the touching document, he spoke to each—to Philip, to Tom, to "well-beloved Nan," to Meg, to Will—even to his daughters-in-law, Mall and "little Bess." In this letter, he advised them to "serve and fear God above all things. I find the point in myself that I have, God forgive me, been negligent in this point. . . ." He emphasized they must love and care for one another and suggested the proper schooling for the younger ones. He had one important suggestion for them. "Beware of high degrees!" he wrote.

Recognizing where his own ambition had led him, he advised his older son to find a "pleasant dwelling of your own" and, with his wife, "withdraw yourself . . . and if your happ may be so good, as you may so live without being called to higher degree. Oh Philip! Philip! then shall you enjoy that blessed life which your woeful father would feign have done, and never could be so happy!" If Philip should doubt him, the Duke suggested he "look into the whole state of the nobility in times past, and into their state now, and then judge whether my lesson be true or not. . . ." He advised that "Meggy and Nan" might go to Lady Sussex who might be entreated to "take them to her as sojourn-ers . . . she is a good lady."

He dwelled little on his own sins, having accepted there was little he could now do about them. He advised Philip "to forget my condemn-ing and forgive, I charge you, my false accusers, as I protest to God I do, *but have nothing to do with them if they live.*" Several of those implicated in the plot had spoken honestly in their confessions, wrote the Duke, but he was obviously bitter at the Bishop of Ross, who "did falsely accuse me and laid his own treasons upon my back. . . ." After writing a solicitous word to each of his "dear and loving children," Norfolk wrote, "I hope ere it be long to be rid out of this wretched world, to follow my dear wives and your mothers in the heavenly joys, whether pray God send me. . . ." Typically, at the end, having had regard to each of his children, the great peer, who had been so beloved of his tenants, spoke of the lease of a farm to one Bowles, "which, if I had lived, I would have performed . . ." as Bowles had been "as honest and true a servant to your father as any that he hath had." Norfolk therefore requested his son Tom to honor his request "that he [Bowles] shall have the lease at your hand."[36]

Then having bequeathed his love and advice to his children—and made his memory sacred to the Bowles family forever—the Duke put aside his writing materials to make his peace with the God whom he professed to have "neglected" and await the moment when his sovereign should order an end to his mortal misery.

It was to be a longer wait than he had anticipated.

Mary Stuart had seemingly repented very little the fact that her cause and her own active conspiring had brought England's only Duke to the scaffold. Blatantly she told the Earl of Shrewsbury, her guar-dian, that the Duke would have to answer for his own doings. She had deliberately been kept ignorant of the true extent of the discoveries which so incriminated her and, therefore, did not realize the revealing deception so obvious when she said, "I have not dealt with him since the time of his restraint . . . neither have I gone about to stir up a rebellion in this realm, nor intended any harm unto the Queen. . . ." She could not refrain from saying that Elizabeth, however, "hath maintained my rebels against me, to the taking of my Crown from my head!" Spiritedly, in telling contrast with the Duke's dejection, she said "that she had come to England as a free Princess relying upon promises which had been repeatedly made to her and instead of friendship and hospitality, she had found a prison." It was true, therefore, that she had applied to the King of Spain to replace her on her throne. Those who said that she had done more were "false villains and lied in their throats." As for the Duke, himself, Mary had little to offer. He was Elizabeth's subject, she said, "and for him she had nothing to say." For herself, "she was a free Princess, the Queen of England's equal, and was answerable neither to her nor to any other person." When confronted with the Bishop of Ross' abject confession, she cried he was but a "flayed and fearful priest, who had done as they would have him do . . ." and reiterated she would not change her own demeanor under pressure. Instead, "they should find her to be a Queen and to have the heart of a Queen. . . ."[37]

Mary found it difficult, if not impossible, to accept that her incessant plotting and intriguing against her cousin Elizabeth—so justified in her own eyes—only contributed to her own hardships. Her guard had been doubled, suspicious servants dismissed and locks removed from her private chambers "that her rooms might be examined at any hour of the day or night. . . ." The Earl of Shrewsbury, Mary's guardian, wrote to Burghley, "It is too plain that her heart is overhardened with deadly hate against the Queen's Majesty. The more, therefore, her Majesty's safety is to be thought upon."[38] Mary's visitors were few, and locked up, deprived of most ordinary means of outside communication, desire for freedom and revenge increased daily. Had she remained silent and uninvolved, in time a renunciation of her rights would almost certainly have resulted in a dishonored freedom. Elizabeth had no desire—and with Mary's ultimate renunciation, no real reason—to keep her imprisoned. It was Mary's own strong and bitter resistance which in effect provided Elizabeth with the key which kept Mary jailed for the remainder of her life. As the true extent of Mary's complicity was unveiled, Elizabeth had shouted that "no sovereign in Europe would sit down under such provocation!" and that "she would count herself unworthy of her realm, Crown and name of Queen if she endured it!"[39]

There was little sympathy for the Scottish Queen either in or out of England. Even her former brother-in-law, King Charles IX of France, angrily declared, "The poor foolish woman will not desist until she loses her head. She will certainly bring about her own execution. If she does so, it will be her own fault. I can do nothing to hinder her. . . ."[40] Elizabeth herself wrote Mary, "Madame, I am no fool to be deceived by your devices," and in words of similar vein had urged Mary to behave herself and protect herself from further retribution. Her concern had gone unheeded. All of Mary's energies were directed toward the goal which made her every waking moment worthwhile: her freedom, her restoration to the Scottish throne and her revenge on her English cousin. Mary recognized what she had lost and, as she often repeated, "the last words she uttered would be those of a Queen of Scotland."

Such demands on her nervous system had resulted in spates of ill health. Outwardly much of the physical agility and dauntless spirit which had so impressed her first guardian, Knollys, were gone, but in the deterioration of her health, her vengeful and careless attitude seemed to grow stronger. Of her health, the Bishop of Ross had stated that "she was much molested with a continual distillation from her head into her stomach whereof hath grown such deviltry and weakness in that part, that she neither hath desire to any meat, neither faculty to retain that long when she doth eat it. She is troubled also with an incessant provocation to vomit . . . without any great or manifest release of her pains, likewise, she is molested with a great inflammation and tension in her left side, under her short ribs, which reacheth so far every way that they yet doubt whether it be inflammation of the stomach, the spleen, the womb or of all those three parts together. . . ."[41]

With the exception of Tutbury Castle, which, surrounded by a moat, was constantly damp as well as inaccessible and lonely on its flat hilltop, Mary's lodgings were usually relatively comfortable. A cloth of estate was permitted over her chair; she had many of her old retainers and ladies-in-waiting around her. Elizabeth maintained Mary and her small court at her own expense, thus allowing Mary to spend her French revenues in bribery and conspiracy against her royal cousin. Her ill health was more the product of a gnawing urgency to be unfettered, the bitter awareness of how much she had lost: freedom, Crown, son, country and subjects. That she was, in her own eyes, unfairly condemned and seemingly to be incarcerated forever, contributed to the mental condition which eventually affected the physical. Nicholas White, an Irish visitor from Waterford, traveling near Chester and "finding the wind contrary," decided to avail himself of the hospitality at Tutbury Castle. He gives a lucid and touching picture of the Scottish Queen in the first years of her long captivity:

The Queen of Scots, understanding by his Lordship [her custodian] that a servant of the Queen's Majesty of some credit was come to the house, seemed desirous to speak with me, and thereupon came forth of her privy chamber into the presence chamber where I was, and in a very courteous manner bade me welcome, and asked of me how her good sister did. I told her Grace that the Queen's Majesty, (God be praised) did very well. . . .

Mary then, according to White, "heard the English service with a book of Psalms in her hand, which she showed me after." At the completion of the service, Mary spoke with White "of sundry matters" for about an hour. She excused her "ill English," saying she was "more willing than apt to learn that language" and how she had used translations "as a means to attain it." Still casting about for mutual conversation, Mary said she understood that Nicholas White was to go into Ireland, "which is a troublesome country," to serve Elizabeth there. White was blunt and replied, "I do so, Madame, and the chiefest trouble of Ireland proceeds from the north of Scotland, through the Earl of Argyll's supportation." At which point, he said, Mary "little answered."

White asked Mary how "she liked the change of air." Mary answered:

She said if it might have pleased her good sister to let her remain where she was, she would not have removed for change of air at this time of the year. But she was the better contented therewith, because she was come so much nearer to her good sister, whom she desired to see above all things, if it might please her to grant the same. I told her Grace that although she had not the actual, yet she had the effectual presence of the Queen's Majesty by her great bounty and kindness, who, in the opinion of us abroad in the world, did ever perform towards her the office of a gracious Prince, a natural kinswoman, a loving sister, and a faithful friend. . . .

Mary nodded at these pious admonitions of White's. His remark that she had much for which to thank her Saviour ("after the passing of so many perils, she was safely arrived into such a realm . . .") she bore with easy grace. Mary could play the same game, and after listening to more statements of the "goodness of the Queen's Majesty" and White's wish that "she meekly bow her mind to God who hath put her into this school to learn to know Him . . ." she very "gently accepted." She added, however, that she required patience, "which she humbly prayed Him to give her." White's letter continues:

I asked her Grace since the weather did cut of all exercises abroad, how she passed the time within. She said that all the day she wrought with her needle, and that the diversity of the colours made the work seem less tedious, and continued so long at it till very pain did make her give over; and with that laid her hand upon her left side and complained of an old grief newly increased there. . . .

Soon after, Mary, tiring of the conversation, "closed up her talk, and bidding me farewell, retired into her chamber." That the Scottish Queen had made a great impression on White is evident in his closing words to Cecil:

But if I, which in the sight of God bear the Queen's Majesty a natural love beside my bounden duty, might give advice, *there should be very few subjects in this land have access to or conference with this Lady.* For beside that she is a goodly personage, and yet in truth not comparable to our sovereign, she hath withal an alluring grace, a pretty Scottish accent, and a searching wit, clouded with mildness. Fame might move some to relieve her, and glory joined to gain might stir others to adventure much for her risk. . . .

An "alluring grace," a "searching wit, clouded with mildness," these had impressed White in spite of himself, and he could not know the uncanny justification of his prophecy that "Fame might move some to relieve her. . . ." At the conclusion of his letter, as if seeking to excuse a momentary lapse into admiration for Mary Stuart, he wrote, somewhat irrelevantly, "Her hair of itself is black and yet Mr. Knollys told me that she wears hair of sundry colours." He had found Mary embroidering a cloth of estate upon which the sentence *En ma fin est mon commencement* ("In the end is my beginning") for which he had a final word. It was, he said, "a riddle I understand not."[42]

The execution of the Duke of Norfolk was scheduled for January 21, but Elizabeth was so wretched at her cousin's plight she could not bring herself to sign the warrant until early February. At eleven o'clock on the evening preceding the execution, she revoked the warrant, earning Burghley's comment: "The Queen's Majesty hath been always a merciful lady, and by mercy she hath taken more harm than justice, and yet she thinks that she is more beloved in doing herself harm! God save her to His honour long among us. . . ." She found many excuses: she had grown up with Norfolk; he was her kinsman; no peer's blood had been shed during her Queenship. And as she talked, unbidden, would come her own dark memories of her incarceration in the Tower, of those long, fearful months when she had never expected to leave her prison alive.

The emotional conflict inevitably affected her health, and in late March she became agonizingly ill. A severe inflammation of the chest and stomach and its subsequent gripping pain were first thought to be poison, although the royal physician wearily proclaimed it yet more evidence of Elizabeth's "contempt for physic, and utter neglect of such potions as they considered necessary to keep her in health." Her distress was such that both Burghley and Leicester passed three nights in her bedchamber as the court waited, in suspense and fear, for the outcome. After five days, the crisis had passed, and when Fénelon saw Elizabeth, she appeared weak and frightened, telling him of the "heavy and vehement pains" she had suffered which had so "straitened her breath and clutched her heart, she thought she was going to die."

Illness, procrastination and excuses, however, could not forgo the necessity of facing up to Norfolk's execution. They were the outward manifestations of a shaken and heartsick woman, shrinking from a responsibility for which she had no real heart. At the same time, she recognized a sovereign's obligation and accepted that Norfolk must die if only to serve as an example to the forces which had worked for her downfall. The Duke had written, "with an overwhelmed heart and a watery cheek," asking for pardon and denying his active participation in pursuing the Scottish marriage. All he had wanted, wrote Norfolk, was "a quiet life." Yet the pressure for his head continued, and despairingly Elizabeth signed the warrant and again, for the fourth time, soon revoked it. Cecil wrote to young Francis Walsingham, an envoy at the French court:

> I cannot write to you what is the inward stay of the Duke of Norfolk's death, only I find her Majesty diversely disposed. Sometimes, when she speaketh of her danger, she concludeth that justice should be done. Another time, when she speaketh of his nearness of blood, of his superiority in honour, she stayeth. On Saturday, she signed a warrant for the writs to the sheriffs of London for his execution on Monday, and so all preparations were made. . . . Suddenly on Sunday, late in the night, the Queen's Majesty sent for me, and entered into a great misliking that the Duke should die the next day. . . . God's will be fulfilled, and aid her Majesty to do herself good![13]

Others were not as charitable, and Lord Hunsdon, another relative, pointed out that the Queen's negligence was dangerous to her own security. "How much more needful is it for her Majesty to take heed, upon whose life depends a whole commonwealth. . . .!" he cried.

Parliament, which was then sitting, insisted that Elizabeth act. They reproved the Queen, saying, "This error has crept into the heads of a number, that there is a person in this land whom no law can touch."[44] They demanded Norfolk's head, and for Mary Stuart, their advice was to "cut off her head and make no more ado about it." She had been warned, they said, "and therefore the axe must give the next warning." Ultimately, a bill was passed pointing the way for Elizabeth to act. The bill stated that any person refusing to recognize Elizabeth's accession as legitimate could not succeed her; it affirmed that the inheritance of the monarchy should be determined by Parliament and the Queen, and to deny any such condition was high treason. Third, a penalty of life imprisonment was ordered for anyone to assert in writing that anyone might succeed the Queen, other than her own lawful issue or a Parliamentary choice.[45] By this means, Parliament sought to protect its sovereign, and its action was a reflection of the English people's concern at the threat to a beloved Queen, as well as the security and safety of the realm. A later Parliament wished to bring in a bill of attainder against Mary Stuart which would have resulted in her immediate execution, but this was vetoed by Elizabeth.

At the same time, a ciphered letter signed by Mary was put into Elizabeth's hands. She exhibited the document to Fénelon, who had come to ask for clemency for the Scottish Queen. In the letter, addressed to the Duke of Alva, Mary had begged that ships be sent to Scotland to capture the person of her son, the young King, "whom she committed to the King of Spain." Mary boasted of the number of her adherents in England "and of the Lords who favoured her cause." She predicted "the Queen of England would not dare touch their lives."[46]

With all the accumulative evidence, with pressure from Parliament and her Council, Elizabeth knew she could delay no longer. The incessant reprieves not only were undermining her own health, but were also creating emotional havoc within the Duke's family. Sadly she signed a warrant for execution on June 2. Her agitation and sorrow were increased by a letter from the Duke in which he asked the Queen to look after his children and stepchildren. Elizabeth designated the man she most trusted, Lord Burghley, to become their guardian, earning Norfolk's grateful reply, for "my unfortunate brats. . . ."

And so, after five months of living from day to day, of wondering whether freedom might yet be his, the proud Norfolk ascended the scaffold on Tower Hill. He had exchanged his worn prison clothing for a doublet of white satin, which he thoughtfully bequeathed to the executioner. Bravely and with a dignity he had often lacked in life, he refused to have his eyes covered and seemed eager to embrace the death he had awaited so long. His last words were: "I fear not death. . . ."[47] With one stroke of the ax, the Duke was dead and his head held up to a lamenting crowd which had assembled to watch the execution. He was later buried in the Chapel of St. Peter-ad-Vincula, in the Tower precincts, not far from his father, the Earl of Surrey and a cousin, Anne Boleyn, all of whom had suffered the same shameful death.

Unknown to Norfolk, on the evening before the execution, Queen Elizabeth had come to the Tower. Troubled, yet resigned to what must be, she had visited the Constable to make sure all was prepared for the morrow and then, aimlessly, had wandered about the area. She had, undoubtedly, planned to vist Norfolk one last time. But there, at the site of the Green, she was reminded of the mother she could barely remember, whose head had been cut off by order of her husband, Elizabeth's father. Farther up the Hill, where the Duke would go on the morrow, her own youthful infatuation, Thomas Seymour, had suffered a similar fate. Fewer than twenty years previously, she herself had come to these melancholy, haunted precincts, sitting firmly on the water stairs in a lashing rain and proclaiming for all to hear, "I am no traitor!" She had never expected to leave the Tower alive.

In the end she became so agitated she did not visit the Duke. And all the next day as the guns boomed that Norfolk's head had at last fallen, she kept to her chambers and, to her ladies, appeared "pensive and sad."

The Pawn

For my own part, I firmly believe that my happiness will be only too great for an old woman to whom paternosters will suffice in place of nuptials.

Chapter Nineteen

As both the Queen of England and the Earl of Leicester approached their fortieth birthdays, their relationship—formerly so tempestuous and indiscreet—had settled into a mutual responsiveness in which their estimation of each other might be compared to the savoring of a vintage wine or "a sweet memory of the past." Sharper jealousies, biting ambitions, impulsive and piqued reactions had softened. Their appreciation—one for the other—was full, yet bore little probing for the new or the unattainable. Each was intensely aware of the other's limitations and, conversely, the other's potentialities. They were still most necessary to each other, but there was now more of each that was available for others. No longer did they sit alone by candlelight, in quiet whispering, while the court thronged about. Their intimacy and knowledge of each other had passed the stage where thoughts needed to be expressed. Leicester could have stated Elizabeth's reaction on almost any subject. Similarly, she knew his nature only too well. What had once been a grand passion had matured to a rewarding affection, a tenderness and respect for each other's capabilities, tempered with the satisfying knowledge—for Elizabeth at least—that it laid no restraint on her, Leicester had long accepted the Queen's restrictions on their association, yet even that awareness had ceased to trouble him. He still wished to marry her but doubted that she would ever accept him or anyone else. Yet every day spent in the company of his sovereign must satisfy him that he was still first in her affections, the source of all his grandeur and it was his constant determination that she did not change in this attitude toward him.

The Queen's indulgence had certainly benefited Leicester. He, with William Cecil, was predominant in her Council, and all the details relevant to the functioning of the kingdom—the state expenditures, the

maintenance of the Army, the Navy and court, the correspondence
dealing with foreign ambassadors and diplomats, the Irish, Scottish,
French and Spanish affairs, the internal problems of education, health,
religion, justice, the political maneuverings within the Council, court
and Parliament—all these now felt the knowledgeable and confident
touch of Robert Dudley. His long exposure to power and influence had
forged a skillful and competent public servant, yet one still possessing
the acquisitive and self-preserving instinct of his earlier days. He and
Cecil, of all Elizabeth's ministers, were so much the direct result of her
beneficence it was unthinkable they would survive under any other
regime. Yet from her earliest arrival in the kingdom, Mary Stuart had
been the recipient of small gifts from Leicester—one including a piece
of an alleged unicorn's horn—indicating the Earl, too, wished "to have
two strings on his bow."

   Neither Elizabeth nor Leicester felt their relationship a hindrance to
seeking the favor and affections of others; Leicester merely had to be
more secretive than the Queen. At forty years of age, Elizabeth Tudor
was still a splendid-looking woman. The red hair was as yet un-
streaked, but following court fashion, the Queen often wore elaborately
curled wigs. These were ordinarily of an even more startling flame,
which she did not hesitate to embellish further with jewels, feathers,
flowers, birds or the tips of green growing plants. The pale skin of
which she was so proud was still a fine testament to her Boleyn heritage; the pits of smallpox were skillfully erased with cosmetics as
blatant as they were dangerous.* Yet tiny lines around the eyes and
mouth indicated that youth had fled. But as her godson would later
say, "when she smiled it was pure sunshine," and one would forget that
the nose above the still-sound teeth had attained a sharper aspect. In
profile this aquiline nose with almost no indentation between the
bridge and the forehead was startlingly like that of her father at a
similar age.

   The resemblance did not end there. Elizabeth had Henry's tremendous vital energy and capacity for hard work. As she grew older, she
exhibited more of her father's characteristics, particularly his
imperiousness, his supreme self-confidence, his courage and inven-
tiveness. In other ways she exceeded his august image, and this could
be laid only to the fact that, combined with all the worthwhile qualities
he had bequeathed her, she possessed the gaudy magnetism, the sensitive and at times outrageously unpredictable result of her sex. As

---

*To preserve her paleness, the Queen used a cosmetic devised of white of egg, powdered
eggshell, alum, borax and white poppy seeds. This, mixed with water, was beaten to a thick froth
but, because of its blanching properties, "was not to be used more than three times a week."[1]

Henry had embodied the masculine image, Elizabeth gloried in the reality of her femininity. She was shrewd enough to make capital of it whenever possible, so that observers were, in fact, compelled to believe that instead of a woman, a Prince stood before them. It did not take visitors long to realize that, as she had often said, "she had the heart and stomach of a King," and "she left no doubt as to whose daughter she was."

This ultimate belief in self, this supreme assurance, was not a pose. The Queen "did play well her tables to gain obedience thus, without constraint," said her godson, Sir John Harrington. Another observer noted that "she did fish for men's souls and had so sweet a bait that no one could escape her network . . . she caught many poor fish who little knew what snare was laid for them!" Elizabeth was a realist and did not allow her passionate instincts to overrule honest wisdom. She brooked no interference from anyone, yet never hesitated to seek advice, particularly in matters of state. Her manner of obtaining it, at times, was unique. "I have seen her smile . . . " continues the observer, "with great semblance of good liking to all around—and cause everyone to open his most inward thought to her. Then, on a sudden, she would ponder in private on what had passed, write down all their opinions, draw them out as occasion required, and sometimes disprove to their faces what had been delivered a month before. . . ."[2] Elizabeth was an organized, disciplined individual. She kept notes, did her homework, filed away facts in an apparently bottomless memory, listened courteously to her ministers' views—and then did exactly what her own common sense and own acute perception dictated. Not one of her ministers—not even Burghley—could honestly state he had swayed or dominated the Queen in any matter about which she felt strongly.

As she grew older, her impatience with others often dissolved into the need for physical action. Should a Councillor or courtier complain of overwork or show resentment at her own officious nature, which often bordered on the dictatorial, Elizabeth did not hesitate to clout more than one unfortunate colleague around the ears or throw the nearest pillow at a lady-in-waiting who had displeased her. Incompetence drove her frantic, and her tolerance of the untutored did not deepen with the years.* Then the famous Tudor temper would blaze out, and her awesome talent for sarcasm and caustic wit would send some hapless maiden, courtier or minister fleeing her presence as the great laugh echoed throughout the chamber. Even Burghley was not

---

*Even so, it was well known that the Queen "did not desert any for age or other infirmity after they were once enrolled in her service." Elizabeth was generous with pensions, as well as keeping retainers about after they had lost their usefulness.[3]

exempt. Once, as he was piously holding forth on some subject, she closed the meeting with reference to her chief minister, "and his Brother Saints" or, on another occasion, "His Brothers in Christ. . . ." Conversely, she could exercise gentle humor, intimate and rapt attention, entrancing others and deprecating herself which—while it fooled no one—allowed her the rather unusual privilege of self-criticism.

This extravaganza was carried on every day at the court of Elizabeth of England, and it became as much an object for visitors from abroad—or from the counties of her realm—to get to see the Queen as it was to accomplish any other object of their journey. To watch the sleekly bejeweled figure in the splendid accouterments of Majesty, the flaming hair and the long fingers, the dead-white skin and the swift, purposeful movements as she walked among her courtiers was a satisfying remembrance to carry home. To hear the high laugh and the great oaths or, inexplicably, to watch Majesty soften and observe the intimate, close and personal attention she might bestow on one who had caught her attention and the dazed and foolishly happy individual she left behind in her wake—all this was the compelling figure of Majesty incarnate. Few who saw Elizabeth in action—in the court, at the Council table, on horseback, on progress or parade—ever forgot the autocratic, vain mien which might crumple at any moment into the bawdy and coarse, depending on her mood and whim.

Elizabeth enjoyed the company of her courtiers, and by the time her fortieth birthday approached, she showed a marked preference for Sir Christopher Hatton. Sir Christopher came of an unremarkable Northamptonshire family, was seven years younger than the Queen, unmarried, and presented, embodied in one figure, all the attributes which Elizabeth so admired in a man: he was "tall and proportionable" with an imposing presence and impeccable manners and possessed great charm. He had been brought up a Catholic and was usually regarded as one who had "strayed from the Faith" not from any lack of belief but rather an acceptance that in no other way could he make his way at court. He had attended Oxford but had not taken a degree. The Queen had first noticed Hatton dancing at a masque at the Inns of Court, where he was a member of the Inner Temple—not primarily to study law as "to acquire a knowledge of the world and of the arts of social intercourse."[4] In addition to his obvious charm, Hatton seems to have possessed a great talent as a dancer. Commenting on his dexterity to Leicester, Elizabeth so provoked her favorite that he petulantly answered that if dancing were so important, he would engage a dancing master to amuse her. To which Elizabeth, brushing him aside impatiently, said, "Pish! I will not see *your* man—it is his *trade!*"[5] Dancing was not Hatton's trade, but it served as his introduction to court life. Elizabeth made him a Gentleman-Pensioner, one of that select group who formed part of her ceremonial bodyguard who were chosen mainly for their height and handsome good looks.

The court was soon agog with the Queen's preference for Christopher Hatton, and wagers were laid on the duration of her interest and its effect on my Lord of Leicester. The usual rumors were soon about—that Hatton was the Queen's newest lover, that she was enriching him unduly with governmental perquisites, and there was more than a modicum of truth in both.*

But Hatton soon found, as Leicester and others had before him, that the fortress of the Queen's virginity was unassailable. Her new favorite intrigued and delighted her, just as courtesy, charm and an amiable disposition—traits always associated with and commented on by contemporaries of Leicester and Hatton—usually impressed the Queen. And a new face and figure was one more challenge to her ability to stir a suitor's ardor. Hatton was to be no exception. His appeal was great, and the Queen took full advantage. But as the handsome young man seemed almost assured of success, he would find himself as loftily put aside as his predecessors, leading one courtier to quip that the Queen was "apter to raise flames than to quench them."[7]

Unlike many who sought and used the Queen's attentions more selfishly, Christopher Hatton seems to have conceived an affection bordering on a genuine passion for Elizabeth Tudor. The Queen certainly recognized all the symptoms and it was not long before she was subjecting her newest conquest to all the jealousies with which Leicester had long since dispensed. When Edward de Vere, the handsome young Earl of Oxford, seventeen years younger than the Queen, was cutting a swath through the court, she momentarily forsook Hatton, "for the Queen's Majesty delighteth more in his [Oxford's] personage and dancing and his valiantness than any other. . . ." When Oxford married Ann Cecil, the fifteen-year-old daughter of William Cecil, there was "great weeping, wailing and sorrowful cheer, of those that hoped to have had that golden day" among the Queen's ladies. The marriage did not deter Elizabeth, and she continued to show him

*In addition to serving as a Gentleman-Pensioner, Hatton was also appointed Keeper of the royal park at Eltham and of Horne Park in Surrey. Lands and manors in and near his home county in Northamptonshire, a farm of the Chapel of Monkton in Pembrokeshire, designation as a Justice of the Peace for the same county, lands in Yorkshire, Dorsetshire, woods in Herefordshire, valuable wardships of several minors—even an inn near Temple Bar called The Ship demonstrate that Elizabeth's favor could be very profitable.[6]

such outright favor, while the young wife sulked, that Lady Cecil was heard to use harsh words about her sovereign "and the Queen has not been a little offended with her." Cecil, who knew his Queen well, "dealeth with matters of the State only, and beareth himself very uprightly . . . at all these love matters [he] winketh only and will not meddle any way . . ." wrote one observer.[8]

But Hatton was not like the wise and prudent Cecil where the Queen was concerned. He was a man in love and could not so easily overlook Elizabeth's defection. And out of his despair he conceived some of the most remarkable love letters the Queen was ever to receive. At the time of her momentary enthrallment with Oxford, Hatton threatened to remonstrate with her. He was mercifully restrained by a friend who wisely advised him that such action would be a good way to lose Elizabeth's affection and regard, once and for all. Hatton accepted the suggestion and contented himself with hurt words in a letter to his royal love, writing that "the time of two days hath drawn me further from you than ten, when I return, can lead me towards you . . . no death, no, nor Hell, no fear of death shall ever win of me my consent so far to wrong myself again as to be absent from you one day. . . ." He told Elizabeth that "to serve you is a heaven, but to lack you is more than Hell's torment. . . . My heart is full of woe. Pardon, (for God's sake) my tedious writing. It doth diminish (for the time) my griefs. I will wash away the faults of these letters with the drops from your 'Poor Lids' and so enclose them." Like others close to her, Elizabeth had bestowed a nickname on Christopher Hatton; he was her "Lids." To this extraordinary example of the adulation the Queen inspired (and insisted on) was his closing: "Would God I were with you but for one hour. My wits are overwrought with thoughts. I find myself amazed. Bear with me, my most dear sweet Lady. Passion overcometh me. I can write no more. Love me, for I love you. . . . Your bondman everlastingly tied. Ch. Hatton." [9]

Clearly the Queen had indulged herself with her dancing Gentleman-Pensioner to the extent that, had he wished to worry, Robert Dudley, the Earl of Leicester, now had sufficient cause. But for the moment, more pressing issues of state and episodes in his own personal life led him to regard Elizabeth's amorous fancies as just that—a fancy. In the end she would return to him, as she always had, and together they would roar with laughter over the foibles and presumption of the late lamented favorite. By the time any relationship had reached that point it mattered little to the Queen or the Earl who got hurt in the process.

One who did get hurt was Douglass, the wife of John, the second Earl of of Sheffield. Douglass was a Howard, the daughter of Elizabeth's great-uncle Lord William Howard. She was a cousin of the executed Katherine Howard, who had been married to Henry VIII, and was very much her duplicate in manner and morals, with Katherine's quick passion and easy virtue. Bored with her older and more demanding husband, she was receptive to the Earl of Leicester's attentions when they met at the Belvoir Castle home of the Earl of Rutland, where Leicester, "being much taken with her perfection, paid court to her and used all the art (in which he was master enough) to debauch her." The twenty-five-year-old Douglass, "who shone like a star in the court, both in respect of her beauty and the richness of her apparel," proved, as her family later acknowledged, "an easy purchase." By the time the visit to Belvoir had ended, Douglass was much in Leicester's thrall and fearful her husband would discover her infidelity. To reassure her, Leicester allegedly wrote that he was aware of what an obstacle the unsuspecting husband was "to the full fruit of their contentment" and told the unhappy woman "that he had endeavored by one expedient already, which had failed. . ." to dispose of Sheffield. But, he said, he would try once more and "doubted not would hit more sure."

This letter, which acknowledged their adultery and obliquely hinted at peril to Lord Sheffield, was dropped by the careless Douglass from her pocket. Frantically she sought to recover it. It had, however, been picked up by her husband's sister, who disdained any knowledge of it before she hurried to show it to Douglass' husband. That night the Lord and Lady Sheffield "parted beds and the next day houses . . ." as Sheffield hurried to London to proclaim the dishonor brought by his wife and the royal favorite. Mysteriously, before he could broadcast his wife's unfaithfulness and seek to set himself free, he was suddenly stricken and died shortly thereafter. It was commonly thought that Leicester had "bribed an Italian physician in whom Lord Knollys had confidence to poison him. . . ." While responsibility for Sheffield's death has been attributed to Leicester, it seems incredible he would take such a chance with the blot of his former wife's death already on his name. Even more important, he had no particular reason for wanting Sheffield out of the way, for he had no intention whatsoever of marrying Douglass. If, therefore, Sheffield's death was deliberate poisoning, it was more likely Douglass herself or members of her family who planned it, hoping that once she were free, the great Earl would wed her. Or Leicester's fears that his indiscretion—which involved two highly placed members of the court—might come to the Queen's notice might have been sufficient for him to risk Sheffield's death.*

When, after a barely suitable period of mourning, Douglass, sure of her reception and hoping to snare the Queen's favorite in marriage, returned to court, she was severely disappointed and disillusioned. Leicester was delighted to continue the liaison, but was definitely disinclined toward matrimony. He recounted Elizabeth's obdurate hatred of and aversion to marriage and told Douglass that if the Queen even knew the true extent of their affair, he would be "undone and disgraced and cast out forever." While he was fond of his new mistress, his affection did not prohibit further attention to other ladies, such as Douglass' sister, Frances Howard, a lady-in-waiting. Gilbert Talbot, son of the Earl of Shrewsbury, recounted court gossip when he wrote to his father: "There are two sisters now in the court that are very far in love with him [Leicester] as they have been long—my Lady Sheffield and Frances Howard. They, of like striving who shall love him, are at great war together, and the Queen thinketh not well of them, and not the better of him. By this means, there are spies over him."[10]

Douglass' attraction for Leicester ultimately proved strongest, however, and he agreed to a contract of marriage at his home in Canon Row in Westminster. The gesture heartened Douglass, who genuinely loved the handsome Earl and would have counted the Queen's wrath small loss for the joy—and the prestige—of being acknowledged the Countess of Leicester. She continued to press her lover to fulfill his contract, and over many months, her efforts mainly wearied and saddened Leicester. He had been more satisfied with Douglass than any other conquest, but she was now becoming a nuisance, and he could not risk the disaster which would inevitably follow a marriage. It would be the end of his favored place at court and possibly the end of his great glory. He could never support his manner of living without Elizabeth's continued indulgence. Eventually, in a brutal interview at Close Arbor in Greenwich at which he hoped to intimidate Douglass, he offered her a generous £700 a year for her promise to forget the marriage contract. Should she refuse, he said, he would not see her again, and neither would he give her another penny. His ultimatum had the predictable effect, and Douglass, overwhelmed at the thought of losing her lover, threw herself into his arms and promised to press him no further. However good her resolve, it could not last, and Leicester, despairing of their relationship, endeavored to give Douglass a choice. In a

*In the *Huntington Library Bulletin* of April, 1936, Conyers Read states: "There is no other evidence that Sheffield was poisoned and nothing to show that any question about his death was raised at the time. It seems likely that, if he had been poisoned and if his sister knew about it, she would have done something about it."

remarkable letter he endeavored to point out the terms on which they had become lovers and offered to release her from the affair. The letter allows great insight into Leicester's personality and into the deadly persuasive charm which engulfed so many:

MY GOOD FRIEND,

Hardly was I brought to write in this sort to you lest you conceive thereof than I mean it, but more loath am I to conceal anything from you that both honest and true goodwill doth bind me to impart unto you.

I have, as you well know, long both loved and liked you, and found always that faithful and earnest affection at your hand again that bound me greatly to you. This good will of mine, whatsoever you have thought, hath not changed from what it was at the beginning toward you. And I trust, after your widowhood began upon the first occasion of my coming to you, I did plainly and truly open to you in what sort my good will should and might always remain to you, and showing you such reasons as then I had for the performance of mine intent, as well as ever since. It seemed that you had fully resolved with yourself to dispose yourself accordingly, without any further expectation or hope of other dealing. From which time you have framed yourself in such toward me as was very much to my contentation.

The affair, so satisfactory to Leicester, could hardly remain so for Douglass Sheffield. Though the Earl had, apparently, stated the terms under which their love for each other would be realized, he recalls "that this last year at one time . . . you pressed me in a further degree than was our condition, wherein I did plainly and truly deal with you." It had ended in a quarrel, and "a great strangeness fell out." After an estrangement of several months, which Douglass took "with great mislike and grief," during which she poured out her love for Leicester in letters, the affair was resumed, and again Leicester impressed on his mistress that there could be no marriage. Douglass accepted the conditions, but soon "it seemed . . . that you have the same mind that you were in last year, which bred then some difference between us." Now the Earl felt he must explain the only way they could proceed in the future. His letter continued:

My affection was never greater toward you otherwise since my first acquaintance with you than it now is. . . . For albeit I have been and yet am a man frail, yet am I not void of conscience toward God, nor honest meaning toward my friend. And having made special choice of you to be one of the dearest to me, so much the more care must I have to discharge the office due unto you. And in this consideration of the case betwixt you and me, I am to weigh of your mind and my mind, to see as near as may be that neither of us be deceived.

Leicester then reiterated that "to proceed to some further degree" was impossible, for it would mean "mine utter overthrow." For Douglass, her lover showed a sensitive awareness of her unhappiness, referring to "the daily accidents that hap by grieving and vexing you, both to the hindrance of your mind and body" and "the subjection you are in to all reports to the touch of your good name and fame." He told his mistress he recognized she might find more legitimate offers of marriage elsewhere. "I know you may have now the best," he wrote, "and as it is not my part to bid you to take them, so were it not mine honesty, considering mine own resolution, to bid you refuse them. . . ." He added: "To carry you away for my own pleasure to your more great and further grief hereafter were too great a shame for me. . . ." And then, to this startlingly frank and honest disclosure, the Earl signed himself "Yours as much as he was, R.L."[11]

However, all his endeavor to placate the enthralled Douglass and to distinguish clearly the restrictions within which their relationship might continue was not enough. Her persistence and the fact that by December, 1573, she was pregnant resulted in a ceremony of marriage at Esher "in the wintertime at night," at which he gave Douglass a ring "set with five pointed diamonds and a table diamond." There, before witnesses, including Giulio Borgherini, the Queen's "Dr. Julio," the royal physician who was thought by most to have been the accommodating gentleman who had disposed of the bride's first husband, Leicester promised, "I vow to take you for my wedded wife." He then advocated the utmost secrecy to all.

Incredibly, the secret was kept, though everyone, including the Queen, knew that Douglass Sheffield was Leicester's mistress. While Elizabeth kept Leicester with her as much as possible, she had few illusions on where and how he spent his time away from court. On August 7, 1574, a son was born. He was named Robert Dudley[12] by the proud parents, and Leicester wrote the triumphant mother that he "did thank God for the birth of their son, who might be the comfort and staff of their old age. . . ," after which he signed himself "Your loving husband." Once Douglass was out of childbed, tearful entreaties and stormy scenes followed. She wanted to proclaim her status and exhibit her son—heir to the earldoms of Leicester and Warwick—to the world. The thought filled Leicester with dread. And instead of binding them more securely, it was the birth of young Robert Dudley, and his mother's ambition, which ultimately allowed their relationship to disintegrate. Leicester was often away with the Queen at the court or on progress. Now he took further care to see that his absences continued. He was not present for the birth of his son, but whatever his thoughts regarding the trying circumstances, he openly acknowledged paternity. About a month after the child's birth, while on progress at Salisbury with the Queen, he met with Douglass on her way to Cornwall and greeted her politely with the query "How do my Lady and my boy?"

When, several months later, Douglass pressed for more open acknowledgment and insisted she was as married as "bed and Bible could make the same," it was eventually disclosed to her unbelieving mind that the Esher ceremony had been somewhat less than legal, a ceremony designed by a weary lover to placate a demanding mistress who had become a nuisance.* Immediately it was brought home to the erstwhile Countess of Leicester that she had had great love, affection, tenderness—and one lusty boy. But she had never possessed the one thing she coveted most: a secure, happy and *legal* place beside the man she loved. Had Elizabeth's relationship with Leicester been other than what it was and permission been granted for a marriage, it is undeniable that Douglass and her husband would have made a happy pair. But faced with the choice of the yielding, clinging woman who loved him so dearly and the unyielding, demanding and fickle female who was his sovereign and the source of all his power, Robert made the only choice possible consistent with his personality and his ambition.

There was also—as there inevitably would be with my Lord of Leicester—another attraction on the horizon. It was an old flame revived in the delectable person of Lettice Knollys, wife of Walter Devereux, Viscount Hereford, whom Leicester had used years previously to make Elizabeth jealous. With a husband absent in Ireland, Lettice, the Viscountess Hereford, was as receptive as Douglass had been in the matter of cuckolding her spouse. But there was a difference. Douglass had been as yielding and pliant as the soft, sensuous nature which had intrigued and fascinated Leicester for so long. Lettice could yield and delight in doing so, but she would never be patiently submissive. She was as demanding, calculating and ambitious as her lover, and it would take Leicester the remainder of his lifetime to know that in Lettice Knollys he had met his match. Outside

*For years thereafter, Douglass Sheffield sought by means of letters, witnesses and her own outraged sense of justice to prove she was the Countess of Leicester. When the Queen learned of the circumstances, she told Douglass she would force Leicester to marry her if the woman could produce evidence of a marriage contract, which Douglass never could do. Ultimately, through sheer lack of interest on the part of the authorities and her failure to produce the necessary documents, she relinquished her claim. She later married the Earl of Stafford, and since she obtained no decree or other legal means to allow her marriage, she must, by that time, have accepted she had never truly been Leicester's wife.

of Elizabeth herself, there was no one more confident, strong and ruthless than Lettice. Between his mistress and his sovereign, Leicester's life, which would have a proportionate share of disappointments and sadness, of elation and despair, would have one notable lack. It would never be dull.

The years following the execution of the Duke of Norfolk saw many new faces at the court of Elizabeth. Old Councillors, relics of her father's appointment, died and were replaced with vigorous, more forward-looking statesmen. Marriages among her ladies-in-waiting brought in fresh replacements, causing an immediate outbreak of renewed interest on the part of the jaded courtiers who had to spend so much time with the Queen's ladies. Among these was dwarfish Lady Mary Grey, whose husband, Thomas Keyes, the giant Sergeant-Porter, had died at Lewisham after several miserable years in the foul Fleet Prison.* Mary herself had spent several years in restraint in various noble houses. She was in the custody of Sir Thomas Gresham at his pleasant house between Bishopsgate and Winchester Street when informed of her husband's death. Sir Thomas wrote Lord Burghley, "His death she very grievously taketh. She hath requested me to write to you to be a means to have the Queen's Majesty to be good to her that she may have her Majesty's leave to keep and bring up his children. . . ." Eventually Lady Mary was released and allowed to live temporarily at Sheen with her stepfather, the former groom Adrian Stokes, who had married another great lady, the widow of Sir Nicholas Throckmorton. Within months, Mary had regained her place at court, presenting Elizabeth at the New Year with "four dozen buttons of gold in each of them a seed pearl and two pairs of sweet [perfumed] gloves." The Queen gave Mary a silver cup and cover weighing eighteen ounces and allowed her to live in a fine house in Aldergate Street with Keyes' vast brood of children.

The Lady Mary's return to royal favor coincided with the return of Elizabeth and her court to the City of London for the first time in two years. During those years as the plague decimated her capital, the Queen had stayed at Westminster or Whitehall or her numerous river palaces but, owing to the infectious nature of the disease, had not ventured east of Temple Bar. In 1570, the anniversary of her accession, November 17, had been made a holiday, and throughout her kingdom,

---

*After as long as five years of imprisonment, Thomas Keyes still wrote petitioning Burghley or the Archbishop of Canterbury to intercede with the Queen "that according to the laws of the country I may be permitted to live with my wife. . . ."[13]

plays, masques, Morris dancing, tournaments and other festivities contributed to the national joy and thanksgiving. Once the City was again judged safe, Elizabeth made a memorable excursion to the Cornhill, where, with royal approval and encouragement, Sir Thomas Gresham had erected a building dedicated to the use of London merchants. Previously, tradesmen had dealt in overly congested Lombard Street or in the central aisle of St. Paul's Cathedral for lack of any central place in which to conduct their affairs. Once the building was complete, Sir Thomas wished his monarch's approval, and the Queen traveled from Temple Bar, along Fleet Street, and Cheapside toward Cornhill. She rode over freshly sanded streets from which all rubbish had been swept and which were hung with banners and bunting; along the way the route was lined with members of the London guilds in new liveries for the occasion. Crowds thronged about, taking advantage of the holiday air which had replaced the pestilent odors of the plague. Many leaned from windows overhanging the street to call and wave handkerchiefs and banners to the Queen as she passed; others waited expectantly on balconies hung with rich arras. A thunderous roar greeted the sight of the monarch who, wrote Fénelon, the French ambassador, "was no less splendid than on the day of her coronation. . . ." Smiling and gesturing to her subjects, Elizabeth acknowledged the acclaim, and many threw up their caps in sheer delight at her response and attempted to run along beside the procession. The sight of the richly clad Gentlemen-Pensioners and all the great lords and ladies on horseback as they clattered past soon worked its magic, and as Elizabeth neared the Cornhill, she whispered to Fénelon, who rode nearby, "to make me remark the affection and devotion with which she is looked upon by this great people."[14] Arriving at the new and costly mansion which Sir Thomas had hung with banners and tradespeople "had set a-glimmer with thousands of wax lights," where the insignia of the Greshams—the Grasshopper—was reflected in the dying January daylight, the Queen expressed her satisfaction at the rooms, "which were plenteously stored with all kinds of rich wares and fine commodities." Summoning her herald and trumpeters, she proclaimed "that the building shall be called the 'Royal Exchange.' " She remained in the building until eight o'clock, examining every part before returning to Whitehall. She was escorted in great state through illuminated streets, where the City residents, supplied with torches, were lined up to "light the Queen home," causing Elizabeth to say to Fénelon "that it did her heart good to see herself so much beloved and desired by her subjects. . . ."[15]

At the court itself the festivities were continued, and the newer ladies-in-waiting—Frances and Katherine Howard, Lady Elizabeth Hastings, Mary Shelton, Elizabeth Stafford, Catherine and Eleanor Bridges and Isabel Holcroft—awaited the arrival of those suitors who had singled them out for intimate attention. Daily, they had been confronted with the risk peculiar to their position—the Queen's known displeasure to marriage, particularly among her ladies. As they traveled between the royal residences or accompanied her on progress or to such a triumph as the opening of the Royal Exchange, they all must attempt to elude the eagle-eyed gaze of their sovereign, which often seemed riveted on them should they attempt to sneak from the royal chambers to meet an impatient lover in the gardens or chambers below. Once they were in the Great Hall with its thronging assembly, it was easier. As the musicians began, the Queen would first dance and then, reclining on cushions at the edge of the room would call gaily from one couple to another to come and converse with her. Once excused, her ladies were more or less free to pursue their own pleasure—games of chess, backgammon, draughts or primero, in which Elizabeth excelled sufficiently so that one courtier, Lord North, would often write in his household account book, "Lost at Play with the Queen" with amounts varying from £28 to £70 for a night's entertainment. Once the music and games were over, the antics of the court fool, Robert Greene, and Elizabeth's dwarf, Mrs. Thompson, added to the merriment. The appearance of another court player, Dick Tarleton, was always eagerly anticipated, for he teased and bullied Elizabeth with remarkable effrontery, and the Queen accepted his taunts with the same ease and affection as her father had endured the jibes of his fool, Will Somers, many years previously. Even in one of her more somber moods, it was noted that Tarleton could "un-dumpish her at his pleasure," and from the moment his ugly, flat-nosed, squint-eyed face was thrust through a pair of magnificent draperies and he came onstage beating a little drum, the court was very gay. Elizabeth was fond of Tarleton; she recognized a genuine wit and talent over the more common buffoonery and indulged the clown by intimate attention to and appreciation of his efforts. One evening, as he jigged and danced around the stage after beating his gaudy drum for attention, the Queen's little dog, who accompanied her everywhere, leaped to the stage unexpectedly to confront Tarleton. The clown, imitating the dog on all fours, confronted the royal pet belligerently and so convulsed the audience "that the Queen bade them take away the knave for making her laugh so excessively."[16]

In the cloistered atmosphere of the court the usual romances soon blossomed, and various suitors joined in the tournaments held at

Whitehall, riding bravely onto the tiltyard before the Queen and her ladies in the gallery at one side, to joust for their honor and their love. Once the heralds had announced their names, the challengers and defenders rode out onto the field, clad in armor, their ostrich plumes decorating their helmets waving in the breeze as they jogged forward on richly caparisoned horses. After making obeisance to the Queen, the participants presented their banners, on which might be found some reference to Elizabeth or the current lady of their choice. After riding once around the enclosure, they stationed themselves at opposite ends and, at a given signal, with visors down and lances couched, galloped full tilt the length of the yard, meeting somewhere in the center in stunning, shocking encounter. Many a lance was shivered and rider unhorsed and many a limb and joint cracked or broken. Once the tournament was ended, the Queen would present jeweled emblems to the victors, and each blushing young lady whose banner had been carried in combat sought out the sweating and shaken victor who had ridden for her favor. Once troths were pledged, it seemed that a veritable fever had engulfed the court when, one by one, Catherine Bridges, Elizabeth Hastings and Isabel Holcroft left to wed. When Mary Shelton, not willing to risk her marriage by asking the Queen's permission, wed James Scudamore secretly, the Queen was so enraged at the discovery that she "dealt liberal with blows and evil words . . . no one ever bought her husband more dearly," wrote Eleanor Bridges. The woman who had to derive her own emotional satisfaction from her subjects' loyalty rather than a husband and family of her own was not likely to be understanding or compassionate when faced with another's unauthorized happiness. Her anger was so deep at the girl who had abused her trust that, in her rage, she handled Mary Shelton so roughly she broke the girl's little finger. Immediately, she was contrite as, common sense asserting itself, she sought to console the terrified bride. Later she forgave her former maid-of-honor and appointed her a Gentlewoman of the Bedchamber.

One who was wiser was Frances Howard, Douglass Sheffield's sister, who, overcoming her passion for the Earl of Leicester, sensibly contracted herself to the Earl of Hertford, the husband of the dead Lady Katherine Grey. Elizabeth was fond of the girl, whom she called "My Frank," and showed little enthusiasm at the prospect of losing her. Hertford, who had spent nine years in prison for the folly of a first marriage, had no wish to duplicate his misfortune, and he left the decision completely up to the Queen. With her recognized inability to make up her mind and her dislike of making a definite decision, it was probably no surprise to either Frances Howard or her fiancé that they had to wait nine years before Elizabeth finally gave her blessing to their marriage.

At the conclusion of one wedding ceremony, Elizabeth was pensive and, retiring early to her chamber, spoke of her ladies, saying "that while so many honourable marriages were making . . . not one of her Council had spoken of a match for her. . . ." Her spinster condition, as her ladies well recognized, was of the Queen's own making, although it had recently been brought home to Elizabeth even more forcibly. For three years she had used the unsettled conditions in England and Scotland, the war in France and her own alleged feminine modesty as an excuse to delay furthering her marriage to the Archduke Charles, and negotiations with the Habsburg court had subsequently foundered on religious differences. Charles' father, the old Emperor, had died, and his brother had ascended the throne as Maximilian II.

When the Huguenots clashed with the Catholics in France, when England's own relationship with Spain was such that the English minister had been recalled and the interfering de Spes dismissed, when the Spanish situation was further aggravated by Elizabeth's high-handed appropriation of its treasure ships, the Queen again felt the clarion call for the protection marriage—or the marriage media-tions—might provide. An emissary was duly dispatched to the Austrian court to reinstate negotiations. There, incredibly, the new Emperor advised "that his brother was very sorry that her Majesty had been so tardy in notifying her good intention to him. . . ." He said that Charles, "not supposing her Majesty would have delayed her answer for three years if she had intended to accept him, had turned his thoughts on another match, and was now engaged to a Princess with whom there could be no disputes on the subject of religion."[17]

Elizabeth was indignant. She said the Emperor had offered her so great an insult that if she had been a man instead of a woman, she would have defied him in single combat. Charles had decided to wed a cousin, a rich Princess of Bavaria noted for her beauty and charm, and Elizabeth petulantly noted that "the Archduke was much obliged to her for refusing him [for] if they could not love each other as spouses, they might love as relations. . . ."[18] For days her courtiers remarked her "grief and vexation," which Elizabeth took little effort to hide, and at one point, outraged, she banged down her fist and, with a great oath, cried "she would show the world she could make a match as great as his. . . ."[19] One observer, however, was more perceptive and aptly in-terpreted his sovereign's attitude. Elizabeth, he said, "was mortified that her beauty and grandeur have been so lightly regarded by him [Charles] and that she has lost this means of amusing her people for the present, and fears that she will now be pressed by her states and her Parliament not to deter taking a husband, which is the principal desire of all her realm."[20]

Parliament, the court, the Council—all would have liked Elizabeth Tudor married. The religious wars in France, between Protestant Huguenots and Catholics, had subsided in an uneasy peace, but the revolt had spread to the Netherlands. The unsettled conditions in Scotland, the recent insurrections in her own country and the continued threat of Mary Stuart's presence—all demanded the union of their Queen with a consort who would provide the realm with the blessed reality of a strong alliance and an heir. Elizabeth listened to her Councillors but proclaimed loudly that in all the conflicts between Spain and the Netherlands, between the two religious factions in France, between France and Spain—and throw in the Vatican and the Pope for good measure—England would remain neutral. With the surreptitious aid she rendered the Dutch Protestants, the moral support sweetened with what monies she could spare sent to the French Huguenots and the commercial exploitation her sailors were making of Spanish possessions overseas, the Queen's actions were not consistent with her announced intention. In all her enterprises with the Huguenots, with the Protestant Netherlanders and particularly with Spain, Elizabeth gambled on the fact that it was still her privilege to swing the balance of power one way or the other. Philip sought to bargain with Elizabeth, recognizing that any overt act on his part would only cause her to look to France for support. Catherine de Medici treated Elizabeth with a wary respect, well aware she might require England's assistance should her relationship with Spain worsen when she attempted to wrest the Netherlands from Spanish domination. Both Elizabeth and Catherine had deep personal grievances against Philip: Elizabeth knew he had condoned an assassination attempt on her, and the French Queen Dowager was convinced that her daughter Elizabeth, Philip's young wife, had been poisoned three years previously. Personal grievances aside, both Catherine and Philip also soberly accepted that owing to Elizabeth's fifteen years of prudent, sensible and thrifty management, the English Treasury was probably richer than their own. Both Spain and France also accepted that invasion of Elizabeth's kingdom would not be easy and would be virtually impossible without internal help and assistance. For the Catholic monarchs—particularly Spain—the Ridolfi conspiracy and the Northern Uprising had demonstrated there was Catholic aid waiting in the realm of the heretic English Queen. The main problem now was to unite, inspire and keep that loyalty alive.

Elizabeth knew a marriage and strong alliance would be the best antidote to the influence of the Scottish Queen and the English Catholics. Shortly after the Hapsburg negotiations ended, she spoke in characteristic fashion to the French ambassador, Fénelon, recalling that at one time his King had been mentioned as a possible suitor. Charles IX had recently wed the beautiful Elizabeth of Austria, a daughter of the Emperor, and as Elizabeth inquired of the marriage, she told Fénelon with a smile, "At all events, he remained true to the name!"[21] She said that "she regretted that she had not thought in time of her want of posterity, and that if she ever did take a husband, it would only be one of a royal house, of suitable rank to her own." As such candidates were not numerous, Fénelon recognized her oblique way of referring to the royal house of France.

Not wishing to be duped as easily as his predecessors, he sparred with the Queen, mentioning the Duke of Anjou, the younger brother of the French King. Elizabeth responded as he had anticipated, saying that she knew "Monsieur was highly esteemed for his excellent qualities." But she had also heard "his thoughts were lodged on a fairer object than her, who was already an old woman and who, unless for the sake of heirs, would be ashamed to speak of a husband. . . ." She then mentioned the many in the past who had aspired to that enviable position but said they had wished to "espouse the kingdom, but not the Queen, as indeed it generally happened among the great who married without seeing one another."

Elizabeth's willingness even to discuss the matter fired Fénelon with great enthusiasm, despite the fact that the Queen was some twenty years older than the Duke. When she said she would have no objection to Anjou but his age, Fénelon replied that "the Prince bore himself already like a man." When Elizabeth replied that he could never "cease to be younger than me," both were interrupted by the retort of the Earl of Leicester, who stood nearby and earned a dark look from the Queen when he laughed outright and said, "So much the better for your Majesty!"

Not to be dissuaded, Fénelon answered that any Princess wishing to acquire perfect felicity in wedlock should "take a consort from the royal house of France." Elizabeth, who kept well informed of court gossip from the Continent, dryly responded that Madame d'Estampes and Madame de Valentinois (two famous courtesans) made her fear "that she would be only honoured by her husband as a Queen and not loved by him as a woman." Chivalrously, Fénelon rose to the occasion, answering that Elizabeth "had resisted the power of time which had taken nothing from her beauty."

Hoping to impress Elizabeth with his good intentions, Fénelon sent the Cardinal de Chastillon to confer with the Queen. The Cardinal advised that "as the affair was of great consequence to the world, she would communicate with her Council on the subject before it went any further." The Queen, however, had had her fill of Councillors' advice; she well knew the furor such a subject would create within the Council ranks. She told Chastillon "that she was a sovereign Queen and did not depend on those of her Council, but rather they on her, as having their lives and their heads in her hand, and that they would, of course, do as she wished...."[22] Elizabeth's optimism was duly challenged the following day, when, pursuing her determination "to make as fine a match" as Charles, she appeared before her Council and recounted the conversations which had taken place. She informed her ministers she was taking them into her confidence only because the Cardinal had pointed out the "inconveniences" which had attended the marriage of her late sister and Philip of Spain because the Council had not been consulted. Her own ministers gaped, amazed at how quickly and how secretly the affair had progressed without their knowledge. One was so incredulous he spoke without thinking, saying, "Monsieur appeared to be very young for your Majesty..." to which Elizabeth rounded on him fiercely, crying scornfully, "And what so, if the Prince be satisfied with me?"

The Council could not believe the Queen was serious, and they listened in astonishment as she berated them. She blamed them for the mismanagement of the Archduke Charles' negotiations which had resulted in his "abandoning her," yet they knew, to a man, how delighted she had been with the respite when it occurred. What they could not understand was the desire of a woman to be loved, cherished and wanted, which warred with the more practical and realistic attitude of a monarch whose sensitive aversion to marriage was predicated on a distrust of anyone who might covet her authority and her Crown. Her imperious attitude reflected her dissatisfaction at their lack of enthusiasm. Constantly they appealed to her to find a husband, and now that she had taken steps in that direction, they must persistently question her judgment and spoil the excitement, pleasure and gratification which came with all marital mediations! Elizabeth needed the assurance that she was still attractive, still sought-after, still desirable. In putting the blame on her ministers' shoulders, she must have known she was actually shifting the blame from herself. It was a game she had played before, which her Councillors now expected her to play again. Yet, previously, she had never taken such an independent initiative in the forwarding of a marriage possibility.

It was also obvious to some that the Queen of England could deceive herself. Returning to her chambers after the enlightening Council session, she spoke peevishly to her ladies, saying "that her people had often pressed her to marry, but her ministers always annexed such hard conditions to the treaty as to keep her from it, and that she should know now who were her good and faithful subjects and they might note well, that she should hold as disloyal those who attempted to cross her in so honourable a match!" When one lady said consolingly that it was a pity Anjou was not a few years older, Elizabeth replied, "He is twenty now, and may be rated twenty-five for everything in his mind and person beseems a man of worth!" Another close friend, Lady Clinton, said that Anjou's youth "ought not to inspire her with fear, for he was virtuous, and her Majesty was better calculated to please him than any other Princess in the world." Their conciliatory attitude encouraged Elizabeth to say blithely that "there was but *ten* years difference" between herself and her suitor; no one present dared tell the Queen she had conveniently lost another ten years in her calculations.

As might have been foreseen, Elizabeth's advisers embraced the subject of her marriage, and the Council chamber rang with their outcries: Whether the union was honorable? Whether it was good for the Protestant religion, Anjou being Catholic? Whether it would provoke the jealousy of other Princes? Was it full of danger for England? When informed that her ministers were picking the subject to pieces in diplomatic niggling, the Queen in tears cried "that if any ill came to her, to her Crown or her subjects, from her not having espoused the Archduke Charles, it ought to be imputed to them, not to her!" She also said "that they had been the cause of giving umbrage to the King of Spain, that they had embroiled her with the Scots, and that, through their intrigues . . . a war with the King of France would have ensued if she had not prevented it!"[23] Again it was her ministers' privilege to experience a dumbfounded amazement coupled with a reluctant appreciation of their sovereign's unique and magnificent talent for simulating offended outrage as she shifted responsibility to shoulders other than her own. They listened as she "prayed them all to assist her now to smooth all these evils in the only way they could, which was by forwarding her marriage with Monsieur, and that she should hold everyone a bad subject, an enemy to this realm, and disloyal to her service, who in any way crossed her in it."[24]

Elizabeth's speech to her Council acknowledged her awareness that not all its members were as conclusive in their actions as they were in their words. Fénelon, incisive and shrewd, noted the condition when he wrote his home court that despite their fine words, several of the

Queen's advisers did not actually wish her to wed. Leicester, for very personal reasons, could scarcely regard any candidate with approval. He told Fénelon that many of the Lords favored an alliance with Spain rather than France and once, in a moment of great confidence, went so far as to say, caustically, that even Lord Burghley himself "did not choose that his royal mistress should have any husband but himself, for he was more the sovereign than she was." Which left the despairing French ambassador to wonder at the superb ability of the Queen and her Council to fool themselves—and each other.

Next to the Queen, the person most concerned was the Duke of Anjou himself. Those who lived in the royal quarters were treated to a thundering reaction as he cursed his mother, brother, ambassadors and the fate which had placed him at the disposal of the Queen of England. Catherine, who had distrusted Elizabeth's enthusiasm in view of her known reluctance to wed, had been completely won over and enjoined her son to make the match for the great glory of France and the House of Valois. Anjou resisted everyone's attempts. He replied gloomily he would be an object of great ridicule, he would offend Catholics everywhere and gain nothing in return "neither honesty, credit, nor safety itself."[25] The young man possessed a ravishing mistress, Mademoiselle Châteauneuf, and the thought of exchanging such enchantment for the cold bed of the Queen of England horrified him. The thought of a bride old enough to be his mother caused his tears to flow as his older brother, the King, threatened to make him "shorter by the head" unless he complied. As a last resort he despairingly exhibited a preoccupation with and an intense attachment to the Catholic faith not previously greatly in evidence, causing one courtier to observe that Anjou's religion "was really fixed on Mlle Châteauneuf. . . ."[26]

In great agitation, Catherine wrote Fénelon of Anjou's disinclination toward Elizabeth, that "even if she be ever so willing to have him, so much had he heard against her honour . . . that he considers he should be utterly dishonoured and lose all the reputation he has acquired," the remark which caused great mirth at the French court, where Anjou "completely dominated by voluptuousness," was also known to enjoy the concerned ministrations of several homosexual partners as well as Mademoiselle Châteauneuf. In England, Fénelon angrily and bravely contradicted the Duke. As the Frenchman was ever as honest and realistic as any ambassador could be in the pursuit of his profession, his words are singularly noteworthy. It was almost an occasion without precedent when the ambassador of a foreign court championed the sovereign of another as Fénelon did when he wrote Catherine:

> They write and speak very differently of this Princess, from the hearsay of men who sometimes cannot forgive the great qualities of their betters. But in her own court, they would see everything in good order, and she is there very greatly honored and understands her affairs so well that the mightiest in her realm, and all ranks of her subjects, fear and revere her, and she rules them with full authority, which, I conceive, could scarcely proceed from a person of evil fame, and where there was a want of virtue. . . .[27]

Faced with defeat, Catherine despairingly wrote that "she had never sobbed so much since the death of her husband . . ." and implored her ambassador to believe "I would give half my lifeblood out of my body could I alter it, but I cannot render him obedient in this matter. . . ."[28] As an alternative to Anjou's continued resistance, the Queen Mother then suggested her sixteen-year-old son, the Duke of Alençon, who, she said, "has the understanding, visage and demeanor of one much older than he is."

Elizabeth had contrived to have Anjou arrive incognito somewhere on the Kentish coast where they might meet and, should the meeting prove unfavorable and disappointing to either, he might then return to France with very few the wiser. The Duke had little enthusiasm to display himself for the Queen's approval and sulkily told his mother "he would not marry her, for she was not only an old creature, but she had a sore leg." Anjou's comment on her infirmity[29] had traveled via the diplomatic grapevine to the English court, and the Queen summoned Fénelon to her presence and repeated the Duke's comment about "her sore leg." She said a "highly-placed person in France" had repeated Monsieur's alleged declaration that should he be made to wed her, "he might administer her a French potion [*un bevrage de France*] which would make him a widower in six months after his marriage and leave him free to marry the Queen of Scots, in whose right he could reign peacefully over the whole island." Incensed, Elizabeth cried that Anjou need not stress her age and told Fénelon it was a pity that he himself had not attended the Marchioness of Northampton's ball, where he might have seen her dance and could then tell Monsieur he "would not find himself cheated in marrying a cripple!" What she neglected to mention was the discomfort the dance had cost her, it being yet another example of her determination not to be regarded as an invalid.[30]

The "highly-placed person" to whom Elizabeth referred was Sir Francis Walsingham, the darkly handsome Puritan minister who had become her Secretary of State when Lord Burghley was elevated to Treasurer. Walsingham was in his forties and came of a family that had given faithful service to the Crown. His father had been an Under-Sheriff of the county of Kent and had acted for Henry VIII as one of the three commissioners investigating the holdings of Cardinal Wolsey when that mighty prelate had fallen from favor. Sir Francis had been brought up as a zealous Protestant. He attended Cambridge and was later admitted as a student of Gray's Inn. During Mary Tudor's reign, he had left England and spent five years on the Continent studying the laws, languages and policies of the chief states of Europe. It was during this self-imposed exile that he had acquired the best possible training for a political and diplomatic career. As a member of Parliament for Lyme Regis, he had caught the attention of William Cecil, who wished to employ Walsingham's foreign experience in the acquisition of secret intelligence from his devoted acquaintances in France and Italy. Later, he had been sent to France as assistant to Sir Henry Norris, the resident English ambassador, a task most congenial to Walsingham as it allowed him to devote his efforts to securing a continued toleration of the French Huguenots.

Elizabeth trusted Walsingham. Her new Secretary was a thin, wiry, straight-backed gentleman with a dark complexion and a heavy-bristled, neatly trimmed black beard, just commencing to gray. He had even, pleasant features and closely cut hair the color of jet, which, combined with heavy black brows over dark eyes, caused Elizabeth, to Sir Francis' dismay, to dub him "Sir Moor." While she knew that anyone as straight-laced, industriously sober, as opinionated and staunch as her conscientious minister could never be deliberately dishonest or disloyal, Elizabeth felt little warmth or affection for Walsingham. She regarded his devotion to the Protestant cause as approaching fanaticism. In turn, Walsingham had small patience with Elizabeth's announced intent to be lenient with the Catholics as long as they gave outward compliance to the national religion and "practiced their own devotion in secret closets." He lamented the royal attitude embodied in Elizabeth's remark that "some think one thing, some another, and only God can say whose judgment is best!"[31] To Walsingham, whose devotion to the Reformed faith was such that he could envision a Protestant League comprising France, Germany, the Netherlands and Scotland, the remark smacked of frivolity.

Yet the Queen respected his ability as she deplored the tinge of the bigot which made for many difficult confrontations. And out of their disharmony, a hard-won respect for each other's integrity and capabilities had evolved. Elizabeth never questioned Walsingham's devotion to England and to his faith. She often questioned his manner of dispensing his obligations. So used to Burghley's talent to bend with the wind and compromise, Elizabeth found Walsingham's stern and unyielding posture a trial over decades of able and faithful service to the Crown.

Walsingham had little heart for the French union, although, as a practiced and sophisticated diplomat, he recognized the value to England of a strong alliance against Spain. Elizabeth's willingness to protract the lengthy bargaining, however, made him disconsolate, and wretchedly he wrote to Cecil to ask for advice and help. When Sir Thomas Smith was sent to assist him, he spoke of the friendliness of Charles IX, the French King, "who was no enemy to the Protestant religion . . . ," and insisted that Elizabeth be made "to take profit of the time." She must not procrastinate further and "must show herself more resolute than she had done . . . or it would breed offence."[32] Elizabeth was muddying the diplomatic waters by hinting that her marriage contract might stipulate the return of the "toy of Calais." The French were asking £ 60,000 a year for the groom for life, the free exercise of the Catholic ritual for himself and his household and the promise that he would be crowned King and rule jointly with the Queen and on behalf of any children should she predecease him. Any one of these major stipulations was enough to quench Elizabeth's enthusiasm, though she still proclaimed her sincerity and, as Burghley wrote Walsingham, "seemed to intend it earnestly." Yet as quickly as one article in the marriage contract was dealt with, other complexities arose, earning Walsingham's vexed comment: "God direct the matter for I have done my uttermost and so hath other Councillors. . . ."[33]

Eventually, negotiations foundered on the religious differences between the Queen and Anjou. Elizabeth professed a "religious conscience" and Anjou a "zeal for the faith." Quixotically, the Queen even remarked to Fénelon "that she would be sorry if Monsieur should abandon his religion, for if he had the heart to desert God, he might desert her!"[34] Recognizing the inevitable, Catherine de Medici acknowledged the face-saving gesture and supported her son's stand, telling Sir Thomas Smith that Elizabeth's husband must be able to worship openly in England. "Why, Madame," said the amused Smith, "then he may require also the four Orders of friars, monks, canons, pilgrimages, pardons, oil and cream, relics and all such trum-

peries. . . ." Yet it was an honorable difference and provided the necessity "to hide the imperfections of both parties," wrote Walsingham
with great relief. In gratitude for her understanding, the King of
France said of Elizabeth "that for her upright dealing, he would
honour the Queen of England during his life."

Eager as she had outwardly shown herself for the French alliance,
even Elizabeth's ambition—had it been sincere—might have recoiled at
the thought of the sixteen-year-old Alençon as a husband. The King's
comment was a fitting epitaph for the months of bargaining, which
were not, however, completely lost. Out of their endeavors, the ambassadors of both countries carved the Treaty of Blois, in which France
and England promised to send 6,000 soldiers to the other's defense,
promised a policy of noninterference in Scottish affairs and help for
opening up new markets for English trade. The Treaty ended forever
England's traditional tie with Spain, which had been strengthened
and emphasized by the marriage of Henry VIII and Catherine of
Aragon, which had given the nation a half-Spanish sovereign in Mary
Tudor. It presented to the world the radical picture of a Catholic and
Protestant nation arrayed together against Spanish might. Again,
through the tired, yet seemingly dependable ruse of an intended
marriage, the Queen of England—now firmly settled into middle
age—had once more swung the balance of power in her country's favor.
Nothing had been lost, except the physical strength, good dispositions
and nervous energy of her overworked ministers, and she could still
pride herself that despite what her mirror had begun to show,
Elizabeth Tudor was still a desirable and agreeable marital contender.
It had been a very satisfactory venture all the way around.

Chapter Twenty

The Queen of England's marital endeavors with France were watched with great interest by the partisans of the former French Queen, Mary Stuart. And from her castle prisons—Tutbury, Sheffield, Bolton, and from Chatsworth—Mary desperately attempted to keep her cause alive in France, as well as in Scotland. Her French revenues were often late or unpaid, and small cash gifts being essential for bribery, she felt the lack of money keenly. What she could spare was sent to her Scottish supporters with pitiful letters beseeching them to remain loyal. She was still "closely kept," and her guardian, the Earl of Shrewsbury, while personally kind, made certain the security was never lax.

Her days had molded themselves into a monotonous repetition of passing months and years, a period in which time literally seemed to stand still. Mary was now well into her thirties, and she, who had once lived each day to its fullest, now had few enjoyable or healthy diversions. There was always the comfort of prayer upon rising; Shrewsbury had "looked through his fingers" at her priest in disguise. Often there was the pleasure of walking outside her chamber when the weather was fit, but hunting, hawking or just riding for the sheer, glorious joy of the sport was limited. She was surrounded by the animals she loved—her turtle doves, small pet dogs and Barbary pigeons—many of which were sent from France. Several of her closest female companions from Scotland had joined her, and together they worked on small hangings and altar cloths; Mary's skill with the needle allowed her to fashion many gifts and supplement her clothing. Her health was a matter of concern for those around the Queen, for the pain in her side had become almost chronic. She suffered from a liver disease and was often plagued with diarrhea, which left her exhausted and weak. The dampness of her castle prisons had contributed to her rheumatism, a condition she recognized was only going to worsen with time. Often, when at Chatsworth, she was permitted to take the healing medicinal baths at nearby Buxton, after which there was always a noted improvement.

But Mary's physical failing was nothing in comparison with the melancholy and depression she constantly strove to throw off as one would shed a physical cover. Her imprisonment had bestowed a degree of maturity formerly lacking in a passionate young woman, and struggling with her circumstances, she recognized the danger of persistent apathy. She had only to recall the magnificent injustices she had suffered both in Scotland and in England to feel once more the bitter desolation and anger at those who had contributed to her downfall. She no longer heard from Bothwell. Few in Scotland wrote to her; there was never any word from her son. She had tried to keep her image alive for him by fashioning small embroidered vests, sending simple jewels for his clothing or a locket with a piece of her hair. None was ever acknowledged. As Mary counted the years, realizing James was now approaching his teens, she felt entirely abandoned. When told that George Buchanan, who had defamed her to the world in his *Detectio*, was her son's tutor, she bitterly accepted that her child was lost to her forever.

Adding up all the injustices, the deprivations, the humiliations she had suffered in the past years, there was always the welcome release of laying the blame on her cousin. Their correspondence was desultory; Elizabeth had long ceased to take Mary's letters seriously. So, by way of keeping her presence alive at the English court, Mary spent days with her needle, skillfully making a pair of sleeves, embroidering a headdress or a small hanging for the English Queen. Dutifully these were sent to Elizabeth, who accepted them with uneasy thanks and asked the messenger to "tell the Queen of Scots that I am older than she is and when people arrive at my age, they take all they can get with both hands, and only give with the little finger!"[1] Viewing the handsome gifts, she recognized Mary's method of intruding in the only way possible.

The Scottish Queen was not Elizabeth's only worry where Scotland was concerned. The Regency had proved a thorn in English politics since Murray's death. The Earl of Lennox had succeeded Murray, and though Elizabeth had ravaged the Border to quell the insurrection which attended his Regency, the inevitable quarreling and greed of the nobles resulted in Lennox's assassination. His successor, the Earl of Mar, sought to complete Lennox's aim in stamping out the main supporters of Mary Stuart. The imprisoned Queen's most prominent adherents were William Maitland, the Laird of Lethington, Kirkcaldy of Grange and several others who had taken possession of Edinburgh Castle. From her former stronghold, they wrote hearteningly to Mary that "her cause would not perish as long as they could keep the Castle." The Regent Mar, anxious to reduce the last remnants of Mary's party, sought the English Queen's aid. Elizabeth's irritating vacillations and endless inconsistencies, combined with her known niggardliness in sending men and money, reduced Mar to despair. From his Castle stronghold, Maitland gloated that the Scottish soldiers would mutiny for lack of pay and do his job for him if Elizabeth would only delay long enough. The comment led Mar, who was becoming more enlightened as each week passed with little assistance from the English, to insist "he was finding nothing but words of which he had already had too much."

Even Leicester urged the Queen to send men and funds to Scotland. He remarked on her "long cold dealing, which had caused many to fall away from the cause when, with hope of maintenance, they would have clung to it."[2] Leicester advised her to send Lord Hunsdon to the Border "that it might appear to her friends there what care she had of them." Elizabeth asked Leicester to write Burghley, who was absent from court, for advice, leading the Earl to beg for the Lord Treasurer's early return, for, as he wrote, "you shall do her Majesty and your country more service in an hour than in all the courts there will be worth this seven years. . . ."[3]

The troubled Scottish conditions gave Elizabeth one more opportunity to rid herself of Mary Stuart's presence, and in this instance, she was urged by Burghley and the Council to negotiate for Mary's return to her native land. Her fate was aptly spelled out by Burghley. He said to keep the Queen of Scots in England was more dangerous than ever, and "if it might be wrought that they [the Scots] themselves would secretly require it, with good assurance to deal with her by way of justice, that she should receive that which she hath deserved, whereby no further peril should ensue . . ." then the English might be agreeable to Mary's return in order that "the realm nor this should be endangered by her hereafter."[4] In short, Mary was to be put to death, but the responsibiity would be the Scottish government's, not the English Queen's. The Regent Mar, scenting a good thing, demanded that Elizabeth provide 3,000 English troops to guarantee order during the actual execution and that the funds which Elizabeth had provided for Mary's support each year must be forwarded to the Scottish Treasury. Elizabeth was incensed by Mar's attitude and, once the offer was made, exhibited great apprehension. She became so ill with nervous tension that several periods of acute hysteria followed. Once the emotional seizures had passed, she realized she could never return Mary for execution, and common sense asserting itself, she exorcised her feelings of guilt by a harsh condemnation of those ministers who had urged the death penalty in the first place.

Her distress was further alleviated with the news that the Regent Mar, dining with the Earl of Morton at Dalkeith Palace, had died suddenly, leading many to whisper of poisoning. In the political crisis which followed, Elizabeth's surreptitious bargaining was forgotten as rivalry among the great clans revived ancient family feuds. When Morton, an implacable foe of Mary Stuart's and a leading representative of the King's party, became Regent, Elizabeth made a definite move. To bolster Morton's authority, England at last recognized the monarchy of James VI. Her recognition of the young King was a blow to Mary Stuart's supporters in Edinburgh Castle, who had hoped to take advantage of the steadily growing sympathy for the incarcerated Queen to work for her freedom and restoration. Many now bowed to the inevitable and swore fealty to young James. But the incident which ultimately proved the death knell for Mary's cause and abolished the last armed resistance to the King was not England's recognition, but an incident which began and ended in France.

Following the Treaty of Blois, which had concluded the marriage negotiations of Elizabeth and Alençon, Catherine de Medici's young and beautiful daughter, the Princess Marguerite, was affianced to the King of Navarre. Another royal wedding was hardly enough to cause a ripple in France's domestic policy, except in this instance, the bridegroom was a Protestant whose followers included the families of Rochefoucault, Montgomery and Montmorency, who, for more than ten years, had fought for the supremacy of the Reformed faith. The Catholics, particularly the Guises, looked with disapproval on the marriage of a royal princess to a heretic, and even the Pope had withheld a dispensation. Many proud and powerful Huguenots arrived in Paris for the festivities, secure in the protection afforded them by the Peace of St.-Germain, blessedly unaware they were to participate in an orgy of death and destruction.

The religious wars in France had had great influence on Catherine de Medici's children, and they had been profoundly influenced by the Admiral Coligny and his heretic group. The young King, Charles IX, was a weakling, very much in his mother's grasp. Catherine disapproved of her son's tendency toward toleration and his almost-unabashed admiration for the indefatigable Coligny. Her years as the Queen Dowager had been blighted by the presence and influence of the powerful Guise family—Mary Stuart's French relatives—and in the simmering undercurrent of tension between Protestant and Catholic, Catherine saw her opportunity of ridding herself of her two enemies, the Guise and Coligny. She engineered an assassination attempt against Coligny, which failed in that he was merely wounded, but the assassin was recognized as a Guise man, shooting from a Guise house and fleeing on a horse belonging to the Guise family. The young King, being apprised of what had happened, sent his own physician to attend the wounded Admiral and asked all the foremost Protestants, particularly Prince Condé and his followers, to go into the Louvre for protection.

Charles correctly guessed the source of the trouble. His suspicions were confirmed by the wounded Coligny when the Admiral told the King his mother and brother the Duke of Anjou "had had too much influence in the management of the State," a remark the King later repeated to Catherine. With a great oath, he dismissed his mother and brother and said, of the wounded Coligny, "by God's death, he spoke true!" Catherine, in great fear she might lose her influence with her son, withdrew and remained out of sight during the next few days while Charles worked to relieve the tension building in Paris. The Huguenots themselves did not help, parading belligerently before the wounded Admiral's house. Up to this point, an admirable restraint on the part of the Catholic King and his advisers and the Protestant leaders and their followers had guaranteed a tenuous peace.

But Catherine was not content. Instead of attaining Coligny's death, she had only incensed his followers. The Duke of Guise, while in momentary disgrace, would soon clear himself once any investigation was made, and then her complicity would be discovered. She sought the aid of several of Charles' Council well known for their fanatical Catholicism and hatred of the Huguenots and later, in the presence of the King, spoke of Protestant retaliation. Charles, still disturbed by what had happened, dreaded a resumption of the religious wars. Catherine had managed to acquire documents—either real or forged —which claimed that the Huguenots were arming with the intention of descending on the Palace the following morning to destroy her and her two younger sons and carry off the King as a hostage for their own safety. Catherine asserted that the conspiracy was nationwide and that Coligny's followers were only waiting throughout France for the signal to rise. The Catholics were aware of the plot, said Catherine, and should Charles refuse to act, would take matters into their own hands. They would not wait to be murdered themselves; they would merely choose another leader, and in the end, he would lose not only his throne, but his life.

When Charles questioned the details, several of his Councillors confirmed his mother's story. Repeatedly Catherine blamed the Admiral Coligny and, for the first time, admitted her responsibility for the attempt on his life. She had only been trying to save her son and her country, she insisted.

The young King was shattered. He found it difficult to believe his mother and spoke of the promise of security he had extended to the Huguenots. Catherine told him it was too late to speak of security and honor. Soon the weak and fearful sovereign was reduced to tears by the immediacy of the intrigue with which he was confronted. As he wavered, Catherine spoke of the danger that might come to her and his brothers because of their own complicity, and contemptuously she asked the King's leave to go. They must "care for themselves," she said and then, before leaving, hissed at her son, "Is it that you are afraid, Sire?"

The taunt was too much for Charles. "By God's death!" he cried. "Since you will kill the Admiral, kill them all! Kill all the Huguenots in France, that none may be left to reproach *me!* Mon Dieu! Kill them all!"[5]

The result was seen the following day, August 24, 1572, St. Bartholomew's Day, in one of the most violent and sickening displays of religious reprisal ever to grip France. The signal for the uprising was the tolling of the great bell at the Palace of Justice and the first man marked for death was the wounded Admiral. He lay at his home, feverish with his wounds, and, hearing the shrieks and curses which followed the bell's tolling in his garden, spoke to his attendant, saying, "Pray for me. I have long expected this. . . ." He offered little resistance when a soldier rushed in with drawn sword, saying only, "Young man, you should respect my age and my wounds. . . ." He was repeatedly stabbed in the breast and beaten around the head. Below in the garden, someone called, "Is it done? Fling him out that we may see!" The bloody body of the Admiral was flung from the balcony to the pavement below, where, still breathing, his head was hacked off by one of the followers of the Duke de Nevers as the corpse was dragged beyond the gates to the howling mob outside.

In the Louvre, followers of the King of Navarre who had gathered for the royal wedding were slaughtered on staircases, halls, chambers, wherever they were found. The example of their betters was not lost on the citizens of Paris. Each Huguenot household was well known, and the Catholics, identifying themselves by a white handkerchief on the left arm and a white cross on their caps, now banded together. In a thronging mass, with the repressed bloodlust of years, they sought, in streets, lanes, boulevards and quays, those who had flaunted their heretical faith. Men, women and children were cornered in houses and the lucky ones slashed to ribbons with swords. Others were flung from their balconies, windows or garret roofs and hacked, garroted, mangled, mutilated and used as objects of target practice for bayonet, pistol or dagger. Zúñiga, the Spanish ambassador, no stranger to violence, wrote with delight, "While I write, they are casting them out naked and dragging them through the streets, pillaging their houses and sparing not a babe." A fervent Catholic, he finished in admiration, "Blessed be God, who has converted the Princes of France to His purpose. May He inspire their hearts to go on as they have begun!"[6]

But any evidence of His divine inspiration was lacking in the sickening scenes which were repeated for days. Babies were strangled or had their brains dashed out on walls or pavements, and the streets and Seine were glutted with parts of human bodies. For three days, the incredible lust for blood and life went on as carts trundled through the streets picking up the mangled remains which littered the pavement. It was impossible to restore order. Soldiers were as busy as the citizens in their assault, and plunder became as desirable as murder. Throughout three days and nights the wholesale carnage was reflected in the glow of houses set afire. The news quickly traveled outside Paris, and the same disastrously bloody drama was played out in Lyons, Orléans, Rouen, Bordeaux, Toulon, Meaux and other small towns and villages.

In Rome, the new Pope, Gregory XIII, struck a medal to commemmorate the event, and in Spain King Philip—noted for his taciturn countenance—was seen to smile broadly for almost the first time in public. And in England, Mary Stuart, hearing of the massacre, cried jubilantly that she had not been so elated since the assassination of her half brother, the Regent Murray.

Could she have seen what was happening in her own country, her elation might have been tempered with knowledge that the brutal scenes in France, her adopted country, were to provide the *coup de grâce* for her hopes in her native land.

In Edinburgh, the Queen of Scots' supporters still held the Castle. Possibly, as time passed, it seemed incongruous to both Kirkcaldy and Lethington that they, who had turned against Mary Stuart at one time or another should, in the end, have chosen the losing side. On the thirty-first, a week after St. Bartholomew's, the aging John Knox, so ill he could no longer walk, was lifted to the pulpit of St. Giles' Church, where he "spoke of the Castle of Edinburgh, that it should run like a sandglass and spew out the Captain with shame. . . ."[7] Several days later, prostrated by a severe paralytic stroke, he remembered his former friends, Lethington and Kirkcaldy and, knowing they had small hope of survival, he summoned a minister, David Lindsay, and said, "Go to yonder man in the Castle, whom you know I have loved so dearly, and tell him that I have sent you yet once more to warn him, in the name of God, to leave that evil cause and give over the Castle. If not, he shall be brought down over the walls with shame, and hung against the sun."

Following Knox's instructions, Lindsay went to the Castle, and while Kirkcaldy appeared impressed, Lethington said with some ridicule, "Go tell Mr. Knox that he is a strutting prophet. . . ."[8] But Knox was almost beyond caring and, on November 24, 1572, as he was asked if he heard his family praying, he said, "I would to God that ye and all men heard them as I have heard them and I praise God of the heavenly sound." And then, with a long sigh, he whispered, "Now it is come," and was gone.

Several weeks later, on a frosty January morning, Scottish guns were trained on Edinburgh Castle. Elizabeth had finally supplied the necessary funds to force Lethington and Kirkcaldy to surrender and acknowledge James VI as King of Scotland. Food was almost gone, and those within the walls knew the Castle well had been poisoned. Lethington was so ill that, for protection and comfort, he had been carried down into the vaults below St. David's Tower. Incredibly, for a month, the Castle held out. Then Lethington and Kirkcaldy attempted to bargain. Lethington wanted to retain the Castle and wished Elizabeth to guarantee that "they should enjoy their lives, lands, rooms, offices and honours, and would give them money to pay their debts." It was all useless. The Regent Morton wanted his countrymen's blood as much as he wanted the Castle; they were the last important allies of Mary Stuart. Morton said that "as long as the Queen of Scots lived, there would be trouble, treason and mischief." In London, Elizabeth was more vacillating than usual. She spoke of the want of ready cash and told Morton "if he could spare her any additional expense, it would be thankfully taken," to which Morton replied that the Castle was being fortified by those inside and "they were expecting help from France before midsummer."

It was ultimately made clear to the Queen that much of the situation in Edinburgh had developed through her own uncertainty. Lethington had gambled on the fact that Elizabeth would not act. Morton had thundered for weeks that he could not support the Scottish Protestants, the loyal Scottish nobles and deter those friendly to France, unless he received aid from England. Eventually, Elizabeth's orders went out to "Her Majesty's Peacemakers"—500 hackbuteers from Berwick—and on May 21 the English guns were secured in the trenches of the High Street.

Inside, Lethington and Kirkcaldy had alternated between despair and an incongruous optimism. Lethington was sure the French fleet would relieve the siege "at any time," and when the Regent asked them to surrender to prevent damage to the Castle, Kirkcaldy hung Mary Stuart's banner out the window by way of answer. It was soon riddled with cannon shot. For six days, the battle went on as well-known ramparts were reduced to rubble and parts of St. Cuthbert's Church and St. David's Tower fell. Inside, the piteous wailing of the women and children was lost in the oaths of the sweaty men committed to fighting such a losing battle. In the streets below the craggy old Castle on its rock, Protestant Scots and English fought together, cheering as the dust from the Castle rock was churned up with each cannon salvo. Some remembered Knox's prophecy that at the end the Castle walls "would be as sand" and ventured that "when going up to watch the firing, they saw the Castle running like a sandy brae."[9]

On the twenty-seventh, a flag of truce was seen hanging from a shattered chamber window. Of the 160 men in the Castle, many were wounded, and some were ill; all were "outwearied having no time to rest." Sir Robert Melville emerged, dusty and worn, to mediate a settlement. Lethington and Kirkcaldy asked for pardon, stating they would go to England or abroad. The Regent insisted they surrender unconditionally and be dealt with at the Queen of England's pleasure; he would expect their answer by nine o'clock that evening.

Inside, each acknowledged the end was near and there was little to do but accept Morton's conditions. To the jeers of their countrymen, the dispirited, ill and wounded occupants of the supposedly impregnable Edinburgh Castle filed out into the purplish twilight—some to freedom and some to prison. Several days later the sick Lethington, unwilling to face the gallows or imprisonment, quietly took poison. The valiant Kirkcaldy of Grange—he who had decimated Mary's troops at Langside—died in her cause at the Market Cross in Edinburgh. Fulfilling John Knox's prophecy, as the wagon was pulled away from the gallows, the wretched body turned and twirled aimlessly about as it faced the setting sun. They were now all gone: Murray, Lennox, Mar, Bothwell, Lethington, Kirkcaldy—all those who at one time or another had fought or assisted the Scottish Queen. When informed of their death, Mary Stuart was wise enough to make no comment. "She makes little show of any grief and yet it nips her very near" wrote her guardian, Shrewsbury. Perhaps she knew then that the last of those willing to bear arms and die for her were gone and that her party and the Catholic religion were finished forever in Scotland.

If Mary Stuart's cause was dead in Scotland, she now faced a greater danger in England. One result of the St. Bartholomew Massacre was a great outpouring of love and concern for Elizabeth Tudor and an equally increased hatred for Mary as a niece of the hated Guise, who, "arrogant as a wolf in a sheep pen," was representative of the faith which had incurred so many deaths. Indignation, horror and fear intermingled in the thoughts of the English Protestants, whose hearts and homes were opened to the terrified Huguenot refugees who crowded English ports, fleeing the brutal fate which had taken so many of their comrades. The exultancy which had poured from Mary's lips at the grim news was soon quenched as she more realistically regarded the reactions of those around her. From the little news which reached her prison quarters, she learned that Portsmouth, Plymouth and Harwich were guarded and the entrance to the Thames was swarming with vessels, many armed to aid the French and Dutch. In Guines, Languedoc and Gascony, the Huguenots were arming for defense, having asked and received Elizabeth's encouragement in the form of money and arms.[10] In the Low Countries and Germany, the heads of the Protestant parties frankly looked to the English Queen for assistance.

Mary heard of the apprehension prevalent in London, and in the barely submerged concern of her English guardians was manifest the Englishman's long memory of the miseries of the Smithfield fires and the Marian persecution. She recognized their determination that France, backed by Spain, must not journey across the "long ditch" to wreak such butcheries in London streets as had bloodied the streets of Paris. And finally, she sadly accepted that, ironically, the Catholic victory in France personified by her family had only made her own position in England more wretched than ever.

The Englishman's fear extended everywhere: court, Church and Queen. The remarkable years of prosperity and a peace marred by French-Scottish conflicts were suddenly viewed as an exceedingly priceless benefaction, one attributed directly to Elizabeth. The Bishop of London, listening to the stories told by white-lipped refugees, wrote Lord Burghley, "The evil times trouble all good men's heads and make their hearts ache, fearing that this barbarous treachery will not cease in France, but will reach over to us. . . . We sore dread the hurt of our head [the Queen] for therein consisteth our life and safety. . . . The citizens of London in these dangerous days had need prudently to be dealt withal."[11]

His solution was simple: "Forthwith to cut off the Scottish Queen's head. . . ." If Elizabeth's Catholic successor was dead, half the urgency of the Catholic cause in England—and the possibility of an occurrence similar to the massacre—was diminished. The Queen accepted, as Burghley had once told her, that as long as she did not wed, Mary's position was strengthened. She had not wed but thought she had solved that problem by keeping Mary in restraint as "a guest," one treated with respect and even some honor. There would have been no honor in returning Mary to death, imprisonment or further ignominy in her own country. There she would have only imperiled her son's monarchy, the Reformed faith and incited further rebellion. To any who had asked for Mary's release, Elizabeth had replied "that she would not be herself the author to hazard her own person, her estate and honour, the quietness of her realm and people, without further consideration how, in doing it, she could maintain her crown and public peace among her subjects."[12] She had felt little remorse over Mary's imprisonment and had hardened her heart toward the woman she blamed for the Northern Uprising and her cousin Norfolk's sad end. She had given haven to a foolish woman, one ill equipped to rule, and, in restraining Mary from seeking French and Spanish aid, had saved that woman and her country from religious wars which bordered on anarchy. Elizabeth did not think of her treatment and the enormous expense of maintaining Mary as ungenerous. She looked on Mary's detention as a matter of statecraft, nothing more. That Mary chose to be ungrateful for her "hospitality" was unfortunate. The Queen of Scots had not learned from previous experiences. She had blundered so badly in her own country she had lost her throne. Now Elizabeth accepted that unless she herself walked warily, she might blunder sufficiently to lose hers. For, after the massacre, Mary's situation had to be regarded differently; the brutal episode had directly affected her royal "guest." Should Spain join forces with France and attempt to free Mary, England would be at the mercy of the two main Catholic powers, and the outcome would determine not only the life of two Queens, but also who would sit upon the throne of England.

Journeying to Woodstock shortly after the massacre, Elizabeth saw apprehension and, for the first time, outright fear apparent in the faces and hushed voices of the people who lined the royal route. At Wood-stock, she met with Fénelon, the French ambassador, who seemed stunned by the news emanating from his capital. He wrote in great distress, to the French King, his grief and annoyance at "what had taken place and the disgraceful light in which it had placed the monarch and people of France. . . ."[13] Elizabeth kept Fénelon waiting three days for his interview during which time she endeavored to ascertain that Sir Francis Walsingham and other English emissaries were safe in Paris. Once their safety was assured, and against the direct advice of her Councillors, she agreed to receive Fénelon. He stepped into her Privy Chamber to find the Queen, surrounded by her Council and all the court, dressed in black of the deepest mourning. An awk-ward silence followed. Then Elizabeth advanced "ten or twelve paces to receive him, with a grave stern countenance, but with her wonted courtesy," and led him alone to a window embrasure, where they talked in low tones. With her unusual perception, Elizabeth recognized the ambassador's painful position. She and Fénelon had a fine regard for each other's capabilities. Her behavior encouraged the ambassador, who later said that Elizabeth's attitude was not duplicated in her court or Council, and he wrote "that no one would speak to him but the Queen who treats him with her accustomed urbanity."[14] Elizabeth told Fénelon that she had been about to send an embassy to France at the birth of King Charles' heir, "but that now she would take care that neither Leicester nor Burghley went, knowing how much their deaths were desired by the persons who were the instigators of what had taken place at Paris."[15] Fénelon assured her, as Leicester later wrote Wal-singham, "that this matter is not the King's and that he doth detest it so much he will make revenge of it." Leicester was doubtful of Fénelon's opinion, but Elizabeth apparently found it inconceivable that any monarch would desire the death of so many of his people, for she told Leicester that if Charles stood in fear of his person or doubted his soldiers' loyalty, she would venture "twenty thousand of her best subjects for him and with him in so good a quarrel."[16]

The St. Bartholomew's Massacre, however, had one result which even the astute Elizabeth or the sorrowing Fénelon could not perceive immediately. It was a signal for a resurgence of Catholic fealty which, once adopted by the more fanatic of that faith, would stop at nothing—murder, imprisonment or torture—to regain the ascendancy forfeited in the years in which the Reformation had gained so much ground. It would mean a coalition of Kings, Queens and Pope whose avowed purpose was the assassination of those adherents of Protestantism such as Elizabeth of England and William of Orange. Such a

murder would carry a papal blessing, lending credence to Burghley's
view "that a Papist with a dispensation from Rome would have few
scruples." Heretofore, English Catholics were not punished for the
practice of their religion; they were punished only if such practice led
to treasonous acts.[17] But the massacre changed the degree of English
forbearance. For the Catholics of England it meant a renewal of hope
which events of the past years had almost expunged: the hope that
Mary, Queen of Scotland might ultimately supplant their heretic
Queen. In short, the religious toleration which Elizabeth had effected
was at last challenged. The stake was no longer just creed, ritual and
belief; it was now her very life.

Chapter Twenty-one

As time passed and familiar faces at Elizabeth's Council table were replaced, as her maids and ladies were removed by illness, accident or death, the Queen of England's relationship with those who still remained became touchingly dependent. Although Elizabeth would have vigorously asserted that Majesty needed only God and her subjects, her reliance on such as Blanche Parry, Anne, the Countess of Warwick, or Kate Carey, now wed to Elizabeth's uncle Lord William Howard was most evident, and it extended in some degree to those who served the Queen in a less intimate manner. Because of increasing blindness, Blanche Parry had relinquished her post to Mary Radcliffe, who, since she rarely left the monarch's side, was known as "the Queen's merry guardian." Lacking a husband and family, Elizabeth transferred her love, attention and supervision to those who were closest to her by birth or rank. While it bestowed on the monarch an assured companionship, as well as an emotional outlet, it preordained a sensitive obligation on the part of her associates and one not always destined for their comfort or happiness.

Elizabeth's goodwill and sympathy were never more apparent than to the bereaved. When Mary Sidney (who had been so monstrously marked during the Queen's siege with smallpox) lost her youngest daughter, Ambrosia, Elizabeth wrote the Sidneys offering to take their older daughter, Mary, into her care. She asked that the girl be removed "from those parts of unpleasant air . . . into these better parts, and if you will send her unto us before Easter . . . assure yourself that we will have a special care of her. . . ."[1] Elizabeth's "special care" culminated in a marriage with the young Earl of Pembroke, after which Mary went to live at Wilton, the Pembroke mansion in Wiltshire.

Others did not fare so happily, as one Mistress Arundel, daughter of

Sir Robert, found to her despair. The young girl, known for her beauty and vivacity, favored one suitor and innocently remarked to the Queen "that she had thought much about marriage, if her father would give his consent." To the surprise of all present, Elizabeth answered, "You seem honest, in faith, and I will sue for you to your father."

Mistress Arundel profusely thanked the Queen, happily content that by her simple frankness and honesty she had solved what everyone had said would be a difficult problem. When, shortly thereafter, Sir Robert Arundel arrived at court, Elizabeth informed him of his daughter's love affair. Sir Robert, unaware of the royal pleasure, hedged. Then, realizing that the Queen seemed affable, he gave his consent. On his doing so, Elizabeth dismissed him, saying, "I will do the rest."

Mistress Arundel answered Elizabeth's summons, shyly apprehensive of her father's reaction, but aware she had a confederate in the Queen. Elizabeth was brief. She had seen Sir Robert, she said, and had persuaded him to leave the matter up to her.

"Then I shall be happy, and it please your Grace . . ." answered the girl with joyful anticipation.

"So thou shalt, but not to be a fool and marry," replied Elizabeth, her voice edged with bitterness and a hard expression on her face. "I have his consent given to me and I vow thou shalt never get it into thy possession. I see thou art a bold one to own thy foolishness so readily."[2] And she waved the stunned girl from her sight.

While the Queen's attitude was undoubtedly accountable for a great deal of heartbreak and disappointment within her maidens' quarters, it was also true that the firm treatment she meted out often saved them from pursuing unwise friendships or more injudicious associations. The Queen felt her ladies had been put into her care and she must guard them with an assiduous devotion which vexed the recipients as much as it often astonished their mothers. Elizabeth also felt that those who lived and spent their days in close association with Majesty should be of untarnished honor and unquestioned virtue. When there were any lapses of grace, the royal wrath was unbounded. Such intense insistence on the circumspection and prudence of her ladies also led to a great deal of inner-chamber rivalry, which caused one disgruntled courtier to write the Earl of Rutland, "You should be here a month before you could learn to speak to one and not offend the other."

This relationship extended to the men closest to the Queen also—to Leicester and to Burghley. As a mark of further distinction for the one for whom the Queen had the most regard, Burghley had been made Lord Treasurer. While other courtiers or ministers were alternately cajoled or bullied, Burghley consistently commanded Elizabeth's re-

spect. She often lost patience with the man she had nicknamed her
"Moor," the Puritan Walsingham, calling him "a scurvy knave" and a
"rogue" to his face and emphasizing her remarks by removing a slipper
which she aimed deftly at the hapless gentleman's ears. Burghley never
suffered such indignities. Elizabeth, however, seemingly did not
realize—or else chose to ignore—the demands she made on her chief
adviser. At his great house in the Strand which backed on Covent
Garden or at his mansion, Theobalds, the man whom she had long
dubbed "Sir Spirit" might be roused at any hour of the day or night in
her Majesty's service. Even the conscientious Lord Treasurer's patience was not inexhaustible, however. At one point, annoyed by political opposition within the Council and Elizabeth's seeming favor of
such opposition, Burghley removed himself from the political arena
and, in a remarkable display of petulance, unusual for him, vowed he
would not return. On being informed of her minister's attitude, the
Queen wrote:

SIR SPIRIT,
   I doubt I do nickname you. For those of your kind (they say) have no
sense (feeling). But I have lately seen an *ecce signum* that if an ass kick you,
you feel it too soon. I will recant you from being *spirit*, if ever I perceive
that you disdain such a feeling. Serve God, fear the King, and be a good
fellow to the rest! Let never care in you appear for such a rumour, but let
them well know that you desire the righting of such wrong, by making
known their error, than you to be so silly a soul, as to foreshow what you
ought to do, or not freely deliver what you think meetest, and pass of no
man so much as not to regard her trust who putteth it in you.
   God bless you and long may you last,
                                                    Omino,
                                                    E.R.[3]

   Receipt of such a missive was usually sufficient to bring a formerly
angry, fearful or sullen subject back to the political bullring which
comprised the English court, full of apologies, relief or enthusiasm. Yet
Elizabeth's favor could be quixotic. Secure in her approbation,
Burghley journeyed to Buxton to take the baths for his gout. Upon his
return, he was suddenly confronted by an angry sovereign, who accused him of visiting Chatsworth in order to see Mary Stuart, "and
hereof at my return to her Majesty's presence, I had very sharp reproofs
. . . with plain charging of me for favouring the Queen of Scots and that
in so earnest sort, as I never looked for, knowing my integrity to her
Majesty . . . !" wrote the amazed Lord Treasurer.[4] If Burghley was
piqued or chagrined, he was certainly later compensated when, on an

occasion of another illness, the Queen visited his home. She was told that because of her high headdress, it would be necessary to stoop to enter the sick room. "For your master only will I stoop . . ." answered the proud Elizabeth as she bent her head and entered the chamber where Burghley lay ill.

Robert Dudley was another who could be certain of the Queen's consideration. To keep her favor, Leicester had forfeited much independence but was never, by any means, weak or submissive. There was still the overwhelming grace, intellect and sheer male strength in Leicester to ensure Elizabeth's love. The Earl did not hesitate to oppose his sovereign in matters of state about which he felt strongly, nor did he decline to use his influence, often to the detriment of others. He regarded Elizabeth's partiality for her new favorites—for the Heneages, the Oxfords, the Hattons—with little jealousy, some concern and much amusement. He had felt more uneasiness over the French marriage negotiations and, tongue in cheek, pointedly wrote Walsingham, "I do believe her Majesty's mind . . . is more resolutely determined than ever. . . . The person of Monsieur is very well liked of. . . . I see her Majesty misliketh not of his estate, for she is of mind to marry with the greatest. . . ." He openly encouraged Fénelon, the French ambassador, while privately encouraging Elizabeth to make almost-impossible marriage demands, which led Burghley to say dryly, "It was strange that any one man should give comfort to the ambassador in the cause and yet the same man to persuade the Queen's Majesty that she would persist. . . ." It was not surprising to those intimately involved when, in a complete about-face, Leicester could write months later, " . . .I am now persuaded that her Majesty's heart is nothing inclined to marry at all . . ." and later to add casually, "For my part, it grieveth my heart to think of it seeing no way, so far as I can think, how she can remain long quiet and safe, without such a strong alliance as marriage must bring. . . ." Elizabeth would have frowned at the ending: "Her Majesty's years, running away so fast, causeth me almost to despair of long quietness. . . ."[5]

Both Elizabeth and Leicester were now in their middle forties, and as the years of duty and devotion to the Crown had given the Queen a thin, almost gaunt appearance, they had bestowed on the Earl a waistline of ample girth, a high color and a receding hairline. Though still handsome and possessed of great presence, Leicester endured the onslaught of middle age, which, in addition to a thickening figure, had resulted in recurring attacks of gout. At one point, he traveled to Buxton for the baths, and Elizabeth's fond supervision of her favorite is apparent in her letter which followed his departure. To Leicester's hosts, she humorously wrote that because of his gout, they were "to cut off some part of the allowance of diet you give him. . . ." Elizabeth advised that the Earl be allowed "by the day for his meat, two ounces of flesh, referring the quality to yourselves . . . and for his drink, the twentieth part of a pint of wine to comfort his stomach and as much of St. Anne's sacred water as he listeth to drink. On festival days, as is meet for a man of his quality, we can be content you shall enlarge his diet by allowing unto him for his dinner the shoulder of a wren, and for his supper, a leg of the same beside his ordinary ounces. . . ."[6]

In addition to the gout which, in part, bore testament to a life well lived (despite the abundance of royal attention), Leicester was enjoying the exquisitely subtle satisfaction of his affair with Lettice Knollys, the former Viscountess Hereford, now the Countess of Essex. Her husband, Walter Devereux, had been created Earl of Essex and was conveniently away in Ireland attempting to consolidate English influence in that unruly country. His absence was directly attributed to Leicester's influence so he might enjoy Lettice's favors unhindered.* If Essex's absence was due to Leicester, it was not held against the Earl by Essex's wife. Lettice Knollys was the daughter of Sir Francis Knollys, who had married a daughter of Mary Boleyn. As such, she was second cousin to the Queen, which often pained Elizabeth, for there was little love lost between them. The Queen regarded the brilliantly beautiful Countess of Essex as shallow, deceitful and too domineeringly ambitious for her own good. Lettice had always been excluded from that tight little circle of devoted ladies about the Queen, and she privately belittled Elizabeth, demeaning the fate which had placed one of her relatives on the throne when it was questionable whether her parents had ever been legally married. Lettice was the mother of four children, Penelope, Dorothy, Walter and little nine-year-old Robert Devereux. She seemingly suffered small remorse or sadness when her husband died in Ireland unexpectedly—and some said unnaturally—while in discharge of his commission. His death left the way clear for a marriage between Leicester and Lettice with only the usual prerequisite of royal approval. It was tacitly understood, however, that because of Leicester's peculiar relationship with his soveriegn, it would be fruitless to ask. And so the affair continued, with everyone—probably including the Queen—well aware of what was going on. Elizabeth had an enviable affinity for closing her eyes to what she did not wish to see, at the same time keeping her ears well open and not disdaining physical

---

*A Privy Council report states that in 1575 the Earl of Essex "threatened the Earl of Leicester" for the latter's behavior toward Lady Essex and that thereupon Leicester used all his influence to get Essex returned to Ireland.[7]

surveillance to acquire whatever information was available. If her Robin wished to consort elsewhere, she wished him good luck with that fool, Lettice. When she wished him by her side, she knew he would not disappoint her.

Leicester also took care to ensure the Queen's continued favor. In July, 1575, Elizabeth and the court journeyed to Kenilworth, the handsome red-brick castle on the vast estate which she had given to the Earl. In a gesture indicative of his ingenuity, Leicester ordered all the clocks in the castle stopped to indicate that time had no meaning during the royal visit. On a previous visit, the Queen had endeared herself to the townspeople of Warwick by her sympathetic treatment of the town Recorder. Mr. Aglionby was a diminutive gentleman and agonizingly nervous over his part in the royal reception, and Elizabeth was told he might be unable to make his address. When she spied the small man, she called graciously, "Come hither, little Recorder. It was told to me that you would be afraid to look upon me, or to speak boldly. But you were not so afraid of me as I was of you, and I now thank you for putting me in mind of my duty, and what should be in me."[8] The dazed official had the presence of mind to kiss the hand so charmingly proffered; the gesture had lost nothing in the retelling. Therefore, there were more than the usual crowds to welcome the Queen to Warwick again. They lined the route to Kenilworth, their cheers and gaiety setting the holiday tone for the remarkable display Leicester had planned for his monarch.

Elizabeth entered Kenilworth through the main gateway over that part of the great mere which bordered on one wall of the castle. The way was lit by blazing torches, and in the moat itself two nymphs disported on a "movable island" also lit by similar flares. Once over the bridge, Elizabeth entered the base court, which Leicester had had converted into a welcoming bower with "seven pairs of pillars . . . with mythological deities standing by them. . . ." The gods offered "live bitterns, curlews, hernshaws and other such dainty birds. . . ." Farther on another pair of pillars were adorned with silver bowls piled high with apples, pears, cherries, filberts and walnuts, and opposite were "two great livery pots of white silver, filled with claret and white wine. . . ."

When Elizabeth entered her chamber, great salvos from the castle cannon were followed by a "profusion of fireworks, with blaze of burning darts flying to and fro, beams of stars coruscant, streams and hail of fiery sparks, lightenings on water and on land, flight and shot of thunderbolts, all with such continuance, tempest and vehemence, that the heavens thundered, the waters surged, the castle shook . . ." said one observer, who added he was "very vengeably afeared."

The welcoming festivities set the tone for the following eighteen days of entertainment unparalleled in length, imagination, expense and magnificence. Each day, after the unusual summer heat had lessened, Elizabeth ventured forth to hunt the great hart, and in forest glade and meadow sunlight, small pageants were devised for her entertainment. There were concerts in holly bowers, picnics in broad meadows and the joy of riding with the one she loved most in the sheer pursuit of nothing but pleasure. At one point, one "savage man, wreathed and girdled with oak leaves. . . ," representing the god Sylvanus, launched a long tedious speech in the Queen's honor and, concluding his remarks, tossed the oak sapling he carried into the air with great relief. It fell, narrowly missing the Queen and the head of the horse she was riding. As the beast reared in frightened protest, Elizabeth called to those who attempted to grasp the bridle, "No hurt! No hurt!" as she skillfully soothed her steed, leading one observer to note, "and this we took to be the best part of the play. . . ."[9]

When showers at last gave respite from the heat, there was entertainment indoors in a vast aviary filled with exotic birds. After the shower, the Queen and her companions walked on the castle terrace "to feel the pleasant whisking wind above and delectable coolness of fountain springs beneath, to taste delicious strawberries, even from their stalks. . . ."[10] As the days melded into weeks, there were bear-baitings, more hunting, "Italian tumblers of extraordinary agility," banquets, players from Coventry, masques and another display of fireworks notable for "three wonderful wheels of scented fire of different colors. . . ." There was indeed such a profusion of fantasy, splendor and brilliance that it inspired a young boy, who had walked from Stratford to see the Queen, to recount it years later in *A Midsummer Night's Dream*. Toward the end of the royal visit, at a water pageant in the great mere, the god Arion was represented astride a dolphin. When it came Arion's turn to make a speech to the Queen, the gentleman, "who had been powerfully refreshed from the Earl of Leicester's cellar in order to qualify his aquatic undertaking, forgot his part and, pulling off his mask, swore " 'He was none of Arion, not he, but honest Harry Goldingham. . . !' " a remark which caused the observers great mirth "and which pleased the Queen more than all the rest of the performance. . . ."[11]

Elizabeth's relaxation and the joy offered by her summer progress were offset by the worsening news from the Low Countries. The flame lit by the St. Bartholomew's Massacre had spread to the Netherlands, where the Spanish Inquisition was at work, and the oppressed Protestants, insisting on their religious privileges, implored Elizabeth's aid. Leicester and the Puritan Walsingham advised outright English assistance for the Dutch States; Burghley and the Queen favored a less definitive policy, although both deplored the "oppressions, violences, burnings, drownings, murderings of them that have always submitted themselves to obedience so they might have their ancient liberties saved. . . ." When her Council seemed to encourage intervention, the Queen banged her fist on the table and shouted, "No war! No war!" Elizabeth inevitably refused to enter any conflict unless it was in what she considered defensive measures or the gain to England was to be very great. She was not about to engage in any holy war to satisfy the Protestants at the expense of the Catholics. Again she was willing to play for time, all the while aware of the very real danger. Should Spain effectively crush Dutch resistance, its army in the Low Countries would present a formidable threat to England. On the other hand, should Spanish forces be temporarily driven out, the success of such an uprising might spill over into England, causing the French to take advantage of the unsettled situation to annex the Netherlands. The Low Countries, opposite the English coastline, were England's "postern gate" at sea, much as Scotland was in the north. The Queen astutely recognized that, short of outright war, she must assist the Dutch rebels as much in her own defense as in theirs. At the same time she must neither encourage France nor offend Spain, a rather delicate procedure under the circumstances.

Therefore, when the Dutch, anxious to obtain Elizabeth's largess, begged her assistance, she demurred. The Netherlands belonged to Spain, she said, and she would never countenance rebellion against an anointed sovereign. She wished to keep England free of any foreign responsibility, for such had been her primary political philosophy since her accession. She would never have the financial resources to fight Spain or France. Ingenuity, sheer gall and duplicity, if necessary, would be needed to keep England free of conflict. One premise, ingrained in the Queen since the days of her father's reign, was that a hostile naval base, close to English shores, must be prevented at all costs. Her country's traditional friendship with the Netherlands—the medieval "Burgundy"—had been predicated on the necessity for mutual protection as much as anything else. Now as flames lit the Dutch cities, the pressure mounted on Elizabeth to assist her old neighbor across the Channel.

It was a perilous situation. The Dutch grievances, particularly their desire for liberty of worship, epitomized the unsettled relationship existing among Spain, France and the Low Countries. The Queen of England was again in the position—enviable or not, as one viewed it—of swinging the balance of power. Her own country was strong. Trade had given England an undreamed-of wealth, and many of those who had been young at Elizabeth's accession were now in comfortable middle age, richer than they had ever believed possible. Prosperity seemed as permanent as it was abundant and welcome. English sailors, "the most arrogant adventurers all around,"[12] had challenged the supremacy of the Holy Roman Empire and Spain as English adventurers named Hawkins, Drake, Gilbert and Frobisher ruthlessly plundered foreign ships in European waters and the New World. Their names became household words, and national pride erupted at their exploits. The booty they brought to England—the spices, sweet wines, dyes, precious metals, jewels and costly materials—guaranteed a free flow of cash into the merchants' pockets and into the coffers of the syndicates which sponsored the voyages. A similar benefit went to the national Treasury, for the English Queen was often a large shareholder in this unlicensed piracy while ships of the Royal Navy shamelessly patrolled the adventurer's sea routes to protect the royal investment.

If Continental observers were vociferously nettled at Elizabeth's patronage and less than understanding at what they considered her unprincipled attitude, it was equally apparent that the Queen of England did not care. Burghley strongly disapproved of Elizabeth's leniency with her seamen. He did not accept her pride in her enterprising sailors, whom she regarded as adjuncts to the Navy and therefore important to England's defense. She, however, gave them an incredible degree of independence and saw to it that they realized the value of royal protection. But that was all. Were they ever to suffer capture, they knew they must disavow her support. If they succeeded —as they invariably did—they knew they would share in the royal approval, as well as in the very considerable treasure. It was a familiar sight to departing seamen bent on commercial expansion—a broad term covering piracy and slave trading—to have the Queen of England wave to them from her chamber window at Greenwich as they sailed down the Thames toward the sea. When one, Francis Drake, wished to sail around the world, Elizabeth personally gave him his commission without informing Burghley or the Council of his intent. Drake sailed on a wintry day in December, 1577. The following August he became the first Englishman ever to sail the Strait of Magellan. He plundered the west coast of South America, helping himself liberally to Spanish storehouses and taking several rich prizes. Instead of returning home, Drake determined to sail west across the Pacific. He reached the Moluccas, Java, crossed the Indian Ocean, sailed around the Cape of Good Hope, arriving home in Plymouth on September 26, 1580, his ships laden with £750,000 of Spanish and Portuguese loot.[13] His first question to those on shore was: "Is the Queen alive and well?"

The following April, Elizabeth boarded Drake's ship, the *Golden*

Hind, to be entertained at a magnificent banquet, after which she endeared herself to every seafaring man by knighting the valiant Drake as he knelt before her on the deck. She was thoughtful enough to advise him to take his £10,000 share at once, "the leaving of which sum in his hands is to be kept most secret to himself alone," should she be made in the future to return any of the stolen plunder.

At the same time, while Drake and Hawkins were ravaging the Spanish treasure ships which came from Panama to Cádiz, King Philip sent an emissary to protest such piracy, as well as the secret aid which Elizabeth was sending to his rebellious subjects in the Netherlands. Publicly, she had offered to mediate the differences between Spain and the Low Countries, while privately she urged the rebels to continue their resistance. Yet when she invited Dutch friendship to the point that they offered her the sovereignty of Holland and Zeeland, she was startled and apprehensive. When informed that one Marnix de Saint-Aldegonde was en route to make the formal offer, she became vastly irritated. Saint-Aldegonde was delinquent in his loyalty to King Philip! cried the Queen, a statement which understandably confused many of her court. She complained to all who would listen of the position in which she was being placed, worked herself up to a fine fit of pique and injured pride and, when the Dutch emissary was announced, "screamed loudly that she was against sending forces openly to Holland. . . ." A Spanish agent in London wrote Philip that Elizabeth was frantic, that "she entered her chamber alone, slamming her door and crying out that they were ruining her over this business. And those who were there, her ladies-in-waiting and others, were much distressed, saying that if she did not open the door they would burst it open. . . ."[14] When they did gain admittance, several of the ladies were sorry, for "the Queen beat at them. . . ."

Once her emotions had subsided, she set to work, and Burghley could write thankfully, "Lord God be thanked, her blasts be not as the storms of other Princes, though they be shrewd sometimes to those she loveth best. . . ." She announced that she would not see Dutch Protestantism extinguished while piously pointing to her refusal to accept a sovereignty as proof of her nonpartisanship. When the pro-Spanish de Champagny, the Governor of Antwerp, arrived to protest her dealings with Saint-Aldegonde, she called the Dutch "trouble breeders" and dwelled nostalgically on England's long friendship with Spain and its King's kindness to her personally while he had lived in England. Yet, she told the emissary, Spain was keeping a perpetual religious war on her very doorstep! When Champagny insinuated that perhaps the war would be over quickly if Elizabeth weren't interfering, she said, "Yes, I know all about that. Your master's intention is to draw a girdle around my realm, thinking he has only to do with a woman, and that England is a nation of women. My father would never have allowed him to go so far as you have done and I, although I am a woman, will also know how to look after myself." When Champagny irascibly mentioned her plundering seamen, the Queen's eyes widened in wonder. *She* was no more responsible for English piracy than the Spanish King was responsible for the Spanish Inquisition! As for stirring up rebellion, wasn't Spain sending Catholic priests to Ireland to foment rebellion in that unruly country?

The Queen had spoken most graciously and smiled with benign friendliness on de Champagny. She emphasized her desire for peace and asked, with a questioning tilt of her head, "what did it matter to the King of Spain if his vassals went to the Devil in their own way?" It was all confusing, bewildering, baffling. De Champagny was charmed in spite of himself and wrote his superior he did not know "whether he was on his head or his heels."

Eventually, King Philip decided to show his mettle and in March, 1576, appointed his illegitimate half brother, Don John of Austria, the twenty-nine-year-old conqueror of the Turks, Governor of the Netherlands. When Don John arrived in the Netherlands, he found the Spanish army had mutinied for lack of pay and sacked Antwerp by way of emphasizing their hardship. The event was sufficient to prod Elizabeth to a definite move. Delay was a refuge, but when Divine opportunity presented itself, she did not, like some of her advisers, recognize it after it had occurred. The Queen knew that once Don John was established in the Low Countries, there were plans afoot, "the Enterprise of England," to use the Netherlands as a springboard to invade England, where, after flinging "the unholy, heretic Elizabeth" from her throne, Don John would wed Mary, Queen of Scots. When Philip buttressed Don John's appointment by sending the Prince of Parma and additional Spanish forces to the Netherlands, Elizabeth offered £ 100,000 and her own jewels as security to obtain German and Swiss mercenaries, with the only proviso being that her aid be kept secret. She persuaded the young Duke of Alençon to work with his brother-in-law the King of Navarre for the Huguenot cause in France and, between her material aid, public words, subversive encouragement and undoubted meddling, vexed the King of Spain's disposition more than when she had carried off his treasure. Her performance puzzled her antagonists, bewildered a good many of her own people, befuddled her Councillors, discouraged the English Protestants and enraged the Catholics. There were many who loudly swore the Queen of England did not know what she was doing, and her behavior often lent credence to their remark. Elizabeth often acted intuitively, yet with certitude; at times foolishly, but always with one thought in mind: the safety of England and its people. With that goal always before her, the opinion of lesser people bothered her not at all.

Her incredible luck held. When Don John died in 1578, an event some laid on his distress and unhappiness with his misfortunes in the Netherlands, the desperate immediacy of the situation lessened, leading Walsingham to say, "God dealeth most lovingly with her Majesty in taking away her enemies. . . ."[15]

The last attempt to acquire a husband for Elizabeth Tudor was a direct outcome of the religious revolt in the Netherlands, a situation complicated by the growing Catholic menace in England. The excesses of the religious wars in France and the Netherlands had fired Catholics with the desire to reinstate that faith in England, where Elizabeth's policy of toleration had been hugely and unexpectedly successful. Missionaries from a Catholic seminary at Douai in the Netherlands and from another at Rome were trained with one object in mind: to provide a religious counteroffensive to the heretics in England, Ireland and Scotland. Pope Gregory XIII gave papal support and blessing to all and singled out the Jesuit order as the main source of recruits. Beginning in 1574, the influx of Catholic priests into England to replace those who had grown old, retired or died increased. It was observed by the English government by means of an espionage system admirably maintained by Walsingham and of proportions unknown even to the Queen. Priests were smuggled into the country in disguise, spirited to noble homes all over England, hidden and protected and then sent on, leaving behind a reservoir of hope and faith. These missionaries came, ostensibly, to save souls, to strengthen, maintain and keep Catholicism alive, and in this endeavor they were willing, if necessary, to die. As long as their ministrations were exclusively religious, they seemed safe. Yet the Papal Bull excommunicating Elizabeth made that almost impossible, and one Papal Secretary embodied Catholic opinion when he wrote, "Since that guilty woman of England rules of two such noble kingdoms of Christendom and is the cause of so much injury to the Catholic faith and loss of so many million souls, there is no doubt that whosoever sends her out of the world with the pious intention of doing God service, not only does not sin, but gains merit."[16] Therefore, the line of demarcation between religious salvation and treason was very thin. The behavior, attitude and desire of some of the faithful were offset by those who encouraged insurrection, rebellion and the murder of Elizabeth Tudor. The situation was further aggravated by the English Puritans, who deplored the fact that since the Queen would not repeat the persecutions of Rome, Geneva or Madrid, she actually encouraged further and total abuse because of such leniency.

In order to combat the threats implicit in the Netherlands situation and subversive papal plots, Elizabeth realized that a husband—or at least the *threat* of a husband accompanied by a strong alliance—might be used to a good purpose one more time. The French King, Charles IX, had died in 1574 after days of illness in which, in a high fever, he complained hysterically of seeing the ghosts of tortured and murdered Huguenots at his bedside. He had been succeeded by Elizabeth's erstwhile wooer, the Duke of Anjou, who became Henri III. While he was King in fact and name, his vicious predisposition to all the abnormal vices, combined with a natural sloth, left the government virtually in the hands of Catherine de Medici. The remaining younger brother, the Duke of Alençon, was barely tolerated by his brother, the King, and, faced with royal resentment and his mother's indifferently superior attitude, looked to the Netherlands as the source of his fortune. It was to this young man that Elizabeth now turned her thoughts. Alençon had been welcomed in the Netherlands and given the fine-sounding name of "Defender of Belgic liberty against the Spanish tyrant." He had little to strengthen his pretensions except his royal birth, and he looked to England for support. He needed money for arms, and Elizabeth might be generous. The English Queen needed time in which the Netherlands situation might be resolved, and if the ambitious Alençon, could provide the means for that time, Elizabeth considered it a good bargain all the way around. In a fervor of gratitude, Alençon offered marriage to the English Queen, and Elizabeth signified her willingness to listen to his protestations of love and devotion. It was an old game, one in which she was most proficient.

And so, once more, marriage was the question. Once more the Queen's prized virginity, which had already rendered her more service than any clutch of royal brides, was to be dangled before a suitor as the courts of Europe gaped in surprise at the prospect of a forty-six-year-old bride and a twenty-three-year-old suitor. Such was Elizabeth's apparent delight in the event, however, her joy in the possibility of being wooed once more that no one, not even the Earl of Leicester or Lord Burghley, could perceive that her intention ended at that point. No one seemed to grasp that again the Queen was about to give evidence that no endeavor of hers, no matter how personal or private, was too great for her country and people.

The first movement in the *divertissement* which was to keep court and country alternately enthralled, enraged—or bewildered—for the next several years occurred with the arrival of the French envoys to discuss Elizabeth's marriage to Alençon. They were received by the Queen on progress at Long Melford and invited to remain with her for dinner, at which Elizabeth was affable and gracious. Once they had left the room, however, all politeness disappeared, and she turned to the Earl of Sussex, pointing with a long finger at the sideboards glittering with gilt bowls, silver tankards, ornamental salts, crystal glassware and the royal plate. In a tight voice, she told him that as Lord Steward and responsible for the display he had been negligent in his duty, that the plate was measly and "insufficient to impress visitors." How could the magnificence of the Queen of England be maintained and "all foreigners reduced to a suitable state of envy" if she was treated so badly by her household?

Sussex, while nonplussed, stood his ground. He was a good many years the Queen's senior, and he answered firmly that he had accompanied her father, her sister and her brother on their progresses and that not even Henry VIII had carried as much plate as she now did, and his tone implied that he thought most of it nonsense. Elizabeth was not to be put off. She answered "that he was a great rogue and that the more good that was done to people like him, the worse they got." Her ill humor needed more venting, and turning to Lord North, she asked if he considered the sideboards as magnificent as they might have been. Lord North, avoiding Sussex's glare, meekly asserted that they might be somewhat lacking. Elizabeth turned away in a huff as North left the room. Sussex followed him, telling him "he had spoken wrongly and falsely in what he said to the Queen, whereupon North replied that if he, Sussex, "did not belong to the Council, he would prove what he said to his teeth."

Sussex complained to the Earl of Leicester, calling North "a great knave," earning Leicester's reprimand that such persons as North's quality should not be spoken of so derogatorily. Sussex contented himself with repeating the churlish remark, and he and North "remained offended with one another as they had been before on other matters."[17] The crucial incident emphasized that now that Elizabeth had put her heart on the line for England, similar sacrifices would be expected of her courtiers, and even a bruised ego or two must not be taken too seriously. All of which led the Spanish ambassador, Mendoza, to write in great humor that it was amusing to see "how easily they may be brought to discord."

Once back at court from progress, great preparations were made for the reception of Jean de Simier, Baron de St. Marc, a close friend of the Duke of Alençon. The Queen had been under great strain during the Netherlands conflict and her irritability was such that even her most devoted ladies found their affection stretched to its breaking point. Now there was the additional pressure of her marriage negotiations and the very real challenge of meeting her suitor's advocate. The Queen's petulance was the result of a hidden uncertainty which caused Elizabeth to wonder if Alençon's interest were sincere. He would be impressed by the Queen, but what would he think of the woman? Such pressures made it difficult for Elizabeth to rest or sleep, and she found herself unable to concentrate. Her distress was such that in one of the rare instances in her long reign, she so neglected her state duties that Sir Thomas Smith complained that she refused to sign letters, attend meetings, meet with ambassadors or conduct any state business whatsoever. Smith implored the ailing Burghley's return to court as soon as possible, implying that presumably one could suffer from gout in a palace as well as in a mansion. Her minister's return had a calming effect on the overwrought sovereign, and within days, the arrival of Jean de Simier at the English court completed the process.

Simier, whom Alençon called "his chief darling," was also a Master of the Wardrobe and a great favorite of Catherine de Medici's. Now, crowning his youthful career at the French court, he was to woo the Queen by proxy. It was a welcome respite for Elizabeth after the many anxious months when she had often felt that, in addition to the Pope, all the world's monarchs were against her. When Simier arrived on January 5, 1579, he brought not only the goodwill and the prestige of the French nation, but 12,000 crowns' worth of jewels—not for the Queen—but for bribery. For Elizabeth, whose curiosity concerning Alençon was boundless, it was a heaven-sent opportunity to find out first hand as much concerning her suitor as possible. Simier was a little man, brown of visage with quick darting movements, and Elizabeth quickly named him her "Monkey" (*le singe*). He was shrewd, perceptive and dedicated to acquiring the aging person of the Queen for his master. Toward that end, he bent all his charm, exercised great guile and displayed every amorous device he possessed. They were considerable. Even those who derided Simier behind his back or laughed at his pretentious, albeit experienced ways, admitted he was "a most choice courtier, exquisitely skilled in love-toys, pleasant conceits and court dalliances." Within twelve days, he became the talk of London and the court. It was all heady wine to the tense, spirited woman who had borne the responsibility of a nation on her thin shoulders for almost a quarter of a century and seemingly had only the prospect of a loveless old age ahead. If the following weeks were to prove revealing where the Frenchman was concerned, they were to prove equally so where the Queen of England was concerned.

Elizabeth had entered into the prospect of the marriage negotiations with a sophisticated, hard-bitten approach, at the same time displaying an eagerness and willingness to prolong the procedure in which she took so much personal pleasure. Soon, however, she found herself relinquishing control of the situation as she enjoyed to the full the attentions of the dapper little Frenchman whose outrageous behavior, backed by a superior charm and boundless self-confidence, continually enraged the Councillors and courtiers who had been schooled in the Queen's own particular brand of subservience to the glory of the English monarchy. Walsingham gloomily echoed everyone's feelings when he said, "The lamb shall be committed to the world, and what will follow afterwards but utter ruin and destruction of this land . . . our remedy must be prayer, for other help I see none!" Walsingham needed all the prayerful protection he could muster in the following months as Simier was allowed a degree of liberty which angered the courtiers, embarrassed the Councillors and lent much extra spice to the gossip which emanated from behind Palace walls to the titillated citizens outside.

For Elizabeth, Simier was nothing less than a source of rejuvenation; the French ambassador noted "she has become more beautiful and blooming that she was fifteen years ago."[18] The Frenchman was unlike anything the Queen had experienced before. He was a welcome relief from responsibility, and she reacted with an unfeigned delight which was as unusual as it was naïve. It was diverting and amusing to have the capering dark man at her side at court festivities, lavishing compliments, engaging in extravagant tomfooleries, whispering extreme and naughty suggestions in her ear while such as Leicester and Hatton glared jealously from the sidelines or Burghley and Sussex looked on in disbelief. She did not even protest when he jauntily presented himself in her bedchamber one morning and, over the startled protests of her ladies-in-waiting, plucked the Queen of England's nightcap from her graying locks. Laughing delightedly, he tore from the chamber, waving the trophy in his hands, which he sent to Alençon as a "love-token."

On another occasion, as the French ambassador wrote Alençon's mother, "she came in her barge to my lodging to fetch him [Simier] before he had read his despatches and when he was not dressed. He was obliged to come out to see her with only his doublet on, and she took him with her...."[19] The Queen's action, in receiving her suitor's emissary while he was en déshabillé riveted the Londoners' attention and added to the wrath of those at court who had till now been the recipient of many royal admonitions on the correctness of their behavior.

Incredibly, the charade went on for weeks, and out of the absurdity grew a genuine and undoubted admiration and respect of each for the other. Simier's charm, courtesy and gracious gallantry soon pierced the tough exterior in which Elizabeth had wrapped herself for years. She had almost forgotten the heady delight of her youthful days when she had engaged in that most satisfying romp with Thomas Seymour, an amour in which she had barely escaped seduction. Since then she had skirmished with such as Leicester, Heneage and Hatton, but they were good proper Englishmen, their sexual appetites somewhat blunted by the knowledge that they were dallying with the Queen without whose goodwill their fortunes might crumple. The irrepressible Simier had no such fears and had only to remember his one great responsibility: to engage sufficiently the attention of the mighty Elizabeth so that a warm reception might await his master. Toward that end, he allowed himself to be fondled in public, danced with tireless grace, spent hours at the Queen's side exchanging sallies and ripostes with the radiant sovereign. And in the end he found great admiration for the elegant woman whose wit, courage and intelligence at times astonished him. They thoroughly enjoyed each other's company while court and country watched the foreplay with an astonishment bordering on incredulity.

The closest person to the Queen, Leicester, was one of the few who dared reproach her for allowing Simier such liberties. Leicester made no secret of his dislike of the proposed French marriage, but the disapproval was somewhat blunted by a secret of his own. Sometime at Kenilworth in early 1578, the Earl had wed Lettice Knollys. While his affair with the almond-eyed Countess of Essex had been common knowledge within the court, no one knew of their marriage. But once Lettice was visibly pregnant, her father, Sir Francis Knollys, remembering the fate of the cast-off Douglass Sheffield, had insisted on a properly witnessed ceremony. Thus, between seven and eight o'clock in the morning on September 21, 1578, at the White House, Leicester's residence at Wanstead, in the presence of Sir Francis, Lord North, the Earls of Warwick and Pembroke and several others, Lettice Knollys

Devereux and Robert Dudley had again been married by a Mr. Tin-
dall. Because of her advanced pregnancy, the Countess had worn a
"loose gown." The guests, on the insistence of the bride's father, had all
sworn before a notary they had witnessed the ceremony. Nothing less
would satisfy Sir Francis.

It had been a happy moment for both the bride and groom, for
Leicester was very much in love with his handsome wife. He had often
voiced a desire for a home with children, and this, combined with
Lettice's persuasive charm and undeniable physical appeal, had led
him to risk endangering his career and fortune by marrying her. For
years, too, his relationship with the Queen had precluded any settled
life. Now he was as determined that his marriage would be a happy one
as he was resolved to preserve his supremacy with Elizabeth. His
marriage would not, he vowed, change his attendance on the monarch
or his attitude toward her. His resolve had soon been put to the test
when, only two days after the wedding, Elizabeth had arrived at
Wanstead for a visit. The ceremony had not been mentioned, and the
Earl had entertained the royal party with a devotion as outstanding as
his guests' discretion. Leicester had soon realized his secret was safe. No
one present had wished to provoke the royal wrath by informing the
Queen of his defection. Lady Leicester had gone at once to Chartley,
her Staffordshire home, a good distance from London, to await the
birth of her child. Elizabeth had never liked Lettice and blessed whatever fortune kept the Countess of Essex from court. Thus, the secret
had been kept.

With the advent of Simier, however, Leicester felt it was his duty to
tell the Queen that the proposed marriage was a disgrace, an affront to
the nation and was highly unpopular with the English people, who
traditionally regarded the French as their enemies. There were many
still alive who could remember the foreign Philip as husband of the
Queen's dead sister, Mary Tudor. She would have a similar difficult
time if she married the Frenchman, Leicester prophesied, well aware as
he talked that though Elizabeth listened soberly, her preoccupation
with Simier's blandishments made his words less effective.

In addition to Leicester's realistic assessment and disapproval of the
French marriage, his influence was strengthened by his support of the
more militant Protestantism becoming known as Puritanism. Two
outstanding Puritans at court were Leicester's father-in-law, Sir Francis Knollys, and Walsingham. They, along with the Earl, were at the
center of a select little circle which included some of Elizabeth's most
illustrious courtiers. Leicester's early flirtation with the Catholics had
met with little success, and he was confronted with a similar lack of

enthusiasm on the part of the Protestants, for he had switched his religious allegiances too often in the past. The Puritan zeal and militancy appealed to the soldier in Leicester, and this, combined with the political clout of those embracing its cause, had quickly drawn him into its ranks. There he was welcomed as much for the luster of his nearness to the Crown and his position as one of the foremost gentlemen of the realm as for his very real energies and talents.

Leicester had earned his party's esteem by the influence he exercised on the Queen to regard the Puritans with the same toleration as she did the Catholics. Elizabeth had little use for what she considered overabundant sanctimony, a narrow-minded intolerance and a lack of respect for Crown and Church as venerable institutions. Now, the Puritans, too, joined in the general censure of the proposed French marriage and added their voices to the popular lament predicting that Elizabeth would die in childbirth and that Alençon would revive the horror of Mary's reign by restoring the Catholic ritual in the churches.

In addition to Leicester's political and religious differences, there was—despite the fact that *he* was married—the satisfying knowledge that Elizabeth was not. He could depend on her esteem and interest; any husband would be bound to make a difference. After listening to one session between the Queen and the Earl, one sympathetic lady-in-waiting, unaware of his marriage, gently reproached Elizabeth that she was making Leicester's life miserable with her apparent eagerness for the French union. Elizabeth angrily replied, "Dost thou think me so unlike myself and unmindful of my own royal majesty that I would prefer my servant, whom I, myself, have raised, before the great Prince of Christendom, in the honour of a husband?" She would hear no talebearing about Simier and told her own ambassador in Paris that "he has shown himself faithful to his master, is safe and discreet beyond his years in the conduct of the case . . ." and ended with a sting undoubtedly aimed at Leicester, "we wish we had such a servant of whom we could make such good use. . . ."[20]

Within several days a mysterious incident added to the common dissatisfaction. While abroad on the Thames, the barge carrying Elizabeth, Simier, Leicester and Hatton was the target of a shot which severely wounded one of the royal bargemen. The stricken attendant had been less than six feet from the Queen. Though she personally believed the shot had been intended for her, Elizabeth did not lose her poise and had, instead, taken her scarf and asked that the bargeman's wounds be bound. She told him "to be of good cheer, for that he should never want . . . for the bullet was meant for her, though it had hit him." Though she was disturbed by the incident, she accepted the explanation of a distraught Thomas Appletree, the culprit, that it had all been an accident. When Appletree's employer, hearing of the incident, moaned that he wished both he and his servant "had never been born," Elizabeth actually intervened so that her careless subject might not lose his employment. She chose to put the best possible face on the incident, saying "that she would not believe anything against her subjects that loving parents would not believe of their children."[21]

Elizabeth had procrastinated in sending a passport to Alençon for the journey to England which many believed never would take place. "I am of the opinion that the wise men of France will never assent thereto . . ." said Sir Francis Walsingham. The Queen was not so certain and apprehensive of the result. If Alençon delayed, it would be an inglorious snub; if he arrived, then the next move would be up to her. The longer she delayed, the more insistent Simier became, and in late July, with all delaying ruses exhausted, the passport was finally issued. The action caused Leicester to retire to his home at Wanstead, professing himself ill with disappointment and grief. Elizabeth, hearing of his sickness, acted as he had anticipated and immediately journeyed to Wanstead to ascertain the true extent of his illness. She remained there for two days, attempting to raise her favorite's spirits. Before she left, she took the precaution of requesting Simier to stay at Greenwich Palace instead of his lodgings in the City. While she was away, she was told that an attempt had been made on his life as he walked in the Greenwich gardens.

Hurrying back to court, she met the aggrieved Frenchman. Simier was certain that Leicester had been behind the attempt, and after two such outrageous incidents, he had little hesitancy in revealing the Earl's great secret. Choosing a propitious moment and aware he was risking Elizabeth's personal censure for his action, he went to the Queen and told her that her great good friend, the Earl of Leicester, had been married for more than a year.

Elizabeth was shocked. She listened to her "Monkey" and then, speechless, waved him away, appalled at the spectacle she must have presented to the entire court in still continuing to lavish attention and devotion on her Robin. Patiently she had listened to his tirades against her marriage, even journeying to his home to alleviate his depression. And all the time that "she-wolf," Lettice Knollys Devereux, had been his wife and given birth to his child! Elizabeth felt abandoned, as though Leicester had physically rejected her, and all the traumatic fears of childhood, the insecurity, injustice and danger, flooded her mind. The more she brooded on the hurt, the more her humiliation deepened, and, wounded to the core, her rage grew as she viewed his action not only as an affront to her personally, but also as an insult to her Crown. At last, she could contain herself no longer. Nearly hysterical, she ordered Leicester to attend her at once and then prepared to meet the man who, in her opinion, had committed the greatest sin in humbling her pride while abusing her trust and love.

The moment Leicester entered the chamber he was aware the Queen knew his secret. Her face was pale, her breathing agitated, and her eyes glittered with an unnatural brightness, unlike anything he had seen before. Approaching him, she swung her arm wide and slapped him broadly across the face. The strength and sting of the blow were nothing compared to the sinking feeling in the Earl's stomach and the perspiration which beaded his brow and palms. He listened as the torrent flowed from tight lips as Elizabeth, raging in her fury, poured abuse on him. Every oath she had ever learned—many from him, he ruefully recalled—every denunciation, every killing, stinging epithet she could muster filled the room as her voice rose to a scream. He could recognize the signs and knew she was fast becoming unmanageable. Savagely, her face contorted, the Queen flung his own words in his face. A fine one he was, she cried, to wish to prohibit *her* marriage when he had been married to that cheap baggage, Lettice, for more than a year! He had flouted her love, abased and abused her trust and insulted her pride. She and she alone had made him what he was—he, who was descended from a line of traitors!—even to the extent of recently lending him £15,000! Never again must he seek anything from her, for she was ashamed of him, and more than that, she cried, she was ashamed of herself, that she, a Prince and a Queen, could have lowered herself to such an extent as to have raised such a one as he to such heights.

As the long outburst ended, the Queen began to stride up and down, threatening Leicester with arrest and imprisonment in the Tower. Elizabeth's voice had rung throughout the Palace corridors during the appalling confrontation, and now one of her most intelligent and capable ministers came forward to end the royal rage. It was Lord Sussex, the Lord Chamberlain, Leicester's bitter enemy, who now attempted to save the Queen from herself. Courageously he entered the chamber and listened to Elizabeth's threats while the ashen-faced Leicester stood by, silently accepting the abuse. Quietly Sussex told her that while she had the power to arrest Leicester, she was in effect only condemning him unjustly, as he was of the opinion "that no man was to be troubled for lawful marriage which amongst all men has ever been held in honour and esteem."[22] Bravely Sussex told the hysterical sovereign she must do nothing, for any action would only redound to her own discredit and be a severe affront to the royal dignity.

Sussex's quiet words reacted on Elizabeth as he had hoped, and gradually, her hysteria lessened. Once she had regained some measure of self-control, she agreed that Leicester should be taken into custody and lodged in a small fort at Greenwich. Sussex summoned a guard, and the Queen gave her orders. Silently, the Earl accompanied the guard from the room, avoiding Elizabeth's eyes as he went. After he had gone, the tears starting again, the Queen clutched Sussex's hand in mute gratitude. Quickly the old courtier left, his heart aching for the shattered woman who had suffered a wound that only one who had known her from childhood could recognize as heartbreakingly painful. Once, years before, he had knelt before the Princess Elizabeth and waited as she wrote an imploring letter to her sister, the Queen, begging not be incarcerated in the Tower. In so doing, the tide had been missed as both Princess and courtier were well aware, and thus, more time had been gained. He could now only hope that time would again work healing wonders for the deeply hurt and embittered woman he left behind.

If Elizabeth had any qualms about further encouraging Alençon, Leicester's defection dispelled them. Simier told the Queen of Alençon's "transports of joy" at receiving the passport, and within days, Elizabeth sought to lessen the ache in her heart by ordering Leicester from his Greenwich chamber to the comparative freedom of his home at Wanstead. Soon the Earl was back at court, he and Elizabeth keeping a wary distance between them or, when they were forced to meet, the royal silence being more provocative than bitter words. The Countess of Leicester did not fare so well. Once her son was born, she returned to court with a magnificent new wardrobe designed to show off her slim figure. The dresses were as ornate and costly as any belonging to Elizabeth, and goaded beyond endurance as the Countess ignored the suggestions that she conduct herself with more meekness, the Queen "soundly boxed the Countess of Leicester's ears, at the same time declaring that as but one sun lighted the earth, so there should be but one at the court—which henceforward would be closed to the Countess of Leicester."[23] The tenuous truce which existed between Leicester and the Queen did not, at any time in the future, include his wife, and from the moment of her banishment, Elizabeth refused to receive Lettice again.

As the weeks passed, Elizabeth gave every evidence of having for-

gotten, if not forgiven, Leicester's unfaithfulness. She impressed the
Spanish ambassador with her sincerity regarding Alençon; until now,
he had been positive Elizabeth was playing her old game. Now he
wrote King Philip he was certain the marriage would take place.
When it was known that the Queen had submitted to a physical
examination to determine if she was capable of bearing children and
that the doctor had stated "that she was a person of pure complexion,
of the largest and goodliest stature of well-shaped women, with all
limbs set and proportioned in the best sort, and one whom in the sight
of all men, nature cannot amend her shape in any part to make her
more likely to conceive and bear children without peril,"[24] there was
genuine dismay at the Spanish court. They did not regard as important that the royal examiners had avoided mentioning the Queen's
almost hysterical aversion to marriage, that she was approaching her
forty-sixth birthday and had a history of scanty menstrual flow. It was
more important to depend on the fact that the constellation under
which she had been born (Virgo) rarely produced sterile women.

In the City, the wagers were two to one against Alençon's actual
coming to England and three to one that the marriage would take
place if he did. Bribery was rampant, and some of the more noted
recipients were Elizabeth's Councillors and courtiers who pocketed
the French crowns while they wore the more tangible proofs of
Spanish influence pinned to their caps or coats. Mendoza, the Spanish
ambassador, sought to utilize Leicester and Hatton's personal dislike
of the marriage so they might, he hoped, influence the Queen. He
wrote King Philip, "Hatton, although attached to your Majesty's
service, has joined Leicester in the French affair, so that if your
Majesty thinks fit, a jewel worth £1,500 may be sent, and he may be
entertained until we see how he goes on. . . . If your Majesty thinks
well, it would be desirable to give something handsome to
Leicester. . . ."[25]

No one need have worried. While the ambassadors intrigued,
courtiers fretted, Councillors debated and preachers thundered
against the union of the Queen with a Catholic Prince, Elizabeth
herself was seeking ways to avoid any responsibility for an affair she
saw rapidly approaching a conclusion. At one point when she asked
her Councillors for their opinion in writing, they each—well aware of
the predicament in which their sovereign had placed herself—declined
to do so. In subsequent meetings, gathering strength from one another,
they formally advised against the marriage, citing the personal unpopularity which would result and the improbability of there being
any children of the marriage. Simier, when informed of their attitude,

saw his many months of work crumbling and, in a fine French rage, accosted the Council. He did not mince words and, his tirade ended, banged the chamber door in their faces as he left. He flew to Elizabeth, who outwardly professed great sorrow at her recalcitrant ministers and told Simier that her suitor must lessen some of his marital demands. Within days, Alençon accommodated her with the one marriage stipulation that he be allowed to observe the Mass in his private apartments and, to demonstrate his cooperation, announced he would come to England soon.

The enthusiasm of her youthful suitor jolted Elizabeth, who had never envisioned that Alençon would actually put himself in the position of being accepted or refused in marriage. Fearfully the panicked woman sought her Councillors' advice, saying, "My Lords, here I am between Scylla and Charybdis. Alençon has agreed to all the terms I sent him and he is asking me to tell him when I wish him to come and marry me. If I do not marry him, I do not know whether he will remain friendly with me, and if I do, I shall not be able to govern the country with the freedom and security that I have hitherto enjoyed. . . ."[26] The Councillors, realizing the collective shoe was now on the other foot, piously stated she could not justifiably or decently withdraw from negotiations without great affront to the French nation. Elizabeth asked Burghley for his opinion, saying that some of her Lords had suggested she "entertain him with half promises." Wisely, Burghley replied, "Madame, I have heard men say that those who would make fools of princes are the fools themselves."

Realizing the decision must be hers, the Queen sought to put the best possible face on the matter. She said she was sure the Duke was seeking her for herself, not for her Crown, and she promised before God "that if he was a good husband to her, she would be the best wife in the world." The remark seemed only further evidence of Elizabeth's need to convince herself as well as others. When it was repeated to Philip by his ambassador, the Spanish King scoffed, saying, "I do not believe the marriage will take place as there can be on either side no great desire for it, but a large amount of pretence." Philip not only was stating a political fact but could, from a greater distance, assess the situation more easily than those closer to Elizabeth. He had one additional advantage. He remembered the young red-haired girl who had been his sister-in-law and the very strong objections she had registered when he had wished to wed her out of England. She had said then that she would never marry, leaving unspoken her own belief that a foreign marriage would endanger her ever attaining the Crown. Philip did not think that now, as overwhelmingly popular as she was, she would imperil her sovereignty by a marriage with the House of Valois—or anyone else.

While awaiting the arrival of Alençon, Elizabeth amused herself with Simier, and her conduct was such that the Frenchman was accused of administering love philters. Mendoza wrote Philip, "She is burning with impatience for his [Alençon's] coming, although her Councillors have laid before her the difficulties which may arise. . . . She herself is largely influenced by the idea that it should be known that her talents and beauty are so great that they have sufficed to cause him to come and visit her without any assurance that he will be her husband."[27] Indeed, Elizabeth's curiosity, now that the die was cast, bordered on obsession. It had been years since any suitor had approached her, daring a rejection, and mixed with her happy anticipation was a backlash from the stinging humiliation of Leicester's marriage. The disclosure of his defection made it all the more important that now *her* opportunity to preen in public with a lover, one who risked his prestige to court her in person, should not lose any predominance.

The enterprising Duke of Alençon arrived in England on the morning of August 17, 1579. He was heavily disguised since the meeting was to be informal, not a state visit, which would have necessitated welcoming ceremonies and endless entertainment. Dust-stained and weary, he quickly sought Simier and implored his emissary that he might meet at once with his splendid bride-to-be. Viewing the tired young man, Simier showed great horror and replied it was impossible as "he would have to pass through a dozen chambers. . . ." He must rest and later present the picture of royal elegance Elizabeth expected. He said the Queen was still asleep and persuaded Alençon "to get between the sheets," telling him also he wished to God Elizabeth was there with him, so he could then "with great facility convey his thoughts. . . ."[28]

The next day the anxious young man was brought to meet the Queen. Elizabeth was agitated, her anticipation edged with an irritableness that plagued her ladies as they attempted to assist her in choosing the right gown and jewels. Now, as she waited for Alençon in the Privy Chamber, she suppressed her excitement, striving for a regalness and poise becoming her Queenship. Hesitantly Alençon approached, and Elizabeth saw a thin man, more youthful-looking than she had expected. His nose was a shade too large and his pockmarks were recognizable. But his appearance was rescued from a swarthy mediocrity by an apparent joviality and self-confidence. He greeted her with great affability, and Elizabeth held out her long bejeweled fingers to be kissed. As the Duke bent over her hand, something of his youthful vulnerability, his dark leanness, which gave him an almost-sinister aspect, reached out to the virginal spinster, and as their eyes met, an immediate *rapprochement* was reached. At once, Elizabeth's anxiety disappeared. She would have nothing to fear from this silly young man; indeed, he would have nothing to fear from her! If the entire prestige and might of the French nation were embodied in the slim form of this dark young Prince, the Queen felt more than equal to the challenge. In the short time he was to be at court, she would be able to show all who watched that it was still possible for the English Queen to divert and enthrall a suitor in the web of her own charm.

Similar thoughts passed through Alençon's mind. The boy had grown up in a court noted for its wanton elegance and lavish display of works of art, of costly jewels, of ornate furniture and hangings. The Duke was not, therefore, interested in the splendor of Elizabeth's chamber or the rich attire of those attending her. Instead, his whole interest centered on the monarch who might soon be his wife. He saw only a woman a shade taller than himself, dressed in exquisite fabrics with jewels blazing at her breast, waist and fingers. She wore what had to be a gaudy red wig, the shade of which only unfortunately accentuated a complexion which, while fair, he felt owed more to the cosmetician's skill than her own good health. Quickly, his eyes swept over her. He saw the aging lines on her neck, the jutting shoulder bones where the fabric met her skin. It would have been more decent to cover up, Alençon decided, and quickly came the thought that his own mother looked younger.

For the next twelve days, Elizabeth Tudor, Queen of England, and François de Valois, Duke of Alençon, played their parts to perfection. The Duke joined the court menagerie when Elizabeth dubbed him her "Frog" (*grenouille*); there were some unkind enough to whisper that, for the first time, a royal nickname aptly fitted the bearer. Whatever her companions' reaction, it was obvious the Queen was enchanted with the witty twenty-three-year-old Frenchman who appeared to see nothing incongruous in wooing a woman approaching her forty-sixth birthday. Elizabeth openly demonstrated her partiality as she fondled and kissed the young man on the slightest provocation and, at all times, gave him every evidence of satisfaction. It was balm to the boy who, with two older brothers in line for the Crown of France, had suffered a bitter childhood rejection and had been made to feel of such little significance that his own mother could scarce abide him. In many ways, Elizabeth and Alençon had a great deal in common. She admired his spirit and his response to her overtures; he was grateful to her for taking the initiative, for honoring him, while at the same time she challenged any adverse reaction from her court. As had happened with Simier, some mysterious alchemy quickly formed so that, within a few days, each affected an honest regard for the other. It had nothing to do with love, although Elizabeth seemingly had convinced herself that the Duke was all she had ever desired in a husband. For Alençon, so used to a sly and deceitful mother or the corrupt brazen females he had known from early youth, Elizabeth's sentimental and open preference touched a wellspring of gratitude, and he openly saluted her courage, wit and cleverness.

The court was, as usual, divided, "everyone fishing to catch the Queen's humour in it. . . ." Alençon had brought the Queen a diamond worth 10,000 crowns, and his generosity extended to her courtiers, who were quick to accept the rich jewels he dispensed so easily. Mendoza wrote Philip, "The Queen is delighted with Alençon and he with her, as she had let out to some of her courtiers, saying that she was pleased to have known him, was much taken with his good parts, and admired him more than any man. She says that for her part she will not stand in the way of his being her husband. . . ." Michel de Castelnau de Mauvissière, the French ambassador, triumphantly wrote Catherine de Medici of her son's performance, saying, "These loving conferences have lasted eight days." He said Elizabeth was captivated and "overcome with love . . . she told me she had never found a man whose nature and actions so suited her."[29]

And so for days the royal spinster and the man young enough to be her son spent much time together while London rang with tales which were exaggerated in every telling. The preachers raged from the pulpits, warning against the union which would corrupt the Church, the state and the Queen. Street crowds listened to the haranguing of speakers who cried of the dastardly plot to wed their monarch to one ridden with "the French disease," a union in which she would probably die in childbirth. While Elizabeth entertained Alençon, Burghley and his fellow Councillors burned the midnight oil, working with Simier and the French ambassador over marriage details. As his reception grew warmer, the Duke's demands had increased.

After twelve days, Alençon had to return to France, and now that the heady delight of seeing her suitor in person had passed, Elizabeth suggested he arrange with his family for more realistic terms concerning her dowry, his religious practices and ruling power. The Duke was convinced Elizabeth was his. From Boulogne he sent a small gold flower, "with a Frog thereon," in which his portrait was ornamented by a pearl pendant. Lord Burghley predicted France would not lessen its demands and, knowing the thin diplomatic ice on which his sovereign was treading, said that "he saw no hope left of the good that was thereby expected." France, said Burghley, would never relent in its terms, and "having lately come hither to see you to be by you reject, it may be taken as quite certain that he will now seek to be revenged upon you." In stern fashion, he held up to Elizabeth the threat that, should she not wed Alençon, that the Duke "will probably marry where we feared [Spain] and France and Spain will unite against us. Our trade will be destroyed, foreign soldiers will be landed in Ireland, and in all likelihood, there will be a rising at home, supported abroad in favor of the King and Queen of Scots. . . ."[30]

Nothing of the sort happened. For months the negotiations dawdled on, during which time Alençon wrote letters, "ardent enough to set fire to the water," in which he swore eternal affection, spoke of the tears he constantly shed at her absence and called himself her affectionate slave. "As such," he wrote, "on the brink of this troublesome sea, I kiss your feet." Simier wrote that "your Frog . . . has done nothing but sigh and weep. And eight o'clock he made me get up to discourse to him of your divine beauty and of his great grief at leaving your Majesty, the jailer of his heart. . . ." Simier said Alençon lived in hope of seeing her again and advised Elizabeth "not to be cruel to him as he desires only to preserve his life so long as you are kind. . . ."

Letters were one thing; reality was another. Lacking Alençon's diverting presence, Elizabeth took stock of the outcry in the City, of the personal unpopularity she was courting in continuing with the proposed marriage. As she read Simier's letters telling of Alençon's unhappiness, she also heard from delegations of churchmen, from her Councillors and from such as the Puritan John Stubbs, who had written a fiery tract against her marriage—and left a right hand at the axman's block for his pains—of the hatred and abhorrence her marriage was causing. When de Mauvissière at Alençon's instigation asked the Queen for a definite answer regarding the marriage, she replied that "it was not a matter which could be settled in such a hurry and she must consult her Council and her people. . . ." De Mauvissière intimated that Alençon himself had a bit of explaining to do at the French court. Rather than lose face over his foolhardiness in coming to England only to be rejected by its Queen, he might be obliged to publish her letters. To which Elizabeth indignantly objected, saying that she was surprised the Duke would think of treating any lady—

much less a Queen—in that way and in great anger closed the interview.

And so it went for another twenty-four months, in which Elizabeth's enthusiasm for the marriage rose and fell with the political conditions in the Netherlands, Spain and Scotland. Sir Francis Walsingham was sent to France to negotiate for the marriage or for a joint league against Spain, but his orders were so contradictory he wrote in despair to Burghley, "When her Majesty is pressed to the marriage, then she seemeth to affect a league. And when the league is yielded to, then she liketh better a marriage. And when thereupon she is moved to assent to a marriage, she hath recourse to the league. And when the motion for the league, or any request is made for money, then her Majesty returneth to the marriage." Walsingham was constantly fearful that if "there ensue a breach of the treaty the blame hereafter might be laid on me."[31]

Elizabeth's main desire, to keep France and Spain fighting for supremacy in the Netherlands, also embraced a strong instinct to keep herself from becoming involved in any war. Sir Francis, fearing the pressure at the French court, heatedly advised the Queen that if she were not going to assist them outright, she should interfere no further. "To give them occasion to think that your Majesty dallies with them both in marriage and league cannot but greatly exasperate them against you, and how your Majesty shall be able to bear alone the malice of Spain, France and Scotland . . . I do not see." Sir Francis's Puritan instincts found Elizabeth's maneuverings distasteful and perilous. "For the love of God, Madame," he wrote in an unusual diatribe, "look to your own estate, and think there can grow no peril so great to you as to have a war break out in your own realm, considering what a number of evil subjects you have. . . ."[32]

Elizabeth "raged and wept" at Walsingham's letter, and her condition was not improved when Alençon received the sovereignty of the Netherlands. He had not consulted her, and she wrote reprovingly to Sir Edward Stafford, her ambassador in France, of the slight, "Let him never procure her harm whose love he seeks to win." She said, "My mortal foe can no ways wish me greater harm than England's hate; neither should death be less welcome unto me, than such a mishap betide me. You see now nearly this matter wringeth me. . . ."[33] She had promised, however, to help her suitor with money and arms, and once her pique was expressed, she wrote the French King, excusing her past irresolution and promising to hasten the marriage negotiations, although, as she stated, "For my own part, I firmly believe that my happiness will be only too great for an old woman to whom paternosters will suffice in place of nuptials."[34] The Spanish ambassador, Mendoza, pretended amusement when he wrote Philip of the splendid ceremonies being planned for the French embassy which would conclude the long protracted mediations. "What will come of it, I cannot pretend to tell your Majesty," he wrote, "but the Queen is chiefly occupied in providing the pageantry. There are serious questions at stake, such as Alençon's relations with the Low Countries, but she is thinking less of these than of tournaments and dancing. . . ."[35] What Elizabeth actually was doing was playing for time. It might take the erection of a magnificent new banqueting house in Whitehall, the building of fourteen new carriages to carry her ladies, the purchase (at cut-rate prices) of much silk, velvet, cloth of gold and silver, but it was all worthwhile to the Queen. It was more painful to Mendoza to relate to King Philip that all this munificence was paid for "with £10,000 of Drake's plunder . . ." and that at the New Year's festivities Elizabeth had worn a crown of diamonds and emeralds fashioned from the confiscated Spanish treasure.*

In the spring of 1581 the French commissioners arrived, accompanied by 500 Frenchmen clad in rich garments. They were met by Philip, Earl of Arundel, the son of the executed Duke of Norfolk, and conducted to Elizabeth's presence. Again the costly court entertainments—the balls, masques, cockfights, the hunting in St. James's and Hyde parks. Upon the Frenchmen's arrival, Leicester flung himself from court, and Hatton remained constantly dissolved in tears as the French King attempted to coerce Elizabeth into marriage. Sir Ralph Sadler, with the prerogative of an aging adviser of Henry VIII, summed up his opinion in few words: "In years the Queen might be his [Alençon's] mother. Doubtfulness of issue more than before. Few old maids escape." Walsingham, believing the decision now made, praised Alençon and said he had an "excellent understanding" and the worst thing about him was an unattractive face. "Then, thou knave, why have thou so many times said ill of him?" cried the Queen in exasperation. "Thou art as changeable as a weathercock!"[37]

The similitude better suited the Queen, for she refused to be cornered. Though she outwardly appeared to combat her Council's advice, not to marry, bewailing that she would leave no "child of her own body to continue the line of Henry VIII!," she had long ago taken Alençon's true measure, and her dallying tactics with his brother, the

---

*None of Elizabeth's investors was backward in accepting a 100 percent return on his investment in Drake's voyage. Only Lord Burghley and the Earl of Sussex refused ten bars of gold as souvenirs, saying, according to Mendoza, "they did not feel they could accept things which had been stolen."[36]

French King, had informed her just how far she might go. Never once in the following months did the man with infinitely more experience than his aging fiancée gain the upper hand. While the French commissioners were deliberating the marriage, Elizabeth wrote Alençon:

> God is my witness that I never use subtleties nor shifts to do good to myself at your expense, as perchance more crafty and less faithful men do often. . . . Monsieur, my dearest, grant pardon to the poor old woman who honours you (I dare say it) as much as any young wench that you will ever find. I thank you a million times for what you write to me from the borders of your country, where the ruler desires to have the grace to be able to serve you in some place, assuring ourselves that England possesses nothing good but what will be dedicated to your use, provided that you treat for it.[38]

The longer Alençon might be diverted, the less chance there was of his brother, Henri III, supporting Spain in the Netherlands. It took many months and excuses, postponements and flattering evasions before the Duke realized he had lost. Even another trip to England, where Elizabeth gave him an "honourable and loving reception," was unsuccessful. The Queen was, by this time, approaching her forty-ninth birthday, and Leicester, Walsingham and Hatton with many of the Council were determined to end the farce which flattered the royal ego but kept international politics at a dangerous and provocative level. One evening, as Elizabeth retired to her private chamber, "all her ladies, who had received their lesson from the anti-matrimonial cabal, got up a concert of weeping and wailing. They surrounded their royal mistress and throwing themselves at her feet, implored her to pause ere she took so fatal a step as contracting marriage, at her time of life, with a youthful husband, by whom she would probably be despised and forsaken." Unsparingly, they recounted her sister Mary's sufferings at the hands of the younger and foreign Philip and entreated her "not to share her power and glory with a foreign spouse," especially a Catholic! Elizabeth said that "by laying errors before her, they had so vexed her mind with anguish that she spent the night in doubtful care without sleep, amongst her women who did nothing but weep." In the morning, still distressed and worn, she called for Alençon and told him that "two more nights such as the last would bring her to the grave." With Hatton standing by for moral support, she told her amazed suitor "that although her love for him was undiminished, she had, after an agonizing struggle, determined to sacrifice her own happiness to the welfare of her people." Distraught, the Duke plucked a ring from his finger with the uncharitable words "that the women of England were as changeable and capricious as their own climate. . . ." Bitterly he flung it to the floor and left the chamber. Later in better humor and unwilling to accept that Elizabeth's decision was firm, he said rather than leave without his royal bride, he would rather they both perished, to which the Queen replied he must not threaten a poor old woman in her own kingdom! When Alençon said he would rather be "cut in pieces" than not to wed and thereby be laughed at by the whole world, it was obvious his leave-taking needed some impetus. Leicester suggested £200,000, which horrified Elizabeth. The Queen said she would never give any such sum, that the Duke could not exchange her goodwill for cash; he would have to make the best of the bargain.

But inevitably, the distressing necessity of parting with some funds was borne upon Elizabeth, and by February, 1582, Alençon was gone, ending a seriocomedy which had kept the English nation and court agitated for months. He took with him, in addition to the devotion of the Queen, some £50,000, and Elizabeth made much of his departure. She experienced a genuine sense of loss, which was as much the product of her emotions as her political percipience. She hated to lose the wooer as much as the political importance attached to his wooing. Everything she had feared about marriage was incarnate in Alençon—the sharing of authority with a foreign power, a discredited religion, to say nothing of the deep personal aversion to marriage formed in her childhood years when her exposure to the married state had been one of implicit and savage danger. The opposition of her Council and subjects had also registered deeply. What Elizabeth had really wanted was a French alliance, not a French marriage,[39] and it took great confidence to end one at the expense of the other. With great courage she told Alençon she would not marry him, but would "ever be a good sister to him." Another attempt on Simier's life only further convinced the Queen of the necessity of disengaging herself from the situation. On this occasion, however, she voiced her suspicions and accused Leicester of responsibility; she told him he was a "murderous poltroon" and should be hanged.[40]

But it was Leicester, along with Howard of Effingham, Fulke Greville and a young man newly arrived at the English court—Walter Raleigh—who escorted Alençon back to the Netherlands. Now that she was safely out of the intricate situation, Elizabeth could be magnanimous. She bade her young suitor farewell with a fervor as warm as it was uncomfortable, for Alençon was now only anxious to put humiliation behind him. In addition to his substantial monies and many public protestations of devotion, the Queen insisted on accompanying him on part of his return journey. She parted from him at Canterbury and, with mournful tears, returned to court. Leicester conveyed his royal charge faithfully to Flushing, where, the tide being out, he later told Elizabeth he had left Alençon "like an old hulk run ashore, high and dry . . . unable to get off a sandbank" on the coast of the Netherlands.

The Queen, still sad, declared she would give £1,000,000 "to have her Frog swimming in the Thames again." Having by then convinced herself she had been martyred in giving up her lover, she quarreled with Leicester for his apparent joy in Alençon's discomfort, bedeviled Walsingham for having encouraged the Duke's departure and even expressed her displeasure to Burghley.

Elizabeth's handling of her relationship with Alençon was her "masterpiece of matrimonial diplomacy."[41] She had been dishonest and evasive, hypocritical and tough. She had risked her popularity with her people, driven her ministers to nerve-racking despair and harangued the courtiers and friends who regarded the marriage with little enthusiasm. But she had used herself as much as she had used Alençon.* And no Englishman had died in what otherwise might have been a grim war. She had parted with good English money in assisting the Duke, lent the luster of her Crown and the hope of her royal person to avert a conflict with France or Spain which she knew she could not win. If, in so doing, she had lost some credibility or honor, Elizabeth was uncaring. She was, by nature, "blessed with a happy degree of fickleness, which, in due time, enabled her to find a fresh and more agreeable source of amusement. . . ."[42]

But for the moment, the Queen's pensiveness and weeping, her antagonism toward those rejoicing over her suitor's departure were real. With the advent of old age the last chance of a husband and children had disappeared, and as the royal tears continued, to the amazement of many within her chamber, it was only the more astute who realized that Elizabeth's tears were perhaps more for herself than for any other reason.

---

*Alençon's career after his return to the Netherlands was disastrous. He was not personally popular and intrigued for more power than the Dutch were willing to give. He finally had to flee to France and died some three years later at Château-Thierry with the inevitable rumors of poisoning.

Chapter Twenty-two

The marital discussions at the English court—and their political consequences—were of especial interest to another Queen, one who was now entering her fourteenth year of captivity. The close restraint in which Mary Stuart had been held following the Duke of Norfolk's execution had, over the years, gradually been relaxed. She changed residences as often as the seasons in order that the castle-prison might be cleansed or "sweetened" from turret to basement. From Wingfield to Sheffield to Chatsworth to Tutbury, and then back in a ceaseless round, the residences all bore one remarkable similarity for Mary: in each she was a prisoner.

Her custodian, George Talbot, the sixth Earl of Shrewsbury, was head of an ancient and illustrious family, one of the richest men in England and one of the influential Northern nobles whose loyalty to the English Queen was unquestioned. In 1569 Elizabeth had placed Mary in the Earl's custody, and from that time, he had not known an anxiety-free moment. Shrewsbury was a kindly man, undistinguished in appearance, mild-mannered but prone to worry. A remarkably ordinary individual for one of her foremost peers, whom Elizabeth referred to as "My faithful Shrewsbury," the Earl was, nevertheless, dependable, honest and conscientious; the Queen was well aware of his value in a court where all three characteristics in one courtier were rare.

Shrewsbury bore a singularly heavy cross in the portly person of his wife, the former Elizabeth Cavendish, widow of the owner of Chatsworth,* an imposing Derbyshire mansion. Bess Shrewsbury was a loud,

*The Countess was to go down in history as the notorious "Bess of Hardwick." In 1590 she commenced the building of Hardwick Hall, one of the most elegant and ornate Elizabethan mansions. It still stands today with her initials "E.S." imposed on its towers against the sky, a testament to her ego, as well as her very considerable artistic judgment.

arrogant, imperious woman, selfish and unfeeling, continually demanding, the opposite of her husband in every way. With the ambitious hardness of a woman who, with only her brains and considerable self-confidence, had through three fortuitous marriages advanced herself from an undistinguished background to one of considerable social prominence, she dominated husband and household alike. While Shrewsbury's kindness toward Mary Stuart was genuine and the product of an honest compassion, his wife's derived more from an instinctive desire to keep in Mary's good graces, all the while preening among the local gentry as the wife of the custodian of the Queen of Scotland.

Under the Shrewsburys, Mary's life had been comfortable, if restricted. In the earliest years of her captivity, the thought that only the life of Elizabeth Tudor prevented this captive Queen from ascending the English throne was a sobering guarantee that any stringent hardship would be absent. Now, after fourteen years, her environment was similar to any highborn or noble lady of means. She had her own personal establishment of servants and other retainers, a steward, ladies-in-waiting, grooms, a smith and a stable of sixteen horses. Her pension from France was sporadically paid, greatly humiliating Mary, for she could not then pay her servants. When it did arrive, there was usually enough for any indulgences she wished for herself, for her household or for generous donations to the neighborhood poor. Mary's Scottish revenues had, at the Regent's insistence, been withheld for years.

Shrewsbury was allowed £52 a week, a goodly sum, to maintain Mary, her retainers and his own staff. When, in 1581, it was cut to £30 a week, the Earl indignantly complained to the Council, and Walsingham felt constrained to write Elizabeth that her predecessors when in peril had not considered expenses, even though "their treasure was neither so great as your Majesty's is nor their subjects so wealthy." He said he prayed that the "abatement of the charges towards that nobleman [Shrewsbury] that had the custody of the bosom serpent [Mary] hath not lessened his care in keeping of her."[1]

Walsingham need not have worried. Realizing he had little alternative, Shrewsbury dipped into his own reserves to maintain Mary appropriately.* The Scottish Queen was grateful. She respected and admired the kindly gray-haired man so much at the mercy of a carping

---

*In the meantime Walsingham worked to acquire some profitable license for exports for Shrewsbury which would reimburse him in whole or in part for his out-of-pocket expenses. This was typical of the Tudor patronage system, which repaid honorable service with perquisites, allowing them, at the same time, the retention of their own funds.

wife and a dictatorial sovereign. She was thankful for the many liberties Shrewsbury permitted, for, within the area close to the Castle,
Mary was allowed to hunt and ride, always, of course, accompanied by
her custodian or other guardians. She could course with greyhounds,
walk in the Castle gardens, play at bowls, exercise her small dogs and
was invariably given privacy to converse with her visitors. In short, she
had a comfortable life lacking only the valuable privilege of freedom.

This freedom was not denied her servants. They had easy and
unquestioned access in and out of the Castle grounds, making it simple
for Mary to forward and receive letters or messages she did not wish to
deliver to the ordinary post or courier. The French ambassador in
London, de Mauvissière, acted as a clearinghouse for the receipt and
disposition of the Scottish Queen's mail. Mary had two secretaries
whom she kept incessantly busy corresponding with her agents in
France, in Scotland, in Spain and at the Vatican. This voluminous
mail, "the occupation of her life," was Mary's one outlet to the outside
world. Innocent letters from her Guise relatives in France, from friends
traveling on the Continent or in England, from ex-retainers in
Scotland—all contributed some interest and warmth to her days.
Elizabeth had honored the privacy of Mary's correspondence, which
was allowed free travel. Up until the middle 1580's it was not tampered
with, even though the English Queen and her ministers knew, from
their own spies, that Mary vigorously maintained her foreign ties,
many of whom were not friendly to England.

Other than the normal daily routine of prayers, correspondence,
perhaps a visit from some of the Catholic gentry in the neighborhood
and an hour or two outside, Mary's day offered little change or
challenge. She had been allowed to keep the prized symbols of her
Queenship—her cloth of estate with the arms of Scotland over the chair
on its dais. The deference of her guardian and the affection of those
who had voluntarily offered to share her exile were touching examples
of the esteem which surrounded the Queen. Mary was well aware that
the emotional climate of her household depended on her, and even
though she was often subject to bouts of melancholy, for the most part
she was amiable to those who had chosen to serve her and, in return,
received from them an affection bordering on veneration. Mary strove
to rise above her periodic depressions, and in a remarkable similarity to
Catherine of Aragon, another imprisoned Queen of a half century
previous, she sought, in the same way, to give some meaning to each
day to those who had given up so much to be with her. Though Mary
usually dressed in black, "as in full mourning," dress patterns arriving
from France were eagerly opened, and later bolts of cloth and or-

naments parceled out to her ladies. Mary's generosity was as instinctive as it was consistent, and within her means, she shared her small luxuries with all. Even Elizabeth was often sent a choice box of French bonbons or a pair of gloves of the softest Spanish leather. These items, the colorful fabrics and accessories, fans and perfumes, once so important to a frivolous young Queen, had lost all meaning to the captive, whose one true luxury seemed to be a superabundance of time.

Mary and the Countess of Shrewsbury often "wrought marvelously with the needle" for hours on end until the darkening light put an end to their labors. Mary needed a continual supply of the silks and other materials she often embroidered to her own design. These and the other parcels which were carried north also served another purpose, for it had been found easy to insert communications in these packages or letters which, for one reason or another, the sender had not wished to trust to the regular post. A small roll of paper might be inserted in the hollow heel of a boot or shoe. A dainty wisp of cambric handkerchief might contain a message written in invisible ink. In this way, those bits of information about plots to help Mary regain her freedom, about the political events in Scotland or England were revealed.

Over the years, the deaths of many she had known and loved had depressed and saddened Mary. Her Guise uncle; her former brother-in-law, Charles, the French King; Marguerite, the Duchess of Savoy, who had shown her such kindness while she was growing up in those faraway happy days at the French court which now seemed only fantasy—all were gone. Many relatives and former playmates, those who had been only slightly older when she left France, had died. When she was informed of Bothwell's death, it was as if the ghost of another younger, happier woman, one not apparent in the face she now saw reflected in a mirror, must die also, for while friends and loved ones disappeared, she remained incarcerated and without hope.

But even with what many would have termed a comfortable existence, the lack of physical freedom and the deprivation of her royal prerogative gnawed at Mary. As she approached her fortieth year, her hatred of Elizabeth Tudor, while not as apparent as in the earlier years when she had wildly threatened and intrigued, had increased to an obsession. Her hostility stemmed not only from the very real tragedy of her captivity, but from the fact that the English Queen had given counsel to those whom Mary considered her enemies, while refusing to meet with Mary herself, a sister Queen and a kinswoman. Indeed it had become impossible to communicate with Elizabeth, who for years had refused to answer most of Mary's letters. They all bore the same theme: Mary's outrage at her restraint and complaints of her treatment. Incensed at one letter, Elizabeth told the French ambassador that when Mary lived in Scotland, she "had no better entertainment or diet, but many times worse or baser!" With Mary's reputation for dishonesty, caprice and the moral weakness which had caused her downfall, Elizabeth felt a response would only give impetus to Mary's considerable troublemaking talents.

Mary Stuart also harbored a similar resentment against the Queen of England's meddling in Scottish affairs, her effort to direct the life of young James Stuart, so that Scotland had become in most respects a mere appanage of England. Mary's foreign agents kept her informed of such developments, and Elizabeth's continued success in Scotland seemed to Mary to have been purchased with her own freedom, the usurpation of her royal privileges and the political independence of her son. Over the years, she had looked to Spain and France for help, enduring a humiliating disappointment as they did nothing to assist her. She had been speechless at Elizabeth's proposed marriage to her own brother-in-law, the Duke of Alençon, and the alliance with France, the beloved nation of which she had once been a proud Queen. It often seemed to Mary that wherever she looked, wherever she turned, either Elizabeth or the English Council blocked the way as surely as Shrewsbury, for all his kindness, prevented her fleeing the Castle gates. She had long given up hope, especially after Lethington's suicide, that any Scottish assistance would be forthcoming. Her son had been too young to provoke any action on her behalf, and she knew the Regent Morton to be intensely vindictive to her cause.

The awareness of her solitary state and her rejection by those still living had given Mary an aloof melancholy which often expressed itself in a restlessness and discontent, in a sighing depression and a faraway look in her eyes as she gazed from a window toward mountains she could not cross. The vivacity which had been so integral a part of the younger Queen had all but disappeared and was revived only in moments of extreme optimism that her position might change. Her soft grace and charm had become muted in resignation; the tones of her personality had changed as swiftly as the gray which had soon sprinkled her abundant dark hair.

Mary's health, too, had worsened during her long captivity. Her lissome figure had thickened and given her a large-boned, more mature aspect. The perfect oval of her face was marred by a prominent double chin, and the long nose had sharpened above lips which seemed to have acquired a permanent tightness. Mary's usual outgoing, capricious nature had disappeared completely; in its place was a taut soberness often tinged with a pathetic resignation.

The high point of Mary's year was her visit to Buxton, the spa in the Derbyshire peaks, where Shrewsbury had built, at his own expense, a house, "a high and symmetrical façade with three towers, but apparently no courtyard,"[2] in which Mary might have privacy and security. The Buxton waters had proved helpful to her rheumatism and the arthritis in her fingers and arm. These aches, together with the chronic pain in her side and her continual catarrh, were greatly relieved by the treatment, and Mary often remained at Buxton for as long as five weeks. Intermittently reports of his indulgence led to sharp remonstrances to Shrewsbury from the English Council, and he would excuse his leniency admitting that his goodwill toward his captive was mixed, as he said, because "her principal object was and is to have some liberty out of the gates."[3] Then, for weeks or months, supervision would be increased, for the Earl dreaded the loss of royal favor. He was well aware of the case which might be made against him when he was forced to be continually absent from court and unable to defend himself.

While the years passed, while her health deteriorated and her hopes were continually dashed, Mary's spiritual resources had increased. Suddenly the faith to which she had paid a devoted lip service all her life acquired an added strengthening substance which gave solace and courage to her thoughts and comfort to her days. In melancholy retrospect, she knew the major part of her life had been lived. The remaining time allotted to her must, therefore, be sublimated in acceptance. Liberation of the body was forbidden, but liberation of the spirit might soar as she knelt before her altar, fingering her rosary and gazing raptly at the cross as her lips moved in frequent prayer. Her empty days were not so long when she could lose herself in the familiar rite which now held a deeper meaning. Shrewsbury was compassionate and tolerated the arrival and departure of several whom he knew to be disguised priests come to inspire and comfort the poor Scottish Queen. Mary often gave thanks for the choice of her kindly guardian, and she was, therefore, understandably fearful when informed that Shrewsbury was relinquishing his custodial role. Her terror increased almost to panic when she realized that his leave-taking carried with it a slight to her honor which she felt powerless to combat and which only brought home to her once more the injustice of her position.

During her years of imprisonment, as they rode outside, embroidered by the hour and even, at times, took their meals together, Mary had formed a friendship with her guardian's wife. Bess Shrewsbury was "an incorrigible intriguer with the tongue of an adder,"[4] a woman of consummate ambition, undisputed malice and small con-

science. She had incurred Queen Elizabeth's anger by allowing the
marriage of her Cavendish daughter to Charles Stuart, the younger
brother of Lord Darnley. With the birth of their child, Arbella, Bess
rejoiced in the fact that now she, too, had a claimant to England's
throne.* After a sojourn in the Tower, she had passed the days of
Elizabeth's displeasure at her Derbyshire domain and, together with
Mary, enjoyed the prattle of the blond, beautiful Arbella as they plied
their needles or conversed with visitors. Under other circumstances,
Mary Stuart and Bess Shrewsbury would have had little in common.
But living now under the same roof, they had each gained from the
other: Bess an enviable luster as companion to the captive Queen, and
for Mary, the talkative woman had proved a boon indeed. Everything
she wished to know about Elizabeth Tudor she had learned from Bess.
Everything she could not gain from other sources about the cousin who
refused to receive her, Bess was only too happy to divulge. Hour by
hour, the Countess regaled the Queen with talk of Elizabeth's conduct
at court with such as Leicester, Hatton "and other lovers." She spoke at
length of Elizabeth's insatiable vanity, her outlandish attire and her
own inestimable opinion of herself. Shrewsbury did not share his wife's
eagerness to gossip and often criticized the malicious tone of her conversation. It was, therefore, of little surprise when, in 1582, after twenty
years of married life, their differences reached the combustion stage,
and, in one outrageous episode, the Countess flung herself from Derbyshire. Traveling to court, she announced she would not be reconciled
with her husband and gave as her reason the fact that he had been
guilty of intimate relations with his prisoner, Mary, Queen of Scots.

Mary was outraged, despairing—and helpless. As Bess Shrewsbury
prattled on in London of the unmentionable goings-on at the Queen of
Scots' prison home, as her tales grew in the telling, so that one enterprising fellow even wrote of the two bastard children Mary had
allegedly borne, she and her guardian looked at each other in horror.
Mary realized the terrible impact such tales would have, and Shrewsbury feared for his honor, his estates and possibly even his head. His
whole reputation was at stake, and indignantly he refuted all the
charges. Before he lost everything, he urgently requested his dismissal
as Mary's custodian. He had been faithful in that capacity for fourteen
years, he wrote Elizabeth, but now he felt unequal to the task, and he
must have relief. He said he lived in hell because of his "wicked and
malicious wife" and his great responsibility for the Scottish Queen's

*As Mary Stuart's right in the succession had passed to her child, James, the son of Lord
Darnley, so the right would ultimately pass (should James leave no children) to the child of
Darnley's brother, in this case the unfortunate Arbella Stuart.

safety. He did not wish to incur the rancor of his own sovereign, and he begged to be delivered of his worrisome charge and given a chance to explain and redeem himself at court.

Mary, too, demanded that the Countess of Shrewsbury and her two older Cavendish sons who had joined in the slander be publicly examined and punished for their contemptible lies. She recognized all too well that few at court were deterred from believing the infamous and hateful tales. This knowledge and her own pent-up anger at Elizabeth caused her to answer the charges in the only way open to her: by demeaning the slanderer. One gray November day she sat incensed at her desk and, caution cast to the winds, wrote the Queen of England, beginning with her first association with the prattling Bess and recounted every miserable piece of gossip which had fallen from the Countess' lips. She told Elizabeth how she was mocked for her incredible vanity, how her ladies, standing behind the throne, often covered their mouths with their hands to keep from laughing while Elizabeth serenely listened to herself being compared with the glory and brightness of the sun, moon and stars. She recounted Bess' version of Elizabeth's adulterous relationship with Leicester and the fact that she had had to seduce Christopher Hatton forcibly. The reason for her insatiable sexual appetite was no secret, wrote Mary, tactlessly administering the *coup de grâce*. It was well known that the English Queen, because of a physical deformity which denied complete sexual union, must satisfy her lusts in different ways. "She says moreover that you are not like other women and it is folly to advance the notion of your marriage with the Duke of Alençon, seeing that such a conjugal union could never be consummated." After this unparalleled frankness, Mary went on to include Elizabeth's unforgivable treatment of her ladies, one of whom she had attacked with a knife and even broken the finger of another, so that they lived in terror of her. Mary mentioned Elizabeth's "sore leg" which was nothing other than evidence of the detestable disease which everyone knew had killed her father. Furthermore, wrote Mary, "Lady Shrewsbury had, by a book of divinations in her possession, predicted that Elizabeth would very soon be cut off by a violent death and Mary would succeed to her throne."[5] Out of many years of captivity and a memory which had nothing to remember of Elizabeth Tudor but injustice, Mary Stuart relieved a tortured spirit. The following day her incredible verbal outpouring was sent to the Queen of England.

Elizabeth never chose to reply to this remarkable document,[6] but her determination to put an end to the rumors was evident in Shrewsbury's recall to court. The Earl explained that his wife had called him a "knave, a fool and a beast to his face and mocked and mowed at him,"[7] and it was obvious to all that his marriage was over. When he appeared at court, Elizabeth did her part to dispel the evil rumors of his wrong-doing by graciously receiving him. Distraught, he heard himself released of his guardianship, and gratefully, he went down on his knees, kissed his sovereign's hand and thanked her for relieving him "of two devils simultaneously."

It was unfortunate for Mary that the domestic upheaval of the Shrewsburys coincided with the threat of a Catholic revival in England. Plots in which honored names such as Throckmorton, Paget, Northumberland and Philip Howard, the Earl of Arundel, the son of the executed Duke of Norfolk, were prominent, made it difficult for Elizabeth to rationalize her continued sufferance of and protection for Mary or to regard her as anything but a provocative menace to her own safety. Following Shrewsbury's dismissal, Elizabeth sent the seventy-seven-year-old Sir Ralph Sadler*, an old and trusted courtier, to remove the Scottish Queen to Tutbury Castle, which, of all her prisons, Mary hated most. It was exceedingly damp, her chamber was over the garderobes which constantly emitted "foul and noxious airs," and its location, being moated and on a hill, made outside exercise difficult. Sir Ralph was a kindly man, albeit not as tolerant as Shrewsbury. He was no stranger to Mary, saying "he had known her from the cradle." On assuming his duties, he wrote the Council, "I find her much altered from what she was when I was first acquainted with her. She is not yet able to strain her left foot to the ground, and to her very great grief, not without tears, findeth it wasted and shrunk of its natural measure."[8] But even a deep sympathy for the imprisoned Queen did not cause him to disregard his stern warning from Elizabeth and the Councillors that Mary must be confined more closely. Sadler did not possess Shrewsbury's wealth, and the expense worried Lord Burghley, who wrote to Walsingham, "I see that her Majesty must be at further charge with her own defrayments than she was by my Lord of Shrewsbury. The argument upon sparing and spending must consist upon her Majesty's resolution how the Scots' Queen shall be hence kept." Wisely, Burghley had recommended a middle road to Elizabeth, saying, "And, therein, no extremity in my opinion is good, neither to keep her with over-much liberty nor with over-much strait-

*Elizabeth's first choice was Lord St. John of Bletsoe who unequivocally refused the commission even when threatened with the Queen's punishment by Leicester and Burghley. St. John said he would "abide any extremity rather than to go." His remark is indicative of the distaste with which many nobles regarded Mary's incarceration, the fear that they might fail in responsibility of keeping her restrained and the inevitable drain on their finances.

ness. The one shall nourish her practice and increase of her party, the other will bring desperation to all her faction."[9]

At Tutbury, Mary's thoughts often centered on her son, James. She had long ago accepted that the boy seemingly had little love for his mother. He had been brought up by her enemy, the Countess of Mar, and with George Buchanan as his tutor, Mary realized his mind had been poisoned against her. In her hopeful naïveté, she believed that if she could meet or communicate with James, she could undo all the wounding effects of the past years to which he had been subjected. Her letters, addressed to the "Prince of Scotland," had always been returned, the Scottish Lords maintaining that such a title insulted their sovereign. It was indicative of Mary's pride that she could not bring herself to address James as "King of Scotland," for despite the abdication made at Lochleven, she still regarded herself as Queen. In the intervening years, as Elizabeth seemed to grow stronger, Mary came to regard James as her one hope of attaining freedom. As he came of age and replaced the Regent, he would, undoubtedly, yearn to shake off English influence and make his peace with France and Spain, and surely he would remember his imprisoned mother! Mary had yearned to remove James from Calvinistic influence in Scotland to be brought up a good Catholic in Spain. But even with their differing religious beliefs, they shared the same blood with the strongest tie two individuals could have. Therefore, Mary reasoned, James would—once he had attained power—certainly challenge Elizabeth and obtain his mother's freedom.

Never was there a more naïve assumption or one so indicative of how truly out of touch Mary Stuart was with current events in Scotland, France, Spain and England. Never was there more obvious a mother's desire to believe the best of her son or one more doomed to failure.

It was while at Tutbury that Mary conceived the plan which she presented to James. Through intermediaries she proposed—as some prelude to acquiring her freedom—a joint rulership, in which James would retain his sovereignty and she would be Scotland's Queen in name and honor only. Mary's thought was that if James would not relinquish his Crown, he might at least be induced to share it. Even though for years she had firmly denied her son's Kingship, by the middle 1580's her distress was such that she was prepared to relinquish her active participation in her country's affairs, if she might be restored as its Queen. Mary's willingness to surrender her sovereign precedence is indicative of her weariness and despair of her long confinement. She was getting old, and suddenly insistence on her royal supremacy did not seem as important as it once had.

In her desperate desire to come to some understanding with her son ("I know the child doth love me and will not deal with the Queen without my advice") Mary acquired the services of Patrick, the Master of Grey. Grey was to urge young James to behave "as a natural and obedient son." Toward that end he visited with the Guises in France and, at their instigation, went to the Scottish court to present the young monarch with his mother's proposal for a joint sovereignty. There, with a fine eye for the quick deal and a perceptive appraisal of what would most benefit him personally, he realized that it would be more to his potential gain to work with James than to represent the discredited and imprisoned Mary. He switched allegiances with a speed that startled even the jaded Scots, whispering small confidences which Mary had told him and so won James' confidence—James who ever loved a "favorite"—that in no time he was en route to Elizabeth's court to intercede, not for Mary, as she thought, but for James.

Mary had commissioned Grey to emphasize strongly to Elizabeth how the goodwill of James Stuart might be obtained by the release of his mother. For the hundredth time she repeated that her detention in England was illegal and detailed how much approbation Elizabeth would win from Scotland and the English Catholics should she voluntarily free Mary. Apparently Mary had some nagging doubts about Grey's capabilities or conscience, and she wrote to de Mauvissière at the English court of the danger to herself and her hopes of freedom if her son was anything less than firm about her release. Any secure alliance with the Scottish people, any recognition of James as England's heir must carry with it the unalterable fact of Mary's sovereignty and her immediate release to rule jointly with her son. What Mary did not realize, of course, was that once Grey had switched his interests, he was in a position of paramount importance to impress on Elizabeth that what James of Scotland *really* wanted was Elizabeth's goodwill, Elizabeth's alliance and, ultimately, Elizabeth's Crown. And if any one of these had to be sacrificed, then the interests and urgings of his mother might be overlooked.

To buttress her chances of success, Mary indicated she was prepared to go to almost any lengths to ensure that Grey's mission would be successful. Once free, she agreed to remain in England for the time being, allowing her restoration to be accomplished gradually and peacefully. She would "forgive" all the wrongs she had suffered. She would denounce the Pope's anathema against Elizabeth and relinquish her claim to the English Crown. James, of course, could hardly be expected to surrender his. And showing the full extent of her despair, she would join in any league against France, provided

England replaced her French dowry, for it was all the money she had in the world. She would direct no efforts against the Protestants in Scotland, and her son's choice of a wife would be at the Queen of England's pleasure. Even Walsingham, never any friend of Mary's, said the concessions "left Elizabeth no more to ask for."

For Elizabeth, too, it seemed a way out. Once her son had come of age, Mary's continued restraint lost its importance and Walsingham said that "if she could be placed in Scotland without any dangerous alteration, England could be glad to be rid of her."[10] Elizabeth recognized a golden opportunity to liberate Mary and, at the same time, hold the English succession as priceless bait to keep James in line. She was sure that the French, who had for years protested Mary's restraint, "would stand as joint guarantor with James for her good conduct."[11] Mary's freedom would provide Elizabeth with a means of uniting England, Scotland and France as never before and would remove the central Catholic pivot from her realm forever.

The tragic fact was that had James at that moment resolutely identified with his imprisoned mother and demanded, with France, some sort of treaty which would release Mary Stuart, Elizabeth almost could not have refused. But in her desperate desire to come to some understanding with her son, Mary had overlooked one thing: his wish to retain what he had and his belief that any hope of succeeding to the English Crown could be acquired only by a complete disregard for Mary's sad and unfortunate position. James had absolutely no desire to share his authority, especially with a dishonored and controversial mother. He had little interest in or affection for Mary. He had no desire to muddy his friendly relations with England by accepting responsibility for a woman and Queen it had kept imprisoned for years. In short, there was never to be any place for Mary Stuart in James of Scotland's future.

James Stuart was now a lad in his middle teens, an "old young man," an undersized insignificant boy with an uncertain manner of speech and an air of perpetual anxiety. Short and stocky, he walked with a peculiar gait, "sprawling and ungainly," completely lacking the tall elegance of both Mary and Darnley, his very awkwardness much at odds with his own good opinion of himself. He was distrustful by nature, yet possessed an intelligent shrewdness by which he appraised those near him. The preservation of his royal status was a prime consideration in all of James' actions. Lacking the love of any parent, he had learned early in his lonely years to replace such love and attention by forming close attachments to "favorites"—servants and other companions—who often used him for their own ends. While the treaty among Mary, Elizabeth and James was in negotiation at the English court, Mary sent M. Fontenay, a French agent who had worked heroically in her behalf, to Scotland to see James. His letter, written to Mary's secretary, Claude Nau, revealed that James seemed a good conversationalist except that "owing to the terrorism under which he had been brought up, he is timid with the great Lords and seldom ventures to contradict them." Fontenay said that James disliked "music, dancing and amorous talk, and curiosity of dress and courtly trivialities . . . he has an especial detestation for ear-rings." Fontenay said that "for want of instruction," James' manners were rough and uncouth. "He speaks, eats, dresses and plays like a boor, and he is no better in the company of women." James apparently masked his lack of self-confidence with loud words, which Fontenay said were "sententious." The Frenchman noted that James preferred hunting to all other amusements, often galloping six hours at a stretch, and that he was "too idle, careless, too easy," often leaving his affairs to be managed by others. When reproached for his idleness, James abruptly told his mother's emissary that he was well aware of what was going on and that "when he attended to business, he could do more in an hour than others could do in a day," that when he tried to force himself to work at his desk without interruption for a long space of time, "he was always ill after it." He likened himself to "a Spanish jennet which could run one course well, but could not hold out."[12]

Indeed all the social graces which had so characterized the vivacious Mary and the handsome Darnley were completely lacking in their son. An unfortunate throwback to the Welsh Tudors—in personality he was not unlike his great-great-grandfather, Henry VII—James was a dour young boy, as ambitious as both parents and possessed of their easy tolerance for any lack of honor or principle. In this he was by no means alone at the Scottish court where betrayal and personal aggrandizement were a way of life. "Money and preferment are the only sirens which charm the Lords of Scotland," wrote Fontenay, "to teach to them of duty to their Prince, of honour, of justice, virtue, noble actions, the memory of an illustrious life which they should bequeath to posterity, they count the merest folly . . . they care nothing for the future and less for the past. . . ."[13]

A good deal of James' easy tolerance of injustice was undoubtedly provided by example and the unfortunate incidents of his childhood. He knew his uncle Murray had been assassinated. He had watched his grandfather, the Earl of Lennox, die as a result of political murder, and he himself had consented to the execution of the Regent Morton, who had governed for him during the years of his minority. The last tragedy had incurred Elizabeth's wrath. The Queen had tried in vain to save Morton, whose friendship toward England was great. When informed of his execution, Elizabeth had cried, "That false Scotch urchin! The night before Morton was taken he could call him 'father!' He could say he had no friend like Morton who had brought him up and that he would protect him. And the next day he had him seized and cut off his head. What must I look for from such a double-tongued scoundrel as this?"[14] It was apparent to Elizabeth that honor and compassion had little meaning for James when his own supremacy was threatened. Where his mother was concerned, they were totally absent. Elizabeth heard he was uncomfortable whenever Mary was mentioned and merely looked at the ground, saying her case "was as strange as any that has ever been heard of in history."[15]

The plan for the restoration of Mary to rule with James was regarded with little enthusiasm in Scotland. For years English money had flowed into that country in the form of bribery and pensions, and Elizabeth had sent James handsome gifts of horses and hounds. The Protestant religion was firmly entrenched, and the English succession loomed large since Elizabeth was now approaching her fifty-first year. Monies and faith were one thing, but a Crown was another. James had been brought up with the knowledge that he was the heir to the English throne, and it seemed doubtful that his religious faith and his filial feelings would be strong enough to reject such a bright future.

Fate then took a hand in solving the perplexity of Elizabeth, Mary and James. Francis Throckmorton, a nephew of the late Sir Nicholas, had returned to England after a year on the Continent and in Madrid, where he had discussed the Catholic "Enterprise" in England, which involved nothing less than the complete overthrow of Protestantism. On his way home, he had made the acquaintance of Mary Stuart's prime agent, Thomas Morgan, who, convinced of the young man's sincerity, disclosed to him the conspiracy involving King Philip and the Guisian party in France. The former would land soldiers in Ireland, meanwhile using his Netherlands bases as ports for embarking further troops into England. The latter would call on Scottish Catholics to assist the French troops landing in Scotland to attack England from the North, while additional soldiers would be landed in Sussex in the South. The plan had the Pope's blessing, as well as that of Mary Stuart, who would gain her freedom as well as Elizabeth's Crown. There were several Catholic nobles at court in addition to Mendoza, the Spanish ambassador, who were privy to the plan. Throckmorton was to make their acquaintance and wait for the signal for the uprising, meanwhile rendering all assistance possible.

Throckmorton was careless and in England was seen leaving Mendoza's lodgings. He was placed under surveillance, and his actions became suspicious enough to waken Walsingham's interest. Orders went out for his arrest, and he was seized at his Paul's Wharf lodgings in the very act of writing a ciphered letter to Mary Stuart. Taken to the Tower, he withstood the torments of the rack the first time but, faced with the grim prospect of a second agonizing session, confessed the plot, giving names, dates and places for the uprising and subsequent invasion. Sobbing miserably, he told of Mary Stuart's knowledge and participation, ending brokenly with: "Now I have disclosed the secrets of her who was the dearest Queen to me in the world, whom I thought no torment could have drawn me so much to have prejudiced. I have broken faith to her and I care not if I were hanged. . . ."[16] Several months later Francis Throckmorton was executed at Tyburn.

Elizabeth was shaken by the extent of the Throckmorton conspiracy and by evidence of the correspondence among the Jesuits, the Pope, the King of Spain, the Queen of Scots, the Spanish ambassador and her own nobles. The scheming had proceeded even as she had considered Mary Stuart's plea to be restored to the Scottish throne to rule jointly with her son. The Throckmorton plot pointed up more than anything else that the prime interest henceforth must be not the restoration of the Queen of Scotland, but the preservation of the Queen of England. And once James had divined the extent of Elizabeth's disillusion, he had small conscience in disclosing that he was prepared to acquiesce to her wishes in the hopes of one day ascending her throne. He asked for a pension of £5,000 a year, leading Elizabeth to say caustically "that her own servants and favourites professed to love her for her good parts, Alençon for her person and the Scots for her Crown . . . but they all ended in the same thing, asking for money!"[17] James also insisted he would be guided by Elizabeth's advice in the selection of a wife and in the administration of his kingdom. In his assent was implicit the understanding that he was more than willing to overlook the interests of his imprisoned mother. And with Elizabeth's subsequent recognition of James' attitude, Mary Stuart's last chance for freedom and restoration was gone. By keeping mother and son separated, Elizabeth held the reins of power over both. While his mother was a physical prisoner of the English Queen, James VI of Scotland was captive also, captive to the elusively tantalizing dream that had contributed to his mother's downfall: the right to wear the Crown of England. As long as he behaved and remained on good terms with Elizabeth Tudor, his chances seemed bright. What would happen to his mother was, seemingly, no concern of his, and her fate would have to be decided by the English Queen.

To keep a proper face on the matter, the negotiations dragged on for months, but by March, 1585, Mary knew she had lost. It was difficult for her to accept. Mercifully, she had not heard James' remarks, which, as the French ambassador wrote, did not appreciate his mother's true intent. James had said he regarded any "association" between him and his mother as "casting a bone to stick between their teeth." He said he wished his mother "would give over her plots and would turn truly to the religion received in the two realms," for she was a "determined Papist and French to the heart. . . ."

The knowledge that James had not fought more vigorously in her defense and had, apparently, succumbed to the blandishments of the English Queen shattered Mary. Not only was her last chance at freedom and restoration gone forever, but she had also lost the son she had never known. She had lost him to the English Queen as surely as she had forfeited the only thing which now gave any hope or meaning to her life: her freedom. When faced with a choice between two Queens, James had not hesitated to choose the stronger, the one who could do the most for him, and in his conscienceless opportunism he pushed his mother to the brink of extremity in anger and a desire for retaliation. Bitterly Mary realized she now had no more "strings to her bow" other than outside Catholic intervention, and should that fail, she was doomed to spend the remainder of her life in captivity.

In outraged dignity, compounded by overwhelming disappointment and hurt, she read James' explanation. He told her she was a prisoner in a foreign country, and he did not consider she was in any position to enter into any agreements or "associations" with him. "I will always recognize you during my life, as Queen-mother," he wrote somewhat defensively. Mary did not reply directly. Instead, she unburdened herself to the French ambassador, writing furiously "that the title of King did not belong to James" and "he will not hold it of me!" She said "that if my son persists in this, you can assure him, by the Justice-Clerk . . . that I will invoke the malediction of God on him, and will give him not only mine, with all circumstances that may touch him to the quick, but say also that I will disinherit him, and deprive him, as an unnatural son, who is ingrate, perfidious, and disobedient, of all the grandeur that he can have through me in this world. . . ."[18]

Writing to James was not enough. Mary felt the need to unburden herself to her archenemy, and in a piteous letter to Elizabeth, she wrote plaintively:

I cannot, Madam, suffer it any longer, and, dying, I must discover the authors of my death. The vilest criminals in your gaols and born under your authority are admitted to be tried for their own justification, and their accusers and the accusation against them are made known to them. Why should not the same privilege be accorded to me, a sovereign Queen, your nearest relative and your legitimate heir? I think that this last quality has been hitherto the principal cause of exciting my enemies against me, and of all their calumnies for creating division between us two, in order to advance their own unjust pretensions. But, alas! they have now little reason and still less need to torment me longer on this account. For I protest to you on mine honour that I now look for no other kingdom than that of my God, whom I see preparing me for the best end of all my sorrows and adversities.

I entreat you, for the honour and grievous passion of our Saviour and Redeemer, Jesus Christ; once more I beseech you to permit me to withdraw from this kingdom to some place of rest, there to seek solace for my poor body, so worn and wearied with unceasing grief, and, with liberty of my conscience, to prepare my soul for God who daily summons me. . . . Give me this contentment before I die that, seeing all things set at rest between us, my soul, delivered from my body, may not be constrained to pour out its complaints before God for the wrong you have suffered to be done me here below. . . .[19]

Unfortunately the malediction of God did not frighten James, nor did the moving appeal of Mary's letter touch Elizabeth. Events in England had passed beyond the point where entreaties or appeals to conscience were important or practical. Her rejection by James had been a "final and profound affront"[20] to Mary, and her subsequent actions were tinged with a recklessness and desperation more reminiscent of the younger Mary than the mature imprisoned Queen. Mary's one grand hope now was to regain her freedom. She had lost her husband, her country, her son, the love of her subjects, her health and the respect of her beloved France. Shattered and despondent, she was ready to grasp any means by which she might acquire her freedom. For one who had lost everything, there was nothing now to take from her but her life.

Chapter Twenty-three

The position of the English Catholics, comprising nearly three-quarters of England's 4,000,000 population, rapidly became untenable as plots and counterplots proliferated. The majority of the Catholics were undisputably loyal to Elizabeth and regarded such cabal with dismay. Under the Act of Uniformity of 1558, the Queen's religious settlement, Catholicism was tolerated, its followers being required only to pay lip service to the state religion. Those who did not feel they could conform were allowed to travel abroad* in search of spiritual comfort and, as long as they behaved themselves, to return home later if they chose. These included not only the Catholics, but also those followers of Calvin and other Counter-Reformation adherents, such as the Puritans, who were noisily demanding additional church reform.

But the Bull of Pius VI and the zeal of his successor, Gregory XIII, encouraged the flow of Jesuit priests into the realm. The papal action emphasized the almost infinitesimal division between loyalty to the state in the person of the Queen and loyalty to the Catholic Church in the person of the Pope. The great Catholic families of the North had made little secret of their preference for Rome, yet most were English first and Catholic second. Since the tragedy of the Northern Uprising, they had given no evidence of forming a political majority to bring down the government, nor did they support any invasion plans which would result in civil war. The majority were personally against any Catholic "protectors" or "deliverers," either French or Spanish. Even Mendoza, the Spanish ambassador, had to admit that any decisive

---

*Several noted Catholics lived abroad during these years, all the while receiving rents from their estates for their maintenance. In all instances the Queen had refused to have their lands confiscated simply because they were living out of England.[1]

Catholic support during an invasion attempt might be less than he would wish.[2]

The prime reason, therefore, for sending the great number of Catholic missionaries to England during the 1580's was to bolster the lagging faith, to imbue some zeal in lapsing Catholics. Known as the "Enterprise," the movement had as its ultimate purpose the overthrow of Protestantism, and it was vigorously opposed by the English government, which had sought to control Catholic influence and infiltration by declaring it a felony to give lodging to any Jesuit or seminary priest. Fines up to £20 a month were often levied against Catholics for nonattendance at church, a far cry from the one shilling per week levied earlier in Elizabeth's reign. When the Pope subsidized forces comprised of Italian, Spanish and French mercenaries to attack Elizabeth's government in Ireland, England's vulnerability to any organized offensive was apparent.[3]

The Queen personally did not feel herself in any great danger, but her confidence was not shared by her intimates. "Nothing in the world grieveth me more than to see her Majesty believes that this increase of Papists in her realm can be no danger to her," wrote Leicester to Walsingham. "The Lord of His mercy can open her eyes to suffer the depths of her wisdom to look into the matter. If she suffer this increase but one year more, as she hath done these two or three past, it will be too late to give or take counsel to help it."[4]

Nor did the Queen fear any great Catholic uprising. She felt the danger had been activated primarily by the missionaries, English exiles and professional troublemakers, and there lay the real difficulty. How was it possible to ascertain those in England or abroad who were promoting the dissension which worked for her overthrow? One result of this difficulty had been the perfection of a superior espionage system, a necessary concomitant of all courts, by Sir Francis Walsingham, the Queen's able Secretary. The system was widespread, and English spies were deemed among the cleverest in Europe. They were a testament to the absolute will, the dedicated Puritan zeal and the complete lack of conscience of Walsingham. The Secretary had succeeded in placing men "in thirteen different parts of France, seven in Holland, nine in Germany, five in Spain and three in Turkey."[5] He had even placed an "observer" in the College of Cardinals in Rome. Many Englishmen in the French and Roman seminaries who professed a conversion to the Roman Catholic faith actually were there to divulge the secrets of priests scheduled to return to England. On their arrival in England these priests were watched from the moment they entered the country, followed to the various Catholic families, where, after performing their service, they were further observed as they traveled throughout the realm. In this way, many Catholic families came under government surveillance. Realizing their danger and disapproving of the Enterprise in general—which they regarded as nothing more than the overthrow of the monarchy and the sacrifice of the nation to the Church—many Catholics even sent emissaries to Rome to plead that the royal tolerance could not be expected to remain unprovoked; they maintained that the "whole policy of the Jesuits was a blunder."[6] Others welcomed the surreptitious visits by those priests, who at times served as not only religious comforters, but political agitators as well. It was unfortunate that under the label of "Catholic" lay two diverse factions which the government itself had no way of separating. The end result was that many loyal English Catholics were to suffer for the dangerous activities of the fanatical few.

By 1584 it had become necessary for Elizabeth's ministers to know primarily the true extent of Catholic persuasion and, secondly, the nature of the Scottish Queen's influence. While none abroad had, in her seventeen years of captivity, outwardly raised a finger to assist Mary Stuart, the success of Catholic infiltration and the discovery of various plots had changed her status accordingly. Suddenly the heiress apparent was viewed with more interest abroad; only the life of Elizabeth, the heretic Queen, lay between Mary and the English throne. The result was the active and public persecution of the Jesuit priests by the government. Quickly they were apprehended and brought to London, often accompanied by members of the families who had received and harbored them.

One of the first was Edmund Campion, a "man of great wit and charm." One hot July evening in 1581, the forty-one-year-old priest was captured in Berkshire. A graduate of Oxford and a former protégé of Leicester's, he had delivered an oration to Elizabeth on the occasion of her visit there. The Council ordered him to London, where he was incarcerated in "Little Ease" in the Tower, a chamber so small there was no room in which to stand up or lie down. Several days later, probably at the instigation of Leicester, he was brought to Leicester House, where he met with his former patron, several of the Council and the Queen herself. Campion had previously written a tract, *Ten Reasons Against the Anglican Church*, which he had addressed to the English Council, foolishly challenging them with the information that the Jesuits have "made a league . . . cheerfully to carry the Cross you shall lay upon us, and never to despair of your recovery, while we have a man left to enjoy your Tyburn, or to be racked with your torments, and consumed with your prisons. The expense is reckoned, the 'Enterprise' is begun! It is of God; it cannot be withstood. So the Faith was planted; so it must be restored." To Elizabeth personally, he had addressed himself: "Make thyself worthy of thy ancestors, worthy of thy genius, worthy of thy praises, worthy of thy fortune. . . ! There will come, Elizabeth, the day which will show thee clearly which have loved thee, the Society of Jesus or the offspring of Luther!"[7]

The priest and the Queen now confronted each other. It had been fifteen years since that glorious royal visit to Oxford when Edmund Campion had last seen Elizabeth Tudor. In those years the reality of his faith and the exaltation of his mission had made the priest one of the noblest representatives of the Catholic religion. Not unlike an earlier devotee of fifty years earlier, Sir Thomas More, he confronted Majesty with the simplicity and zealous enthusiasm for his own spiritual belief which would not be shaken. He willingly, almost eagerly, answered the Council's questions, but in his very docility was evident a dogged determination not to be swayed. When it was obvious his interrogators were getting nowhere, Elizabeth herself asked the man if he acknowledged her as his Queen? Gently and with conviction, Campion answered that he did, saying, "Not only for Queen, but for my *lawful* Queen!" Elizabeth then asked "if he considered that the Pope could excommunicate her lawfully?" Evasively, Campion stated that "it was not for him to decide in a controversy between her Majesty and the Pope. . . ."[8] Lord Burghley then leaned forward to ask what later captive priests would call the "bloody question." In essence, it asked the priest if a Catholic invasion should be attempted in England, whom would he support—Pope or Queen? Campion refused a direct answer, merely stating, "I would do as God would give me grace," and he reiterated he was a priest with a mission to save souls and not engage in seditious activities.

The Queen realized that very likely Campion was speaking the truth. He himself was not a political agitator, but a gentle, honest spiritual being, intent only on strengthening the faith which was his life. Quickly, she told him she did not believe he meant to endanger her personally, but he must also recognize the threat he presented to the English church. She had a proposition for Campion, she said, and she hoped he would listen. She wished him no harm, but he must show that he wished *her* no harm. If he would attend one Protestant church service, and it need only be *one,* the Queen emphasized, then he might go free. She had no more than finished her words, however, when she realized Campion was a lost man. He disdained the bargain, refusing to answer, merely gazing at her with a penetrating stare that made her acutely uncomfortable. Quickly, the Queen arose, signifying the interview was at an end, and Campion was returned to the Tower.

There he was racked unmercifully in an effort to gain information of his activities and the names of those who had given him shelter. Later he was brought to trial in Westminster Hall, where, because of his dislocated joints, he could neither raise his hand nor stand without assistance. In his own defense, he uttered the memorable words which must have made many present, who had once professed Catholicism, ill at ease: "The only thing that we have now to say is that, if our religion do make us traitors, then we are worthy to be condemned, but otherwise are and have been as true subjects as ever the Queen had. In condemning us, you condemn all your own ancestors, all the ancient priests, bishops and kings—all that was once the glory of England—the island of saints and the most devoted child of the See of Peter. For what has he taught, however you may qualify with the odious name of treason, that they did not uniformly teach? To be condemned with these old lights not of England only, but of the world by their degenerate descendants is both glory and gladness to us. God lives; posterity will live; their judgment is not so liable to corruption as that of you who are now going to torture us to death. . . ."[9] And with the ending of his words, he and his companions commenced to chant the "Te Deum."

Several days later, Edmund Campion and his fellow priests were taken to Tyburn to suffer the monstrous fate of traitors. Again like their fellow martyr Sir Thomas More, they approached the hour of their death with joy and almost humorous exaltation. Several were even seen to kiss the executioner's bloody hands. Always before, when nearing Tyburn, Campion "would pass bare-headed and making a deep bow, both because of the sign of the Cross and in honour of those martyrs who had suffered there, and also because he used to say that he would have his own combat there." Now, as he prepared to experience the first dreadful part of his punishment, he stopped under the gallows to pray for the Queen. Someone in the crowd called out, "Which Queen?" to which Campion answered, "For Elizabeth! For your Queen and mine!" The rope was then put around his neck, and then, mercifully, he was left there to dangle in space. Instead of having him cut down alive, to experience the disemboweling and quartering while still conscious, someone in authority had quietly given the word to wait until Campion was dead before carrying out the last part of the sentence.*

Someone, either Leicester or the Queen, had remembered from an earlier time the bright, beautiful face and spirit of Edmund Campion.

*Edmund Campion was beatified by Leo XIII in 1886.

Even though he had not chosen to cooperate with them, preferring the martyr's fate, in memory of that happier time, they apparently had granted one last mercy to the man who would do nothing to help himself.

News of the martyred Catholic priests spread swiftly, evoking memories of Mary Tudor's persecution of the Protestants twenty-five years previously. In vain did Burghley protest that no Catholic had been or would be punished for Catholic *opinion*. In vain did Elizabeth command "that never a Catholic should be troubled for religion or supremacy so long as they lived like good subjects."[10] Unfortunately, the degree of difference between politics and religion was tiny indeed, and with the exposure of intrigue and purported treason, absolute allegiance was considered necessary for the preservation of the Crown and the safety of the monarch. There were to be no exceptions.

One who chose to consider himself an exception was soon called before the Council, where Lord Burghley, particularly, found the session painful. Burghley had always favored Spain over France; his early training and background could hardly have made it otherwise. With the full disclosure of the Catholic conspiracies, however, Burghley was forced to listen to the Council's diatribe directed to Mendoza, the Spanish ambassador, with whom the Queen professed herself to be greatly dissatisfied "regarding his conduct." His transgressions were spelled out: "He had communicated with the Queen of Scots, encouraging her to rely on Spain, and contrived with her to escape. He had helped the Jesuits, corresponding with such traitors as Throckmorton and Northumberland, aided others, his home had also been a rendezvous for priests." All this, he was told, her Majesty had tolerated, but she would tolerate it no longer and he was ordered to quit the country in fifteen days.

Outraged, Mendoza protested his innocence and angrily challenged Walsingham to prove his charges. Rather than insult *him*, cried the volatile Spaniard, the English Queen should look to her own actions! She had lent money to revolutionaries in the Netherlands, protected sailors who looted Spanish vessels and retained stolen Spanish monies. He protested he could not possibly leave England unless King Philip commanded him to do so. Whereupon the English Council rose as one body and, leaving no doubt of their sincerity, informed the embattled ambassador he must leave at once. He was a disgrace to his King, they said and he "should congratulate himself that her Majesty had not ordered him to be chastised."[11]

This was too much for the almost-speechless Mendoza. Affronted, he answered that he would be responsible to Philip for his own conduct and that "none else should touch him unless with sword in hand." He accused the Queen of sacrificing her best friend, "but being a woman, she was acting after her kind." Bitterly, he strode from the room, saying since he had not pleased her as a minister of peace, perhaps he would in the future satisfy her better as a minister of war. Later he comforted himself, writing to Spain, "The insolence of these people so exasperates me that I desire to live only to be revenged upon them. I hope in God the time will soon come and that He will give me grace to be an instrument in their punishment. I will walk barefoot over Europe to compass it...."[12]

Another possessing a similar desire was William Parry. Parry held a minor court position, possibly obtained through the influence of a near kinsman, Thomas Parry, Elizabeth's late Comptroller. As a result of a quarrel and the subsequent murder of a creditor, Parry was convicted, but influential intervention at court allowed him to go abroad until his crime was conveniently forgotten. There, to recover some degree of favor, he agreed to act as a spy for Sir Francis Walsingham. He insinuated himself into the good graces of the Jesuits and, in so doing, seems to have experienced some measure of compunction for his unsavory past. In a wave of remorseful enthusiasm, he agreed to expatiate his sins by returning to England, where, because of his entry at court and his knowledge of Elizabeth's habits, he would find it easy to assassinate her. On his way home he met Thomas Morgan, Mary Stuart's Paris agent, who encouraged him in the plan, even introducing him to the Papal Nuncio, who promised Parry a Papal dispensation for the act.

Once back in England, this scoundrel, whose mental processes were even then deteriorating, returned to court to be near the Queen. He bided his time, waiting for the auspicious moment—and sufficient courage—to dispatch his sovereign. Daily he watched Elizabeth as she walked in nearby St. James's Park or in the Palace gardens. Later, as conscience asserted itself, he said that "he had felt so strong an impulse to murder the Queen that he had ... left his dagger at home when summoned to her presence, lest he should set upon and slay her!"[13] On another occasion, as he came close enough to stab her easily, he said he had been so appalled by her likeness to Henry VIII that he could not strike the fatal blow.

For more than a year this semi-fanatic calmly walked the halls of Westminster and Whitehall, and finally, through the influence of friends of his former wives, whose dowries he had dissipated, he obtained a seat in Parliament. During one session while there was discussion of a bill recommending that all Jesuits and seminary priests be ordered to quit the realm in forty days, after which they would "suffer as traitors" and those who harbored them would be "hanged as felons," Parry remembered his friends abroad, and torn between loyalty and expediency, he became visibly distraught. He rose and argued that the bill was "full of blood, danger, despair and terror to the English subjects of this realm. . . ." It was also "full of confiscations—but unto whom?" he cried. Indignantly, Parry was asked to state the reasons for his behavior. Whereupon he merely repeated his former words. His reasoning bore more than a modicum of truth and sat uneasily on the consciences of several of his fellow lawmakers. Nevertheless, he was brought for questioning to the bar, where he weakly pleaded ignorance of Parliamentary procedure and, with a stern warning, was soon discharged.

He spent the summer with another malcontent, Edmund Neville, to whom he babbled of his Catholic friends on the Continent. He even showed the Papal dispensation which he had received for the Queen's murder. Bitterly he spoke of his treatment in the Parliament and again turned to the assassination of Elizabeth, which he predicted would be welcome, "for the world was weary of her." Neville listened with an eye to his own profit. At last he determined that more would be forthcoming if he played the role of the informer. Therefore, for the "discharge of his conscience" he went to the Council and revealed the "traitorous and abominable intention."[14]

Parry's instant arrest followed, and threatened with the rack, he disclosed everything. He spoke of his connection with Thomas Morgan; he admitted the receipt of a Papal dispensation and his communication with other priests and cardinals. Tried before a special commission, he pleaded guilty. Several days later, before a howling mob in Palace Yard, he "summoned Queen Elizabeth's answer for my blood before God!"[15] before he was hanged, drawn and quartered.

The extent of the Catholic conspiracy was emphasized by a second and this time successful attempt on the life of William of Orange, the great Protestant leader in the Netherlands. A full account of the religious plots against Elizabeth had been circulated throughout England and abroad, and with the death of Orange, the Queen of England, Defender of the Faith, now took her place as the next foremost target.

The shock of Orange's death, the disclosure of the Throckmorton and Parry plots left little doubt of the Queen's constant danger. "I know of no creature that breathes whose life standeth hourly in more peril for religion than mine own," she said.[16] Yet she refused to listen to the remonstrances of her ladies, of Burghley or Leicester or to the pleadings of Hatton, to take more security for her person. She went her way as before with that fatalistic disdain which is the burden of all royalty. She disregarded advice that her bodyguard be enlarged, that her public audiences be diminished or done away with altogether, declaring that she'd as soon be dead if she were to be held such a captive or deprived of that close communication with her people which was her very breath of life. Her own stalwart courage and determination not to be undone by rumors were evident as she defiantly walked in the Westminster and Whitehall parks and gardens, as she continued to receive visitors or rode through the City streets. Her associates did not help. When Walsingham brought a sheaf of espionage reports detailing stray bits of information about allegedly seditious activities at home and abroad, Elizabeth glanced at them and soberly advised him "not to let his imagination run away with him." To those who professed admiration for her unquenchable courage, the hardening of her face and firm gaze answered the unasked question: What would they have her do otherwise?

Yet Elizabeth was human enough to know fear. She knew Pope Gregory XIII had upheld the Bull of his predecessor and had further said that "as touching the taking away of that impious Jezebel . . . know ye we do not only approve the act, but think the doer, if he suffer death simply for that, to be worthy of canonisation!"[17] Now, as Elizabeth walked the Palace corridors, she experienced an odd insecurity. Abroad on the river she remembered the day that fool Appletree had discharged a shot wounding her bargeman. She felt uneasy as she walked in ceremonies or rode on horseback or wandered in the very park where Parry had lost his nerve. If such malcontents had infiltrated her very court, where could she be safe?

The result was an increase in nervous strain which had been growing for years. It caused a shortness of breath, made sleep difficult and resulted in a sharpened restlessness which Walsingham said made it difficult for Elizabeth to listen to long speeches or read lengthy dispatches or letters. The Queen had never suffered fools gladly; now they were merely waved away with little show of graciousness lucky to evade more formidable oaths or biting sarcasm. She was ill-humored with her ladies; only those closest to her recognized the hysteria which lay just below the surface of her ill humor.

Fear also gripped the Queen's subjects. They showed an unusual concern for the woman who now appeared frail and vulnerable. They thronged about the Palace gates at the full disclosure of the Jesuit threat and of the Parry plot. One bitterly cold December day, as Elizabeth rode to London from Hampton Court, she and the French ambassador gazed at rows and rows of people as they knelt in the snow and mud and called "a thousand blessings" to the monarch as she passed. Many urged caution and gave stout evidence of their loyalty by wishing her enemies might be destroyed while she was mercifully protected. To which Elizabeth, greatly moved, frequently stopped to thank them "for the affection they manifested for her." To the ambassador she said, as they rode on, she "saw clearly that she was not disliked by all," ending somewhat grimly with her gratitude that not *everyone* wished her dead.

The Queen refused to be deterred from opening her Parliament in 1584 and, clad in crimson gown and robe, rode through the streets in a coach drawn by six magnificent grays, their manes and tails dyed a flaming orange. The jewels in their bridles equaled the flash and glimmer of the pearls and diamonds on the Queen's person. The national feeling for Elizabeth's safety was again evident in the unusual multitude lining the route, cheering the great procession as it clattered by. Their concern was reflected in the stirring opening addresses which caused the Recorder to say, "Before this time I never heard in Parliament the like. . . ." The speeches emphasized the national pride in the Queen under whom they "had enjoyed peace now full twenty-six years, the like whereof, so long together, hath not been seen in any age. . . ."[18] The speakers noted the "civil and intestine troubles" which plagued other nations and peoples. They derided the Pope and "his impudent and most blasphemous Bull," accusing him of "dreaming that he is the monarch of the whole world and that the kingdoms of the earth are in his disposition to be given . . . at his will." Other nations with their murderous wars and personal atrocities were no example to England, they cried. They stressed that should Elizabeth be assassinated, chaos and anarchy would replace decent constitutional government. All those who held their commissions from the Queen—Councillors, Judges, Lord Lieutenants, Justices and countless others—would be powerless. Some measure for the protection of the governmental hierarchy and function, as well as for the person of the Queen herself, must be devised.

The answer was the passage in Parliament of the famous Bond of Association of the Privy Council by which, as Lord Burghley wrote, "all noblemen and other principal gentlemen and officers . . . voluntarily bind themselves to her Majesty's person against all evil willers. . . ." The Bond, which was later formalized by statute, An Act for the Security of the Queen's Royal Person and the Continuance in the Realm of the Peace, forbade acceptance of "any such pretended successor by whom or for whom any such detestable act [*i.e.*, the murder of the Queen] shall be attempted or committed." Such guilty person or persons "would be prosecuted to the death," and those who signed bound themselves "to take the uttermost revenge upon them . . . by any possible means . . . for their utter overthrow and extirpation."[19] The Act itself put it even more bluntly, asserting that "all persons against whom such sentence or judgment shall be given [who] pretend to have or claim the Crown of this realm . . . her Highness's subjects shall . . . pursue to the death every such wicked person. . . ." It further stated that if "any such detestable act shall be executed against her Highness's most royal person, whereby her Majesty's life shall be taken away . . . then every person by or for whom any such act shall be executed . . . shall by virtue of this Act be excluded and disabled forever to have or claim . . . the Crown of this realm."[20] There was little doubt at whom the document was aimed. Henceforth not only would the actual perpetrator of any crime against Elizabeth be condemned to death, but also the beneficiary of that crime would be considered equally guilty. In the Act, the Council served notice to Mary Stuart and those working in her behalf that her royalty would no longer protect her should any danger come to Elizabeth. She would be denied the Crown, and those who supported her claim would be declared traitors, and all would be held responsible for Elizabeth's death.

The Queen professed herself greatly touched at her Parliament's concern. She insisted, however, that no one in England must be judged for acts committed by another without a formal trial. The Bill was reworded to grant such protection; it further stated that it must be proven that the beneficiary had given consent to any crime committed against the Queen.

When the Bond of Association was formalized by statute, Mary Stuart startled everyone by offering to sign as an indication that she wished Elizabeth no harm. She personally wrote to Burghley and Walsingham that she, above everyone else, most desired the English Queen's welfare and prosperity. She wrote to Elizabeth "not to reject the hand of a kinswoman which was frankly and lovingly extended to her."[21]

It is revealing of Mary's natural tendency toward intrigue and her reckless lack of caution engendered by her son's abandonment that at the same time she was offering to sign the Bond of Association and disclaiming all knowledge of any Catholic invasion plan, she was writing the Catholic Sir Francis Englefield in Spain, asking him to inform the Pope and King Philip "that she desired the execution of the great plot and designment to go forward without respect of peril and danger to herself, stating "that she would account her life happily bestowed if by losing it, she would help and relieve the oppressed children of the Church."[22]

Elizabeth had no such aspiration; her own religious feelings were always more political than spiritual. William Allen, founder of the Jesuit college at Douai, said she had no religion at all.[23] Yet many of Elizabeth's commentaries and particularly her written prayers indicate that the Queen believed in a very personal God, and the way to His mercy was unencumbered, as far as she was concerned, by any articles or creeds, sacramental mysteries or "other schemes of salvation." The little shades of difference which others regarded as so important left Elizabeth unmoved.

She had as little tolerance of and respect for many of her own Anglican clergymen as she did for the Catholic priests. When criticism of the inept preachers who cluttered her Church reached a voluble high point, the Queen ordered the removal of "those who have offended." The Bishop of Rochester reminded Elizabeth there were 13,000 parishes in England, and it would be impossible to find a competent preacher for each. "Jesu!" cried the Queen impatiently. "Thirteen thousand is not to be looked for. . . !" She said she knew they were "not to be found," and therefore the Bishops were to find "honest, sober and wise men . . . such as can read the Scriptures and the Homilies unto the people. . . ."[24]

The Queen had long accepted, however, that for national safety and the political security of the country, there must be *one* state religion. The circumstances of her birth had placed her squarely on the side of the Reformation, for it had been her mother's marriage which had caused the rupture with the Roman Church. But Elizabeth had no personal distaste or strong conscience for or against Catholicism. Obviously she distrusted the troublemaking element in her country and the horror the Catholics were perpetrating in the Netherlands. But she just as heartily disliked the sanctimony of the professional Protestant as much as she detested the bigotry of the overzealous Puritan.

With the death of William of Orange, "the deliverer of Holland," the power of Spain in the person of Alessandro Farnese, the Duke of Parma, had become stronger and constituted a greater and more imminent danger to England. There was a tremendous wave of enthusiasm for the persecuted Dutch in their struggle against the

Spanish Inquisition, and pressure was strong for Elizabeth to accept the sovereignty of Holland, Zeeland and Utrecht or an active "protectorship" of the Dutch Republic.

With her own religious sophistication, the Queen had no desire to fight a religious war. In addition, there was her strong reluctance to render open assistance to subjects rebelling against their monarch. Yet it was obvious that she considered subversive assistance something else again. Her main desire where the Netherlands was concerned had always been to keep Philip so diverted he would have little time, money or enthusiasm to work against England. At the same time, she recognized that should Philip lose his sovereignty over the Low Countries, the French might ally with the Dutch and constitute an active hostile power across the "broad ditch" which separated it from England. Yet instinctively the Queen had felt an outright declaration of war would bring disaster to her own nation. It was best to let others do the fighting for her, while she rendered such assistance as would do the most good for England.

With Orange's death, however, and Parma's decision to besiege Antwerp a few weeks later, the situation was presumed lost unless England actively intervened. Burghley firmly recommended that England had little alternative other than outright participation in the Dutch conflict, for with the loss of Orange, "who of all living hath been the greatest stay of his [Philip's] conquest," the valiant Dutch were liable to be ground under the Spanish heel. Once Holland and Zeeland were subjugated, he warned, England would be next. He recommended quick intervention and, to be effective, advised the Queen that her assistance must be given openly, not secretly.

The situation appalled Elizabeth. It meant nothing less than challenging the combined power of Spain, Portugal, Italy and the Pope. Her own ally would be a small nation, now leaderless and growing steadily poorer as its richest cities fell to the Spanish might. She would have to send Englishmen to fight on foreign soil with uncertain odds in their favor. English trade was sure to suffer for the Low Countries were England's principal market. In addition, the question of money plagued Elizabeth. Through her own direction and native thrift, the Queen had scrimped and saved and stolen to amass the funds which constituted her remarkable solvency.* In the years she had saved, she had built up the Navy, strengthened her coastal

*It says much for Elizabeth's careful husbanding of her finances that her credit rating with the Antwerp moneylenders stood so high that she could, on short notice, borrow any amount of money at 5 percent. Philip of Spain, on the other hand, could not borrow any amount of money on any terms.[25]

defenses and established a militia for the defense of the realm.[26] The
thought of dissipating that carefully hoarded money pained the
Queen. There were some who urged that she "meddle no more in the
matter of the Netherlands" and conserve her finances as she reinforced
her borders against a future confrontation. Elizabeth was tempted.
The self-preserving instinct of the Tudor was strong, however, and the
peril of a victorious Spain so near her own borders far outweighed all
arguments. While it went against the grain of the woman who passionately hated war, particularly its cost, it left the sovereign little
alternative but to espouse the Dutch cause.

With the fall of Antwerp, the decision became easier. She told the
Dutch she would assist them "in money and men and must be repaid to
the last farthing when the war is over and until that period must have
solid pledges in the name of a town in each province." She was practical in her approach, stating that if she were to help them, they must
also help themselves to the ultimate of their resources. "You see,
gentlemen," she told their emissaries, "that I have opened the door,
that I am embarking once and for all with you in a war against the
King of Spain. Very well, I am not anxious about the matter. I hope
God will aid us and that we will strike a good blow in your cause."[27]
More important, she informed the Dutch they would have 4,000 soldiers and 400 horses, with the cities of Flushing, Brill and Rammikens
for security.

It was paramount in Dutch minds that the English forces must be
led by someone who would carry the prestige of the English Crown to
inspire the armies to give their best in the battle against Spain. As far as
the Dutch were concerned, there was only one gentleman of the realm
who fulfilled every attribute they had in mind, and that was Robert
Dudley, the Earl of Leicester. Leicester was known throughout Europe
as a very great Lord, a man of tremendous influence and one occupying
an unusual and notable intimacy with the Queen of England. His very
presence in the Netherlands would be a tremendous psychological
deterrent to the enemy and would indicate a determination of
Elizabeth's part that minor political maneuvering and evasionary
tactics were no longer part of the game. Leicester's presence would be a
significant guarantee that England was there to win.

Leicester was eager and anxious to go. The distribution in England
of a debatably unsavory book which came to be known as *Leicester's
Commonwealth* had made the Earl an uncomfortable focal point. The
book mixed salacious gossip and vindictive presumptions with just
enough known fact to present a deadly and defamatory diatribe. First
issued in Antwerp, copies had been smuggled into England to be

eagerly read by Leicester's friends and foes alike. Its pages contained a resume of Robert Dudley's alleged crimes, beginning with the murder of his wife, Amy Robsart, continuing through the poisoning of Sir Nicholas Throckmorton, the attempts on Simier's life and the poisoning of the Earl of Essex so he, Dudley, might wed Essex's widow. The Earl was accused of high-handed practices in placing his friends, relatives and associates in positions of power, of thwarting the Queen's marriage plans, of switching his religious affiliations with ever an eye to his own welfare, of debauching Douglass Sheffield and of continually preying on Elizabeth's goodwill and affection. The book was careful to praise the Queen for having the good sense not to marry him. After accusing Leicester of every known crime from theft through murder and treason, it concluded with: "He hath nothing of his own, either from his ancestors or out of himself, to stay upon in men's hearts or conceits; he hath not ancient nobility as others of our realm have, whereby men's affections are greatly moved." And as for courage, the book was succinct: "He hath as much as a mouse."[28]

In addition to the enormity of the charges, of which he was well aware there was some justification, Leicester was eager to leave England for other reasons. He was happy enough in his marriage, but his wife's behavior had often angered and worried him as it bore directly on his relationship with Elizabeth. Lettice was still denied admittance to the royal chambers, where her husband was eagerly awaited each day. Instead of acting as a restraint, Elizabeth's decree that the Countess of Leicester was unwelcome at court seems only to have encouraged Lettice to goad the Queen in other ways. One observer has left a picture of the Countess, reveling in her position as wife of one of the foremost peers: "She rides through Cheapside drawn by four milk-white steeds with four footmen in black velvet jackets and silver bars on their backs and breasts, two knights and thirty gentlemen before her, and coaches of gentlewomen, pages and servants behind her, so that it might be supposed to be the Queen or some foreign Prince or ambassador. . . ."[29] Leicester had even gone so far as to plead with Lord Burghley to intercede for Lettice. Even though her minister's remonstrances had not softened Elizabeth's attitude, Leicester wrote his thanks "that it please you so friendly and honourably to deal in the behalf of my poor wife. For truly, my Lord, in all reason, she is hardly dealt with. God must only help it with her Majesty . . . for which, My Lord, you shall be assured to find us most thankful to the uttermost of our powers. . . ."[30]

In addition to the deep rancor existing between his wife and Queen, the death of his little son, the four-year-old Lord Denbigh, a few weeks after Orange's assassination had saddened Leicester. It was the only child of his marriage to Lettice, and he realized there were not liable to be any more. He was nearly fifty-two, and his wife some eight years younger. He yearned to be away from the atmosphere of the court which had suddenly grown stale. But he soon realized the largest part of the challenge facing him was not the advancing of England's cause in the Netherlands, but the actual withdrawal from the side of his sovereign.

It was not easy. For Elizabeth it was an extremely agonizing decision. The knowledge that she was going against her oft-expressed refusal to assist rebels against their monarch, that English blood and English money must be spent tormented the Queen night and day. She had promised £125,000 to maintain her soldiers and their beasts, and in addition to compromising her innermost beliefs and the dispersal of her hoarded monies, she was now faced with the loss of Leicester. The fact that the Earl had little military experience seemed to bother no one, least of all the gentleman himself. If Elizabeth wondered at his competence, she did not say so. As for the Dutch, they wanted a symbol of Elizabeth's resolve to help, and in the Earl of Leicester, they knew they had one.

But any grandeur inherent in her intervention in the Netherlands was lost on Elizabeth. To the intrigues and plots against her life, the worsening plight of Mary, Queen of Scots, the usual everday responsibility of running her realm were now added the tension of war preparation and its existing responsibilities. She saw her Councillors and minor underlings puffed with their own importance as they grandly spent her money in a campaign which would challenge the might of Spain, and she knew she must exert all her energy and efforts to keep the situation under control. But the fact that her Robin, her "Two Eyes," was leaving was almost too much. In one of those several moments in her life when Majesty and sovereignty fell from her like a discarded cloak, Elizabeth became a woman losing her man to the wars. She collapsed; she wept; she raged; she became childlike with tears which gave ample evidence of her suffering. Each episode would be followed by a period of melancholy and depressed withdrawal which galled her ministers, as well as Leicester himself. She kept him constantly uncertain. One day he would go; the next he would stay. And in the Netherlands, a commander, Saint-Aldegonde, bitterly complained "that it was foolishness to expect help from a woman and that woman the most variable and uncertain in the world!"[31]

In addition, the "variable woman" must know Leicester's exact intentions. She must approve the circumstances of his going, the strength of his train, and the brilliance of the spectacle he would present. It accounted for hours of discussion and weeks of delay. And always Elizabeth refused to pay for anything but the barest minimum. When Leicester had had his fill of Majesty's parsimony, he wrote to Burghley, "For if her Majesty be not persuaded and fully resolved that the cause is of other importance than, as it were, to make a show and become only a scarecrow, it were better never to enter into it." When he realized that Elizabeth was not going to underwrite the project to the extent he thought necessary, he mortgaged part of his lands to her for funds which went toward equipping and outfitting a proper entourage.

Leicester said the money lent by the Queen on his "prize lands" made her the gainer and him the loser. He guessed that Elizabeth had hoped to make it difficult for him and thus "discourage me from her service." But the ruse had not worked. However, he allowed himself the luxury of sarcasm in a letter to Walsingham, saying, "I pray you to remember that I have not had one penny of her Majesty towards all these charges of mine—not one penny—and by all truth I have already laid out about £5,000. Well, let all this go. It is like I shall be the last shall bear this, and some must suffer for the people." And with this pious admonition, Leicester closed the letter with the comment "Good Mr. Secretary, let her Majesty know this, for I deserve God-a-mercy at least!"[32]

When the Queen had about given in, she heard that Lettice was planning to accompany her husband to the Netherlands, and she used the episode to stay the endeavor once more. Walsingham wrote to William Davison in the Low Countries, "I see not her Majesty disposed to use the services of My Lord of Leicester. There is great offense taken at the conveying down of his Lady." Leicester hurried to court to see the Queen.

He found her frail and tearful. As he later wrote to Walsingham:

> She makes the cause not only the doubtfulness of her own self, by reason of her oft disease taking her of late and this last night worst of all. She used very pitiful words to me for her fear that she shall not live and would not have me from her. You can consider the manner of persuasion this must be to me from her. . . . I would not say for any matter, but did comfort her as well as I could, only I did let her know how far I had gone in preparation. I do think for all this that if she be well tonight, she will let me go, for she would not have me speak of it to the contrary to anybody. . . .[33]

For six days Leicester waited, vexed, changing plans, writing letters to those he wished with him, arranging for armor, horses, steel saddles, tents, munitions and the vessels to convey them, all the while cognizant that the whimpering woman who was his Queen might cancel the plans at the very last moment. Elizabeth's depression and fear were real. "Unless God give her Majesty another mind," wrote Walsingham to Leicester, "it will work her and her subjects' ruin." To which Leicester wrote dejectedly in reply, "This is the strangest dealing in the world . . . for my own part I am weary of life and all."

It took two months for Elizabeth to make up her mind. At last, on December 8, 1585, Leicester was given permission to embark. He had, however, the natural caution and worry of one who would be absent for so long a period. A fall from a horse had given him a "shrewd wrench" and kept him in bed for several days, and he had assessed the disadvantages of absence from the Council, where influences he would be powerless to combat might be used against him. He put his thoughts to paper in a letter to Lord Burghley startling in its frankness. He reminded Burghley that he and the Council had agreed "how meet and necessary it was for her Highness to yield aid and assistance for the relief of those afflicted countries. . . ." Leicester was candid, stating that "in so great an absence and such a service," he hoped to rely "upon your particular good will and regard of myself." His knowledge and tolerance of Elizabeth's vacillation were evident in his words: "Her Majesty, I see, My Lord, often time doth fall into mislike of this cause and sundry opinions it may breed in her withal, but I trust in the Lord, seeing her Highness hath thus far resolved and grown also to this far execution. . . ." He was comforted by Burghley's reply assuring him "no less a portion of my care and travail for many respects to the furtherance of your own honour than if I were a most near kinsman in blood. . . ."[34]

And so, with his wife sulking in enforced retirement at home, his heart aching for the loss of his son, his monarch petulant, ill and wavering in her Palace, the Earl of Leicester set forth on December 8, 1585, from Harwich. It was a mission outwardly for the advancement of religion, the security of England and the relief of the Dutch. Anyone who knew the Earl well, however, was convinced the expedition would in some way also further enhance the fortunes and fame of Robert Dudley.

Chapter Twenty-four

Once the Earl of Shrewsbury had departed his post, Elizabeth appointed Sir Amyas Paulet as custodian for Mary, Queen of Scots. Paulet ("my Amyas" as Elizabeth called him) was a fanatical Puritan whose rank, Mary Stuart protested, was not sufficient. Rank, as she would later learn, would be the least of her complaints where her new guardian was concerned. Paulet, who had served Elizabeth well as an ambassador to France, was a strict and efficient jailer and one whom his fellow Puritan Walsingham thought especially right for the task.

No choice would have been more unfortuante, however, from the point of view of both captive and custodian. Paulet had no sympathy for Mary's plight, no tolerance of her religion and no compassion for a human spirit as confined and degraded as Mary was, now that her complicity in the Catholic Enterprise was known. A harsh, humorless man, highly conscious of his responsibility, Paulet looked no further than the letter of his commission, aware that he himself would gain in stature with Elizabeth by a keen and inflexible attention to his duties. Both Shrewsbury and Sadler had stretched their commissions to the utmost to provide Mary with as much comfort, homage and small favors as were consistent with their responsibility. Paulet was their exact opposite, and his prime objective, other than the dispensing of Elizabeth's commission, was to rob Mary of every last shred of dignity and honor. The fact that she was royal, sick and under restraint only lent more satisfaction to his task. He wrote Elizabeth with a gratified air, "The indisposition of this Queen's body and the great infirmity of her legs, which is so desperate as herself doth not hope of any recovery, is no small advantage to her keeper who shall not need to stand in great fear of her running away if he can foresee that she be not taken from him by force."

His first step in the subordination of Mary's spirit was to deprive her of the one small remnant of her sovereignty which she so cherished. He ordered the removal of her cloth of estate, which hung above the chair on its dais. Mary watched, quivering with rage, as Paulet's servants silently removed it. Demanding an explanation, she was told that it must be removed since, officially, it had never been allowed. In vain did Mary protest, and finally, collapsing in tears, she reprimanded them until the dais and the chair, minus its cloth, were returned. Defiantly she hung the arms of Scotland on the chair's back.

Once he had indicated in every way possible that Mary was no different in his eyes from any other prisoner of the Queen, Paulet proceeded to treat her like one. Her servants, who had heretofore passed easily in and out of the castle-prisons, were now forbidden to venture outside without a special pass and were searched going out and on their return. Those of her own small retinue, her ladies-in-waiting, secretaries and steward, could not go abroad without a special permit and then only when accompanied by a guard. Mary was ordered to cease dispensing alms to the neighborhood poor by which, said Paulet, "she hath won the hearts of the people. . . ." Her horses were transferred elsewhere, and she herself commanded to remain indoors, deprived of fresh air, exercise and free conversation with other occupants of the Castle. Paulet was gratified by a communication from Elizabeth in which she said, "If you knew, my dear Amyas, how much indebted I feel to you for your unparalleled care, how thankfully I recognize the flawlessness of your arrangements, how I approve your wise orders and safe measures in the performance of a task so dangerous and difficult, it would lighten your cares and rejoice your heart."[1]

The "wise orders and safe measures" also embraced the subject of Mary's mail, and soon it, too, came under severe inspection. Each parcel was opened and thoroughly scrutinized; her letters were read before being passed on to her. Correspondence with her agent and ambassador in France, even her personal friends, was strictly forbidden. She was to be allowed only official correspondence with the French ambassador; no private mail was to be sent or received. With the deprivation of her mail, Mary's one link with the outside world, it was apparent that the Scottish Queen was to be made to realize the extent of her imprisonment and isolation.

Each day a new restriction caused distress among the Queen's staff and disheartened and enraged Mary. She called Paulet "one of the strangest and most *farouche* men she had ever known." There was little in her experience, except for her past association with John Knox, to lend understanding of the stern man who was now her guardian.

During her long captivity, she had not experienced deliberate ill will from those around her or cruelty from such as Paulet, who, in handing her a letter he had first read, would tell her the bad news of her friends which, as he later reported, "was as grateful to her as salt to her eyes."[2]

Mary protested to her jailer and to Elizabeth about her incarceration at Tutbury; the cheerless, forbidding rooms and incessant damp only contributed to her depression and ill health. Paulet wrote Elizabeth that Mary had sworn "she would die in her bad lodgings" and complained of conditions "with other bitter words wherein she was no niggard when moved with passion." It was, therefore, with some degree of pleasure for the Scottish Queen and incredulity for Paulet when Mary was ordered to be removed to Chartley Manor in Staffordshire.

Chartley Manor was especially chosen by Sir Francis Walsingham and was the first step in his deliberate objective of ensnaring Mary Stuart in a web of sufficient strength and complexity to remove her once and for all as any threat to Queen Elizabeth. Chartley was the former home of Lettice Knollys Devereux when she was the Countess of Essex. It was now the inheritance of Lettice's son, the eighteen-year-old Robert Devereux, the Earl of Essex. Robert had been born at Chartley and was especially fond of the timbered manor house set among fields and orchards with a view of distant forests. When his father died in Ireland, young Robert had lived for a time in the household of William Cecil, Lord Burghley, where he had the company of Burghley's young son, Robert Cecil. At the age of ten he had been sent to Cambridge, receiving his Master of Arts degree in 1581 at the age of fourteen. During his absences from school, Robert had visited his mother and stepfather at their London home or at Wanstead, but he spent an equal amount of time at Chartley, consulting with his stewards, supervising his tenant farmers and in most respects fulfilling the duties of a young Lord of the manor. He accompanied his stepfather, Leicester, to the Netherlands and, before his departure, violently protested the proposal of the Council to place the Queen of Scots in his residence during his absence. The house and estate were too small for the increased guard, he noted, and since there was no other source of fuel, he worried that he would lose many of the fine trees of which he was so proud. In case Elizabeth and the Council remained unsympathetic, however, he took the precautions of removing "all the beds, hangings, and such like stuffs" to be sent to Lichfield before Mary arrived.

Mary was, to Paulet's disgust, delighted with the change from the formidable Tutbury. Even the rigor of the journey during an exceedingly cold and windy Christmas Eve in 1585, the shabby furniture and her "stained and ill-flavoured bed" which she found upon arrival could not deprive her of the joy of the dry and more spacious rooms. The distance from Tutbury to Chartley was only twelve miles, but the slowness of the horses owing to the icy road conditions was such that the Queen and her ladies arrived weary and half-frozen, and Mary spent the next several weeks in bed with a bad cold. Paulet recorded his disapproval of the move. "You would hardly believe the baggage that this Queen and her company have of books, apparel, and other like trash," he wrote to Walsingham.[3] It took eighty carts to transport the Queen of Scotland satisfactorily to her new residence, reported Paulet, and his tone indicated he clearly considered the whole move sheer nonsense.

Walsingham did not choose to enlighten Sir Amyas of his motive for removing Mary to Chartley. It was more important to the Secretary that the Chartley estates joined those of a Catholic family named Gifford, minor relatives of the Throckmortons, and that access to Chartley was much easier than at Tutbury. While Sir Amyas, puzzled and resentful, wondered at the degree of security he could provide at Chartley, Sir Francis Walsingham, "the most sharp minister of purer religion, a most diligent searcher of hidden secrets,"[4] was making the acquaintance of a "ruined rake," one Gilbert Gifford. Gifford had, at one time, studied at the Jesuit seminaries in Rome and Rheims and, because of his unsavory mode of life, managed to get himself expelled, He joined a small group of expatriate Englishmen, malcontents all, who moved in Catholic circles abroad, urging invasion and alternately threatening to murder the Queen of England, talking with others of similar intent and conjuring up visions of great reward and recognition could they pull off the infamous task to which they had set themselves. With many it remained just talk: "loud brags" and little action. Others, with more than a modicum of serious intent, were fair prey for such as Walsingham, who recognized a rascal when he met one and was quick to ascertain how he might best be used.

In Paris, Gilbert Gifford had met Thomas Morgan, Mary Stuart's agent, and was aptly assessed as one who might be employed to further any scheme "to remove the beast that troubles all the world." Gifford agreed to act in Mary's behalf. Arriving in England to ascertain how he might communicate with the Scottish Queen, he was arrested by Walsingham's agents and brought before the Secretary. He was quick to discern the situation and, with an eye to his own pocket and freedom, decided to double-cross Morgan. It is also possible that he had been in Walsingham's employ when he contacted Morgan in

Paris. In any event, he agreed to act as an *agent-provocateur*, to appear as Mary's friend, gain her confidence, as well as that of her friends, and so help lure her into Walsingham's trap.

It was almost pitifully easy. Gifford was introduced to another of Walsingham's spies, Thomas Phelippes, a man "of low stature, slender every way, eaten in the face with small pocks, of short sight, thirty years of age. . . ."[5] Phelippes was well traveled and educated, a man adept in ciphers, not only in English, but also in Latin, French and Italian. He was also an accomplished forger. He and Gifford obtained lodgings in Leadenhall Market, and within days, Gifford called at the French embassy, where a postbag of Mary Stuart's mail had awaited delivery for almost a year. Despite his credentials from such as Mary's Archbishop of Glasgow, Gifford was regarded with some suspicion. Ultimately, however, his avowals of sympathy for the Scottish Queen and the fact that his knowledge of Chartley and the nearby village gleaned from his youth might prove valuable, he was given a large packet of mail which he promised to deliver to Mary personally.

Mary was less strictly kept at Chartley than she had been at Tutbury. There were, to be sure, thirty-eight armed soldiers on the premises at all times. Because Paulet wished Mary to be unable to signal anyone, he had, much to her chagrin, put her in apartments which overlooked the inner court rather than the fields and meadows. As Mary was granted small privileges, Paulet worried about security, vexed with Walsingham and the Council who had not dared apprise him that only with fewer precautions might Mary have the opportunity to implicate herself thoroughly and finally. There was, to the guardian's dismay, even a priest in disguise on the premises. Paulet hesitated to act against the intruder, because as he wrote Walsingham, Elizabeth "so dandled the Catholics" he felt she would do nothing. In this he was correct. When the English Queen was informed of the situation, she bade the disgusted Paulet "to let the priest be."[6]

Very soon after Gifford and Phelippes traveled to Chartley, a small miracle occurred. A letter pierced the isolationist barrier which had surrounded Mary Stuart for so many months. The letter, from Thomas Morgan in Paris, informed Mary that Gifford would act as his agent, that she must trust him, and by his assistance, some means of communication might be devised despite the vigilance of Paulet.

Mary was thoroughly unsuspecting and, after months of deprivation and virtually starved for news of her friends and the world outside her prison, could only gaze at the letter with the greatest delight. When she questioned her secretary, Claude Nau, about the method of its arrival, she was told that it had come via a casket of beer from a brewer in nearby Burton. The bunghole of the barrel was stopped by a large cork, and to this it was found easy to attach an innocent-looking waterproof tube which seemed part of the cork itself. In this way, letters might be sent to the Castle, for although the brewer and the barrels were observed upon arrival, no one had ever thought to look *inside* the barrels themselves. Once the barrels were emptied and called for, correspondence might be put in the tube and so sent away from the Castle. The brewer was happy to accommodate and received money not only from Gifford, who had instigated the plan, but also from Mary Stuart's steward, who actually purloined the tube at the first opportunity. He received money from Paulet himself when he threatened to reveal to Mary the danger she was risking by such furtive correspondence.* He also increased the price of beer, scandalizing Paulet, who wrote Walsingham, "The honest man plays the harlot . . . but I must yield to his asking or lose his service. . . ."[8]

The bribery was of small importance, however. The success of the plan was instantaneous, and Mary, excited and buoyed by hope after months of disappointment and illness, replied to Morgan, asking that her mail be forwarded to her. Soon the backlog of letters which had accumulated in London was forwarded, and for the first time in many months, Mary had the priceless privilege of communication with the world outside her courtyard windows. What she did not know was that every letter arriving was first opened, deciphered, read, copied by Phelippes, resealed by another expert, Arthur Gregory, and the copy sent to Walsingham, while the original was then inserted in the beer barrel. The same procedure was adopted for every letter she wrote in reply.

For months, Mary dictated her letters to Claude Nau, her secretary, who then read them to her in French before putting them in cipher, sealing the letter, which was then handed to the steward who would insert it in the beer barrel. Off to Rome, Madrid, Glasgow and Paris went the Scottish Queen's communications. She offered her rights in the English Crown and the Crown of Scotland to Philip if he would help her escape. In letters to the Continent, she urged a Spanish and French invasion, derided her son for his lack of support and begged all who would listen to remain faithful to her.

Although the Queen made little secret of her unhappiness, depression and hatred of her restraint, there was nothing in her correspon-

---

*Not only did the brewer obtain additional money, but so did Gifford, who wrote Mary that while he was "honoured to be of use to her, he was risking his life and deserved a pension" which again scandalized the Puritan Paulet, who wrote Walsingham, "He hath played the wanton in writing to this Queen. . . ."[7]

dence which might be considered treasonous. Cries for help and for-
feiture of Crown rights meant little from a semi-crippled and ailing
prisoner. For several months, Walsingham read Mary's correspondence and on one occasion, while Gifford was in London, complained
that while the communications ruse had worked, there was little in
Mary's letters to implicate her. Apparently, she needed some impetus
to inveigle her more deeply into a position from which she would be
unable to extricate herself and with which Elizabeth and the English
Council would find it impossible to forbear.

Thomas Morgan unwittingly provided that impetus. Among the
Paris acquaintances of Mary's agent was John Ballard, an ex-priest
who had obtained the sanction of the Pope to kill Queen Elizabeth.
Ready to do any bidding for money or as a tribute to whomsoever
could purchase his skill, Ballard violently proclaimed he wished only
Elizabeth's death. He even visited Mendoza, now the Spanish ambassador in France, informing him of the vast number of Catholics in
England who allegedly would rise on the death of the English Queen.
Charles Paget, acting in Morgan's behalf, wrote to Mary. Calling
Ballard "discreet and honest," he advised that many noblemen and
knights "in the North parts, in Lancashire, the West-country and
divers other shires besides" were only waiting to take arms in Mary's
cause. He stressed that Leicester had "taken all the best Protestants,
captains and soldiers . . ." to the Netherlands, the people were "much
grieved . . . and discontented . . . and the time was now very fit and
proper to give them relief." Inevitably, Ballard was introduced to
Gifford, who, acting the double agent to perfection, revealed the plot to
Walsingham. Immediately, the brain of the minister was aflame with
the possibilities. Mary might use the beer-barrel method for relatively
harmless communications forever. Ballard might be the means of
bringing her to a much-desired end.

With the unerring eye of the conspirator, Ballard picked Sir
Anthony Babington, a twenty-five-year-old Derbyshire gentleman, as
the catalyst by which the plot might be forwarded. Babington was rich,
well educated and well traveled, as enduring a Catholic as he was an
idealistic dreamer. He was a familiar sight at court, where, with "his
enchanting manners and wit" and despite his Catholicism, he was very
welcome. The personable Babington was an easy prey for Ballard; the
ex-priest soon revealed the plot to rescue Mary and so instigate a
Catholic uprising in England. Babington was typical of the younger
Catholic generation, who did not remember Kirk o' Field or the
Catholic compromise in Scotland, and he regarded Mary, Queen of
Scots, as a martyr to the Catholic faith in England as much as to the

personal animosity of the heretic Elizabeth. The two conspirators met often in Babington's lodgings in Herne's Rents, and soon the impressionable young gentleman's energies and pocketbook were firmly committed.

Ballard told Babington that not only was Queen Mary aware and eager for the conspiracy to proceed, but also the Duke de Guise, the Prince of Parma and the Pope all were engaged in raising troops to assist Mary once Elizabeth was in her grave. When Babington asked who was to murder the Queen of England, he was told that John Savage, an ex-soldier, had "vowed the performance." Within days, moved by no motive other than devotion to his religion, chivalry toward Mary Stuart and an overdose of honorable intention, Babington was drawn into the plot. He brought with him several other attractive young gentlemen from about the court: Thomas Salisbury, Chidiock Tichborne, Charles Tilney, Robert Barnwell and Edward Abington. All were equally blinded by religious sincerity and devotion to the Scottish Queen from realizing the futility of the mad undertaking to which they had pledged themselves.

Walsingham was delighted with Gifford's revelations. He could, of course, have arrested the conspirators then and there, but the Secretary was pursuing a larger quarry than a group of young hotheaded zealots. Mary *might* be deemed guilty under the Bond of Association simply because the men were working in her behalf, but Walsingham doubted he could make a strong enough case on the proceedings thus far. He wanted Mary's assent to Babington's suggestions, and he prodded Gifford, who, amply supplied by funds from Walsingham, in turn prodded Babington. He passed many an evening with Sir Anthony and his companions in the Cheapside taverns, encouraging them as they argued the merits of their scheme. And suddenly the amateurish plot, which might have dissolved through sheer lack of enterprise if let alone, took on the polish of the professional.

By the end of June Babington had written to Mary Stuart informing her of two packets of mail which the obliging Gifford had acquired from the French embassy. Mary wrote in reply, calling Babington "my very good friend," and in a wave of enthusiasm at her communication, Babington answered the innocent note from the Queen, whom he addressed as "Most Mighty, most Excellent, most Dread Sovereign Lady and Queen. . . ." He spoke of her desperate situation "in the custody of a wicked Puritan" and his plans to relieve her. His remedy encompassed pages of plans which had been discussed in his lodgings and taverns with his fellow conspirators: the planned invasion, the ports to be used, those who would assist the invaders, the "deliverance"

of Mary and, most important, "the despatch of the usurping competitor, Elizabeth." He asked for Mary's thoughts and advice, assuring her
that "myself with ten gentlemen and a hundred of followers will
undertake the delivery of your royal person from the hands of your
enemies" and noted that "for the despatch of the usurper . . . there will
be six noble gentlemen, all my private friends who, for the zeal they
bear to the Catholic cause and your Majesty's service, will undertake
the tragical execution." He said he would be at Lichfield on July 12 to
await Mary's answer.[9]

Mary could scarcely believe the words which promised everything
she desired—freedom and a resumption of her sovereign power. She did
not question the intent of the ardent young gentleman from that
segment which still held the Catholic faith dear. Through him might
lie her path to *freedom*. Even the importunities of her secretary, Claude
Nau, not to answer the letter made little impression, for even he could
not state clearly the reasons for his foreboding.

Mary did not share Nau's apprehensions. Elizabeth had immured
her for years, had rendered her helpless and ineffective, had seduced
her son from her cause and degraded her before the eyes of the world.
She, a Queen of Scotland and a former Queen of France, had every
right to pursue any cause which would result in her freedom. She
regarded Babington's letter not primarily as an instrument for
Elizabeth's execution but as a means of regaining that freedom. If an
assassination happened as a by-product of her struggle to be free, it was
no more than the English Queen deserved. Mary did not think of
herself as conspiring for Elizabeth's life; she was conspiring for her own
liberty. She was doing nothing which any good English Catholic and
every Catholic abroad, English or otherwise, would not feel justified in
doing.

And so, over Nau's objections, Mary answered Babington's letter.
Never once did it occur to her that everything the conspirators suggested could be carried out without her permission. Never once did it
occur to her that in making her privy to their plans, they were placing
her in great jeopardy. Even Morgan was imprudent enough to write
Mary's secretary, saying, "There be many means at hand to remove the
beast that troubles all the world," and to Mary herself he wrote plainly
"that there were good members attending upon opportunity to do the
Queen of England a piece of service which, if it pleased God to lend
assistance, he trusted would quiet many things."

While Mary deliberated over her reply to Babington, in an adjoining chamber, Thomas Phelippes deciphered other communications
and, on July 14, wrote to Walsingham, "We attain her very heart at the

next." In a mood of quiet jubilation and in order that he might not be misunderstood, he drew the sign of the gallows ⌐⌐ on the covering fold of the letter.

In her reply, which took several days to write, Mary Stuart sealed her fate. After urging Babington to keep in communication, she referred to the numbers of "foot and horse" to be involved in the enterprise, the nobles who might help and the towns and ports of which Babington must make certain. She noted the foreign assistance needed, the provision of "money and armour" which had been made, the plans of his accomplices and advised that such information be sent to the Spanish ambassador, Mendoza, in France. She then wrote, "The affairs being thus prepared and forces in readiness both without and within the realm, then it shall be time to set the six gentlemen to work, taking order that, upon the accomplishment of their design, I may be suddenly transported out of this place, and that all of your forces in the same time be on the field to meet me in tarrying for the arrival of the foreign aid, which then must be hastened with all diligence."[10]

Once Mary had dictated her thoughts to Claude Nau, the secretary rendered them back to her in French before putting them into cipher. During that time, Mary had pondered how matters might proceed up to her very deliverance without Elizabeth's actual removal from power. She suggested to Babington that once free, she must "be set in the midst of a good army or in some very good strength" to await for "foreign succours" or else Elizabeth might recapture her and "in catching me . . . to enclose me forever in some hole, forth of the which I should never escape, if she did use me no worse, and to pursue with all extremity those that have assisted me, which would grieve me more than all the unhap which might fall upon myself." The words are pathetic evidence of just how completely out of touch the Scottish Queen actually was with world affairs. In her desperation, she found it easy to believe that—after eighteen years of imprisonment—the Duke of Parma, the Duke of Guise and hundreds of Catholics were awaiting only her release to rise against Elizabeth.

Mary then suggested an appropriate route near Chartley where "fifty or three score men, well-horsed and armed" might provide a successful ambush. If the barns or stables were set afire to divert Paulet and his soldiers, Mary said she could make her escape, while "you and your company might surprise the house. . . ." The guards' lodgings were half a mile away, Mary wrote, and other diversions, such as delivery carts upset near the entrance, might be utilized, after which other gentlemen, concealed in bushes, "might rush in." Then, having given her benefactor her advice, Mary ordered him to burn her letter immediately. The letter was then sealed and passed to the steward for insertion in the beer barrel. Within moments it was in Phelippes' hands.

As he deciphered the words, however, he felt something was needed. Mary had compromised herself, but he wished the impact of her words to be without any doubt. Therefore, at the very end, copying Nau's script with great dexterity, he inserted a postscript, "I would be glad to know the names and qualities of the six gentlemen which are to accomplish the designment, for it may be I shall be able upon knowledge of the parties to give you some further advice necessary. . . ."

When informed of the letter's contents, Paulet, who had considered the nefarious scheme an affront to his Puritan ethics, cried elatedly, "God has blessed my exertions and I rejoice that He has thus rewarded my faithful service!" Phelippes, too, was jubilant, for Mary had recently written to Paris asking Sir Edward Stafford to intercede with Lord Burghley to provide her with another guardian, "more inclined toward her." Phelippes had written to Walsingham that Mary was "weary of her keeper. She is very bold to make way to the great personages and I fear he [Burghley] will be too forward in satisfying her for her change till he see the Babington treasons!" Phelippes' comments provide undisputable evidence that at this stage of the conspiracy, even Lord Burghley had not been informed of Walsingham's intentions.[11]

At last Walsingham was satisfied. The letter in his hands proved Mary's awareness of, as well as her consent to, the plot to murder Queen Elizabeth. It had taken seven months, during which time the Secretary had often despaired that Mary would ever rise to the bait or that Babington would remain constant. It was a justifiable fear, for on several occasions, Sir Anthony had seemed to lose enthusiasm and only the encouragement of his fellow conspirators kept him to the task. When Babington at last received Mary's letter some ten days after Walsingham had seen it, an uneasy fear had gripped him. For the past several weeks he and his garrulous accomplices had continued their plans as if they were attempting nothing less than the success of a great youthful escapade. Babington had even commissioned a portrait of the group he was certain would later be immortalized as "the deliverers of their country." Beneath the portrait were the words "My comrades these, whom very peril draws!" Now, however, with Mary's letter in his hands, he felt uncomfortable and less confident and, within hours, had decided to talk with Mendoza in Paris. He applied for a passport to the gentleman whose business it was to dispatch such items: Sir Francis

Walsingham. It tantalizes the imagination to wonder at the Secretary's thoughts as he confronted the young man whose correspondence he had been reading for months. On one pretext or another, he detained Babington and by the first week in August was ready to strike.

The first taken was Ballard on the charge that he was a seminary priest in disguise. Fearful that everything would be discovered, Babington rushed to John Savage and ordered that, before Ballard disclosed everything, Savage should make good the deed of which he had been boasting for months—the murder of Queen Elizabeth. Savage replied that he did not have the proper clothing and would, therefore, not be admitted at court. Babington flung him a purse of coins, bade him buy the right clothes and accomplish the deed while there was still little security about the Queen. Then, deducing that Walsingham was more likely now privy to the plot, Babington lost his composure. With four others, he rode in great haste to St. John's Wood, some distance from the City and, disguised as a laborer with his face dyed with walnut juice, ultimately concealed himself in a barn at Harrow.

Walsingham had to act fast. As he wrote Leicester, still in the Netherlands, "My only fear is that her Majesty will not use the matter with that secrecy that appertaineth." The Secretary's fear was justified. He had informed the Queen of as much as he wished her to know, and her attitude had alarmed the minister, for he saw his cunning stratagem jeopardized by her reaction. At one point, before Mary Stuart had written the damning letter which rendered her as guilty as the others, Elizabeth had told the French ambassador, "Sir, you are in frequent communication with the Queen of Scotland. I would give you to know that I am aware of all that goes on in my kingdom. I have myself been a prisoner in the days when my sister Mary ruled this land as Queen and I am, therefore, familiar with the strange expedients used by prisoners to corrupt servants and effect secret communications." Her words may have been a sop to her conscience, but they had to be said. Elizabeth also had a superstitious feeling that "it was her duty to put an end to the evil designs of her enemies while it was in her power to do so, lest, by not doing it, she should seem to tempt God's mercy, rather than manifest her trust in His protection."[12] She had, however, given Walsingham his head, but the minister still did not trust her to pursue the unpleasant business to its logical end.

To acquaint Elizabeth with the seriousness of the plot, she was shown the portrait of Babington and his fellow conspirators which Gifford obligingly brought for her inspection. She recognized several faces usually seen on the fringes of court gatherings. One day, as she walked in Richmond Park with Christopher Hatton and several of her ladies, she saw the Irishman Barnwell loitering nearby. While she did not remember his name, she recognized the swarthy countenance as one of the sitters in the Babington portrait. Quickly she walked in his direction, and looking at him with the penetrating stare, "the piercing eye, wherewith she used to touch what metal strangers were made of. . . ,"[13] she said in a loud voice, "Am I not well guarded today, with no man near me who wears a sword at his side?" The taunt and stare were too much for Barnwell. Whatever mission had brought him to the Queen's presence was quickly forgotten, and as he fled, he was further humiliated to hear Elizabeth's high laugh. The Queen did not divulge his identity to her companions.*

Rumors of assassination, invasion by Parma at Newcastle and Guise at Sussex "and a conspiracy to burn the City of London and murder the Queen" were soon abroad in the City with the predictable result of security preparation among the militia and an angry and frightened excitement among the people. Elizabeth went to Windsor, where she inevitably repaired in time of crisis since it was the one royal residence where a siege might be successfully withstood. The Protestants were fearful of the Catholic invasion, and the Catholics were alarmed because of further persecution if the undertaking proved unsuccessful. The ports were closed as bonfires and the bells of London signaled that once more Elizabeth, the Queen, had escaped an infamous plot to end her life, one designed to put England under foreign jurisdiction. Quickly the conspirators were rounded up, although Babington successfully eluded capture for ten days. After arrest, they were led through the London streets in chains, their arrogance evaporating as the crowd followed them, shouting epithets and curses. Within hours they were locked in the Tower of London, and over the City and the Thames the victorious bells pealed a triumphant coda to their sad and misguided ambition.

With Walsingham's disclosure of Mary Stuart's participation in the plot against her life and Crown, Elizabeth faced the distressing reality of a situation which, in many ways, she had allowed to worsen. Throughout the years of Mary's long captivity, by means not always understood or approved by her Councillors or subjects, she had protected her sister sovereign from English persecution or Scottish reprisal. In championing Mary, especially by her rephrasing of the

*Barnwell recounted this incident in his trial, and Hatton stated that if he had known Barnwell's identity, "he would not have got away as he did."[14]

Bond of Association, she had incurred "the misliking and discontent-ments of our best devoted subjects," she said. The Bond had been formalized by statute; there was now a law without precedent in England, a law which safeguarded its sovereign's life, and Elizabeth knew the grim actuality could be evaded no longer. She, no more than any other, could afford to regard Mary's pathetically misguided at-tempt at freedom as anything other than a bold and unscrupulous move against England's Queen and English law.

In addition, Elizabeth was painfully aware that her tolerance had bred treason within her own household. Of the apprehended con-spirators, Tilney was one of her Gentlemen-Pensioners; Abington was the son of her Under-Treasurer. Jones was the son of her Master of the Wardrobe, and several others had connections in and about the court. She was told that Savage had confessed that he planned to "lurk in her gallery, and stab her with his dagger, or if she should walk in her garden, he might shoot her with his dagg; or, if she should walk abroad to take the air, as she often did, accompanied rather with women than men, and those men slenderly weaponed, then might he assault her with his arming sword, and make sure work; and though he might hazard his own life, he would be sure to gain Heaven thereby."[15]

This knowledge, together with the strain of the war in the Netherlands, left Elizabeth severely depressed. If Mary Stuart's baleful influence were allowed to continue, how long would her own private chambers remain free of conspiracy and intrigue? She spent her fifty-third birthday at Windsor, melancholy, tearful and so quarrelsome that any who could avoided her presence. From all sides, she was besieged with briefs and depositions from Walsingham, whom she regarded with mixed emotions. She hated the Secretary's methods, which, little by little, were coming to light. Elizabeth had had enough experience of plots gained through the sad proceedings of her own youth to wonder: had he not meddled, would the plot have advanced thus far? Then, following on her reflections about Walsingham's methods, dishonest and calculating as they were, was the knowledge that they had also very possibly saved her from what might have been a genuine and successful attempt on her life. With it came the awareness of just how much she owed the minister who continued to place the conspirators' confessions beneath her weary eyes.*

Day after day, as she read the confessions, Elizabeth reviewed the past. She had suffered the Ridolfi plot, tolerated the Throckmorton

---

*All except that of Gifford, who, because of his superlative services was allowed to flee. He went to Paris, where he eventually was ordained a priest with a £100 annual pension from Elizabeth. In December, 1587, he was arrested in a brothel and imprisoned until his death four years later.[16]

plot, fought the Northern Uprising with the consequent loss of many of her noblemen, including that of her kinsman the Duke of Norfolk. She was no longer young, and both she and those around her were destined to be continued prey for the unscrupulous and ruthless ones who would aim at her very throne. All the good and worthwhile for which she had striven to benefit her people was at the constant mercy of anyone who might conspire against her. And if that were not enough, the captive Catholic Queen would remain, apparently, a sad symbol, awaiting only that release which might be obtained through the murderous effort of some of Elizabeth's own subjects.

The more Elizabeth dwelled on the unhappy past, the more her distress and anxiety grew. She reviewed the danger to which she had been subjected, and terror and fright—hugely enlarged in her imagination—suddenly engulfed her. All the many months of risk to which she had exposed herself were remembered. And with that rememberance came an unusual and vindictive desire for revenge. In extreme agitation, she summoned Lord Burghley and ordered that "some new device" be contrived for the prisoners' punishment. Burghley assured the Queen there was nothing more hideous than the hanging, drawing and quartering which all English traitors suffered and advised his royal mistress to content herself with that, with word to the "executioner to take care to protract the extremity of their pains in the sight of the multitude."[17]

On September 20, 1586, Babington and his accomplices were drawn on hurdles to St.-Giles-in-the-Fields. An unusually large crowd had gathered to revile and spit on the prisoners who had dared envision the murder of their Queen. Shouts and curses greeted their last words. Ballard said he had sought "only the advancement of what he called the 'true religion.' " Babington noted that the murder of the Queen had been held up to him as "a deed lawful and meritorious." Tichborne poignantly said he had honestly expected Elizabeth's pardon. All three, secure in their martyrdom, if not in their goal, professed themselves ardent Catholics to the end. Then they were seized, and with the especial instructions that their suffering be long, they were quickly hung, then cut down, thrown to the ground as their bodies were ripped open from neck to groin, their entrails flung into the street, then castrated and slowly hacked to pieces. What might have been done quickly and skillfully to dispatch the unfortunate men under the knife was now prolonged and deliberate. For three hours attention was paid "with due precaution for the protraction of pain." Babington was heard to cry "Jesus!" three times as his heart rested in the executioner's hands.[18] At last, even the crowd, sickened and outraged at the needless

suffering, cursed and threatened the executioner. When the incident
was reported to the Queen, she became ill. Wretchedly, she turned
away but not before ordering that the remaining prisoners scheduled
to die the following day should be hung until dead before they were
mutilated.

Even as the unfortunate conspirators were being racked in the
Tower, word had gone north from Walsingham to secure all possible
evidence which would further implicate the Queen of Scots. Elizabeth,
on the other hand, was equally as desirous that Mary *not* be involved
personally, for she could then foresee she would be forced to act in a
situation which she knew would redound to her own discredit. Yet
even though she had wished only enough evidence to "maintain the
indictment" against the prisoners, Walsingham's evidence proved the
futility and impracticality of any further attempt to shield Mary.

On August 8, therefore, as Walsingham had moved to capture the
conspirators, Sir Amyas Paulet accompanied Mary Stuart on a stag
hunt to be held in the park of Sir Walter Aston of nearby Tixall. With
her guardian, her secretaries, Claude Nau and Gilbert Curle, and
several others of the royal party, the Queen had galloped in high
spirits, pounding over the dry turf in sheer exhilaration at being away
from her restricted quarters. At one point, she thoughtfully stopped to
wait for Sir Amyas to join her, remarking that she had forgotten he was
not feeling well.

Some distance from Tixall, a small group of strangers were seen
approaching. Mary's first thoughts were that they might be Babington's supporters come to set her free. But her hopes were dashed as
Paulet greeted the leader whom he presented as Sir Thomas Gorges, a
Gentleman-Pensioner of Elizabeth's. The stranger dismounted,
walked to where the puzzled Mary sat astride her horse and said,
"Madame, my Queen, my mistress finds it very strange that you,
against the agreement which you made together, have undertaken
against her and her estate what she never would have thought of if she
had not seen it with her own eyes. And as she knows that some of your
servants are guilty, you will not take it ill if they are separated from
you. . . ."[19] As Nau and Curle attempted to ride to Mary, they were
apprehended. Gorges shouted to his companions, "Take them away . . .
take them away! Do not allow them to speak to her!" The secretaries
were quickly surrounded by Paulet's soldiers, who urged them away
from the Queen. Dazed and fearful, Mary watched them go. She could
not know she would never see them again.

Enraged, Mary protested, but to little avail. She was taken to Tixall, where, realizing now how she had been lured deliberately from Chartley, she remained for nine days. Mute and helpless, except for those releasing moments when tears came, she tried to ignore Paulet, whose inexorable gaze held contempt mixed with a touch of triumph. She was refused writing materials and, with nothing to do, could only guess at what must be taking place at Chartley and in London. She had no change of clothing, the house was small and inadequate, and she had no company except her guardian and her conscience. Mixed with fear for her own safety was the sickening awareness that Babington and all those who had assisted her, probably even the brewer at Burton, were now suffering royal condemnation. The knowledge bore on Mary's spirits, which had risen in the previous months, and is apparent in the remark made upon her removal from Tixall. As her presence in the neighborhood had become known, groups of beggars waited at the gates, for Mary's generosity was well known. Weary and despondent, disheveled in her rumpled riding habit, the Queen of Scotland emerged from the courtyard and, in obvious misery, said to the assembled group, "I have nothing for you for I am a beggar as well as you. All is taken from me. . . ."

At Chartley, she found her escritoires, boxes and all her secretaries' possessions thoroughly ransacked. Copies of letters, secretarial notes, lists of ciphers—some sixty in all—had been packed and sent to Walsingham. The chamber was bare of everything she had used and cherished in the eighteen years of her imprisonment. Small pictures of her family, of her French relatives, even of Elizabeth were gone. Her jewelry, such as it was, had been confiscated. Every scrap of paper, much of it innocent, had vanished. Only a small sum of money had been left untouched. Angrily she confronted Paulet and said, in tears, "Two things you cannot take from me—my English blood and the Catholic religion which I will keep 'till my death!"

Paulet was pleased to find a note from his sovereign: "Amyas, my most faithful and careful servant, God reward thee treblefold in the double for thy most troublesome charges so well discharged. If you knew, my Amyas, how kindly, besides most dutifully, my grateful heart accepts and prizes your spotless endeavours and faultless actions, your wise orders and safe regard, performed in so dangerous and crafty a charge, it would ease your travails and rejoice your heart. . . ." Elizabeth advised Paulet to "let your wicked murderess know how, with hearty sorrow, her vile deserts compel these orders and bid her from me, ask God's forgiveness for her treacherous dealing towards the saviour of her life many a year. . . ."[20]

Within days, Elizabeth wrote to Mary herself, a secret communication in which she said that if Mary would confess her guilt and ask forgiveness, no further action would be taken against her. "It was not to entrap her," Elizabeth later stated, and there is little reason to doubt the English Queen's sincerity. Such a confession from Mary would preclude what Elizabeth most dreaded: the trial of Mary in an open court. Such an admission of guilt would spare Mary public humiliation and release Elizabeth from the onus of persecutor. Such a confession of complicity with the Babington conspirators—and the knowledge of their terrible fate—almost guaranteed a cessation of similar attempts in the future.

But as Elizabeth waited for Mary's reply, the Scottish Queen recognized her sister sovereign's vulnerability. Elizabeth was obviously looking for a way out of the dilemma which, no matter what the end, could do nothing but redound to her, Mary's, disadvantage. If Mary accepted Elizabeth's offer, she would still spend the rest of her life in prison, while the English Queen flaunted her "confession" and piously and justifiably reaped the plaudits for her tolerance in letting Mary live.

But if she, Mary, were to die? There was little left for which to live. She had nothing—no Crown, no country, no home, no child, and her health was a daily trial. She faced nothing but imprisonment, dishonor, ill health and, now that she was in such ill repute, probably harsher restrictions. If she were to die, Elizabeth would be compelled to take the responsibility for her death. And Mary inherently recognized that such responsibility was just what Elizabeth was attempting to evade.

Thus, in her moment of deepest despair, Mary Stuart felt a resurgence of triumph and elation. She had two reasons to wish for death: the moral justification of her Catholic faith and the fact that she had nothing really worthwhile left for which to live. She possessed no valid excuse for taking advantage of Elizabeth's offer. It would gain her nothing and would be the easiest way out for the English Queen.

On that note, she cast aside Elizabeth's offer of compromise. She had nothing further to say.

Several weeks later, she was transferred to Fotheringhay Castle in Northamptonshire. She knew it would be her last prison.

Chapter Twenty-five

The Queen of England's predominating anxiety, overshadowing the seriousness of the Netherland's campaign and her anger at Mary Stuart, was the question of money. England's resources never approached those of Spain and France. Elizabeth's annual revenues amounted to just under £300,000, and out of this sum, the Queen was expected to run the government, maintain her court and pay her own expenses. Over and above this, the Crown had little recourse but to call on Parliament for additional funds. Since these were obtained by levying taxes, which the commonalty considered odious, both Parliament and Queen hesitated. Heavy taxation was an admission of failure to deal with one's normal income and, to one who cherished her popularity as Elizabeth did, to be employed only as a last resort.

Yet week in and week out the matter of money—where it might be obtained, how it might best be spent—plagued the Queen and her Councillors. Early in her reign with the funds then available to her, Elizabeth had settled many of her sister Mary's state debts. Later she had expelled the French from Scotland, fought a losing war in France and mustered an army costing £93,000 for the quelling of the Northern rebellion alone. The needed funds had been obtained by Parliamentary subsidies, by loans and, most hurtful of all, by a considerable sale of Crown lands. Such sales did nothing to improve the economic stability since they depreciated the royal income further by the loss of rents. Elizabeth had been meticulous about repayment of all debts and loans. She was scrupulous about undertaking any unnecessary debt. The Queen's rigid economic practices, her inborn frugality and stubborn insistence on proper account keeping were the outgrowth of a lesson well learned in a straitened adolescence. The discriminating use of her money which had given England its remarkable solvency had

509

won the respect even of her adversaries. The new Pope, Sixtus V, said, "She certainly is a great Queen and were she only a Catholic she would be our dearly beloved. Just look how well she governs! She is only a woman, only mistress of half an island and yet she makes herself feared by Spain, by France, by the Empire, by all!"[1]

The Queen's natural vigilance regarding money was not helped by her ministers such as Walsingham, who, staunch Puritan as he was, had hoped the Netherlands campaign might result in an outright attack on Catholic Spain. He deplored what he considered an exaggerated parsimony, saying that "she greatly presumeth on fortune which is but a very weak foundation to build upon. I would she did build and depend upon God!" Elizabeth was content to depend on her Saviour, but she also privately considered He helped those who helped themselves. She kept a wary eye on the Exchequer, the very lifeblood of her nation, protecting it from the depredations of those with more ambitions than the state purse would stand.

The Queen was, therefore, understandably nervous over the progress of the war in the Netherlands. Her policy of ensuring that all hostile powers be kept as far as possible from the borders of her realm was proving expensive. Elizabeth hated the outflow of money as much as she hated the spilling of blood; waste in any form always appalled her. She was equally uneasy about public opinion abroad, so much so that she had published a pamphlet in which she declared England sought no additional territory in the Netherlands. She was merely being a "good neighbor" to the Protestant Dutch in helping them in their fight to retain those religious and civil liberties Spain wished to destroy. The deaths of Alençon and Orange had left the Dutch leaderless, said the Queen, and no one had offered to help them. She had tried to interest Henri III of France, writing, "Jesus! Was there ever a Prince so smitten by the snares of traitors without the courage or counsel to reply to it? . . . for the love of God, rouse yourself from this too long sleep!"[2] Henri, embroiled in civil wars, had done nothing. Repeatedly Elizabeth said she had refused the sovereignty of Holland and Zeeland out of traditional respect for the ruler *in absentia*, Philip of Spain. She would not govern there, but she would help protect. Her motives did not go unrecognized, and in great admiration, the King of Sweden said, "Elizabeth of England was extraordinarily brave to risk her Crown when no one else in Europe would do so."[3]

She had sought to impress her philosophy on the Earl of Leicester before his departure. Leicester was only too well aware of Elizabeth's thrift, a virtue he recognized as practically nonexistent in himself. He had left her a New Year's gift of a pearl necklace "with one hundred and one jewels hanging thereat, a great table diamond in the midst and two rubies on each side of it," which greatly pleased the Queen but did not for one moment cause her to view the campaign any differently. Much to Leicester's chagrin and annoyance, he had departed with considerably less authority than he had anticipated and was heard to comment derisively that he hoped she would "never send a general again as I am sent—and yet I will do what I can for her and her country."

The Earl's reception in the Netherlands more than atoned for his Queen's restraint. Through The Hague, Rotterdam, Amsterdam and Delft, his reception was replete with cannonades, fireworks, processions and other triumphant displays of welcome. It compensated somewhat for the lack of full control and the scantiness of the retinue with which Elizabeth had seen fit to equip him. The Dutch were almost hysterically glad to see him. They called Leicester their "Messiah," blessed his appearance and the Queen who had sent him to be their deliverer, calling her name "as if she herself had been in Cheapside!" The adulation and ovations, the splendid masques and pageants worked their magic on the impressionable Earl, who wrote home, "I like this matter twenty times better than I did in England. . . ."* He regarded the forthcoming campaign optimistically, never doubting he would free the Dutch from Spanish tyranny. Their gratitude—which would redound to the benefit of England, Elizabeth and him-self—where would it end? Visions of a permanent suzerainty danced before his eyes, and he wrote Burghley exultantly that "the Dutch would serve under me with a better will than ever under the Prince of Orange . . . [though] they loved him well and never hoped of the liberty of their country until now."[4]

The accuracy of the Earl's words was soon demonstrated. Some three weeks after his arrival, a delegation appeared and, "with many good words for her Majesty's sake," offered Leicester the "absolute government of the whole provinces," wishing to proclaim immediately that Elizabeth's representative would be the "Governor-General of the United States of the Netherlands." The Dutch recognized the need for a central power with control over the civil, religious, military and financial forces, with the power of appointment of officials and dis-position of all revenues.[5] The office carried as great an authority as that

---

*In one moment of elation and exaggerated self-esteem, Leicester jolted even the stolid Dutch by stating that when Lady Jane Grey, who had been married to his brother Guildford Dudley, was overthrown by Henry VIII's daughter, Mary Tudor, his family had been deprived of the Crown of England.

borne by any other leader and as much as Elizabeth would have possessed had she accepted the sovereignty.

Leicester's ego was such that while he was not overwhelmed at the offer, it did not seem either that he should reject it. In England, he had always been favored as the "Queen's creature" with little opportunity to forget that she was the source of his wealth and his power. Regarding the campaign itself, Elizabeth held him on a narrow rein. She insisted on being consulted on all decisions. It was *her* money being spent, and the outcome in the Netherlands would evolve in *her* name, she had emphasized repeatedly. Just such prerogatives as were implicit in the Governor-Generalship had been the basis of many of the arguments which had delayed his departure. The Dutch had been anxious that Leicester have as much power as possible, but Elizabeth, knowing her "sweet Robin" better, had been firm.

However, the Dutch offer was too tantalizing to reject. The Earl's ego was solaced and his pride increased as he deliberated and, looking for moral support, consulted William Davison, Walsingham's principal-secretary in the Netherlands. He was pleased when Davison and others of his staff concurred that some supreme authority was indeed desirable. And so, with their approbation ringing in his ears and confirming his own innermost desire, he accepted the Governor-Generalship in direct opposition to his royal mistress' clearly stated wishes.

Elizabeth was stunned—a condition which soon gave way to "extreme choler and dislike." She knew Leicester's pride and ambition only too well; she had spelled out clearly the terms on which he had been allowed to go to the Netherlands. Her reaction was not helped by the fact that having heard of Leicester's great honor, his Countess, the hateful Lettice, was preparing "to go over presently . . . with such a train of ladies and gentlemen, and such rich coaches, litters and side-saddles, that her Majesty had none such, and that there should be such a court of ladies and gentlemen as should far surpass her Majesty's court here. . . ."[6] There was more "extreme choler at all the vain doings," a courtier wrote Leicester, informing him that Elizabeth had forbidden the Countess' departure, saying "she would have no more courts under her obeisance, but her own, and would revoke you from thence with all speed. . . ."

The Queen's anger was justified. She had refused the sovereignty herself and had proclaimed her truthful intent to all Europe. She felt Leicester's action only discredited her. Elizabeth was also certain that once Leicester possessed sufficient authority, he would instigate a more

Queen Elizabeth
at age thirty-eight

Robert Dudley
Earl of Leicester
Age forty-four

Miniatures by Nicholas Hilliard,
the Queen's foremost painter

Sir Walter Raleigh

Sir Francis Drake

Sir Christopher Hatton
Artist unknown
*The National Portrait
Gallery, London*

Charles Howard
Lord Admiral and
Earl of Nottingham
The Queen's uncle
*The National Portrait
Gallery, London*

Sir Francis Walsingham
Artist unknown
*The National Portrait
Gallery, London*

Mary, Queen of Scots
Painted during
her captivity
*The National
Portrait Gallery,
London*

Elizabeth Talbot
The Countess
of Shrewsbury
*The National Trust
Hardwick Hall*

George Talbot
Earl of Shrewsbury
*The National Trust
Hardwick Hall*

Robert Devereux
Earl of Essex
*The National
Portrait Gallery,
London*

Lettice Knollys
The Countess
of Leicester
Mother of
Robert Devereux,
Earl of Essex
Courtesy of
The Marquess of Bath
and The Courtauld
Institute of Art

Sir John Harrington
Queen Elizabeth's
godson

Artist unknown
*The National Portrait
Gallery, London*

Sir Robert Cecil
Artist unknown
*The National Portrait
Gallery, London*

Philip II
By Coëllo
*Kunsthistorisches
Museum, Vienna*

The Duke of
Medina Sidonia
*Thomson
Newspapers Ltd.*

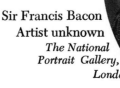

Sir Francis Bacon
Artist unknown
*The National
Portrait Gallery,
London*

Queen Elizabeth
Artist unknown
*Pinocoteca di
Siena, Italy*

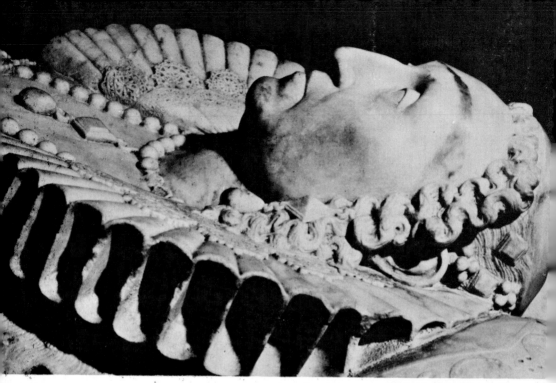

Photograph by Werner Foreman
Courtesy of Weidenfeld and Nicolson

Queen Elizabeth
Tomb effigy in Westminster Abbey

James Stuart
Son of Mary,
Queen of Scots
James VI of Scotland
James I of England
*The National
Portrait Gallery,
London*

aggressive campaign than she could afford. When William Davison arrived in England with Leicester's belated explanation, she asked what the Earl was to be called. When told he was to be addressed as "Excellency," her wrath boiled over. "Excellency," she was informed, had been installed by solemn proclamation on January 25, 1586, as "the highest and supreme commandment and absolute authority above and in all matters of warfare" and was now traveling throughout the Protestant provinces with a canopy usually reserved for royalty over his head.

It was too much for the Queen. Although her Councillors pointed out the advantages of the appointment, as Burghley wrote Leicester, "we find her Majesty so discontent with your acceptance of the government there before you had her Majesty's opinion, that although I, for my own part, judge this action both honourable and profitable, yet her Majesty will not endure to hear any speech in defence thereof. . . ." Burghley's intervention for Leicester was limited, for the sixty-six-year-old minister was laid up at Theobalds after a bad fall. He wrote that he was forced to write from his bed, "which I have kept these two days not . . . for pain of my gout, but indeed having some days past rubbed off a good deal of skin upon my shin. . . ."[7]

Relieving her frustration, Elizabeth wrote to Thomas Heneage in the Netherlands, "You shall let the Earl understand how highly upon just cause we are affected . . . you shall let him understand that we hold our honour greatly touched by the said acceptance of that government and least as we may not without honour endure, for that it carrieth a manifest appearance of repugnancy to our protestation set out in print by the which we declare that our only intent in sending him over into those parts was to direct and govern the English troops that we had granted to the States for their aid. . . ." She then demanded that Leicester "make an open and public resignation in the place where he accepted the same absolute government." Nor did the Dutch them-selves escape the royal wrath. Elizabeth angrily informed them they had wronged her "by provoking a minister of ours to commit so notorious a contempt against us, the other in that they show them-selves to have a very slender and weak concept of our judgment by pressing a minister of ours to accept of that which we refused. . . ." When Heneage wrote protesting her decision to make Leicester resign, she wrote heatedly in reply, "Jesus! What availeth wit when it fails the owner at greatest need? Do that you are bidden and leave your con-siderations for your own affairs. . . . I am assured of your dutiful thoughts, but I am utterly at squares with this childish dealing."[8]

In the Netherlands, Leicester received a letter from his brother, the Earl of Warwick, informing him of the emotional climate at court and indirectly urging him to be steadfast.

> Well our mistress's extreme rage doth increase rather than diminish, and she giveth out great threatening words against you. Therefore, make the best assurance you can for yourself, and trust not her oath, for that her malice is great and unquenchable is the wisest of their opinions here. . . .
>
> And let this be a great comfort to you . . . that you were never so honoured and loved in your life amongst all good people as you are at this day, only for dealing so nobly and wisely in this action, as you have done; so that whatever cometh of it, you have done your part. . . .
>
> Once again, have great care for yourself (I mean for your safety) and if she will needs revoke you to the overthrowing of the cause, if I were as you, if I could be assured *there* [*i.e.*, the Netherlands] *I would go to the farthest part of Christendom, rather than ever come into England again.* Take heed whom you trust, for that *you have some false boys around you.* . . .[9]

And then, touchingly demonstrative of the goodwill between Ambrose and Robert Dudley, Warwick ended, "Advise me what to do, for I mean to take such part as you do."

Burghley had returned to court to intercede for Leicester, but the Queen brooked no interference. She had written to the Earl, and Thomas Heneage was about to depart with the reply. In the letter, she left little doubt of her feeling. "How contemptuously we conceive ourself to have been used by you, you shall by this bearer understand, whom we have expressly sent unto you to charge you withal. We could never have imagined had we not seen it fall out in experience that a man raised up by ourself and extraordinarily favoured by us above any other subject of this land, would have in so contemptible a sort broken our commandment, in a cause that so greatly toucheth us in honour. . . ."[10]

The tone of the letter appalled Leicester. He had expected anger, recrimination, even a mild threat or so. But not this calm, icy abuse and peremptory demand that he lay aside his new glory. He asked to resign, "finding myself very unfit and unable to wade in so weighty a cause as this, which ought to have much more comfort than I shall find or receive. . . ." He told Elizabeth that to prove his allegiance, she might send him to the Indies, where "by my humble and daily prayer, which shall never cease for her most happy presentation and long continuance," he would serve her without offending her by sight of him. Remorsefully, he said, since it was evident his usefulness to her was limited, perhaps Elizabeth would allow him to work in the royal stables, "where I can at least rub your horses' heels, a service which would be much more welcome to me than this, with all that these men may give me!"[11]

The letter had the predictable effect. Burghley wrote Leicester that Elizabeth "found her princely heart touched with favourable interpretation of your actions, affirming them to be only offensive to her in that she was not made privy to them; not now misliking that you had authority." He was puzzled by Elizabeth's protracted anger and wrote Leicester, "Surely there is some treachery amongst ourselves, for I cannot think she would do this out of her own head."[12] He privately suspected the handsome Sir Walter Raleigh of using the opportunity of Leicester's absence and misdemeanor to further his own cause with the Queen.

Ultimately it was Burghley who tempered the Queen's wrath. His skinned leg having recovered, he was then stricken with gout, which led him to say, "I might wish my body or my feet were of iron or steel, for with flesh and blood, I cannot long endure...."[13] Nevertheless, he dragged himself to court to reason with Elizabeth, and inevitably his good sense won out over the Queen's hurt pride and disappointment. Burghley said it would be a disaster if she humiliated Leicester by making him resign the Governorship. When Elizabeth remained resolute, he said before he allowed her to so demean herself, he would resign his office. It was not an idle threat, and the Queen glared balefully at the aging minister, who tottered on his gouty legs, daring to touch that imperious will with his own. He pointed out that the Dutch were already regarding their newly appointed "Excellency" with puzzlement, for apparently the English Queen had sent her greatest noble to fight an aggressive war. Yet she denied him adequate power, a proper title and sufficient money. He was obviously no better than a puppet peer whose movement and action were designed to be manipulated by the Queen of England.

Sensitive to criticism and loss of prestige, Elizabeth allowed herself to be convinced, especially when Burghley reiterated that public renunciation of the honor the Dutch had conveyed on Leicester would do more damage than anything else in insulting the very people she was attempting to help. In the end, Burghley took his painful body home, certain he had prevented the Queen from making a fatal mistake.

If, at that point, Leicester had also been firm, reiterating Burghley's admonitions, he might indeed have won a far more impressive authority. But knowing Elizabeth's variable moods and the continued effect of his absence on the court, the Earl chose the safer path. In letters which continued to pass between them in which he addressed his "Most Gracious Lady," to "consider my long, true and faithful heart toward you," he implored that his absence would not deprive him "of that which, above all the world I esteem . . . which is your favour and your presence. . . ." While "prostrate at your feet," he begged leave to return home, writing, "If your Majesty shall refuse me this, I shall think all grace clean gone from me and I know my days will not be long."[14] With such clever and propitiatory offerings, the Earl soon redeemed himself. It saved his honor since it allowed him to keep his debatable title, which he now knew to be meaningless and empty.

But the beginning foretold the end. Elizabeth had no intention of waging the offensive, expensive war her ministers, Leicester and the Dutch wished. Almost at once, she attempted to negotiate a peace with Parma and bring her army home before it bankrupted her. Her action did not endear her to the Dutch. However, impressed by her logic, the Duke of Parma, almost as ill supplied by Philip as Leicester was by Elizabeth, advised Philip to let the Spanish troops withdraw. The Spanish King did not agree. If nothing else, he might exhaust England's resources so that, should he attempt the invasion he was rapidly coming to view as inevitable, its defense would be limited. While Leicester and the Dutch were thinking of aggressive campaigns and victory, the English Queen was thinking of money, defensive deployment and getting her army and its arrogant commander home as soon as possible. The division in intent between the Queen and her commander guaranteed an early and unsettling defeat.

Also, as would soon be proved, the Earl of Leicester simply was not competent for the task. While he applied himself diligently, going among his men, climbing in and out of trenches and supervising the work, while he often displayed great personal courage, the fact remained that he was a poor administrator. He found it difficult, if not impossible, to delegate authority, and his lack of tact soon pricked the Dutch pride and irritated the professional English and Dutch soldier. Ordered to fight a "good sharp war," which was what he wanted, the result might have been different. But after his inauspicious beginning, Elizabeth doled out small amounts of men and money, so the Earl was hamstrung. The Dutch, once apprised of Elizabeth's bargaining with Parma without their knowledge, were angry and disillusioned. They felt cheated of the victory they were sure English intervention would bring and censured both Queen and Earl.

Corruption, that constant disease of the era, was widespread within the ranks, and tales of starvation and hardship among the English troops were rampant. "Give me leave to speak for the poor soldiers,"

Leicester wrote, "if they be not better maintained, being in this strange country, there will be neither good service done, nor be without great dishonour to her Majesty." When it appeared that Leicester had done little to alleviate the suffering, Elizabeth wrote that she had sent him £20,000 to pay the soldiers' wages, which did not seem to be enough. The Queen was unsuccessful when she demanded an accounting of her funds. "It is continually alleged," Elizabeth wrote fretfully, "that great sums are due, yet why such sums are due or to whom they are due, and who are paid and not paid . . . is never certified. . . ."[15] Against her express command, Leicester had increased his and his officers' pay and was the last man in the world to answer. Dishonest paymasters, officers who loaded the muster sheets with excess names for which they received payment or provisions which they then unscrupulously sold were numerous. Through Burghley, Elizabeth commanded that the soldiers' wages be paid them directly instead of to their captains, with whom the money inevitably remained; her command was ignored. When no adequate accounting was provided, she stubbornly refused to send additional funds, only making the bad situation worse. The misappropriation of the English monies committed to the Dutch defense approached a national scandal, and as reports of overspending reached the Queen, she found it difficult to stave off panic. More than half her yearly income was wiped out in five months, and she said, depressed and embittered, "It is a sieve that spends as it receives to no little purpose. . . ."

When word of the Queen's condemnation reached Leicester, he wrote angrily that he hoped to live long enough "to see you employ some of them that are thus careless of me, to see whether they will spend £20,000 of their own for you in seven months. . . ." It was all she could do to restrain herself from a stinging reply that the money had come from her in the first place. The fact that many able-bodied men had deserted and returned home and that her army was now comprised mainly of "tosspots and ruffians, rogues and vagabonds" did not help. Leicester let Walsingham know his opinion: "I am ashamed to think, much more to speak, of the young men that have come over. Believe me, you will all repent the cockney kind of bringing up at this day of young men. . . . Our simplest men in show have been our best and your gallant blood and ruffian men the worst of all others."[16]

At home, Elizabeth sought to placate her favorite and, in a remarkably informal letter, so in contrast with her more usual tortuous prose, indicated his past indiscretion had been forgiven. The letter also conveys the unusual blend of personality and spirit which characterized the Elizabeth Leicester knew. It was written at the height of the Netherlands campaign in July, 1586.

> Rob,
>
>   I am afraid you will suppose, by my wandering writings, that a mid-summer's moon hath taken large possession of my brains this month; but you must needs take things as they come in my head, though order be left behind me. When I remember your request to have a discreet and honest man that may carry my mind, and see how all goes there, I have chosen this bearer (Thomas Wilkes) whom you know and have made good trial of. I have fraught him full of my conceits of those country matters and imparted what way I mind to take, and what is fit for you to use.

Elizabeth then spoke of several of Leicester's officers and of their Dutch counterparts of whom the Earl had complained. She said that since they had "ventured their lives and won our nation honour," Leicester should settle his differences with them. If, however, they were responsible for the disastrous condition of the common soldier, "let them hear of it without open shame and doubt not I will well chasten them therefore." Her letter continued:

>   It frets me not a little that the poor soldiers that hourly venture life should want their due, that well deserve rather reward; and look in whom the fault may truly be proved, let them smart therefore. And if the Treasurer be found untrue or negligent, according to his desert, he shall be used. But you know my old wont that love not to discharge from office without desert. God forbid! . . .
>
>   Now I will end that do imagine I talk still with you ⊙⊙ and therefore loathly say farewell one hundred thousand times though ever I pray God bless you from all harm and save you from all foes, with my million and legion of thanks for all your pains and cares.
>
> As you know, EveR, the same,
E.R.[17]

With ill-trained and half-starved soldiers, greedy officers and an incompetent Governor-General, the outcome was predictable. A few minor victories were forgotten in the general debacle. Unable to face staggering losses and all-around inadequacy, Leicester, in a frenzied pique and hoping to cast blame elsewhere, had one garrison commander hanged for treason. The result was a general disillusionment, constant quarreling within the Dutch and English advisory ranks and always, at home, Elizabeth holding tight to power and the purse strings. Between them, and with the help of his thieving officers, they managed to bring the campaign to a disastrous end. By November, weary and despairing, Leicester sailed for home. His reputation, which had suffered severely with the publication of the libelous *Leicester's Commonwealth*, was now the target of even greater censure. All except from the Queen. Elizabeth staunchly defended her "sweet Robin." Even the Earl admitted, "Never since I was born did I receive a more gracious welcome!"

With Leicester came his stepson, the eighteen-year-old Robert Devereux, the Earl of Essex. Elizabeth soothed Leicester's feelings, greeted Essex and sent her favorite off to take the healing waters of Bath. Young Essex remained at court until Mary Stuart was removed from his Chartley Manor home to Fotheringhay. In those few months, as he followed the court to Richmond and Greenwich, he realized his future lay near the sovereign and he must do as his stepfather before him: seek the wealth, power and authority which came from the Crown. In this, he expected little difficulty, for he realized the Queen liked him despite the fact that his mother, Lettice, was still forbidden her presence. However, given sufficient time, he might be able to sway even Queen Elizabeth's feelings so his mother would once again move in the illustrious circles to which she had been born. With youthful confidence and a natural arrogance, he did not realize that the position of the Queen's favorite needed additional attributes to a handsome form, a swaggering manner and a compelling charm. It would take him the next fifteen years—all that remained of his life—to accept what Leicester had learned very early in his youth. Which was that, in addition to a courtier's grace, Queen Elizabeth demanded something else which Essex was never to possess: humility.

Elizabeth had been overwhelmed by the evidence Walsingham gained from Mary Stuart's confiscated letters—evidence which proved the Scottish Queen's awareness of the plots against Elizabeth's life and Crown. Even as she recognized the impasse that now confronted her, Elizabeth knew she could no longer tolerate the threat Mary's continued existence entailed. Yet both Burghley and Walsingham were driven to distraction in getting the Queen to act. Elizabeth simply could not face what her ministers obviously had in mind. The only retributive action to take against the imprisoned Queen of Scots was death, and Elizabeth shrank from contemplating such a step. She would gladly have left Mary at Fotheringhay, increased the guard and used every precaution to prevent the Scottish Queen's conspiring against her. But she was well aware that *outside* those prison walls and *inside* her own court, others might intrigue in Mary's behalf, with her own life as the prize. Weeks before, as she had been proceeding to Chapel, her mind on many things, she suddenly remembered the words of a letter from Davison to Burghley, "that a Dutchman, newly arrived from Paris . . . had begged him to advise her Majesty to beware of one who will present a petition to her on her way to Chapel or walking abroad. . . ." Normally, Elizabeth would have treated the words with contempt and a joking aside about so many worried old men at court. But suddenly, there in the sunlight, she was "overcome by a shock of fear . . ." and had felt herself almost stumble. Her ladies had run to her side and guided her back to her chambers, an event which was "greatly to the wonder of those present." Only Elizabeth knew the cause. *Fear*, an unusual and unwonted, yet recognizable *fear*, had gripped her with a reeling intensity. Even as she acknowledged her terror, she despised not only herself for her reaction, but also the woman who was the cause: Mary Stuart.

William Davison, returned from the Netherlands to be Walsingham's principal secretary, voiced the concern of many that Elizabeth "will keep the course as she held with the Duke of Norfolk, which is not to take her [Mary's] life, unless extreme fear compel her."[18] But Walsingham had not worked so assiduously for such a disappointing end to his efforts. He had enlisted Burghley's help, and between them they brought Elizabeth, "variable as the weather," to agree that Mary must be examined at Fotheringhay. The Queen was persuaded to write Mary that although she had professed ignorance of the Babington plot, "we find by clear and most evident proof that the contrary will be verified." Noblemen and Councillors would be appointed to debate her guilt or innocence, said Elizabeth, and since Mary lived "within our protection and therefore subject to the laws of the realm . . ." Mary would do well to cooperate with the commissioners. When Mary, through the French ambassador, sought counsel, Elizabeth replied "that she [Mary] required not the advice or schooling of foreign powers to instruct her how she ought to act" and said she considered "the Scottish Queen unworthy of counsel."[19]

At Fotheringhay, Mary had continued staunch that she had never sought the English Queen's life, only "that she had endeavored to gain her liberty and would continue to do so as long as she lived." She said that if Elizabeth "chose to question her in person, she would declare the truth, but would reply to no inferior." And to buttress her statement, she added that since Elizabeth had no jurisdiction over an anointed sovereign, she would reject the authority of anyone appointed to try her.

It was, therefore, with considerable misgiving during the first week of October, 1586, that Elizabeth watched the departure of the commission for Fotheringhay. The delegation was headed by Sir Thomas Bromley, the Lord Chancellor, and Burghley. Accompanying them were Walsingham, Sir Christopher Hatton and some eight Earls and thirty other clerks, attorneys, judges and Privy Councillors. Elizabeth had found fault with everything pertaining to the commission: the number of personnel which removed everyone of influence from the court; the title used to designate Mary; the fact that Mary would be tried under the Bond of Association with its punishment so amply spelled out. Hidden behind the impassive faces of those assembled to hear her instructions, she knew, was a determination to bring her face to face with the problem of the Scottish Queen. Elizabeth meddled so much that Walsingham lost patience and, once out of the royal hearing, cried, "I would to God her Majesty would be content to refer these things to them that can best judge of them as other princes do!"[20]

Fotheringhay Castle in the small Northamptonshire village of Fotheringhay sat, shrouded in autumnal fogs, high on its mound above the Nene River. The huge old complex of Great Hall, Chapel, drafty chambers and inner courtyard was medieval, with a formidable keep and towers visible for miles around. The Castle was girdled by a double moat on three sides with the river on the fourth. It was with relief that Burghley and his companions glimpsed the great towers, for the journey north had been distressing with storms and gale wind. They were no sooner in residence than they received a letter from Elizabeth, who, beset by doubts in their absence, ordered the commission "to forbear passing sentence on the Scottish Queen till they had returned to her presence and made their report to herself." She softened this command, which she recognized deterred them effectively, by stating that in view of the dreadful weather, she longed "to hear how her 'Spirit' and her 'Moor' do find themselves after so foul and wearisome a journey. . . ."

The commission carried a letter from Elizabeth to Mary Stuart. It was short and to the point:

You have, in various ways and manners, attempted to take my life, and to bring my kingdom to destruction by bloodshed. I have never proceeded so harshly against you, but have, on the contrary, protected and maintained you like myself. These treasons will be proved to you, and all made manifest.

Yet it is my will, that you answer the nobles and peers of the kingdom as if I were myself present. I therefore require, charge and command that you make answer, for I have been well informed of your arrogance.

Act plainly, without reserve, and you will sooner be able to obtain favour of me.

ELIZABETH[21]

Mary was summoned from her apartments. She had been given small, inferior chambers and, from the unusual activity among Paulet's servants, correctly guessed she was to have visitors. She read Elizabeth's letter and, smiling faintly, told Burghley as she returned it to him, that she found Elizabeth's tone "strange," that she, born a Queen, should be expected to answer such a command. She also ignored Elizabeth's message conveyed by one of the delegation that "if she showed a disposition to confess in private, one or more of the Council would hear her." She would not, she said, "prejudice her rank, her royal blood or the right of her son" or "set so poor a precedent for other princes by submitting to such an indignity."[22] She had come to England for help and succor, she said, and instead had remained a prisoner for eighteen years. Since the laws of the country had been so little protection to her, she would not now obey them, for they had no jurisdiction over her.

Burghley attempted to explain. She was in England as heir to the Crown, and by her place in the succession, she possessed certain rights which the English Queen had recognized in that she had never allowed them to be impugned. In turn, England possessed corresponding rights over her. Though her obligations were not defined by law, Mary nonetheless possessed them; she could not possess these obligations while disclaiming responsibility. Elizabeth had shown amazing forbearance, the Lord Treasurer emphasized, but it was this very forbearance which had led to activities resulting in a disastrous confrontation between the two Queens. Mary listened but appeared unimpressed.

It took two days before a decision was reached. Mary said she would appear before the commissioners, provided she did not appear as a criminal and one subject to English jurisdiction. She would acknowledge such jurisdiction only if Parliament named her next in succession or the Queen declared her next of kin. Otherwise, she would not appear or submit to the commissioners' judgment.

"Then," said Burghley, "we will proceed . . . in this cause, though you be absent and continue contumacious." To which Mary replied, "Search your conscience, look well to your honour and God reward you and yours for your judgment against me."[23]

During the evening, Mary looked over the list of peers, Privy Councillors and judges. She saw many familiar names, names she knew had been friendly to her in the past, such as old Sir Ralph Sadler, and many Catholic names, such as Rutland, Cumberland and Montague. Before departing earlier, Sir Christopher Hatton impressed Mary when he told her that neither civil law, canon law nor "the law of Nature" exempted her from appearing and that, if she were truly innocent, she would only damage her cause further by refusing to cooperate. It seemed sensible to the woman who had no alternative advice or counsel on which to depend, and after further thought, she summoned Burghley and told him she would appear "if the court allowed a protest." Burghley said that was impossible, but it would be "enrolled." Hesitatingly, Mary indicated she would appear.

She entered the Great Hall of Fotheringhay Castle the next morning, October 15, leaning on the arm of her steward, Andrew Melville. Mary had chosen her usual attire of black velvet, with a peaked cap and its white mantle flowing over her shoulders. If the picture of the fiery and proud Queen of Scots who had been considered incarnate of every evil did not coincide with the tall, aging woman who dragged a painful leg across the floor, certainly the set faces of the English aristocracy must have caused Mary some reflection. As they rose and uncovered their heads at her entrance, she gazed at the Englishmen—more than she had ever seen in eighteen years—and was as plainly curious of them as they were of her. She could not resist a bitter jest, however, and said to Melville, "Alas, there is a great number of Councillors here and yet not one of them is for me!"[24] She passed a thronelike chair, symbolically representing the presence of the English Queen, on which were embroidered the arms of England. She paused a moment before settling herself in the small crimson chair set a bit lower. "I am a Queen by right of my birth and my place should be there. . . ." She gestured toward the empty chair on its dais. A moment later she brightened as she saw the face of the Earl of Shrewsbury among the spectators.*

Mary was charged on two counts: the first, conspiring with known traitors and foreigners to encourage invasion and second, conspiring the death of Elizabeth. The Queen's Sergeant, Sir Thomas Gawdy, rose and explained the plot contrived by Babington and his six confederates to accomplish Elizabeth's murder. Mary denied that she had ever met Babington and said she knew nothing of his six gentlemen.

---

*Shrewsbury had attempted to evade sitting on the commission formed to try the woman he had guarded so faithfully for so long. The Lord Chancellor sent word, however: "I advise you not to be absent."

She had no way of knowing, of course, how much had been discovered against her, and it must have been with a sinking heart that she listened to the prisoners' depositions and then the reading of the letters between herself and the dead Babington. She said, as the commissioners studied the correspondence circulating among them, "It may be that Babington wrote those letters, but let it be proved that I received them . . . if they say so, I say they lie openly!" She denied knowledge of the papers which were copies of the originals and demanded to see the originals and copies side by side. "It is quite possible that my ciphers have been tampered with by my enemies," she said. "I cannot reply to this accusation without full knowledge!"[25] Mary did not disclaim her efforts for freedom: "I do not deny that I have earnestly wished for liberty and done my utmost to procure it for myself. In this I acted from a very natural wish." But she utterly refused to admit that she had worked for Elizabeth's death. She cried, "Can I be responsible for the criminal actions of a few desperate men, which they planned without my knowledge?" Since the letters were written in cipher, there was no proof that they had come from *her*, she said passionately. Anyone could write cipher and then, pointing to Walsingham, cried, "that even *he* might have composed the damning documents!" Shaken, Walsingham arose and said, "I call to God to record that as a private person I have done nothing unbecoming an honest man, nor as I bear the place of a public person, have I done anything unworthy of my place!"[26] He confessed only to being careful of the safety of Queen Elizabeth and the realm.

Queen Mary took particular exception to the paragraph in her reply to Babington in which she mentioned the "enterprise" and the speed with which she herself must be freed before Paulet was informed of the "execution." Mary insisted, "on the word of a Princess," that by "execution" she meant execution of the plan to rescue her, not the execution of the Queen. Indignantly she insisted that the notes of her two secretaries, Nau and Curle, would show this. "Bring my own handwriting," she said, "anything to suit a purpose may be put in what be called copies. . . ."[27] At which Walsingham rose and, clearing his throat, said, in a sad tone, "he wished to God" the secretaries' notes could be found. Since it is incredible to believe that the cautious Secretary who had pursued Mary with deadly seriousness for two years would let vital evidence be lost or misplaced, it is certain that the particular paragraph to which Mary objected was an interpolation. Mary saw the effect on the judges and, suddenly frightened, burst into tears, crying, "Do not believe I have consented to the Queen's destruction! I would never make shipwreck of my soul by conspiring the destruction of my dearest sister!"[28]

The followng day presented little more reason for Mary to hope. She appeared pale and anxiously drawn, limping again to the little red velvet chair. She had slept badly and had found it difficult to compose her mind at her morning prayers. She recognized too late that though she had agreed to appear in order to clear herself of treasonous charges, she was actually *defending* herself before a commission which gave every indication of having prejudged her as guilty. She had no lawyer, no advocate. None of her original papers, not even the copies, had been shown her, yet they were freely circulated among the commissioners. It was not possible to defend oneself against evidence one was not allowed to see. "What becomes of the majesty of princes," she asked the commissioners, "if the oaths or attestations of their secretaries are to be taken against their solemn protestations?" Again, for the hundredth time, she opposed the trial and the manner in which it was being conducted. "I am held in chains," she cried, "I have no counsel. You have deprived me of my papers and all means of preparing my defence. . . ." She objected to the implications being made against her, "a Prince anointed," and affirmed that she was being made to appear as a criminal before a .court of justice. She concluded, somewhat plaintively, "that there is not one, I think, among you, let him be the cleverest man you will, but would be incapable of resisting or defending himself were he in my place." Then, with a spark of Stuart temper, she said, somewhat sarcastically, "God forgive you lawyers, for you are so sore fellows. God bless me and my cause from your laws, for it is a very good matter that they cannot make seem bad."[29]

As Mary listened to further discussion of the damning evidence, discussion directed to the Lords and which gave her little opportunity to say anything in her own defense, she became visibly perturbed. At one point, the pressure became too much, and she said scathingly, holding out her arms, "I cannot walk without assistance nor use my arms, and I spend most of my time confined to bed by sickness." That she would work in such an underhanded fashion to regain a Crown was ludicrous, she intimated. "My advancing age and bodily weakness both prevent me from wishing to resume the reins of government," she cried. "I have perhaps only two or three years to live in this world and I do not aspire to public position. . . ."[30]

Burghley wrote Davison of what followed:

The Queen of the Castle was content to appear again afore us in public to be heard, but in truth not to be heard for her defence, for she could say nothing but negatively—that the points of the letter that concerned the practice against the Queen's person was never by her written, nor of her knowledge. The rest, for invasion, for escaping by force, she said she would neither deny nor affirm. But her intention was, by long artificial speeches, to move pity, to lay all the blame upon the Queen's Majesty, or rather upon the Council, that all the troubles past did ensue. . . . I did so encounter her with reasons out of my knowledge and experience as she had not the advantage she looked for. . . . The auditory did find her case not pitiable, her allegations untrue. Whereby great debate fell yesternight very long and this day renewed with great stomaching. . . .[31]

Burghley had been firm, and Mary, who had counted on some objectivity from the Queen's great minister, was disappointed. He had rebuked Mary for insinuations he said were not valid and noted she had intrigued to send her son to Spain, had transferred her rights in the English Crown to Philip and had continued sponsoring Thomas Morgan in Paris, even after she knew he had been conspiring Elizabeth's death. Because of his past tolerance and the fact that he had played no part in Walsingham's efforts, his words had great effect on the others and on Mary, who appeared crumpled by his reaction. She said sadly and almost in a whisper, "Then I see you are my adversary. . . ."

"I am adversary to Queen Elizabeth's adversaries . . ." Burghley had replied sternly. To this Mary, rising, said she had often disapproved of the efforts of others, but ill and restrained, she could hardly be held responsible for them. She said that since she had no advocate for her cause, she would be heard by only Parliament or the Queen of England. She whispered something to Walsingham which seemed to anger him deeply and then, turning, spoke to the foremost peers of England. "My lords and gentlemen, I place my cause in the hands of God. . . ." With great calm, she asked a heavenly pardon for the way they had treated her and, with a semblance of a smile, said, "May God keep me from having to do with you all again."[32] Even the commissioners glanced at each other and smiled at the Queen's humor as she walked from the chamber as quickly as her leg allowed.

To Paulet, who bore little admiration for Mary Stuart, she appeared "utterly void of all fear of harm. . . ." To others once friendly to her cause, her bold denials and staunch conviction, plus an engaging charm which even illness and restraint had not banished completely, had a curious effect. Several of the commissioners appeared shaken, and, as Walsingham wrote to Stafford in Paris, "they wished the matter to be more advisedly considered. . . ." They were almost relieved when Burghley received a letter from Elizabeth which justified the minister's fear of royal interference. At any crisis in the Queen's life—and this was to be no different—Burghley might have noted, "I am greatly discouraged by her lack of resolution." With the absence of her dependable Lord Treasurer, Elizabeth, obviously overwrought and fearful that some definitive action from which she would find no escape might take place at Fotheringhay, recalled the commission to London. Her fears and doubts had grown to gigantic proportions, and once the pressure had become unbearable, she brought her nobles home in the hope that she might exert some influence on their decision.

On October 25, the commissioners reassembled in the Star Chamber, and Claude Nau and Gilbert Curle were produced in person, there "frankly and voluntarily" to substantiate the testimony read at Fotheringhay. Walsingham wrote in a complacent tone to Stafford in Paris that the evidence "brought a great satisfaction to all the commissioners, insomuch that albeit some of them, as you know, stood well affected to her [Mary], yet considering the plainness and evidence of the proofs, every one of them after this gave his sentence against her, finding her not only accessory and privy to the conspiracy, but also an imaginer and encompasser of Her Majesty's destruction."[33] Walsingham omitted to mention that one young peer—Lord Zouch—disturbed at the evidence, bravely announced himself as "not satisfied," boldly saying it had not been proved that the Scottish Queen "had compassed, practised or imagined the death of Elizabeth."

It remained now only to pass sentence, and both Walsingham and Burghley—whose initiative had brought the proceedings thus far—knew Elizabeth herself to be incapable of that. They convinced her, therefore, that the matter should be settled by Parliament, which "the Queen misliketh but we do all persist to make the burden better borne and the world abroad better satisfied." Elizabeth refused to attend the opening ceremonies, not wishing, she insisted, to participate in any proceedings against her sister sovereign. To emphasize her point, she remained in Richmond during the entire session, disconcerting Burghley, who signified he would attend, saying he "would bring the gout with me in my foot, which nobody either here or there will accept from me I am sure. But I thank God my heart is free."

With Burghley in the House of Lords and Sir Christopher Hatton in the Commons, the story of the Scottish Queen was twice told. Labeling Mary "by nationality a Scot, by upbringing a Frenchwoman, by blood a Guise, in practice a Spaniard and in religion a Papist,"[34] Hatton hoped Divine intervention might influence Elizabeth to "take away this most wicked and filthy woman." Mary was called "the hope of idolatry," and it was alleged she had "thirsted after this Crown" to such an extent that only one end was possible. Both Houses, "with one assent," adopted an address to the Queen advising there were "no other means to provide for your Majesty's safety, but by the just and speedy execution of the said Queen. . . ." A deputation was sent on November 12 to the Queen at Richmond. She acknowledged Parliament's efforts and answered "in a manner as princely, wise and grave . . . not only to the admiration of all that heard it, but to the drawing out of the tears out of many eyes. . . ."[35] It is obvious, however, that Elizabeth was still looking for a loophole. On the following Monday, November 14, Hatton spoke to the Commons and declared that "her Majesty would be glad to spare the taking of her [Mary's] blood if by any other means to be devised by her Highness's great Council of this realm, the safety of her Majesty's own person and of the state might be preserved." The Commons remained unmoved and confirmed their earlier verdict that Mary must die.

The decision was presented to the Queen on the twenty-fourth at Richmond. She had, of course, been apprised of Parliament's opinion and, in a speech remarkable for its frankness, proclaimed many of her own fears. She gave thanks to her lawmakers for their work, saying that "as I came to the Crown with the willing hearts of subjects, so do I now, after twenty-eight years reign, perceive in you no diminution of good wills, which, if haply I should want, well might I breathe but never think I lived." Elizabeth then proceeded to the heart of her speech: "And now, albeit I find my life hath been dangerously sought, and death contrived by such as no desert procured it, yet am I thereof so clear from malice . . . as I protest it is and hath been my grievous thought that one, not different in sex, of like estate, and my near kin, should be fallen into so great a crime. Yea, I had so little purpose to pursue her with any colour of malice, that as it is not unknown to some of my Lords here—for now I will play the blab—I secretly wrote her a letter upon the discovery of sundry treasons, that if she would confess them, and privately acknowledge them by her letters unto myself, she never should need be called for them into so public question. Neither did I . . . it of mind to circumvent her, for then I knew as much as she could confess and so did I write."

Elizabeth said she would gladly give her own life if it were best for the kingdom, but assured her listeners it was for their sakes she desired to live "to keep you from a worse." She said she had had much "good experience and trial of this world. I know what it is to be a subject, what to be a sovereign, what to have good neighbors and sometimes, evil-willers." She said the Bond of Association had not been made "to entrap" Mary but was, "rather, an admonition to warn the danger thereof." Elizabeth then permitted herself a touch of humor. She compared her lawyers, "who are so nice and so precise in shifting and scanning every word and letter, that many times you stand more upon form than matter, upon syllables than the sense of the law . . ." to the higher status of Majesty. She spoke slowly, "For we Princes, I tell you, are set on stages, in the sight and view of all the world duly observed. The eyes of many behold our actions; a spot is soon spied in our garments, a blemish quickly noted in our doings. It behoveth us, therefore, to be careful that our proceedings be just and honourable." Warming to the task, she said the Parliamentary action had "laid an hard hand on me—that I must give direction for her death, which cannot be but most grievous, and an irksome burden to me. And lest you might mistake mine absence from this Parliament . . . it hath not been the doubt of any such danger or occasion that kept me from thence, but only the great grief to hear this cause spoken of, especially that such one of state and kin should need so open a declaration, and that this nation should be so spotted with blots of disloyalty."

The Queen then stated she thought "it very requisite with earnest prayer to beseech His Divine Majesty so to illumine mine understanding and inspire me with His grace, as I may do and determine that which shall serve to the establishment of His Church, preservation of your estates and prosperity of this Commonwealth under my charge. . . ."[36] And then, retiring from her chair on its dais, she thanked her Parliamentarians and left. Other than acknowledging their action, justifying her own—and leaving the matter in the hands of her Saviour—Elizabeth had not committed herself in any way.

Several days later, November 29, the assembled lawmakers passed sentence on Mary. The penalty under the Bond of Association was death to anyone who conspired against the Queen of England's life and Crown. Burghley carried the proclamation to Elizabeth at Richmond, writing Walsingham, who was ill at home, "I passed through the City and Southwark afore daylight . . ." but he found his urgency wasted. Elizabeth was unwilling or unable to act further. "God must direct her therein which I most desire to be for her honour and safety," wrote Burghley. The Lord Treasurer had assumed that once the proclamation of the sentence was signed and published, the warrant for the execution would automatically follow. But some inkling of the delay which was to follow was in Elizabeth's insistence that the record of the proceedings be not deposited with the records of Parliament.* However, the sentence was made public, and Parliament was merely adjourned, not prorogued, and it was obvious to everyone that the next move was now up to the Queen.

For Elizabeth herself the swift course of Mary's trial and sentencing meant a wretchedly despairing time which depleted her energies, assaulted her emotional health and left her sick and apprehensive. Each step in her ministers' remorseless quest for Mary Stuart's head only pushed her, the Queen of England, into a position from which she saw no escape. The bad temper with which she struck out at those around her was outward manifestation of an inner torment, as pride, fear, anger and conscience assailed her. Her concern with the financial drain of the Netherlands campaign, her fear for her own personal safety which still would not be quenched were nothing compared to the spiritual war within. Everything in Elizabeth's background had inexorably led to this moment as she was confronted with another sovereign who challenged everything she held dear: her Crown, her life and the future of her beloved England. It was easy for her ministers to speak of punishment for the Queen of Scots. Well might they prophesy her own evil fate if she did not make an end of Mary Stuart soon. *They* had not suffered imprisonment and deprivation and the patronizing ministrations of a hawk-eyed guardian who watched every movement. Elizabeth did not speak lightly when she said that during the eighteen years of Mary's imprisonment, she knew the innermost secrets of captivity which Mary was experiencing. She also knew the prisoner's fears and longings, and she could now, too easily for comfort, put herself in Mary's place and, with vivid imagery, conjure up the reactions of her sick, despairing cousin. It did not make for restful nights or comfortable days. And always, no matter how her ministers defended their actions in bringing Mary to bay, there remained the fact that it would be she, Elizabeth, Queen of England, who alone would suffer responsibility for the fate of Mary, Queen of Scotland.

Young King James had vigorously protested his mother's sentencing and sent an embassy to the English court to plead for her. It was soon apparent, however, that James was more concerned about his rights to the throne and whether they would be compromised by his mother's being condemned as a common criminal. One of the Scots' representatives, Archibald Douglas, sought the Earl of Leicester's opinion and

---

*Sir John Neale, Elizabeth's famous biographer, has conjectured this action was followed so there would be no "infamous memorial" in the archives when Mary Queen of Scots' son, James, ultimately came to the throne.[17]

then wrote to James, "I rode back from the court with my Lord of Leicester, who repeated to me that it was to your Majesty's interest that your mother should suffer justice. I assured him your Majesty would receive that persuasion in good part. He made many protestations of service to your Majesty for which I thanked him heartily. . . ." James did not scruple to accept the hint and wrote Leicester in reply, "How fond and inconstant I were if I should prefer my mother to the title, let all men judge. My religion ever moved me to hate her course, although my honour constrains me to insist for her life. . . ."[38] Sir William Keith, the Scottish ambassador, nevertheless loyally begged Elizabeth to consider reprieving Mary, to which the Queen answered stoutly, "I swear by the living God that I would give one of my own arms to be cut off, so that any means could be found for us both to live in assurance." The Master of Grey, who had accompanied the Scottish delegation, suggested that Mary should remit her rights in the English succession to her son, and because he was a Protestant, "the hopes of the Catholics would be cut off."

Elizabeth had not spent nearly twenty-eight years evading the naming of a successor to accept such a suggestion placidly, and she pretended not to understand. Leicester, standing nearby, hastened to explain it meant simply that the King of Scots would be named in his mother's place as her successor. "Is it so?" cried the Queen as she turned on her startled favorite. Unknown to him, she had been shown much of his early correspondence with Mary Stuart, from the years when he had sought the Scottish Queen's friendship in order to have "two strings to his bow." With an oath, Elizabeth cried, "Get rid of one and have a worse in her place! Nay, then I put myself in a worse place than before!" Her voice shaking with anger, the words revealed the constant fear which made even those closest to her suspect. "By God's passion, that were to cut my own throat—and for a duchy or an earldom for yourself, you, or such as you, would cause some of your desperate knaves to kill me!" The impassioned outburst caused even the confident Leicester to back away in silence.

On December 6, 1586, a public proclamation was made in the City of London whereby Mary Stuart, the Scottish Queen, was declared "a traitress incapable of succeeding to the Crown and worthy of death." The Earl of Pembroke, the Mayor and aldermen of the City assisted as the proclamation was cried at Paul's Cross and other gathering places. At the same instant, all the bells in the City began to ring. This was followed throughout the realm as the bells of England pealed continuously for twenty-four hours. The Londoners, delighted as the phantom of civil war and a disputed succession disappeared, built huge bonfires. They locked hands and, singing psalms, danced and rejoiced that their Queen had at last determined on the destruction of one who had conspired against her life and throne.

On hearing that Elizabeth was proceeding "to urge extremities to the Queen of Scots," the French King, Henri III, sent M. de Pomponne de Bellivre, his Minister of Finance, to plead with Elizabeth for Mary's life. Elizabeth received the visitor at Richmond and listened as he likened Mary to a "stone that you hold in your hand." De Bellivre was explicit. "Fling it at your enemy and it is gone; you can threaten with it no more. Kill her as some advise you, and her death will arm your adversaries with despair and will give them a more plausible ground on which to assail you." He said that Mary's brother-in-law, the French King, had "for nineteen years" observed Elizabeth closely and that she had used Mary's pretensions to the throne "as your strongest protection." Now was not the time to change, said de Bellivre. Mendoza, in Paris, was openly gloating that it would be to Philip's advantage "if the Queen of Scots is destroyed," for then the English Catholics would give *him*, Philip and Spain, their undivided allegiance.[39] He asked that Elizabeth spare Mary, that she "think of the judgment of posterity and of the name which you will leave behind. . . ."

De Bellivre's comment strongly voiced many of Elizabeth's innermost fears, and in a tone "so loud the archers of her guard could hear" she told him, "I am very sorry that you have not come on a better occasion, that I have been compelled to come to the resolution I have taken because it is impossible to save my own life if I preserve the Queen of Scots. . . ." She then added poignantly "that she had never shed so many tears at the death of her father, of her brother, King Edward, or her sister Mary, as she had done for this unfortunate affair." Elizabeth said that if the French could think of "some means whereby she could preserve the Princess's life without being in danger of her own . . ." she would be greatly obliged to them. When, in a subsequent interview, they could produce no definite guarantees, Elizabeth said "she could not be cruel to herself" and suggested that the French King "ought not to consider it just that she, who is innocent, should die and that the Queen of Scotland, who is guilty, should be saved. . . ." When de Bellivre impassionedly defended Mary as "a persecuted supplicant, in very great affliction . . . so humiliated and abased that her greatest enemies must view her with compassion . . ." with nothing to look forward to but a "miserable life of a few sad days," Elizabeth appeared moved. But when he continued that "surely no one can believe that your Majesty can resolve to cut those short by a rigorous execution," the Queen repeated her grievances and ended the interview saying that out of respect for the French King, she would delay twelve days "before proceeding to the execution of the judgment. . . ."[40]

During the following twelve days, Elizabeth could find no solution. To put Mary to death might be viewed as private revenge rather than political expediency. Her Councillors, seeing Elizabeth's perplexity only increased by the Scottish and French embassies' visits, spoke of the futility of granting such audiences, but with her sure instinct for public approval, Elizabeth realized she must listen to all such pleas for Mary's life, while still maintaining her right to execute her cousin for her treasonous acts. Also, a personal confrontation with the representatives of James of Scotland and Henri of France was valuable, and in subsequent audiences, Elizabeth eventually realized neither country would actively seek revenge should Mary die. James would not risk his rights in the succession, and Henri could not afford to attack his neighbor across the Channel. When de Bellivre had exhausted his efforts, disappointed his King and wearied himself in Mary's behalf and yet saw no change in Elizabeth's attitude, he made plans to return to France. With a heavy heart he realized that all hope for Mary Stuart was gone. Her son had abandoned her; Philip of Spain and the Pope had done nothing.

He could not know as he made ready to depart that many more than the twelve days Elizabeth had granted would elapse before any definite action against the Scottish Queen would be taken. The one who had protested the loudest and longest, the Queen of England herself, was—despite the glad bells pealing over England—as uncertain, as reluctant and full of misgiving as the disappointed Frenchman. Sentencing was one thing; execution another.

With the departure of the foreign ambassadors, Elizabeth was left to face her dilemma alone. Burghley, ill at Theobalds, dragged himself to court from time to time, and Walsingham remained at Barn Elms. The Queen had shown nothing but animosity toward her Secretary, and she turned a deaf ear to Burghley's contention that she owed her life to Walsingham's careful diligence. The minister, greatly in debt, had hoped to be awarded Anthony Babington's estates, and Burghley expressly told his sovereign, "it would be a great dishonour to her if she allowed him [Walsingham] to be crushed." Leicester, anxious to settle some small grudge against Walsingham, persuaded her otherwise, but was somewhat abashed when the Queen gave the estates instead to Sir Walter Raleigh. Walsingham did not take his defeat lightly. He wrote

Burghley, "Her Majesty's unkind dealing towards me has so wounded me, as I could take no comfort to stay. . . ."[41]

Walsingham was not the only one dismissed from her presence. The Councillors, at first demanding that Elizabeth act on Parliament's sentence, "were dismissed, all unsatisfied, with no other reason but that it [Mary's execution] . . . was utterly repugnant to her mind."[42] Once the court had moved to Greenwich for the holidays, London became ominously quiet as her subjects waited. The inevitable rumors commenced. "False bruits were spread abroad," wrote Walsingham, "that the Queen of Scots was broken out of prison, that the City of London was fired, that many thousand Spaniards were landed in Wales, that certain noblemen were fled, and such like. . . ." The tension in the court, where everyone expected Elizabeth to act, was broken when a letter from Mary Stuart was handed to the Queen.

Mary addressed her cousin as "Madame," She said she had experienced great difficulty in getting permission to write,* and she hoped Elizabeth would "credit or disbelieve my discourse as it seems best." She had been apprised of the sentence against her and admonished "to prepare for the end of my long and weary pilgrimage," and for that she was grateful. She wrote, "I would willingly return you thanks, and supplicate still further, as a last request . . . which I ought to ask of you alone, that you will accord this ultimate grace, for which I should like not to be indebted to any other, since I have no hope of finding aught but cruelty from the Puritans, who are, at this time, God knows wherefore, the first in authority, and the most bitter against me. . . ."

For her unfortunate position, Mary said she accused no one, but she did not say this to excuse Elizabeth, who, "more than anyone, ought to feel the honour or dishonour of your own blood. . . ." She then requested that "when my enemies have slaked their black thirst for my innocent blood, you will permit my poor desolated servants altogether to carry away my corpse to bury it in holy ground with the other Queens of France, my predecessors, especially near the late Queen, my mother. . . ." Mary said in Scotland the bodies of the Catholic Kings had been "outraged," and dying as she would in England, "I shall not be given place near the Kings, your predecessors. . . ."

Mary thanked Elizabeth for the concession of a priest and said she hoped "you will refuse me not this my last request, that you will permit me free sepulchre to this body when the soul is separated, which, when

*Mary had an equally difficult time acquiring the writing materials, and Paulet accepted the letter only when she had wiped her face with both sheets of paper to show that the stationery was not poisoned.[43]

united, could never obtain liberty to live in repose such as you would procure for yourself. . . ." Mary said she "dreaded the tyranny of those to whose power you have abandoned me," and she entreated Elizabeth "not to permit the execution to be done on me without your own knowledge, not for the fear of the torment, which I am most ready to suffer, but on account of the reports which will be raised concerning my death without other witnesses than those who would inflict it, who, I am persuaded, would be of very different qualities from those parties who I require (being my servants) to be my spectators. . . ." Mary's great pride in her manner of death and her equally great fear that she would be done away with privately and ignominiously, with no witnesses to the fact that she died "in the faith of our sacrament, of my Saviour and in obedience to His church," are evident throughout the letter. She said she hoped Elizabeth would allow her such privilege "after all is over, that they (my servants) together may carry away my poor corpse, (as secretly as you please) and speedily withdraw without taking with them any of my goods, except those which, in dying, I may leave to them . . . which are little enough for their long and good service."

Mary then asked permission to send a small jewel and a "last adieu" to her son and told Elizabeth her cloth of estate and dais had been removed by her jailers who "had done all in their power to degrade me from my rank . . . they told me 'that I was a mere dead woman, incapable of dignity.' God be praised!"

Mary then asked that Elizabeth receive all the papers she might leave so that "it may be manifest to you that the sole care of your safety was not confined to those who are so prompt to persecute me." And then, arriving at the end of the letter, she frankly put in words the fear she knew must be haunting her cousin:

To conclude, I pray God, the just Judge, of his mercy, that he will enlighten you with His holy Spirit, and that he will give me grace to die in the perfect charity I am disposed to do, and to pardon all those who have caused or who have cooperated in my death. Such will be my last prayer to the end, which I esteem myself happy will precede the persecution which I foresee menaces this isle, where God is no longer seriously feared and revered, but vanity and worldly policy rule and govern all. . . .

Yet while abandoning this world and preparing myself for a better, *I must remind you that one day you will have to answer for your charge* [author's italics], and for all those whom you doom, and that I desire that my blood and my country may be remembered in that time. For why? From the first days of our capacity to comprehend our duties, we ought to bend our minds to make the things of this world yield to those of eternity!

From Fotheringhay, this 19th of December, 1586.
Your sister and cousin, prisoner wrongfully,
MARIE, Queen[44]

The letter prostrated Elizabeth. Leicester, who saw its effect, wrote Walsingham, "There is a letter from the Scottish Queen that hath wrought tears, but I trust shall do no further therein, albeit the delay is too dangerous." Elizabeth's tears were her only outlet against the pressure to conclude Mary's sentence. Parliament was not prorogued, merely adjourned—and waiting. Ringing in her ears were her law-makers' final words: "We, your most loving and dutiful subjects, shall thereby be brought to utter despair of the continuance amongst us of the true religion of Almighty God and of your Majesty's life . . ." if she did not at once order Mary's execution.

As the Queen played her part in the Christmas festivities, as she accepted the rich and rare gifts tendered the monarch at the beginning of the New Year, the heartbreaking problem evaded solution. To execute Mary was against all tradition. Crowned, anointed monarchs did not lay their heads on a block, yet Elizabeth could scarcely forget her own mother had been a notable exception. It was more fitting and charitable, if they must be done away with, to have them dispatched by poison, stabbing or smothered in cloistered horror. Anything was preferable to judicial trial and public execution.

No one was at hand to help in this most painful decision of her life. The Queen felt abandoned. Her reluctance to dispose of Mary was unfeigned. Yet, at the same time, there was little doubt that she desperately wanted Mary out of the way—if only she herself did not have to suffer censure for the death. Her ministers did not help, merely informing her that, with the rumors abounding, "with such scarecrows and affrighting arguments," they could not understand her indecision. Only Burghley and Leicester realized the soul-searing agony their sovereign was experiencing, and Burghley noted, "Her Majesty keepeth herself more privately than she was wont." Those in her chamber could hear her often mutter to herself as she paced the floor, "Either bear with her or smite her," and, after a moment, adding bitterly, "Strike, lest thou be stricken."[45]

At last Elizabeth could delay no longer; there remained nothing but the signing of the warrant which she hoped would placate her ministers for the moment. It would, at least, show her good intention. By signing the warrant, she might also help to quell the disquiet in the City, and she could wait for any period of time before actually putting it into effect. After a long conference with her uncle Lord William Howard, who implored her "to have more regard to the surety of herself and the state," Elizabeth, absorbing some of his strong confidence and realistic determination, sent word that the warrant be brought to her. William Davison, the Secretary substituting for the absent Walsingham, was found in Greenwich Park and hurried back to the Palace. Howard told Davison the Queen "was now fully resolved to proceed to the accomplishment thereof, and had commanded him to send expressly . . . to bring the warrant unto her to be signed, that it might be forthwith despatched and deferred no longer," words Elizabeth would later deny. Accordingly, Davison, warrant in hand, soon entered the Queen's Privy Chamber.

Elizabeth was pleasantly casual. She asked, as Davison later reported, "whether I had been abroad this fair morning?" She talked briefly on the merits of early-morning exercise to which she herself was devoted, and she advised Davison to "use it oftener." She glanced at the papers and asked, "What I had in my hands. . . ?" Davison answered, "Divers things to be signed that concerned her service." She asked if the Lord Admiral had mentioned the warrant, and Davison placed it in her hands. She told the Secretary she had neglected signing it for so long as evidence of her extreme reluctance to proceed against Mary. She glanced at it carefully and then, calling for pen and ink, signed it, unexpectedly asking Davison "if he were not heartily sorry to see it done?" The Secretary, taken aback by her frankness, answered that "seeing the life of that Queen threatened her Majesty's death . . . this act of hers, in all men's opinions, was of that justice and necessity that she could not defer it. . . ." The answer seemed to satisfy Elizabeth, and she asked, smiling faintly, 'What else have you to sign?" After the Queen had finished with other minor papers, she commanded Davison to take the warrant to the Lord Chancellor "to use it as secretly as might be, lest the divulging thereof before the execution might increase her danger." It was also Elizabeth's wish that on the way to the Lord Chancellor, Davison was to stop at Walsingham's London house and tell him what she had done. Elizabeth's hard tone turned to one of ironic humor as she said tersely, "The grief thereof would go near to kill him outright."[46]

As Davison prepared to leave, Elizabeth had other suggestions. She commanded that the execution be private in the Great Hall of Fotheringhay, and then she said, complainingly, that Sir Amyas Paulet and his co-custodian, Sir Drue Drury, might "have eased her of this burden." When Davison professed ignorance of her meaning, she ordered that Walsingham should write to Mary's guardians that the intent of the Bond of Association was that her noblemen should protect her, their Queen, from all designs on her life. Her meaning was clear. She had signed the warrant, which showed her intent, but she expected Paulet and Drury to dispose of the Queen of Scots themselves. Bravely, Davison said that "albeit I had before excused myself from meddling therein," he would now assure Elizabeth that "it would be so much labour lost, knowing the wisdom and integrity of the gentlemen whom I thought would not do so unlawful an act for any respect in the world," and he told the Queen that the bond would protect them only if they acted on Elizabeth's express orders. Even at the end Elizabeth's desperation was such that she hoped someone such as Paulet would spare her the responsibility of taking Mary's life. Her surreptitious plea to Paulet was the act of an anguished and frightened woman, one who hoped to conceal her real desire for Mary's death as she anxiously struggled to preserve her own life and good reputation.

Davison, however, did as he was ordered. The warrant went to the Lord Chancellor for sealing, "which was done between the hours of four and five in the afternoon," and then to Secretary Walsingham. The next day Walsingham dutifully wrote Paulet and Drury, informing them of Elizabeth's contention that she had noted in both "a lack of that care and zeal for her service . . . in that you have not, in all this time . . . found out some way of shortening the life of the Scots' Queen, considering the great peril she, Queen Elizabeth, is hourly subjected to so long as the said Queen shall live. . . ." Walsingham appealed to the "satisfaction of your consciences towards God and the discharge of your credit and reputation towards the world" and mentioned the oath they had taken under the Bond of Association. He said Elizabeth "taketh it most unkindly towards her that men professing that love towards her that you do, should in any kind of sort, for lack of the discharge of your duties, cast the burden upon her, knowing as you do her indisposition to shed blood, especially of one of that sex and quality and so near to her in blood as the said Queen is."[47] Davison was so fearful of the letter that he sent it enclosed in one of his own and at the bottom wrote, "I pray let this and the enclosed be committed to the fire. . . ."

By five o'clock the next afternoon the letter was at Fotheringhay. The Puritan Paulet was aghast at the Queen's implication, and with that careful thought which attended his meticulous nature—especially when it could prove the difference between life and death—he did not burn the letter. He noted the date of its receipt in his letter-register and then, with little waste of time, neatly answered that he would have nothing to do with the matter. Professing "great grief and bitterness of mind, in that I am so unhappy to have lived to see this unhappy day in which I am required by my most gracious sovereign to do an act which God and the law forbiddeth," Paulet replied, "his good livings and life are at her Majesty's disposition . . . but God forbid that I should make so foul a shipwreck of my conscience, or leave so great a blot to my poor posterity, to shed blood without law or warrant!" He said that Sir Drue Drury "subscribeth in heart to my opinion."[48]

All of which left Elizabeth exactly back where she had been at the beginning. Except she had now signed the warrant and had only to order its express dispatch to rid herself once and for all of the challenge of the Queen of Scots.

The next day, February 2, Davison attended the Queen, and she asked idly if the warrant had been sealed. When told it had, she turned and said brusquely, "What needeth that haste?" to which the surprised Secretary, fearing her displeasure, nevertheless frankly reminded her that he had made "no more haste than she herself commanded."

"Well, I think that it might have been otherwise handled for the form . . ." Elizabeth said noncommittally, leaving Davison uneasy. He mumbled that what had been done was the "honourable and just way" if the Queen meant to proceed at all, and then, leaving her presence, he proceeded to Sir Christopher Hatton, whom he apprised of all that had happened. He reminded Hatton of Elizabeth's vacillation at the time of Norfolk's execution and her animosity toward those who had insisted on his death. He could foresee something of that nature facing him and wishing "to do nothing that might give her any advantage to cast a burden of so great weight upon my single and weak shoulders . . ." implied he would go no further unless Hatton and others of the Council shared the responsibility. Hatton agreed and said he was pleased "the matter was brought thus far. . . ."

Together, the two went to visit Lord Burghley, still ill with his old ailment at his home. The signed warrant was put into his hands, "God be praised!" said the Lord Treasurer. "The Queen hath done her part." He was told of Elizabeth's wavering and Davison's fear of acting alone. In spite of her command for secrecy, he called a meeting, and the following morning Howard, Hunsdon and Sir Francis Knollys answered his summons. They listened to Burghley's assertions that the danger to the Queen and the realm was such that the execution must be proceeded with immediately. He showed them the warrant, and afraid that Elizabeth might retract it at any time, the Council voted unanimously that the warrant should be sent to Fotheringhay at once. Robert Beale, the Clerk of the Council, was delegated to carry it to the Earl of Kent and the Earl of Shrewsbury to see that it was acted on.

Then, their business finished, the Lords went to their dinner between one and two in the afternoon.

The following morning, February 4, Davison saw the Queen and Burghley in her chambers. Nothing was mentioned of the previous day's proceedings. Elizabeth, however, as if asking an answer to a question she dared not ask aloud, commented that "she had been troubled that night upon a dream she had that the Scottish Queen was executed," and she told Davison she was so angry with him "that she would have run him through with a sword." As it was said in a smiling fashion, Davison merely replied "that it was good for me I was not near her, so long as that humor lasted!" However, his general anxiety was such that he asked her "what it meant?" She had signed the warrant. Did she not expect to go through with it?

"Yes," answered the Queen, knowing that she ultimately would have to proceed, yet she stated once more that she "thought that it might have received a better form because this threw all the responsibility upon herself." There must be a better way of accomplishing the same end. For herself, she would be glad to have Mary strictly incarcerated. If the country and government expected anything more of her, they should assist her in such a great event where she might be accused of personal vindictiveness.[49] Davison soothed the Queen, saying she had acted "as the law required," and such law "could not well be altered without any honesty, justice or surety." He said he did not think there were sound reasons "to prove it either honourable or safe for her Majesty to take any other course than that which standeth with law and justice." When, a day or so afterward, she read Paulet's letter in which he bluntly refused to do away with Mary, Elizabeth allowed herself the luxury of an outburst, angrily flinging the letter from her and complaining of "the daintiness and perjury of him and the others who, contrary to their Oath, did cast the burden upon herself!" In Paulet's refusal, the Queen recognized she alone must take responsibility for Mary's death. In great disappointment, she walked hastily around the chamber for several moments as if to dissipate an intolerable anxiety. She muttered against "the niceness of those precise fellows who in words would do great things for her surety, but in deed perform nothing," and she concluded by saying "that she could have it well enough done without them!" If they could or would not soil their hands, Elizabeth said, she knew several in court who would. Certainly, "one Wingfield" would undertake Mary's secret murder. Her words, as Davison later said, "gave me occasion to show unto her Majesty how dishonourable, in my poor opinion, any such course would be. . . ."[50]

Elizabeth evinced no further information about "one Wingfield" but contented herself with further denunciation of Paulet and Drury.

The following morning Davison again appeared in the Privy Chamber with documents to be signed and noticed that Elizabeth's agitation had increased. Almost at once the Queen opened the conversation and said that because "of the danger she daily lived in, how it was more than time this matter were despatched." Several days had passed since she had signed the warrant, and she had now persuaded herself it would have to be discharged. Turning to Davison, with a great oath, she ordered the Secretary "to have a letter written to Mr. Paulet for the despatch thereof, because the longer it was deferred, the more her danger had increased." Davison, knowing the warrant had already gone to Fotheringhay, was momentarily tongue-tied, as he perceived his predicament and then, hoping to ease the situation said, that he "thought there was no necessity for such a letter, the warrant being so general and sufficient as it was." Remembering Paulet's "daintiness and preciseness," however, the Queen was not so sure. "No," she said abruptly, "Mr. Paulet will look for it."

At that point, several of her ladies entered "to hear her Majesty's pleasure about dinner," and Davison was left with the solitary knowledge that it was February 8, 1587, the morning the Council had ordered for the execution of Mary, Queen of Scots, at Fotheringhay.

Chapter Twenty-six

By February, 1587, Mary had passed six weeks under sentence of death. She had spent that time writing farewells to her son, to the Pope, to Henri III and to Philip of Spain. Her great concern was her servants' fate after she was gone and how, in the meantime, she might best tolerate the daily abuse by Paulet and those visiting from the English court. At Chartley, Mary's dais and cloth of estate had been restored. But, once under sentence, as she wrote Archbishop Beaton, "Paulet came again to me with Drury, who is much more modest and civil to tell me that since I had . . . neither shown contrition nor any sense of fault, she [Elizabeth] had commanded him to take down my dais, to signify to me that I was a dead woman, deprived of the honours and dignity of a Queen." Her servants had refused to do Paulet's bidding, and amid their cries of protest, he had called "seven or eight of his own creatures and, having knocked down the dais, he seated himself, covered his head and told me 'that as there was no longer any time for leisure for me to waste in idle recreation,' he should take away my billiard table. . . ." Later Paulet was forced to admit he had acted in anger without Elizabeth's permission, but "at the suggestion of one of the Council." Mary listened and then, as she wrote a relative in France, "I showed them the Cross in the place where my dais had been. . . ."[1]

As the weeks passed, Paulet wrote to Walsingham of his displeasure "of the unseasonable delays" in proceeding further against Mary. He said that "Fotheringhay was forgotten, although the Lady under his charge had given all her Majesty's true and unfaithful subjects cause not to sleep soundly till the head and seed-plot of all practices and conspiracies was utterly extirpated." He said Mary "was ill in one of her knees, but that is no new thing." His encounters with the Scottish Queen continued to anger him. "I see no change in her from her former quietness . . ." he wrote. Mary's unrepentant and proud attitude so disturbed him he eventually stopped visiting her apartments each day. He told Walsingham, "I pray you let me hear from you whether it is expected that I should see my charge often, which as I do not desire to do so, so I do not see that any good can come of it."[2]

As her reprieve continued, Mary's hopes began to rise, and her first assumption that Elizabeth would never dare to execute her became stronger. Whenever the threat of death did return, she would cling to her conviction that she would die for the faith which made her such a powerful threat to England's Queen. If she became too optimistic, the sound of soldiers' footsteps beneath her window and outside her chamber reminded her of the suspense and dread with which she lived. Her servants appeared worried, distracted and sad. There was no news to be had, and she remained in her room, the desolate weather precluding any exercise, even if it had been allowed. Her health had worsened under the mental strain and physical deprivation, and she asked Bourgoing, her physician, for medicine which might alleviate her discomfort. There was also another reason. "When the summons for my death comes," Mary said, "I would not willingly be so circumstanced that my incapacity to rise from my bed might be construed into reluctance or fear." Bourgoing sought Paulet for the necessary permission to go into the village and fields for the requisite herbs and simples, only to be refused. When Mary protested, Paulet told her evasively, "Peradventure, you will not require it . . ." for daily he expected the arrival of the warrant. When Mary heard that Robert Beale, the Clerk of the Council, had arrived at Fotheringhay and that the household "was in a terrible state of apprehension," she realized there was only one mission which would have brought him. When she was told to expect visitors later, her fears were confirmed; then her strongest desire was to accept her fate calmly, with the dignity worthy of a Queen.

Several hours later Mary was seated in a small chair at the foot of her bed when the chamber door opened to admit the Earl of Kent, Beale, Sir Drue Drury and her old friend the Earl of Shrewsbury. While Shrewsbury courteously uncovered his head, the others pointedly kept their hats on. Mary waited, silent, her hands clenched in the folds of her gown to hide their trembling.

Shrewsbury spoke first. It was with a sorrowful voice that he said, "Madame, I would have desired greatly that another than I should announce to you such sad intelligence as that which I now bring on the part of the Queen of England." Pointing to Kent, he said, "He and I being both faithful servants . . . could but obey the commandment she gave me." And after telling Mary she must "undergo the sentence of death" pronounced against her, he nodded to Beale to produce the warrant from which dangled the yellow waxen Great Seal of England.

After listening to Beale's sententious reading of the warrant and guessing at Shrewsbury's discomfort, Mary said calmly, "I am thankful to you for such welcome news! You will do me great good in withdrawing me from this world, out of which I am very glad to go, on account of the miseries I see in it, and of being myself in continual affliction. I am of no use or profit to anyone. From day to day for eighteen years, I have expected this moment. . . ."[3] She then asked when she was to suffer, and, being told it would be at eight o'clock the next morning, seemed stunned, saying, "The time is very short." In one corner of her chamber, Jane Kennedy, her maid, began to weep.

The Earl of Kent, silent until then, told Mary she might have "the solace of the Dean of Peterborough . . . who would be able to show her the errors of the false religion in which she had been brought up. . . ." His words brought a smile to Mary's lips, and she replied that "she had both heard and read much on the subject, especially since her detention in England, but her mind was fully made up that she would die in the religion in which she had been baptized. . . ."

"Madame," said the Protestant Earl of Kent, not realizing the great import of his words or the comfort he would give to the condemned woman, "your life would be the death of our religion. Your death will be its preservation!" A happy smile enhanced Mary's wan features. "Ah!" she exclaimed, "I did not flatter myself with the thought that I was worthy of such a death and I humbly receive it as an earnest of my acceptance into the number of God's chosen servants!"[4]

Mary had not finished, however. As Kent remained silent, she placed her hand on the New Testament which lay on a nearby table. "I take God to witness that I never desired, sought nor consented to the death of your Queen!"

"That book is a Popish Testament!" cried Kent, "and your oath is of no value!" To which Mary, stung by his attitude, answered sharply, "If I swear on the Book which I believe to be the true version, will your Lordship not believe my oath more than if I were to swear on a translation in which I do not believe?"

There was an awkward silence for a moment, and then Mary asked if Elizabeth had sent any final word. "None," replied the Earls. She asked if the English Queen had given any instructions for the disposition of her body and was told only that Elizabeth had been firm that she would not be buried in France. She was relieved to hear Shrewsbury tell Paulet, "Sir Amyas, we remit this lady into your hands. . . ."

At least she knew what to expect from Paulet. Hateful as he was, she could have been delivered into other more brutal hands.

At the Earls' departure, Mary summoned all her strength and resources to deal with her servants, cowering in the candlelight in the far corner of her chamber. They were weeping, crossing themselves and showing all evidence of the strain they, too, had lived under for so many weeks. Mary arose and, as her physician came to her side, called to the group. Jane Kennedy, coming forward, flung herself at Mary's knees, clasping the rheumatic legs as if she would never let go.

Mary looked down at the woman fondly. "Up, Jane Kennedy!" she said, attempting a touch of humor and sternness. "Leave weeping and be doing, for the time is short. Did I not tell you that it would come to this?" And then, almost as if speaking to herself, she said, "Blessed God that it has come and fear and sorrow are at an end!"

Mary spent the remainder of the evening accomplishing the small tasks for which she had so little time. Elizabeth had returned her money confiscated at Chartley, and Mary now divided the coins into little sacks, writing down the name of a servant on each little bundle. One thing kept bearing on her mind, and as she wrote, she pondered on it, later mentioning it to Bourgoing. "They said," she noted reflectively, "I was to die for attempting the life of the Queen of England, of which you know I am innocent. But now this Earl [Kent] lets out the fact that it is on account of my religion! Oh, glorious thought, that I should be chosen to die for such a cause!"

And thus, from the chance remark of an embittered Earl, came the solace and comfort which were to remain with the Queen throughout the long night as she waited in the cold darkness of her chamber, listening to the hammering in the Great Hall as the execution scaffold was erected.

She did not sleep throughout the evening. Instead, she had caused a large cup to be filled with wine, and she drank a toast to each of those who had shared her imprisonment, asking them to drink one to her in return. Shakenly, they had come closer to the Queen, begging her forgiveness for small sins, as Mary smiled and said, "With all my heart, my children, even as I pray you to forgive me of any harshness of which I may have been guilty towards you." With Bourgoing's aid, she went to her desk, where she had written an inventory of everything she possessed. On his insistence, she seated herself and each item was then brought forth to her—garments, insignificant jewels, plate, a few pieces of silver. She gave the physician two small silver boxes, two lutes, her music book bound in velvet and the crimson hangings of her bed. To Elizabeth Curle she gave a gold and enameled tablet with miniatures of herself, her son, James, and her first husband, François II. Other mementos were set aside for Catherine de Medici, the King of Spain and other relatives and friends.[5] She then wrote her chaplain, confessing "the gravity of her sins." Calmly and unemotionally, she then picked up her pen and wrote her will. In its pages were mentioned all who had been faithful, Jane Kennedy, Elizabeth Curle, Sebastian Pages, Martin her cook, Andrew Melville, her steward, now forbidden her presence, and her faithful Bourgoing. Even her absent secretaries, Claude Nau and Gilbert Curle, were not forgotten. She then wrote a short letter to Henri III of France asking that a Requiem Mass be held and that wages and pensions be paid to those of her servants who wished to return to France.

At two o'clock in the morning, tired with the strain of attempting to remember everything, she lay down on her bed and listened to Jane Kennedy read from *The Lives of the Saints*. Slowly the tapers in the chamber burned down as the Queen of Scotland, with eyes closed, though not sleeping, listened to the pounding in the Great Hall and the soldiers' noises outside. In the chamber, several of her servants, reluctant to leave, dozed through their tears. Only once did Mary rouse them. She wished an especially fine handkerchief with a gold embroidered edge to lay on the pillow beside her. It would do well to cover her eyes on the morrow, she said.

At six o'clock on February 8, Mary rose from the bed and submitted to the ministrations of her servingwoman. Washed, coiffed in a fine wig, she selected blue stockings attached to silken garters to be worn inside drawers of white fustian. A scarlet petticoat went beneath her traditional dress of black satin edged with black velvet. Atop the petticoat, for modesty's sake, she had donned a fine crimson camisole to cover the upper part of her body when the dress was removed, as she knew it would be. On her head she wore the peaked cap with a long flowing white veil "of the most delicate texture, edged with lace," which descended over her shoulders almost to the ground. A pomander chain and an Agnus Dei were put about her neck, while a pair of beads with a cross was looped around her waist. As she touched the cross dangling from its chain, the terrible significance of the moment became overwhelmingly real, and turning to her women, she said fearfully, "I shall be incapable of thinking of this poor body or bestowing any care upon it. Oh, then, for the love of our Blessed Saviour, abandon me not while under the hands of the executioner!"[6]

Struggling to compose herself, she then went into her Oratory to pray in the little time left.

Returning, she gathered her ladies about her for one final embrace. One by one, her menservants—Gervais, the apothecary; Stouvart, the valet; Didier, her old butler; and several others—all entered to kiss her hand. As her physician handed her a little bread and wine, she asked that her will be read so that her servants would know she had tried to the best of her ability to care for them at the end. She then asked that they all stay together until her own body had been disposed of and ended by stating she had left her coach and her horses and furniture to be sold for sufficient money for their return either to Scotland or France. "Now," she said, "I have finished with the world. Let us all kneel and pray together for the last time." At that moment, a shout and loud banging on the door interrupted the devotions. Being told that "Her Majesty was engaged in prayers with her servants," Sheriff Thomas Andrews departed. In fifteen minutes, he returned with Paulet, Shrewsbury, Kent and several others. This time the door was opened, and the group was confronted with the moving picture of Mary and her servants in silent prayer. After a moment, the Sheriff said in a faltering voice, "Madame, the Lords have sent me for you."

Mary rose, gesturing her servants to follow, at which two of Paulet's men came forward to say they had been chosen to assist her. Loyally, Mary's servants clustered around the Queen, but at the door they were stopped and told they must go no farther. Bourgoing protested "the cruelty of the proceeding" as the cries of the women could be heard outside in the Hall. Mary then asked that "her poor servants might be present with me at my death. . . ," to which the unfeeling Kent brutally said, "Madame, that which you have desired cannot be conveniently granted, for if it should, it were to be feared lest some of them, with speeches and other behaviour, would both be grievous to your Grace, and troublesome and unpleasing to us and our company. . . ." He ended by saying that some of them "might not even stick to put some superstitious trumpery in practice if it were but in dipping their handkerchief in your Graces's blood. . . ."[7]

Mary protested, "My Lord, I will give you my word, although it be but dead, that they shall do none of these things." She said she was sure "Her Majesty hath not given you such straight commission but that you might grant me a far greater courtesy than this. . . ." Then the strain breaking through, she burst into tears, at the same time, with a touch of Stuart and Tudor temper, crying, "Remember! I am cousin to your Queen, descended of the blood royal of Henry VII, a married Queen of

France, and the anointed Queen of Scotland!" Then, angrily, her tears forgotten, she demanded that her servants be allowed to accompany her.

The strength of Mary's tone, coupled with the majesty of the tall, imperious figure, quelled those who opposed her. Ultimately, Jane Kennedy and Elizabeth Curle, Melville, her steward, Bourgoing, her physician, and Jacques Gervais, the apothecary, were allowed to accompany her. She turned and once more embraced those she must leave behind, kissing them tenderly and raising those who cast themselves at her feet. Then, with the sound of their weeping still in her ears, she indicated the processsion should continue.

At the foot of the stairs she met, for the first time in several weeks, the absent Melville, and as he advanced to join her, the tearful scene was repeated. "Weep not, Melville, my good and faithful servant," said the Queen, "thou should rather rejoice that thou shalt now see the end of the long troubles of Mary Stuart . . ." and she leaned gratefully on his strong arm. She took the opportunity of her last few moments with Melville to ask that he seek out her son and tell James she had "done nothing to prejudice him in his realm, nor to disparage his dignity. . . . Tell him, from my example, never to rely too much on human aid, but to seek that which is from above. . . ."

As she proceeded toward the Hall, others, such as Sir William FitzWilliam, a former resident who held the lease of Fotheringhay, came forward to kiss her hand, and Mary thanked him "for his gentle entreatment of her while in his house. . . ." Knowing she had omitted him from her will, she asked that he accept a portrait of the King, her son, "which he would find hanging at her bed's head, being her last remaining possession she had not bequeathed."[8] At the entrance to the Great Hall, she stopped and said to Melville, "Farewell, good Melville . . . pray for thy Queen and mistress."

In the Great Hall, a fire blazed in the huge fireplace, and around the room more than 300 spectators—knights and gentlemen of the county—had gathered to watch the execution. In the center, Mary saw a platform, twelve feet square and two and a half feet high, covered with black cloth and surrounded with a railing. In one corner of the platform were two masked, black-clad figures, one of them holding an ax. If Mary saw them—and she could hardly have avoided doing so—she gave no sign. She noted the block covered in black serge. Nearby were a small chair for her and two stools for Shrewsbury and Kent. Ignoring the spectators, who seemed awed by her calm, she advanced almost eagerly toward the scaffold. Paulet was waiting at the steps erected for easy ascending. He offered his arm to assist her, and Mary accepted, saying, "I thank you for your courtesy, Sir Amyas. This will be the last trouble I shall give you and the most agreeable service you have ever rendered me."[9] Ascending the platform, Mary sat down in the chair and listened once more to the warrant being read by Robert Beale. At its completion, she crossed herself, saying, "*Judica me, Deus, et discerne causam meam*," and then folded her hands in her lap and waited.

With obvious difficulty, the Earl of Shrewsbury arose and spoke, "Now Madame, you see what you have to do." To which Mary replied, "Do your duty . . ." and then, quickly, before Shrewsbury sat down, asked if she might have her priest. Instead, to her extreme consternation, Dr. Fletcher, the Dean of Peterborough, shouldered his way through the crowd and ascended the platform, approached Mary in her chair and, bending over, spoke to her. Mary looked at him and said, "Mr. Dean, trouble not yourself nor me, for know that I am settled in the ancient Catholic and Roman faith. . . ." The Dean implored Mary to change her mind "and repent of your former wickedness." Mary answered, advising the Dean to "trouble not yourself any more about this matter," saying she meant "to shed her blood for her faith." The Dean was insistent and, as Mary turned away, persisted in following her so he faced her again. Continuing in his remonstrances, he so irritated Mary, who was endeavoring to compose her mind with one last prayer, that she lay the crucifix against her breast and closed her eyes so she might not see him. Shrewsbury, jolted by the Dean's persistent haranguing, ordered him to discontinue, at which the prelate went to the scaffold steps and commenced to pray loudly, his words intermingling with the Queen's. As Mary, at one point, touched her crucifix, the Earl of Kent called, "You had better, Madame, leave such Popish trumperies and carry Christ in your heart."[10] To which Mary turned and, with a level gaze fixed on Kent, asked in a firm voice, "Can I hold the representation of the sufferings of my crucified Redeemer in my hand without bearing Him, at the same time, in my heart?"[11]

As Mary rose from her seat, the two executioners came forward to beg forgiveness. "I forgive you and all the world with all mine heart, for now I hope you shall make an end of all my trouble," Mary replied. When they offered to assist her in removing her headgear and outer dress, she said, with a touch of humor, "I have not been accustomed to be served by such pages of honour, not to disrobe before so numerous a company." She summoned Jane Kennedy and Elizabeth Curle, who quickly climbed the scaffold and, almost undone with emotion, proceeded to help Mary with her cap. Their eyes blinded with tears, they were clumsy, and Mary herself commenced to take out the pins.

"Do not weep," she said softly to them, "I am very happy to leave this world. . . . Are you not ashamed to weep? . . . if you do not give over these lamentations, I must send you away, for you know I have promised for you!"[12] When she took the necklace from her neck and handed it to Jane Kennedy, the executioner suddenly snatched it from the weeping woman. Mary gestured to him, saying, "My friend, let her have it. She will give you more than its value in money," to which the executioner replied sullenly, "It is my right." Mary then kissed the two women as they finished removing her upper garments and helped her draw on a pair of crimson sleeves. When the black dress was removed, Mary was seen in her crimson velvet petticoat, crimson sleeves and the red camisole, thus presenting a blood-red picture from head to foot, a stark contrast with the black-clad executioners, the black-draped Hall and scaffold. As the handkerchief was handed to Jane Kennedy, she wept so profusely she could scarcely see, and again Mary reproved her, saying, "I have promised for you. Weep not, but pray for me." Together Jane Kennedy and Elizabeth Curle pinned the handkerchief around Mary's brow, at which point they were led from the scaffold.

After a short prayer, Mary was guided to the block, where she lay her head, whispering as she did, "Into thy hands, Oh Lord, I commend my spirit!" Shrewsbury stood up and, waving his wand of office, prepared to signal the executioner. As he did so, the executioner noticed that Mary had grasped the block firmly with her hands, which might be cut or mangled at the fatal blow, and he motioned to his assistant to remove them to her side. The assistant grasped her hands, drawing them forward to the front, and again Shrewsbury held his wand of office high as, his face agitated, he swung the wand to the floor with a resounding thud.

The raised ax crashed upon the defenseless woman, but being put off his aim by the momentary pause to remove her hands, the executioner missed the neck and struck a glancing blow at the skull. Mary did not react. Mercifully the blow may have stunned her, although several witnesses later swore they heard the whispered words "Sweet Jesus!" Quickly, the ax was raised, swung downward and the head rolled to one side, with only one strong tendon still remaining. With a sawing motion, the executioner severed the head completely, and it rolled into the sawdust below. Perspiring and grimly exultant, aware he had not performed upon royalty too well, the executioner snatched up the head and shouted, "God save the Queen!" To which the rejected Dean of Peterborough, not to be outdone, cried, "So perish all enemies of the Queen!" The assembled spectators, awed by the display of raw courage, gaped at the bloody relic and reiterated the cry. Shrewsbury, speechless, his face wet with tears, made ready to leave the platform when a cry of horror arose from the crowd. Out of the wig of dark curls which the executioner held, the head of Mary Stuart fell to the floor once more, and the onlookers noted it "appeared perfectly gray, being polled very short. . . ." As the executioners prepared to take anything else of value from the still-warm corpse, a small animal, Mary's favorite Skye terrier, crept from beneath her undergarments and settled near the bloodied neck. He had come with the Queen, enveloped in the voluminous folds of her skirts, into the Hall and to the very block itself. Quickly, he was snatched up and taken away to be washed.

As Mary's body was borne away, as the bloody block and the clothing were carried outside to be burned so no martyr's relics might remain, Gilbert Talbot, Shrewsbury's son, passed out of Fotheringhay's courtyard to ride throughout the night to London. He carried the Dean of Peterborough's remarks on the day's events. "The eighth day of February, that judgment was repaid home to her, which on the tenth of the same month, twenty years past, she measured to her husband."

On Thursday, February 9, Talbot reached Greenwich and hurried at once to Burghley. The minister and his fellow Councillors forbade Talbot to inform Elizabeth of the execution, for, as Burghley said, "it would be better for time to break it cautiously to her by degrees." Therefore, what was known to many inside Greenwich Palace in a matter of moments was unknown to the Queen as, surrounded by her equerries and ladies, she rode forth from the park for a day of hunting. On her return late in the afternoon she received Don Antonio, the claimant for the disputed Crown of Portugal, and then, returning to her chamber, heard the pealing of the City's bells. As their clamor was wafted down the river, she asked one of her ladies "why the bells rang out so merrily?" and was told, "because of the death of the Queen of Scots."

Elizabeth's first thought was that Paulet had not waited for the letter she had signed the day before but, putting his "precise daintiness" aside had relieved his sovereign of the responsibility; the second was that Mary, infirm in health and burdened by stress, might have expired naturally. Her optimism was short-lived. When informed of the truth, she seemed stunned, "her countenance altered, her speech faltered and failed her and, through excessive sorrow, she stood in a manner astonished, insomuch that she gave herself over to passionate grief, putting herself into a mourning habit and shedding abundance of tears. . . ."[13]

Elizabeth's emotionalism was not unexpected. Her predilection for hysteria when tension became intolerable was well known. Certainly her Councillors had girded themselves for the inevitable impressive fireworks. But even they were silenced in the appalling display of passionate grief which Elizabeth Tudor revealed at the news of her cousin's execution.

The Queen had closeted herself in her chamber and there, susceptible to a vivid imagination, evoked for herself the scene in the Great Hall at Fotheringhay as related by her informants. She had, to be sure, signed a warrant for Mary's death, but she had done so merely to show her intentions and to satisfy her Councillors; she had not meant to have it acted on without her express authority. She had also written a letter to Paulet, but no one had cleared its dispatch with her. Soon Elizabeth convinced herself that inevitably she would have recalled the letter. Warrants and letters were easily rescinded; she had meant to go no further, at least not for the time being. To put to death a crowned Queen was an infamous deed; to do so publicly, as one would execute a common criminal, was shocking.

The following morning, Friday, Elizabeth summoned Sir Christopher Hatton to her chamber, and there she bitterly castigated William Davison for usurping her authority and effecting the death of the Queen of Scots. Hatton hurried from the royal presence to advise Davison to keep out of Elizabeth's sight until her anger had subsided.

Two days after the news had reached Greenwich, the Council was summoned to the Queen's presence. They entered the Withdrawing Chamber, where a pale Elizabeth, her eyes swollen and red-rimmed, awaited them. There was a silence for a moment, and then, as she cast all ceremony aside, the Queen's wrath exploded, and she "rebuked us all exceedingly for our concealing from her our proceeding in the Queen of Scots' case . . ." as one observer wrote to Leicester absent in the Netherlands. She thundered at her Councillors. The signed warrant would have been a powerful deterrent to Catholic aggression or any political move to aid Mary Stuart, she cried; *that was all she had meant it to be!* Davison, particularly, had exceeded his authority in allowing it to pass from his hands. As the white-faced Davison said nothing, the Queen turned her attention to Burghley and scathingly denounced him for dispatching the warrant. When Burghley, judging it prudent to remain silent, made no defense, Elizabeth loudly condemned Davison to the Tower. Aghast, the Councillors went en masse on their knees "to pray for the contrary" for the relief of the hapless

Secretary, who had so correctly foreseen his danger. As he later said, "he did not much marvel, considering what he had before observed of her desire to cast it [the responsibility] from herself." When the Council rose, Elizabeth repeated Davison would go to the Tower, and Burghley was ordered to his home. In great relief, the Council heard itself dismissed, and as Leicester's friends wrote to the absent Earl, "I think your Lordship happy to be absent from these broils. . . ."[14]

It was soon apparent, however, that the Queen's reaction was more than a "broil" which would disappear in a day or so. By royal order, all ports were closed so the news might not escape the country, and as word of Elizabeth's reaction seeped into the City, the blazing bonfires, the jubilant dancing, feasting and merriment ceased. Elizabeth's grief then engulfed court and country, and as she continued to deny all responsibility in the death of the Queen of Scots, toughened Councillors were reduced to tears. Others felt small stirrings of fear. In the Tower, Davison wondered—too late—at the comparative ease with which he, a minor Secretary, had apparently been selected as the scapegoat.

In the next several weeks, amid the taut atmosphere of her court, Elizabeth sought to deal with the political results of Mary's execution. The first and foremost premise in any explanation continued to be that she, the Queen of England, was not responsible. Circumstances had been such that a Secretary and a group of Councillors had taken a warrant she had signed as a threat and dispatched it without her express command. Technically, the Queen was absolutely correct, and she continually shied away from any assertion of what her future directions might have been. Instead, she presented the picture of a horrified monarch, heartbroken and distraught at the shocking death of her cousin the Catholic Queen, and in her persistent denial lies a germ of truth.

For many weeks, Elizabeth had been under tremendous psychological pressure from the Council to effect Parliament's sentence against Mary Stuart. Her reluctance to submit to that pressure was coupled with the frustrating knowledge that her ministers were driving her to effect an act too terrible for her to contemplate. Her actions in signing both warrant and letter may have been the ploy of a woman desperately playing for time, willing to show her good intent, deceiving herself that something—*anything*—might happen before the deed was done. She always had the privilege of recalling both warrant and letter.

Now, the more she reviewed what had happened, the more she convinced herself that she had *never* intended Mary's death and that her Council and Secretary had betrayed her. The event at

Fotheringhay had come as a shocking surprise rather than a dreaded inevitability, and it revived and released those long-hidden evils which had permeated her lonely and dangerous childhood. Again Elizabeth experienced that unsettling vulnerability and defenselessness which the years of power and privilege had effectively masked, and this, as much as anything else, combined to strengthen and justify her scandalous treatment of her ministers.

For days, the Council remained in disgrace. Walsingham, prudently ill at home, wrote Leicester, "Her Majesty doth wholly bend herself to devise further means to disgrace her poor Council . . . and in respect thereof, she neglects all other causes."[15] Indeed, Elizabeth could not deal with her sovereign responsibilities while so aware that the world's judgment was upon her. Her every waking moment was given over to reflecting how she might redeem herself with other monarchs for having put to death one of their own. Her first concern was young James Stuart, Mary's son.

Within days the stormy reaction of the Scottish people was known in London. Having done nothing in eighteen years to assist their former Queen, they considered the manner of Mary's death as an affront to their national pride. Lord Scrope wrote to Walsingham of James' reaction: "When the King understood . . . that his mother was in truth put to death, he did not only take that news very grievous and offensively, but also gave out in secret speeches that he could not digest the same, nor leave it unrevenged. . . ." Threats of Border raids, of burning Newcastle and other reprisals against the murdering English were carried to London. James wavered first with one group who advised action, then with another which counseled compromise. Always his lack of genuine sorrow at his mother's tragic end was mixed with dismay and worry as to how the manner of her death would affect his rights in the succession.

Elizabeth correctly guessed James' anxiety and, eager to placate, sent Lord Hunsdon's son, Sir Robert Carey, to Scotland to see James. He carried a message from the Queen. In the letter, Elizabeth addressed the King as "My dear brother," and she wrote, "I would you knew (though not felt) the extreme dolour that overwhelms my mind for that miserable accident which, far contrary to my meaning, hath befallen." She explained she sent Carey "to instruct you truly of that which is irksome for my pen to tell you"—that Davison had acted improperly in showing the warrant to the Council, which had overreached its authority in dispatching it. Her desire to appease James is apparent in her lines: "I beseech you, that as God, and many more know how innocent I am in this case, so you will believe me, that, if I had bid aught, I would have abided by it . . . I would never lay it on others' shoulders. . . ."[16]

James, ultimately, had an exquisite revenge. In a self-righteous parody of the tone Elizabeth had long adopted with Mary Stuart, he said he would like to believe her, but he must first "have a trial of her innocency. He would not condemn her unheard, but he could do no less than suspend his judgment from cleansing or condemning till further trial, for proofs that she had yet given of her innocency, he remitted to her own judgment, whether she had yet satisfied the world to her honour in that matter or not. . . ."[17] Stung, Elizabeth replied "that she found by the King's articles, a disposition to suspend his intelligence until he might be better satisfied of her innocency." She decried that he used words such as "trial" and "cleansing" as though he were a judge! She said she considered them absurd and "unmeet to be applied to her, being a Queen and a Prince Sovereign, answerable to none for her actions. . . ." Elizabeth did not remember—or chose to forget—that such had been Mary's reaction and defense before the York inquiry and the Fotheringhay trial.

Whatever James' secret beliefs, he could do little other than accept what Elizabeth told him, and within weeks, Walsingham wrote to Stafford in Paris that "the part of your letter where you say the King of Scots excuses her of the blame of the late execution, and lays the same upon her Council, did wonderfully content her Majesty, who desires nothing more than to have it generally conceived that she had the least part in the action. . . ."[18] Walsingham's return to court had exposed him to the same trial by fire the other Councillors had experienced, and he wrote, ". . . behind my back her Majesty giveth out very hard speeches of myself, which I the easier credit for that I find in dealing with her, I am nothing gracious. . . ."[19]

To complete her self-justification, Elizabeth continued the punishment of her Council. Davison remained in the Tower, where he obstinately clung to his story, appealing "to God and her Majesty's conscience for the knowledge of truth. . . ." Since he would acknowledge no fault, he was brought before a Star Chamber inquiry on charges of revealing secret communications of the Queen to "others of her ministers." The commissioners listened to the wretchedly tearful Davison beg them not to "urge the matter further" since he would not "contest with the Queen. . . ." He had no real defense except that he had acted as he conceived "for the best interests of his mistress and the realm." Well aware of where their duty lay and recognizing Davison's acquittal was a virtual condemnation of the Queen, the commissioners replied that while "the thing done was good, the manner was evil" and ordered the Secretary fined 10,000 marks* and to remain imprisoned at the royal pleasure. Undoubtedly at the end, Davison felt himself fortunate to have a head on his shoulders.

As the weeks of Elizabeth's disfavor continued and word of her continued grief was brought him, Lord Burghley, concerned about the effect on the high-strung woman he knew so well, wrote to the Queen, beseeching her "in your great wisdom, though you will yet continue offended against us, yet cease to grieve yourself with thinking of that which can never be revoked and let us bear your offence to our griefs until it please your Majesty either to hear us for our defense or to change your mind. . . ." When Elizabeth remained unmoved, Burghley offered to resign his offices. He said he was ready "to wear out the short and weak thread of my old, painful and irksome days as your Majesty shall limit them. . . ."[20] Several weeks later he was summoned to court.

He arrived expecting to find himself reinstated in the Queen's good graces. Instead, Elizabeth expressed her displeasure of events in the Low Countries and berated her Lord Treasurer with such vehemence that Burghley became fearful. He wrote to Sir Christopher Hatton, "I am so wounded by the late sharp and most heavy speech of her Majesty to myself in the hearing of Lord Leicester and Mr. Secretary Walsingham. . . ." The sight of the white-haired and gouty old minister had not softened Elizabeth's attitude, and Burghley was forced to listen, in humiliating fashion, as the Queen called him a "false dissembler, a traitor and a wicked wretch." He told Hatton he found her resentment "so settled and increased" that "without my heart bleeding to abide the countenance of such her displeasure, I am most careful how by any means to me possible, I may shun all increase of this, her Majesty's weighty offence, knowing it very true that was said by the wise King, '*Indignatio principis mors est*,' ('The wrath of the King is death.')." That he had received nothing but censure for taking a responsibility she herself had shirked galled Burghley, however, and he wrote, "My chief sickness is grounded upon ingratitude, which is worse than a continual fever. . . ."[21]

Burghley returned to his home, where he did not disdain writing the abject letters he knew would most impress the Queen. When Elizabeth did not respond, he felt his career was over and wrote, with some spirit, to Walsingham, saying, "I do imagine that her Majesty hath some further intention to my misliking than for my grief you will utter to me. But herein you may be bold to let me know the worse, for I am, thank

*He was released one year later. His fine was remitted, and a salary paid to him for the rest of his life. His career, however, was at an end.

God, provided of an armour of proof to defend my conscience from all assaults. . . . I see no cause to return to any love of court. . . ." To Leicester, he put it more simply, "Why her Majesty useth me thus sharply, I know not. To some she saith that she meant not that I should have gone from the court, to some she saith she may not admit me nor give me an audience. I shall dispose myself to enjoy God's favour and shall do nothing to deserve her disfavour. And if I be suffered to be a stranger to her affairs, I shall live a quiet life."[22]

The Queen's denunciation of her Council was meant to be regarded as part of her own defense. One month after Mary's death, she told de Châteauneuf, the French ambassador, that "she had experienced one of the greatest misfortunes and vexations that had ever befallen her . . ." and reiterated she had never meant to execute Mary "except in the case of a foreign invasion or a formidable insurrection of her own [Catholic] subjects." She said that her Council "had played her a trick which she could never forgive" and that "but for their long services and for the supposition that they had acted out of consideration for the welfare and safety of her person and state, they should all have lost their heads."[23] Telling the ambassador she personally was "deeply afflicted" by the execution, she promised the French King all aid in the form of men and arms with ample gifts of money to aid Henri in his fight against the Guises and the Catholic Holy League. De Châteauneuf, knowing his King would and could do little to avenge his sister-in-law's death, said little, but his expression plainly indicated he considered Elizabeth's words nonsense. Perhaps, as he gazed at the English court and the Queen, all clad in deepest mourning and listened to plans for the magnificent state funeral for Mary at Peterborough, he ironically remembered the treatment of his predecessor upon his first visit to the English court after the St. Bartholomew's Massacre.

When de Châteauneuf returned to France, where obsequies for the Queen of Scots were to be held on March 13 in the great Cathedral of Notre Dame, Elizabeth knew the worst was over. While the consequences of Mary's death had been shattering to her personally, it was apparent no great physical harm threatened her nation. Mary's son would not avenge her, and her French relatives would offer no gesture other than a magnificent Mass.

It remained for one from whom Mary Stuart might have expected more to effect the final flagrant denouement. "What a glorious Princess!" cried Pope Sixtus V when he heard of Mary's execution. He was not referring to the Scottish Queen. "It is a pity that Elizabeth and I cannot marry—our children would have mastered the whole world!" Later he would say that there were only three sovereigns in Europe who understood the art of governing—Henri of France, himself and Elizabeth of England.

And so the death of the Queen of Scots did not move armies or religious factions in vengeful retribution. Her son viewed the Crown of England and privately thought one less threat to its realization had been removed. Her brother-in-law the French King realistically accepted the situation knowing his country—torn by civil war—could do little else. Only one other brother-in-law, Philip of Spain,* regarded Mary's death as an important element in what he was coming to see as a regrettable necessity. Mendoza in Paris had echoed his thoughts when he wrote to Philip, "I pray that your Majesty will hasten the Enterprise of England to the earliest possible date, for it would seem to be God's obvious design to bestow upon your Majesty the crown of these two kingdoms."[24] Philip had written to the Pope, "I am grieved since she [Mary] would have been the most suitable instrument for leading those countries [England and Scotland] back to the Catholic faith. But since God in His wisdom has ordained otherwise, He will raise up other instruments for the triumph of His cause."[25] Philip had been trying, unsuccessfully, to receive a papal subsidy for an invasion of England, but the Pope, familiar with the King's delaying tactics, said he would get not one scudo until a Spanish soldier set foot in England.

In the past, Philip had excused his lack of formal action against Elizabeth by insisting that any invasion attempt would result in Mary's death. Even if the Scottish Queen were saved and an invasion successful, he would have achieved little. Mary, a thorough Frenchwoman and a Guise and one he regarded as emotionally immature, would undoubtedly have allied with France against Spain. But with Mary's death—and a death which was an insult to all the reigning monarchies—Philip's attitude underwent a strong change. He had found, by virtue of his descent from John of Gaunt, that he might make as good a claim to the English Crown as James of Scotland. It would make a throne for his daughter, the Infanta, Isabella Eugenia, to whom, he was sure, the English Catholics would rush to pay homage. It would be a satisfying moment to replace a heretic Queen with a representative of the only true faith and apt repayment for the inglorious instances of Elizabeth's humiliating exploits. For years she had provoked him, lied to him, taunted him, stolen his money, financed armies to aid his rebels, thrown his ambassador out of England and flaunted her heresy in the face of more godly nations.

In the letters and instructions which now issued from the Escorial

*Philip's third wife was Elizabeth of Valois, the sister of Mary Stuart's husband, François.

was evidence of Philip's conviction that the moment for the great Enterprise had arrived. During the next few months, as preparations continued in Lisbon and Cádiz, the greatest challenge ever to face Elizabeth of England, as a woman and as a sovereign, would become a stunning reality.

In England rumors of Philip's building and repair activity in the Tagus River shipyards at Lisbon and at Cádiz had been rife for months, and Elizabeth's procrastination in actively dealing with the threat led Walsingham to write disconsolately to Burghley that if she did not act quickly, "she shall have good cause to say, 'Farewell, my days of peace.' "[26]

The Queen did not doubt that at last the Spanish King's tolerance was at an end. Yet, in the aftermath of Mary Stuart's death, she had sent negotiators to the Low Countries in a desperate attempt to stave off the inevitable. Elizabeth did not relish her defensive position; she had everything to lose and little to gain materially in any direct confrontation with Philip.

Both sovereigns were realists and very similar in the evasive methods by which they had avoided conflict during the past thirty years. But it is doubtful, as their ministers haggled over the fine points of diplomatic protocol, if Elizabeth and Philip realized just how much *was* at stake.

For fifty-odd years, as the Reformation had flourished in England, there had been no decisive challenge to its growth. Scotland's King was Protestant because it was politically important that he be so; he was not likely to chance any religious encounter with England. France and the Netherlands were torn with religious dissension and unable to challenge England. The Pope had contented himself with excommunicating Elizabeth, and he remained impassive to the Spanish King's pleas for men and money to fight her increasing power. No other country or monarch would or could assume any chastening of England's heretic Queen. It remained, therefore, for Philip and Elizabeth, brother- and sister-in-law, who had not seen each other in more than thirty years, to become active combatants in this fight for men's souls. It would have taken the intelligence of a dullard—and neither Philip nor Elizabeth was obtuse—to appreciate the quixotic fate which cast them as participants in a conflict which would decide the way people as yet unborn would worship and live. The nations of Europe, therefore, settled back to watch the conflict which would affect all Christendom. There were no neutrals in 1588.[27]

An important part of Spanish strategy included transporting the

Duke of Parma and his forces from Flanders across the Channel to effect the invasion of England. At one point in mid-1587 had Parma had the necessary barges and an adequate protective convoy, he might have been successful. But he was ordered to wait for the coming of the Spanish fleet to reinforce his troops and act as escort, and within that time, England's strength increased, while Parma's army, sitting through a wet winter on short rations, lost 50 percent of its strength through disease and desertion.

Queen Elizabeth used the time to good advantage. A Scottish captain, hauled in from his ship as it passed Greenwich Palace, told the Queen that at Lisbon he had seen "floating fortresses" meant to be used against England. When she commented on this to Walsingham, who was in the room, he answered in such a way that she removed her slipper and angrily flung it in his face. Constantly, her ministers had remonstrated with her and she had listened to the windy opinions of such as Leicester, who had recently returned from another excursion in the Netherlands so disastrous it had taken all her support to keep him from being impeached.* Attack before we are attacked, was the gist of her Council's advice, and in this her seamen, straining at the leash, were eager to confront the Spaniard in his home waters.

The Queen did not agree. She pointed to the unheroic results of her soldiers' fighting in the Low Countries. England was unique in that it was an island, and its best defense must be made on the sea, not on the land! Elizabeth was adamant that she would not leave her sea borders exposed while the major part of the Royal Navy was absent. Therefore, during 1587 and the first months of 1588 ships of the fleet, only half-victualed and manned by skeleton crews, rode at anchor in the harbors of England. The Queen remembered that ships absent from their home ports for a long period invariably returned in poor condition. The crews, hemmed together in small areas and fed mostly on salt beef and stockfish, stale biscuits and rancid beer, were depleted and at times mortally ill with typhus. The ships would need repair and new crews, and that took not only money, but time. Time was now precious. So, in contrast with Philip, Elizabeth kept her ships in port, her crews on land and her money in the Treasury. If the Spaniards came, she meant England to be ready.

To give emphasis to her words, a system of beacons across England was implemented with new additions to warn when the Spanish fleet

---

*He had been sent at the insistence of Walsingham and Burghley who decided that the damage the Earl could do in the Netherlands was less than he could do in England at the sensitive time preceding the Armada's arrival. They had found that "she [Elizabeth] was more manageable and reasonable in his absence than in his presence."[28]

was sighted. Musters were held in villages and towns throughout the realm, and everywhere yeomen, squires and gentry responded. In the coastal towns, ditches were dug and existing ones cleaned and repaired. Fortifications such as city walls and ramparts were inspected and improved. The spirit of the English people in early 1588 was evident in the response of the City of London on being requested by her Majesty's ministers to furnish the needed men and ships. After asking the necessary amount, they were told, "Five thousand men and fifteen ships." Two days later the Lord Mayor reported, in the name of his fellow citizens, that the Queen might expect "ten thousand men and thirty ships." All over England, individual towns emulated the City's example as nobles and gentry mustered their considerable resources in supplying men, armor and money for the Queen's cause.

However, if wagers had been drawn in 1588, it would have been difficult not to favor the monarch who ruled more of the earth's surface than anyone before in history.[29] Even in London fear was present and is evident in the letter received by a London merchant which told of rumors emanating from the Continent of the great preparation being made by Parma and Philip for invasion. "God help England!" noted the writer, "for a destruction is preparing if God stay it not. . . ."[30]

Both Philip and Parma had agreed that the element of surprise was an important factor in their planning, although how the assembling of so large a fleet which must sail through the English Channel could be kept secret, no one could say. Parma was doubtful of his chances of securing a port with sufficient depth to allow the huge Spanish galleons to draw sufficient water. The swift Dutch flyboats under the capable direction of the wily Justin of Nassau constantly patrolled the coastline. It was enough, thought King Philip, to leave the success of the undertaking to Divine Providence. With such protection, the magnitude of the Spanish fleet and the intensity of its fighting men almost guaranteed a great victory. This attitude was summed up by a Spanish officer who, when asked if the English gave battle in the Channel did the Spaniards expect to win the contest, replied, "It is very simple. It is well known that we fight in God's cause. So, when we meet the English, God will surely arrange matters so that we can grapple and board them, either by sending some strange freak of weather, or, more likely, by depriving the English of their wits." He admitted the English ships were faster and their guns of longer range and said they, the Spaniards, were therefore "sailing against England in the confident hope of a miracle."[31]

Elizabeth remembered the advice Philip had given when he had lived in England as Mary Tudor's husband: "The kingdom of England is and must always remain strong at sea, since on this the safety of the realm depends." In the months following Mary Stuart's death, as her ministers one by one returned to a somewhat testy royal favor,* they listened to the pleading of Sir Francis Drake that he be allowed "to impeach the purpose of the Spanish fleet and stop their meeting at Lisbon." Elizabeth was doubtful of how such an intention to ravage and despoil in Spanish harbors would be regarded by her peace negotiators. For years she had, to Burghley's disgust, been disclaiming all responsibility for Sir Francis' actions, yet had never hesitated to claim the lion's share of his spoils. Yet even Burghley had to admit that the exploits of such as Drake, Frobisher and Hawkins had contributed immeasurably to the skill of the British fleet, and he said that "the ships of her subjects are also at this day both in number, in strength, in captains and mariners, stronger than ever they were in the memory of man." It was the nearest Lord Burghley ever came in tribute to the Queen's sea pirates.

Elizabeth at last was convinced. She gave tentative approval—and six ships—provided the other costs were underwritten by London merchants who would supply additional vessels. It was tacitly understood that Drake would bring back some return on the investment. The Queen's agreement had been so tenuous, however, that Drake, not trusting her to remain consistent, hurried to Plymouth. There, before she had second thoughts, he lost no time in sailing, writing to Walsingham from the cabin of his flagship, the *Elizabeth Bonaventure*. "The wind commands me away! Our ships are under sail. God grant we may so live in His fear as the enemy may have cause to say that God doth fight for her Majesty as well abroad as at home. Haste!"[32] Within days word arrived at Plymouth that the Queen indeed had changed her mind, and Drake was instructed "to forbear to enter forcibly any of the said King's [Philip's] ports or towns. . . ." By that time he was well on his way. There were many who viewed Elizabeth's change of heart with a jaundiced eye. At least she could always say she had tried to avoid nettling the King of Spain.

On Wednesday, April 29, eighteen days after leaving Plymouth, Sir Francis Drake passed the Pillars of Hercules and sailed into Cádiz Harbor. Amid the pealing of trumpets and the breaking out of the English banners, a salvo from the *Elizabeth Bonaventure* caught the unguarded harbor and townspeople by surprise. The bay was filled with ships from the Mediterranean, the Netherlands and France;

---

*"When I am absent, she complaineth thereof, but when I come I see her Majesty otherwise occupied," wrote an indignant Lord Burghley. Middle age did not make Elizabeth any easier to live with.

others were vessels bound for the Armada assembling at Lisbon. With twenty-five galleys, Drake's seamen sped between the moored freighters, galleons and merchantmen. The holocaust was tremendous. Speedily and seemingly favored by holy protection, he fired and scuttled some thirty vessels, ignoring the fire from the Cádiz fort on shore. When one large Genoese ship, laden with hides, wool, cochineal and logwood for Italy, attempted to protect its valuable cargo by firing, Drake returned the onslaught so vigorously the ship began to sink. At this point, other ships in the harbor ceased to fight back, and the English, anchoring their vessels, set about boarding and looting and towing other hulks out to sea to be fired or else cast them adrift. At night the Bay of Cádiz and the walls of the adjacent town were lit up like daylight in the glow of the flames.

The following day Drake entered the upper bay, where captive prisoners had told of a great galleon destined to be the flagship of the Armada. The English set upon the defenseless ship, which was soon in flames. From time to time, guns from the harbor fort would blaze, but the English fleet suffered little damage. At night, the Spaniards stuffed small ships with combustibles and let them drift toward the English fleet. But the venture was fruitless, for the ships were deflected and led Drake to the humorous remark that the Spaniard was doing the Englishman's work in burning their own ships.[33]

By Friday morning Drake was finished. "The loss was not very great," said King Philip when told of the disaster, "but the daring of the attempt was very great indeed." Exultantly, Drake turned toward the open sea, crying he had "singed the King of Spain's beard!" He ravaged the Spanish and Portuguese coasts, and in these plundering actions he accomplished a far greater harm to the Armada than the destruction of the Cádiz vessels. Philip was dependent on the supplies of fish, oil, nets, barrel staves, casks and kegs and other such items without which the Spanish fleet could never sail. Many were supplied from these very villages. In the smoke of the pillaged ruins lay evidence that the Armada would not sail soon. The next day Drake sailed northwest to the harbor of Lisbon, where he could see at first hand the tremendous activity taking place. Unable to provoke any action and having lost the advantage of surprise, he did not enter the harbor but wisely sailed on.

There was also another reason. Drake had heard of a magnificent carrack, the San Felipe, laden with spices and goods from Goa homeward bound for Lisbon. On the morning of June 18, he encountered the San Felipe off São Miguel in the Azores. The crew of the San Felipe, ailing from the rigors of their long voyage, were no match for the English. After a few salvos, the ship was surrendered, and after captain and crew were put ashore, Drake turned his fleet and its pirated prize homeward.

Drake knew the value of the carrack itself would soften any royal wrath awaiting him at home; it would also provide an adequate return on the London merchants' investment. But even he was surprised at the magnitude of the plunder. Once back in Plymouth, the holds spilled forth ivories, cinnamon, pepper and cloves, bolts of cloth, silks and calicoes, in addition to gold, silver and caskets of jewels. Nearly £114,000 of loot was stuffed into the *San Felipe*. Drake received £17,000, the London merchants some £50,000, and the Queen's anger was appeased with £40,000. Altogether the value of the carrack alone made the venture worthwhile and was three times the value of all the ships burned or sunk in Cádiz Bay.[34]

Drake's reconnoitering in Lisbon Harbor led him to advise the Queen, "Prepare England strongly and most by sea!" His advice agreed with Elizabeth's own intuitive assertion that she must fight a defensive, not an aggressive, battle. Drake's activities at Cádiz and the devastation of the supply villages had set the sailing of the Armada back for many months, but by spring of 1588 both Spain and England were ready again. Elizabeth had used the interim to good advantage, accumulating money to build, repair and buy ships, purchase powder and shot and grappling hooks. The Queen's biggest worry was the maintenance of her ships until the Spanish struck. It cost the Treasury £12,000 a month to feed, arm and keep the fleet in fighting condition.[35] Elizabeth's anxiety is evident in Lord Burghley's comment that "a man would wish, if peace cannot be had, that the enemy would no longer delay, but prove, as I trust, his evil fortune." To those who advised that the fleet should sail forth to meet the enemy, the Queen reiterated: her ships would stay in coastal waters and protect the nation. It was this decision, as much as anything else, which guaranteed the ultimate English victory.

Elizabeth's insistence in keeping her ships in home ports and her crews maintained largely on land had also resulted in such improvement that her uncle Charles Howard of Effingham, whom she had appointed Lord High Admiral, wrote exultantly to Walsingham, "I protest it before God that were it not for her Majesty's presence, I had rather live in the company of these noble ships than in any place!"[36] The Admiral was plainly delighted with the condition of the ships and crews, and riding at anchor in a well-fitted vessel, he could agree with his cousin Sir Henry Seymour's statement: "Our ships do show themselves like gallants here. . . ."

As the early spring storms of 1588 abated, a tension hung over the nation, awaiting the arrival of the Spanish Armada. At court, a confident Elizabeth worked with Burghley, Walsingham and her Council from morning until night. The Queen had authorized the publication of a "news-paper," the *English Mercury*, the first of its kind, to be printed daily to combat the rumors which flew about London; a series of these journals were published all during the Armada's voyage. The information of the enemy's movements contained in these little publications helped coalesce a remarkable national feeling, particularly evident in the City. All sectarian jealousies and personal feuds were laid aside as Catholic and Protestant forgot their differences and bowed to the emergency which might precipitate a foreign ruler on their native soil.

At the Palace, there was excitement as courtiers bid farewell to the Queen and her ladies-in-waiting. The Earl of Leicester, as Lieutenant and Captain General of the Army, was dispatched to Tilbury, where he was to direct the building of a blockade across the Thames to Gravesend. The Earl of Hunsdon accompanied the Queen to Windsor Castle, where, with 23,000 soldiers, he was prepared to withstand a siege. Rumor had reached England that Philip had received instructions from the Pope that after capturing Elizabeth, she was to be sent to Rome "to the purpose that his Holiness, the Pope, should dispose thereof, in such sort as it should please him." English roads were dusty with the tramp of the militia which left for various coastal towns and "at every rumour of the approach of the foe, and the prospect of doing battle with them," the troops were elated and "rejoiced like as lusty giants about to run a race!"[37]

It was, therefore, almost a relief when finally the Invincible Armada was sighted off the Lizard, where "the English descried the Spanish ships, with lofty turrets, like castles, in front like a half-moon, with wings thereof spreading out about the length of seven miles, sailing very slowly, though with full sails, the winds being, as it were, tired with carrying them, and the ocean groaning with the weight of them."[38] Quickly a courier left for London with the news of the sighting.

As the signal beacons flared throughout the realm and as the bells of the City pealed that the enemy was at hand, Queen Elizabeth, safe behind the walls of Windsor, composed a prayer for her threatened church and nation.

We do instantly beseech Thee of thy gracious goodness, to be merciful to the Church militant here upon earth, and at this time compassed about with most strong and subtle adversaries. O, let thine enemies know that Thou hast received England, which they most of all for Thy gospels' sake do malign, into Thine own protection. Set a wall about it, O Lord, and evermore mightily defend it. . . .[39]

If, as the Spaniards said, they were sailing "in the confident hope of a miracle," it is apparent the English Queen also expected the Almighty's help. However, were a heavenly blessing to be withheld, she had done her part in keeping her fleet at hand and in fighting condition. In the end it was to make the difference between depending on a miracle and depending on oneself.

The Warrior

*I would have you know that this kingdom
of mine is not so scant of men but that there
may be a rogue or two among them.*

Chapter Twenty-seven

The building of the Spanish Aramada had commenced under the direction of the Marqués Santa Cruz. At his death Philip had appointed Don Alonso Pérez de Guzmán el Bueno, the Duke of Medina Sidonia, to its command. The thirty-eight-year-old Castilian grandee, one of the richest men in Spain, was totally ignorant of naval warfare and aghast at Philip's action. In February, 1588, he wrote the King, asking that he reconsider. "My health is not equal to such a voyage for I know by experience of the little I have been at sea, I am always seasick and catch cold. . . ."[1] Philip remained unmoved, and at royal insistence, the courtly Medina Sidonia bowed to the inevitable, writing, "As I shall be doing God's work, I may hope that He will help me. . . ." He spent many months bringing order out of Santa Cruz's chaos at Lisbon and Cádiz, a task for which he was eminently endowed by persistence, efficiency and capability. If, in the pursuit of his command, he was constantly overridden by the innumerable suggestions from Philip pertaining to the diet, habits, religious responsibilities and moral outlook of the crew, he was too loyal to say so.

The Armada consisted of six squadrons, each with its own Vice Admiral, Captain and flagship. The ships were as varied in size as they were in condition. There were the great galleons, the merchantmen used for soldiers' transport, the *urcas* or freighters and many auxiliary craft such as dispatch boats, picket boats and small scouting cruisers. Forty galleys and 6 Italian galleasses completed the greatest sea force Europe had ever seen.[2] Altogether about 130 vessels, many old and in poor condition, carried the 26,000 Spanish and Portuguese soldiers, the 8,500 sailors and 600 others consisting of priests, doctors, officers, volunteers, monks and a representative of every noble house in Spain and Portugal.

Medina Sidonia's orders had been precise. He was to make straight for the English Channel to a port as yet unnamed, where he would meet with Parma, and together their forces would effect the English invasion. He was to keep to the English side of the Channel, where the water was deepest, said King Philip, and he must not engage the enemy beforehand unless forced to do so. The Invincible Armada was not essentially a fleet prepared to fight a sea battle, but a convoying expedition to precipitate a land victory. England, on the other hand, had approximately 200 ships, smaller than the Spaniards, but these were heavily armed with guns of longer range than the enemy's. Not all the 200 ships were in one place. The prudent Elizabeth had ordered 5 galleons and 30 merchantmen and pinnaces under Sir Henry Seymour to patrol between England and Dunkirk and Nieuport should Parma attempt any sea action. The Lord High Admiral and Sir Francis Drake, with 14 great galleons and some 50 smaller vessels, were to remain at Plymouth, where Sir Francis had chafed for weeks waiting for the Spaniards' appearance. Nevertheless, at the first sighting of the proud Armada, a speck on the horizon which became larger as it assumed the shape of a crescent or spread eagle, Drake remained calm. Legend has it that, when informed of the sighting at a game of bowls on Plymouth Hoe, he said, "We have time enough to finish the game and beat the Spaniards too." His composure was not duplicated by the English sailors. From the *Ark Royal*, flagship of the Lord High Admiral, Howard of Effingham, the crew "shouted for joy."

In the late afternoon of July 30, 1588,* the Spanish Armada anchored just off Dodman Point, and the English sailors, hoisting themselves into the topmost shrouds of their ships, returned to deck to speak with awe of the size of the half-moon fleet which measured seven miles from tip to tip. During the evening, the English ships stood out from the harbor and by morning had the wind in their favor.

Aboard the Spanish vessels, a council of squadron commanders had been held. Some had hoped to engage the English before they left Plymouth Harbor and thus revenge Drake's triumph at Cádiz. But Medina Sidonia, aware of his instructions, did not agree. Already, on the journey from Lisbon, he had lost several vessels in stormy weather, and the ships were beset with problems of leaking barrels, food spoilage and such impossible drawbacks as cannonballs in the holds the wrong size for the cannon on the decks.

On the morning of the thirty-first, as the Spaniards approached the Eddystone, Medina Sidonia ordered the Armada's banner to be

*New Style Calendar.

hoisted on high. The emblem depicted the imperial arms of Spain and the figure of the crucified Christ on one side and Mary, the Virgin, with the words "Arise O Lord and vindicate Thy cause!" on the other. On the deck of each ship, the Spaniards knelt to pray. As they neared Plymouth Harbor, Howard of Effingham sent his personal pinnace, appropriately named the *Disdain*, to challenge Medina Sidonia and, that propriety observed, led the English fleet *en hilera*, as the Spaniards described single file, to attack the half-moon's nearest tip. At the same time, Drake in the *Revenge*, Hawkins in the *Victory* and Frobisher in the *Triumph* sailed toward the other southernmost tip. Here was where the heaviest and strongest of the Spanish vessels were concentrated; here was where the English chose to test the mettle of the enemy.

The action off the Eddystone was revealing to both sides. The English stood off from the Spaniards and pounded their ships with their long-range culverins. Because of the rapid and deadly fire, the Spaniards could not effect the strategy on which their whole undertaking was founded: to close in, grapple a ship with large hooks and board. Hand-to-hand fighting would then decide the issue. It was a technique they had brought to a high art, but now, when it should have counted the most, it seemed to mean little. The English rarely came closer than 300 yards, and the Spanish ships, firing their shorter-range guns, wasted their powder as they struggled to maintain the formation which was their strength. The entry in the Spaniards' official logbook for that first day of battle tells the story. "The enemy having opened the range, the Duke collected the fleet, but found he could do nothing more, for they still kept the weather gauge, and their ships are so fast and so nimble, they can do anything they like with them."[3] On both sides, admiration for the enemy's prowess and skill was evident.

The first day's damage to the Spanish fleet was slight, but the ineffectiveness of their strategy lay revealed. The English had hoped to cause a melee in which individual ships would be a fair target. Their inability to shatter, harass or weaken the Armada's formation, or deflect it from its course, was alarming. The English regarded the Spanish vessels as clumsy but gave grudging respect to the sailors' discipline and seamanship. After the first encounter, an ebullient Drake wrote to Walsingham: "We have the army of Spain before us and mind, with the grace of God, to wrestle a pull with them. There was never anything pleased better than seeing the enemy flying with a southerly wind to the northwards. God grant we have a good eye to the Duke of Parma! For, with the grace of God, if we live, I doubt it not, but were it be long, so to handle the matters with the Duke of Sidonia as he shall wish himself at St. Mary Port among his vineyards. . . ."[4] To Sir Henry Seymour, whose fleet lay ahead, he wrote that "there hath passed some cannon shot between some of our fleet and some of them. . . . [They] are determined to sell their lives with blows."

The English fleet followed the Spaniards as they sailed in splendid undulating formation toward their destination. They did not, unfortunately, know as yet just where that destination would be. Frantic appeals to the Duke of Parma had yielded the name of no port where any army lay waiting. In the meantime, the English kept in pursuit to deter any landing on the southern coast, hoping that some freakish chance would give them the opportunity of disrupting the Armada's close formation, a formation which was at once a protection and a disadvantage.

From Plymouth to Portland Bill, results were the same. Musket fire and shots were exchanged, cannon roared, a few Spanish ships were taken prisoner and looted, but in each instance the aim of both sides was unrealized. The English attempted to dislodge the Spanish formation; the Spaniards attempted to grapple and board the English vessels. But the Spaniards could not get close to the English ships without being pounded to pieces, and their supplies were getting lower with each incident.

As the Armada kept to its course toward the Dover Strait, the English fleet was reinforced with volunteers from ports all along southern England. There were minor skirmishes which kept both sides in fighting condition on the third and fourth, and as they approached the Isle of Wight, the Spanish commander, Medina Sidonia, held a council meeting aboard his flagship, the *San Martín*. King Philip had instructed that he "gain and fortify" the Isle of Wight to await Parma's instructions. However, as they neared the Isle, they evaded one of the greatest dangers confronting the seafarer. Medina Sidonia, aboard the ship nearest the tip of the crescent formation, noticed the water's color with tips of rocks showing in the distance. They were off the Owers, a deadly reef, and the English, in pursuing them, had been attempting to force the Spaniards upon the shoal. In time, Medina Sidonia fired an alert gun to veer south-southeast, and soon, amid a fresh shaking out of canvas, the Armada was in safer depths.

On August 5, the Spanish fleet left the English Channel and entered the Dover Strait, its destination still unknown. It had successfully evaded the English, had coped with its battle scars and maintained its formation. Medina Sidonia was sure he had inflicted damage to enemy ships, killed enemy seamen and damaged enemy morale. Yet the English were constantly sustained and reinforced by fresh volunteers, food and supplies from the shore. While his own stores were almost exhausted, it did not help to accept that they had been spent firing at smaller more maneuverable ships manned by experts who had successfully eluded much damage.

By the afternoon of Saturday, the sixth, the Spanish fleet dropped anchor in Calais Roads, beyond which point Medina Sidonia dared not proceed. At this time the Spanish commander might have wondered at the fate which had brought the world's greatest sea expedition to a port where no welcoming confederate awaited him. Ahead was the North Sea, and behind him was the constantly increasing might of the English fleet. Across the Channel lay the tempting ports of Dover and Margate, but in between were the Dutch flyboats and English forces under Sir Henry Seymour. If Parma did not come soon—and with ample supplies of ammunition, food and water—there was no way the Armada could fulfill its destiny.

The same thoughts were occurring to the English. Their strength had been increased with thirty-five of Seymour's vessels. A mile and a half away they could see small boats leaving the Armada for the shore and inferred that Parma's arrival was imminent. If his army was of any reasonable size at all, once combined with the Spanish soldiers and sailors aboard the enemy vessels, it would constitute a mighty invasion threat. The English were confident of their capability on the sea; they were also very aware that their land forces might be a poor match for Parma's seasoned veterans.

On Sunday, August 7, a council of war met aboard the Lord High Admiral's *Ark Royal*, attended by Howard, Drake, Hawkins, Seymour and Frobisher. It was agreed that to attempt a bombardment of the Spanish fleet would be wasteful, for even English supplies were now at a low point. Remembering the flagrant abuse of her funds in the Netherlands and the disinclination of her officers to remedy the situation, the Queen had insisted that she personally examine all charges. She would give no authority to anyone to spend money or supplies without her knowledge and acted "as if every officer she possessed were in a conspiracy to ruin her." This dictatorial attitude had been greeted with little enthusiasm. Her uncle Lord Admiral Howard grunted, "Sparing and war have no affinity together,"[5] while sailors muttered of ships being lost "for a pennyworth of tar."

In view of their short supplies and well aware of the freshening wind from the south-southeast and the flood tide running in their favor, the English spent the next several hours discussing alternative strategy

which, once evolved, encompassed the use of the deadliest weapon one
fleet could send against another: the fireship. Once the orders were out,
the captains scrounged, begged, commandeered and stuffed every
available hulk and vessel from 90 to 250 tons, acquiring eight in all.
After emptying them of their gear and stores, they were filled with
anything combustible, their spars, roping and sails covered with pitch
and their guns double-shotted so that in the intense heat they would
add to the general destruction by firing.

Aboard the *San Martín*, Medina Sidonia had accepted a welcome
present of fresh fruit from the Governor of Calais, who warned him the
Spanish fleet's position was extremely vulnerable. Medina Sidonia had
used the opportunity to send the purveyor ashore for fresh supplies and
gave orders for cleaning and restoring the damaged vessels. He had
sent word to Parma, "I am anchored here, two leagues from Calais
with the enemy's fleet on my flank. They can cannonade me whenever
they like, and I shall be unable to do them much harm in return. If you
can send me forty or fifty flyboats . . . I can, with their help, defend
myself here until you are ready to come out."[6]

It was just as well that the Spanish commander did not know that
Parma's "fleet" consisted of fewer than a dozen flyboats and a few
small canalboats, flat-bottomed and clumsy and used mainly for the
transporting of cattle. There was no way he could have supplied
Medina Sidonia. Between Dunkirk and Nieuport and Ostend, the
murderous flyboats of Justin of Nassau patrolled diligently. His soldiers were helpless, frustrated and ill. If Medina Sidonia was puzzled
by Parma's apparent lack of cooperation, Parma himself was outraged.
He had repeatedly informed Philip that he should not advance his
forces until a deepwater port to receive the Armada was secured. He
had advised, as diplomatically as possible, that the Armada be delayed
until such had been accomplished. But Philip had insisted on the
sailing, suggesting that he rendezvous with the fleet at sea near Margate. But because of the presence of the Dutch and English and Parma's appalling lack of supplies, there could be no conjunction of forces.
The fleet that had sailed "in the confident hope of a miracle" had
failed.

The Duke of Medina Sidonia, an optimistic man, could not as yet
concede that the Invincible Armada was beaten. It was not until
midnight on Sunday, August 7, that one of his strongest fears was
realized. He had discussed the danger of fire to the anchored fleet and
had ordered several pinnaces and ships' boats to act as a screen to
deflect and tow away any enemy fireships. Only in the extremest
emergency, he stressed, must the Armada lose its close formation. Only

if the fireships proved hazardous were they to slip their cables and sail out to sea.

When, therefore, shortly after midnight, eight brilliant flaming objects appeared near the edge of the English vessels, the Spaniards were not surprised. But they became frantic at observing that the wind and tide were bringing the fireships directly toward them. Their speed was such that in order to deflect them in the short distance between the English and Spanish fleet, the rescuing pinnaces had to work under a tremendous barrage of gunfire from the English batteries. The perfect formation of the fireships made it difficult for the Spaniards' grappling hooks to catch onto the flaming decks, and their size, the height of their blazing rigging and the heat from the flames made deflection difficult. Ultimately, two fireships were grappled and maneuvered out of line, but at that moment, the guns, which had been set, shot skyward a belching roar of flame. The explosion and the subsequent shot which fell hissing in spraylike fragments into the boiling water caused the pinnaces to flee for safety, and the remainder of the six fireships bore down on the helpless Armada.

A melee occurred close to shore. The firing of the signal gun awoke any soldier or sailor who might have been asleep, and at once, captains cut their cables and stood out into the Channel. In their haste, several battered each other, and the danger of collision became as great as that of the fireships. From the English vessels, a mile and a half away, a great cheer arose from the decks as they saw the might of the Spanish crescent dissolve in the glow of flames under Calais Cliffs. Now each and every ship would be an easy target for English seamanship.

It was impossible—though he tried—for Medina Sidonia to reassemble his fleet. Those ships which had collided sustained such damage they were useless; some ultimately drifted as far as six miles and were captured by the English. Others were driven ashore. Signaling as many as possible to follow, Medina Sidonia hoisted anchor and sailed defiantly into the Strait with the English not far behind. He recognized at last that Parma could not save him. Now there was only one thought: to preserve as many lives and ships as possible. And to hope, if Providence should so ordain, to find some way home.

The pursuing English came upon the Spanish fleet off Gravelines, and as the clumsy high-pooped vessels lumbered toward the North Sea, the guns of Medina Sidonia's *San Martín* exchanged shots with Drake's *Revenge*. In the meantime, laggard ships, the galleons of Portugal and Castile, the great carracks and Florentine galleasses, had slowly and at great risk from English fire rejoined the main part of the fleet. One by one, as the smaller vessels sought their place within the protecting area of the greater ships, another crescent emerged. "They went," says an English observer, "into the proportion of a half-moon, their Admiral and Vice-Admiral in the midst. . . ." It was an exploit which impressed the English as "a remarkable feat of Spanish discipline and seamanship."[7]

Spanish courage was also greatly evident. The darting nimbleness of the English ships with their superior guns and marksmanship led to an easy outflanking of the Spanish vessels, which continued to give a good defense. The crippled Spaniards, however, were hampered not only by their battered condition, but by their lack of ammunition. There was also the constant danger of running aground. The English had at last realized that to do any great damage they would have to venture closer, and in an engagement which lasted five hours, they ruthlessly pounded the Armada. The wooden decks offered no defense for the shot which went through them with force "enough to shatter to pieces a rock." The slaughter was tremendous, and amid shot, smoke and flying fragments, priests groped their way, crucifixes in hand, toward the injured and dying. Yet still the Spaniards fought on, ignoring the cries of their comrades and the blood dripping from the scuppers.

At the battle's end, the Armada ships were pummeled and leaking, their crews mangled or dead; many were drifting toward the Flemish shore. Others, so crippled they could not bear their canvas, drifted dangerously near the enemy. The night was spent in throwing the dead overboard, examining the damage to the supplies in each ship's hold, while the captains and Medina Sidonia held a hasty meeting aboard the battered *San Martín*. The reports were not heartening. Hundreds of soldiers and sailors had been injured, casks of drinking water punctured, and other supplies blown to bits. About seventy vessels—a little more than half the original number—were all that remained of the proud Armada fleet.

The English did not hurry to the attack the next morning, for their own supply of ammunition was short, and more than one unseemly word on Queen Elizabeth's parsimony was muttered among command and crew. Instead, the English watched the Armada vessels drifting inexorably toward the coastal sandbars. And then, about noon, the wind changed, a change both English and Spanish described—for different reasons—as a miracle. The wind, backing to the southwest, suddenly steadied and kept the great Spanish galleons from being smashed upon the shoals. "God was pleased to work a miracle," wrote one aboard a Spanish vessel. He had not deserted them "through the most terrible cannonade ever seen in the history of the world." The wind kept rising and, by four o'clock, had become a storm of hurricane proportions. Violent rains, blinding in the wind, allowed Medina Sidonia the opportunity he needed. Even as the English struggled to keep out of each other's way, they saw the great galleons racing to join the *San Martín*. The last glimpse the English had of the Invincible Armada before the mists and fogs of the North Sea enclosed it forever was of the receding tip of a half-arc rim as the Spanish crescent, once again in perfect formation, disappeared from sight.*

Before the Armada sighting, the Queen of England had kept herself, her ministers and her court in a constant state of readiness. Her uncle the Lord High Admiral had chastised her for what he considered an unforgivable lack of precaution against assassination. "For the love of Jesus Christ, Madame, awaken thoroughly!" he advised. Dutifully, she had gone to Windsor, where, tense and nervous, she hectored Burghley and Walsingham and drove more than one lady-in-waiting to tearful despair. There she chafed through several wretched weeks, dispatching orders, surveying muster sheets and their charges and tallying the long list of disbursements from the Treasury. She dearly wished to be nearer the excitement of war preparations and finally returned to the heavily guarded St. James's Palace in London. She kept herself informed of Leicester's activities at Tilbury and, missing him more each day, proposed that she visit the camp.

At Tilbury, Leicester had satisfied himself that the 10,000 men under his command "were as forward and willing men as ever he saw" although, as usual, the government which could put a vast fleet on the sea still seemed unable to cope with the comparatively easier task of getting food and drink to the common foot soldier. When the men of Essex, some 4,000 in all, marched into the West Tilbury encampment, there was "not a barrel of beer nor a loaf of bread among them," and Leicester complained that "someone had blundered." The "someone" most probably was the Queen, whose economy had caused privation among her soldiers for victuals and her seamen for ammunition. The Earl was in no mood to entertain the Queen and, as gently as possible, attempted to dissuade her from her plan. Addressing her as "My most Dear and Gracious Lady," he told Elizabeth he well understood her

---

*The fate of the Armada is well known. Ships foundered off Norway, Scotland and Ireland with a disastrous loss of life. Those who did not drown were slaughtered when they waded ashore. Only about sixty vessels ultimately returned to Spain, and more than 10,000 men had perished. Hardly one noble family did not suffer some casualty. The country went into national mourning over the catastrophe.

desire "to employ your own person in this dangerous action." However, it was his opinion that she should gather some part of the Army for her own protection and remain where she was. "Now for your person, being the most dainty and sacred thing we have in the world to care for . . . a man must tremble when he thinks of it, specially finding your Majesty to have that princely courage to transport yourself to your utmost confines of your realm to meet your enemies and to defend your subjects. I cannot, most dear Queen, consent to that, for upon your well-doing consists all and some for your whole kingdom, and therefore, preserve that above all!"[8] He suggested that Elizabeth "withdraw yourself to your house at Havering," for the Army, which lay at East Ham and Hackney "and the villages thereabout," would constitute a real defense.

By the first week in August, when the Armada was passing the Isle of Wight, Elizabeth could restrain herself no longer. To wait, hushed and expectant, as everyone else seemed to be doing, was agonizing to the woman who did not suffer patience gladly. *She* was responsible for England and its people! *She* had guided her country's destiny for almost thirty years, and now if her ministers expected her to sit like a cloistered matron while its enemy appeared at the very borders of her realm, it only proved what she had always suspected and often expressed: that mere clerks did not necessarily make wise men. Danger had never prevented her from exercising her royal prerogative; now it seemed almost to excite her.

She also longed to see Leicester. Ultimately, knowing he could delay her no longer, he obliged, "Good sweet Queen—alter not your purpose if God give you good health!"[9] Though some of her older ministers looked askance, young Robert Cecil, Lord Burghley's son, understood his mistress' restlessness. "It is a comfort to see how great magnanimity her Majesty shows, who is not a whit dismayed," he said. All during the Armada's passage through the Channel, Elizabeth's confidence had been very evident. She had beseeched God to "set a wall" about England, and she had helped Him in every tangible way with ships, money and men. If ever doubt rose within the royal breast, it never manifested itself to those around her. Her insistence on going to Tilbury to see Leicester and review the troops was to inspire those who would fight the ground battle and to make clear that she expected England to win.

On August 18 the Queen traveled by water to Tilbury. The great barge was replete with her ladies, courtiers and minstrels. In its wake came several other boats carrying servants, the Queen's coach and the great white gelding she expected to ride at review. Leicester and other officers were on the dock near the Block House, and as the royal barge approached just after noon, they knelt to receive the Queen. As she set foot on land, cannon were discharged, and in the distance, drums and fifes began to play. Several miles away, the booming cannon could be heard in the encampment itself, whereupon all the company flags were hoisted high. Sir Roger Williams and 2,000 horsemen waited as the Queen and her party stepped ashore. One thousand of these were sent ahead, and the other thousand rode behind with Elizabeth in her coach, "painted chequer-fashion to simulate jewels," in the center. The great procession left for Ardern Hall, "one Master Rich's house," some three miles away from the camp, where the Queen was to rest overnight.

The following morning the 2,000 horsemen, who had spent the night in Master Rich's grounds, escorted Elizabeth to Tilbury camp, the envy of the Dorset Regiment, which had offered £500 for the honor of accompanying the Queen. Days had been spent in cleaning the area of the rubbish of martial occupancy, and now the checkered and particolored pavilions of the nobles and gentlemen were bright, and their banners were taut in the wind. The soldiers were in their cleanest clothing, and as the Queen approached, "they couched their pikes and bowed their ensigns down." Cries of "Lord preserve our Queen!" and "God save your Grace!" commenced in a small ripple, to which Elizabeth, smiling and pleased, held out her hands and replied, "Lord bless you all!" The shouts and cries became louder as she approached until finally the entire camp was waving and calling in a tremendous roar of devotion and pride.

Elizabeth's appearance commenced a memorable afternoon for the thousands who stood on Tilbury plain. Accompanied by the Earl of Leicester, his stepson the young Earl of Essex and several others, she had mounted the great white horse with its dappled gray flanks. She waited as a deputy rode toward her and, in the name of the troops, welcomed her to their midst. With evident excitement, the Queen replied she had "come to see the army." She further intimated she did not intend to see it from a distance, surrounded by the plumed helmets of her courtiers. When it looked as though Leicester might protest, one glance from Elizabeth silenced him. The Earl, who knew her moods so well, nodded and, with himself and several others, formed a small circle around the Queen. One more glance, and they fell behind as Elizabeth rode forward alone.

For such a momentous event, the Queen had carefully chosen a dress of the virginal white velvet which she so often preferred. She wore the most fiery red of her many wigs and had thrust two white plumes into the curls. For the past several years, adequate security for her royal person had been a worry; everyone had pointed out the risk from some fanatic or foreign agent in the vast assembly on the field. Someone had insisted that Elizabeth wear a breastplate, and it glinted, sending silvery streaks of lightning toward the massed militia as she rode forward. The troops saw the regal woman, erect and proud, a silver truncheon chased in gold in one hand as she advanced. When the men saw she meant to come among them with only a small escort, which she was obviously keeping at a distance, the ranks exploded in cheers. Henry Tudor had often done the same thing, and he would have been proud of his daughter's performance. Elizabeth well knew the merit of the gesture; happily, it also fitted in with her own desire. These were her people, and she still, with her fifty-fifth birthday less than three weeks off, meant them to recognize their sovereign's vigilance. The wild cheers and the applause were just as exhilarating to the Queen as they had been to the young girl who had accepted such homage thirty years previously. She acknowledged their cheers by reining in her horse and stopped to accept the acclaim.

The shouting continued for several moments, and the troops' goodwill caught at the Queen's heart. She saw the faces which looked up at her, eager and expectant, young and old, sick and well, some in tatters, others well dressed. Men of England they were, from all walks of life and from all corners of her realm. Obviously moved, she spoke and the words came from her heart.

"My loving people!" she cried, and instantly all other sounds ceased. No one wished to miss a word. "My loving people! We have been persuaded by some that are careful of our safety, to take heed how we commit ourselves to armed multitudes for fear of treachery. But I do assure you, I do not desire to live to distrust my faithful and loving people." That explained the incongruous breastplate of which the Queen was apparently disdainful and which had startled many of her soldiers. She continued:

"Let tyrants fear! I have always so behaved myself that, under God, I have placed my chiefest strength and safeguard in the loyal hearts and goodwill of my subjects. Therefore, I am come amongst you as you see at this time, not for my recreation and disport, but being resolved, in the midst and heat of the battle, to live or die amongst you all—to lay down for my God and for my kingdoms, and for my people, my honour and my blood even in the dust!" A loud roar of approval from the troops caused her horse to become skittish. Quickly, the Queen quieted the beast even as she spoke:

"I know I have the body of a weak and feeble woman, but I have the heart and stomach of a King, and of a King of England too, and think foul scorn that Parma or Spain, or any Prince of Europe should dare to invade the borders of my realm, to which, rather than any dishonour should grow by me, I myself will take up arms."

Elizabeth checked the great outcry which greeted her challenge and, instead, told her soldiers they deserved "rewards and crowns and we do assure you, on the word of a Prince, they shall be duly paid you." She said that Leicester, "whom never Prince commanded a more noble or worthy subject," would be her Lieutenant General in the field, and "by your obedience to my General, by your concord in the camp and your valour in the field, we shall shortly have a famous victory over these enemies of my God, of my kingdoms and of my people!" As she finished, out of breath and exultant, she thrust the truncheon forward, and the camp erupted in a sea of waving pikes, ensigns, cheers and caps thrown in the air. Others wept unashamedly. Behind the Queen, Leicester and Essex exchanged glances, each with the same thought. The "weak and feeble woman," whom they had dared not encourage to venture too close for safety's sake, had, with a few words and a majestic air, conquered the field more than any stringent supervision or harsh commands could possibly have done. If Parma's veterans should arrive soon—the shouting mob on the field, with the Queen's words ringing in their ears—would make short work of them.

That evening, as Elizabeth dined with Leicester in his tent, news of the great victory over the Armada was received, and throughout the camp, bonfires burned far into the night as the troops rejoiced. "God be thanked," wrote Leicester to the Earl of Shrewsbury, "the most difficulties are past which lay most upon mine own hand and our gracious mistress hath been here with me to see her camp and people which so inflamed the hearts of her good subjects, as I think the weakest person amongst them is able to match the proudest Spaniard that dares land in England. . . ."[10] It was still felt that Parma might attempt a landing, and Elizabeth refused to return to London "in case there were any likelihood that the enemy should attempt anything. . . ."

When it was obvious the immediate danger was past, Elizabeth prepared to leave Tilbury. She rode once more through every corner of the camp, talking with the soldiers and thanking them for their good-will. At her departure, as the troops lined up in farewell, she was accompanied by Leicester and Essex. There were those among the observers with longer memories than most who noted the differences in the trio. Leicester, his height diminished by an overample girth, looked an old man with his white hair and beard, which only accented his florid, coarsened complexion. By comparison, the Queen had kept her fine skin, which was enhanced with the latest cosmetics; she had also kept her figure. Though her wig was false, she still retained most of her teeth, and she moved with the same rapid agility which had so characterized her as a young girl.

Many glances lingered on the tall and graceful figure of Robert Devereux, the Earl of Essex. The twenty-two-year-old son of Lettice Knollys had his mother's dark and expressive eyes and her fair complexion. The high and attractive forehead was covered with a thatch of curly reddish-brown hair which no cap could tame, and a neat beard covered the strong chin. Essex was a handsome courtier, graceful with the Queen, obviously respectful toward his stepfather. He had acquitted himself well during the royal visit.

As the two men knelt and kissed her hand in departing, as she settled back gratefully to enjoy the long luxurious ride up the Thames, Elizabeth's gaze lingered on the white head so close to the darker one, and as the barge pulled away from the shore, her eyes misted suddenly. It was just as well that in the hour of her greatest personal triumph, a capricious fate did not warn the Queen that from this day forward her life would be changed and that within weeks the man on whom she had leaned for almost a lifetime would be taken from her. And that from the graceful courtier by his side would come the greatest personal challenge to her throne and Crown.

By the time Elizabeth returned to St. James's, all London was celebrating the Armada's defeat. Everywhere people lined the streets, which had been draped in blue cloth to greet and cheer the Queen, to salute her as a bold leader and a defender of her country and people. They "did nothing but talk of the great Queen she was and how they would die for her," said one observer. Elizabeth rode in a great gold coach with the lion and dragon upholding the arms of England in the front, while four columns held the canopy in the shape of a crown. The City Companies lined one side of the route with the Inns of Court gentlemen on the opposite. Among those was young Francis Bacon, Burghley's nephew, who said to his companions, "Mark the courtiers. Those who bow first to the citizens are in debt. Those who bow first to us are at law."[11] There were services at St. Paul's and sermons at Paul's Cross, where an exhibit of captured Spanish banners caused a great crowd to assemble, and throughout England, bonfires and dancing, psalm singing and tournaments celebrated the great victory. The formal thanksgiving was to be held on November 17, 1588, the thirtieth observance of Elizabeth's accession to the throne.

Leicester also returned to London after visiting with Lettice at Wanstead. "He was accompanied," said a witness, "by as many gentlemen as if he were a King and followed by his household and a troop of light horse. He was going from his country house to St. James's and was quite alone in the coach."

Elizabeth had warmly welcomed the Earl and, in a flood of enthusiasm and gratitude, proposed to make him Lord Lieutenant of England and Ireland, an appointment of unprecedented power. Burghley, Walsingham and Hatton bravely opposed the Queen, noting the position was that of a Viceroy and too influential for any one person. The Council was so vigorously insistent that "in time she foresaw the danger of too great power in one man" and withdrew the patent. Her action mortified Leicester. He was unwell and suffering from a fever caught in the Tilbury marshes; the Queen's acquiescence to the Council did not help his disposition, and a bitter quarrel ensued. Elizabeth, who had expended much of her emotional reserves during the previous several months, did not feel too well herself. She recommended some "specifics" for Leicester and suggested he take the healing waters at Buxton. Still gravely disappointed, he joined the court toward the end of August at the Whitehall tiltyard, where the Earl of Essex had organized a review of the troops. It was a day of martial display so favored by the court, during which each noble tried to excel all others in the elegance and skill of his forces. When Leicester's troops had left the field, those of the Earl of Essex marched forward and in the finale eclipsed all others. Essex had "six musketters and sixty mounted harquebussiers in orange-tawney with white silk facings, and two hundred light horsemen all in orange velvet and silver. . . ."[12] The occasion in which his stepson had taken the honors for the day was almost prophetic, for it was the last public appearance of the Earl of Leicester, and the onlookers saw him "in a window with the Queen."

He left London soon afterward, taking Elizabeth's advice to proceed, in easy stages, to Buxton. On the twenty-ninth he was at the Rycote home of Sir John Norris, where he and the Queen had lodged many times before. Elizabeth had sent him a token, and their quarrel forgotten, he wrote the Queen:

> I most humbly beseech your Majesty to pardon your p(•)(•)r (poor) old servant to be thus bold in sending to know how my gracious Lady doth and what ease of her late pain she finds, being the chiefest thing in this

world I do pray for, for her to have good health and long life. For my own poor case, I continue still your medicine and find it amend much better than with any other thing that hath been given me. Thus hoping to find perfect cure at the bath with the continuance of my wonted prayer for your Majesty's most happy preservation, I humbly kiss your foot, from your old lodging at Rycote this Thursday morning, ready to take on my journey, by your Majesty's most faithful and obedient servant,

R. LEICESTER[13]

On September 4 his illness overtook him, and he died "of the continual fever" or "cold rheums." Lettice had joined him en route and was with him at Cornbury, not too far from Amy Robsart Dudley's lodging at Cumnor Hall, where, almost twenty-eight years to the day, she had been found at the foot of the stairs with a broken neck. It was three days before Leicester and Elizabeth's fifty-fifth birthday.

The news was soon brought to London although history does not record who first informed the Queen of Leicester's death.[14] Elizabeth had been drained by the suspense of the past weeks and the seemingly unending celebrations at court, and her poise and stoicism deserted her. Before she disgraced herself in public, she fled to her chamber, ordered her ladies away and shut her door to mourn the loss of her favorite apart from the prying eyes that would note her grief. Even in Paris, Mendoza heard, "The Queen is sorry for his death, but no other person [is]. . . . She was so grieved that for some days she shut herself in her chamber alone and refused to speak to anyone. . . ."[15] Food was taken in and brought out hardly touched as worried groups of ladies-in-waiting and Councillors gathered in the corridors. They spoke of the Queen, overwhelmed and prostrate on her bed, her eyes swollen with weeping. The atmosphere in the City and the court alike was one of great shock. The Earl was unpopular with most, but he had dominated the court scene by sheer virtue of his personality and his influence with the sovereign; it seemed unthinkable he should have passed away in so unspectacular a manner.

At last, concern for the middle-aged woman whom he knew had suffered a most devastating loss caused Lord Burghley to act. He pounded on the door and insisted that Elizabeth come out. When the Queen did not obey, the old minister gave orders that the door be broken down. It was soon under way, and the smashing blows which rended the door brought the Queen to her senses. She had mourned and grieved, but life must go on. Her responsibilities did not include the luxury of prolonged sorrow.

She arose from her bed, signaled that her ladies be admitted and prepared to face the rest of her days without Robert Dudley. Her grief was very evident when, several weeks later, she was presented with his last gift, a splendid rope of 600 pearls from which hung a jewel with three great emeralds and a large, fair table diamond in the middle. He had left the necklace for Elizabeth in his will, for, he wrote, "first of all and above all persons, it is my duty to remember my most dear and gracious Princess, whose creature under God I have been and who hath been a most bountiful and princely mistress to me."[16]

The Queen's grief did not extend to Leicester's widow. Within several months, Lettice married Sir Christopher Blount. Elizabeth was devastated at the lack of respect and feeling toward Leicester's memory, and she did not hesitate to sue his estate for all the thousands of pounds he owed the English Crown, rather than see the money go to the hateful Lettice and her new husband.[17]

Her devotion to Leicester's memory was such that she took the letter he had written her and on the back, in a faintly wavering hand, wrote "His last letter." She put it carefully in the box beside her bed where, as she had told James Melville, the Scottish emissary many years before, she always put her most valuable things.

It was still there fifteen years later when Elizabeth herself died.

Chapter Twenty-eight

While the courts of Europe settled back to view the incredible happenings in the Dover Strait during which a small insular nation had withstood the proud ships of the most powerful ruler in the world, it pleased Elizabeth to regard the Armada victory as the work of the Almighty, rather than the skill of her seamen. Learning the fleet was nearing Scotland, she wrote King James: "Now may appear, my dear brother, how malice conjoined with might strivest to make a shameful end to a villainous beginning, for, by God's singular favour, having the fleet well beaten in our Narrow Seas, and pressing with all violence to achieve some watering place, to continue their pretended invasion, the winds have carried them to your coasts. . . ." Elizabeth expressed her hope that there "they shall receive small succour and less welcome. . . ." Her view of Philip was concise: "You may assure yourself that, for my part, I doubt no whit but that all this tyrannical, proud and brainsick attempt will be the beginning, though not the end of the ruin of that King, that most unkingly, even in the midst of treating peace, begins this wrongful war. He hath procured my greatest glory that meant my sorest wrack. . . ."[1]

Esteem for England and its Queen was never higher. The "Protestant wind" which blew the Armada northward might be attributed to Divine interference. Nevertheless, the ships patrolling the coastline and the spirit of the seamen aboard them were a tribute to the woman who had mastered the complexities of sovereignty, of imbuing respect and devotion among her subjects, as well as her ministers, and thus preserved the unity of England.[2] It was a tremendous satisfaction to Elizabeth personally that during the hazardous week of the Armada threat, the English Catholics (upon whose support Philip had placed so

much importance) had not risen in his cause.* Apparently a heretic
English Queen was preferable to a foreign Catholic King. The Queen
had been further heartened when informed that English Catholic
students at work in the Jesuit seminary at Douai had burst into cheers
upon hearing of the Armada's defeat.

Elizabeth's public appearances had always drawn spectators, but
now the close feeling of pride and love for their monarch approached
reverence whenever she went abroad. On her coronation anniversary,
she traveled by the river to dine with her uncle the Lord High Admiral
in Chelsea. When informed that a large number of people carrying
torchlights lined the road to await her return to Whitehall, she chose to
travel by coach rather than disappoint her wildly cheering subjects. A
young boy who later became Bishop Goodman has left an illuminating
account of the emotional and physical appeal which Elizabeth could
always inspire by her mere appearance:

> I did then live in the Strand near St. Clement's Church when suddenly
> there was a report (it was then December, about five and very dark) that
> the Queen was gone to Council. And I was told "If you will see the Queen,
> you must come quickly!" Then we all ran, when the court gates were set
> open and no man hindered us from coming in. There we stayed for an
> hour and a half, and the yard was full, there being a great number of
> torches, when the Queen came out in great state. Then we cried, "God
> save your Majesty!" and the Queen turned to us, and said, "God bless you
> all, my good people!"
> Then we cried again, "God save your Majesty!" And the Queen said to
> us, "Ye may well have a greater Prince, but ye shall never have a more
> loving Prince!" And so the Queen and the crowd there, looking one upon
> another, while her Majesty departed. This wrought such an impression on
> us, for shows and pageants are best seen by torchlight, that all the long
> way we did nothing but talk of what an admirable Queen she was and how
> we would all adventure our lives in her service.[4]

In the months after Leicester's death, Elizabeth had turned more to
other court gentlemen for companionship. She had, for years, successfully played one against the other, and many, such as Sir Christopher
Hatton, had risen to great prominence in the process. Over the years
this remarkable courtier seemingly asked nothing other than the
privilege of a perpetual attendance on and a genuine devotion to his
monarch. Once out of sight, he continued to pen his lavish and adoring
letters, and although he rarely ventured beyond the prudent, his un-

---

*Sir Francis Walsingham noted, "Nothing so much displeased the King of Spain as the loyalty
of the Catholics to their Queen during the late enterprise."[3]

doubted loyalty and dependability had paid large dividends. Several years previously, he had coveted property near Ely Place in Holborn stretching from Leather Lane to the Holborn River. The main part of the property comprised the ecclesiastical residence of the Bishop of Ely. Traditionally, it belonged to the See of Ely and was exempt from Crown or City jurisdiction. Adjoining the Bishop's residence were nine cottages, a large mansion, the little Church of St. Etheldreda, a vineyard and kitchen garden. Nearby a meadow and orchard bordered a rose garden famed in an area where such retreats were numerous. In the past, many of Henry VIII's nobles had cast a longing eye on the Bishop's town house; there were numerous instances along the Strand of episcopal palaces having been converted to private residences. None succeeded until Sir Christopher Hatton sought possession of the pastoral setting at Holborn Hill and, by means somewhat questionable, actually obtained a lease from the Bishop for twenty-one years. Since the house was inhabited only occasionally by Richard Cox, the Bishop of Ely, Hatton thought he might also reside there. But Cox took a different view. Plaintively he wrote Burghley that he had refused other offers of tenancy, "So when God shall call me, my successor shall [not] be driven to make suit for his own house." He said that the place was convenient for him when he visited London and Westminster and that "he had furniture there which would be a nuisance to a tenant who would have to remove it." On receiving this letter and realizing who was urging the Bishop's removal, Burghley tactfully referred the matter to the Queen. She dispatched the following terse letter to Bishop Cox:

> "Proud Prelate! I understand you are backward in complying with your Agreement, but I would have you know that I who made you what you are can unmake you and if you do not forthwith fulfil your engagement, by God, I will immediately unfrock you!"[5]

The letter was followed by one from Lord North, who reminded Cox that the Queen had promoted him to the richest Bishopric in the country, worth £3,000. Recalling for Cox "how tenderly and heartily her Majesty wrote this summer," he proclaimed, "it is more than marvelous to know with what face you could deny her." Both the Queen and North knew that many of the Bishop's own methods of dealing with the See's tenants were questionable. North listed them:

> It will not like you that the world know of your decayed house, of the lead and brick that you sell from them, of the leases that you pull violently

from many, of the copyholds that you lawlessly enter into, of the free land
which you wrongfully possess, of the tolls and imposes which you raise of
God's good ministers that you ceaselessly displace. You suffer so many to
live longer under you than you like him. And to be flat, you nourish the ill
and discourage the good.

The Queen and her gentlemen had known how to proceed. The
terrified Bishop had little recourse but to yield, and the twenty-one-
year lease was eventually made over to Hatton for the Palace of Ely
with a rental of ten loads of hay, £10 a year for the ground and one red
rose for the gatehouse and garden.* Cox had the last word, however,
and reserved the right to walk unmolested in the garden and to gather
some twenty bushels of roses each year.[6]

Sir Christopher Hatton had distinguished himself in the Queen's
service. He was a patron of literature and exploration and a great
promoter and sponsor of England's famed sea dogs. He had been one of
the originators of the Bond of Association and a noted speaker in
Parliament. From Captain of the Queen's guard to Vice-Chamberlain,
Elizabeth had finally given him the Chancellorship of Oxford
University. In 1587 she did even better and delivered to Hatton the
Great Seal and made him Lord Chancellor of England. Despite the
ensuing sneers directed at the Queen's favorite dancing partner, Hatton had emerged as a talented administrator and an influential
statesman. His capacity for work was almost equal that of Burghley's
and his loyalty as unquestioned. He had also—after one brief venture in
the direction of Elizabeth Cavendish, the Countess of Shrewsbury's
daughter—wisely decided to remain unwed.

As her indulgence of Hatton had galled Leicester while he was alive,
so the new Lord Chancellor had his own nemesis in the person of
thirty-year-old Walter Raleigh, a West-country man, a distant relative
of Elizabeth's old governess, Kate Ashley. Walter Raleigh had been
born at Hayes Barton in East Budleigh, Devon, and was kin of many
distinguished Devon and Cornwall families—the Carews, Champer-
nownes, Grenvilles and even Sir Francis Drake. His father had married
three times and his mother twice. One of his half brothers was the
noted mariner Sir Humphrey Gilbert, some fourteen years his senior,
whose ancient family seat, Compton Castle near Torquay, was as
familiar to young Walter as the thatched farmhouse in which he had
been born. When Hayes Barton was sold during a period of financial
strain, young Walter was sent to Oxford, where his lack of indus-

*The name of the area is still extant in modern London in Hatton Gardens, and the Church of
St. Etheldreda is open to visitors.

triousness was equaled only by his poverty. Money, honors and privileges seemed the right of many others, but not for the awkward and often threadbare boy with only the illustrious relatives to recommend him. They were undoubtedly embarrassing and uncomfortable years for young Raleigh, whose pride was as fierce as his ambition.

On leaving Oxford, Raleigh went to London, took up residence in the Temple and, seemingly destined to be a soldier, fought in the Huguenot wars in France and later with Leicester in the Netherlands. Certainly soldiering seemed an agreeable way for a penniless provincial to earn his living; Raleigh had great energy, courage and good health to recommend him. A rare and artistic intelligence was to be discovered later.

In 1580 Raleigh was sent to Ireland, where he served with distinction in the Irish bogs which had been the burial ground for so many English gentlemen and as many English fortunes. He was personally courageous and aggressive, and his distinctive leadership inspired great confidence in his men. Where the enemy was concerned, he was pitiless, and the extermination of the Irish or of the Spanish and Italian prisoners sent to foment rebellion was attended to without compunction or conscience.

In 1581 he returned from Ireland, his military reputation secure. He became the expert adviser on Irish affairs for Lord Burghley and Sir Francis Walsingham, who privately expressed his opinion on the subject by saying "he wished Ireland in the sea." Raleigh had obtained the post with a typical Raleigh maneuver. He severely censured Lord Arthur Grey de Wilton, the head English Deputy in Ireland, stating in no uncertain terms that Grey was too lax in dealing with the recalcitrant Irish, and accused Grey of making Ireland "a lost land—not a commonwealth, but a common woe."[7] In circumstances already noted for bestial cruelty, Raleigh's solution was to effect even greater suffering on the unfortunate Irish. He noted that after two years of Grey's administration, "there are at this instance, a thousand traitors more than there were the first day."[8] On hearing the comment, Grey sniffed and replied that Raleigh was a small loss. "I liked neither his carriage nor his company . . ." he said. Burghley and Walsingham had little liking for Raleigh personally, but his blunt outspokenness had not gone unappreciated, for, said one observer, "He had gotten the Queen's ear at a trice and she began to be taken with his elocution and loved to hear his reasons to her demands." She wrote Grey that Raleigh would not return to Ireland but would remain at court, "for it is our pleasure to have our servant, Walter Raleigh, trained some time longer in that our realm for his better experience in martial affairs. . . ." The

Queen was apparently impressed with the man who had "a good presence, in a handsome and well compacted person, a strong natural wit and a better judgment; with a bold and plausible tongue, whereby he could set out his parts to best advantage."[9]

There is little doubt that Elizabeth was also charmed by Walter Raleigh. She had always liked men of unusual height, and Raleigh was very tall, with sensitive hands and a neat, trim foot. His swarthy complexion, heavy-lidded deep-blue eyes, the springy dark hair, mustache and beard—all contributed to a somewhat rakish appearance which his reputation—"he loved a wench well" said one friend—did nothing to lessen. He spoke in the soft burr of the West-country and could affect moments of startling gentleness as unexpected as they were gratifying. His delight in ornate clothing equaled Elizabeth's. The boy who had clambered barefoot over the rocks of the Devon and Cornish coast during childhood and spent his adolescence in shabby clothing at Oxford soon acquired a wardrobe of gold and silver tissue, satins, silks, brocades, jeweled caps, soft laces and velvets, which were the envy of many a wealthier gentleman. In a court where extravagance in dress was the norm, Walter Raleigh shone in prodigal splendor; he became almost at once the butt of many a contemptuous remark about the "new man" who had risen so quickly. In the confident manner in which he wore his newly acquired finery—and well aware he presented a more pleasing picture than many of more eminent background—was Raleigh's ill-concealed disdain.

Elizabeth was nearly twenty years older than Raleigh, but it was understood by all the Queen's favorites that once royal favor had been bestowed, age made little or no difference. She reveled in Raleigh's facile mind, his great wit and consistently agreeable manner. He was unmarried, a delight to the eye and more than willing to devote every waking moment to her. That was enough for Elizabeth. To the disgust of his colleagues, the Queen even gave him a nickname, "Water," and she called Raleigh, "the gentleman with the bold face."

The Queen was also generous to Raleigh. In 1584 he was knighted and in the following year appointed to the lucrative office of Lord Warden of the Stannaries (tin mines) in Devon and Cornwall, was made Lord Lieutenant of Devon and Vice Admiral of Cornwall. He was given 40,000 acres in Cork and Ireland, the manor of Sherborne in Dorset and the great estates of the executed Sir Anthony Babington. Elizabeth gave him further recognition and wealth in numerous licenses to export playing cards, cloth and wines, which contributed greatly to his financial security. Such success did not deter him from soliciting even further honors, and one day Elizabeth, impatient at his attitude, said irritably, "When will you cease to be a beggar, Raleigh?" Her courtier's answer was quick and frank. "When, Madame, you cease to be a benefactress!" he replied, as the Queen smiled indulgently.[10]

In pursuit of a long ambition, Raleigh obtained the Queen's patent to send several expeditions to the New World, even as he recognized Elizabeth would refuse to let him go personally. She later consented that one landing, the Isle of Roanoke, be called Virginia, in her honor. Though the results of the Virginia voyages were financially unsuccessful, the most notable and enduring consequence was mundane: the discovery of the pleasing properties of tobacco. Leaves of tobacco acquired from the Indians were ground for smoking in a pipe, and it commenced a fancy which took Europe and England by storm. At court, one evening, Sir Walter even induced the Queen to try her hand. While Elizabeth was experimenting with Raleigh's distinctive silver-mounted pipe, he nonchalantly bet his sovereign he could tell the weight of the tobacco smoke issuing from her lips. Eagerly the Queen accepted the wager, whereupon after weighing a new pipeful of tobacco, he smoked it, emptied the pipe of its ashes and soberly weighed them as the court erupted in laughter. Elizabeth greatly appreciated the joke, waving a fist at his head in feigned anger as she paid the wager and commenting, "she had heard of many who had turned gold into smoke, but that Raleigh was the first who had turned smoke into gold."[11] It was one more instance of the easy and ingratiating manner which had so won Elizabeth's fancy. His success with the Queen—and the valuable material perquisites which had followed—soon led to many snobbish sneers at Raleigh's "bloody pride" and the arrogance that led one courtier to write that he "was the best-hated man in the world, in court, city and country."

As if in defiance of such attitudes, Elizabeth made Raleigh her Captain of the Guard. She had learned through long experience there was much to recommend in an unpopular appointment to her service. In playing one gentleman off against the other, she encouraged rivalry, which not only gratified her vanity but curtailed the formation of any political factions. She kept everyone on his mettle looking to his own advantage and, at the same time, made certain that others—who had yet to gain—looked only to the Crown for their advancement. It was a device Elizabeth had wielded with great deftness, and it had rarely failed her.

Raleigh was eminently suited to his new position, not only for his extraordinary good looks, but by his willingness to spend cloistered hours attending his sovereign. He was given Durham House in the

Strand as his residence, and whenever he could leave the court, he went straight to the little turret room which was his favorite. "I well remember his study there," wrote a friend, "which was a little turret that looked into and over the Thames, and had the prospect which is as pleasant as any in the world, and which not only refreshes the eyesight, but cheers the spirits and (to speak my mind) I believe enlarges an ingenious man's thoughts. . . ."[12] In the past, Durham House had sheltered many: Sir Thomas Seymour, the Bishop de Quadra, the great Leicester, even Elizabeth herself. Yet few had experienced the days of pleasurable solitude Raleigh enjoyed by isolating himself in his study and composing the verses he would later read and dispose of with prodigal abandon among his friends, such as Christopher Marlowe and other habitués of the Mermaid Tavern and the inns of Cheapside and the Strand.

Sir Walter Raleigh was proof positive that the Queen's appreciative eye for the graceful and accomplished courtier was not waning. Indeed, even in her sixties, her indulgence with and tolerance of handsome young blades seemed even stronger. There were dozens of young men about the court, the offspring, in many instances, of relatives or older courtiers who had served their monarch well. Elizabeth had, for many years, cast an indulgent eye on her godson, the ingratiating Sir John Harrington, who, with irrepressible good humor, had tried the royal patience on more than one occasion. Harrington well knew how to reinstate himself in Elizabeth's favor. "I must go in at an early hour before her Highness hath special matters brought to counsel on. I must go before the breakfasting covers are placed and stand uncovered as her Highness cometh forth her chamber. Then kneel and say, 'God save your Majesty! I crave your ear, at what hour may suit for your servant to meet your blessed countenance!' " Thus, said Harrington, "will I gain her favor to the auditory."[13]

It was the affectionate behavior between Harrington and his young wife which caused the Queen to ask of Lady Harrington "how she kept her husband's goodwill and love?" Lady Harrington replied that "she had confidence in her husband's understanding and courage, well founded on her own steadfastness not to offend or thwart, but to cherish and obey." It was by such example, she said, that she convinced her husband of her own affection, "and in so doing did command his." Elizabeth was pleased by the answer. "Go to! Go to! mistress!" she cried, "you are wisely bent, I find. After such sort do I keep the goodwill of all my husbands—my good people. For if they did not rest assured of some special love towards them, they would not readily yield me such good obedience."[14]

Sir John Harrington was given to poetry, as well as mechanical contrivances, and one of his earliest experiments was the Ajax, a mechanical flush toilet which replaced the outside privy, the close stool and the chamber pot. He asked the Queen's permission to install one in the royal chambers, and calling him a "saucy poet of the laystow," Elizabeth consented. She soon summoned young Harrington to her presence, said the sound of the privy waters were enough to upset her digestion for a week and he might remove his contraption. "Go to, Sir Jakes, your jest will be the ruin of my bowels and is unfit for all but savages! Take a patent upon it and sell it to the Irish or blackamoors. But not in my kingdom!"[15]

Harrington was always clever enough to discern the royal mood before entering Elizabeth's presence. One day, on meeting Sir Christopher Hatton as he emerged from the Privy Chamber, he asked Hatton the Queen's disposition and was told, "If you have any suit today, I pray you put it aside; the sun doth not shine. . . ." When he ultimately did see his royal godmother, she complimented him on his clothing. Harrington later reported, "The Queen loveth to see me in my last frieze jerkin and saith 'Tis well cut.' . . ." Harrington recalled another courtier who had not fared so well. When Sir Matthew Arundel arrived at court in a new fashion, the fringed cloth, the Queen took one look at the ragged-appearing edges of the cloth strips and said nothing. Arundel attempted in every way he could think of to call attention to his new costume. Finally he had the Queen's answer. Harrington relates, "She spat on Sir Matthew's fringed cloth and said, 'the fool's wit has gone to rags!' " Yet she could, a moment later, become unusually gentle and tell the gout-ridden Burghley he must not rise or stand in her presence, adding the softening remark, "My Lord, we make use of you not for your bad legs, but for your good head."[16]

Elizabeth had some ten years previously attempted to check the "presumptuous disposition of her subjects" who strove to emulate the lavishness of court dress. An act was passed in Parliament allowing certain officials to stand at street corners, armed with scissors, for the purposes of clipping all ruffs that exceeded the size allowed by law.[17] Yet as she grew older, her own taste in clothing became more elaborate, overloaded with symbolic and theatrical devices and expensive frivolities. Simple linen nightcaps became "night-coifs of cambric cut-work and spangles . . . with bone lace." Her tooth cloths, normally of Holland cloth, were "wrought with black silk and edged with bone lace of silver and black silk."[18] Dress materials were involved, being "worked all over with sundry fowls, beasts and worms, in silks of divers colors. ...." Others bore ears and eyes, snakes, swords, snails embroidered into rich fabrics. Elizabeth chose the stark colors of black and white, vivid crimson or the richer shades of violet when she wished to be seen at a distance, the softer shades for intimate use in the Privy Chamber. In the royal wardrobes were some 125 petticoats, 67 round gowns in Peachflower, Maiden's Blush, Gingerline and Marigold,[19] hundreds of kirtles, foreparts, mantles, veils, French gowns with flowers and beasts of Venice gold, with rainbows and "pomegranates, pineapples and the Nine Muses in the same border." There were also Dutch cloaks of black velvet, "embroidered all over with flowers and grasshoppers of Venice gold silver and silk, lined with a tawney sarcanet, furred with sables ...", another embroidered with a device showing "raised moss work embroidered with stubs of dead trees, set with fourteen buttons embroidered like butterflies."[20] Many of these items of clothing were given to the Queen as New Year's presents, and with them she used numerous fans, some with a handle of gold, having two snakes winding about it, garnished with a ball of diamonds in each end ...", others of gold enamel, of crystal or of "elitropia, garnished with gold. ...."[21] Elizabeth was not content with all this finery; into some small place at her bosom, waist, hair or ear, she invariably tucked a fresh flower, a plume of fern, at times perhaps even small fruits such as cherries or strawberries.*

It was again her godson, John Harrington, who related that the Queen, with the pique of a schoolgirl, was jealous of her finery and brooked no challenge from her ladies-in-waiting. "I could relate," said Harrington, "many pleasant tales of her Majesty outwitting the wittiest ones, for few knew how to aim their shafts against her cunning." He said that Elizabeth "did love rich clothing, but often chid those that bought more finery than became their state. It happened that Lady Mary Howard was possessed of a rich border (or flounce) powdered with gold and pearls and a velvet suit belonging thereto, which moved many to envy. Nor did it please the Queen who thought it exceeded her own. One day the Queen did send privately and got the Lady's rich vesture which she put on herself and came forth from the chamber among her ladies. The kirtle and border being far too short for her Majesty's height, she asked everyone 'How they liked her new-fancied suit?' At length, she asked the owner herself, 'If it were not made too short and ill-becoming?' To which the poor lady agreed, 'Why then,' rejoined the Queen, 'if it becomes not me as being too

*They are difficult to find amidst the ornate embroidery, ribbons and pearls, but many portraits of Elizabeth show some flower such as in the simple miniature in the second section of portraits showing the Queen at age thirty-eight with a white rose pinned to her left shoulder.

short, it shall never become thee as being too fine.' " Harrington reported "that this sharp rebuke abashed the Lady and the vestment was laid up till after the Queen's death."

Elizabeth's high-handedness, as she grew older, was one of the lesser crosses her faithful ladies bore in patience. "She was subject," said an observer, "to be vehemently transported with anger, and when she was so, she would show it by her voice, her countenance and her hand. She would chide her familiar servants so loud that they who stood afar off might sometimes hear her voice. And it was reported that for small offences she would strike her maids of honour with her hand."[22]

As Elizabeth approached her sixties, her dependence on those closest to her became more noticeable. In 1589 the blind and sickly Blanche Parry died. The eighty-two-year-old woman had rocked the baby Elizabeth in her arms, and the Queen was desolate at her loss, a sore trial so shortly after Leicester's death. Her own health, which always suffered under any emotional stress, also worried many. Her eyes had become severely strained from shortsightedness and the diligence with which she daily studied state papers, correspondence, or worked at her embroidery; such strain only increased the intensity of occasional migraine headaches. At times she suffered attacks of rheumatism but quickly brushed aside any assistance in walking or riding. When she was well, her stride was as vigorous as ever. A lifelong fondness for sweets had resulted in torturing toothaches, as her amazingly sturdy teeth gave way to decay. One particularly agonizing session of several days, during which she had obtained no relief from the usual remedies, was severe enough to enlist her Councillors' aid. They sent for a physician, John Anthony Fenatus. Fenatus had not treated the Queen previously and was told he might not for safety's sake see her Majesty, for "he might possibly be a Jew or even a Papist." He might instead write a prescription. Fenatus demurred, saying he would have to examine the tooth, for "if it were hollow, when all was said and done, it was best to have it drawn, though at the cost of some short pain."

The Councillors were nonplussed. The Queen, as she had often stated, had the body of a woman and the heart and mind of a King, but such fortitude usually failed at the thoughts of being subjected to any instruments. She would, said Elizabeth, forbid any such treatment and suffer the toothache's pain instead. Her terror of the operation was so obvious that John Aylmer, the Bishop of London,* who was present as the Council pleaded with Elizabeth to submit, came forward and said that "although he was an old man and had not many teeth to spare, she

---

*Readers of the author's *Crown for Elizabeth* will remember John Aylmer as the kindly tutor of Lady Jane Grey who made her schoolroom hours such a pleasant refuge.

would see a practical experiment of it on himself." Whereupon the surgeon came forward and, apparently quite skilled, drew the Bishop's tooth as Elizabeth grimaced in sympathetic admiration. After such a brave display of valor, she allowed Fenatus to draw her own tooth also.

While her fondness for sweets was responsible for such fearful encounters, in other instances of diet, Elizabeth remained frugal. She had always eaten little; now she ate even less and took care to mix a greater proportion of water to her wine, so "her faculties might remain unclouded." In the summer, "she reposed herself for a short time on an Indian couch . . . but in the winter, she omitted her noon sleep."[23] She still kept the late hours so popular with the court when strolling musicians, players or jugglers entertained. She played at cards or chess, always asking for her winnings at once, after which she conversed with different groups or, if desiring privacy, taking a particularly favored person to a window embrasure or a deserted corner for a personal conversation.

The politics of the court and the behavior of its people were the favorite topic of interest with the masses outside the Palace walls, and the court jesters were one quick source of information. In their evening performances before the thronging court they might also, if they chose, quickly and deftly inform their monarch of the populace's attitude. One such jester, Pace, had been banished for several days for exceeding the bounds of good taste and wisdom in his ribald comments to the court and Queen. Eventually, Elizabeth agreed he might return. Still brooding from the royal snub, he stalked through the door one evening before the full assembly as Elizabeth, sensing his belligerence, spoke up in a friendly tone. "Come on Pace, now we shall hear our faults. . . ." The old jester rose to the bait but eluded the reproach, saying, "What is the use of speaking of what all the town is talking about?"[24]

Elizabeth rarely concerned herself with City gossip unless it involved her authority. It mattered even less when it dealt with her relationship to various courtiers. By the early 1590's everyone at court, as well as in the City, was aware her attention had shifted from Sir Walter Raleigh to Robert Devereux, the Earl of Essex. It was a cause of some concern about the court. The arrival of a new favorite always upset the established factions, as rivalry and jealousy once more became predominant.

Essex had been brought to court as an eighteen-year-old boy by his stepfather, the Earl of Leicester, in an effort to moderate Raleigh's influence with the Queen. He was now twenty-four, and the tall, gangling youth had become a powerfully built man with a shock of russet hair, a high intelligent forehead and the large eyes, straight nose

and sensual, well-formed lips of his mother, Lettice Knollys, the
Countess of Leicester. If he was one of the youngest and most attractive
courtiers, he was also the poorest, and his lack of funds considerably
embarrassed the young noble. He was spared the knowledge that his
current poverty was the beginning of a lifetime handicap. Debt was
preferable to disgrace, and his solution was to spend anyway. When
Burghley reprimanded him, he wrote penitently, "I hope your
Lordship in courtesy will pardon my youth if I have, through want of
experience, in some sort passed the bounds of frugality."[25] Burghley
was not placated, as Essex had meant him to be. The great minister
could remember hearing his father, a court official, speak of the extravagance of the Boleyn family. Essex's great-grandmother had been
Mary Boleyn, a sister of the ill-fated Anne. Both women had been
extravagant, thoughtless, proud and possessed of that quicksilver
charm and vivaciousness that were so much a part of Lettice—characteristics which she had passed on to her son. When
Leicester brought Essex to court, he had also hoped to set in process the
means by which the penniless Earl might recoup some part of his
family fortune. For the next several years, Essex had devoted every
waking moment toward that purpose.

Essex had a great example to follow in the pursuit of his goal.
Leicester had always been frank to admit that all his authority, glory
and wealth had come from the Queen. She was his dear Princess, his
mighty sovereign for whom he would lay down his life and his only
desire was to serve her always. Essex proclaimed likewise and, on
accompanying his stepfather to his disastrous campaign in the
Netherlands, had equipped his own followers in handsome uniforms,
the cost of which entailed more than £1,000 on his estates. His shocked
grandfather, Sir Francis Knollys, chided him "that wasteful
prodigality hath devoured and will consume all noble men that be
wilful in expenses. . . . You are so far off from being beforehand in land
and living left by your father to you, that by unhappy occasions your
father hath not left you sufficient lands for to maintain the state of the
poorest Earl in England. . . ."[26]

Essex's introduction at court had been more wildly successful than
either he or Leicester had dreamed. The physical impact of the tall
young man with the superb figure and the steady gaze, with the odd
ambling gait redeemed from clumsiness by an arrogant self-confidence, impressed Elizabeth. Essex could recite poetry, possessed a
pleasant singing voice, danced gracefully and could speak with ease on
many subjects. Elizabeth admired the Earl's courtesy and gracious
good manners, and in return, Essex found he liked the Queen. It was

understood, of course, that the monarch was always venerated, but the young man discovered he *liked* Elizabeth, the woman. Her great oaths, disarming frankness and blunt unpredictability appealed to his own youthful masculinity. Essex realized he could flatter with the best and was rewarded by an appreciative look in the Queen's dark eyes. He found it was easy to play the cavalier and not feel foolish, even as Elizabeth—despite the fact that she was older than his own mother —accepted such homage as completely her due.

For Elizabeth, Essex was nothing short of a revelation. Not only was he so brilliantly handsome and adoring that his very presence proved a goad to others who might yet take her favors for granted, but his impact on the ambassadors and court dignitaries was a delight to see. Elizabeth had only to look throughout any gathering when Essex appeared to see the electric current of awareness that passed through the throng. The young girls smiled and sidled by to gain attention; the men looked wary and thoughtful. It took only a word from the Queen to bring him to his knees, to kneel subserviently at her velvet-clad feet and kiss the still-slender bejeweled fingers. His handsome youthfulness vividly recalled the poignant vulnerability of those years when she and Robert Dudley, also short of funds, proper clothing and even hope, had faced a court filled with animosity.

Because of his youth—and her age—Elizabeth trusted Essex more readily and was certainly more tolerant than she might have been with other aspiring young men in the past. The Queen had always followed Burghley's advice to "gratify your nobility and the principal persons of your realm, whereby you shall have all men of value in the realm depend only upon yourself."[27] Now Elizabeth was so powerful—and Essex so powerless—that it pleased her to play the fairy godmother, as long as he was the adoring courtier who might provide diversion, feed her still insatiable vanity and charm in the process. So, as Hatton and Raleigh looked on from the sidelines, the Queen danced a pavane or a galliard with the young Earl, flirting with him from behind a fan or whispering in his ear, her hand on his shoulder. They rode together out the Palace gates for a day's hunting, and on the return, Essex remained to sup lightly with his sovereign, to listen to a tired minstrel's tale of lovers' trials and earthly woes. In the year before the Armada, his servant, wide-eyed at the instant success of his master, wrote his Shropshire father in wonder: "When she is abroad, nobody near her but my Lord of Essex and at night my Lord is at cards, or one game or another with her, that he cometh not to his own lodging till birds sing in the morning. . . ."[28]

A momentary infatuation would have been nothing new for the

Queen. The court was filled with nine-day wonders who had, at one time or another, caught Elizabeth's attention. But such continued favoritism was something else again, and propinquity could work wonders. To ensure that such propinquity did not lead to indifference and to guarantee Essex's constant attendance, Elizabeth had given him Leicester's old position as Master of the Horse, with £1,500 per year, care of his own horses and patronage perquisites in underappointments. It was one of the first instances of Essex's handling direct authority; he found the process quite satisfying. If there were those who thought a young, penniless Earl an unsuitable choice for such an honor, they said nothing. If the Queen wished to spoil the handsome young man who seemed so passionately eager to please, they were forced to admit at the same time that as far as appearance was concerned, she could hardly have bettered the selection. Dressed in fine new clothes, Essex was a study in magnificence as he rode with the Queen whenever she went abroad.

His self-confidence, however, led to an early quarrel. The Queen's regard for Essex had not changed her opinion of his mother, Lettice. Nor did the Queen like Dorothy Devereux, Essex's sister, whose frank opinion of Majesty, combined with a headstrong, impetuous behavior which had resulted in a runaway marriage, led to her being forbidden Elizabeth's presence. When the Queen proposed to visit Leicester's brother, the Earl of Warwick, at North Hall, Essex hurried to inform her that his sister was also a guest of the Warwicks. Elizabeth appeared unconcerned, saying that "she would treat her well." But on her arrival, she had second thoughts and commanded that Dorothy "keep her chamber." Essex angrily hurried to the Queen. There was little or no subterfuge in the young Earl, his very bluntness had always appealed to Elizabeth, and he now, with more than a show of bad temper, complained of the royal treatment. Elizabeth heard him out patiently and then attempted to explain, saying that "if she received his sister, the world would say it was for love of him" and not an act of her own prerogative. Her words should have warned the young man that he was venturing into that private world of Majesty, privilege and authority in which the Queen alone was supreme. But he continued indignantly, making little effort to see Elizabeth's point of view or graciously accepting the fact that the Queen even bothered to make any explanation at all.

Instead, knowing that Sir Walter Raleigh as Captain of the Guard was on duty outside her chamber door, he attempted to turn the quarrel into a larger issue and loudly accused Elizabeth of acting thus "to please that knave Raleigh!" To do so, he charged, she would disgrace him, Essex, before everyone. The Queen turned and looked at him in amazement. Angrily, she defended Raleigh, replying that Essex was showing the same absurd behavior that had caused his mother's banishment. That was enough for Essex. He would leave, he said—and his sister with him. Leave and be damned, was the Queen's reply and she turned to speak to the Countess of Warwick, giving every indication she had already forgotten the matter.

By morning Essex and his sister were gone, and on returning to London, Elizabeth found Essex had left the court, determined to join the fighting in the Netherlands. By then her temper had cooled and, even amused, she sent young Robert Carey posting after him. Essex was at Sandwich and, the gesture made, belligerently returned to court. As he made his way to the royal presence and ultimate forgiveness, he met young Charles Blount emerging from an audience. Blount wore a golden chessman tied with a crimson scarf to his arm. Essex noticed the unusual decoration and asked a companion its meaning. On being told the Queen had awarded it to Blount for distinguishing himself in the tiltyard the previous day, Essex replied, "Now I see every fool must have his favor." The remark being carried to Blount, Essex was challenged to a duel, which was fought several days later in Marylebone Park, where Blount disarmed him and wounded him in the thigh. When Elizabeth was informed of the incident, she swore in exasperation: "By God's death, it is fit that someone or other should take him down and teach him better manners, otherwise, there would be no rule with him."[29]

Elizabeth had a lifetime's experience to augment her own inborn ability to assess individual strengths, capacities and liabilities. From the first she had recognized flaws in young Essex. He was impetuous, eager and acquisitive; yet he also had elegance, idealism and superb self-confidence. Experience had also shown his tendency to petulance and a curious lack of judgment when he was crossed. He was neither as malleable nor dependable as Leicester, Hatton or Raleigh; he needed tempering. Elizabeth had quickly determined that she would shape and form young Robert Devereux, as she had Robert Dudley.

Elizabeth's attitude to Essex differed from her feelings for other courtiers who had given her devoted attention, and this was due, in a large part, to her age. Elizabeth was thirty-four years older than Essex. With Leicester and Hatton, sex—or the possibility of sexual encounters—had always played a part. With Raleigh, advancement for him and faithful service to her were the foundation of their relationship, and the bargain struck, she had not hesitated to bestow many preferments with the absolute conviction that her Captain of the Guard would serve her capably and honorably. But almost from the first—and despite his ardent protestations—there had been little assurance Essex would do the same. In years past, one of his difficult temperament would have been relegated to the fringes at court or suffered a banishment similar to his mother and sister's. That he prospered instead was due primarily to Elizabeth's being older, wiser and, in truth, more lonely. Personable young men willing to spend much time with their sovereign were numerous at court, but the Queen could not suffer the majority, whom she privately considered overweening, brainless and overprivileged. A young man as attractive and bright as Essex was a rarity, and he provided a pleasant opportunity for her to play the fairy godmother, the solicitous aunt or a benign and generous sovereign.

If the Queen had visions of a lasting friendship and courtly devotion from Essex, he, in turn, had greater dreams of political supremacy embellished with wealth and power. As events were shaping up, however, the conflicts that were to govern the last years of Elizabeth's reign were to test the wisdom of her choice and to challenge the mettle of the young man who had sought his fortune from the aging hand of his Queen.

It was unfortunate for a Queen who had always preferred peace to war that the latter years of her long reign were marred by conflict. There was little doubt that Philip would send future Armadas to England or that Parma might yet make an invasion attempt. In 1589, Henri III, the last Valois King of France, was assassinated; the heir, the Bourbon Henri of Navarre, was a Huguenot. The Catholic League and Spain worked furiously to dethrone the heretic monarch and, in their effort, was a serious threat to England. Should Henri IV be defeated, the Netherlands revolt would collapse, and Spain would then be predominant in France as well. Elizabeth had, therefore, little recourse but to aid Henri IV with money, which, as it grew in substance, was wrested from a reluctant and at times hostile Parliament. It angered the Queen that solid citizens and lawmakers could not understand what was so plainly evident: English intervention kept Flemish and French coastal cities and ports from falling into Spanish hands. If some viewed her strategy as a mere stopgap measure, it was the kind of maneuver which best suited the English Queen who had spent a lifetime avoiding definite confrontations.

Even with a Parliamentary subsidy, Elizabeth found that the money would pay only one year's war expense. A normal prewar expenditure of £150,000 had jumped to £367,000 in 1587 and to £420,000 in the

Armada year. It was the prospect of increased war demands on her finances which led the Queen to venture more deeply into a previous source of immense profit: piracy on the high seas. Drake and his fellow sea captains all urged their sovereign to confront the enemy, Spain, in its home seas and ports, to destroy the vessels which might be used against England. In the years preceding the Armada, London's merchant adventurers had formed companies to challenge Spain's right to conquest and exploitation of the riches of North, Central and South America. As these merchant ships went in search of foreign markets—or as English sea captains sailed toward an enemy shore—who was to prevent a foreign ship passing their way from being taken as a prize? Inevitably, such ships were filled with gold, silver, tin, jewels, copper, spices—at times, even slaves—and they were a source of great potential wealth to whoever captured them. To take the ship itself was a blow to the enemy; to capture the booty of the Spanish empire beyond the seas served to quench the Englishmen's thirst for retaliation against King Philip even as it struck at the very source of his power.

So the Queen let her sea dogs loose. Sir Francis Drake was to undertake a voyage to Portugal, and the Queen's orders were firm: he would raid Corunna and other ports destroying Armada remnants and all Spanish shipping. He was to attack the Azores and await the Spanish treasure ships from the Americas and, while in Lisbon, attempt to reinstate the exiled Don Antonio, the Portuguese pretender whose throne King Philip had claimed. The expedition was financed by private subscription among wealthy nobles and merchants, with the Queen contributing £50,000 and a number of ships.

The Earl of Essex was eager to join the expedition, but Elizabeth refused to listen to his pleas. He had been living well beyond his means and was greatly in debt. The opportunity to share in the plunder was alluring, and he resolved to go despite the Queen's attitude. He wrote his grandfather, Sir Francis Knollys, that his precarious financial position left him little alternative, for "Her Majesty's goodness hath been so great as I could not ask more of her." He said there was "no way left to repair myself but mine own adventure. . . . If I should speed well, I will adventure to be rich; if not, I will never live to see the end of my poverty." Once the letter was on its way, he quickly left for Plymouth, riding 220 miles in thirty-six hours. Incensed, Elizabeth sent the aging Sir Francis after his disobedient grandson to command his return. She wrote, "As we have authority to rule, so we look to be obeyed!" and she ordered Essex home immediately. "These be no childish actions," wrote the Queen angrily, "nor matters wherein you are to deal by cunning of devices to seek evasions as the custom of lawyers is. . . ."[30]

But she was too late. Essex had foreseen her actions and, quickly boarding the *Swiftsure* under the command of his good friend Sir Roger Williams, had hastily put out to sea. It was not until some six weeks later that they joined the English fleet itself under the command of Drake and Sir John Norris. With arrogant self-confidence and to the ill-concealed dismay of Drake and Norris, Essex, as the highest in rank, claimed an unjustified share of the command. He had ignored the pinnaces bearing letters from the Queen insisting on his return. In Portugal, he leaped ashore with the abandon of a high-spirited schoolboy "and was the first that landed, who by reason the billows were so great, waded to the shoulders to come ashore."[31] After a few forays and skirmishes, instead of sailing to Lisbon, some 60 miles away, he insisted that the troops march by land, hoping to gather Portuguese support for Don Antonio along the way.

From the beginning the campaign was a dismal failure. The Portuguese were apathetic in acknowledging their Pretender. At Lisbon, most of the natives had fled inside the city walls, and the English forces were too small to effect great damage. At night the flames from the houses on the walls lit up the area as the resident Spaniards burned them lest the English attempt to occupy them. Several assaults by the enemy followed, and weary with such maneuvering which only depleted his forces, Norris, the military commander, proposed to abandon Lisbon. The disappointed Essex, in a bravura performance, contented himself riding to the city gates, "demanding aloud if any Spaniard mewed therein durst adventure forth in favour of his mistress to break a lance."[32] There was no reply, and in a bad temper, the Earl drove his pike into the great gate before riding to rejoin his men.

Several days later the arrival of Drake and the remainder of the fleet and the subsequent capture of several Hanseatic vessels loaded with copper, corn, wax, masts and cables somewhat redeemed the expedition. Supply ships from England also brought a letter from Elizabeth, now nearly two months old, in which she spoke of his "sudden and undutiful departure" and how offensive it had been. "Our great favours, bestowed on you without deserts, hath drawn you thus to neglect and forget your duty . . ." said the Queen. Essex had no excuse now but to obey the royal command, especially on reading her final words: "whereof see you fail not, as you will be loath to incur our indignation, and will answer for the contrary at your uttermost peril."[33] He arrived in London to the acclaim of people always ready to embrace a new hero and, since he had at last obeyed her command, to the smiles of a Queen. Elizabeth chose to view his behavior as a great youthful prank, while Sir Francis Drake went into momentary disgrace for the poor return on her investment. Yet in the Queen's indulgence lay one fact which the young adventurer himself did not overlook. Essex had braved her wrath and done as he wished, returning to challenge her retaliation with apparent impunity. He had turned her anger into welcome. It was a deed well observed not only by Essex but others at a court where few could claim a similar privilege.

Though the Lisbon expedition had been a financial failure, the daring enterprise led to Elizabeth being hailed as "The Lady of the Sea" and "Queen of the Seas." The acclaim coincided with a renaissance encompassing a fresh consciousness beginning to be evident throughout England. The printing press had brought books and other printing to a nation of 4,000,000 men and women, many of whose parents had been unable to read. In literature, the theater and the arts, this spirit of revival and learning was as dominant as the spirit of exploration and exploitation which sent the Elizabethan sailor to sea. Among the myriad farmers, wool manufacturers, lead merchants, shipbuilders, weavers, journeymen and yeomen, hop growers, printers, geographers and doctors were the architects and builders struggling to raise the great mansions which would dominate the English landscape for centuries. And in London especially, Nicholas Hilliard, the brilliant court painter, could hardly keep up with demands for his jewellike miniatures, while young Will Shakespeare, dramatist and poet, was struggling through an apprenticeship which would prove the shining pinnacle of his English heritage.

Nowhere was this new spirit more apparent than in the Anglican Church. But it was a spirit less welcome to Elizabeth and the majority of her Council, for it derived from the increasing influence of the Puritans in her court and country, as well as in her Church. The Calvinistic doctrine in England expressed itself in the Puritan desire for a Church differing from Elizabeth's Anglican hierarchy in that its governing officials, from ministers through "elders" were elected. It replaced the Queen's authority with that of a synod at the apex of various committees. Elizabeth had little interest in or tolerance of the alleged "purifying" aspects of the Puritan tenet. She abhorred "excercises" and "prophesyings" and three-hour sermons in which lay members might speak on equal terms with the clergy. She resented the challenge to her authority as much as she deplored the impracticability of a system which poked an inquisitorial nose into the privacy of men's consciences and laid a heavy burden of sanctimonious conformity on each individual soul. Elizabeth was determined that the Church she had established should be allowed to grow and shape itself in accordance with the nation's needs, and for this purpose, time was required. She knew intolerance had not worked in the past and was certain it would not work in the future. "Those kinds of platforms and devices which they speak of are absurd," she noted angrily. The Queen did not like change. A royal reactionary, she regarded innovation, especially religious innovation, as the work of the devil. She said frankly that such practices would only lead to further religious tyranny. She suspected that many of the religious "innovators" actually were political agitators, using—not for the first time—religion as a cause for their differences. "I see many," she scolded in Parliament, "overbold with God Almighty, asking too many subtle scannings of His blessed will, as lawyers do with human testaments." Elizabeth said she had no perfectionist's view of her Church. There was a great need for improvement, but, she was insistent, "If I were not certain that mine were the true way to God's will, God forbid that I should live to prescribe it to you."[34] She had no use for the rigid Puritan discipline, she said, and she knew her people too well to think they could live with it.

In 1583 Elizabeth had appointed John Whitgift as Archbishop of Canterbury. She sensed the strong discipline and dictatorial will of "her little black husband," as she called Whitgift, might prove a realistic deterrent to the Puritan movement. Both Queen and Archbishop were shaken when Whitgift eventually unearthed the true extent of the Puritan advance throughout the realm as well as in the Church itself. The reformers of the already supposedly reformed Church had infiltrated small towns and cities. In Parliament, also, voices were raised in opposition to Whitgift's cleansing methods, which included a system of exorbitant fines and even imprisonment in dealing with ecclesiastics of doubtful orthodoxy. Even Burghley daringly denounced Whitgift's methods as "Romish." "Now my Lord," he wrote Whitgift, "bear with my scribbling. . . . I desire peace of the Church, I desire concord and unity in the exercise of our religion. But I conclude that, according to my simple judgment, this kind of proceeding is too much savoring of the Roman inquisition and is rather a device to seek for offenders than to reform any. This is not the charitable instruction that I thought was intended. . . ." Whitgift, conscious of the Queen's powerful protection, soothed Burghley but was not intimidated or swayed, saying, reproachfully, ". . . in these public actions I see no cause why I should seek friends, seeing they to whom the care of the commonwealth is committed ought therein to

join with me."[35] Even that staunch Puritan Walsingham was so outraged at Whitgift that he urged the other Councillors to write reproving letters to the Archbishop.

Elizabeth had always held the view that, provided it rendered the
monarch indisputable support and loyalty, the sovereign should allow
the Church independence. She had no desire to meddle with it, as
her predecessors had done, and was willing for the Bishops to govern
within the existing framework of the law.[36] Her position was that of a
watchful protector, and the Archbishop was her appointed representative. To make the point to her subjects and Councillors, she appointed Whitgift to the Privy Council, the only instance in her entire
reign of an ecclesiastic serving in such an office.[37] In his appointment
was implicit the Queen's answer to the growing Puritan movement,
and it served to check temporarily the movement which would gain so
much political power in the future as to wreak a vengeful havoc on her
successors.

It was to be Elizabeth's sad fate that as she grew older, one by one,
her close associates were taken from her. After Blanche Parry's loss, Sir
Francis Walsingham died. The sixty-year-old minister had been unwell for years, and a lifetime of frustration and disappointment, added
to his monarch's abuse, had saddened his last years. The man who had
said, "Knowledge is never too dear," had paid huge sums of his own
money to garner the foreign intelligence that was the foundation of his
work. Walsingham was not wealthy, and some ten years before his
death, he had asked Sir Christopher Hatton "to put her Majesty in
mind that in 8 years time wherein I have served her, I have never yet
troubled her for the benefiting of any that belonged to me, either by
kindred or otherwise; which I think never any other could say that
served in that place." Elizabeth had responded with several
remunerative posts for Walsingham, but he was, in many instances, a
prisoner of the system of his own making. The espionage monies were
his responsibility, and he continued to spend his own resources. This,
combined with the death of his son-in-law, the renowned Sir Philip
Sidney in the Netherlands, completed his financial ruin, for he was the
target of all of Sidney's creditors. He had hoped for the Queen's
compassion, as well as the estates of the executed Sir Anthony
Babington, but they had gone, instead, to Sir Walter Raleigh. The
depressed Walsingham retired from the court and died in his home
near Seething Lane on April 5, 1590. A man of few illusions, he asked
that because of the "greatness of his debts and the mean state he left his

wife and heir in," he "be buried without any such extraordinary ceremonies. . . ." Burghley wrote a friend in Italy informing him of Walsingham's death, saying, "The Queen's Majesty and her realm and I and others . . . have had a great loss, both for the public use of his good and painful long services and for the private comfort I had by his mutual friendship."[38] The Queen honored Walsingham's request, and so creditors might not seize his body, about ten o'clock the next evening, with no fuss whatsoever, the man who had served so faithfully was buried in St. Paul's "without solemnity."

It followed shortly after Walsingham's death that his daughter, the widowed Lady Sidney, married again. This in itself was not surprising, for with her father's death, the penniless widow faced actual hardship. The choice of bridegroom, however, left the court in shock, for Lady Frances Sidney wed none other than Robert Devereux, the Earl of Essex. It is doubtful that Essex was very much in love with Lady Frances. In his will, Sir Philip Sidney had left his valuable sword to his best friend Essex, and presumably, it was understood that Essex would look after Sidney's widow also. Lady Frances was no belle, but that she captured two of the most dashing heroes of the day demonstrates she was not without attractions. Essex, whose affairs in and out of the court were notorious and whose relationship with the Queen was as unique as Leicester's, possibly even seduced his dead friend's widow and then felt it imperative to redeem her honor, as well as his, by marrying her, It was a measure of Elizabeth's mellowing age that, after her first outburst of disbelief and fury, the tempest soon subsided, and one of her Privy Chamber gentlemen could write, "If she could overcome her passion against my Lord of Essex for his marriage, no doubt she would be much the quieter; yet doth she use it more temperately than was thought for and, God be thanked, does not strike *all* she threatens!"[39] Undoubtedly her temper cooled somewhat when Essex, frankly admitting his marriage, agreed that "for her Majesty's satisfaction" he would be pleased that "my Lady, my wife, shall live very retired in her mother's house."

The following year Elizabeth endured another painful loss in the death of Sir Christopher Hatton. Her "dancing Chancellor" had suffered for years with kidney trouble and a painful cystitis, and by 1591, depleted in energy and his large, handsome form wasted, he took to his bed in Ely Place. Elizabeth had been tart in her comments to Hatton regarding his enormous debt to her, even insinuating that he repay some part of her loans. Unfortunately, his last illness followed her demand, and full of compunction, the Queen hastened to Hatton's home, where, tearful and saddened, she remained for five days. At her arrival, she had carried canisters of "cordial broths," which she fed to Hatton with her own hand. Even the royal ministrations were useless, and on November 11, six days before her Accession Day festivities, Sir Christopher Hatton died. Though he was £42,000 in debt to the Queen, he was given a splendid funeral in St. Paul's Cathedral, and seven months later, his nephew and heir, Sir William Hatton, erected an elaborate monument to his memory.*

With Hatton and Walsingham gone, and Burghley often ill at Theobalds, the Earl of Essex became more prominent at court and in the City, where his popularity was immense. The Londoners recounted with delight the adventures abroad that had hardened his youthful figure and given it a muscular strength and vitality. He was a familiar sight ambling with his strange rolling gait among the gardens and corridors of Whitehall Palace or striding into the courtyard of Essex House, formerly Leicester House, in the Strand. Once Elizabeth had graciously consented to receive his wife, Lady Essex appeared little at court, and his amatory affairs were the subject of great interest with those who noted he was "continually grateful to the ladies."[41]

His finances were still a strain. Though his income from his estates and his position as Master of the Horse might have been sufficient for someone of more sober tastes, they were inadequate for the Earl. The maintenance of Essex House was expensive. Its master demanded the finest livery for his servants and clothing for himself and his family, and it had cost him £7,000 alone to participate in the Lisbon raid. He was soon over £20,000 in debt to the Queen, and in sympathy, she lent him £3,000 more shortly after his return. Elizabeth could be changeable, however, and within weeks, her own worrisome expenditures caused her to ask for repayment. Essex was shocked and begged for a delay, but the Queen was adamant. She would lend her nobles money when she could she said, but when *she* needed it back, the money or land in its equivalent value must be paid immediately. Essex had little recourse other than to accede, and he wrote: "Now that your Majesty repents yourself of the favour you thought to do me, I would I could, with the loss of all the land I have, as well repair the break which your unkind answer hath made in my heart, as I can with the sale of one poor manor answer the sum which your Majesty takes of me." It may have given Essex small pleasure to have the last word, and as a fine

*It was so imposing and so in contrast with the modest tombs of Sir Francis Walsingham and Sir Philip Sidney that Londoners quipped, "Sir Philip and Sir Francis have no tomb. For great Christopher takes all the room."[40]

Huntingdonshire manor "of mine ancient inheritance, free from in-
cumbrance, a great circuit of grounds in a very good soil" passed to the
Queen, he wrote, "Money and land are base things, but love and
kindness are excellent things and cannot be measured by themselves."[42]

To lessen the blow, Elizabeth gave Essex the right to the farm of the
customs (taxes) of the sweet wines imported from the Mediterranean.
In such a manner did the Crown, which could afford small salaries for
court positions or appointments, recompense its loyal servants.
Monopolies, patents, wardships, pensions, leases and grants of Crown
land were carefully dispensed with due regard for their worth by the
Queen. Not only did they compensate for services rendered, but they
also, as Elizabeth was well aware, further bound the loyalty of the
recipient to the Crown. The farm of sweet wines customs was one of the
most substantial, and Essex's financial condition improved considerably. Not only did he have ready cash, but since most of his lands were
mortgaged, the sweet wine monies were a principal source of security
when he wished to raise additional funds.

Essex was keenly interested in the progress of the religious wars in
France. Henri IV's great difficulty in holding onto his Crown came to
a head in late 1591 with the advancement of the Duke of Parma's
troops throughout Picardy, as other Spanish forces entered Brittany.
Elizabeth was greatly concerned for the safety of the Brittany ports and
other Channel provinces so favorably located for invasion of England.
King Henri, well aware of the Queen's alarm, begged the English for
assistance, and eventually Elizabeth sent Sir Roger Williams and Sir
John Norris with a small expeditionary force to join the French. With
several thousand men, they overpowered enemy garrisons and, needing further assistance to ensure their conquest, asked for additional
troops.

The Earl of Essex had been one of the first to beg leave to go to
France, and the Queen, taking a perverse delight in punishing him for
his marriage, had refused. Elizabeth had heard Essex proclaiming his
love of martial life and his pleasure in being among soldiers and
officers. "I love them for mine own sake," he said, "for I find sweetness
in their conversation, strong assistance in their employment, and happiness in their friendship. I love them for virtues' sake and for their
greatness of mind. . . . I love them for my country's sake, for they are
England's best armour of defence and weapon of office. If we may
manage peace, they have purchased it; if we must have war, they must
manage it."[43] To one of such enthusiasm, a royal veto was not to be
tolerated, and on three occasions, Essex went to court for the express

purpose of insisting on Elizabeth's permission to go to France; at one point he pleaded on his knees for two hours. Gradually he wore down the royal reluctance and was given his first command with three definite provisos: that he would help King Henri in the siege of Rouen; that Elizabeth would pay the troops for two months only; and that in order not to debase the worth of a title, Essex would bestow knighthood sparingly. Although he was nominally in command of the forces, Elizabeth regarded her young noble with a calculating eye and appointed three experienced gentlemen, Sir Thomas Leighton, Sir Henry Killigrew and Sir Henry Unton, to act as his advisers and "tutors." The Queen's indulgence of Essex is apparent in Unton's instructions, for he was particularly ordered to have "special regard to the actions of the Earl of Essex" and to "deal plainly with him."

In great exhilaration Essex landed at Dieppe on August 3. He met Sir Roger Williams, who had recently returned from visiting the French King at Compiègne. Henri IV was overjoyed at Essex's arrival and wished to meet the daring young noble whose reputation had spread to the French court. Essex's orders were not to leave Dieppe until Henri had agreed to Elizabeth's terms for the two-month loan of her armies and the promise of an attack on Rouen. Once he heard of the French King's eagerness to meet him, however, he was eager to be off. The fact that the route lay about 100 miles inside enemy country heavily armed with patrols only lent extra spice to the adventure. Essex persuaded himself he had little alternative than to obey Henri's wishes, and giving little heed to his own monarch's instructions or the fact that he was leaving his troops behind, he rashly set off on the dangerous mission which could accomplish little but a personal gratification. Taking 100 horsemen garbed in the Devereux colors of tangerine and tawny velvet trimmed with gold, he soon arrived at Compiègne. "He had before him six pages mounted on chargers and dressed in orange velvet all embroidered with gold. And he himself had a military cloak of orange velvet covered all with jewels. His saddle, bridle and the rest of his horse's harness were in like sort. His dress and the furniture on his horse alone were worth 60,000 crowns. He had twelve tall bodysquires and six trumpets sounding before him,"[44] wrote one observer.

Essex's arrival had an electric effect on the French King, and for several days, Henri outdid himself providing entertainment for the visiting nobleman and every demonstration of cordiality far into the night, with dancing and music "and other evidences of mutual accord." On one occasion there was even a leaping contest in which the two young men—King and Earl—participated, and Essex, because of his great height "over-leapt them all." For two weeks the festivities went on despite the fact that an army was waiting at Dieppe eating up expenses while a Queen waited for word of how her money was being spent.

On Essex's return he again traveled through enemy territory. On this occasion word of his presence at Compiègne had spread to the enemy, and his return journey was even more hazardous. At one point, he narrowly missed a force of 700 horsemen commanded by the Governor of Rouen. Later he wrote a lengthy letter to the Queen and Council informing them of Henri's plans ultimately to besiege Rouen and dwelling on the dangers he had encountered, "I have passed sometimes within caliver shot of his [the Governor's] scouts. . . ."[45]

Elizabeth, aware of the loss of time, the knowledge that the French King was ignoring his promise and that her prestige and money were being lost to no purpose, was angry. In addition, Essex was acting like a great schoolboy on a long-overdue holiday. She said "that the Earl of Essex would have it thought that he ruled her realm, but that nothing was more untrue; that she would make him the most pitiful fellow . . . and instead of sending more troops, she would recall all. . . ." She sent a scathing letter to those officers who were to act as his "judges," saying, "Where he is, or what he doth, or what he is to do, we are ignorant. . . ." She complained that the Rouen expedition was already a month late, and, as Essex later wrote, "I was blamed as negligent, undutiful, rash in going, slow in returning, indiscreet in dividing the horse from the foot, faulty in all things, because I was not fortunate to please."[46] A minor skirmish outside Rouen's walls had resulted in the death of his younger brother, Walter. Essex, ill and sad at the loss, was insulted at the Council's recrimination that he had risked his life with "trailing a pike like a common soldier," throughout enemy-held territory. Shortly thereafter Essex was ordered to turn over his command to Sir Thomas Leighton and return to England. Before he left on October 8, he reviewed his troops from a hill outside Rouen, making a moving farewell speech. And then, to the amazement of all who knew of the Queen's pronounced disclination to grant honors unless for notable service, he knighted twenty-four of his officers for their "good will." They had hardly had the opportunity to perform any great martial feat.

His reception at home was as he expected. The Queen was aloof and critical and, after a thorough harangue on the bestowal of knighthoods, waved him away. From Essex House, he wrote petulantly, "I see your Majesty is constant to ruin me. . . . I appeal to all men that saw my parting from France, or the manner of my coming hither, whether I deserved such a welcome or not." When she learned that the French King was now ready to besiege Rouen, hoping to teach Essex a lesson, the Queen ordered him back to France with the biting comment that he behave like a general and not some "soldier or executioner." On arrival Essex was aghast at the decimation of his forces by illness and desertion; only about half remained, he wrote the Privy Council. Well aware that he might not perform too admirably with such small troops, he wrote the Queen a letter contrived to remind her of the devotion they had shared. He wrote that "he wished to do something which shall be worthy of the name of your servant. At my return, I will humbly beseech your Majesty that no cause but a great action of your own may draw me out of your sight, for the two windows of your privy chamber shall be the poles of my sphere, where, as long as your Majesty will please to have me, I am fixed and unmoveable. When your Majesty thinks that heaven too good for me, I will not fall like a star, but be consumed like a vapour by the same sun that drew me up to such a height. . . ."[48]

The siege of Rouen finally commenced some two months later. The first week in November trenches were dug around St. Katherine's Castle, Rouen's chief defense, with Essex vigorously directing the action "and showing such enthusiasm and energy that his personal followers were tired out, and agreed among themselves to take it in turns to escort him."[49] On the thirteenth, King Henri himself came to watch the siege, at which point the trenches had been dug so close to the enemy's that the soldiers could talk across the intervening space. Essex had fewer than 800 men; the French King's troops were busy elsewhere. The enemy was well provisioned, and Essex's were not. His men had not been paid, for Elizabeth's time limit had expired, and they were now the responsibility of Henri IV, whose own troops were mutinying for lack of pay. There was general discouragement as supplies ran lower, as ladders to scale the garrison's walls were found to be too short and as sickness and the mortality rate increased.

By January Elizabeth had had enough. In great disgust, she said the whole campaign was "rather a jest than a victory" and her monies were being dissipated by a youthful, energetic King and Earl with little awareness of her own responsibility to her subjects, who already were murmuring against the loss of life and increased taxation. In January her patience was at an end, and she angrily ordered Essex home in order to stay further slaughter of "divers gentlemen of good quality, dear to their parents and blood . . .", saying that as far as Essex was concerned, "we shall right well allow of your judgment to return as a thing very fit and necessary to be performed ... without putting Sir Thomas Leighton to any further trouble in this hard time of the winter...."[30]

So, for the second time, the Earl of Essex took leave of his depleted and ill troops. Before departing, he challenged the Governor of Rouen to personal combat, saying that "if you wish to fight yourself on horseback or on foot, armed or in your doublet, I will maintain that the King's quarrel is juster than the League's, that I am better than you and that my Mistress is fairer than yours...!"[51] Such bombast had little effect on the inmates of the Rouen garrison, and the Governor was heard to sneer "that as to the beauty of their mistresses, it was scarcely worth his while to put himself to much trouble...!"[52]

The campaign that Essex was to have brought to a close within two months ended six months later, when on January 8, 1592, he boarded a ship for home. Before leaving, he drew his sword and, dramatically kissing the hilt, handed over his command to Sir Roger Williams.

Chapter Twenty-nine

The return of the Earl of Essex to England coincided with the fall from favor of Sir Walter Raleigh. For years the two antagonists had contested as Queen's favorite; when one was in the ascendant, the other was invariably on the wane. When the Lisbon raid brought Essex great prominence, Raleigh had retired to his Irish estates, and he arrived back in England in the wake of Essex's momentary eclipse after the Rouen debacle. He was soon involved in a liaison with Elizabeth Throckmorton, one of the Queen's maids-of-honor. One courtier wrote to a friend on the Continent, "Sir Walter Raleigh, as it seemeth, has been too inward with one of her Majesty's maids. . . . The matter hath only now been apparent to all eyes and the lady hath been sent away. . . . Sir Walter Raleigh hath escaped from London for a time. He will be speedily sent for and brought back. . . . All think the Tower will be his dwelling. . . . It is affirmed that they are married, but the Queen is most fiercely incensed and, as the bruit goes, threateneth the most bitter punishment to both offenders. . . ."[1]

Elizabeth Throckmorton, the tall, blond, blue-eyed daughter of the late distinguished Sir Nicholas Throckmorton, was undeniably pregnant. The Queen was maddened, not only by the easy desertion of a close friend, but also at the inroads courtiers such as Raleigh were making on the supposedly impeccable morals of the virginal cluster which had been entrusted to her care. A good deal of the Queen's relentless attitude toward her ladies' marriages was not directed at the marriage itself but rather at the sexual dalliance which usually preceded the ceremony. There was more than one plumply pregnant bride among Elizabeth's ladies, and since the young girls had been put in her care, she regarded the offense not only as a lack of manners and morals but a careless disrespect for the Crown itself.

Sir Walter Raleigh had not, as was suspected, attempted to escape his responsibility toward Mistress Throckmorton. He had persuaded the Queen to participate in an expedition designed to attack Panama and surprise the Spanish plate fleet which, several times yearly, brought the treasures of Spanish conquest to King Philip. Eventually some thirteen ships were outfitted, but at the last moment the Queen, delighted with Raleigh's presence, refused him the active command. Instead, he was permitted only to lead his fleet out to sea, where he turned it over to Sir Martin Frobisher.

In his absence, Elizabeth Throckmorton's condition became known. Upon Raleigh's return both were sent to the Tower. It was there he heard that the expedition he had put together, in which he had invested every penny he had in the world, had provided Elizabeth with the greatest pirating prize England was ever to take on the high seas. While he languished in the Tower, writing despairing and abject love letters and a poem to "The Lady of the Sea" in an anxious attempt to regain his freedom, his fleet was engaged in a battle off the Azores. After several hours, Raleigh's own flagship, the *Roebuck,* commanded by Sir John Borough, captured the Lisbon-bound Portuguese East Indian carrack *Madre de Dios.* It was a gilded, towering ship of 1,600 tons, high-pooped and lumbering, manned by a tough crew which was subdued with sword and shot and, after boarding, by hand-to-hand combat. On investigation, the marauding English were speechless at the cargoes' wealth. Gold, silver, diamonds, emeralds, musk, ambergris, spices—the pepper alone later brought £102,000—perfumes and ivory carvings all were packed away in the hold. The English went wild with the plunder. Loose-fingered sailors and equally nimble-fingered officers pocketed and pilfered and nearly set the ship afire on three different occasions as they wandered, candles in hand, from compartment to compartment, stuffing their shoes, doublets and hose with whatever small objects they could hide.

A pinnace from the fleet was eventually dispatched with news of the capture. Thus, when the *Madre de Dios* was towed into Dartmouth, merchants who had ridden hard from London, clogging the roads in their haste to be among the first to board in order to protect their investment, were waiting. When the returning seamen were informed that their commander Raleigh was in prison—*and for getting married!* —they stormed the decks, plundering outright what they had been pilfering secretly for days. Chains of gold, pearls the size of peas, lavishly jeweled spoons, velvet pouches filled with rubies and emeralds disappeared from the dockside to be sold at one-tenth their value to the speculators waiting to obtain some part of the fabulous hoard.

In London the Queen was informed of the mutiny and spoiling of the carrack. Robert Cecil wisely advised that Raleigh be released from the Tower as the one man able to control the unruly seamen. Within hours, Sir Walter was riding hard for Devon, directly after Cecil himself, who later wrote that everyone he passed smelled of musk or ambergris or had bulging pockets, which led Raleigh, enraged, to cry that if he came upon any of them, "I mean to strip them naked as ever they were born!"

At Dartmouth, Raleigh went directly to the docks. Robert Cecil watched his arrival and wrote his father, Lord Burghley, "I assure you, Sir, his poor servants, to the number of 140 godly men, and all the mariners came to him with such shouts and joy as I never saw a man more troubled to quiet them in my life." Cecil had advised Raleigh to give the impression he had been permanently released by the Queen, but Raleigh disdained the ruse and told everyone who congratulated him, "No, I am still the Queen of England's poor captive," to which the mariners responded ominously. Raleigh had never been liked at court—such was the price the Queen's favorite inevitably paid—and Cecil apparently found it difficult to credit the seamen's affection for their commander. He wrote his father, "I vow to you before God [it] is greater amongst the mariners than I thought for. . . ."[2]

In the end, the great prize, worth some £300,000 originally, had some £141,000 left for the investors, and Sir Walter used the riches to effect his release. He wrote Lord Burghley that in assembling the great expedition to honor his Queen, he had brought her the great prize. Surely such riches were worth something? He would buy not his bondage, but his freedom, he said, and he generously offered the Queen, who had contributed only one-tenth of his expenses, the lion's share of £80,000. "Four score thousand pounds is more than ever a man presented to her Majesty as yet," he said. "If God has sent it for my ransom, I hope her Majesty will accept it."[3]

Majesty was pleased to accept; Elizabeth also relished the cleverly defiant gesture. Raleigh had made bargains before, and this was the handsomest yet. Without hesitation, she took the greater share, salving any twinges of conscience with the knowledge that her courtier, after a token return to the Tower, would gain his freedom. The London merchants doubled their investment, and Sir Walter Raleigh lost everything—except his liberty. He was banished to Sherborne Manor, where his son, "Wat," was born. Unlike Essex who had retained his influence in spite of a marriage, Sir Walter never regained the affection

of his Queen. She was later to use his abilities, but never again was the "man with the bold face" in a position to be bold with his sovereign.*
Perhaps in some way, Elizabeth recognized she had met her match in Raleigh, who could equal her defiance with the keen, penetrating wit and the intelligence Essex lacked. He was unique in her court, and she must have missed him.

Other faces were also disappearing. Again death took several near the Queen—Leicester's brother Ambrose Dudley, the Earl of Warwick, although his passing brought a warm comfort in the return of his wife, Ann, to serve as lady-in-waiting. Death also claimed Elizabeth's cousin Lord Hunsdon, Mary Stuart's faithful guardian the Earl of Shrewsbury, as well as Thomas Randolph, who had spent many months at her court. Often it seemed to the Queen that wherever she looked, there were newer—and younger—faces. Positions of prominence remained open because the normally vacillating Elizabeth seemed unable to replace the familiar loved ones who had given her decades of faithful service. The thirty-year-old Robert Cecil had taken on many of his father's duties, yet he had no title. The frail, pale-faced young man with the hunched back and the thin, pursed lips above a neatly trimmed beard bore little resemblance to Lord Burghley, except in his devotion to his work and loyalty to his sovereign. The young man spoke and wrote well and possessed a great administrative capacity. For years, Burghley had conscientiously groomed his son to replace him, and Robert's outstanding ambition was to honor his father and Queen—and further his own career in the process. Unlike Essex, he did not court popularity. To charges that he was too youthful for such an aging monarch, he told the Queen, "Time which catcheth everybody leaves only you untouched"; he knew how to exercise that precise blend of subtle flattery mixed with respect which for years his father had found effective. Robert Cecil was prudent and temperate in all things and possessed an exceedingly fine intelligence. If he was not heartily disliked, neither did his cool confidence and fastidious disdain encourage any real warmth. Because of his diminutive size, Elizabeth called him her "Pygmy." If it irked the deformed little man, he had better sense than to show it.

The Secretaryship vacated by Walsingham's death still remained open. Though Robert Cecil was the obvious choice, the Earl of Essex had attempted to obtain the position for William Davison. It was

---

*He was bold enough to say, years later when Elizabeth was in her grave, that "howsoever she seemed a great and good mistress to him in the eyes of the world, yet she was unjust and tyrannous enough to him to lay many of her oppressions on him, besides seizing on the best part of everything he took at sea for herself. . . ."[1]

typical of Essex's proclivity to sponsor lost causes that he proposed the man now released from the Tower for his part in the Queen of Scots' execution. Honor seemed to demand he make the gesture. In any event, it was always a challenge to test his influence with the Queen or, as he put it, "to do the Queen good against her will." Often she unexpectedly humored her favorite, but in this instance, he was disappointed. Elizabeth, aware of the rivalry between the Essex and Cecil factions, wisely left the position vacant. In any event, Cecil was fulfilling the duties and shouldering the responsibilities; the title could come later.

Essex was becoming something of a problem at court. There was a perpetual friction between the Queen and the nobleman which kept others edgy and uncertain. She still reveled in his comeliness, his grace and his unstinting willingness to serve her. Yet his lack of tact, impetuosity and obstinacy irritated; his ambition could be viewed only as foolhardy. He was not above using his attraction for the younger ladies to incur royal jealousy, and he succeeded frequently enough to arouse the Queen's wrath. There were many at court who cautioned Essex to emulate Leicester and Hatton and not be indiscreetly careless in his attitude toward the Queen; above all, he must never take her affection or favor for granted. Even his enemies were amazed at the breadth of the Queen's tolerance. They acknowledged that she handled him with great dexterity and wisdom, often without the not-too-perceptive Earl's awareness of just *how* he was being manipulated. It was this ignorance, this reluctance or inability to see exactly to what extent the Queen indulged him, that inevitably led him to make the biggest mistake of all.

Essex was the constant target of place seekers, and two who had sought him for preference were Anthony and Francis Bacon, the sons of Elizabeth's first Lord Keeper, Sir Nicholas Bacon. Their mother was the sister of Lady Burghley, and as nephews of Lord Burghley and first cousins of Robert Cecil, the Bacons might have expected to rise in prominence in court positions consistent with their intelligence, background and ambition. But Burghley gave them "fair words, with no show of real kindness." He tossed no plums their way, especially with his own son to look out for. Anthony Bacon was a chronic invalid who had left England in his twenties and for some twelve years lived abroad, where he had served as one of Walsingham's intelligence agents. He had many friends in foreign capitals who were later to prove invaluable. His brother, Francis, was a Cambridge graduate, more studious than Anthony and with pronounced homosexual tendencies. He was pursuing a career in the law and served as a Member of

Parliament, and all, friend and foe alike, agreed he possessed a rare intelligence and "occupied his leisure with literary exercises and philosophical speculations."[5]

It was a fitting tribute to Essex that when it was obvious that Lord Burghley was not going to assist his Bacon nephews, they sought him out as the one most likely "to do good to the State." Essex liked the Bacon brothers, and he sympathized with their plight; the Cecil family had thwarted him on more than one occasion. Francis Bacon had brought Thomas Phelippes, the cipher expert who had worked at Chartley against Mary Stuart, into Essex's employ, and with Anthony's important connections on the Continent and his knowledge of foreign diplomacy, it seemed wise to build up an intelligence system which would rival anything the Cecils could produce. Soon four secretaries were hired to handle correspondence which flowed in from all the foreign capitals. Visitors from Scotland, France, Holland, Spain, Italy and Bohemia mingled with agent-spies at Essex House. The somewhat raffish lot attracted many malcontents from court fringes, as well as the more adventurous nobility, among whom none was more prominent than Henry Wriothesely, the Earl of Southampton. Southampton, a friend of Francis Bacon's, was the patron of the up-and-coming young poet and playwright William Shakespeare, who had dedicated his new poem, *The Rape of Lucrece,* to Southampton, saying, "The love I dedicate to your Lordship is without end. . . . What I have is yours; what I have to do is yours; being part in all I have, devoted yours." Southampton was a great champion of the London theater, now under fire from the Puritans for despoiling the Sabbath, and he was being acclaimed as "a dear lover and cherisher as well of the lovers of poets as of the poets themselves."[6] Southampton, a particular friend of the Earl, was in his element at Essex House. Both were remarkably alike; they easily attracted others to their cause, even as their exciting magnetism detracted from the lack of any real substance in their characters.

From his efforts, it was obvious that Essex wished to place himself at the head of a faction in opposition to the Cecils. Such faction would have little or nothing to do with the graybeards still left at court but would attract younger recruits for the positions of prominence as they became available. Essex paid an oblique compliment to old Lord Burghley when he said, "Things do remain in the same state as they did. They who are most in appetite are not yet satisfied, whereof there is great disappointment." That he was hoping for Burghley's resignation or death is apparent in his final comment: "If it stand at this stay awhile longer, they will despair, for their chief hour-glass hath little sand left in it and doth run out still."[7]

It was not long before the busy activities at Essex House were known to the Queen, and at first she was amused at what seemed presumption. Later she was impressed by the extent of Essex's knowledge and information and the memoranda and recommendations which, for the most part, were the direct result of the Bacon brothers' efforts. She had nothing to lose and everything to gain in accepting their information; much of it she already knew, but much she did not. Then in acknowledgment of Essex's efforts, she made him a member of the Privy Council. The effect on my Lord of Essex was instantaneous. "His Lordship is a new man," reported his steward, "clean forsaking all his former youthful tricks, carrying himself with honourable gravity. . . ." The twenty-five-year-old Essex was delighted, and the Queen was pleased. If nothing else, she was now certain he would not use the agents and information at his disposal to go off on some harebrained tangent of his own or someone else's making.

Essex had promised the Bacons his strong support, and when the office of the Attorney General was vacated by Sir Thomas Egerton, he bent every effort to obtain it for Francis Bacon. Unfortunately, the younger Bacon brother had spoken in Parliament, tilting with the Cecil faction, against a subsidy the Queen desperately needed. His speech had preceded his knowledge that he might be considered for the appointment, and he had worked hand in glove with Members of Parliament returned by direct order of the Earl of Essex from his estates around Lichfield, Stafford, Tamworth and Newcastle. It was one of the first overt instances of Essex pitting his political strength against the Cecil party, and there was little doubt he had won an important victory. As far as Essex was concerned, the Queen's disappointment and anger were less important than the fact that he had caused Robert Cecil a considerable setback. But both Elizabeth and Cecil were to have their revenge sooner than Essex anticipated.

When Essex suggested Francis Bacon for the Attorney Generalship, Elizabeth demurred. Bacon had given her no support in Parliament, she said, and was hardly to have such a plum at her hand! When the Earl persisted, Elizabeth told him outright there were other considerations—Bacon was nine years younger than Sir Edward Coke, the other candidate, and many thought Coke himself too young. When Essex would not desist and continually dwelled on Bacon's talents, Elizabeth became piqued and told him "she would have her own way." She said she would depend on her own judgment. When she mentioned again his offense in Parliament and said that "if it had been in the King her father's time, a less offense than that would have made a man be banished from his presence forever,"[8] Essex had Bacon write an apologetic letter explaining his conduct. Elizabeth was outraged at his presumption. When Essex pretended not to hear her denunciation, the Queen lost patience and, in a bad temper, brushed him away saying he must leave such selections to Lord Burghley, whose judgment she trusted more than his!

Her tone would have warned anyone more sensitive or less confident than the Earl. Robert Cecil, apparently extending a peace feeler from the Queen, said that possibly Francis Bacon might be considered for a lesser position, that of Solicitor General, since "it might be of easier digestion to her Majesty." Essex replied in ill humor, "Digest me no digestions! For the Attorneyship for Francis is what I must have. And in that I will spend all my power, might, authority and amity and with tooth and nail defend and procure the same for him against whosoever! And whosoever getteth the office out of my hands for any other, before he have it, it shall cost him the coming by!"[9] Cecil could scarce believe what he was hearing.

Nor could Essex believe Elizabeth would persist in her refusal. But the Queen took advantage of Robert's various absences to knight Robert Cecil and to make Sir Edward Coke the Attorney General. For eighteen months after Essex's return from France, he then attempted to secure the previously scorned Solicitorship for Francis Bacon. When Elizabeth refused to listen to his entreaties, he wrote Sir Robert Cecil, saying "Her Majesty never in her reign had so able and proper an instrument to do her honourable and great services as she hath now, if she will use him." Then, back at court, he would plead with the Queen once more. One old courtier who had seen many ambitious young bloods was aghast at Essex's persistence, saying that "he must continually be pulled by the ear." When Elizabeth had had enough, she huffily told him to be off and go to bed if he could talk of nothing else, and when he flung himself from court, she made no overtures in his direction. A more discerning man would have tried to retrieve a bad situation before it worsened. Essex did not. While no one disputed his physical bravery, he sorely lacked moral courage and, like a spoiled child, found it easier to sulk than to admit error or defeat.

But one closer to him recognized the situation and its eventual outcome quite clearly. Francis Bacon realized that if he had spoiled his chances by an unfortunately timed Parliamentary speech, Essex had made it almost impossible for him to serve the Queen. And when, after eighteen months, Elizabeth gave the Solicitorship to a "Mr. Fleming,"

Essex, too, realized he had forfeited Bacon's chances. He told his friend, "You fare ill because you have chosen me for your mean and dependence and you have spent your time and thoughts in my matters." Characteristically, he gave Bacon a gift of his own land, which Bacon accepted, intimating at the same time, it left him under no obligation to Essex.

It seemed almost as if Francis Bacon could read the future more clearly than the Earl himself.

As the Queen grew older, those in positions of responsibility fervently hoped her love of travel might lessen. But no such thought occurred to Elizabeth as, week after week throughout the summer, she prepared for her progresses and visits to the neighboring gentry. Seemingly she never tired of the long, dusty roads over which the royal coach and wagons rumbled, and from Theobalds to Cowdray Castle, to Rycote to Elvetham, where the Earl of Hertford had employed 300 "artificers" to make arrangements for her reception, her subjects, who rarely came to London, were given a glimpse of their Queen. Once, in Huntingdonshire, one rough-clad individual stepped from the verge at the roadside and approached the royal coach. With no trace of self-consciousness he asked, "May I speak with the Queen?" and a delighted Elizabeth, stifling her laughter, stopped the procession and withdrew her glove so that her visitor might kiss her hand. Often her journeys were shorter—to her palaces of Hatfield or Richmond or merely to dine with her Lord Keeper at his house in Kew. Wherever the royal party passed, the Queen remained enthusiastic and pleased with the unending receptions, the flowers, the cheering throngs, the pageants and picnics, the hunting, fireworks, music and parading. Nor did she ever tire of the gifts provided by eager hosts or the bags or containers of money presented by nervous Lord Mayors or aldermen. "Look to it—that is £100!" she sharply told one awestruck equerry when he hesitated in accepting an ornate compote filled with great gold coins. Her nobles willingly impoverished themselves to entertain her as she cheekily prolonged her visits to save the expense of maintaining them at court. One observer has left a picture of Elizabeth as she passed in procession:

> Next came the Queen, in the sixty-fifth year of her age, as we were told, very majestic; her face oblong, fair, but wrinkled; her eyes, small, yet black and pleasant; her nose a little hooked; her lips narrow and her teeth black; (a defect the English seem subject to, from their too great usage of sugar).

She had in her ears two pearls, with very rich drops; she wore false hair, and that red. Upon her head she had a small crown . . . her bosom was uncovered, as all the English ladies have it, till they marry; she had on a necklace of exceeding fine jewels. Her hands were small, her fingers long, and her stature neither tall nor low; her air was stately, her manner of speaking mild and obliging.

That day she was dressed in white silk bordered with pearls of the size of beans and over it a mantle of black silk, shot with silver thread. Her train was very long, the end of it borne by a marchioness. Instead of a chain, she had an oblong collar of gold and jewels. As she went along, in all this state and magnificence, she spoke very graciously, first to one, then to another, whether foreign minister or those who attended for different reasons, in English, French and Italian. For besides being well skilled in Greek, Latin and the languages I have mentioned, she is mistress of Spanish, Scotch and Dutch. Whoever speaks to her, it is kneeling; now and then she raises some by her hand. . . .[10]

In addition to tiring her associates with her progresses and processions, the Queen's disinclination to make up her mind did not change with age, and it often affected the lower as well as the high echelons of court personnel. Thus one day as a carter came to the gate for the Queen's belongings, he was told—for the third time—that she had changed her mind. The carter slapped his thigh, swore loudly and exclaimed, "Now I see that the Queen is a woman as well as my wife!" He was thunderstruck to hear a laugh from above. "What a villain is this!" someone cried, and gazing up, he saw Majesty herself, leaning from the window to throw three gold coins at his feet.

At sixty-five, Elizabeth Tudor was, for her time, an old woman or, as Sir Walter Raleigh more gracefully said, "A Lady whom Time hath surprised." But the surrender of self to age did not come easily to the Queen. She attempted to hide the wrinkles in her skin by an extra application of cosmetics. The loss of several of her teeth lent a not unattractive sibilance to her speech. Her refusal to dose herself with the noxious physics and emulsions so popular at court contributed to a good digestion and an astonishing energy, which her insistence on walking and other exercise only increased. She had ceased to use hand mirrors, saying they were "so far from niceness," as near as she would ever come to admitting she did not like her aging reflection. Instead, she trusted to her ladies for the "comeliness of her attire."[11] She was proud of her resilience and "thanked God that neither her stomach, nor her strength, nor her voice for singing, nor fingering her instruments, nor lastly her sight, was any whit decayed."[12] She still received much affection from the older courtiers, one especially who, gazing at her during the Twelfth Night festivities said, "She was as beautiful to my old sight as ever I saw her."[13]

Lord Burghley, with his son neatly launched at court, would dearly have loved to resign the Treasurer's office and enjoy his remaining years of feeble health with some measure of peace, but the Queen would not hear of it. She acknowledged his discomfort and the seriousness of his condition but told him that "she did entreat Heaven daily for his longer life—else would her people, nay herself, stand in need of cordials, too!"[14] When Burghley's granddaughter, one of her maids-of-honor, Ann, was to wed the Earl of Derby, Elizabeth was sufficiently interested in the wedding plans to arrange that the ceremony take place at Greenwich Palace, where, she wrote Burghley, she expected him to come and dance with her. He replied to his son, "For her hope to have me dance, I must have longer time to learn to go, but I will be ready in mind to dance with my heart, when I shall behold her favorable disposition to do such honour to her maid for the old man's sake."[15] The wedding festivities, spun out over several days, were highlighted by the presentation of *A Midsummer Night's Dream* by the new young dramatist all London was talking about, William Shakespeare.

Elizabeth still spent countless hours dealing with public affairs—reading and answering her correspondence, attending meetings, conferring with her Council, receiving ambassadors and reading innumerable documents, often making notes in her own hand for future discussion. Her mind was as keen as ever, perhaps keener, for she possessed an almost total recall that was the envy and at times the despair of many around her. Foreign ambassadors, usually considerably younger men, came to Elizabeth's court prepared to scoff at "petticoat government." After the brilliant ceremonial of the Queen's arrival in the Presence Chamber, the presentation of credentials and the princely greeting, the Queen would then converse with her visitor. One day, as she spoke knowledgeably on the complexity of European politics, skillfully weaving in known bits of information with such intelligence as she had gleaned from her own private sources, she noticed a blank expression on the face of one ambassador. She stopped short, thinking he had lost the drift of her conversation and asked if he understood her meaning? Shaking himself, as if from some hypnotic spell, the ambassador frankly admitted he was so impressed with Elizabeth's grasp of affairs and her logical and forthright manner of presenting them that he had been spellbound. With a satisfied smile, the Queen continued.

Not all confrontations were so pleasant. Sir Robert Cecil wrote early in 1597 of the Polish ambassador's visit to England. From her canopy of state, the Queen had extended a gracious greeting as the ambassador advanced. After kissing her hand, Elizabeth settled back to hear his reply. The ambassador spoke in Latin, and instead of the courtly and politic phrases usually preceding the essential reason for his visit, he charged the Queen of England with assuming a "maritime superiority" over other nations and implied that because of England's size, it was undeserving. He accused her of meddling in the Spanish-Netherlands-France conflict which was disturbing the trade of neutral nations. He said his master (whose display of courage in sending the ambassador in the first place owed something to a recent marital affiliation with the Hapsburgs), would accept it no longer. He, said the ambassador, had come all the way to England to inform her of his sovereign's ultimatum.

The Queen had listened silently, one of the few present who could follow his Latin speech easily. Under the thick white makeup on the lined skin, a flush of red shone. When he had finished, she caught at the rings on her hands to dispel some of her anger before she replied to the shocking disregard of diplomatic protocol. Then, having digested the meaning of the ambassador's Latin phrases to her satisfaction, she answered him in the same language.

> Is this the business that your King has sent you about? Surely I can hardly believe that if the King himself were present, he would have used such language. For, if he should, I must have thought that he, being a King not of many years, and that not by right of blood but by right of election, they, haply, have not informed him of that course which his father and ancestors have taken with us, and which, peradventure, shall be observed by those that shall live to come after him.

The Queen then said, gesturing to the ambassador, "And, as for you, although I perceive you have read many books to fortify your arguments . . . I am apt to believe that you have not lighted upon that chapter which prescribes the forms to be observed between kings and princes. . . ." Elizabeth said that if he did not enjoy diplomatic protection, she would have answered him "in another style." Rising, she suggested the ambassador's withdrawal, telling him he had shown himself "a herald rather than an ambassador."[16] On departing, he was treated to Elizabeth's high piercing laugh as she rose and, turning to the shocked court, exclaimed, "God's death, my Lords! I have been enforced this day to scour up my old Latin, that hath lain long rusting!" As several clustered around her to express their anger, it was

ncounter. With the spots of red
still bright in her cheeks she said she "was sorry that Essex had not
heard her Latin that day." She still wore a pleased air as she left the
chamber, the diatribe forgotten, her satisfaction in her Latin very
evident.

Philip of Spain had vowed to avenge the Armada disaster, even if, as
he said, it cost him his last candlestick. In the past, there had been more
than a modicum of truth in the international jest that the reason Spain
and England had not clashed sooner was that neither Spain's King nor
England's Queen could make up his or her mind. Now, however,
although Hawkins and Drake had perished on their last fateful journey
to the Caribbean, English assaults on Spain's treasure fleets continued
to be crippling. Philip had been enraged when Elizabeth had meddled
in France, accommodating that fool Henri IV and, with her peculiar
insular strength, helping to secure Channel ports against Parma. She
had become antagonistic in her attitude toward the English Catholics
and, while she had shown tolerance in the past, now seemed eager to
persecute those who would challenge her religious authority. Burghley
insisted that the only Catholics suffering the death penalty were those
"who profess themselves by obedience to the Pope to be no subjects of
the Queen . . . ,"[17] an undoubted reference to the Jesuits, particularly,
who seemed destined for martyrs' deaths.* Resentment of Elizabeth's
success and her prolonged heresy was clear in the vigorous preparations
Philip now made to launch yet another formidable expedition to
invade England.

The Spanish King's desire for revenge was no secret at the English
court, and many urged that England strike first. The greatest
proponent of an aggressive English thrust was Essex. Having cut his
teeth on the Lisbon raid, he was desperately eager to carry the battle to
the enemy's shore. In this he had enlisted the support of Lord Burghley,
and the great minister wondered if England—and particularly its
Queen—could stand the financial strain and psychological trauma of
another pre-Armada defense movement.

In France, Calais had fallen to the enemy. Characteristically,
Elizabeth had waited too long before rendering any assistance. But
when the guns bombarding Calais could clearly be heard in Greenwich
Palace, she reluctantly surrendered to her Council's advice, and an
expedition was readied to meet the Spaniard in his own waters before

*Two-thirds of the Catholics who suffered death as a result of government persecution were
foreign-trained ecclesiastics dedicated to martyrdom.[18]

an assault could be made on England. Eventually, it was decided that the fleet, under the joint command of the Lord Admiral Charles Howard and the Earl of Essex, would consist of four squadrons. Accompanying them, each with their own squadron, were the Lord Admiral's nephew Sir Thomas Howard and Sir Walter Raleigh. Raleigh had recently returned from a voyage to Guiana, the success of which had goaded Essex for months. Rank, precedence and short tempers accompanied all preparations for the great military and naval campaign as the four commanders bickered among themselves. Elizabeth did not help. One courtier wrote, "The Queen is daily changing her humour about my Lord's voyage and was yesterday almost resolute to stay it. . . ."[19] Later they would go; the next day they would stay. When Essex learned she proposed to recall two commanders and send only half the fleet, he said, in a moment of rare maturity, "Of my own interest, I will not speak, since every day I do more and more incline to the Stoics' opinion, and will, if I can attain unto it, bring myself to their temper."[20]

To take his mind off the Queen's "daily changing her humour," Essex worked hard. His zeal was evident in the long hours spent compiling lists, signing requisitions, overseeing the loading of vessels, watching the soldiers and sailors training. He used much of his own money in the process, even as Elizabeth constantly harassed her commanders to be gone and save *her* expenses! Essex was exasperated at her attitude. He said had they intended merely to cross the Channel instead of the sea, the Queen would act the same. "She would then fear as much the issue there as she doth our intended journey," he noted. "I know I shall never do her service but against her will." If she canceled the expedition at that late point, he threatened that "he would become a monk upon an hour's warning."[21] Her attitude had irritated the other commanders, and when a joint communication was sent to the Queen, Essex quickly signed his name above that of the Lord Admiral. The Admiral, Elizabeth's cousin, was so exasperated he later cut out the offending signature with his penknife before dispatching it.

It was with relief all around that the expedition finally sailed the first week in May, 1596. With Elizabeth's farewell came a prayer addressed to the Lord Admiral: "I make this humble bill of requests to Him that all makes and does, that with His benign hand He will shadow you so as all harm may light beside you, and all that may be best hap to your share; that your return may make you better and me gladder." Noting the absence of Essex's name in her communication and guessing why and by whom the signature had been cut out, she added humorously, "Let your companion, my most faithful Charles, be sure that his name is not left out in this petition. God bless you both, as I would be if I were there, which, whether I wish or not, He alone doth know."[22]

The fleet bound for Cádiz was almost the size of the original Armada, with more than 100 vessels carrying 11,000 souls. Each of its four commanders sailed with varying motives. Howard in the *Ark Royal* was anxious to uphold the reputation made during the Armada disaster, particularly as he was forced to compete with the zeal and youthful vigor of such as Essex. In the *Mere Honour*, Lord Thomas Howard hoped to do well himself, perhaps fitting himself for the aging Lord Admiral's honors when he should die. In the *Warspite*, Sir Walter Raleigh hoped the Cádiz venture would reinstate him in the former intimacy and affectionate graces of his Queen. And in the *Due Repulse*, Essex hoped to demonstrate his courage and enthusiasm for the great cause, to bring further honor and luster to his name. In a long letter to the Council, he explained the blow by which he hoped to cripple Spain: ". . . we shall cut his sinews, and make war upon him with his own money, and to beat him, or at least discontinue him by sea. . . ." He hoped to seize and maintain a port, "a thorn sticking in the foot of Spain," where, he said, English ships might prey further on the treasure ships of the Indies. He asked that his suggestions not be criticized until he could defend them in person, "for as the nature of my place is subject to envy and detraction, so a little body full of sharp humors is hardliest kept in temper. . . ."[23]

On Sunday, June 20, the English surprised the town of Cádiz, situated at the end of a six-mile-long isthmus. By virtue of his rank, Essex had defiantly claimed the right to land first by an assault on the beaches. The sea was rough with a rising wind, and in the first attempt, two boatloads of fifteen soldiers, clumsy in armor and carrying heavy weapons, were overturned by the high waves and drowned. This setback and the bad weather caused a change in plan. Waiting until the following day, Raleigh decided to attack the town by sea. Essex, impatient at the delay, agreed to join him, while Lord Howard was to see to the restraint of several galleons and Spanish merchantmen floating in the harbor. For the next three hours, as the guns blazed forth, as Spanish ships cut their cables to escape, the English pounded them unmercifully. Some were caught by the tide and swept ashore; others were captured. But before the English could board the captive vessels, the Spanish crews set the masts and sails aflame as the sailors attempted to flee the blazing infernos. Sir Walter Raleigh later described the spectacle as "lamentable." He said, "many drowned themselves, many half-burnt, leaped into the water, very many hanging by the ropes' ends . . . under the water even to the lips . . . many swimming with grievous wounds . . . and withal so huge a fire and such tearing of the ordnance . . . and the rest, when the fire came to them, as, if any man had desire to see Hell itself, it was there most lively figured."[24]

Once the sea battle was ended, Essex took advantage of the calmer seas to effect a landing. Raleigh had figured prominently in the sea battle, and Essex was eager to make his own charge. A drum on the deck of the *Due Repulse* began a somber ominous beat, which was then picked up by the rest of the flotilla. Small boats carrying 2,000 men, the oarsmen dipping together to the drum's sound, left the mother ships and rowed toward the shore. Once on land, they fell into formation and marched on the town, which was defended by only 500 cavalryman. The hand-to-hand combat was relieved in dramatic fashion by the timely arrival of Lord Howard, who had remembered the Queen's strict order that "Essex was not to expose himself to danger unnecessarily." Instead of seeing to the custody of the Spanish merchant ships, Howard had decided instead to follow Essex. With him came Sir Walter Raleigh, who "was not able to march so fast as the rest by reason that he was hurt in the leg with a splinter. . . ."[25]

In a magnificent coincidence of fate, the commander of the Cádiz fort, the Duke of Medina Sidonia, had watched the battle from the nearby heights of St. Mary's Port, overlooking the bay. He had seen the forty Spanish vessels flee to the inner harbor for protection, and he sent an offer of 2,000,000 ducats for the safety of the ships. Howard disagreed; he would accept the ransom for the ships' cargoes, he maintained, but the ships themselves would be secured as prizes of war. At the same time, he did nothing to see to their safety. There was a delay of several hours before Howard had an answer, and the result must have given Medina Sidonia tremendous satisfaction. As Howard, Essex and others held a council of war in the Cádiz fort, a great column of black smoke appeared over the Bay of Cádiz. The Spaniards were burning their own fleet rather than let the English capture it, and soon more than forty vessels in prime condition and worth more than 12,000,000 ducats lay at the bottom of the harbor. It left the English in possession of a Spanish city and £120,000, which the inhabitants had raised for their ransom before they streamed over the Puente de Suazo Bridge to the mainland. Once the townspeople had left, the English troops were let loose to plunder, and the sunny town of Cádiz was soon a welter of brawling, cursing soldiers, busily throwing contents of houses into the streets, looking for jewels, money, ornaments or other valuables they could carry home.

Individually, the soldiers fared better than the expedition as a whole. The pride of the Spanish fleet lay at the bottom of the bay, and its destruction was "the greatest blow ever dealt to the power of Spain." Yet they had taken no great booty, and Essex, therefore, proposed to remain in Cádiz and await the arrival of the Spanish plate fleet. In the meantime, he named himself Governor of Cádiz and conferred some sixty-eight knighthoods on his officers.

Essex's enthusiasm to remain at Cádiz was not shared by others. Several pinnaces filled with deserters had left the fleet, and the commanders themselves could not agree on the procedures to be taken. If they left Cádiz, Essex advised that they sail to Lisbon or the Azores, where they might intercept the Spanish plate fleet. Eventually, he was persuaded that lack of provisions, leaking ships and the disease taking its toll of the crews demanded a swift return home. On July 1 the town of Cádiz was ruthlessly burned, and the English fleet then cruised along the Portuguese coast, making several token raids which netted some insignificant plunder. Again Essex advised waiting for the Spaniards, and again he was overruled by the other commanders, each anxious to return to the Queen before conditions worsened. On August 6, as Essex raged at being balked, the English headed for Plymouth.

Forty-eight hours after the English had passed Lisbon, the great Spanish plate fleet, laden with treasures worth £20,000,000, proudly sailed into the Tagus River, having just missed the marauders. Treasure excelling that of the *Madre de Dios* had been lost because four commanders of the English fleet had wasted time—and endangered the health of their crews and the safety of their ships—because of their chronic disagreement.

Essex had been justifiably uneasy about his return, for the plunder he was bringing home was little in comparison with the Queen's investment. In order to pave the way for a more amiable reception, he prepared a document *A True Relation of the Action at Cádiz on the 21st of June Under the Earl of Essex and Lord Admiral Sent to a Gentleman in Court from One That Served There.* It was given to one of Essex's agents with instructions to post to London, where it was to be printed and distributed before Essex himself arrived at court. The Queen and Council learned of the document and forbade its publication. Word had reached Elizabeth of the scarcity of booty and the disappearance of much of what had been taken. On August 11, she appointed commissioners to "search the ships which are come up the Thames for all goods, money, jewels or other commodities taken in the spoil of Cádiz to be reserved towards defraying the charge of voyage. . . ."[26]*

On the eleventh, the Earl returned to court, and the royal reception for the victor of Cádiz was decidedly cool. Since Essex had insisted his rank gave him precedence, he was the first to hear Elizabeth's comments that so many knights had been made that she should "not hereafter be troubled with beggars, all were become so rich . . . !" But where was the £50,000 she had given? When Essex, as well as several Councillors, attempted to explain the blow to King Philip's sea power and prestige, as well as his Treasury, Elizabeth remained unimpressed, and Essex later wrote, "I see the fruits of these kinds of employment and I assure you I am as distasted with the glorious greatness of a favourite as I was before the supposed happiness of a courtier. . . ."[28] To make matters worse, the Queen had knighted Robert Cecil and, while Essex was absent at Cádiz, had given him Walsingham's post as Secretary. Now that his thirty-three-year-old son had obtained the coveted position, Lord Burghley could be generous, and he interceded with the Queen on Essex's behalf, earning her ringing accusation, "My Lord Treasurer! Either for fear or favour, you regard my Lord of Essex more than myself. You are a miscreant! You are a coward!" After which both Essex and Burghley did the only thing possible. They silently left the court, and Elizabeth remained to nurse her disappointment alone.

If Essex's favor with the Queen was on a momentary wane, in London it was never higher. The glorious sack of Cádiz gave my Lord of Essex a popular appeal lacking in former royal favorites. He was the darling of the court and City hotbloods; even the preachers spoke of his daring exploits. Couriers leaving the realm were eagerly greeted in foreign capitals, and Essex's feat lost nothing in the retelling. Abroad in the streets, mobs soon formed to follow him. They clustered about Essex House in the Strand, cheering when he appeared, and later drank his health in the inns and taverns of Cheapside. His journey to Wanstead, where he had gone in a fit of pique, was attended by throngs, whose greetings made him forget Francis Bacon's warning that "the wrath of a prince is as the roaring of a lion." It did not help, while at Wanstead, to hear the Queen had reinstated Sir Walter Raleigh as Captain of the Guard.

Ultimately Essex returned to court and some reconciliation with

*The fleet returned to Plymouth, but the Queen had found that "certain ships followed the English fleet . . . to make private gain by buying from captains and soldiers commodities which they had got by spoils. . . ." It was these other ships, putting into London Pool, which were searched.[27]

Elizabeth. A more astute man would have recognized a difference in their relationship, but Essex was not one to ponder the attitude or motives of another too closely. Francis Bacon *did* see the subtle shift in Elizabeth's regard, and he wrote Essex that the tremendous popularity he was enjoying was his greatest danger, for "it maketh her Majesty more fearful and shadowy, as not knowing her own strength."[29] He said Essex's aggressive thrust for popularity and his pleasure as a soldier could hardly endear him to his sovereign. "I demand," he asked, "whether there can be a more dangerous image than this represented to any monarch living, much more to a lady and of her Majesty's apprehension?" Bacon also said Essex's attitude toward the Queen was too cursory; he should emulate Leicester and Hatton and not be so certain of Elizabeth's continued favor. He should show less ambition and use more sense in the expenditure of the monies that had come to him as a direct gift from the Crown. It was the best advice Essex could have received, even as it was absolutely impossible for him to accept or follow it.

It was also his peculiar inclination continually to underestimate the Queen. That Elizabeth was still fascinated with Essex, that she depended on him and still hoped to mold him into a mature statesman was apparent to all. Yet she was very aware of his faults, erring only in thinking she could control and guide him. She was certain that her hold on him, both personal and political, was such that it would outweigh his ambition and arrogance. There was also the very poignant fact, where she personally was concerned, that Essex had few real competitors. She had lost Leicester and Hatton. Raleigh was married and happy with his Bess when he was not sailing off to look for the profits that eluded Essex. It was the tragedy of Elizabeth's old age that at a time when she most needed the compassionate goodwill of a loving friend, the position was filled by one who felt the Queen's will subject to his own, even as he himself did as he pleased.

Hearing the Spaniards were assembling troops and supplies to be either launched at England's southern coast or sent to Ireland, Essex pleaded that he and Raleigh be allowed to sail to the Azores in the hope of waylaying the fleet. Elizabeth was tart in her refusal, and chagrined, Essex flung himself from court and angrily rode to Wanstead, where he professed himself too ill to return. As his absence continued, Elizabeth, sensing a silent challenge, cried, "I shall break him of his will and pull down his great heart!" adding irrelevantly that he acquired his obstinacy "from his mother's side." The silence continued for days, and eventually several of the Council advised that Essex be permitted to intercept the Spanish fleet. With a coolness still existing between Queen and Earl, the fleet sailed for the Azores on July 7, 1597. A storm overtook them at sea, and at first all were thought lost. Ultimately, the ships returned to Plymouth for massive repairs, and when informed of her favorite's safety, Elizabeth cried with relief. Sir Robert Cecil in a moment of rare impudence wrote Essex, "The Queen is so disposed to have us all love you, that she and I do every night talk like angels of you."[30]

At last, one month later, under the command of Essex and Sir Walter Raleigh, the Islands Voyage commenced. It was not a success, and it foundered as much on the egos of its commanders as anything else. Essex was very popular with the seamen, many of whom were his own followers, while Raleigh was known as a hard disciplinarian. Through sheer luck and a bit more use of his intelligence, Raleigh acquitted himself better than Essex, capturing a town in the Azores, and when the Earl's followers advised Essex to bring him to a court-martial on alleged misconduct, Essex replied grimly, "I would had he been one of my friends."[31] Through a comedy of errors in which both Essex and Raleigh worked seemingly independent of the other, they again missed the Spanish plate fleet. Finally, in mid-October, it was decided to return to England, with both commanders wondering what excuse to present the Queen for the great waste of time, energy and money. In the meantime, King Philip, recognizing England's vulnerability with the major part of its fleet absent, attempted another attack on the southern coast. When Essex landed at Plymouth on October 26, he learned the warning beacons had been prepared, the militia had been organized and money was waiting to revictual and repair his ships. There was also a note from a grim Elizabeth commenting on the failure of the voyage and accusing Essex of giving the enemy "leisure and courage to attack us." Luckily, storms again scattered the Spanish vessels, breaking many of them up on the French coast and forcing others, leaking and battered, to return home. It was in this climate of relief, combined with the Queen's irritation, that Essex returned to court.

He found Raleigh had preceded him and somewhat stolen his thunder in explaining the Islands Voyage fiasco. He also learned that Sir Robert Cecil had been named to the Chancellorship of the Duchy of Lancaster, a remunerative post. But the incident which galled and infuriated the Earl beyond measure was the Queen's conferring of the Earldom of Nottingham on her uncle Howard of Effingham. It was an affectionate gesture and all the more meaningful, for the Queen "honoured her honours by bestowing them sparingly."[32]* The patent

*During her entire reign, Elizabeth created, restored or recognized no more than eighteen titles, and of these only Burghley and Compton belonged to "new" families.[33]

not only named Howard's contribution during the Armada crisis, but mentioned his exploits at Cádiz, a campaign Essex considered peculiarly his own. In addition, Howard had been designated Steward of the next Parliament and, as such, would walk in procession ahead of Essex. Many of the Earl's friends felt the last appointment a deliberate insult to Essex, and they played on his inherent vanity and pride until he found it impossible to remain at court. Within days he left again for Wanstead and, severely depressed, shut himself up in his room, refusing to see anyone. His behavior, always inconsistent, now took a more eccentric turn, and brooding and sullen, he refused to listen to any word from the court, even when Lord Burghley reminded him that November 17 was the fortieth observance of Elizabeth's accession and another courtier hinted that the Queen "rather imagined you should look into the state of the realm as a Councillor rather than respect your private state. . . ."[34]

For several weeks, he remained at Wanstead. His followers described the Queen as rapidly losing patience, declaring that "a Prince was not to be contended withal by a subject." His return to London was made more dramatic by not appearing at court. In the meantime, the Queen had spoken with several others who had accompanied Essex on the Islands Voyage and given a more charitable account of Essex's conduct than she had heard from Raleigh. Immediately she made a gesture of peace toward her disgruntled nobleman, but foolishly, Essex remained aloof. Instead of accepting Elizabeth's gracious gesture, he offered to fight Nottingham or his sons for the slight the Lord Admiral's patent cast on his own contribution at Cádiz.

The whole situation had got tremendously out of hand, and at last Elizabeth acted. She needed Essex at court; his extreme obstinacy and absence from the Council table were embarrassing. Yet her eventual decision only prolonged the incredible idiocy of Essex's behavior as he blundered even more foolishly along his arrogant path. Elizabeth's policy, however, was one of conciliation. Therefore, on December 18, she granted Essex the title Earl Marshal of England, one which gave him precedence over Nottingham on public occasions. It was now Nottingham's turn to remain at his Chelsea home and practice the sulkiness Essex adopted so effectively.

Miraculously, Essex's sullenness disappeared, and he returned to court. But the stress and tension had told on the Queen and many of the Council. Elizabeth had made the peace but at some cost to her pride, and she no longer had any illusions of the Earl's worth as a selfless adviser; she knew he would never be a statesman. Yet the exultant Essex saw only the momentary victory over his sovereign. For the sake of a childish pride, he had compounded an already bad situation by accepting a title almost forced from his Queen and not bestowed on a useful public servant. He did not recognize that he had lost dignity, endangered his worth at court or, more important, lost the Queen's respect. Essex was, as the French ambassador noted, "a man who in no wise contents himself with a petty fortune and aspires to greatness." What the ambassador did not add was that the source of Essex's great prominence, Elizabeth Tudor, no longer had any illusions where her young Earl Marshal was concerned. The main thing now would be to bridle him before he brought himself to an extravagant and ignoble end and tarnished her own Crown in the process.

He did not make it any easier. Secure in his hold over the Queen, Essex treated her with the same willful caprice he exhibited to his mother, Lettice Knollys, the Countess of Leicester, who wrote her son complaining he was "slothful . . . somewhat sparing of the pen." Lettice dearly wished to be reinstated in the royal favor, and flushed with the success of his return to court, Essex made a concerted effort to compel Elizabeth to meet with Lettice. The Queen's attitude left little doubt of her reluctance to see the Countess, but Essex insisted. Lettice had found life at Drayton Basset in Staffordshire tiresome and said "country life is fittest only for the disgraced."[35] While Essex remonstrated with the Queen, Lettice arrived in London and went to her son's house in the Strand. In order to encourage Elizabeth, Essex told her the meeting need not be long or formal. He might, for instance, have his mother in the Privy Gallery as Elizabeth walked through, and all she need do would be to greet Lettice. When the Queen did not reply, Essex took her silence for consent, but the day Lettice Knollys waited in the Privy Gallery, the Queen did not pass by. Lettice's brother, Sir William Knollys, Elizabeth's Comptroller, then prepared a great banquet on Shrove Monday at the Tilt End, and Lettice waited with a jewel worth £300 since the Queen had agreed to attend. The Queen's coach was made ready when "upon a sudden, she resolved not to go and so sent word." When Essex heard of her behavior, he became so distressed he came to intercede on his mother's behalf "but could not carry his point." Within days, however, he had so pressured Elizabeth that the two cousins were ultimately brought face to face for a temporary reconciliation. "My Lady of Leicester was at court," wrote an observer, "and kissed the Queen's hand . . . and did embrace her, and the Queen kissed her. . . . Lady Leicester departed the court exceedingly contented. . . ."[36] Several days later, when Lettice signified she wished to return once more, the Queen threw up her hands and, with a great oath, signified she wished to hear nothing more of the matter. Lettice had had her moment, and it had cost her the £300 jewel. That was all there was to be.

Elizabeth's irritation with Essex and her short temper with petty court rivalries were reflections of concern over the larger issues with which she was daily confronted. For the first time in her long reign, the Queen was aware that her popularity was waning. Many of the younger members of the court complained of an aging ruler's caprices. Those who had handled Elizabeth so skillfully in the past were dying off, and their replacements, with the exception of Sir Robert Cecil, who had been blessed with a very flexible father to coach him, bore the royal will with less equanimity. The long war and its toll in lives, increased taxation and interrupted trade had set many subjects to grumbling. To make matters worse, England had suffered catastrophic weather conditions for the past several years; the raging storms brought ruined harvests and inflated food prices which had resulted in outright rioting and hardship. The people blamed "the government," the two parties comprising the followers of Essex and Cecil, for friction within the Council. Implicit in their attitude was criticism of the Queen, who supposedly could not control these factions. Elizabeth sought to keep a firm grip on her Council, but their personal and interfamily rivalries did not make the task any easier.

The Queen was also beginning to suffer the small twinges and ailments of old age. She caught cold more easily with "hands so burning hot, her complaint of distemperature in all parts, with the feeling of a soreness in her body, back and legs." Her arthritic right thumb gave her a great deal of trouble. Even though one ambassador said, "It is not possible to see a woman of so fine and vigorous disposition both in mind and body,"[37] for the first time, the psychological implications of old age were present. When she met de Maisse, the French ambassador, she shocked the old gentleman, for "she kept the front of her dress open, and one could see the whole of her bosom and, passing low and often, she would open the front of this robe with her hands, as if she were too hot. . . ." De Maisse recounted that "all the time she spoke she would often rise from her chair and appear to be very impatient with what I was saying. She would complain that the fire was hurting her eyes, though there was a great screen before it and that six or seven feet away. Yet did she give orders to have it extinguished, making them bring water to pour upon it." Some infirmity having been aknowledged, the royal pride would assert itself, and Elizabeth would then boast of how formerly she had always stood to speak with ambassadors "and used sometimes to tire them of which they would on occasion complain." The ambassador remembered he "begged her not to over-tire herself in any way and I rose when she did and then she sat down again and so did I." Elizabeth had postponed the audience because of a sore throat, and as she accompanied the ambassador "to that place where she had come to receive me," she said she "was grieved that all the gentlemen I had brought with me should see her in that condition and she called to see them. They made their reverence before her, one after the other, and she embraced them all with great charm and smiling countenance."[38]

Her awareness of old age caught the Queen at odd moments. When the admirable Lord Keeper Puckering died, Elizabeth asked Sir Thomas Egerton to fill his place. At the ceremony, the Queen felt obliged to explain to Sir Thomas why he should not have the title of Lord Chancellor, which she had not given to anyone since Sir Christopher Hatton's death. With a winning smile, she said, "I *began* with a Lord Keeper and he was a wise man, I tell you." And then, faltering she. said, "And I shall *end* with a Lord Keeper." Lord Burghley, sitting nearby, saw her distress and loyally called out, "God forbid, Madame! I hope you shall bury four or five more!" At his words, Elizabeth lost her composure. "No, this is the last . . ." she whispered, and then, to the amazement of everyone present, the Queen burst into tears and hurriedly left the room. For days the court rang with the tale of Elizabeth's odd performance, so unusual in one of such composure and self-assurance. Few could imagine what an aging woman, beginning for the first time to acknowledge her mortality, might feel. It was Elizabeth's triumph that she had put off the confrontation so long.

Chapter Thirty

In 1598, Henri IV of France was ready to come to terms with Spain. King Philip, bankrupt from his various Armada attempts, sick and facing death, finally accepted he could not continue to bleed his empire. The first step toward resolving the long conflict had been the conversion of Henri to the Catholic faith. "Paris," he said, "is worth a Mass." Blithely, he disregarded his treaty obligations to England, earning Elizabeth's comment that he was the "Anti-Christ of Ingratitude." From 1589 to 1595 her assistance to France had cost nearly £300,000, and while these monies were being spent, the Queen was also financing maritime expeditions against Spain. Critics of Elizabeth's financial policy did not appreciate how she had to juggle figures, dispose of Crown lands and frequently resort to unpopular taxation, loans and subsidies to keep going. Considering that her own yearly revenues rarely exceeded £300,000, the wonder is not what she did not accomplish, but the fact that she accomplished as much as she did.[1]

However, with peace in the air, the Queen and Council were optimistic, especially if the government of the Low Countries was maintained and their ancient liberties and religion were guaranteed. In every debate for peace versus war, few put forth good reasons for continuing the conflict. The lone dissenter was the Earl of Essex, and he spoke so strongly and enthusiastically for prolonging hostilities that at one point a disgusted Lord Burghley, maintaining that Essex "breathed nothing but war, slaughter and blood," pulled out his Prayer Book and pointed a shaking finger at the 55th Psalm: "Blood thirsty and deceitful men shall not live out half their days."[2] One notable result of the war's end would be reflected in Ireland and the West-country. Spanish depredations on the English coast had increased in past years, and an actual landing had been made at

Penzance, where the countryside had been burned and ravaged. Ireland's proximity to England rendered it dangerous as a base of operations for Catholic and foreign military influences. By the latter years of Elizabeth's reign the Jesuits had made a remarkable infiltration into the country, and religion had become the *raison d'être* by which the Irish leaders hoped to inspire their people to spill their blood in ousting the English from their land. One leader, James Fitzmaurice Fitzgerald, had appealed to Rome for protection, and earlier in Elizabeth's reign, the Pope had actually sent two separate military expeditions to Ireland. The second of Philip's ill-fated Armadas had had Ireland as its destination.

Of even greater concern was the state of English supremacy in Ireland. For generations, England had kept token forces in the English Pale, comprising the counties of Dublin, Meath, Westmeath, Kildare and Louth.[3] The English in Ireland had given little thought to Irish law, language, Irish institutions beyond the Pale or the Irish people themselves. It was easier to exterminate the native and turn his land over to the Englishman willing to live in the land of mists and bogs who might bring his Protestantism and "civilized" ways to the unruly Celts. The Irish had, of course, fought back; they also fought among themselves. There was as little unity among the Irish as there was among the English sent to govern them, and the result was seen in a desolate, war-scarred country of infinite beauty, inhabited by a tough, resolute, illiterate people dedicated to freedom of self, tribe and religion.

The chief Irish leader was Hugh O'Neill, the Earl of Tyrone. When news arrived in England of Tyrone's defeat in Armagh of Sir Henry Bagenal, Marshal of the English Army, and his force of 3,500, the immediate problem confronting the Queen and her advisers was who to send to Ireland to chasten the rebel Earl whose victory threatened the always-shaky English government in the Pale. Several names, including those of Sir George Carew, Sir William Knollys and Sir Charles Blount, were suggested. Essex, back in attendance at the Council table, favored Carew, while the Queen wished to have Knollys. Elizabeth dismissed the Earl's nominee with a knowing laugh; Essex merely wished Carew exiled from court since he was a great supporter of the Cecilian party. Essex, angered at her attitude, began to argue, at which point the Queen, impatient at his continual insistence that he have his own way, indicated she'd had enough. Enraged, Essex gave her a scornful look before turning his back on her, an insult in itself before royalty. Elizabeth was furious and heatedly "gave him a cuff on the ear and bade him be gone and be hanged!"

Such scenes had happened before between Essex and the Queen or between the Queen and others. But Essex went one step further. The light blow at his ear seemed to madden him, and his face distorted with anger, he made a menacing gesture as if to draw his sword from its sheath. Quickly, the Earl of Nottingham stepped forward and stood with outstretched arms between Elizabeth and Essex. The silence was broken by a gasp from Sir Robert Cecil, the only other witness present. It seemed to bring Essex to his senses. He backed away from the Queen and "swore a great oath that he neither would nor could put up with so great an affront and indignity, neither would he have taken it at King Henry VIII's own hands. . . !"[4] Quickly he strode from the room and rode immediately to Wanstead.

There he strove to make his peace in a halfhearted attempt at a letter which placed the blame squarely on Elizabeth. "I was never proud 'til you sought to make me too base," he wrote, and he emphasized the "intolerable wrong you have done both me and yourself." Elizabeth was still angry and ignored the letter. She said, "He hath played long enough upon me and now I mean to play awhile with him and stand as much upon my greatness as he hath upon his stomach."[5] She was salved by the remark of one courtier who spoke of Essex's enemies and friends: "I will tell you," said the gentleman, "I know but one friend and one enemy my Lord hath. That one friend is the Queen and that one enemy is himself."[6]

For days Essex nursed his injured pride as courtiers rode from court and begged him to make his peace with the Queen. She wished it, they emphasized, but the first gesture must come from him. Lettice Knollys, remembering her former husband's confinement upon their marriage, frantically wrote her "sweet Robin" from the country, where, she said, she and her husband "cannot but be troubled with this news and do wish ourselves with you, as we would soon be, if we thought our service needful, or that you would have it so. . . ." She signed the letter "Your mother, dearliest loving you, Lettice Leicester."* Her brother Sir William Knollys wrote, "Between her Majesty's running into her princely power and your Lordship persisting in your settled resolution, I am so confounded as I know not how nor what to persuade." He cautioned Essex to remember "that there is no contesting between sovereignty and obedience" and, having fulfilled his obligations, stated he would, therefore, "leave it to God's work, to Whom I heartily pray you to settle your heart in a right course. . . ."[7]

The "right course" eluded Essex. As his absence continued, even Lord Keeper Egerton felt compelled to advise Essex that he was only

*Lettice, who had remarried, apparently still preferred to use her former, more illustrious name.

helping his enemies "do that . . . which they could never do for themselves." Essex's attitude was no secret. He still did not feel remorseful and merely wrote belligerently he could "never serve her Majesty as a villein or slave. . . ." He asked, "What! Cannot Princes err? Cannot subjects receive wrong? Is an earthly power or authority infinite? Pardon me, pardon me . . . I can never subscribe to these principles. . . ."[8]

It was not any change of heart, but rather the death of Lord Burghley that brought the Earl's return to court. Burghley, depressed by the deaths of so many of his contemporaries, had offered to resign his offices, but Elizabeth would not hear of it. He had been more ill than usual for months and at last told the Queen he wished to remain home to take the physic. In the past, Elizabeth had called him a "froward old fool" for undertaking such ministrations. At times it seemed almost as if she were deliberately refusing to acknowledge his precarious physical condition. After he had gone, Elizabeth's uncle Nottingham wrote to Burghley, "Yet are you to her in all things and shall be Alpha and Omega. . . ." The Queen had spoken so warmly of her minister and his son Sir Robert Cecil that, said Nottingham, "my heart was so filled with her kind speeches as I watered my eyes."

When Elizabeth was informed Burghley's condition had worsened, she visited him at Cecil House in the Convent Garden. She had brought him some broth and, seeing his frail, wasted body propped up in bed, spoke comfortingly to him. Later she sought to restrain the tears as she fed him teaspoons of the soup. Calling him "Sir Spirit," she repeated a remark which brought tears to the eyes of the old gentleman when she told him she did not wish to live any longer than she had him by her side.[9] In his last letter, Burghley wrote to his son, "Only I pray you diligently and effectually, let her Majesty understand how her singular kindness doth overcome my power to acquit it, who though she will not be a mother, yet she showeth herself by feeding me with her own princely hand, as a careful nurse, and if I may be weaned to feed myself, I shall be more ready to serve her on earth, if not, I hope to be in heaven a servitor for her and God's Church." Knowing these might be his last words to his son, he wrote a postscript which embodied the philosophy of a lifetime: "Serve God by serving of the Queen, for all other service is indeed bondage to the Devil."[10] When Elizabeth learned of the letter, she said that "her comfort had been in her people's happiness, and their happiness in his [Burghley's] discretion."[11]

By the third of August, several weeks after the Queen's visit, Burghley knew his end was near. He had been restless, "which caused him often times with tears to wish for death." His children and grandchildren were summoned to his bedside, where he cautioned them to love and serve the Queen and each other. He then handed his will to his steward, Thomas Billot, saying, "I have ever found thee true to me and I now trust thee with all." Then, quietly, he whispered, "Now, the Lord be praised, the time is come," and as his chaplain prayed, he lapsed into unconsciousness. At four in the morning, as the doctors, "by infusions of hot waters into the mouth," attempted to revive him, he cried, "Oh what heart have I that will not die. . . !" and he rebuked the onlookers, "Oh, ye torment me . . . for God's sake let me die quietly. . . !" At last, between seven and eight o'clock in the morning of August 4, 1598, William Cecil, Lord Burghley, died. Those at his bedside noted death had been peaceful. His last words were: "Lord receive my spirit—Lord have mercy upon me," as observers noted, "he lay looking so sweetly and went away so mildly as in a sleep, that it could scarce be perceived when the breath went out of the body."[12] It was just a few weeks short of his seventy-eighth birthday.

The news was sent immediately to the Queen, who ordered the court into mourning and then, in great grief, retired to her own chamber. Burghley's death was hardly unexpected, but his actual passing was a painful and biting realization that now all the great ones who had once surrounded her were gone. Burghley had been her mainstay, her guide, the source of much of her strength, wisdom and power for more than forty years. His conscientiousness, devotion, loyalty and dependability were almost unique among her advisers. During the past years, Elizabeth had lost many friends, relatives and courtiers, but in Burghley's death, her loss was measured by the depth of her sorrow. In the months that followed, it was not without good reason that the Councillors agreed among themselves—and urged others also—not to mention Burghley's name in her presence. If they did, the Queen's vulnerability was most obvious, and she would turn her face away as she fought gamely to withhold her tears.

The death of Lord Burghley resulted in much additional work for the Council, and it was noted that "the absence of the Earl of Essex at this time is very unseasonable both for the common good and his own private good. . . ." Two weeks later King Philip of Spain died, and the deaths which removed two giant figures from the political arena caused much speculation at the English Council table and only emphasized the silent battle of wills between Essex and the Queen. The quarrel had now lasted nearly two months, and everyone from Sir Robert Cecil to Essex's many friends had contrived to effect a reconciliation. Particularly pressing was the appointment of the new Lord Deputy for Ireland. When it became known that Elizabeth still preferred Charles Blount, of "golden chessman" fame, Essex could hardly contain himself. He appeared at court, claiming that "duty was strong enough to rouse me out of my deadest melancholy," but since he had not apologized for his outrageous behavior, the Queen refused to see him. Recognizing the shifting sands that comprised the royal favor, he returned to Wanstead, where he became legitimately ill. For the next several weeks his friends worked assiduously on the Queen in his behalf, and eventually she sent her own physician to attend him. Elizabeth's sympathy was aroused, and this, combined with the urgency of Council matters which needed Essex's presence, turned the tide. She indicated she would receive him when he was well, and in little time, Essex was back at court and outwardly reconciled with his sovereign.

Those who had worked so carefully for his restoration had misgivings. They impressed on the Earl that he should upset her no further or "he would have more reason for grief than if he lost her favour." They said if Elizabeth were forced once more, "she would never forget it"; such tactics would only make his enemies stronger and his friends weaker. Essex also had Francis Bacon's sensible advice to "exercise compliance and respect," even as Essex insisted that "necessity and authority" were good for the Queen. In the past when Elizabeth had yielded, he would bait Bacon, exuberantly saying, "Now, Sir, whose principles be true?" To which Bacon would reply, "My Lord, these courses be like to hot waters. They will help at a pang, but if you use them you shall spoil the stomach and you shall be fain still to make them stronger and stronger and yet in the end they will lose their operation."[13] Even Elizabeth could see that though Essex bent in graceful submission at her feet, there was little humility in the gesture. Bacon could never impress Essex with the fact that while Elizabeth outwardly yielded, she was not fooled and that in yielding, she exhibited greater poise and common sense than the Earl.

Immediately Essex set about to regain the Queen's lost favor and recoup any prestige or authority lost in his several months' absence. He attempted to gain Burghley's post as Lord Treasurer, as well as the lucrative Master of the Wards office. The Queen pointedly left both vacant. And when news arrived that the Earl of Tyrone had increased his influence in the central and eastern portions of Ulster, the northernmost province, it became imperative to name a new Lord Deputy to Ireland. Essex again insisted on Sir George Carew. The Queen and Council suggested Sir Charles Blount, whom Essex pronounced "too bookish." Wearily, Elizabeth watched him parry all other suggestions and then said, tartly, if he could not approve of any others, he might as well go himself. In that way there would be no further criticism of her or her Councillors, and since he seemed to know what the position demanded, she would have *him* as her new Lord Deputy. Essex appeared dumbfounded, and the Councillors could scarce conceal their joy at her tactics. The Earl had hoped to influence the choice of Lord Deputy, but few believed he actually wished the post himself. Suddenly, through his own presumption, he was now in a position where he could do little but accept. The Queen and Council were watching him, and he sought to hide his dismay, even as Elizabeth reflected that his reputation would ensure little difficulty in mustering sufficient forces for Ireland. Every soldier would be eager to serve under the glorious Essex.

As the Council adjourned, there were many who wondered how much of Elizabeth's spontaneous endorsement of Essex was a gesture of trust; there were some who even wondered whether the spontaneity was genuine or a deliberate means of removing a troublesome influence from court. As one courtier wrote, "If the Lord Deputy Essex perform in the field what he hath promised the Council, all will be well. But, though the Queen hath granted forgiveness for his late demeanour in her presence, we know not what to think thereof. . . ."[14] Many thought Essex now had a great opportunity to redeem himself with honor and regain the close trust and affection of the Queen. His last public appearance, however, seemed only to emphasize his determination to keep the limelight no matter what the cost. On November 17, Elizabeth's Accession Day, Sir Walter Raleigh celebrated his reappointment as Captain of the Guard by parading a modest number of his followers garbed in new orange livery in the tiltyard. They were enthusiastically received, and the cheers had hardly ceased before the appearance of Essex, whose followers in identical tangerine and tawny and numbering an unusual 2,000, marched onto the field. Elizabeth was so exasperated at Essex's childish arrogance that she closed the proceedings earlier than usual.[15]

On March 27, 1599, at two o'clock in the afternoon, the Earl set out from Essex House on the first step of his journey to Ireland. He rode up Seething Lane accompanied by other noblemen and officers, and from all sides, the people of the City responded, crying, "God save your Lordship!" and "God preserve your Honour!" Many followed Essex for almost four miles outside the City walls and were only turned back at Islington when a shower quickly turned to hail. Their loyalty had cheered Essex. His last few weeks had given him plenty of opportunity to reflect on what lay ahead, and his lack of enthusiasm for the venture was apparent in his last letter to Elizabeth. Signing himself "Your

Majesty's exiled servant, Robert Essex," he asked the Queen, "What service can your Majesty expect, since any service past deserves no more than banishment and proscription to the cursedest of all islands?" To the Council, he wrote, "What my body and mind will suffice to, I will, by God's grace, discharge with industry and faith. But neither can a rheumatic body promise itself that health in a moist, rotten country, nor a sad mind vigour and quietness in a discomfortable voyage. . . ."[16] Essex regarded his position as unenviable, even as he conveniently forgot he had no one but himself to blame for it. It was very much on the Earl's mind that Ireland had ruined his father's estates and health and had finally taken his very life. He had more than a slight suspicion that his enemies were rejoicing openly at his appointment, was certain they would work against him in his absence and proclaimed that "it amazeth me . . . to see myself sent on such an errand, at such a time with so little comfort or ability from the Court of England. . . ."[17]

His departure from the Queen had been gracious, if strained. Elizabeth had given him the title of Lieutenant and Governor-General of Ireland, and she promised 16,000 men and 1,300 horse, her unstinted support and all England's blessing. Her instructions were to march into Ulster in the north and subdue the forces of the Earl of Tyrone. He must assemble the Irish Council, "learn the state of the country" and work with officers already within the English Pale. As Lieutenant and Governor-General, Essex would have "the fullest powers ever conferred upon an Irish Deputy"[18] to continue the war, make the peace, pardon crime and treasons and, with the exception of the Irish Master of the Horse, make his own appointments. Essex had wanted the mercurial Earl of Southampton for the post, but Southampton had had the court in an uproar all summer by his seduction of Elizabeth Vernon, one of the Queen's maids-of-honor, and had been hauled back from France to marry the pregnant girl. Elizabeth had subsequently forbidden his appointment. Keeping Essex's past performances in mind, the Queen also specifically cautioned that he was to confer no knighthoods except for extraordinary service.

Essex chafed at Elizabeth's restrictions, and his opinion of the royal dictum was scarcely concealed in his comment "I sued her Majesty to grant it [the appointment of Southampton] out of favour, but I speak a language that was not understood, or to a goddess not at leisure to hear prayers. . . ."[19] To others he said, "Methinks it is the fairer choice to command armies than humours. . . !"[20]

Essex arrived in Dublin on April 14, 1599, and his campaign was a disaster from start to finish. Elizabeth had specifically instructed him to march north to Ulster, where the main concentration of Irish forces were based. Once these forces and the rebel leader, Tyrone, were taken, it would be relatively easy to subdue smaller detachments of Irish strength in the west and south. The Irish Council did not agree with the Queen. They insisted that Tyrone was dissipating his strength by sending small regiments to the isolated pockets of resistance, which they advised should be wiped out first. Also, mid-June or July would be more agreeable for a northern campaign since rivers would have lowered from the spring thaw and thus be more easily forded and more pastureland would be available as feed for the horses. Essex, therefore, wrote the English Council requesting 2,000 additional men and 200 horse. Before the campaign had begun, he dubbed two knights and, against the express command of the Queen, made the Earl of Southampton his Master of the Horse.

The Irish Council's advice to attack Tyrone later coincided with Essex's desire to make general sorties outside the English Pale, and on May 9, 1599, he left Dublin with some 3,000 soldiers and 300 horse and marched south. Essex had been to the Azores, to Spain, to Portugal, France and the Netherlands, but Ireland confounded him. It was due, in a larger sense, to the land itself, "uneven, mountainous, soft, watery, woody and open to winds and floods of rain, and so fenny as it hath bogs upon the very tops of mountains, not bearing man or beast, but dangerous to pass, and such bogs are frequent all over Ireland. . . ."[21] This treacherous country was inhabited by a people, said one of Essex's advisers, who excel in "skirmishes in passes, bogs, woods, fords and in all places of advantage. And they hold it no dishonour to run away. For the best sconce and castle for their security is their feet." The Irish had had fifty years of dealing with the invading British, and they had honed their skills in the fine art of survival; outright brigandage and a cutthroat technique were the trademark of the Celts. They were abysmally poor. "Their ordinary food is a kind of grass. Neither clothes nor houses generally do they care for. With this their savage life, they are able to wear out any army that seeketh to conquer them. It is no more possible to defeat them at once than to destroy so many wolves and foxes . . ."[22] wrote one tired campaigner.

From Athy, to Maryborough, to Ballyragget, Essex met the enemy in skirmishes, forays and charges in bogs, mountain pass, over muddy roads and woods, an enemy which seemed to melt into the mists of a steep defile, on terrain as familiar to them as it was hazardous to the English trained for Continental warfare. One soldier wrote, "On the bog, they likewise presume with naked celerity to come as near our foot and horse as is possible and then fly off again, knowing we cannot or indeed dare not follow them."[23] The English, however, had their revenge on the poor Irish peasant. Daily horseboys were sent out to forage for the horses. Often horseloads of corn were taken from the natives, and, wrote one Bishop, "they [the Irish poor], having no other sustenance to relieve them and their families than a little cow about which they have taken great pains and travail, and if they come to rescue it . . . they [the horseboys] fall upon them and beat them and cut them in the heads most lamentable to see."[24]

From Kilkenny to Clonmel to Limerick, the quagmires, trenches, ambushes and detours left weary, discouraged soldiers and a disheartened Lord Lieutenant. Essex was following in the wake of Englishmen who had never realized or chose to ignore that their raids, pillaging and murders accomplished nothing. There was no lessening of Irish hatred or Irish determination to effect reprisals at the first opportunity. By the time he reached Waterford in mid-June, the majority of his soldiers were sick with malaria or dysentery and more than 500 men lay dead in the fenny fields and dripping woods through which they had passed in the two-month campaign. They had captured but one castle, and the soldiers' morale was not helped by the Queen's comment that they had merely taken "an Irish hold from a rabble of rogues."[25] Before his return to Dublin, Essex reported to the English Council, and his discouragement is apparent in his admission that "the only gloss I can make upon the plain and true text I send is this—that if so much hath not been here performed, as is there by her Majesty expected, either it hath been because she made a choice of an insufficient minister, or else because it hath pleased her to match him with a weak and insufficient Council. . . ." Hoping again to cast some blame upon the Council, he wrote, "I know that those who are guilty of them will confidently deny, and cunningly distinguish to excuse themselves."[26] To the Queen he wrote directly, "What talk I of victory or success? Is it not known that from England I receive only soul's wounds?" and to Lord Keeper Egerton, he wrote in exasperation, "What can you expect from this accursed country but unfortunate news?"[27]

Elizabeth was explicit in her complaints. Previously she had said that Essex's campaign might be compared to the wake of a ship at sea; as he had passed through Leinster toward Munster, there seemed to be great embroilment. But after he had passed, everything quieted, and nothing was gained. She garnished her remark with the further observation that she was allowing my Lord of Essex £1,000 a day to go on progress.[28] Elizabeth had ordered that Ulster and Tyrone be attacked first in order that the major part of her monies be spent in rooting out the rebel, "as the axe may be put to the root of that tree. . . ." It was hoped, then, the "poisoned plants and grafts"—the pockets of resistance outside the Pale—would collapse. Instead, months later, Tyrone was still supreme, and she had spent £90,000 to no avail.

The Queen did not mince her words to Essex. She deplored the knighthoods and the appointment of Southampton, but mainly, she rejected any explanation for Essex's contrary behavior. She spoke of the "excessive charges" and of the people of England, "who groan under the burden of continual levies and impositions." She mentioned her own position "that has the eyes of foreign Princes upon our actions. . . ." She chided Essex angrily that "you have now learned, upon our expenses, by knowledge of the country that those things are true, which we have heretofore told you. If you would have believed us, how far different things would prove from your expectation. . . !" She said what especially displeased her was that she, a Queen of a small insular power, who "had held down the greatest enemy she ever had" (Spain), could not seem to subdue "a base bush kern," the Earl of Tyrone. She deplored that "regiments should be committed to young gentlemen that rather desire to do well than know how to perform . . ." and suggested, after more numerous venting of her indignation, that Essex "with all speed pass thither [north]. . . ."[29] When Essex sent word he would need more men, horses and supplies to attack Tyrone, the Queen refused. Men were needed for defense at home, she said, and she again berated Essex: "You have broken the heart of our best troops and weakened your strength upon inferior rebels, and run out the glass of time which can hardly be recovered."[30]

But the English Council, badgered with the Earl's complaints and suspicions that they were working against his interests, convinced the Queen that 2,000 more soldiers might be sent, and with their order went their pious admonition that Essex's suspicions "are so improper to us, as we will neither do your Lordship that wrong to take them so intended, nor ourselves that injury to go about to excuse them. . . ."[31] Elizabeth had the last word. Well aware of Essex's impetuousness and knowing he might use consultation with the Council as a device for delay, she stated that, under no circumstances, must he return home. There must be no more delay; he must take her additional troops and money and head north at once.

On August 21 he summoned a general council of war at Dublin Castle and found the Irish Council had little heart for the northern campaign. Senior offices revealed that many soldiers had deserted and others of Irish extraction had gone over to the enemy side. Those who had accompanied Essex on his forays had had a taste of what Irish warfare was like and had no enthusiasm for the northern expedition, especially on hearing it was the Irish Councillors' opinion the rebel forces would outnumber the English, that the "course was full of danger and of little or no hope. . . ." The officials were so adamant that "we could not with duty to her Majesty and safety to this kingdom advise or assent to the undertaking of any journey far north"[32] that Essex incorporated their declaration in a communication to the Queen in London.

The Earl was in an unenviable position. His own instincts and the more experienced Irish officers advised against the northern campaign. He was aware that had he followed Elizabeth's original instructions to proceed against Tyrone, he would now have a fresh army, sufficient supplies and a less strong enemy. Yet at the end of August he knew he could delay no longer, and heartsick with his decimated forces, he sent his secretary, Henry Cuffe, to England to announce his departure. He was further depressed and angered when word reached him that in his absence, the Queen had appointed Lord Buckhurst to Burghley's post of Lord Treasurer and Sir Robert Cecil had received the profitable appointment as Master of the Wards. More than once it occurred to the Earl that the Queen and Council had turned his own actions to good account by removing him from court and sending him upon a lost cause. His attitude did not make for an auspicious beginning to the venture. He remembered, somewhat ironically, his boast that he had beaten Knollys and Blount to the Irish command "and, by God, I will beat Tyrone in the field, for nothing worthy of her Majesty's honour hath yet been achieved!"[33]

The Earl of Tyrone had spent the spring and summer in Ulster awaiting the Earl of Essex. Hugh O'Neill was some twenty years older than Essex, but in many ways, they were very much alike. Both were personally courageous and ambitious, and each had a like dose of arrogance. O'Neill had spent his boyhood in England and had served in the household of the Earl of Leicester. At twenty-eight, his brother was murdered and he returned to Ireland and succeeded to the barony. At once his "Irishry" rose to the front, and he repudiated England and the Earldom of Tyrone, which Elizabeth had given him in 1587. When he succeeded as "the O'Neill," head of the clan, he became a symbol of Irish rebellion and the target of English retaliation. He was clever, sly, half dreamer and visionary, yet a capable soldier and a leader feared and respected by his men. For five years he had evaded capture as a traitor to the English Queen and in that time legendary stories had grown up about "the O'Neill." He was as elusive and as dissembling as his brothers-in-arms and twice as confident that he could handle anyone the English Queen sent to escalate the misery already heaped on a war-torn island and a miserably destitute people. It was no secret he had sought Spanish assistance in establishing an Irish kingdom with himself as King.

This was the man Essex was to subdue with an army decimated by disease, desertions and casualties. To give some encouragement to his men and boost his own popularity in the process, Essex had created some fifty-nine new knights to accompany him to Ulster. By the first week in September, 1599, they had confronted the rebel army on a hill a mile and a half outside Ardolph. Essex did not offer battle; he could see Tyrone's forces greatly outnumbered his own. The next day he marched farther north, seeking a more strategic position. Here a messenger arrived from Tyrone requesting a parley, which Essex refused. Two days later the same messenger reappeared with the information that Tyrone was seeking the Queen's mercy and again asked to speak with Essex. This was more definite, and when the messenger said Tyrone would be at the ford of Bellaclynthe within the hour, Essex agreed to appear.

Neither side really trusted the other; an ambush by the Irish particularly would be miserably easy. Essex took a company of officers and remained on high ground overlooking the ford as the Earl of Tyrone rode into the water up to his horse's belly. "With great reverence," he saluted Essex, who could scarce conceal his curiosity at seeing the symbol of Irish resistance to the Crown in the flesh. Tyrone was a compelling and majestic figure with strong features, long, luxuriant black hair and a heavy beard who sat astride his horse, a flowing black cloak about his shoulders. In spite of himself, Essex was impressed, as Tyrone had meant him to be. The Irish Earl's spies had brought him news of Essex's misfortune, and he was well aware the English constituted little threat to him at the moment. In a lilting brogue, Tyrone said he "craved the Queen's mercy, and that his Lordship would be a mean to it; that the grievances of the country might be heard; that he bore no arms but for his own defense against the oppression of her ministers."[34] Tyrone offered terms to the English: cessation of arms for six weeks, to be renewed for periods of six weeks until May Day or to be broken on fourteen days' warning on either side. Tyrone said he did not wish to put his submission in writing, he would give Essex his word and Essex would give his oath. He implied it was a good deal more sensible to resolve their differences in this manner, and Essex, greatly encouraged, thought it an admirable way out of his dilemma. He was certain Tyrone knew the disastrous condition of the English army.

Essex convinced himself Tyrone's submission was an honorable and wise solution. It was, of course, nothing of the sort and only a device by which the English were saved from defeat. Essex chose to overlook that the truce was a compromise with a rebel whom he had been sent—at considerable expense—either to kill or to imprison. Once Essex had accepted the terms, however, Tyrone was in a position to keep his army intact and let time—and the Queen—inform the young English Earl *he* was the one who had, in fact, surrendered. By the time Elizabeth sent another expedition to Ireland Tyrone expected to have help from Spain.

Elizabeth had been angered at the Irish Council's declaration. She was shocked at Essex's acceptance of their authority and advice while disregarding her own. She had not as yet been informed that he had finally moved against Tyrone. In a stinging letter, she denounced him, saying, "You have, even to this hour, possessed us with expectation that you would proceed as we have directed you, but your actions always show the contrary, though carried in such a sort as we were sure to have no time to countermand them."[35] She reviewed his activities, the monies spent, the men and beasts sent to Ireland, all to no apparent avail. "You had your asking," she said, "you had your choice of times, you had power and authority more ample than ever any had, or ever shall have."[36] Referring to the fact that Essex had disregarded her timing for subduing Tyrone, Elizabeth allowed herself the privilege of sarcasm: "If the spring were too soon and the summer that followed otherwise spent, if the harvest that succeeded were so neglected as nothing hath been done, then surely we must conclude that none of the four quarters of the year will be in season for you and that Council to agree of Tyrone's persecution, for which all our charge is intended."[37] Elizabeth castigated Essex for "filling his papers with impertinent arguments" and said she and the Council "wondered at your indiscretion to subscribe to letters which concern our public service, and directed to our Council table, which is not wont to handle things of such small importance."

Essex read the letter in a blind fury. If the Queen could not accept the Irish Council's advice, how could she accept the fact that he had guaranteed a truce with Tyrone? The Earl was now more certain than ever that her advisers, Cecil particularly, were using his absence to undermine him. Essex's pride was stung, and he spoke of returning to London. He was encouraged by Southampton, who further suggested taking 1,000 picked soldiers to accompany him and march on London and the Queen. Aghast at such implication, Essex's stepfather Sir Christopher Blount wisely dissuaded him from the scheme. On September 24, in direct defiance of Elizabeth's instructions prohibiting his return to England, Essex bade the Irish Council farewell, handed his sword of state to Archbishop Loftus and, with Sir George Carew, Southampton and a handful of newly dubbed knights, boarded a ship for home.

Four days later, on Friday, September 28, the Earl and his friends arrived in London. They learned the Queen was still at Nonsuch Palace a few miles south of London. They did not stop at Essex House to change their soiled, mud-spattered clothing but hastily crossed the Thames by the horse ferry at Westminster and, arriving at Lambeth Palace water stairs, did not even wait for their own horses to cross. Instead, they seized six other beasts waiting for their owners, who were on the opposite shore. They learned en route that Lord Grey was just ahead and quickly rode in the same direction. As Essex had hoped to have the advantage of time and a personal interview with the Queen to give his explanation of the truce, he wanted to beat Grey to the Palace. One of his companions, Sir Christopher St. Laurence, offered to ride ahead alone and kill Grey, but Essex waved him aside. On arriving at Nonsuch, he was told that Grey had arrived fifteen minutes earlier and was with Sir Robert Cecil. Frantic that they both might see the Queen before he did, Essex vaulted up the stone steps to the royal apartments. It was ten o'clock in the morning, and few of the court, with the exception of some pages and grooms were about; they explained that the Queen had not yet arisen. Impatiently, he brushed them aside and strode toward the Privy Chamber. It was empty. He did not hesitate for a moment but quickly walked to Elizabeth's bedchamber and, disdaining the gestures of the guard, who could scarce believe what he was seeing, flung the door open wide.

Inside, the Queen had just arisen, and her ladies were busy with her toilette. She wore a simple robe over her nightdress, her wrinkled skin was free of cosmetics and, for the first time in their eleven-year association, the Earl saw Elizabeth without her wig, with just wisps of thinning gray hair "hanging about her ears." The Queen raised startled eyes at the commotion at her door and was speechless when Essex flung himself, repentent and subdued, at her feet. As she looked at the rumpled clothing and dusty figure of the proud Earl whom she had thought safely in Ireland, she might have wondered if he had brought his entire army with him to challenge his sixty-six-year-old monarch and if indeed, the Palace were not in his hands. She was relieved when Essex covered her hands with kisses and commenced to mumble an explanation for his outrageous appearance and behavior. Immediately Elizabeth, acutely aware of her haggard appearance and sensing from his attitude there was more to hear than she wished to know at the moment, suggested a later interview. With some of her old friendliness, she gently asked him to leave. Joyfully, the Earl arose, kissed her hands once more and left to find suitable clothing himself. Outside, he told a startled Sir Robert Sidney, who looked as though he were seeing a ghost, that he "thanked God that after so many troublous storms abroad, he had found a sweet calm at home."[38]

The "sweet calm" did not last. Sir Robert Cecil soon arrived with the true extent of Essex's defection, the terms of the truce, the number of knighthoods conferred and the debilitated condition of the army. Within the hour, secure in her pearls, diamonds, ruff and wig, the Queen summoned the Earl and questioned him more closely. At the noonday meal, changed into clean clothing, Essex was the center of interest, as many flocked around him to hear the state of things in Ireland. Sir Robert Cecil, Sir Walter Raleigh, the Earl of Nottingham and others pointedly dined apart. After the meal, Essex again returned to the Queen, who appeared more disturbed. She "began to call him in question for his coming away and leaving all things at so great a hazard."[39] After hearing his explanation, she appeared even more deeply troubled.

The next day he met with the Council and Mr. Secretary Cecil. All rose and saluted when he arrived, but though he was also a Councillor, he was not asked to be seated. He remained standing while Cecil asked for an explanation for "his contemptuous disobedience of her Majesty's letter and will in returning . . . his proceedings in Ireland contrary to the points resolved upon in England, 'ere he went; his rash manner of coming away from Ireland, and his overbold going the day before to her Majesty's presence to her bedchamber, and his making of so many idle knights. . . ."[40] Essex explained as best he could and was told the Queen "would pause and consider his answers." Later he was told to "keep to his chamber."

He remained in his room all day Sunday, and on Monday he was informed it was the Queen's pleasure that he should be committed to the charge of Lord Keeper Egerton at York House with two servants to attend him. He left for London immediately, and the Queen went to Richmond. Neither realized they would never see each other again.

The Arbiter

*I rely only on the favour of God, the estate
that I hold from Him and on the goodwill
my subjects bear me as a result of benefits
and good treatment.*

Chapter Thirty-one

For the Queen, the following months were reminiscent of the wretched years of Mary Stuart's restraint. Again Elizabeth was faced with the distressing responsibility for one who, in this instance, had been dear to her personally, as well as an outstanding national figure. Aware of the Queen's disinclination to come firmly to grips with a situation, many realized the decision—far-reaching in its implications—would not come easily. Regarding Mary, public opinion had been all on her, Elizabeth's, side. But Essex had, for years, been the darling of her subjects, and that popularity was now emphasized as many of his captains, officers and soldiers returned from Ireland "so that the City was full of them to the great discontent of her Majesty that they are suffered to leave their charge."[1] Strong in their allegiance to their commander, they flocked to York House in the hope of seeing Essex. There, as they thronged within the courtyard, they threatened bodily harm to Sir Robert Cecil and others of his party. They were quick to challenge all dissenters, dueled openly in the streets, sang inflammatory songs in the taverns and scrawled scurrilous remarks and obscenities on the very walls of Whitehall. Elizabeth was stung at this evidence of the Earl's popularity and reacted more quickly than she might have under other circumstances.

The Queen had made one gesture in Essex's favor. She had insisted he not be charged with treason, although to leave one's command against express orders might be so interpreted. Presumably he had effected the truce with Tyrone in good faith, convinced he was doing the right thing.

She still could not bring herself to see him. It would have helped if Essex had made some initial conciliatory gesture, some acknowledgment of personal failure and repentence. But he did nothing.

Instead, during the first weeks of his confinement, he harangued the English Council, Cecil and Raleigh for working for his downfall and, when Elizabeth persisted in her refusal to see him, blamed their influence. It was psychologically impossible for Essex to admit to a mistake; it was equally hopeless for him to recognize the continual danger he courted.

It was the growing pressure of public opinion which finally determined Elizabeth to take some action. Therefore, on November 29, 1599, in the Star Chamber, Lord Keeper Egerton, in whose house Essex was confined, attempted to satisfy public curiosity. He spoke of the seditious people who mistakenly spread false rumors, encouraged rebellion and, by their speeches, slandered the Queen, court and nation. He spoke of the fiasco Essex had made of the Irish campaign: he had disobeyed instructions, decimated one of the largest armies ever taken abroad, made many "idle knights" and effected a compromising truce, before returning home against his sovereign's command. He revealed the Crown's great expense and Elizabeth's unusual tolerance in merely confining and not imprisoning him in the Tower. The open disclosure had the remarkable effect of stilling rumors in the City, and many of Essex's more responsible adherents quietly withdrew their allegiance.

Two results followed the inquiry. Essex House was formally closed, and 160 servants were dispersed to find new employment. The Countess of Essex, newly out of childbed, had petitioned the Queen to see her husband and been refused. At last, "all dressed in black of the meanest price," she visited the court, "the most sorrowful creature for her husband's captivity," but still Elizabeth would not receive her.

As the weeks wore on, Essex suffered a long-delayed nervous reaction from the tremendous pressure of the previous months. He became listless and melancholy, and a severe dysentery only added to his general misery. He ate little, slept hardly at all, appearing gaunt and ill-groomed. Elizabeth's silence particularly unnerved him. It was a device he had used with great effectiveness in the past, and the irony of the Queen's adopting it now was not lost on him.

By December Essex's distress had increased. The confinement, the lack of male companionship, which had been the very breath of life to him, the loss of easy access to court and power resulted in a deep depression, and seeking release in an unusual religious fervor, he turned to his Bible, kneeling for hours on end as he read. His piety would then dissolve into a wild agitation, and such onslaughts of emotion continued to weaken him physically. He kept to his chamber, his face turned to the wall, and appeared so frail that when his bed was made, he had to be "lifted out in the sheets." Everywhere the concerned and the curious gathered together in small knots to discuss the stricken Earl, and the City churches offered prayers for his recovery, which greatly annoyed the Queen. Yet when she was informed of his condition, her eyes filled with tears, and she sent him a message that he "should comfort himself." She said she would like to visit him, but such a gesture was not "consistent with her honour."

The Queen found her kinder instincts constantly warring with her awareness of Essex's defections and her determination to teach him a lesson. Many viewed her leniency as a miracle. However, the decision to maintain his confinement, which would have been difficult for a younger woman to whom he had been attached, wore upon the older woman, who missed the solace and satisfaction their relationship had provided. With the exception of some of her older ladies-in-waiting, Elizabeth's daily routine now brought her few who could provide personal warmth and affection. There was simply no one left to tender the attentive, worshipful devotion she had received for so long from such as Leicester and Hatton.

Her disappointment and hurt inevitably turned to anger, as Sir John Harrington, newly returned from Ireland, found when he visited his royal godmother. Catching sight of her "saucy poet," the Queen frowned and, "in the very heat and height of all displeasures," threatened him with the Fleet Prison. "What! Did that fool bring you, too? Go back to your business!" she cried. Swearing loudly, she complained "that we were all idle knaves, and the Lord Deputy Essex worse, for wasting our time and her commands. . . ." As Harrington attempted an explanation, Elizabeth "walked fastly to and fro, looked with discomposure in her visage and, I remember, catched my girdle when I kneeled to her and swore, 'By God's son, I am no Queen! That man is above me! Who gave him command to come here so soon! I did send him on other business!'" Her rage increased as she dwelled on the subject, and when she once more impatiently urged Harrington to leave, he confessed, "I did not stay to be bidden twice. If all the Irish rebels had been at my heels, I should not have made better speed, for I did now flee from one whom I both loved and feared!"[2]

When Essex's condition worsened, Elizabeth sent her physicians to see him. He had used his health before as a means of arousing her sympathy, and she was not going to be deceived again. The doctors reassured the Queen that the Earl was not going to die. They found "his liver stopped and perished . . . his entrails and guts exulcerated. . . ."[3] He needed rest, a "quiet mind" and, when recovered, some recreation or exercise. Elizabeth, "pensive and grieved" at their information, sent him some broth. She said that "she meant only to correct him, not to ruin him," and gave permission that he might walk in his garden and have his Countess visit him from seven in the morning until six at night. Her decision brought forth a letter from the Earl in which he asked that she hear "the sighs, the groans and read the lamentations and humble petitions of the afflicted." He offered to resign his offices and said that if he must continue exiled from court, "no death can be so speedy as it shall be welcome to me." Elizabeth did not accept his resignations, a gesture interpreted by the more optimistic that Essex's restoration to favor was merely a matter of time.

For the first time in years, the Earl of Essex was missing from the Christmas festivities at Greenwich, where a new play by William Shakespeare, *Twelfth Night,* was presented and "where almost every night her Majesty is in presence to see the ladies dance the new and old country-dances with tabor and pipe."[4] Both Essex's mother and his sister Penelope, Lady Rich, sent lavish New Year's presents, one a "curious fine gown" which Elizabeth liked well, but "things standing as they did, she did not accept or refuse it. . . ."[5] Neither mother nor sister was yet permitted to visit Essex, so they often went to a house overlooking the garden in which he walked "in a cloth gown, cloth jerkin, cloth hose, cloth stockings, and cloth mittens" to wave and call to him.

As the year 1599 ended and a new century began, conditions in Ireland had reached a disastrous point. Nightly raids into the English Pale by the natives had been so successful that the Council expected Tyrone to attack Dublin at any time. Strong measures were called for, and when the Council cast about for a replacement for Essex, Elizabeth again named her original choice, Sir Charles Blount, now Lord Mountjoy. A humorous moment occurred after a Council meeting when Elizabeth mentioned Mountjoy's appointment to Francis Bacon and asked his opinion. "Surely, Madame, you cannot make a better choice, unless you send over my Lord Essex . . ." Bacon said. "Essex!" exclaimed the Queen vehemently. "When I send Essex back to Ireland, I will marry you. Claim it of me!"[6]

Before his departure, Mountjoy had, with Essex's knowledge, sent an incredible proposal to James Stuart, King of Scotland, that James demand a declaration of his rights to the succession. Later he, Mountjoy, might return from Ireland with the army, and this, combined with Essex's supporters in London and tenants from his estates, would constitute a considerable force which might establish Essex in power to form a new Parliament and declare James heir to the throne.[7] In the meantime, Mountjoy left for Ireland and there, suddenly, became a new man. The energies he had previously dissipated in court intrigues, in supporting or defending Essex were now dedicated to the complex task of doing his job. His arrival was timely, the army was desperate for new leadership, and the "golden chessman," Mountjoy, now found his true vocation. He had a great capacity to inspire enthusiasm, to delegate responsibility and listen to competent advice. Efficient and hardworking, he soon proved to be a brilliant strategist and technician, as well as a valorous soldier and a sound example of Elizabeth's discerning shrewdness. She had wanted to send him two years previously.*

On March 21, 1600, the Earl was removed to Essex House under the care of Sir Richard Berkley with two servants to attend him. He was now well enough to walk in his garden, play an occasional game of tennis with Henry Cuffe, his secretary, and meet with friends. He again petitioned the Queen, saying he had received her words "that you meant to correct and not to ruin." He said that his troubles "and the increase of your indignation have made all men so afraid of me as my own poor state is ruined, and my friends and servants like to die in prison, because I cannot help myself with my own. . . ." He told the Queen, "I not only feel the weight of your indignation, and am subject to their malicious informations that first envied me your favour . . . as if I were thrown into a corner like a dead carcass, I am gnawed on and torn by the basest creatures on earth. The prating tavern haunter speaks of me what he lists; they print me and make me speak to the world. . . ." He said that in the eight months of his close confinement the Queen had rejected his letters and refused to hear him, "which to traitors you never did. . . ." He asked that Elizabeth conclude his punishment, "that I may go to my Saviour, Who had paid Himself a ransom for me, and Whom (me thinks) I still hear calling me out of this unkind world. . . ."[9]

Elizabeth was moved to tears by the letter. For the first time she appeared to relent, saying that "she would have him again in her service when he knew himself and his duty." Her words provided some cheer to the frantic Essex but only dismayed others at court such as Sir Robert Cecil, Nottingham and Raleigh. While Essex firmly believed Cecil was the prime mover for his continued restraint, Sir Robert had actually remained noncommittal. He had a lifetime observation of his father's wise example of "bending with the wind," of keeping himself

*Mountjoy eventually overcame the Earl of Tyrone and compelled him to surrender. Tyrone was en route to England to beg Elizabeth's pardon when she died. In 1607 he was suspected of further intrigue and fled to Brussels and later to Rome, where he passed the remainder of his life, living on a small stipend furnished jointly by the Pope and the King of Spain.[8]

apart from court factions, in remembering that all power and authority was in the Queen's gift. He had continued to remain aloof in the Essex affair, and his unwillingness to use his influence with the Queen galled Sir Walter Raleigh. Ever the blunt soldier, Raleigh put on paper what many others were thinking when he wrote that if Cecil should "relent towards this tyrant, you will repent it when it shall be too late." He said, "The less you make of him, the less he shall be able to harm you and yours; and if her Majesty's favour fail him, he will again decline to a common person. . . . Lose not your advantage! If you do, I read your destiny." And in case Cecil missed the point, Raleigh ended with a postscript: "He will ever be the canker of the Queen's estate and safety—I have seen the last of her good days and all ours after his liberty."[10]

By June the situation had become untenable, and daily Elizabeth was reminded of her irresoluteness. When she went abroad, she was without a Master of the Horse. Essex's place in the Council remained vacant, and his other offices had been suspended. Since she had refused him a trial, Essex's supporters were charging that he had been "condemned unheard." Elizabeth, always touchy where her popularity was concerned, now insisted on a public airing of the case, "where his fault shall be laid open to him. . . ." She appointed a special commission of eighteen Councillors and judges, and on June 5, 1600, the hearing began.

In essence, the proceedings were a mere formality. The judges were aware that the Queen wanted no condemnation, but merely a chastening after which, presumably, she would take some action. As far as the Earl was concerned, total submission and admittance of guilt were all that was required. Essex was brought to the chamber, where he knelt at the end of a long table, and "the Lords did admire his discretion and carriage" in remaining kneeling until Archbishop Whitgift whispered that the Earl might have a cushion for his knees. Lord Keeper Egerton reiterated the charges—the decimation of the army, his misconduct in Ireland and the farce of his truce with Tyrone. Many of the spectators who saw the Earl on his knees "wept at the pitiful and lamentable sight to see him that was the minion of Fortune now unworthy of the least honour he had of many."[11] One who did not weep was Francis Bacon. It was none other than Essex's great and erstwhile good friend, now serving on the commission, who used the opportunity to quote from some private correspondence from Essex while the Earl had sulked away from court. Bacon had drawn up the declaration against Essex, and when taken to the Queen for signature, she had said that "whatever she did should be for his chastisement, not for his destruction. . . ." Bacon's reply had been to insinuate she had lost a good deal of impact by delay. He said, "Certainly it is now far too late. The matter is old and hath taken too much wind. . . ."[12]

Essex was given an opportunity to answer the charges and did so brilliantly, saying he had come "not to justify himself, but to acknowledge his transgressions, how that his honour and loyalty was touched. . . ." He spoke feelingly of the Queen and her graciousness in sparing him the ordeal and humiliation of a public trial. He spoke of his great afflictions, of the sorry weight on his conscience, of his offense against her Majesty, admitting all crimes of "error, negligence or inconsiderate rashness, which his youth, folly or manifold infirmities" had led him.[13] Considerably chastened, he made a great impression on everyone until, erratic as always, he then proceeded to argue the charges that his actions had been disloyal. At once the Lord Keeper interrupted. No one, noted Egerton, said the Earl had been disloyal. He had merely been "contemptuous and disobedient," and this was why he was being censured. Contritely, the Earl remained silent. At length, Egerton delivered his opinion that Essex deserved imprisonment, a heavy fine and the removal of all offices. Lord Buckhurst moved that he be forgiven the fine; Nottingham that he be excused from imprisonment. Mr. Secretary Cecil made "a wise, grave speech," and eleven hours later, the commission formally adjourned, and the Earl, still a prisoner, was removed to Essex House.

Elizabeth read the commission's report with mixed feelings. No one could now accuse her of unfair treatment. Her condemnation of Essex had been publicly justified; he had been publicly censured. She felt vindicated, if unsatisfied, and, realizing that definite action must now be taken, finally gave the Earl his freedom. Two months from the date of the hearing and almost a year after his return from Ireland, Essex was brought to York House, where Cecil announced "that though her Majesty was content that he should remain under no guard, save that of duty and discretion, yet he must in no sort suppose himself to be freed from her indignation; neither must he presume to approach her court or person."[14] Joyously, Essex made ready to leave London, saying he would go "into honourable retirement" at Gray's, the Oxfordshire home of his uncle, the Comptroller Sir William Knollys.

At this point, having acknowledged and repented his faults, there was the slimmest chance that, given time, through prudent and quiet behavior, Essex might have retrieved some remnants of his blasted career and gained some reinstatement at court. But the months of frustration, isolation and brooding melancholy had only aggravated a personality at once contradictory and eccentric. Instead of admitting the Queen's generosity, he convinced himself he was a martyr to the ambitions of others. The great events occurring in Ireland, where Mountjoy was reaping the success Essex felt should have been his, the English victories in the Netherlands, a growing national prosperity that had eluded England for years—all served to demonstrate to Essex the great daily issues in which he had no part. Added to that, the malcontents, the "swordsmen, bold confident fellows . . . discontented persons and such as saucily use their tongues in remarking against all men," with whom he was soon surrounded, made it almost impossible for any realistic assessment on his part. His friends left him little peace, seeking through Essex, a way to improve their own fortunes. Frustrated and bored, he was more than vulnerable to the whispered suggestions and taunts of his secretary, Cuffe, who insinuated that in observing the terms of his freedom, he was "low-spirited and faint-hearted." Contemplating rebellion, Essex reminded Mountjoy of the scheme to bring the army home should James of Scotland prove receptive to pressuring Elizabeth to name a successor; Mountjoy was now less than enthusiastic. He had had great success in Ireland and had little desire to assist one so publicly censured as Essex. He said he wanted only to return to court "in such peace as a dog should not wag his tongue against him."[15]

Essex had other cause for worry. His finances, always in dire straits, now approached the catastrophic. He was more than £16,000 in debt, and his farm of the sweet wine fees was about to expire. The farm, the one great financial mainstay of Essex's fortune, had been granted ten years previously at the beginning of his career, as an example of Majesty's esteem. It was ironic that at the moment of his deepest despair, it should come up for renewal. Essex wrote Elizabeth that "he would be undone" if she did not renew the lease in his favor. He tried, as of old, with persuasive intimacy, to impress the Queen. "Haste paper to that happy presence, whence only unhappy I am banished. Kiss that fair correcting hand which lays new plasters to my lighter hurts, but to my greatest wound applieth nothing. Say thou comest from shaming, languishing, despairing SX."

Lady Scrope delivered the letter, and after reading it, Elizabeth sighed. Heartened, Lady Scrope reminded Elizabeth that Essex's punishment had lasted more than a year and said she hoped the Queen might look with favor on the exiled Earl. Elizabeth sighed again and replied, "Indeed, it is so," but did not commit herself. The past year had been a great strain on the sixty-eight-year-old Queen, and she, too, had suffered unusual bouts of depression, which the Essex affair had not mitigated. Her courtiers often found her melancholy, and one, Sir

Robert Sidney, wrote to Sir John Harrington, "I do see the Queen often. She doth wax weak since the late troubles and Burghley's death doth often draw tears down her goodly cheeks. She walketh out but little, meditates much alone and sometimes writes in private to her best friends." Sidney said Elizabeth had honored him in visiting his home, "and she seemed much pleased at what we did to please her." He spoke of the reception and entertainment, "at which she did . . . eat two morsels of the rich comfit-cake and drank a small cordial from a golden cup." Later, walking about the premises, "she called for a staff . . . and said she was much wearied in walking . . . and would come again another day." On riding home it was obvious "that her years make her unable to travel . . . she always complaineth of the uneasy going of her horse and when she is taken down, her legs are so benumbed that she is unable to stand, till the footmen, falling down, having a long time by earnest rubbing brought them to a better temper."[16] It was evident to all that that vital spark which had previously been so much a part of the Queen's disposition had diminished, partly by age and, many were coming to suspect, partly by the excessive demands on her emotions and the disappointments she had suffered in the past months.

By September Elizabeth had done nothing about the renewal of his sweet wine lease, and Essex was desperate. He wrote again to the Queen, and this time he did not mince words or attempt to flatter. He said the lease was "the means of satisfying a great number of hungry and annoying creditors which suffer me in my retired life to have no credit." He reminded her that the lease "is both my chiefest maintenance and mine only means of compounding with the merchants to whom I am indebted. . . ." He said if his blood would satisfy his creditors, "Your Majesty should never hear of this suit . . ." but even his blood would not do. In closing, he begged, "that you will once again look with gracious eyes unto your Majesty's humblest, faithfullest and more than most devoted vassal."[17]

The Queen let him wait. She told Francis Bacon that Essex "had written some very dutiful letters and that she had been moved by them, and when she took it to be the abundance of the heart, she found it to be but a preparative to a suit for the renewing of his farm of sweet wines."[18] By October 18 Essex had returned to London, and presumably being advised by Bacon, he tried one last appeal. He did not mention the wine lease. Instead, his letter was more personal; he said he hoped for a return to court, where he might ask his favors in person. "Out of that passion my soul cries out unto your Majesty for grace, for access, and for an end of this exile. If your Majesty grant this suit, you are most gracious, whatsoever else you deny or take away." Essex wrote that if he were denied, "time itself is a perpetual night, and the whole world but a sepulchre. . . ."[19]

In the meantime, Elizabeth had inquired into the value of the wine lease and found it amounted to £50,000 a year. Saying that "when horses become unmanageable, it was necessary to tame them by stinting them in the quantity of their food,"[20] she decided to let the lease revert to the Crown.

The Queen's action constituted a catastrophe at Essex House. The Earl had convinced himself that Elizabeth was merely punishing him further but would, in the end, renew the lease. Now he felt not only the crushing weight of her prolonged disfavor, but the panic of staving off his creditors and providing for his family and servants. He had never been wealthy, but the yield from the posts he held by Elizabeth's generosity were sufficient to support him in considerable style. His inherited lands, such as they were, were heavily mortgaged. He was thirty-three, one of the foremost nobles of the realm, married and with a family—and he had nothing. He was bankrupt in every sense of the word, and his situation was doubly disastrous since he had no recourse to the only source from which he might expect aid: the court and the Queen. "Much vexed at heart and all on fire with indignation," he was only too vulnerable to suggestions that might forestall the doom awaiting him.

And there were, unfortunately, only too many willing to oblige him with schemes for recouping his fortune. While several of his former partisans such as Lord Mountjoy had withdrawn their support, his stepfather, Sir Christopher Blount; his secretary, Henry Cuffe; his steward, the "fiery Welshman," Sir Gilly Merrick; Sir Henry Danvers, the Earl of Southampton; and a host of lesser characters worked on his emotions. Nightly, as the heavy curtains at Essex House were drawn against the river wind, "they insinuated to him . . . that the Queen, the Council and his adversaries are resolved to thrust him down into that extremity of poverty that he shall be forced to live upon the alms basket. . . ." Essex listened as his friends promised that "once become a poor man and neglected by the Queen, he will soon be neglected and slighted by all men. . . ." He was only too ready to believe the wild charges and rumors his friends brought from court—such as that Cecil was plotting to bring the Spanish Infanta to the throne when Elizabeth died. Essex wrote James of Scotland, advising him again to send an ambassador to confront Elizabeth with determining the succession, and ultimately a short handwritten note arrived from the King, which the Earl put in a small leather bag he wore around his throat. Daily more exaggerated charges issued from his raffish companions, and those who came to see him, such as Sir John Harrington, were appalled as Essex shifted "from sorrow and repentance to rage and rebellion." Harrington said, "He hath ill advisers and much evil hath sprung from this source. . . . His speeches of the Queen becometh no man. . . ." Harrington said he had no desire to pursue a friendship with the Earl, for he himself "had nearly been wrecked on the Essex coast."[21]

The activities at Essex House had not gone unnoticed at court. It was observed that the Earl's doors "are set open to all comers" and, joining Essex and his companions were such as Rutland, Bedford, Lords Mounteagle, Cromwell and Sandys, all young, hot-blooded, fractious, not-very-bright sprigs of illustrious fathers who had rendered Elizabeth and her predecessors notable service. They were representative of a growing segment in London: young men of good background whose memories of the Armada were childish, who could not remember the earlier years of Elizabeth's reign, the triumphs of Burghley or Leicester or, farther back, the persecutions and intrigues of Queen Mary's day. Privileged and in debt, their loyalty and attachment to the Crown were, in most instances, as loose as their morals. To them, Elizabeth was an aging woman, verging on incapability and intent on destroying their idol.

Urged on by his friends, Essex approached the zenith of folly. He cried, "The Queen has pushed me down in private life. I will not be a vile obsequious slave!" He showed his contempt for the court and the Queen, and, said one visitor, he "would not listen to the wiser counsels of his friends. These things are brought to the Queen's ears and alienate her affection for him more and more, and especially one speech inflameth her most of all, for he said that being now an old woman, she is no less crooked and distorted in mind than she is in body."[22]

Essex's words are evidence that a mind always somewhat unbalanced was now suffering a disintegrating process which panic and fear only accelerated. Early in January, 1601, it was obvious there were two armed camps in London. One was at Whitehall with the Queen, the court, and Council. The other was at Essex House, less than a mile away, where the Earl, devoured by his grievances, met with his companions to plot a coup in which the Queen would be forced to subjugate his enemies, particularly Cecil and Raleigh, a new Parliament would be summoned and James named as successor. There were several at court, once Essex's friends, who could see where he was heading. Lord Buckhurst, who had succeeded to Burghley's post, sent the Earl a friendly note, advising him against keeping such "base and desperate men" about him and noted that by courting popularity again, he was making it difficult for those who still remained his true friends to help him. Essex replied with a flash of his former hauteur "that he knew no rascals who resorted to him," and since he was a free man, "he saw no reason to withdraw himself. . . ."[23]

Elizabeth, too, fell prey to the fears her Councillors daily discussed in her presence. Sir John Harrington said, "She is quite disfavoured and unattired and these troubles waste her much." He said he had seen dish after dish brought to her table, but she had eaten little. "Every new message from the City disturbs her and she frowns on all her ladies." When she glimpsed him at court, she told Lord Buckhurst, "Go tell that witty fellow, my godson, to get home. It is no season to fool it here!" Harrington said he "took to his boots . . ." all the while lamenting that "the many evil plots and designs have overcome all her Highness's sweet temper."[24]

It was not only age which was making Elizabeth victim of a fear she would have spurned as little as five years previously, but a supreme disappointment in the Earl of Essex. His defection and absurd behavior only emphasized that she had again been played for the fool. She had given great authority and prominence to someone manifestly unfit and unable to handle authority, and her soul shriveled as she realized how she, usually so quick to judge the worth of a man, had erred. She had made no mistakes with Leicester or Hatton. To the end, they had remained her adoring servants and protectors. Her pride in them, "her creatures," had been passed to Essex, and she had depended on him for all the myriad satisfactions Leicester and Hatton had given with such grace. And he had failed her. It was in that failure that Elizabeth felt her own self-esteem touched and her own emotional resources diminished—that a young man given such indulgence by his sovereign had held it of so little value.

Her behavior continued to give daily evidence that tension was taking its toll. "She walks much in her privy chamber," Sir John Harrington wrote, "and stamps her foot at ill news. . . ." He said she kept a sword by her at all times, even at the table, and it was not unusual for her to grasp it and "thrust it into the arras in a great rage." Harrington concluded, "So disordered is all order, that her Highness hath worn but one change of raiment for many days, and swears much at those that cause her griefs in such wise, to the no small discomfiture of all about her. . . ."[25] The actions of Essex and his friends had reacted on the court, particularly the Queen; to those who watched her grappling with discontent, the wonder was that she had tolerated it so long.

By early February, 1601, the activity at Essex House, the corres-pondence with James Stuart, the plan to secure the Queen and the Palace were known to Sir Robert Cecil and the Council. Sir Chris-topher Blount and Sir Charles Danvers were to be placed at strategic posts within Whitehall, while others would be placed in the Tower and Mint. At a given signal, Essex and his followers would rush from the Royal Mews just north of the Cross at Charing to confront the Queen.* Once Whitehall was secured, special couriers would be sent to proclaim Essex's victory within the City, where he was sure his popularity was such that the Londoners would at once rush to his aid.

On Friday, February 7, Lord Mounteagle and several others were rowed across the Thames to the Globe Playhouse, where they per-suaded the Lord Chamberlain's Players to stage a special performance of *Richard II*. The Players complained it "was so old and so long out of use" that only a forty-shilling guarantee induced them to stage the play in which the Divine right of Kings is questioned and a King is eventually deposed. Presumably the play would whet public accep-tance of Essex's coup.

Previously, the Council had discussed how best to deal with the provocative element at Essex House, and the inflammatory play was the last straw. A hurried meeting held at Lord Buckhurst's home resulted in a summons being sent to Essex requesting him to appear before the Privy Council. When the summons was delivered, those who had returned from witnessing *Richard II* greeted the courier with jeers and epithets, while Essex surlily "excused himself." John Herbert, a secretary of the Council, was then dispatched to Essex House and reiterated the request to the Earl himself. Essex complained that he was not well, "that his life had been attempted by Lord Grey in the Strand" and he felt himself in such danger as he might "be murdered in his bed this night," and he refused to comply with the Council's request. By midnight Herbert was back with his answer, and the Council adjourned.

Essex and his followers realized that with the Council's awareness of their activities, the element of surprise was lost. Many now felt their courage slipping away and said the plan to secure the Palace was foolhardy and impracticable. Others argued it was feasible. Essex had more than 300 followers, and the Sheriff of London had promised 1,000 armed soldiers. Surely the City would rise in the Earl's support!

*The Royal Mews were just north of Charing Cross on the site where the National Portrait Gallery stands today. The monarch's falcons had been housed there since Plantagenet times. During the reign of Henry VIII, the stables (in what is now the Bloomsbury section of London) were damaged by fire, and the royal horses were moved into the mews.

Eventually those who were most eager—of whom Essex was predominant—overbore the others, and at long past midnight, as the Council was adjourning less than a mile away, Essex House and its ill-matched occupants settled down for the night. Tomorrow the City —and the Queen—would be theirs.

Elizabeth had been kept informed of Essex's activities, and she now commanded that Lord Keeper Egerton, the Earl of Worcester, Sir William Knollys and several others bring Essex before the Council. At ten o'clock the next morning they rode to Essex House to find the courtyard swarming with men "in a tumultuous sort." As they rode in, the Earl and several companions came forward. The Lord Keeper told Essex they had been sent by her Majesty "to understand the cause of their present assemblage." At first, Essex appeared unperturbed, but as he spoke, he became more agitated and declared "that his life was sought, that he should have been murdered in his bed, and that he had been perfidiously dealt with. . . ." Egerton replied that Essex should accompany him as ordered and that if he had any complaints, they should be heard and he would have justice. His words brought a reaction from the throng and cries of anger, of "Away my Lord!" and "They abuse you!" and "They will betray you!" were shouted from all sides. Egerton asked if the deputation might speak with Essex in private. "You lose time!" someone called out, and for a moment, Essex appeared uncertain. Then he motioned the visitors inside as cries of "Kill them!" and "Cast the Great Seal out the window!" followed in their wake. As the Councillors went into the small "book chamber," or library, Essex suddenly turned quickly, shut the door and locked it behind them, crying, "My Lords, be patient awhile and stay here and I will go into London and take order with the Mayor and Sheriffs for the City and will be here again in half an hour."[26] In a few moments, the stunned and angry Councillors could hear the mob departing from outside.

They thronged out into the Strand, some brandishing rapiers and pistols. The majority wished to go to the Palace as originally planned, and had they had their way, the result might have been different. While the guard had been increased at Whitehall, it was still relatively undefended against a mob of 300. Instead, Essex turned east into the Strand toward the City, where he hoped the citizens who had so doted on him would join him. Raising his sword, he cried, "For the Queen! A plot is laid for my life! For the Queen!" Behind him, the great throng poured along the usually crowded street, which now, on a quiet Sunday morning, was devoid of life. Essex "had been given to understand" that the Sheriffs would have 1,000 "trained bands" to assist him, though incredibly he had never spoken with the Sheriffs themselves. He now made for Sheriff Smith's house in Fenchurch Street. Overhead windows were thrown open as sleepy citizens looked with disbelief at the shrieking mob below. Cries of "England is sold to Spain by Cecil and Raleigh!" and "They will give the Crown to the Infanta!" or "Citizens of London, arm for England and the Queen!" filled the air.

The citizens watched, mouths agape. Some cheered as others slammed their windows and hurriedly drew their curtains. Few ventured outside, and those who did came mainly from curiosity. Hurrying to overtake the citizens who had assembled to hear the Sunday-morning sermon at Paul's Cross, the rioters met with a similar lack of enthusiasm, although Essex "besought them to arm themselves else they would be of no use to him. . . ." Onward down the Poultry and Lombard Street to Sheriff Smith's house he ran, only to find that that good man had "straightway withdrew himself by a back door to the Lord Mayor." There was no sight of the 1,000 armed soldiers.

By now the riot had lost much of its initial bravado. Not one man had joined the rebel throng, and Essex, "with a melancholic and downcast countenance" had sweated so profusely in his sortie down the Strand that he was "fain to shift his shirt" in the cold February air. For two hours, he remained at the Sheriff's house, even sitting down to a meal, while the nucleus of the mob waited outside. Then, anxious to return to Essex House and his prisoners "and go with them to the Queen to intercede for a pardon," he departed. So far no blood had been spilled, and the abortive rally might somehow be explained away.

In the meantime, the rioters' noise could clearly be heard downriver at the Palace, and Sir Thomas Cecil, now Lord Burghley, the Earl of Cumberland and several others had entered the City and, with heralds and a dozen horsemen, had proclaimed the Earl of Essex and his followers as traitors. Near the west gate of St. Paul's a chain had been drawn across the street, and soldiers with pikes and muskets were waiting. As the bedraggled mob approached them, Essex asked for passage. Being refused, he challenged the soldiers, and a few shots were fired. Sir Christopher Blount attacked one officer with his sword before being wounded and taken prisoner. In the general melee that followed, several others were wounded or killed as Essex, slipping away, dashed down a side street toward Queenhithe, hoping to return home by the river. He commandeered a boat floating in the murky tide and in a moment was dashing up his own water stairs. He tore into the library from which the Councillors had been released and "broke open a casket . . . and burnt diver papers and a book, observing they should tell no tales to hurt his friends. . . ." The little bag at his neck containing James Stuart's note was also consigned to the flames.

Essex knew all was lost. The place was in an uproar as stragglers from his "army" returned, some staunching blood from their wounds. On the third floor, the women—his wife, sister and female servants—were hysterical. The house was rapidly being surrounded by the Queen's soldiers. As Essex prepared to withstand siege, the Earl of Nottingham sent a message "that for sparing the weaker sex, he would permit the Countess, his wife, and the Lady Rich and their waiting gentlewomen, who filled all places with their shrieks and womanish cries, to come forth. . . ."[27] Then he would set cannon to the place if Essex did not surrender. From the leads, "holding all things for lost and desperate," Essex cried that "it was more honourable to die fighting than by the hand of the executioner." Others such as Southampton were not so eager, and eventually they persuaded the Earl to yield on three conditions—that they be "civilly dealt withal," that they be justly and fully heard and that a minister, Mr. Ashton, accompany Essex to his detention. Nottingham answered that for all these things "he would make intercession unto the Queen."

Therefore, at ten o'clock that night, as the mist from the river began to disperse in a cold drizzle, one by one, the shattered members of Essex House streamed out to surrender their swords to Nottingham. Essex and Southampton were taken to Lambeth Palace instead of the Tower, for the tide was rising and no one wished to "shoot the bridge" in the dark. Early in the morning, before many were abroad on the river, Essex and his companion were removed to the Tower of London, and the City, aghast at the previous day's activities, settled back to await the royal retaliation against one of its favorite sons.

At Whitehall, barricades of coaches had been flung across the street below the Cross at Charing, and weapons collected as the citizens of Westminster and even the little village of Chelsea rushed to protect the Queen. Unlike her sister, Mary, who had endured several risings, Elizabeth had never been a mere mile away from those eager to snatch at her Crown. But suddenly, the very immediacy of the situation and the release from anxiety acted as a tonic, and her blood rose in anger at those who would depose or kill her. She had been at dinner when news of the rising was brought to her; indeed, the shouts and cries in the City could clearly be heard. But she appeared untroubled, merely saying "that He that had placed her in that seat would preserve her in it," and continued with her meal, "not showing any sign of fear or distraction of mind, nor omitting anything this day that she hath been accustomed to do at other times."[28] Later when it was feared the rioters might come to the Palace gates, Elizabeth spoke of going out to meet them, saying "that not one of them would dare to meet a single glance of her eyes—they would flee at the very notice of her approach."[29]

The following day she was lavish in her praise of her Council, soldiers and especially her subjects. In a proclamation, she declared "not only in how thankful part she doth accept the loyal persisting of her subjects in their duty, and doth promise on her part that whatsoever she shall have cause to show it, they shall find her more careful over them than for herself."[30] Regarding Essex, she told the French ambassador that "a senseless ingrate had at last revealed what had long been in his mind," leading the ambassador to believe that Elizabeth had for some time suspected that Essex might attempt force and only the catalyst of the reversion of the sweet wine lease had brought it to a head. Within days, the Council acted to clear the City, which, now the danger was past, was proving a haven for gossips. The "great multitude of base and loose people . . . listening after news and stirs and spreading rumours" were advised "to get them down into the country upon pain of death by martial law."[31]

On February 19 the trial of the Earls of Essex and Southampton took place in Westminster Hall. Lord Buckhurst, as Lord High Steward, presided over the special court which was set up in the form of a square in the Hall's center. He was surrounded by clerks, judges, Councillors and twenty-six Peers of the realm and their attendants. When Southampton and Essex met at the bar, they embraced each other, and as the peers' names were being read, both Earls appeared almost jaunty. When Lord Grey's name was read, "Essex laughed upon Southampton and jogged him by the sleeve. . . ."

The law defining treason was read, and Essex and his companion were charged with "working to deprive and depose the Queen's Majesty from her royal state and dignity and to procure her death and destruction. . . ." Both Earls pleaded not guilty, with Essex insisting, "I bear a true heart to her Majesty and my country and have done nothing but that which the law of nature commanded me to do in my own defence, and which any reasonable man would have done in the like case."[32]

Sir Edward Coke, the Attorney General, then rose and rebutted Essex's statement as he recapitulated the details of the rising.

Disregarding Essex's assumption that had he been successful, he would have called a Parliament, Coke maintained that "a bloody Parliament would that have been where my Lord of Essex, that now stands all in black, would have worn a bloody robe! But now in God's last judgment, he of his Earldom shall be Robert the Last, that of a Kingdom thought to be Robert the First!"[33] Depositions from other prisoners, as well as from the Councillors Essex had shut up in his house, were read. Sir Walter Raleigh was then called, and as he was given the oath, Essex called out loudly, "What booteth it to call the fox?" Raleigh, who had rowed to Essex House on the day of the rising, recounted his conversation with one of the Earl's followers, who had told him that "you are likely to have a bloody day of it."[34]

Southampton then spoke, attempting to show that while there had been talk of securing the court and Tower, nothing had actually been accomplished and he asked if an action not carried through could be adjudged treasonous? When Attorney General Coke dryly interrupted to state that Southampton had been observed with a pistol in his hand during the riot, Southampton petulantly turned on the lawyer and said, "Mr. Attorney, it is the uncivillest thing in the world to interrupt a man who is speaking for his life!" He maintained he had taken the pistol from a man in the street, but "it had no flint and could not hurt a fly."[35]

Other confessions from Danvers, Blount, Rutland, Cromwell, Sandys and Mounteagle were read. Francis Bacon then arose and, confronting his former patron and friend, said "that my Lord of Essex was like Pisistratus, that had a purpose to procure the subversion of a kingdom . . ." and that "all that my Lord could answer to the charges were but shadows and, therefore, it were best to confess and not to justify."[36] When Essex challenged Bacon on their past friendship, which had included composing eloquent letters which he had been advised to write her Majesty, Bacon answered, "I loved my Lord as long as he continued a dutiful subject and spent more hours in making him a good servant than ever I did about my own business." To which Essex answered caustically, "I acknowledge all your gifts. . . ."[37]

When, a few moments later, Essex accused Sir Robert Cecil of stating he believed the Infanta of Spain had a better title to the Crown of England than anyone else, there was an appalled silence in the Hall. Cecil had been listening to the trial from a small room outside. He hurriedly appeared before the judges and knelt on one knee to beg Lord Buckhurst's permission to answer the slanderous charge. Buckhurst indicated the whole assemblage considered Essex's words nonsense, but Cecil would not be stayed. Small, frail and hunchbacked, his pale face quivering with rage, he turned and cried, "My Lord of Essex, the difference between you and me is great. For wit I give you the pre-eminence, you have it abundantly. For nobility, I give you place—I am not noble, yet a gentleman. I am no swordsman—there you also have the odds. But I have innocence, conscience, truth and honesty to defend me against the scandal and sting of slanderous tongues and in this court I stand as an upright man and your Lordship as a delinquent. I protest before God I have loved your person and justified your virtues and I appeal to God and the Queen, that I told her Majesty your afflictions would make you a fit servant for her, attending but a fit time to move her Majesty to call you to court again. . . ." Cecil said he would have gone on his knees to Elizabeth in Essex's defense, but now that the Earl had shown his "wolf's head in a sheep's garment" he washed his hands of him. "God be thanked, we now know you . . ." he cried. He challenged Essex to name the Councillor to whom he had spoken such a damning statement. Essex, white and subdued, demurred, and Cecil replied that it was "an invented fiction. . . ." Southampton then spoke and said the Councillor to whom Cecil had ventured the information was Sir William Knollys. Eventually, Knollys was sent for and, mystified at his summons, was aghast at being asked if Sir Robert Cecil had ever proclaimed the validity of the Spanish Infanta's claim to the Crown of England? The entire Hall held its breath as Knollys said that he remembered Mr. Secretary talking of a book where the titles to the throne were set down, but that Cecil had called it "*a strange impudence* that the Infanta was given equal right to the succession of the Crown as any other." The remark had almost the exact opposite meaning, and a vast sigh of relief swept the Hall while Essex protested the words "had been reported to him in another sense."

Cecil, still pale but composed, turned to Essex and said, "No, my Lord, your Lordship out of malice towards me, desires to make me odious, having no other true ground than the breach between us about the peace with Spain, which I labored for the profit and quiet of my country. But with you it hath ever been a maxim to prefer the war before peace, in respect of the importance it gave to your Lordship and such as followed you. . . ." He turned away, doubtless blessing the good fortune which caused him to be present, and said, to Essex, that "as to my affection to advance the Spanish title in England, I am so far from it that my mind is astonished to think of it. . . . I beseech God to forgive you for this open wrong done unto me. . . ."[38]

One by one the peers and judges then filed out to make their decision. After "refreshing themselves with beer, confections and taking their tobacco," they returned to the Hall, where each peer was asked to stand and answer the question "My Lord . . . is Robert, Earl of Essex, guilty of this treason. . . ?" Each stood and replied, "Guilty, my Lord, of high treason, upon my honour." Both Essex and Southampton were then returned to hear judgment. Essex, composed, said, "My Lords, I am not at all dismayed to receive this sentence, for death is far more welcome to me than life and I shall die as cheerful a death as ever man did. And I think it fitting that my poor quarters, which have done her Majesty true service in divers parts of the world, should now at the last be sacrificed and disposed of at her Majesty's pleasure. Whereunto with all willingness of heart, I do submit myself."[39] He then asked the Queen's clemency for Southampton, and the young Earl, quick to take advantage, "spake somewhat more earnestly for pardon, and with such sweet favor and winning expressions and such ingenuous modesty that he moved the hearts of all standers-by to pity."[40]

Pity aside, the Lord High Steward pronounced sentence. Each Earl was condemned to suffer the fate of traitors: death by hanging, drawing and quartering. Essex asked for the services of a minister and begged the pardon of Lord de la Ware and Lord Morley "for involving their sons in his troubles."

At six o'clock against the darkening sky, as news spread abroad that the trial had ended, "Many forsook their suppers and ran hastily into the streets to see the Earl of Essex as he was led back to the Tower, the blade of the axe turned towards him." The day had been long, and Essex was spent. It was noted that he "passed with a swift pace, bending his face towards the earth and would not look upon any of them, though some spake directly to him."[41]

The next morning Essex waited in his cell for the Reverend Abdy Ashton. Overnight he had reviewed the previous day which had wrought him from a self-styled deliverer of the Queen to a condemned traitor. He was disappointed to see his first visitor was not Ashton, but Dr. Thomas Dove, Dean of Norwich. Unknown to Essex, Dove arrived fresh from a meeting with the Council, which had, with disarming frankness, informed the minister that a fuller confession was needed from the prisoner. At his trial Essex had insisted he intended no violence to the Queen and had refused to implicate anyone else. The sympathy for Essex, already abroad in the City, could be counteracted only by a strong case against him, the Councillors said. While his condemnation had been perfectly legal and justified, Essex appeared

more as scapegoat of the plot than its prime mover, and to proceed
further would only redound to the Council and Queen's discredit.

When, therefore, Dr. Dove advised the prisoner to "acknowledge his
offenses," to lay his proud spirit aside and confess the full conspiracy,
Essex became impatient and replied resentfully, "If you knew how
many motions have been made to me to do my best to remove such
evils as the commonwealth is burdened with, you would greatly
wonder!" But he gave no indication of cooperating and turned his back
on the Dean, gazing out his cell window, his shoulders hunched and
tense. Quietly the minister withdrew to report his failure.

Later in the day Dr. Ashton arrived. He, too, had been informed of
the Council's urgent need of a complete confession. The Earl, still
smarting from what he considered presumption on Dr. Dove's part,
commenced to denounce the Dean. Hurriedly Ashton interrupted
Essex. "My Lord," he exclaimed, "I am unfeignedly sorry to see no
more sense in you of these and other fearful sins, into which you have
fallen, whereby you have dishonoured God, shamed your profession,
offended your sovereign, and pulled upon yourself many notes of
infamy!" Warming to his task, the minister denounced Essex for "an
ambitious seeking of the Crown," of using "men of no means . . . or
base persons that you had raised." He warned that "if by a true
confession and unfeigned repentance you do not unburden yourself of
these sins, you shall carry out of the world a guilty soul before God and
leave upon your memorial an infamous name to posterity."

Essex was astonished at Ashton's remarks and vigorously defended
himself, saying he had only wished access to Elizabeth to compel her to
remove the "evil instruments" about her and settle the succession. "No,
no, Master Ashton!" he cried, "I have never desired any other condition than the state of a subject, but only to my sovereign—not to so base
and unworthy vassals under her."

Dr. Ashton told Essex he did not believe him. "My Lord . . . you
must remember you are going out of the world. You know what it is to
receive sentence of death here, but yet you know not what it is to stand
before God's judgment seat, and to receive the sentence of eternal
condemnation." He advised Essex to "leave . . . all glorious pretenses,
free your conscience from the burden of your grievous sins, for I protest
I cannot believe that you had any other pretence than I have told
you. . . ." Then Ashton adroitly challenged Essex to name one man
who believed the Earl's motives as he had described them.

Ashton had been the Earl's religious adviser for some time, and
Essex trusted him completely. Without thinking, he now spoke fast.
Anxious to vindicate himself, he quickly named everyone remotely

connected with the rising. He described the plan to take the Palace and the Tower and, thinking he had justified himself, even offered to write it all out. But Ashton had heard enough. He replied, "These be great matters your Lordship hath opened to me and the concealing them may touch my life. . . ." Subtly, he attempted to solace the Earl, saying that by his revealing the true information, "it may give satisfaction to many that hold the same opinion of your courses which I did."[42]

Instead of realizing how truly he had been beguiled, Essex felt only the tremendous relief of confession. He had explained his motives, purged his soul and conscience and, for the first time, come face to face with himself. Ashton's words had been doubly revealing, for they had stripped the self-delusion with which Essex had always regarded his actions. Where previously he had gloried in his position as one closest to the Queen, he now realized, with a stunning ferocity, he had, by his own foolish and irresponsible behavior, forfeited everything. He had lost honor, respect and the love of his Queen and her subjects. His own self-esteem plummeted, and despairing, he felt debased and unworthy. The urgency of his confession removed the prop of self-righteousness, and he spent the night in a frenzy of religious expiation. Though a miserable sinner, there was some comfort in the fact that he could face the scaffold with a clear conscience.

When, the following day, Sir Robert Cecil and the Earl of Nottingham came to the Tower, Essex could hardly wait to recount his experience with Dr. Ashton. "For this man in a few hours hath made me know my sins unto her Majesty and to my God. I must confess to you that I am the greatest, the most vilest, and most unthankfullest traitor that ever was born in this land. And, therefore, if it shall please you, I will deliver now the truth. . . ." And in four sheets of close writing, he detailed the plot, accusing Blount, Cuffe, Mountjoy, Danvers and even his sister, Lady Rich, "who did continually urge me on with telling me how all my friends and followers thought me a coward and that I had lost all my valour." Essex said, "She must be looked to, for she hath a proud spirit."[43] Essex's written confession was his last task. Never once did it occur to him to write his wife, mother or sister, nor did he make a will.

The following day two other ministers, Dr. Mountford and Dr. Barlow, attended Essex. The Earl was pitifully glad to see them, so anxious was he now to abandon all earthly issues and devote his remaining time to the welfare of his soul. Dr. Mountford had difficulty reconciling the arrogant young man he had seen at the trial with the abject, repentant creature now awaiting him. Essex recounted his confession and said he had "now become another man." He said he thanked his Saviour that the rising had been unsuccessful, for "the Queen could not be safe so long as he lived on earth."

Dr. Mountford and Dr. Barlow accompanied the Earl of Essex when he left his cell at eight o'clock in the morning on Ash Wednesday, February 25, 1601. He was dressed in a gown of wrought black velvet, a satin suit and felt hat and seemed calm and resigned as he came to the scaffold on Tower Green. Because of his rank, Essex was not to suffer the traitor's hanging, drawing and quartering. The upturned faces of many of the peers, knights, gentlemen and Tower officials, all of whom he knew well, did not appear to disturb him. The crowd had been momentarily nettled by the arrival of Sir Walter Raleigh. Many muttered "that he came to feed his eyes with the sight of the Earl's blood. . . ." Raleigh retorted he wished to be present "if anything should be objected against him by the Earl. . . ." His statement did not convince the spectators, and the stir continued as someone admonished him "not to press the Earl at his death." Their resentment was so strong that Raleigh ultimately withdrew to the Armory in the White Tower and watched through a window.

Essex ascended the scaffold resigned and seemingly at peace. He spoke to the ministers who stood beside him and then, removing his hat and "making reverence to the Lords," made a speech in which he called himself a "most wretched sinner," whose sins "were more in number than the hairs of my head. . . ." He asked pardon and forgiveness for his "pride, lust, uncleanness, vainglory and divers other sins . . ." and called God's blessing on the Queen, the Church and the state. He asked that everyone have a "charitable opinion" of him, for he had never desired violence or the death of his sovereign.

Then, asking everyone to pray for him, he removed his ruff and gown and, calling for the executioner, who came forward and knelt on one knee for pardon, told the man, "Thou art welcome to me. I forgive thee. Thou art a minister of justice." Essex then knelt in the straw and "with his eyes fixed to Heaven and with long and passionate pauses . . . prayed. . . ." As his words floated out on the icy morning air, many of those present joined him in the Lord's Prayer with "floods of tears and lamentations."

Essex stood, removed his doublet, revealing a scarlet waistcoat, and bowed before the block, saying, "Oh God, give me true humility and patience to endure to the end, and I pray you all to pray with me and for me. . . ." He lay his head on the block and stretched out his hands, whispering, "Lord have mercy upon me, Thy prostrate servant," and then, "Executioner, strike home. Come Lord Jesus and receive my soul." As he finished, the executioner struck, and though he struck three times, "neither arms, body nor head stirred. . . ." When the great dark head finally rolled into the straw, the executioner grasped it, holding it high, and shouted, "God Save the Queen!" while many in the crowd recoiled from the sight.

As the executioner departed from the Tower, his bloody work finished, the citizens of London set about him, and "he was beaten by the people so that the Sheriffs of London were called to assist and rescue him, else he had been murdered," wrote one observer.[44] Inside the little Tower church of St. Peter's-ad-Vincula, the body of the thirty-four-year-old Robert Devereux was buried near the headless corpse of his great-aunt, Anne Boleyn, the Queen's mother.

Of the other ninety prisoners implicated in the Essex conspiracy, only four others suffered death.* Sir Gilly Merrick and Henry Cuffe were hanged, drawn and quartered at Tyburn and, five days later, Sir Charles Danvers and Sir Christopher Blount, Essex's stepfather, were beheaded on Tower Hill. Blount had attempted to lessen his guilt even to the block itself by insisting he had prevented Essex from leaving Ireland with an army of 3,000 instead of the few soldiers who actually accompanied him. It made little difference to the authorities, and in the traitorous executions, Lettice Knollys lost not only her handsome erratic son, but the husband, which of all three, seems to have given her the most happiness. She retired at once from court to live another thirty-three years in the country, a life she had once described "as fittest only for the disgraced."

---

*The Earl of Southampton remained in the Tower for the rest of Elizabeth's reign. He was released in 1603 by James I, became very popular at the Stuart court and even gained the profitable farm of sweet wines. The other young nobles were all exorbitantly fined; many were in debt for the rest of their lives. Elizabeth was kind to Essex's widow and helped her financially until she later married the Earl of Clanrickard.

Chapter Thirty-two

The remaining years of Elizabeth Tudor's life were overshadowed by the poignant wastefulness of Essex's death. She had quickly realized that to delay his execution, as she had in the Norfolk conspiracy, would show indecision on her part and reflect on the truth of the Earl's guilt. She had signed his death warrant with no visible emotion and, calling on the fortitude gleaned through similar childhood experiences, received the news of his death with seeming indifference. She had been playing the virginals when the message was officially presented. She stopped playing for a moment as a hush fell over the room. The Earl of Oxford looked at Sir Walter Raleigh, and several ladies-in-waiting dabbed at their eyes, but no one spoke. For only a moment the silence lingered, and then, calmly and capably, the Queen continued to play.

Inwardly, however, Elizabeth was badly shaken, and her grief was the more intense since it had to be hidden. And to admit that a vicious uprising had formed within the shadow of her Palace walls with her foremost noble at its head made her grief defensive. However, as the news spread throughout the country and to the Continent, respect for Elizabeth's courage was widespread. Henri IV of France cried, "She, only, is a King! She, only, knows how to rule!" From York, Sir Robert Cecil's brother, Lord Burghley, wrote that the Queen's clemency toward the remaining rioters "was a thing the like was never read in any chronicle!" She relished the satisfaction of writing James Stuart, whom she knew to have been in touch with Essex, that it had taken only twelve hours to quell a plot "which was in hatching divers years."[1]

Yet Essex's spirit seemed to live over the City which had reveled in his exploits, and for the remainder of her life, Elizabeth knew the sadness of his end was strong among her people. Eighteen months after his death, citizens were still singing the sad "Essex's Last Goodnight" in the taverns and, out of the Queen's hearing, in the Palace itself. Visitors to the Tower were shown the place on the Green where he had perished, and at Whitehall, shields from his victories on the tiltyard were exhibited to awestruck ambassadors and their companions.[2]

In time, Elizabeth could discuss the tragedy with some objectivity. She told the French ambassador she would willingly have spared Essex's life had she been certain of the safety of her state and Crown. She said in addition to becoming insolent and ungovernable, he had attempted to strengthen his own following by conferring knighthoods with indiscriminate haste. He himself had said he and the Queen could not exist in England together. She told the ambassador she had warned him two years previously that "since he took every occasion of displeasing her and insolently despising her person, he should be careful not to touch her sceptre, so that she would be compelled to punish him according to the laws of England. . . ."[3] And she added, "He who touches the sceptre of a Prince lays hold of a firebrand which must destroy him. . . ."

If the loss of Essex, "England's Sweet Pride," continued to linger in the City, it was also felt by the Queen. Loneliness now became her abiding companion. Her memory often lingered on the golden days—was it only thirty or forty years ago?—when the court had rung with the laughter, dancing, jousts and tilts, of picnics and hunting with my Lord of Leicester at her side or, at other times, a host of handsome, witty fellows who were now becoming mere shades in her memory. She recalled the days of Burghley's triumphs and remembered the host of creatures who crowded the canvas of decades—Philip, Catherine de Medici, Charles, Alençon, Norfolk and that foolish, foolish cousin Mary Stuart. All were now gone, and only she was left. Now she was surrounded by young and foolish maids-of-honor, bubbling with health and energy, or older ladies-in-waiting, many who had grown old in her service or buried their husbands and returned to court to become as aging and creaky as herself. She had them all in a flurry one day when she suddenly asked for a hand mirror. There was a great silence as a timid young maid approached and handed the Queen a heavy silver glass. Everyone knew that Elizabeth, loftily disdaining such vanity, had refused to look into a mirror for years. She had left her toilette to her ladies, several of whom present had more than once impudently rouged a withered cheek a shade too brightly. Suddenly, with a great apprehension of her own age and decline, she took the mirror and gazed at her countenance, "truly represented to her in a glass. . . ." Everyone held her breath as the Queen for the first time in years regarded her face, "then lean and full of wrinkles." She looked long and hard and then handed the mirror to her maid, saying "how often she had been abused by flatterers whom she held in too great estimation, that had informed her the contrary."[4] Though her voice was strong, her ladies could see there were tears in the Queen's eyes.

As if to deny the evidence in the mirror, Elizabeth spent her summer on short progresses and, released from tension and worry, appeared to have recaptured some of her old vigor. She observed May Day by going a-Maying in the green forests of Lewisham, then entertained the Duc de Nevers with a great ball at Richmond. She opened the dancing with him in a galliard "and danced with wonderful agility for her time of life." She visited the Earl of Nottingham at his country home and hinted broadly she would like the magnificent tapestries depicting the Armada victory in which he had played so important a part. However, both the Earl and his lady were disinclined to such generosity, and the Queen left emptyhanded. On hearing that Henri IV was at Calais, Elizabeth traveled to Dover and invited the French King to come for a visit, "as she greatly desired to see him." But the man who had been the recipient of hundreds of thousands of English pounds, in whose cause thousands of Englishmen had lost their lives, had little desire to pay court to a sixty-nine-year-old monarch and declined the invitation. Elizabeth felt the snub keenly.

By September it was noted that the Queen appeared more frail, and in one moment of rare frankness, she confessed to the French ambassador that "she was a-weary of life." Yet her spirit was such that in an effort to remove the gloom that constantly threatened, she entered into court festivities with such vigor that the aging Earl of Worcester could write, "We are frolic here at court, much dancing in the Privy Chamber of country-dances before the Queen's Majesty who is exceedingly pleased therein. Irish tunes are at this time most liked but in winter, *Lullaby,* an old song of Mr. Byrd's, will be more in request, I think,"[5] a slight allusion to the fact that Elizabeth's powers were slowly diminishing.

When the Queen did not feel up to dancing, she would sit on cushions on her chair of state and beat the time with her hand and foot. Her arthritic hand still bothered her. She had been greatly depressed when the coronation ring, which she had worn continually for almost forty-five years, was found to have grown into the flesh and had to be filed off. For days she looked at the bare spot on her finger with something akin to horror.

If dwindling good health and loneliness at times overwhelmed her, Elizabeth at least had peace of mind in knowing that her country's affairs had taken an upturn. In Ireland, Lord Mountjoy was successfully shoring up the English government and beating the rebel Tyrone in the process. In the Netherlands, the Battle of Nieuport had signaled Dutch gains, and the nation was enjoying an impressive commercial success. Another Spanish invasion attempt at Kinsale in Ireland had been thwarted, after which the Queen delivered herself of the caustic comment: "I shall never fear the threat of a Prince who was twelve years in learning his alphabet,"[6] a not too oblique reference to the known mental deficiencies of the Spanish King, the young dullard Philip III.

The English sailor, having served a fiery apprenticeship in the pursuit of piracy and war, had made increasingly confident efforts toward a genuine maritime supremacy. English ships carrying English cloth and other exports now plowed the seas from Archangel to the Guinea coast, to the Caspian Sea and the lonely shores of the New World. It was a matter of great pride to Elizabeth that these ventures were financed by English merchant companies.

Sir Robert Cecil had successfully walked the political tightrope between the old nobility and the "new man" and now enjoyed absolute authority with the Queen and Council. He was competent and deferential, though lacking the warmth and humor which had made Elizabeth's long association with his father so satisfying. The Queen never doubted Cecil's loyalty, even when he begged an additional £2,000 pension for the King of Scotland. Although she had kept in close touch with James over the years since his mother's execution, she had never given him any assurance—except by her consistent attention—that he would be her successor. Even now, in her declining years, Elizabeth could not bring herself to make the concession, yet it was not entirely selfish. To name James would give her enemies—and his— sufficient time to plan against his assumption of the Crown. There were many who realized Elizabeth's preference, however, and the foremost was Robert Cecil. He had kept in close contact with James and intended to be the bridge by which a smooth transition of government from the Tudor to the Stuart would be achieved.

So, wisely maintaining her silence, Elizabeth agreed to the increased pension. But when Sir Roger Ashton, the Scottish ambassador, arrived for his appointment, he was kept waiting in a small room adjoining the Presence Chamber, where, by listening to music and peering around a drapery, he might see the Queen of England dancing to a lively tune with only a nearby fiddler present. Elizabeth intended James to hear he must not count on the Crown too soon.

To help the Dutch, to subdue the Irish and thwart the Spaniard,

Elizabeth had been forced to sell Crown lands and jewels. Expenditures had been such that even the Queen's financial prudence could not stave off a grave emergency, and in late October, 1601, she summoned Parliament. During all her reign, there had been only fourteen Parliaments. Elizabeth had, over the years, tilted with her lawmakers on many subjects dealing with subsidies, the succession, her marriage and her own royal prerogative. Her last Parliament differed from others only in the attitude of many of its younger members. Those who attended were shocked at the Queen's frail appearance at the opening session, where she was seen to totter under the weight of her heavy ceremonial robes before someone lent a strong arm. And as she departed, many of the younger, more independent members were lax to move quickly when the Gentlemen-Ushers cried, "Make way for the Queen!"

Elizabeth was quick to sense the hostility and was soon informed of the members' grievance. In a previous Parliament she had promised to look into the matter of monopolies, the royal grants which gave to one person the whole right to make or sell certain articles. The articles were not luxury items, but such basics as salt, starch, coal and vinegar. Elizabeth, feeling her prerogative touched, had done little about reforming the practice. In the five years which had elapsed, however, the monopoly abuse had become extravagant, and the surly mood of the Commons was evident in their ultimatum: no monopoly reform, no subsidy.

Had the Queen been younger, she might have enjoyed a good lusty session in which all hostilities were aired and a peace—with the monarch the victor!—was achieved. Now, however, she asked her Clerk Comptroller, Richard Brown, to look into the matter by analyzing her own household expenditures for the present year versus the third. The Queen was appalled at the increased charges shown by her own books, and she lashed out at Brown, "And shall I suffer this? Did I not tell you, Brown, what we would find...? I will not suffer this dishonourable spoil and increase that no Prince before me did to the offence of God and the great grievance of my loving subjects.... And now, myself understanding it, they may justly accuse me to suffer it.... But my speedy order for reformation shall satisfy my loving subjects.... For I will end as I began with my subjects' love...!"[7] Very soon thereafter she had repealed many of the patents and suspended others, promising that in the future the monopoly practice would be more equitable "for the good of the people."

While the Queen had been inquiring into her household accounts,

Sir Robert Cecil and Francis Bacon were busy defending the royal prerogative in the Commons. They were hectored to such an extent that Cecil informed the members they were more like schoolchildren than her Majesty's Parliamentarians. In the midst of the debates, the Queen issued the proclamation revoking the existing monopolies, and suddenly the hostile Parliament was once more overflowing with goodwill and affection for their sovereign. They asked if they might send a deputation to render their formal thanks, and on November 30, at three o'clock in the afternoon, 140 members of Parliament crowded into the Council chamber at Whitehall to see the Queen. There, on their knees, they said, "that no words would be sufficient for so great goodness . . . prostrate at your feet we present our most loyal and thankful hearts. . . ."

Elizabeth had not expected the number which had pushed and shuffled its way into the small room, but on receiving the royal invitation, not one member had wished to be left out. In the meantime, the Queen had been busy. She realized this would probably be her last Parliament and, therefore, her only opportunity to put into words the essence of her regard for her subjects and her country which in turn would epitomize the whole meaning of her long reign. She had put her words to paper and committed them to memory so she might speak naturally and fully. She waited until the room was silent before commencing the speech which, later in life, many of those present would recount to their children and grandchildren.

"Mr. Speaker," the Queen began as a hush fell over the room. "We have heard your declaration and perceive your care of our estate, by falling into a consideration of a grateful acknowledgment of such benefits as you have received, and that your coming is to present thanks to us, which I accept with no less joy than your loves can have desire to offer such a present."

Elizabeth paused and glanced about the room. She had their undivided and rapt attention, and warming to her task, she continued. "I do assure you there is no Prince that loves his subjects better, or whose love can countervail our love. There is no jewel, be it of never so rich a price, which I set before this jewel—I mean your love. For I do esteem it more than any treasure or riches, for that we know how to prize, but *love* and *thanks*, I count invaluable! And though God hath raised me high, yet this I count the glory of my Crown—that I have reigned with your loves. This makes me that I do not so much rejoice that God hath made me to be a Queen, as to be a Queen over so thankful a people. . . . Neither do I desire to live longer days than I may see your prosperity and that is my only desire."

The Queen was aware her kneeling subjects might be experiencing some discomfort and asked the Speaker that they stand, "for I shall yet trouble you with longer speech." Thankfully, the audience arose and the Queen continued:

"Of myself I must say this—I never was any greedy, scraping grasper, nor a strait, fast-holding Prince nor yet a waster. My heart was never set on any worldly goods, but only for my subjects' good. What you bestow on me, I will not hoard it up, but receive it to bestow on you again. Yea, mine own properties I account yours, to be expended for your good. . . ." Referring to the monopolies, she said, "Since I was Queen, yet did I never put my pen to any grant but that . . . it was both good and beneficial to the subject and in general, though a private profit, to some of my ancient servants who had deserved well at my hands. *But the contrary being found by experience, I am exceedingly beholding to such subjects as would move the same at the first. . . .*" Elizabeth said she was "exceedingly grateful" to know the extent of abuse the monopolies had entailed, and "that my grants should be grievous to my people and oppressions under colour of our patents, our kingly dignity shall not suffer it. . . ."

Then, remembering that when this Parliament was adjourned, its members would leave for their homes and holidays, she left them with words close to her heart. "I know the title of a King is a glorious title. But assure yourself that the shining glory of princely authority hath not so dazzled the eyes of our understanding but that we well know and remember that we are also to yield an account of our actions before the great Judge. To be a King and wear a Crown is a thing more glorious to them that see it than it is pleasant to them that bear it. For myself, I was never so much enticed with the glorious name of a King or royal authority of a Queen, as delighted that God hath made me His instrument to maintain His truth and glory and to defend this kingdom . . . from peril, dishonour, tyranny and oppression. There will never Queen sit in my seat with more zeal to my country, care for my subjects, and that will sooner with willingness venture her life for your good and safety, than myself. For it is my desire to live nor reign no longer than my life and reign shall be for your good. And though you have had and may have many Princes more mighty and wise sitting in this seat, yet you never had nor shall have any that will be more careful and loving."[8]

It had been a long speech but had passed as only a moment to the breathless audience in the small room at Whitehall. The occupants had entered in varying moods—some curious, some hostile, some friendly. But at the conclusion of what they later called "Queen

Elizabeth's Golden Speech" there were few who did not feel an increased awe and respect, at times tinged with tears, as they cleared their throats and made ready to leave, waiting only for the Queen to dismiss them.

But Elizabeth had one more request. "Mr. Speaker!" Her high voice floated over the room, and again silence fell, and she asked that her Council should bring forth each visitor "to kiss her hand before leaving." As each went forward and put his lips to the still-beautiful long-fingered hand held graciously out to him, the Queen, still a regal Gloriana in one of the most memorable moments at the end of her long reign, looked satisfied, happy and pleased with herself and her visitors.

Before the holidays of 1602 approached, Sir John Harrington paid a visit to court and wrote an account to his wife:

Our dear Queen, my royal godmother and this State's natural mother, doth now bear show of human infirmity, too fast for that evil which we shall get by her death, and too slow for that good which she shall get by her releasement from her pains and misery.

I was bidden to her presence. I blessed the happy moment, and found her in a most pitiable state. She bade the Archbishop ask me if I had seen Tyrone? I replied, with reverence, "that I had seen him with the Lord-Deputy" [Essex]. She looked up, with much choler and grief in her countenance and said, "Oh! Now it mindeth me that you were the one who saw that man elsewhere. . . ." And hereat she dropped a tear and smote her bosom.

She held in her hand a golden cup, which she oft put to her lips, but in sooth, her heart seemeth too full to lack more filling. This sight moved me to think of what passed in Ireland, and I trust she did not less think on *some*, who were busier there than myself. She gave me a message to the Lord-Deputy [Mountjoy] and bade me come to the chamber at seven o'clock.

Her Majesty inquired of some matters which I had written and, as she was pleased to note my fanciful brain, I was not unheedful to feed her humour and read some verses. Whereat she smiled once and was pleased to say, "When thou dost feel Time creeping at thy gate, these fooleries will please thee less. I am past my relish for such matters. Thou seest my bodily meat doth not suit me well. I have eaten but one ill-tasted cake since yesternight."

Harrington said the Queen had then called some servants and "rated them most grievously" because of alleged laxness which, in truth, was only an example of Elizabeth's aged forgetfulness. "But who, dearest Moll," asked Harrington, "shall say 'Your Highness hath forgotten'?"[9]

In January Elizabeth's arthritis had extended from her fingers to her arm, and although she rarely complained aloud, she ordered the court to Richmond, which she called "the warm winter-box to shelter her old age." On January 21 she left London for the last time, going on the river in "the sharpest season" that many could recall. She had not dressed as warmly as she might have for the chill blasts from the icy waterway, receiving the stern admonition of her uncle the Earl of Nottingham that she should realize "that she is old and to have more care of herself, and that there is no contentment to a young mind in an old body." She suffered a slight cold but recovered sufficiently to receive Giovanni Scaramelli, the Venetian ambassador, on Sunday, February 6. As if to refute her uncle's statement, she chose a summery silver and white taffeta gown, trimmed with gold and wore the imperial crown on her hair, which, as the ambassador later said, "was of a light color never made by nature." Elizabeth had covered herself with "pearls like pears" and a "vast quantity of gems" and had the satisfaction of seeing the ambassador's face momentarily awestruck by the brilliance. After reproving him for the Venetian Republic's laxness in waiting so long to send an ambassador to her court, she softened and spoke more graciously, saying, "I do not know if I have spoken Italian well. Still I think so, for I learnt it when a child and believe I have not forgotten it." Despite her age, Scaramelli wrote his home court that he could well believe her "fame of past, though never quite lost, beauty."[10]

Shortly afterward her greatest friend of childhood days, Kate Carey Howard, the Countess of Nottingham, died. Elizabeth was beside herself with grief. As inevitably happened as she grew older, each death increased her melancholy, and she reviewed once more the many she had lost. One courtier found her alone in the dark, "bewailing my Lord of Essex's death." All state appointments were canceled that the Queen might mourn in private, but it was evident to many that it was not only grief that beset her. Her cold symptoms had returned, and when Robert Carey, son of her late cousin Lord Hunsdon visited her, he wrote, "I found her in one of the withdrawing chambers, sitting low upon her cushions. She called me to her. I kissed her hand and told her it was my chiefest happiness to see her in safety and in health, which I wished might long continue. She took me by the hand and wrung it hard and said, 'No, Robin, *I am not well.*' "

The Queen told her visitor she had been "sad and heavy" for the twelve days following Lady Nottingham's death, and he said she "fetched not so few as forty or fifty great sighs." Carey said he had never known her to sigh so much "but when the Queen of Scots was beheaded."

For the next fourteen days, Elizabeth remained among the cushions, refusing to go to bed. A day later the French ambassador wrote Henri IV "that Queen Elizabeth had been much indisposed for the last fourteen days, having scarcely slept at all during that period and eaten much less than usual, being seized with such a restlessness that, though she had no decided fever, she felt a great heat in her stomach and a continual thirst, which obliged her every moment to take something to abate it, and to prevent the phlegm, with which she was oppressed, from choking her."[11]

Obstinately she refused all medication, and her attitude wearied her attendants. "The Queen," said one, "had fallen into a state of moping, sighing and weeping melancholy. . . ." When one of her ladies asked if there was some "secret cause of grief," Elizabeth answered that "there was nothing in this world worthy of troubling her." She had moments or hours of feeling better, but, with little or no rest or food, did not improve. Sir Robert Carey, hearing of her continued weakness, said, "The Queen grew worse because she would be so, none about her being able to persuade her to go to bed."

News of the Queen's condition was soon abroad, and a silence fell over London, Westminster and Whitehall. Soon the Privy Council forbade news of Elizabeth's health from being made public in order to allay concern, but their action had only the opposite effect. Silent groups of people from the neighboring villages gathered around Richmond Palace, waiting on the icy edges of the tiltyard to observe the arrivals and departures, noting the concern on some faces and the quiet resignation on others.

The Earl of Nottingham arrived wearing mourning for his late wife, which caused a great outburst of weeping from the Queen. Both Sir Robert Cecil and Archbishop Whitgift informed him of Elizabeth's refusal to go to her bed or take medication and said the Queen had told them angrily "that she knew her own constitution better than they did and that she was not in so much danger as they imagined." The Earl came to her presence and knelt among the cushions, kissed the hot, thin hands and asked her to take some broth. When she agreed, he fed her himself. But when he asked her to go to bed, she pushed away the spoon and said that "if he were in the habit of seeing such things in his bed as she did when in hers, he would not persuade her to go there."

Sir Robert Cecil, standing by, could not resist asking, "If her Majesty had seen any spirits?" Elizabeth, realizing she was being baited, "scorned to answer *him* such a question!" She had her revenge a moment later when Cecil added his entreaties to those of Nottingham, saying that "to content the people, she must go to bed." Elizabeth looked at him sternly and said that "the word *must* was not to be used to Princes!" She went on, "Little man, little man—if your father had lived, ye durst not have said so much! But ye know I must die and that makes ye so presumptuous." And she waved the chastened minister away. Once alone with her uncle Nottingham, she said tearfully, her defenses down. "My Lord, I am tied with a chain about my neck." When he attempted to soothe her, she said despairingly, "I am tied, I am tied, and the case is altered with me. . . ."

At length, Nottingham persuaded her to be carried to bed. Daily she grew worse as her voice failed, and for four straight days, she sat on cushions in the bed "without rising or resting herself." She refused to eat, keeping one finger constantly in her mouth, and "was greatly emaciated by her long watching and fasting."

By March 23 it was obvious the end was near. The physicians, marveling at the Queen's tenacious hold on life, had given her up three days previously. She had not spoken for days, and her body "had long lain in a cold sweat." A small abscess had burst in her throat, which had momentarily restored her speech, and weakly she told her ladies, "I wish not to live any longer, but desire to die." Afterward her mind "had some slight wanderings at intervals."

By late afternoon the Council, despairing of receiving any recognition of the Queen's successor, gathered around her bed and, since her throat troubled her, suggested she hold up a finger when they named the claimants to her throne. When James Stuart's name was mentioned, Elizabeth did more than hold up her finger; instead, she clasped her hands around her sweating forehead in the shape of a Crown.

The Archbishop of Canterbury, John Whitgift, whom the Queen called her "little black husband," had remained in the Palace day and night. On the Council's departure, he entered the sick chamber with several prelates, and Elizabeth, momentarily aroused by the sight of her churchmen, recovered her voice and "bid them be packing." She whispered that she was no atheist, "but she knew full well they were but hedge-priests." By six o'clock she had changed her mind and "made signs for the Archbishop and his chaplains to come to her." She lay on her back "with one hand in the bed and the other without." Whitgift kneeled by the bed, speaking to her of her faith, and she signaled that she heard him by opening and closing her eyes, and weakly lifting up a hand. He told her she had been a great Queen, but she was about to die and "must yield on account of her stewardship to the great King of Kings."

A hush fell over the bedchamber at the communication—silent where one was concerned—between the Queen of England and the foremost prelate of the land. Whitgift prayed earnestly for his sovereign's soul, which Elizabeth acknowledged and then closed her eyes. Weary and thinking she had passed into a coma or light sleep, Whitgift made as if to arise, whereupon Elizabeth gestured to him to continue. For half an hour the Archbishop prayed for the soul of his monarch. Again he made as if to leave, and again the Queen signaled him to remain. Once more he knelt and "with earnest cries to God for her soul's health, which he uttered with that fervency of spirit that the Queen, to all our sights, rejoiced thereat." At the very end, she put her weak fingers in his before slipping into a coma. Her father, on his deathbed, half a century previously, had made the same gesture to another Archbishop of Canterbury, Thomas Cranmer.

It was well past midnight when the tired Archbishop rose from his labors and, with the others, left the chamber. The candles were burning low as the women who remained in attendance wearily sought a chair or cushion to receive their tired bodies. As the night wore on, one attendant, Lady Scrope, awakened about three o'clock in the morning and, stealing to the bedside, looked at the gaunt and shrunken face in the pillows "and discovered that the Queen had ceased to breathe." Sadly, she awakened her companions, and they knelt in prayer beside the body of their sovereign who had departed this life Thursday, March 24, 1603, on the Eve of the Festival of the Annunciation, sometimes called Lady Day.[12]

One last duty remained before the Councillors were called and the news made public. Lady Scrope lifted the wrinkled hand, still warm, and removed from the long finger a blue sapphire ring which the Earl of Essex had given to Elizabeth in happier days and which she had used to replace the coronation ring. Cecil had horses posted all along the route to Scotland and had commissioned Sir Robert Carey, Lady Scrope's brother, to inform James of Scotland of Elizabeth's death. When Carey entered the chamber at daylight, he found all the ladies weeping bitterly, and silently, his sister handed him the ring.

The body of the Queen was taken by water to Whitehall, where, watched over by her ladies, it lay in state for five weeks. On April 28, as spring came once more to the City she had loved and served so well, Elizabeth passed through its streets to her final resting place in Westminster Abbey. John Stow, who witnessed the funeral, wrote that "the

City of Westminster was surcharged with multitudes of all sorts of people, in the streets, houses, windows, leads and gutters, who came to see the obsequy. And when they beheld her statue, or effigy, lying on the coffin, set forth in royal robes, having a Crown upon the head thereof, and a ball and sceptre in either hand, there was such a general sighing, groaning and weeping, as the like hath not been seen or known in the memory of man; neither doth any history mention any people, time or state, to make like lamentation for the death of their sovereign."[13]

Only after Elizabeth was interred with her sister, Mary, at Westminster Abbey could her brokenhearted godson, Sir John Harrington, write what was in his heart. "Here now will rest my troubled mind," he said, referring to his retirement into the countryside, where, he wrote, he desired "to tend my sheep like an Arcadian swain that hath lost his fair mistress. For in sooth, I have lost the best and fairest love that ever shepherd knew, even my gracious Queen. And, sith my good mistress is gone, I shall not hastily put forth for a new master. . . ."[14]

And, at the Holyroodhouse in Edinburgh, the son of Lord Darnley and Mary Stuart received the ring and title for which he had waited for thirty-seven years. Once the funeral of Elizabeth was over, James VI of Scotland commenced his journey south. As he made his way over the roads of the kingdom he had never seen, he might possibly have reflected on the words of the Venetian ambassador, who had said of the dead Queen, "She was the most remarkable Princess that has appeared in the world for these many centuries . . . she possessed, in the highest degree, all the qualities which are required in a great Prince."[15]

It is more likely he thought of the strange irony of fate which decreed that this "remarkable Princess," who had bullied and beguiled him for decades, had, with her death, been the means of uniting Scotland and England in one Great Britain in which he, as James I of England, would found a new dynasty. And even more remarkable, in James' opinion, was that in denying the Crown to his mother, Elizabeth had actually preserved it for him.

Bibliography

Bibliography

BECKINGSALE, B. W., *Burghley: Tudor Statesman,* London, 1967.
———, *Elizabeth I.* London, 1963.
BELLOC, HILLAIRE, *Elizabeth, Creature of Circumstances.* London, 1942.
BESANT, SIR WALTER, *London in the Time of the Tudors.* London, 1904.
BINDOFF, S. T., *Tudor England.* London, 1950.
BLACK, ADAM AND CHARLES, *Maps of Old London.* London, 1908.
BOWEN, MARJORIE, *Mary, Queen of Scots.* London, 1934.
BREWER, H. D., *Old London.* London, 1962.
BROOKS, ERIC ST. JOHN, *Sir Christopher Hatton.* London, 1946.
BYRD, ELIZABETH, *Immortal Queen* [Mary Stuart]. London, 1965.
BYRNE, MURIEL ST. CLARE, *Elizabethan Life in Town and Country.* London, 1925.

CAMDEN, WILLIAM, *History of Princess Elizabeth, Late Queen of England.* London, 1675.
CHAMBERLIN, FREDERICK, *The Private Character of Queen Elizabeth.* London, 1921.
———, *Sayings of Queen Elizabeth.* London, 1923.
CLAPHAM, JOHN, *Elizabeth of England,* ed. by Evelyn Plummer Read and Conyers Read. Philadelphia, 1951.
CONSTANT, T., *The Reformation in England.* New York, 1966.
CREIGHTON, MANDELL, *Queen Elizabeth.* London, 1908.

DAVEY, RICHARD, *Sisters of Lady Jane Grey.* London, 1911.
DENT, JOHN, *The Quest for Nonesuch,* London, 1970.
DUNLOP, IAN, *Palaces and Progresses of Elizabeth I.* London, 1962.

EMMISON, F. G., *Tudor Food and Pastimes, Life at Ingatestone Hall.* London, 1964.
Encyclopedia Americana, New York, 1953.

FRASER, ANTONIA, *Mary, Queen of Scots.* London, 1969.
FROUDE, J. A., *History of England,* Vols. 7–12. London, 1870.
——, *The Spanish Story of the Armada.* London, 1892.

GARRETT, GEORGE, *Deat ʃ the Fox* ⌊Sir Walter Raleigh]. London, 1972.
GIROUARD, MARK, *Robe ı Smythson and the Architecture of the Elizabethan Era.* New York, n.d.
GORMAN, HERBERT, *The Scottish Queen.* New York, 1932.
GRIERSON, EDWARD, *The Fatal Inheritance* [Philip of Spain]. London, 1969.

HANSON, MICHAEL, *Two Thousand Years of London.* London, 1969.
HARRISON, G. B., *The Elizabethan Journals,* London, 1938. 3 pts.
——, *Letters of Queen Elizabeth.* London, 1935.
——, *Life and Death of Robert Devereux, The Earl of Essex.* London, 1937.
HOLMES, MARTIN, *Elizabethan London.* London, 1969.
HUGHES, PAUL, AND FRIES, ROBERT F., *Crown and Parliament in Tudor-Stuart England.* New York, 1959.
HUME, MARTIN, *The Courtships of Queen Elizabeth.* London, 1904.
——, *The Great Lord Burghley.* London, 1906.
——, *The Love Affairs of Mary, Queen of Scots.* London, 1903.
HURSTFIELD, JOEL, *Elizabeth I and the Unity of England.* London, 1960.

INNES, ARTHUR D., *England Under the Tudors.* London, 1950.
IRWIN, MARGARET, *The Great Lucifer* [Sir Walter Raleigh]. London, 1960.

JENKINS, ELIZABETH, *Elizabeth and Leicester.* London, 1961.
——, *Elizabeth, the Great.* London, 1958.

KLARWILL, VICTOR VON, *Queen Elizabeth and Some Foreigners.* London, 1928.

LACEY, ROBERT, *Robert, Earl of Essex.* London, 1971.
LEMON, ROBERT, ed., *Calendar of State Papers, Domestic Series, 1547–1601.* London, 1856.
LETTON, JENNETTE AND FRANCIS, *The Robsart Affair.* London, 1957.

MACNALTY, SIR ARTHUR S., *Elizabeth Tudor: The Lonely Queen.* London, 1954.
MARSHALL, BEATRICE, *Queen Elizabeth.* London, 1920.
MATTINGLY, GARRETT, *The Defeat of the Spanish Armada.* London, 1959.
MAYNARD, THEODORE, *Queen Elizabeth.* London, 1943.
MINNEY, R. J., *Hampton Court.* London, 1972.
MORRIS, CHRISTOPHER, *The Tudors.* London, 1966.
MUMBY, F. A., *Elizabeth and Mary Stuart.* London, 1914.
——, *The Fall of Mary Stuart.* London, 1921.
——, *The Girlhood of Queen Elizabeth.* London, 1909.

NEALE, SIR JOHN, *Elizabeth I and Her Parliaments.* London, 1953. 2 vols.
——, *Queen Elizabeth.* London, 1934.

POLLARD, A. F., *Political History of England,* Vol. 6, 1547–1603. London, 1910.

READ, CONYERS, "A Letter from Robert, Earl of Leicester to a Lady," *Huntington* [California] *Library Bulletin* (April, 1936).
——, *Lord Burghley and Queen Elizabeth.* London, 1960.
——, *Mr. Secretary Cecil and Queen Elizabeth.* London, 1955.
——, *The Tudors.* London, 1936.
RICHARDSON, MRS. AUBREY, *The Lover of Queen Elizabeth* [Leicester]. London, 1907.
ROBERTSON, A. G., *Tudor London.* London, 1968.
ROWSE, A. L., *An Elizabethan Garland.* London, 1953.
——, *The England of Elizabeth.* London, 1950.
——, *Raleigh and the Throckmortons.* London, 1962.

SALAMAN, MALCOLM, *London, Past and Present.* London, 1916.
SALZMAN, L. F., *England in Tudor Times.* London, 1969.
SARGENT, RALPH M., *Life and Lyrics of Sir Edward Dyer.* Oxford, 1968.
SITWELL, EDITH, *The Queens and the Hive.* London, 1962.
SMITH, A. G. R., *Government of Elizabethan England.* London, 1967.
SMITH, LACEY BALDWIN, *The Horizon Book of the Elizabethan World.* London, 1967.
STRACHEY, LYTTON, *Elizabeth and Essex.* London, 1928.
STRICKLAND, AGNES, *Lives of the Queens of England,* Vols. 7 and 8. London, 1851.
——, *Lives of the Queens of Scotland,* Vol. 7. London, 1859.
STRONG, ROY, *Portraits of Queen Elizabeth.* Oxford, 1963.
STRONG, ROY, with OMAN, JULIA TREVELYAN, *Elizabeth R.* London, 1971.

THOMPSON, EDWARD, *Sir Walter Raleigh, Last of the Elizabethans.* London, 1935.
TYTLER, PATRICK FRASER, *England Under the Reign of Edward and Mary.* London, 1839. 2 vols.

WALDMAN, MILTON, *Elizabeth and Leicester.* London, 1944.
——, *Elizabeth, Queen of England.* London, 1933.
——, *Sir Walter Raleigh.* London, 1928.
WHEATELY, H. B., *London Past and Present.* London, 1891. 3 vols.
WILLIAMS, NEVILLE, *All the Queen's Men: Elizabeth I and Her Courtiers.* London. 1972.
——, *Elizabeth, Queen of England.* London, 1967.
——, *Henry VIII and His Court* London, 1971.

——, *The Life and Times of Elizabeth I.* London, 1972.

——, *Thomas Howard, The Fourth Duke of Norfolk.* London, 1964.

WILLIAMS, PENRY, *Life in Tudor England.* London, 1964.

WILSON, VIOLET A., *Queen Elizabeth's Maids of Honor.* London, 1922.

WRIGHT, LOUIS B., AND LAMAR, VIRGINIA A., *Life and Letters in Tudor and Stuart England.* New York, 1962.

WRIGHT, THOMAS, *Queen Elizabeth and Her Times.* London, 1838. 2 vols.

ZWEIG, STEFAN, *The Queen of Scots.* London, 1935.

Notes

Notes

CHAPTER 1

1. Froude, *History of England*, vol. 7, p. 14.
2. Strickland, *Lives of the Queens of England*, vol. 7, p. 90.
3. Froude, *History of England*, vol. 7, p. 16.
4. Smith, A. G. R., *The Government of Elizabethan England*, p. 13.
5. Froude, *History of England*, vol. 7, p. 17.
6. *Ibid.*
7. Beckingsale, *Burghley: Tudor Statesman*, p. 38.
8. *Ibid.*, p. 64. William Cecil served as a Justice of the Peace in Lincolnshire during his retirement years. While he was undoubtedly gratefully aware of his good fortune in escaping with life and property intact from a venture which cost others their heads, the inactivity must have been galling. His relief at the end of Mary's reign is apparent in his diary in which he wrote: "Queen Mary reigned five years, five months and twenty-two days." As one biographer says, "He had been counting the days," knowing full well that as long as Mary was Queen, there would be no place for him at court.
9. Waldman, *England's Elizabeth*, p. 18.
10. Mumby, *The Girlhood of Queen Elizabeth*, p. 278.
11. Froude, *History of England*, vol. 7, p. 22.
12. *Ibid.*, vol. 8, p. 8.
13. Jenkins, *Elizabeth the Great*, pp. 55–60.
14. Waldman, *England's Elizabeth*, p. 37.
15. Hughes, *Crown and Parliament in Tudor-Stuart England*, p. 106.
16. Mumby, *Elizabeth and Mary Stuart*, p. 17.
17. Neale, *Queen Elizabeth*, p. 57.
18. Neville Williams, *Elizabeth I: Queen of England*, p. 66.
19. Strickland, *Lives of the Queens of England*, vol. 7, pp. 159–60.

CHAPTER 2

1. Froude, *History of England*, vol. 7, p. 32.
2. Strickland, *Lives of the Queens of England*, vol. 7, p. 151.
3. *Ibid.*, p. 152.
4. *Ibid.*, p. 155.
5. *Ibid.*, p. 156.
6. *Ibid.*
7. Waldman, *England's Elizabeth*, p. 39.
8. Creighton, *Queen Elizabeth*, p. 40.
9. Mumby, *The Girlhood of Queen Elizabeth*, pp. 250–53.
10. *Ibid.*, pp. 274–75.
11. Froude, *History of England*, vol. 7, p. 31.
12. *Ibid.*, p. 29.
13. *Ibid.*, p. 36.
14. *Ibid.*
15. Hume, *Courtships of Queen Elizabeth*, p. 26.
16. Froude, *History of England*, vol. 7, p. 58.
17. Neale, *Queen Elizabeth*, p. 71.

CHAPTER 3

1. Strickland, *Lives of the Queens of England*, vol. 7, p. 168.
2. Chamberlin, *Sayings of Queen Elizabeth*, p. 130.
3. Mumby, *Elizabeth and Mary Stuart*, p. 33.
4. Chamberlin, *Sayings of Queen Elizabeth*, p. 262.
5. Froude, *History of England*, vol. 7, p. 26.
6. *Ibid.*, p. 7.
7. Chamberlin, *Sayings of Queen Elizabeth*, p. 131.
8. Froude, *History of England*, vol. 7, p. 71.
9. Neale, *Queen Elizabeth*, p. 56.
10. Strickland, *Lives of the Queens of England*, vol. 7, p. 163.
11. Mumby, *Girlhood of Queen Elizabeth*, p. 321.
12. Richardson, *The Lover of Queen Elizabeth*, pp. 39–40.

13. Strickland, *Lives of the Queens of England,* vol. 7, p. 161.

14. Chamberlin, *Sayings of Queen Elizabeth,* p. 32.

15. Strickland, *Lives of the Queens of England,* vol. 5, p. 263.

16. Tytler, *England Under the Reign of Edward and Mary,* vol. 1, p. 70.

CHAPTER 4

1. Mumby, *Courtships of Queen Elizabeth,* p. 23.

2. Nonsuch was one of the most extraordinary palaces in England. In 1538 Henry VIII demolished the village of Cuddington near Ewell in Surrey to rear a palace relatively small in comparison with other royal dwellings, but a monument to the "excellent artificers, sculptors" and others skillful builders who worked there. The King "built with so great sumptuousness and rare workmanship that it aspireth to the very top of ostentation for show ... that most worthily it may have ... this name of Nonsuch." In 1959 the remains of Nonsuch Palace were unearthed by a dedicated group headed by John Dent, borough librarian of Epsom and Newell, who compiled the results of his findings, with photographs, in a remarkable book, *The Quest for Nonsuch.*

3. Mumby, *Elizabeth and Mary Stuart,* p. 64.

4. Read, *Mr. Secretary Cecil and Queen Elizabeth,* p. 155.

5. Hurstfield, *Elizabeth I and the Unity of England,* p. 8.

6. Hume, *Courtships of Queen Elizabeth,* p. 36.

7. Mumby, *Elizabeth and Mary Stuart,* p. 51.

8. Froude, *History of England,* vol. 7, p. 99.

9. Mumby, *Elizabeth and Mary Stuart,* p. 13.

10. Waldman, *Elizabeth and Leicester,* p. 35.

11. *Ibid.,* p. 38.

12. Jenkins, *Elizabeth and Leicester,* p.5.

13. *Ibid.,* p. 40.

14. Waldman, *Elizabeth and Leicester,* p. 51.

15. Richardson, *The Lover of Queen Elizabeth,* p. 34.

16. *Ibid.,* p. 7.

17. *Ibid.,* p. 36.

18. Froude, *History of England,* vol. 7, p. 99.

19. Mumby, *Elizabeth and Mary Stuart,* p. 67.

20. Hume, *Courtships of Queen Elizabeth,* p. 33.

21. Hurstfield, *Queen Elizabeth and the Unity of England,* pp. 36-37.

22. Mumby, *Elizabeth and Mary Stuart,* p. 8.

23. Jenkins, *Elizabeth the Great,* p. 76.

24. Jenkins, *Elizabeth and Leicester,* p. 50.

CHAPTER 5

1. Mumby, *Elizabeth and Mary Stuart,* p. 33.

2. *Ibid.,* pp. 39-40.

3. *Ibid.,* pp. 46-47.

4. *Ibid.,* p. 50.

5. *Ibid.,* p. 39.

6. MacNalty, *Elizabeth Tudor: The Lonely Queen,* p. 49.

7. Mumby, *Elizabeth and Mary Stuart,* p. 49.

8. Hume, *Courtships of Queen Elizabeth,* pp. 41-45.

9. Richardson, *The Lover of Queen Elizabeth,* p. 49.

10. *Ibid.*

11. Froude, *History of England,* vol. 7, p. 152.

12. *Ibid.*

13. Mumby, *Elizabeth and Mary Stuart,* p. 61.

14. Froude, *History of England,* pp. 181-82.

15. *Ibid.,* p. 187.

16. Wright, *Queen Elizabeth and Her Times,* vol. 1, p. 24.

17. MacNalty, *Elizabeth Tudor: The Lonely Queen,* p. 108.

18. Froude, *History of England,* vol. 7, p. 193.

19. *Ibid.,* pp. 157-58.

20. Mumby, *Elizabeth and Mary Stuart,* p. 51.

21. *Ibid.,* p. 177.

22. *Ibid.,* p. 162.

23. Froude, *History of England,* vol. 7, pp. 225-26.

24. *Ibid.,* p. 218.

25. Mumby, *Elizabeth and Mary Stuart,* p. 119.

26. *Ibid.,* pp. 119-20.

27. Froude, *History of England,* vol. 7, p. 245.

CHAPTER 6

1. Mumby, *Elizabeth and Mary Stuart,* pp. 126-27.

2. Froude, *History of England,* vol. 7, p. 265.

3. Mumby, *Elizabeth and Mary Stuart,* p. 139.

4. Waldman, *Elizabeth and Leicester,* p. 92.

5. Hume, *The Great Lord Burghley,* p. 99.

6. Froude, *History of England,* vol. 7, p. 281.

7. Read, *Mr. Secretary Cecil and Queen Elizabeth,* p. 199.

8. Froude, *History of England,* vol. 7, pp. 283-87.

9. Several historians deny or negate this letter's credibility, yet—in the absence of anything else—invariably use it. For all its possible inaccuracies, deliberate or otherwise, it has a ring of truth. *Something* took place between de Quadra and Cecil. It would have

been beyond the bounds of reason for de
Quadra to have invented the whole episode.
How much the Spaniard embroidered the letter, how much information he withheld or
elaborated upon, will never be known. In this
important circumstance, it is also possible that
de Quadra told the truth as he saw it.

10. Mumby, *Elizabeth and Mary Stuart*, p. 15.
11. MacNalty, *Elizabeth Tudor: The Lonely Queen*, p. 89.
12. Mumby, *Elizabeth and Mary Stuart*, pp. 144–45.
13. *Ibid.*, pp. 145–48.
14. Seven years later John Appleyard, Amy's half brother, revived the tragedy by ac-cusing Dudley of shielding Anthony Forster, whom, he said, had caused Amy's murder. Dudley reacted quickly, answering, "that it was not fit to deal any further in the matter considering that by order of law it was already found otherwise...." Appleyard went to the Fleet Prison for his action and there, after reading a copy of the inquest, including the testimony of fifteen persons, announced him-self satisfied with the verdict. Allegedly, Appleyard was approached by enemies of Dudley, who "promised he would lack neither gold nor silver if he would join them in charg-ing Dudley with the death of his wife...." (Mumby, *Elizabeth and Mary Stuart*, pp. 149–50.)
15. Froude, *History of England*, vol. 7, pp. 297–98.

CHAPTER 7

1. Froude, *History of England*, vol. 7, p. 300.
2. Mumby, *Elizabeth and Mary Stuart*, p. 66.
3. The author has been told by one who witnessed the incident of the bombing of St. Mary's Church by the Germans during World War II. The spire was badly damaged, as were parts of the church. After viewing the destruc-tion, the authorities told of discovering the tomb of Amy Robsart Dudley, and "when the coffin was examined, *it was found to be full of stones.*" The theory was that in this instance (not unusual in Tudor times) when the coffin and body might be desecrated, a "public burial" took place and the body was privately and decently interred elsewhere. There is, of course, always the alternate theory that the body was disposed of so it might never be examined at a later date. The site was sealed and is still shown as the tomb of Amy Dudley.
4. Strickland, *Lives of the Queens of England*, vol. 7, pp. 196–97.

5. *Ibid.*, p. 196.
6. Froude, *History of England*, vol. 7, p. 305.
7. *Ibid.*, p. 301.
8. Waldman, *England's Elizabeth*, p. 75.
9. Mumby, *Elizabeth and Mary Stuart*, p. 154.
10. Froude, *History of England*, vol. 7, p. 308.
11. Mumby, *Elizabeth and Mary Stuart*, p. 158.
12. *Ibid.*, p. 159.
13. Froude, *History of England*, vol. 7, p. 307.
14. *Ibid.*, pp. 312–14.
15. Mumby, *Elizabeth and Mary Stuart*, p. 163.
16. Waldman, *Elizabeth and Leicester*, p. 88.
17. Mumby, *Elizabeth and Mary Stuart*, p. 177.
18. Hume, *The Great Lord Burghley*, p. 106.
19. Hume, *Courtships of Queen Elizabeth*, p. 55.
20. Mumby, *Elizabeth and Mary Stuart*, p. 168.
21. *Ibid.*, p. 169.
22. Elizabeth's anxiety stemmed from the example of several formerly illustrious court ladies who had wed beneath them. There was Frances Brandon, the mother of Lady Jane Grey, who had married her Groom of the Horse, Adrian Stokes, nineteen years her junior. Then Catherine Willoughby Brandon, daughter of Catherine of Aragon's great friend Maria de Salinas, had married a mere "gentleman of her household," a Mr. Bertie, after the death of Charles Brandon. Most shocking of all was the marriage of the for-merly powerful Duchess of Somerset, the Protector's widow, who wed the commoner, Francis Newdigate.
23. Mumby, *Elizabeth and Mary Stuart*, p. 71.
24. *Ibid.*, p. 171.
25. *Ibid.*, p. 173.
26. *Ibid.*
27. *Ibid.*, p. 174.
28. Froude, *History of England*, vol. 7, p. 346.
29. Waldman, *Elizabeth and Leicester*, p. 98.
30. In an effort to avoid the tragedies and religious casualties of the previous reign, Elizabeth had assisted in the actual drawing up of regulations which declared the supreme power of the Crown. However, the Oath of Supremacy was administered only to those in office. Citizens who wrote or spoke against the supremacy were liable to the death penalty, but only on the third conviction.
31. Froude, *History of England*, vol. 7, p. 347.
32. *Ibid.*, p. 351.
33. Hume, *The Great Lord Burghley*, p. 105.

34. *Ibid.*
35. Read, *Mr. Secretary Cecil and Queen Elizabeth,* pp. 210–11.

CHAPTER 8
1. Brewer, *Old London,* pp. 25–26. The original City wall was laid out by the Romans, the earliest part in 102 A.D. Succeeding generations built upon the original base so that by Tudor times the work was mostly medieval. Though the great gates have all disappeared, there are many traces of the Old Wall—both Roman and medieval—still to be seen. One is in Cooper's Row, Trinity Place. Another is in the mail van yard of the King Edward Post Office in Newgate Street. Other remnants are in the churchyards of St. Alphage and All-Hallows-on-the-Wall in the street called, appropriately enough, London Wall. Cripplegate Church and 41 Ludgate Hill also have a portion of the wall, and a piece may be seen within the Tower of London precincts.
2. Hanson, *Two Thousand Years of London,* p. 57.
3. Robertson, *Tudor London,* p. 34.
4. With the exceptions caused mainly by modern rebuilding following the London Blitz of World War II, the street plan of Elizabethan London is similar to that of today. The overlay of a modern map on the old City and West-minster and Whitehall areas shows a remarkable and startling retention of street routes, directions and names.
5. Robertson, *Tudor London,* p. 95.
6. Greenwich was a favorite dwelling place of all the Tudor sovereigns. It was the nearest palace, being but a few miles down the river. The Tower and St. Paul's could easily be seen from Greenwich. Known as Pleasaunce or Placentia, it was already ancient when Henry VIII was born there. His daughters, Mary and Elizabeth, were also born at Greenwich, and his son, Edward VI, died there. Greenwich Palace's last days of glory ended with the Tudors. It was neglected by the Stuarts. At one point it served as a biscuit factory, and in 1664 "its ruins were tipped into the river" and the modern building which serves as the Royal Naval College was built near its site.
7. Strickland, *Lives of the Queens of England,* vol. 7, p. 190.
8. *Ibid.,* p. 172.
9. *Ibid.,* p. 199.
10. *Ibid.,* pp. 192–93.
11. Strong, *Elizabeth R.,* p. 27.
12. *Ibid.,* p. 65.
13. Strickland, *Lives of the Queens of England,* vol. 7, p. 204.

14. Strong, *Elizabeth R.,* p. 72.
15. Read, *Mr. Secretary Cecil and Queen Elizabeth,* p. 194.
16. Jenkins, *Elizabeth the Great,* p. 83.
17. Strickland, *Lives of the Queens of England,* vol. 7, p. 200.
18. *Ibid.,* p. 205.
19. *Ibid.,* p. 206.

CHAPTER 9
1. MacNalty, *Elizabeth Tudor: The Lonely Queen,* p. 12.
2. Wilson, *Queen Elizabeth's Maids of Honor,* p. 7.
3. Davey, *Sisters of Lady Jane Grey,* p. 139.
4. Wilson, *Queen Elizabeth's Maids of Honor,* p. 29.
5. Froude, *History of England,* vol. 7, p. 308.
6. Mumby, *Elizabeth and Mary Stuart,* pp. 187–88.
7. *Ibid.,* pp. 189–90.
8. Strickland, *Lives of the Queens of England,* vol. 7, p. 210.
9. Mumby, *Elizabeth and Mary Stuart,* pp. 196–201.
10. *Ibid.,* p. 202.
11. *Ibid.,* p. 213.
12. Mumby, *Elizabeth and Mary Stuart,* p. 210.
13. *Ibid.,* p. 215.
14. Strickland, *Lives of the Queens of England,* vol. 7, p. 209.
15. Richardson, *The Lover of Queen Elizabeth,* p. 33.
16. Jenkins, *Elizabeth and Leicester,* p. 87.
17. Mumby, *Elizabeth and Mary Stuart,* p. 216.

CHAPTER 10
1. Strickland, *Lives of the Queens of England,* vol. 7, p. 214.
2. MacNalty, *Elizabeth Tudor: The Lonely Queen,* p. 111.
3. Mumby, *Elizabeth and Mary Stuart,* p. 227.
4. *Ibid.,* p. 243.
5. *Ibid.,* pp. 219–21.
6. *Ibid.,* p. 237.
7. Hume, *Mary, Queen of Scots,* p. 140.
8. Froude, *History of England,* vol. 7, p. 427.
9. Mumby, *Elizabeth and Mary Stuart,* p. 244.
10. *Ibid.,* pp. 245–46.
11. *Ibid.,* p. 258.
12. *Ibid.,* p. 296.
13. Neale, *Queen Elizabeth,* p. 116.
14. *Ibid.,* p. 88.

15. *Ibid.*, pp. 108–9.
16. Froude, *History of England*, vol. 7, p. 507.
17. Mumby, *Elizabeth and Mary Stuart*, p. 205.
18. *Ibid.*, p. 207.
19. Hume, *Mary, Queen of Scots*, p. 130.
20. Zweig, *Mary, Queen of Scotland and the Isles*, p. 4.
21. *Ibid.*, p. 6.
22. Neale, *Queen Elizabeth*, p. 123.
23. Read, *Mr. Secretary Cecil and Queen Elizabeth*, p. 229.
24. Neale, *Queen Elizabeth*, p. 108.
25. MacNalty, *Elizabeth Tudor: The Lonely Queen*, p. 120.
26. Zweig, *Mary, Queen of Scotland and the Isles*, p. 85.
27. Mumby, *Elizabeth and Mary Stuart*, pp. 271–74.
28. Hume, *Mary, Queen of Scots*, pp. 155–56.
29. Mumby, *Elizabeth and Mary Stuart*, p. 289.

CHAPTER 11

1. Mumby, *Elizabeth and Mary Stuart*, p. 307.
2. Hume, *Mary, Queen of Scots*, p. 193.
3. Froude, *History of England*, vol. 8, pp. 86–87.
4. Mumby, *Elizabeth and Mary Stuart*, p. 333.
5. Chamberlin, *Sayings of Queen Elizabeth*, p. 199.
6. Hume, *Mary, Queen of Scots*, p. 143.
7. *Ibid.*, p. 184.
8. *Ibid.*, p. 204.
9. Mumby, *Elizabeth and Mary Stuart*, p. 319.
10. Strickland, *Lives of the Queens of England*, vol. 7, pp. 227–30.
11. Mumby, *Elizabeth and Mary Stuart*, p. 319.
12. *Ibid.*, pp. 319–20.
13. *Ibid.*, p. 323.
14. Hume, *Mary, Queen of Scots*, p. 210.
15. *Ibid.*, p. 221.
16. *Ibid.*, p. 217.
17. Mumby, *Elizabeth and Mary Stuart*, pp. 334–44.
18. Hume, *Mary, Queen of Scots*, p. 218.

CHAPTER 12

1. Strong, *Elizabeth R.*, p. 25.
2. Wilson, *Queen Elizabeth's Maids of Honor*, p. 41.
3. *Ibid.*, p. 60.
4. *Ibid.*, p. 44.

5. Strickland, *Lives of the Queens of England*, vol. 7, p. 203.
6. Chamberlin, *Sayings of Queen Elizabeth*, p. 64.
7. *Ibid.*, p. 200.
8. Mumby, *Elizabeth and Mary Stuart*, pp. 336–37.
9. Read, *Mr. Secretary Cecil and Queen Elizabeth*, p. 315.
10. *Ibid.*, p. 339.
11. *Ibid.*, p. 342.
12. Waldman, *Elizabeth and Leicester*, p. 110.
13. Mumby, *Elizabeth and Mary Stuart*, p. 348.
14. *Ibid.*, p. 350.
15. Hume, *Mary, Queen of Scots*, pp. 227–28.
16. Mumby, *Elizabeth and Mary Stuart*, p. 353.
17. *Ibid.*, pp. 355–56.
18. Hume, *Mary, Queen of Scots*, p. 223.
19. Mumby, *Elizabeth and Mary Stuart*, pp. 360–61.
20. *Ibid.*, p. 367.
21. Hume, *Mary, Queen of Scots*, p. 240.
22. Mumby, *Elizabeth and Mary Stuart*, pp. 374–75.
23. Read, *Mr. Secretary Cecil and Queen Elizabeth*, p. 317.
24. Mumby, *Elizabeth and Mary Stuart*, pp. 375–76.
25. Hume, *Mary, Queen of Scots*, p. 257.
26. Gorman, *The Scottish Queen*, p. 232.
27. Jenkins, *Elizabeth, the Great*, p. 115.
28. Neville Williams, *Elizabeth I, Queen of England*, p. 127.
29. Mumby, *Elizabeth and Mary Stuart*, p. 382.
30. Neale, *Queen Elizabeth*, p. 205.

CHAPTER 13

1. Mumby, *The Fall of Mary Stuart*, p. 17.
2. Bowen, *Mary, Queen of Scots*, p. 161.
3. Read, *Mr. Secretary Cecil and Queen Elizabeth*, p. 345.
4. Davey, *The Sisters of Lady Jane Grey*, p. 264.
5. Strickland, *Lives of the Queens of England*, vol. 7, p. 244.
6. Mumby, *The Fall of Mary Stuart*, p. 63.
7. Waldman, *Elizabeth and Leicester*, p. 114.
8. Read, *Mr. Secretary Cecil and Queen Elizabeth*, pp. 331–32.
9. Waldman, *Elizabeth and Leicester*, p. 116.
10. Mumby, *The Fall of Mary Stuart*, p. 18.
11. *Ibid.*, p. 21.
12. *Ibid.*, p. 64.
13. Jenkins, *Elizabeth, the Great*, p. 122.

14. Froude, *History of England*, vol. 8, p. 289.

15. Hume, *Mary, Queen of Scots*, p. 301.

16. Bowen, *Mary, Queen of Scots*, p. 161.

17. Mumby, *The Fall of Mary Stuart*, p. 36.

18. Zweig, *Mary, Queen of Scotland and the Isles*, p. 116.

19. Mumby, *The Fall of Mary Stuart*, p. 37.

20. Hume, *Mary, Queen of Scots*, p. 304.

21. Gorman, *The Scottish Queen*, p. 267.

22. Pollard, *Political History of England*, vol. VI, p. 266.

23. Mumby, *The Fall of Mary Stuart*, p. 71.

24. *Ibid.*, p. 69.

25. Strickland, *Lives of the Queens of England*, p. 249.

26. *Ibid.*

27. Chamberlin, *Sayings of Queen Elizabeth*, p. 39.

28. *Ibid.*, p. 30.

29. Mumby, *The Fall of Mary Stuart*, p. 81.

30. Neale, *Elizabeth and Her Parliaments*, vol. 1, p. 133.

31. Waldman, *England's Elizabeth*, p. 126.

32. Mumby, *The Fall of Mary Stuart*, p. 102.

33. Read, *Mr. Secretary Cecil and Queen Elizabeth*, p. 362.

34. Neale, *Elizabeth and Her Parliaments*, vol. 1, p. 146.

35. Strickland, *Lives of the Queens of England*, vol. 7, p. 263.

36. *Ibid.*, p. 264.

37. *Ibid.*

38. Waldman, *England's Elizabeth*, p. 131.

CHAPTER 14

1. Mumby, *The Fall of Mary Stuart*, p. 83.

2. *Ibid.*, pp. 88–89.

3. *Ibid.*, p. 67.

4. Hume, *Mary, Queen of Scots*, p. 335.

5. *Ibid.*, p. 318.

6. Mumby, *The Fall of Mary Stuart*, pp. 115–23.

7. *Ibid.*, p. 8.

8. Zweig, *Mary, Queen of Scotland and the Isles*, p. 146.

9. Hume, *Mary, Queen of Scots*, p. 349.

10. Mumby, *The Fall of Mary Stuart*, p. 135.

11. Hume, *Mary, Queen of Scots*, pp. 342–43.

12. The Queen's letters, the famed "Casket Letters," were found under Bothwell's bed in a silver casket with chased "F's" which had belonged to Mary's first husband, the young Francis. The authenticity of the letters has been in dispute for generations. In the main, however, they seem to be letters written by the Scottish Queen. Much of their substance, particularly conversation, was later corroborated by some of Lennox's servants. There was also, literally, almost no one else at the Scottish court with the knowledge and literary talent, plus what Pollard calls the "diabolical ingenuity and psychological insight," to forge the letters. The documents themselves also bear witness that they were written by someone in the severe spiritual and moral distress such as Mary was experiencing. It is always possible, of course, that *parts* of the letters were forged, but this also has never been proved.

13. Mumby, *The Fall of Mary Stuart*, pp. 161–62.

14. *Ibid.*, pp. 170–71.

15. *Ibid.*, pp. 181–82.

16. Pollard, *Political History of England*, vol. VI, p. 266.

17. Bowen, *Mary, Queen of Scots*, p. 249.

18. Neville Williams, *Elizabeth I, Queen of England*, pp. 146–47.

19. Bowen, *Mary, Queen of Scots*, p. 256.

20. Mumby, *The Fall of Mary Stuart*, pp. 219–20.

21. Hume, *Mary, Queen of Scots*, p. 378.

22. Bowen, *Mary, Queen of Scots*, p. 266.

23. Hume, *Mary, Queen of Scots*, p. 386.

CHAPTER 15

1. Mumby, *The Fall of Mary Stuart*, p. 351.

2. Strickland, *Lives of the Queens of England*, vol. 7, p. 275.

3. Jenkins, *Elizabeth and Leicester*, p. 149.

4. Richardson, *The Lover of Queen Elizabeth*, p. 164.

5. *Ibid.*, p. 166.

6. Read, *Mr. Secretary Cecil and Queen Elizabeth*, p. 292.

7. Froude, *History of England*, vol. 8, pp. 448–49.

8. *Ibid.*, p. 495.

9. Hume, *Mary, Queen of Scots*, p. 389.

10. Mumby, *The Fall of Mary Stuart*, p. 252.

11. *Ibid.*, p. 254.

12. Hume, *Mary, Queen of Scots*, p. 396.

13. Mumby, *The Fall of Mary Stuart*, p. 258.

14. *Ibid.*, pp. 255–60.

15. Froude, *History of England*, vol. 9, p. 94.

16. Mumby, *The Fall of Mary Stuart*, p. 262.

17. *Ibid.*, p. 271.

18. Froude, *History of England*, vol. 9, pp. 109–10.

19. Bowen, *Mary, Queen of Scots*, p. 249.

20. *Ibid.*, p. 256.

21. Hume, *The Fall of Mary Stuart*, pp. 219–20.

22. *Ibid.*, p. 293.

23. Mumby, *The Fall of Mary Stuart*, p. 268.
24., *Ibid.*, p. 277.
25. *Ibid.*, p. 283.
26. *Ibid.*, p. 292.
27. *Ibid.*
28. *Ibid.*, p. 275.
29. *Ibid.*, p. 287.
30. *Ibid.*, p. 291.
31. *Ibid.*, pp. 297–98.

CHAPTER 16
1. MacNalty, *Elizabeth Tudor: The Lonely Queen*, p. 170.
2. Chamberlin, *The Private Character of Queen Elizabeth*, p. 155.
3. *Ibid.*, p. 32.
4. Strickland, *Lives of the Queens of England*, vol. 7, p. 265.
5. Wilson, *Queen Elizabeth's Maids of Honor*, p. 97.
6. Strickland, *Lives of the Queens of England*, p. 266.
7. *Ibid.*, p. 298.
8. Waldman, *Elizabeth and Leicester*, p. 119.
9. Richardson, *The Lover of Queen Elizabeth*, p. 123.
10. Waldman, *Elizabeth and Leicester*, p. 124.
11. *Ibid.*, pp. 137–39.
12. Davey, *The Sisters of Lady Jane Grey*, pp. 200–1.
13. *Ibid.*, p. 219.
14. *Ibid.*, pp. 231–35.
15. Katherine's husband, the Earl of Hertford, remained in custody for about another year. In August, 1571, he was permitted to return to Cambridge and take his degree as Master of Arts. Several years later he married a daughter of Lord Howard and regained Elizabeth's favor to the extent that he entertained her at his Hampshire estate in 1591. He later incurred the royal displeasure by attempting to prove the legitimacy of Lady Katherine Grey's oldest son and did not actually do so until some eighteen years after Elizabeth's death.
16. Mumby, *The Fall of Mary Stuart*, p. 323.
17. Fraser, *Mary, Queen of Scots*, p. 348.
18. Mumby, *The Fall of Mary Stuart*, p. 328.
19. *Ibid.*, p. 329.
20. Bowen, *Mary, Queen of Scots*, p. 323.
21. Zweig, *Mary, Queen of Scotland and the Isles*, p. 253.
22. Read, *Mr. Secretary Cecil and Queen Elizabeth*, p. 397.
23. Camden, *History of Princess Elizabeth, Late Queen of England*, pp. 109–10.

24. Wright, *Queen Elizabeth and Her Times*, vol. 1, pp. 276–78.
25. *Ibid.*, pp. 279–80.
26. Mumby, *The Fall of Mary Stuart*, p. 342.
27. Hume, *Mary, Queen of Scots*, pp. 430–31.
28. Mumby, *The Fall of Mary Stuart*, pp. 343–44.
29. Waldman, *England's Elizabeth*, p. 142.

CHAPTER 17
1. Neville Williams, *Elizabeth I, Queen of England*, p. 149.
2. Read, *Mr. Secretary Cecil and Queen Elizabeth*, p. 402.
3. Mumby, *The Fall of Mary Stuart*, p. 347.
4. Wright, *Queen Elizabeth and Her Times*, vol. 1, pp. 280–84.
5. Read, *Mr. Secretary Cecil and Queen Elizabeth*, p. 404.
6. Wright, *Queen Elizabeth and Her Times*, Vol. 1, pp. 286–87.
7. Waldman, *England's Elizabeth*, p. 142.
8. *Ibid.*, p. 270.
9. *Ibid.*, p. 272.
10. Beckingsale, *Burghley: Tudor Statesman*, p. 114.
11. Froude, *History of England*, vol. 9, p. 249.
12. *Ibid.*, p. 278.
13. Jenkins, *Elizabeth the Great*, p. 139.
14. Neville Williams, *Thomas Howard, The Fourth Duke of Norfolk*, p. 104.
15. *Ibid.*, p. 137.
16. *Ibid.*, p. 140.
17. Froude, *History of England*, vol. 9, p. 338.
18. *Ibid.*, p. 341.
19. *Ibid.*, p. 427.
20. Antonia Fraser in her remarkable *Mary, Queen of Scots* has given perhaps the most complete analysis of the famous Casket Letters, "those debatable documents which were so damning to Mary Stuart." Lady Fraser presents a plausible argument that many of the letters—of which no originals survive—were undated, unsigned, and, in many instances, were at complete odds with Mary's known actions at the time. It is her opinion that in the casket found under Bothwell's bed were not only letters from Mary, *but also other letters from women with whom he had had notorious love affairs*, but which Murray and his associates insisted belonged to Mary. In those letters which were unquestionably Mary's, it is Lady Fraser's contention that dates were later added and gross interpolations included which rendered the letters even more sinister.
21. Froude, *History of England*, vol. 9, p. 351.
22. *Ibid.*

23. *Ibid.*, p. 381.
24. *Ibid.*, p. 397.
25. *Ibid.*, p. 396.
26. Zweig, *Mary, Queen of Scotland and the Isles*, p. 258.
27. *Ibid.*, p. 276.
28. Neville Williams, *Thomas Howard, The Fourth Duke of Norfolk*, p. 144.
29. Froude, *History of England*, vol. 9, p. 461.
30. Fraser, *Mary, Queen of Scots*, p. 418.
31. Froude, *History of England*, vol. 9, pp. 326–33.
32. Neale, *Queen Elizabeth*, p. 176.
33. Froude, *History of England*, vol. 9, p. 377.
34. *Ibid.*, p. 378.
35. Strickland, *Lives of the Queens of England*, vol. 7, pp. 287–88.
36. Froude, *History of England*, vol. 9, p. 426.
37. Read, *Mr. Secretary Cecil and Queen Elizabeth*, p. 444.
38. Strickland, *Lives of the Queens of England*, pp. 291–92.
39. Jenkins, *Elizabeth and Leicester*, p. 165.
40. Strickland, *Lives of the Queens of England*, vol. 7, p. 301.
41. *Ibid.*, p. 302.
42. Froude, *History of England*, vol. 9, p. 488.
43. *Ibid.*, p. 489.
44. *Ibid.*, p. 490.

CHAPTER 18

1. Froude, *History of England*, vol. 9, p. 522.
2. *Ibid.*, p. 529.
3. Wright, *Queen Elizabeth and Her Times*, vol. 1, p. 358. The Duchess of Westmorland who had urged and prodded her husband every step of his treasonous way was a sister of the Duke of Norfolk. After her husband had fled, she was the first to write Elizabeth "to give me leave to come to her royal presence, which although my Lord's doings have been such as they much abase me so to do, yet mine own innocency and the great desire I have had to do my humble duty to her Highness . . . embold-eneth me to continue this my suit. . . ." Elizabeth did not receive the Duchess. West-morland was so thoroughly stripped of his vast estates that his family was virtually penniless. The Duchess was removed to her brother's es-tate, where she lived on an annuity of £300 which Queen Elizabeth granted for her sub-sistence. Upon her death twenty-three years later, she was buried in Kenninghall Church.
4. Pollard, *Political History of England*, vol. 6, p. 294.
5. Neville Williams, *Thomas Howard, The Fourth Duke of Norfolk*, p. 166.
6. Strickland, *Lives of the Queens of England*, vol. 7, p. 302.
7. Froude, *History of England*, vol. 9, p. 586.
8. *Ibid.*, pp. 601–2.
9. Jenkins, *Elizabeth the Great*, p. 157.
10. Pollard, *Political History of England*, vol. 6, p. 297.
11. Froude, *History of England*, vol. 9, p. 569.
12. Jenkins, *Elizabeth the Great*, p. 155.
13. Strickland, *Lives of the Queens of England*, vol. 7, p. 311.
14. Read, *Lord Burghley and Queen Elizabeth*, p. 34.
15. Wright, *Queen Elizabeth and Her Times*, vol. 1, p. 391.
16. Hume, *The Great Lord Burghley*, p. 255.
17. Beckingsale, *Burghley: Tudor Statesman*, p. 128.
18. Neville Williams, *Thomas Howard, The Fourth Duke of Norfolk*, p. 191.
19. *Ibid.*, p. 196.
20. *Ibid.*, p. 197.
21. Maynard, *Queen Elizabeth*, p. 207.
22. Neville Williams, *Thomas Howard, The Fourth Duke of Norfolk*, p. 199.
23. Hume, *The Great Lord Burghley*, pp. 226–27.
24. Wright, *Queen Elizabeth and Her Times*, vol. 1, p. 399.
25. Neville Williams, *Thomas Howard, The Fourth Duke of Norfolk*, p. 213.
26. Froude, *History of England*, vol. 10, p. 302.
27. Neville Williams, *Thomas Howard, The Fourth Duke of Norfolk*, p. 215.
28. Froude, *History of England*, vol. 10, p. 15.
29. Hume, *Mary, Queen of Scots*, p. 456.
30. Wright, *Queen Elizabeth and Her Times*, vol. 1, pp. 380–81.
31. Froude, *History of England*, vol. 10, p. 41.
32. Read, *Lord Burghley and Queen Elizabeth*, p. 28.
33. Waldman, *England's Elizabeth*, p. 181.
34. Read, *Lord Burghley and Queen Elizabeth*, p. 50.
35. Read, *The Tudors*, p. 180.
36. Wright, *Queen Elizabeth and Her Times*, vol. 1, pp. 402–12.
37. Froude, *History of England*, vol. 10, p. 301.
38. MacNalty, *Elizabeth Tudor: The Lonely Queen*, p. 147.
39. Waldman, *England's Elizabeth*, p. 184.
40. Zweig, *Mary, Queen of Scotland and the Isles*, p. 286.
41. Gorman, *The Scottish Queen*, pp. 433–34.
42. Wright, *Queen Elizabeth and Her Times*, vol. 1, pp. 307–11.

43. Strickland, *Lives of the Queens of England,* vol. 7, p. 358.

44. Neale, *Queen Elizabeth,* p. 198.

45. MacNalty, *Elizabeth Tudor: The Lonely Queen,* p. 144.

46. Strickland, *Lives of the Queens of England,* vol. 7, p. 359.

47. Neville Williams, *Thomas Howard, The Fourth Duke of Norfolk,* p. 254.

CHAPTER 19

1. Jenkins, *Elizabeth the Great,* p. 158.

2. Neale, *Queen Elizabeth,* p. 213.

3. Jenkins, *Elizabeth the Great,* p. 208.

4. Brooks, *Sir Christopher Hatton,* p. 29.

5. Strickland, *Lives of the Queens of England,* vol. 7, p. 318.

6. Brooks, *Sir Christopher Hatton,* pp. 57–58.

7. Jenkins, *Elizabeth the Great,* p. 166.

8. Strickland, *Lives of the Queens of England,* vol. 7, p. 396.

9. Brooks, *Sir Christopher Hatton,* pp. 96–97.

10. Waldman, *England's Elizabeth,* p. 146.

11. Read, *Huntington Library Bulletin,* April, 1936.

12. Waldman, *Elizabeth and Leicester,* pp. 153–55. Douglass Sheffield kept her baby for about two years, and then Leicester took the child, who was brought up in the home of a relative in Stoke Newington. Leicester maintained an interest in and kept in contact with the boy all through his childhood and adolescence, and young Robert Dudley was always treated with the care and deference due an Earl's son. In 1584 he was being tutored near the neighborhood home of his uncle, the Earl of Warwick, where Leicester visited him and declared to one of the attendants, "Owen, thou knowest that Robin my boy is my lawful son, and as I do and have charged thee to keep it secret, so I charge thee not to forget it, and there see thou be careful of him."

Robert Dudley attended Oxford, matriculated as *Filius Comiti* (Earl's son) in 1588 and was left considerable property upon Leicester's death. He married a Cavendish, went to sea and served later with the Earl of Essex during his legendary raid of Cádiz, after which he was knighted. A year after Elizabeth's death (apparently realizing how pointless it would be during the Queen's lifetime) he brought suit in the Court of the Star Chamber to have his mother's alleged marriage acknowledged and his claim to the Leicester title and his uncle Ambrose, the Earl of Warwick's estates, made legitimate. Though Douglass bore witness to her marriage, she could not produce the necessary documents, and many of those attending had died; the claim was disallowed. In disgust, Sir Robert Dudley quit his native land forever, and deserting his second wife and a string of daughters, he took a younger cousin, Elizabeth Southwell, disguised as a page, and settled in Florence, turned Catholic and, out of his despair, carved a remarkable career as a shipbuilder and engineer. He was made a Papal Count, given the Warwick and Northumberland titles he was refused at home and, at his death in 1649 at the age of seventy-five, left thirteen children.

13. Davey, *The Sisters of Lady Jane Grey,* p. 281.

14. Strickland, *Lives of the Queens of England,* vol. 7, p. 315.

15. *Ibid.,* p. 317.

16. Wilson, *Queen Elizabeth's Maids of Honor,* pp. 578–81.

17. Strickland, *Lives of the Queens of England,* vol. 7, p. 308.

18. *Ibid.,* p. 314.

19. Waldman, *England's Elizabeth,* p. 189.

20. Strickland, *Lives of the Queens of England,* vol. 7, pp. 308–9.

21. MacNalty, *Elizabeth Tudor: The Lonely Queen,* p. 94.

22. Strickland, *Lives of the Queens of England,* vol. 7, p. 312.

23. *Ibid.,* p. 322.

24. *Ibid.*

25. Froude, *History of England,* vol. 10, p. 227.

26. Hume, *Courtships of the Queen of England,* p. 145.

27. Strickland, *Lives of the Queens of England,* vol. 7, p. 327.

28. *Ibid.,* p. 325.

29. Elizabeth suffered for years with a running ulcer just above the ankle, a condition associated with varicose veins and aggravated by her refusal to give the ailment proper care. It was a painful infirmity of which she was very conscious and sought to belittle. She was not helped by her doctors, who advocated the contemporary treatment of keeping the ulcer in a discharging condition and, several years later, when it commenced to dry up naturally, the physicians "did not know how to find a remedy for this mishap!"

30. MacNalty, *Elizabeth Tudor: The Lonely Queen,* p. 239.

31. Jenkins, *Elizabeth the Great,* p. 169.

32. Froude, *History of England,* vol. 10, p. 353.

33. *Ibid.,* p. 230.

34. Waldman, *England's Elizabeth,* p. 192.

CHAPTER 20

1. Chamberlin, *Sayings of Queen Elizabeth,* p. 34.
2. Froude, *History of England,* vol. 10, p. 450.
3. Read, *Lord Burghley and Queen Elizabeth,* p. 105.
4. *Ibid.,* p. 88.
5. Froude, *History of England,* vol. 10, pp. 397–403.
6. Jenkins, *Elizabeth the Great,* p. 184.
7. Froude, *History of England,* vol. 10, p. 444.
8. *Ibid.,* p. 455.
9. *Ibid.,* p. 469.
10. Hume, *The Great Lord Burghley,* p. 278.
11. Read, *Lord Burghley and Queen Elizabeth,* p. 87.
12. Richardson, *The Lover of Queen Elizabeth,* p. 223.
13. Strickland, *Lives of the Queens of England,* vol. 7, p. 381.
14. *Ibid.,* p. 383.
15. *Ibid.*
16. Richardson, *The Lover of Queen Elizabeth,* p. 246.
17. Beckingsale, *Queen Elizabeth,* p. 79.

CHAPTER 21

1. Wilson, *Queen Elizabeth's Maids of Honor,* p. 102.
2. *Ibid.,* p. 42.
3. Chamberlin, *Sayings of Queen Elizabeth,* p. 35.
4. Hume, *The Great Lord Burghley,* p. 310.
5. Richardson, *The Lover of Queen Elizabeth,* pp. 233–38.
6. Chamberlin, *Sayings of Queen Elizabeth,* p. 35–36.
7. Jenkins, *Elizabeth and Leicester,* p. 203.
8. Strickland, *Lives of the Queens of England,* vol. 7, p. 375.
9. *Ibid.,* vol. 8, pp. 27–28.
10. Jenkins, *Elizabeth the Great,* p. 200.
11. Strickland, *Lives of the Queens of England,* vol. 8, p. 30.
12. Waldman, *England's Elizabeth,* p. 201.
13. MacNalty, *Elizabeth Tudor: The Lonely Queen,* p. 184.
14. Read, *Lord Burghley and Queen Elizabeth,* p. 162.
15. Neale, *Queen Elizabeth,* p. 233.
16. Strickland, *Lives of the Queens of England,* vol. 8, p. 41.
17. Wilson, *Queen Elizabeth's Maids of Honor,* pp. 117–18.
18. Richardson, *The Lover of Queen Elizabeth,* p. 256.
19. Hume, *Courtships of Queen Elizabeth,* p. 208.
20. Neville Williams, *Elizabeth I: Queen of England,* p. 198.
21. Strickland, *Lives of the Queens of England,* vol. 8, p. 43.
22. Wilson, *Queen Elizabeth's Maids of Honor,* p. 122.
23. *Ibid.,* p. 123.
24. Neale, *Queen Elizabeth,* p. 237.
25. Richardson, *The Lover of Queen Elizabeth,* pp. 258–59.
26. Read, *Lord Burghley and Queen Elizabeth,* p. 226.
27. Hume, *Courtships of Queen Elizabeth,* pp. 208-9.
28. *Ibid.,* pp. 211–12.
29. *Ibid.,* p. 212.
30. Waldman, *England's Elizabeth,* p. 225.
31. Froude, *History of England,* vol. 11, p. 454.
32. *Ibid.,* p. 456.
33. Strickland, *Lives of the Queens of England,* vol. 8, p. 58. .
34. Chamberlin, *Sayings of Queen Elizabeth,* p. 89.
35. Froude, *History of England,* vol.ˆ11, p. 440.
36. Jenkins, *Elizabeth the Great,* p. 233.
37. Froude, *History of England,* vol. 11, pp. 471–72.
38. Harrison, *Letters of Queen Elizabeth,* pp. 147–48.
39. Maynard, *Queen Elizabeth,* p. 235.
40. Neville Williams, *Elizabeth I, Queen of England,* p. 211.
41. Waldman, *England's Elizabeth,* p. 228.
42. Strickland, *Lives of the Queens of England,* vol. 8, p. 65.

CHAPTER 22

1. Strickland, *Lives of the Queens of England,* vol. 8, pp. 85–86.
2. Girouard, *Robert Smythson and the Architecture of the Elizabethan Era,* p. 103.
3. Fraser, *Mary, Queen of Scots,* p. 443.
4. Neale, *Queen Elizabeth,* p. 256.
5. Strickland, *Lives of the Queens of England,* vol. 8, p. 128.
6. There is some question among historians whether Elizabeth ever received this letter. It was found among the papers of Lord Burghley, which does not necessarily indicate that the Queen never read it. It would be inconceivable that when her Councillors were looking for any reason to blacken Mary's name or further incriminate her with the Queen, such a letter would be withheld. It would be equally understandable that once she had seen

it, Burghley might have retrieved it so it might never come under the scrutiny of anyone else. Had he wished the Queen to remain unaware of it, it could easily have been destroyed since obviously it could not go into the State Archives.

7. Girouard, *Robert Smythson and the Architecture of the Elizabethan Era*, p. 118.
8. Strickland, *Lives of the Queens of England*, vol. 8, p. 107.
9. Read, *Lord Burghley and Queen Elizabeth*, p. 341.
10. Froude, *History of England*, vol. 11, p. 584.
11. Neale, *Queen Elizabeth*, p. 258.
12. Froude, *History of England*, vol. 11, p. 696.
13. *Ibid.*, p. 701.
14. *Ibid.*, p. 496.
15. Bowen, *Mary, Queen of Scots*, p. 389.
16. Froude, *History of England*, vol. 11, p. 645.
17. Read, *Lord Burghley and Queen Elizabeth*, p. 283.
18. Gorman, *The Scottish Queen*, p. 464.
19. Zweig, *Mary, Queen of Scotland and the Isles*, p. 292.
20. *Ibid.*, p. 293.

CHAPTER 23

1. Froude, *History of England*, vol. 11, p. 638.
2. Jenkins, *Elizabeth the Great*, p. 242.
3. *Ibid.*, p. 266.
4. Neale, *Elizabeth I and Her Parliaments*, vol. 2, p. 13.
5. Maynard, *Queen Elizabeth*, p. 227.
6. Froude, *History of England*, vol. 12, p. 226.
7. Maynard, *Queen Elizabeth*, pp. 221-22.
8. Strickland, *Lives of the Queens of England*, vol. 8, p. 66.
9. Maynard, *Queen Elizabeth*, p. 222.
10. Neale, *Elizabeth I and Her Parliaments*, vol. 2, p. 41.
11. Froude, *History of England*, vol. 11, p. 654.
12. *Ibid.*, p. 655.
13. Strickland, *Lives of the Queens of England*, vol. 8, p. 100.
14. Froude, *History of England*, vol. 12, p. 83.
15. *Ibid.*, p. 85.
16. Jenkins, *Elizabeth and Leicester*, p. 288.
17. Richardson, *The Lover of Queen Elizabeth*, pp. 316-17.
18. Neale, *Elizabeth I and Her Parliaments*, vol. 2, p. 28.
19. *Ibid.*, p. 17.
20. Hughes, *Crown and Parliament in Tudor-Stuart England*, pp. 122-23.
21. Froude, *History of England*, vol. 12, p. 55.
22. *Ibid.*, p. 56.
23. Jenkins, *Elizabeth the Great*, p. 263.

24. *Ibid.*
25. Froude, *History of England*, vol. 11, p. 60.
26. MacNalty, *Elizabeth Tudor: The Lonely Queen*, p. 180.
27. Waldman, *England's Elizabeth*, pp. 243-44.
28. Jenkins, *Elizabeth and Leicester*, pp. 293-94.
29. Read, *Lord Burghley and Queen Elizabeth*, p. 286.
30. *Ibid.*, p. 316.
31. Froude, *History of England*, vol. 12, p. 154.
32. Richardson, *The Lover of Queen Elizabeth*, pp. 325-26.
33. Froude, *History of England*, vol. 12, p. 157.
34. Read, *Lord Burghley and Queen Elizabeth*, p. 327.

CHAPTER 24

1. Zweig, *Mary, Queen of Scotland and the Isles*, p. 305.
2. Bowen, *Mary, Queen of Scots*, p. 397.
3. Froude, *History of England*, vol. 12, p. 236.
4. Neville Williams, *Elizabeth I: Queen of England*, p. 261.
5. Gorman, *The Scottish Queen*, p. 471.
6. Froude, *History of England*, vol. 12, p. 115.
7. *Ibid.*, p. 238.
8. *Ibid.*, p. 237.
9. *Ibid.*, p. 256.
10. Zweig, *Mary, Queen of Scotland and the Isles*, p. 316.
11. Froude, *History of England*, vol. 12, pp. 257-58.
12. Strickland, *Lives of the Queens of England*, vol. 8, p. 110.
13. Morris, *The Tudors*, p. 170.
14. Jenkins, *Elizabeth the Great*, p. 270.
15. Strickland, *Lives of the Queens of England*, vol. 8, p. 112.
16. Gorman, *The Scottish Queen*, p. 497.
17. Strickland, *Lives of the Queens of England*, vol. 8, p. 113.
18. Maynard, *Queen Elizabeth*, p. 279.
19. Gorman, *The Scottish Queen*, p. 498.
20. Harrison, *Letters of Queen Elizabeth*, p. 180.

CHAPTER 25

1. Neale, *Queen Elizabeth*, p. 282.
2. Neville Williams, *Elizabeth I: Queen of England*, p. 288.
3. Jenkins, *Elizabeth and Leicester*, p. 308.
4. *Ibid.*
5. Richardson, *The Lover of Queen Elizabeth*, p. 333.

6. Strickland, *Lives of the Queens of England,* vol. 8, p. 94.
7. Read, *Lord Burghley and Queen Elizabeth,* p. 328.
8. Neale, *Queen Elizabeth,* p. 287.
9. Richardson, *The Lover of Queen Elizabeth,* p. 346.
10. Harrison, *Letters of Queen Elizabeth,* p. 174.
11. Richardson, *The Lover of Queen Elizabeth,* p. 351.
12. Hume, *The Great Lord Burghley,* p. 401.
13. Read, *Lord Burghley and Queen Elizabeth,* p. 329.
14. Richardson, *The Lover of Queen Elizabeth,* pp. 351–52.
15. Neale, *Queen Elizabeth,* p. 289.
16. Waldman, *England's Elizabeth,* p. 189.
17. Harrison, *Letters of Queen Elizabeth,* pp. 178–79.
18. Read, *Lord Burghley and Queen Elizabeth,* p. 351.
19. Strickland, *Lives of the Queens of England,* vol. 8, p. 116.
20. Read, *Lord Burghley and Queen Elizabeth,* p. 351.
21. Strickland, *Lives of the Queens of England,* vol. 8, pp. 116–17.
22. Froude, *History of England,* vol. 12, p. 298.
23. Gorman, *The Scottish Queen,* p. 517.
24. *Ibid.,* p. 521.
25. *Ibid.,* p. 523.
26. Read, *Lord Burghley and Queen Elizabeth,* p. 355.
27. Strickland, *Lives of the Queens of Scotland,* vol. 7, p. 401.
28. Froude, *History of England,* vol. 12, p. 303.
29. Neale, *Queen Elizabeth,* p. 273.
30. Fraser, *Mary, Queen of Scots,* p. 511.
31. Read, *Lord Burghley and Queen Elizabeth,* p. 358.
32. Fraser, *Mary, Queen of Scots,* p. 516.
33. Read, *Lord Burghley and Queen Elizabeth,* p. 359.
34. Neville Williams, *All the Queen's Men,* p. 202.
35. Read, *Lord Burghley and Queen Elizabeth,* p. 362.
36. Neale, *Elizabeth I and Her Parliaments,* pp. 116–20.
37. *Ibid.,* p. 133.
38. Neale, *Queen Elizabeth,* p. 276.
39. Froude, *History of England,* vol. 12, pp. 319–20.
40. Strickland, *Lives of the Queens of England,* vol. 8, p. 132.
41. Froude, *History of England,* vol. 12, p. 335.
42. Neale, *Elizabeth I and Her Parliaments,* p. 136.
43. Fraser, *Mary, Queen of Scots,* p. 525.
44. Strickland, *Lives of the Queens of England,* vol. 8, p. 127.
45. *Ibid.,* p. 140.
46. *Ibid.,* pp. 141–42.
47. Gorman, *The Scottish Queen,* pp. 535–36.
48. *Ibid.,* p. 536.
49. Froude, *History of England,* vol. 12, p. 348.
50. Strickland, *Lives of the Queens of England,* vol. 8, p. 148.

CHAPTER 26
1. Strickland, *Lives of the Queens of Scotland,* vol. 7, pp. 415–16.
2. Fraser, *Mary, Queen of Scots,* p. 519.
3. Gorman, *The Scottish Queen,* p. 540.
4. Strickland, *Lives of the Queens of Scotland,* vol. 7, p. 435.
5. *Ibid.,* pp. 439–40.
6. *Ibid.,* p. 442.
7. *Ibid.,* p. 447.
8. *Ibid.,* p. 450.
9. Gorman, *The Scottish Queen,* p. 553.
10. *Ibid.,* p. 555.
11. Strickland, *Lives of the Queens of Scotland,* vol. 7, p. 453.
12. *Ibid.,* p. 453.
13. Strickland, *Lives of the Queens of England,* vol. 8, p. 151.
14. Wright, *Queen Elizabeth and Her Times,* vol. 2, p. 332.
15. Froude, *History of England,* vol. 12, p. 371.
16. Strickland, *Lives of the Queens of England,* vol. 8, p. 159.
17. Froude, *History of England,* vol. 12, p. 377.
18. MacNalty, *Elizabeth Tudor: The Lonely Queen,* p. 162.
19. Wright, *Queen Elizabeth and Her Times,* vol. 2, p. 335.
20. Read, *Lord Burghley and Queen Elizabeth,* p. 371.
21. *Ibid.,* p. 374.
22. *Ibid.,* pp. 377–78.
23. Strickland, *Lives of the Queens of England,* vol. 8, p. 163.
24. Mattingly, *The Armada,* p. 40.
25. *Ibid.,* p. 81.
26. Wright, *Queen Elizabeth and Her Times,* vol. 2, p. 347.
27. Mattingly, *The Armada,* p. 5, Preface.
28. Read, *Lord Burghley and Queen Elizabeth,* p. 329.
29. Mattingly, *The Armada,* p. 70.
30. Wright, *Queen Elizabeth and Her Times,* vol. 2, p. 352.

31. Mattingly, *The Armada*, p. 217.
32. *Ibid.*, pp. 90–91.
33. *Ibid.*, p. 107.
34. *Ibid.*, p. 126.
35. Lacey Baldwin Smith, *The Elizabethan World*, p. 280.
36. Mattingly, *The Armada*, p. 199.
37. Strickland, *Lives of the Queens of England*, vol. 8, p. 177.
38. Wilson, *Queen Elizabeth's Maids of Honor*, p. 164.
39. Strickland, *Lives of the Queens of England*, vol. 8, p. 179.

CHAPTER 27
1. Froude, *The Spanish Story of the Armada*, p. 20.
2. Mattingly, *The Armada*, p. 76.
3. *Ibid.*, p. 282.
4. Wright, *Queen Elizabeth and Her Times*, vol. 2, p. 382.
5. Froude, *History of England*, vol. 12, p. 461.
6. Mattingly, *The Armada*, p. 318.
7. *Ibid.*, p. 332.
8. Strickland, *Lives of the Queens of England*, vol. 8, pp. 181–83.
9. Richardson, *The Lover of Queen Elizabeth*, p. 377.
10. Wright, *Queen Elizabeth and Her Times*, vol. 2, p. 391.
11. Wilson, *Queen Elizabeth's Maids of Honor*, p. 165.
12. Hume, *The Great Lord Burghley*, p. 432.
13. Richardson, *The Lover of Queen Elizabeth*, pp. 382–83.
14. There were the inevitable rumors at Leicester's unexpected death, the most prevalent being that, unhappy with her attention to young Sir Christopher Blount, the Earl had prepared a poisoned cordial for Lettice, recommending that she use it "in time of faintness." Unsuspectingly, Lettice gave the Earl the cordial from which he expired. The second version of the story was that Lettice *knew* the cordial was poisoned and deliberately gave it to Leicester. However, a postmortem examination concluded that death came from natural causes.
15. Wilson, *Queen Elizabeth's Maids of Honor*, p. 166.
16. Waldman, *Elizabeth and Leicester*, p. 200.
17. Although the treasures which spilled forth from Kenilworth, Leicester House and Wanstead were numerous, they did not cover Leicester's debt to the Crown, and at Elizabeth's death, a good part of the debt was still unpaid. Lettice did not honor his several bequests to charity, and her new husband made considerable inroads on her fortune. Lettice lived to be ninety-two, dying on Christmas Eve in 1614.

CHAPTER 28
1. Harrison, *Letters of Queen Elizabeth*, pp. 193–94.
2. Hurstfield, *Elizabeth I and the Unity of England*, pp. 158–59.
3. Jenkins, *Elizabeth the Great*, p. 285.
4. Strickland, *Lives of the Queens of England*, vol. 8, pp. 199–200.
5. Brooks, *Sir Christopher Hatton*, p. 147.
6. *Ibid.*, pp. 145–50.
7. Irwin, *The Great Lucifer*, p. 21.
8. Waldman, *Sir Walter Raleigh*, p. 22.
9. *Ibid.*, pp. 25–26.
10. Strickland, *Lives of the Queens of England*, vol. 8, p. 69.
11. Waldman, *Sir Walter Raleigh*, p. 45.
12. *Ibid.*, p. 54.
13. Strickland, *Lives of the Queens of England*, vol. 8, p. 16.
14. *Ibid.*, pp. 72–73.
15. Garrett, *Death of the Fox*, p. 201.
16. Strickland, *Lives of the Queens of England*, vol. 8, p. 203.
17. *Ibid.*, p. 54.
18. *Ibid.*, p. 18.
19. Garrett, *Death of the Fox*, p. 320.
20. Strong, *Elizabeth R.*, p. 35.
21. *Ibid.*, pp. 30–31.
22. Strickland, *Lives of the Queens of England*, vol. 8, p. 205.
23. *Ibid.*, p. 201.
24. *Ibid.*, p. 202.
25. Lacey, *Robert, Earl of Essex*, p. 22.
26. Harrison, *Robert Devereux, Earl of Essex*, p. 10.
27. Lacey, *Robert, Earl of Essex*, p. 42.
28. Creighton, *Queen Elizabeth*, p. 243.
29. *Ibid.*
30. Harrison, *Robert Devereux, Earl of Essex*, p. 37.
31. Lacey, *Robert, Earl of Essex*, p. 67.
32. Strachey, *Elizabeth and Essex*, p. 34.
33. Harrison, *Robert Devereux, Earl of Essex*, pp. 43–44.
34. Neale, *Queen Elizabeth*, p. 307.
35. Read, *Lord Burghley and Queen Elizabeth*, p. 295.
36. Creighton, *Queen Elizabeth*, p. 264.
37. Neale, *Queen Elizabeth*, p. 310.
38. Read, *Lord Burghley and Queen Elizabeth*, p. 464.

39. Strickland, *Lives of the Queens of England*, vol. 8, p. 221.

40. Brooks, *Sir Christopher Hatton*, p. 354.

41. Lacey, *Robert, Earl of Essex*, p. 79.

42. Strachey, *Elizabeth and Essex*, p. 36.

43. Neale, *Queen Elizabeth*, p. 320.

44. Lacey, *Robert, Earl of Essex*, p. 84.

45. Harrison, *Robert Devereux, Earl of Essex*, p. 53.

46. Strickland, *Lives of the Queens of England*, vol. 8, p. 233.

47. Lacey, *Robert, Earl of Essex*, p. 88.

48. Harrison, *Robert Devereux, Earl of Essex*, p. 61.

49. *Ibid.*, p. 64.

50. *Ibid.*, p. 67.

51. *Ibid.*, p. 62.

52. Strickland, *Lives of the Queens of England*, vol. 8, p. 234.

CHAPTER 29

1. Waldman, *Sir Walter Raleigh*, p. 73.

2. *Ibid.*, p. 76.

3. Irwin, *The Great Lucifer*, p. 85.

4. Strickland, *Lives of the Queens of England*, vol. 8, p. 270.

5. Strachey, *Elizabeth and Essex*, p. 49.

6. Wilson, *Queen Elizabeth's Maids of Honor*, p. 229.

7. Hume, *The Great Lord Burghley*, p. 445.

8. Lacey, *Robert, Earl of Essex*, p. 107.

9. Harrison, *Robert Devereux, Earl of Essex*, p. 85.

10. Wilson, *Queen Elizabeth's Maids of Honor*, p. 237.

11. *Ibid.*, p. 199.

12. Strickland, *Lives of the Queens of England*, vol. 8, p. 274.

13. Strachey, *Elizabeth and Essex*, p. 57.

14. Wilson, *Queen Elizabeth's Maids of Honor*, p. 203.

15. *Ibid.*, p. 204.

16. Strickland, *Lives of the Queens of England*, vol. 8, p. 293.

17. Hume, *The Great Lord Burghley*, p. 450.

18. Beckingsale, *Elizabeth I*, p. 116.

19. Hume, *The Great Lord Burghley*, p. 481.

20. Harrison, *Robert Devereux, Earl of Essex*, p. 106.

21. Strachey, *Elizabeth and Essex*, p. 98.

22. Harrison, *Robert Devereux, Earl of Essex*, p. 107.

23. *Ibid.*, p. 109.

24. Waldman, *Sir Walter Raleigh*, p. 126.

25. Harrison, *The Elizabethan Journals, 1596*, p. 382.

26. *Ibid.*, p. 388.

27. *Ibid.*, p. 389.

28. Lacey, *Robert, Earl of Essex*, p. 167.

29. Neale, *Queen Elizabeth*, p. 343.

30. *Ibid.*, p. 344.

31. MacNalty, *Elizabeth Tudor: The Lonely Queen*, p. 211.

32. Neville Williams, *Elizabeth I: Queen of England*, p. 330.

33. *Ibid.*

34. Neville Williams, *The Life and Times of Elizabeth I*, p. 230.

35. Wilson, *Queen Elizabeth's Maids of Honor*, p. 233.

36. Strickland, *Lives of the Queens of England*, vol. 8, p. 297.

37. Neale, *Queen Elizabeth*, p. 342.

38. Harrison, *Robert Devereux, Earl of Essex*, p. 179.

CHAPTER 30

1. Read, *The Tudors*, p. 226.

2. Neville Williams, *Elizabeth I: Queen of England*, p. 331.

3. Lacey, *Robert, Earl of Essex*, p. 220.

4. Harrison, *The Elizabethan Journals, 1598*, p. 38.

5. *Ibid.*, p. 51.

6. *Ibid.*, p. 40.

7. Harrison, *Robert Devereux, Earl of Essex*, p. 195.

8. Harrison, *The Elizabethan Journals, 1598*, p. 42.

9. Neale, *Queen Elizabeth*, p. 349.

10. Wright, *Queen Elizabeth and Her Times*, vol. 2, p. 488.

11. Creighton, *Queen Elizabeth*, p. 280.

12. Harrison, *The Elizabethan Journals, 1598*, p. 46.

13. Neale, *Queen Elizabeth*, p. 351.

14. Strickland, *Lives of the Queens of England*, vol. 8, p. 318.

15. Neville Williams, *Elizabeth I: Queen of England*, p. 335.

16. Harrison, *Robert Devereux, Earl of Essex*, p. 217.

17. *Ibid.*, p. 218.

18. MacNalty, *Elizabeth Tudor: The Lonely Queen*, p. 213.

19. Harrison, *Robert Devereux, Earl of Essex*, p. 218.

20. Neville Williams, *All the Queen's Men*, p. 233.

21. Lacey, *Robert, Earl of Essex*, p. 220.

22. *Ibid.*, p. 222.

23. *Ibid.*

24. *Ibid.*, p. 229.

25. Harrison, *Robert Devereux, Earl of Essex*, p. 230.

26. *Ibid.*, pp. 226–28.

27. Jenkins, *Elizabeth the Great*, p. 308.

28. Neale, *Queen Elizabeth*, p. 357.

29. Harrison, *Robert Devereux, Earl of Essex*, pp. 229–33.

30. *Ibid.*, p. 235.

31. *Ibid.*, p. 236.

32. *Ibid.*, pp. 238–39.

33. Strachey, *Elizabeth and Essex*, p. 190.

34. Harrison, *The Elizabethan Journals, 1599*, p. 115.

35. Harrison, *Robert Devereux, Earl of Essex*, p. 243.

36. Neale, *Queen Elizabeth*, p. 362.

37. Harrison, *Robert Devereux, Earl of Essex*, p. 245.

38. Strickland, *Lives of the Queens of England*, vol. 8, p. 323.

39. Wilson, *Queen Elizabeth's Maids of Honor*, p. 246.

40. *Ibid.*

CHAPTER 31

1. Harrison, *The Elizabethan Journals, 1599*, p. 118.

2. Strickland, *Lives of the Queens of England*, vol. 8, pp. 324–25.

3. Harrison, *The Elizabethan Journals, 1599*, p. 132.

4. *Ibid., 1600*, p. 136.

5. Wilson, *Queen Elizabeth's Maids of Honor*, p. 252.

6. Strickland, *Lives of the Queens of England*, vol. 8, p. 343.

7. Neale, *Queen Elizabeth*, p. 369.

8. *Encyclopedia Americana*, vol. 27, p. 246.

9. Harrison, *The Elizabethan Journals, 1600*, p.155.

10. Neale, *Queen Elizabeth*, p. 367.

11. Harrison, *The Elizabethan Journals, 1600*, p. 160.

12. Strickland, *Lives of the Queens of England*, vol. 8, p. 339.

13. Harrison, *Robert Devereux, Earl of Essex*, p. 264.

14. Strickland, *Lives of the Queens of England*, vol. 8, p. 342.

15. Neale, *Queen Elizabeth*, p. 370.

16. Harrison, *The Elizabethan Journals, 1599*, p. 104.

17. Harrison, *Robert Devereux, Earl of Essex*, p. 271.

18. Neale, *Queen Elizabeth*, p. 371.

19. Harrison, *Robert Devereux, Earl of Essex*, pp. 272–73.

20. Strickland, *Lives of the Queens of England*, vol. 8, p. 345.

21. *Ibid.*, p. 346.

22. Harrison, *The Elizabethan Journals, 1600*, p. 199.

23. Harrison, *Robert Devereux, Earl of Essex*, p. 279.

24. Strickland, *Lives of the Queens of England*, vol. 8, p. 348.

25. *Ibid.*

26. Harrison, *The Elizabethan Journals, 1601*, pp. 210-11.

27. *Ibid.*, p. 213.

28. *Ibid.*, p. 214.

29. Strickland, *Lives of the Queens of England*, vol. 8, p. 300.

30. Harrison, *The Elizabethan Journals, 1601*, p. 215.

31. *Ibid.*, p. 217.

32. Harrison, *Robert Devereux, Earl of Essex*, p. 297.

33. Lacey, *Robert, Earl of Essex*, p. 303.

34. Harrison, *Rober Devereux, Earl of Essex*, p. 301.

35. *Ibid.*, p. 302.

36. *Ibid.*, p. 305.

37. Harrison, *The Elizabethan Journals, 1601*, p. 222.

38. Harrison, *Robert Devereux, Earl of Essex*, pp. 307-10.

39. *Ibid.*, p. 313.

40. Harrison, *The Elizabethan Journals, 1601*, p. 224.

41. *Ibid.*, pp. 223-24.

42. Harrison, *Robert Devereux, Earl of Essex*, pp. 315-18.

43. *Ibid.*

44. Harrison. *The Elizabethan Journals, 1601*, pp. 228-29.

CHAPTER 32

1. Neville Williams, *Elizabeth I: Queen of England*, p. 342.

2. Neale, *Queen Elizabeth*, p. 381.

3. Chamberlin, *The Private Character of Queen Elizabeth*, p. 152.

4. Hurstfield, *Elizabeth I and the Unity of England*, p. 190.

5. Strickland, *Lives of the Queens of England*, vol. 8, p. 368.

6. *Ibid.*, p. 363.

7. Hurstfield, *Elizabeth I and the Unity of England*, p. 195.

8. Neale, *Elizabeth I and Her Parliaments*, vol. 2, pp. 388–91.

9. Strickland, *Lives of the Queens of England*, vol. 8, p. 371.

10. Neville Williams, *Elizabeth I: Queen of England,* p. 351.

11. Marshall, *Queen Elizabeth,* p. 185.

12. Strickland, *Lives of the Queens of England,* vol. 8, p. 377-88.

13. Marshall, *Queen Elizabeth,* p. 189.

14. Hurstfield, *Elizabeth I and the Unity of England,* p. 217.

15. Chamberlin, *The Private Character of Queen Elizabeth,* p. 157.

Index

726